KU-246-739

Learning in Doing: Social, Cognitive, and
Computational Perspectives

Series Editor Emeritus
JOHN SEELY BROWN, *Xerox Palo Alto Research Center*

General Editors
ROY PEA, *Professor of Education and the Learning
Sciences and Director, Stanford Center for Innovations in
Learning, Stanford University*
CHRISTIAN HEATH, *The Management Centre,
King's College, London*
LUCY A. SUCHMAN, *Centre for Science Studies and
Department of Sociology, Lancaster University, UK*

Continued following the Index

Vygotsky's Educational Theory in Cultural Context

Edited by

ALEX KOZULIN

*International Center for the Enhancement of
Learning Potential*

BORIS GINDIS

Touro College

VLADIMIR S. AGEYEV

The University at Buffalo, State University of New York

SUZANNE M. MILLER

The University at Buffalo, State University of New York

CAMBRIDGE
UNIVERSITY PRESS

CAMBRIDGE UNIVERSITY PRESS
Cambridge, New York, Melbourne, Madrid, Cape Town, Singapore, São Paulo, Delhi

Cambridge University Press
32 Avenue of the Americas, New York, NY 10013-2473, USA

www.cambridge.org
Information on this title: www.cambridge.org/9780521821315

© Cambridge University Press 2003

This publication is in copyright. Subject to statutory exception
and to the provisions of relevant collective licensing agreements,
no reproduction of any part may take place without
the written permission of Cambridge University Press.

First published 2003
Reprinted 2004, 2005, 2006, 2007

Printed in the United States of America   2 00 6 004 082

A catalog record for this publication is available from the British Library.

Library of Congress Cataloging in Publication Data

Vygotsky's educational theory in cultural context / edited by Alex Kozulin ... [et al.].
  p. cm. – (Learning in doing)
Includes bibliographical references and index.
ISBN 0-521-82131-2 (hardback) – ISBN 0-521-52883-6 (pbk.)
1. Learning, Psychology of. 2. Cognition and culture. 3. Vyotskiæ, L. S.
(Lev Semenovich), 1896–1934 – Contributions in education. 1. Kozulin, Alex. II. Series.
LB1051.V943 2003
370.15'23 – dc21   2002042902

ISBN 978-0-521-82131-5 hardback
ISBN 978-0-521-52883-2 paperback

Cambridge University Press has no responsibility for
the persistence or accuracy of URLs for external or
third-party Internet Web sites referred to in this publication
and does not guarantee that any content on such
Web sites is, or will remain, accurate or appropriate.

Vygotsky's Educational Theory in Cultural Context

This book comprehensively covers all major topics of Vygotskian educational theory and its classroom applications. Particular attention is paid to the Vygotskian idea of child development as a consequence rather than premise of learning experiences. Such a reversal allows for new interpretations of the relationships between cognitive development and education at different junctions of the human life span. It also opens new perspectives on atypical development, learning disabilities, and assessment of children's learning potential. Classroom applications of Vygotskian theory, teacher preparation, and the changing role of a teacher in a sociocultural classroom are discussed in addition to the issues of learning activities and peer interaction. Relevant research findings from the United States, Western Europe, and Russia are considered together to clarify the possible new applications of Vygotskian ideas in different disciplinary areas. The sociocultural orientation of Vygotskian theory helps to reveal learning patterns that become obscured in more traditional research.

Dr. Alex Kozulin is Research Director at the International Center for the Enhancement of Learning Potential and an Invited Lecturer at Hebrew University, School of Education, in Jerusalem. Dr. Kozulin is author of *Vygotsky's Psychology: A Biography of Ideas* (1990) and *Psychological Tools: A Sociocultural Approach to Education* (1998).

Dr. Boris Gindis is Professor of Psychology and Director of Bilingual Programs at Touro College, Graduate School of Psychology and Education, in New York. He is the author of many articles and book chapters on Lev Vygotsky's scientific legacy, and in 1995–1996 he was guest editor of special issues of two journals, *Educational Psychologist* and *School Psychology International*, devoted to Vygotsky's theory and practice.

Dr. Vladimir S. Ageyev is Associate Director of the Urban Education Institute and Clinical Professor of Psychology in the Graduate School of Education at the University at Buffalo, State University of New York. He was an Editorial Board member of the journals *Conflict and Peace: Journal of Peace Psychology* and *Politics and Individual*.

Dr. Suzanne M. Miller is Associate Professor in the Graduate School of Education at the University at Buffalo, State University of New York. She is a coeditor of the book *Multicultural Literature and Literacies* (1993) and has published numerous articles in journals such as *Research in the Teaching of English, American Educational Research Journal*, and *English Education*.

Contents

Contributors

Vladimir S. Ageyev, Graduate School of Education, University at Buffalo, State University of New York, Buffalo, New York

Elena Bodrova, Mid-Continent Research for Education and Learning, Colorado

Seth Chaiklin, Department of Psychology, University of Aarhus, Risskov, Denmark

Anne DiPardo, University of Iowa, Iowa City, Iowa

Kieran Egan, Faculty of Education, Simon Fraser University, British Columbia, Canada

Natalia Gajdamaschko, Faculty of Education, Simon Fraser University, British Columbia, Canada

Hartmut Giest, Institute for Primary Education, University of Potsdam, Potsdam, Germany

Boris Gindis, Graduate School of Education and Psychology, Touro College, New York, New York

Jacques Haenen, IVLOS Institute of Education, Utrecht University, The Netherlands

Yuriy V. Karpov, Graduate School of Education and Psychology, Touro College, New York, New York

Alex Kozulin, The International Center for the Enhancement of Learning Potential, Jerusalem, Israel

James P. Lantolf, Center for Language Acquisition, Penn State University, University Park, Pennsylvania

Carol D. Lee, School of Education and Social Policy, Northwestern University, Chicago, Illinois

Deborah J. Leong, Department of Psychology, Metropolitan State College of Denver, Denver, Colorado

Carol S. Lidz, Freidman Associates, New Hope, Pennsylvania

Joachim Lompscher, Institute for Primary Education, University of Potsdam, Potsdam, Germany

Holbrook Mahn, College of Education, University of New Mexico, Albuquerque, New Mexico

Suzanne M. Miller, Graduate School of Education, University at Buffalo, State University of New York, Buffalo, New York

Carolyn P. Panofsky, Department of Educational Studies, Rhode Island College, Providence, Rhode Island

Pedro R. Portes, College of Education, University of Louisville, Louisville, Kentucky

Christine Potter, Language, Literacy and Culture Division of Curriculum & Instruction, University of Iowa, Iowa City, Iowa

Jean Schmittau, School of Education and Development, State University of New York at Binghamton, Binghamton, New York

Hubert Schrijnemakers, IVLOS Institute of Education, Utrecht University, Utrecht, The Netherlands

Job Stufkens, IVLOS Institute of Education, Utrecht University, Utrecht, The Netherlands

Jennifer A. Vadeboncoeur, School of Education, The University of Queensland, St. Lucia, Queensland, Australia

Galina Zuckerman, Psychological Institute, Russian Academy of Education, Moscow, Russia

Series Foreword

This series for Cambridge University Press is becoming widely known as an international forum for studies of situated learning and cognition.

Innovative contributions are being made by anthropology; by cognitive, developmental, and cultural psychology; by computer science; by education; and by social theory. These contributions are providing the basis for new ways of understanding the social, historical, and contextual nature of learning, thinking, and practice that emerges from human activity. The empirical settings of these research inquiries range from the classroom to the workplace, to the high-technology office, and to learning in the streets and in other communities of practice.

The situated nature of learning and remembering through activity is a central fact. It may appear obvious that human minds develop in social situations and extend their sphere of activity and communicative competencies. But cognitive theories of knowledge representation and learning alone have not provided sufficient insight into these relationships.

This series was born of the conviction that new and exciting interdisciplinary syntheses are under way as scholars and practitioners from diverse fields seek to develop theory and empirical investigations adequate for characterizing the complex relations of social and mental life and for understanding successful learning wherever it occurs. The series invites contributions that advance our understanding of these seminal issues.

Roy Pea
Christian Heath
Lucy Suchman

Introduction

Sociocultural Theory and Education: Students, Teachers, and Knowledge

Alex Kozulin, Boris Gindis, Vladimir S. Ageyev, and Suzanne M. Miller

What are the differences among American, German, and Japanese classrooms? If we take as a cue the anecdote told by Stiegler and Hiebert (1999) in their book *The Teaching Gap*, in a Japanese classroom there are students and there is knowledge and the teacher serves as a mediator between them. In a German classroom there are also knowledge and students, but teachers perceive this knowledge as their property and dispense it to students as they think best. In the American classroom there are teachers and there are students, but the status of knowledge is uncertain.

In this book we are offering a perspective that is different from those mentioned, yet poses the same fundamental question of the relationships among students, teachers, and knowledge. Our perspective is grounded in the theory of Lev Vygotsky (1896–1934), whose ideas turned out to be instrumental in shaping the learning processes in a growing number of classrooms in Russia, Europe, and the United States. At the heart of Vygotsky's theory lies the understanding of human cognition and learning as social and cultural rather than individual phenomena. During his tragically short lifetime Vygotsky developed this central thesis in a variety of areas including the theory of child development and educational psychology. He explored relationships between language and thought, instruction and development, everyday and academic concept formation, and a host of others. For a number of decades his theory inspired only a relatively small group of followers in Russia and Eastern Europe. And yet with the passage of time instead of disappearing from the scientific and educational horizon, Vygotsky's theory began attracting more and more attention in different countries.

What is the secret of the vitality of Vygotskian ideas? What causes contemporary Vygotskians to continue arguing about concepts and hypotheses first advanced in the 1920s? Returning to the opening anecdote we may suggest that instead of offering a definitive model, Vygotsky prompts us to inquire into the nature of knowledge used in the classroom, for example,

1

knowledge as information versus knowledge as concept formation. His theory makes us aware of our vision of students, for example, children defined by their age and IQ versus culturally and socially situated learners. It forces us to formulate our ideal of a teacher, for example, role model versus source of knowledge versus mediator, and so on. Such an inquiry does not produce educational prescriptions or recipes. What we present here is a collective dialogue of researchers-cum-practitioners from different countries concerned with deeper understanding of social and cultural underpinnings of the modern classroom.

Each of us has "discovered" Vygotsky's theory in his or her own way. Some of the authors studied in Russia and acquired Vygotsky's theory directly from people who knew Vygotsky and worked with him. Other authors became initiated by reading translations of Vygotsky's works and applying his ideas in sociocultural contexts very different from those in which these ideas were originally conceived. As a result, the theme of cultural diversity in understanding and applying Vygotsky's theory becomes a strong leitmotif of the entire volume.

Our aim is to present all major concepts of Vygotskian theory of learning and development, explore the transformation and adaptation of these concepts to different educational frameworks, review research on specific classroom applications of sociocultural ideas, and attend to the diversity of learners and learning situations. The book has four clearly defined parts: Part I, Concepts and Paradigms; Part II, Development and Learning; Part III, Classroom Applications; Part IV, Diverse Learners and Contexts of Education.

Part I covers such central concepts of Vygotskian theory as psychological tools, mediation, learning activity, zone of proximal development, and scientific and everyday concepts. One reason for the delayed recognition of Vygotsky's theory is that it offered answers to the questions only recently formulated in Western psychology and education. One of these is the question of the agency of learning. For a long time it seemed obvious that an individual learner constituted a natural agency of learning. More recently this "obvious" interpretation received a critical reappraisal partly prompted by the spectacular success of nonindividualistic learning models prevalent in Far Eastern societies and partly by the failure of more radical individualistic approaches. Unlike the individualistic theory of learning, the Vygotskian approach emphasizes the importance of sociocultural forces in shaping the situation of a child's development and learning and points to the crucial role played by parents, teachers, peers, and the community in defining the types of interaction occurring between children and their environments. As a result, the "obvious" individualistic identification of the agency of learning was challenged. Two concepts emerged as central in redefining the agency of learning: mediation and psychological tools. The concept of mediation emphasizes the role played by human and symbolic intermediaries placed between the individual learner and the material to be learned. Psychological tools are those symbolic systems specific for a given culture that when internalized by individual learners become their inner cognitive tools. Beyond their theoretical role the concepts of mediation and psychological tools also have an important applied function, serving as a basis for a number of applied programs offering new techniques for the enhancement of students' cognitive functions, development of metacognition, and integration of cognitive elements into instructional practice. The chapter by Alex Kozulin provides a systematic comparison of the Vygotskian approach to other theories of mediation, such as Feuerstein's theory of mediated learning experience. The complementary nature of symbolic and human mediators is discussed, as well as the question of which elements of mediation are universal and which are socioculturally specific. Content-based cognitive education programs are contrasted with cognitive programs that are content-neutral.

Vygotsky's notion of the zone of proximal development (ZPD) became the most popular of Vygotskian concepts used in contemporary educational theory, and yet it remains rather poorly understood. The problematic nature of ZPD can be explained by the fact that Vygotsky used this concept in three different contexts. In the developmental context ZPD is used for explaining the emerging psychological functions of the child. In the applied context ZPD explains the difference between the child's individual and aided performances, both in situations of assessment and in classroom learning. Finally, ZPD is used as a metaphoric "space" where everyday concepts of the child meet "scientific" concepts provided by teachers or other mediators of learning.

The chapter by Seth Chaiklin provides a systematic analysis of Vygotsky's original writings on ZPD, as well as the existing secondary research. The historical discussion of Vygotsky's concept emphasizes the metaphorical quality of the concept, and therefore the possibility of applying the concept to a wide range of phenomena from learning a specific concept to developing capabilities that may take months or years (e.g., professional training). Furthermore, the concept of ZPD can be applied to groups as well as individuals. ZPD is often defined as existing only in the interaction between children and others, and in this way a common misunderstanding of ZPD as a property of the child is revealed. It is also argued that the true meaning of ZPD can be understood only if it is taken in the broader context of Vygotsky's theory of child development and learning.

Although the notion of ZPD has been a success with American readers, the idea of students' scientific concepts as differing in principle from their everyday ones is still taking its first steps in American education. In his chapter Yuriy V. Karpov demonstrates how this original idea of Vygotsky's has been elaborated by Russian psychologists and educators into two different types of learning. These are *empirical learning*, which results in students' acquisition of spontaneous concepts, and *theoretical learning*, which results in their acquisition of scientific concepts. The results of more than 30 years of research activity by Russian Vygotskians have demonstrated the numerous advantages of theoretical learning over empirical learning for the development of students' learning skills and cognitive development. The notion of two types of learning (empirical and theoretical) can serve as a powerful tool for the analysis of different approaches to instruction. The analysis shows that the traditional system of school instruction promotes empirical learning. Surprisingly enough, some of the innovative approaches in American education that have been developed to overcome the shortcomings of the traditional system of school instruction promote empirical learning as well.

The chapter by Carol S. Lidz and Boris Gindis focuses on current practices in the application of ZPD as a basis for dynamic assessment (DA) of learning potential. They show that this methodology capitalizes on the cultural context for children's development of higher mental processes and the mediating role of adults serving as experienced collaborators to create ZPDs in their interactions with children. Whereas traditional approaches to assessment offer information about "yesterday's" functioning and provide limited information that is useful for planning for the future, DA simulates the process of development in the planned creation of ZPD that represents the intent of a more experienced collaborator to elicit information that bridges the "yesterday" of learners with their potential for "tomorrow." In this way, DA connects assessment with intervention with the intention of facilitating the learner's movement to the next higher level of functioning. The chapter contends that "test–intervene–retest" procedures, known as DA, with their focus on learning processes, cognitive modifiability, responsiveness to an adult's mediation, and amenability to instructions and guidance, are particularly suited for individuals who require individualized learning experiences, such as children with special needs and learners with atypical educational backgrounds. Vygotsky's idea of evaluation in the developmental and sociocultural context that results in effective remediation is examined through practical creation of ZPD within an assessment situation.

One of the innovative contributions made by Vygotsky was his idea that our sense of the world is shaped by symbolic tools acquired in the course of education and learning. He understood intellectual development in terms of intellectual tools, such as language, that we accumulate as we grow up in a society and that mediate the kind of understanding that we can form or construct. Though symbolic tools can be of a different nature, language in its different forms undoubtedly constitutes the major symbolic tool appropriated by children that shapes their understanding of the world. In their chapter Kieran Egan and Natalia Gajdamaschko argue that both on a historical and on an individual plane we can discern the successive development of oral language, literacy, theoretical abstractions, and self-conscious reflection about the language one uses. Vygotsky also perceptively observed that language forms do not replace one another but coexist in the human mind; similarly new forms of understanding do not dislodge the previous ones but complement them. Literacy in its different forms not only supports logicomathematical thinking but also provides tools for students' imagination and emotional development. The theoretical perspective presented here proposes the recognition of the educational process as an acquisition of symbolic tools that make the different forms of understanding possible. The chapter also provides examples of how to shape classroom lessons in accord with these principles.

Part II of the book focuses on Vygotsky's concepts of development and learning and their neo-Vygotskian interpretations. Vygotsky strongly believed in the close relationship between learning and development and in the sociocultural nature of both. He proposed that a child's development depends on the interaction between a child's individual maturation and a system of symbolic tools and activities that the child appropriates from his or her sociocultural environment. Learning in its systematic, organized, and intentional form appears in sociocultural theory as a driving force of development, as a consequence rather than a premise of learning experiences. Such a reversal from a dominant Piagetian position allows for new interpretations of the relationships between cognitive development and education; it also opens new perspectives on atypical development (delays and disabilities). Vygotsky discovered the systemic interrelationships and interdependencies between development and learning/teaching through examining the origins and phases of child development and through analyzing the qualitative transformations in a child's development.

Holbrook Mahn's chapter explores Vygotsky's original concepts of stages and crises in childhood as well as the dynamics of the relationships between teaching/learning processes and development. Vygotsky considered development as a process marked by qualitative transformations. He investigated both the functions that had matured and those emergent functions that just were coming into existence. Development, according to Vygotsky, is marked by periods of stability transitioning into qualitative transformations ("crises") in which there are both integration and disintegration of mental functions and structures. As shown by Holbrook Mahn, Vygotsky's examination of child development relied heavily on his theory of concept formation, which helped him explain the structural and functional transformations that occur when language is acquired, when children start formal education, and when children enter adolescence.

Learning and development of preschool children from the Vygotskian perspective are elaborated in the chapter by Elena Bodrova and Deborah J. Leong. This complex issue is analyzed in the context of the changing social situation of development accompanying the onset of formal school instruction. With the changes in society that have occurred since Vygotsky's time, one could expect certain changes in the meaning of preschool years for an individual's development; therefore, the authors examine the relevance of Vygotsky's ideas in the changing social context. In addition to the ideas expressed by Vygotsky himself (e.g., the role of self-regulatory inner speech in cognitive development and the role of play in creating a child's Zone of Proximal Development), the later contributions of Vygotsky's colleagues and students are critically discussed.

The authors describe the relationships that exist between fundamental theoretical concepts such as psychological tools and higher mental functions and the specific applications of these concepts to the development of preschool children in the works of the prominent Russian Vygotskians D. Elkonin, P. Galperin, A. Zaporozhets, and L. Venger. Of utmost interest, the authors' current research in the United States is used to illustrate the application of these ideas and their efficacy in promoting the development of preschool children in formal settings (e.g., Head Start classrooms) as well in informal adult–child interactions taking place in the family.

In her chapter Galina Zuckerman elaborates further the same topic of post-Vygotskian development of sociocultural theory, concentrating on one of the most important contributions made by Russian neo-Vygotskians (specifically, Daniel Elkonin and Vasilii Davydov), namely, their development of the notion of learning activity. The neo-Vygotskian theory distinguishes specially designed learning activity from learning in a generic sense. Learning in a generic sense is a part of many human activities, such as play, practical activity, and interpersonal interactions. Being an important component of these activities, learning, however, does not constitute their goal. What distinguishes learning as a special kind of activity is its focus on changes produced in the learner himself or herself. The learning activity was perceived by Russian followers of Vygotsky as a new cultural tool that amplifies the students' tendency toward independent, reflective, and critical thinking and acting. Elkonin, Davydov, and their students produced a strong body of evidence to substantiate the claim that when education in the elementary school is organized in the form of the learning activity, for the majority of elementary school children it creates the opportunity of becoming reflective thinkers and learners who know how to learn. Galina Zuckerman provides illustrations of the application of the notion of learning activity in Russian and Western primary school contexts and argues that when the instructional process is organized on a basis other than that of learning activity, the education in the elementary school is successful in developing valuable skills only in a relatively small number of gifted students. Only these students can distinguish between already mastered and not yet acquired skills, between already known and unknown concepts; they can hypothesize on the unknown and test their hypotheses. The same abilities are demonstrated by the majority of children in the learning activity classrooms.

Yet another view of neo-Vygotskian theory of learning and development is offered by Yuriy V. Karpov. Russian followers of Vygotsky have elaborated his developmental ideas into a theory that integrates cognitive, motivational, and social aspects of child development. The major determinant of development in this theory is the children's leading activity, that is, their age-specific joint action with adults and peers oriented toward the external world. In the course of this leading activity, children develop new mental processes, abilities, and motives, which outgrow their current leading activity. As a result, children switch to the new leading activity, which is characteristic of the next period of their development. Russian Vygotskians identified the sequence of children's leading activities in modern industrialized societies from infancy to adolescence and studied the mechanisms of children's transition from one leading activity to the next. As Yuriy V. Karpov states, the neo-Vygotskians' theory seems to present the most comprehensive approach to the problem of determinants of child development known in contemporary developmental psychology.

Children with special needs constitute a relatively new topic in Vygotskian literature in the West, although Vygotsky's contribution to the special education domain is prominent. The chapter by Boris Gindis starts with a review of Vygotsky's theory of disontogenesis (distorted or atypical development) in the context of sociocultural theory. The interrelationships between cognition and language in the process of the qualitative transformations during child development, both typical and atypical, and the role of socialization in the formation of human activities are the bases for the analysis. Vygotsky considered handicaps as sociocultural developmental phenomena in which compensation arises from socialization and enculturation. He demonstrated that a disability varies psychologically in different cultural and social environments. He introduced concepts of primary defects (organic impairment) and secondary defects (distortions of higher psychological functions due to sociocultural factors) in their dialectical interaction. In the area of psychoeducational assessment of children with special needs, Vygotsky created the foundation for the development of alternative methods, currently known as the family of dynamic assessment procedures. In Vygotsky's view, the main objective of special education should be the creation of a "positive differential approach" that can fully develop a handicapped child's higher psychological functions and overall personality. This concept is discussed in the context of the current debates about the notion of inclusion as a prospect for development in special education. Vygotsky's idea that a disabled child's development is determined by the social implications of his or her organic impairment creates a new perspective for socialization–acculturation and cognitive development of children with special needs. The chapter includes discussion of international experiences by scientists and practitioners working within a Vygotskian paradigm of special education. It concludes with a brief review of those remedial methodologies, general (e.g., cognitive education) as well as disability-specific (e.g., deafness), that either are based on a Vygotskian approach or have incorporated his major ideas. It is suggested that Vygotsky's socially, culturally, and developmentally oriented scientific legacy has the potential to unify, restructure, and promote special education as a science, profession, and social institution.

Part III addresses sociocultural approaches (1) to understanding of teacher development in teacher education classes and in schools and (2) to pedagogy in four disciplines – math, science, history, and literature. A major theme here is conceptual change, particularly in science, mathematics, and history. Using Vygotsky's distinction between everyday (i.e., spontaneous, empirical, practical) concepts and scientific (i.e., academic, theoretical) concepts, the authors examine the pedagogical means of developing students' deep disciplinary understanding through sequenced instructional activity.

In those efforts, almost every chapter addresses the current stance toward the nature of knowing in its discipline. The crossover to constructivist epistemologies is elaborated in the chapters on literature, history, and science but contested in mathematics, in favor of a specific cultural historical approach. The power of Vygotsky's concept of the zone of proximal development as a framework for understanding teaching and learning in mathematics, history, science, and literature is profoundly illustrated in this section. Each chapter also suggests the kinds of social interactions that move inward to become students' psychological tools, with extensive illustration of students' initiating use of those thinking tools in the chapter on literature. Finally, the impact of teachers' emotional lives in collaboration and crisis is also taken up in both theoretical formulations and in case study examples.

In her chapter Jean Schmittau proposes a Vygotskian-based curriculum as an alternative to the current constructivist reform movement in mathematics education. She critiques the pervasive practice of basing school mathematics on the activity of counting, demonstrating how such spontaneous concepts need to be replaced by the scientific concept of measurement. Drawing on her work with Davydov in Russia and using his mathematics curriculum in U.S. classrooms, she provides evidence that a Vygotskian learning paradigm for numbers and multiplication based on measurement better reflects mathematics in its essence – "the science of quantity and relation." She provides evidence that this inquiry focus promotes not only a deep understanding of mathematics, but also the ability to think theoretically.

The chapter by Jacques Haenen, Hubert Schrijnemakers, and Job Stufkens provides a Vygotsky–Galperin model for the acquisition of historical concepts. Galperin's mental action theory, they argue, extends Vygotsky into the specific steps of instruction. Its usefulness is examined and illustrated through a school-based implementation and in teacher education. The question of how prior or "practice-based" knowledge can best be used in the teaching and learning of historical concepts is a central issue. According to Galperin, the formation of mental actions at four basic levels of abstraction must be a focus of the teaching–learning process. The authors extend Galperin's approach in teaching preservice teachers historical concepts through the use of visual models and dialogue to study concepts as categories. The sequence of activities is demonstrated through school-based lessons on historical concepts, using everyday concepts to build understanding of academic concepts, such as democracy and monarchy.

Hartmut Giest and Joachim Lompscher examine the issue of how conceptual problems in science learning can be overcome by the formation of learning activity ascending from the abstract to the concrete to promote the development of theoretical thinking in students. Examples from studies of how learning was arranged as a process of problem solving demonstrate what this means for students in science classes and also for teachers in preparation. The idea of formation of learning activity that allows creation of a real unity between learning and instruction, self-regulation and systemic learning, under a teacher's guidance is an important pedagogical approach that requires attention to two zones of development: current and proximal. The concrete activity in the classroom requires support by teachers, as is demonstrated by an extended example of the vortex study showing how using a heuristic provides the opportunity for students to begin thinking dialectically.

Suzanne Miller synthesizes more than a decade of ethnographic research on how classroom discussion in social constructivist literature pedagogy shapes students' knowing and thinking. Innovative secondary-school English teachers in diverse contexts created zones of proximal development through discussion and other dialectical activities to develop their students' narrative and critical thinking. The most effective teachers provided narrative and reflective strategies at students' points of need, using more instructional assistance for students with greater needs. In this way all teachers lent their structuring consciousness to students' interpretive activity. Over time, these varied ways of questioning and making sense – these assisted ways of talking – were appropriated by students, moving inward to become students' conscious strategies for narrative reflection and critical thinking about texts. In all, the studies provide evidence that teacher mediation in problem-posing contexts contributes to specific forms of critically reflective literacy practice.

In the context of school reform Anne DiPardo and Christine Potter remind us that whenever we want students to engage in new practices, we must also attend to teachers who need supported opportunities to internalize those practices deeply. In this chapter the authors draw on and expand Vygotskian theory beyond its well-known cognitive aspects to provide a theoretical analysis of "the role of emotions in informal thought and action," particularly in the working lives of teachers. Through two extended case study examples, they develop, also, a narrative argument for enhanced attention to emotions in the professional lives of teachers, demonstrating that stress and burnout are not individually but socially constituted. Their full assessment of implications for teacher development suggests the importance of this topic at a time when external accountability of teachers may undermine the courage, the passion, the energy to teach.

In the last two decades, the Vygotskian theoretical framework has been steadily expanding into several neighboring areas of research and practice, such as cultural diversity and multicultural education. Though Vygotsky pioneered some cross-cultural studies of cognition, in vain would a contemporary reader seek direct references in Vygotsky's texts to "cultural funds of knowledge," culturally appropriate, or culturally compatible pedagogies, and so many other important concepts related to modern multicultural education. At the same time, in its very essence, Vygotsky's approach does contain, potentially, one of the best theoretical frameworks for educating culturally and socially diverse learners. Part IV is dedicated entirely to the exploration of these potentials.

Does child–adult interaction differ, depending on socioeconomic status (SES)? In what ways do these differences influence cognitive development? How do these differences come into play in teacher–student interactions in and out of the classroom? In which ways does the lack of awareness of those differences perpetuate the disparity and achievement gap of low-income and minority students? Two chapters address these important questions. Pedro R. Portes and Jennifer A. Vadeboncoeur summarize a broad spectrum of theory and research, providing a comprehensive picture of data on the SES differences in socialization processes, in general, and in child–adult interaction, in particular. Carolyn P. Panofsky, on the other hand, focuses on a relatively few, in-depth studies that undertake detailed analyses of how differences in teacher–student interaction in classrooms, which sometimes are very subtle and of which teachers themselves are unaware, may convey lowered expectations and impede the learning process of low-income and minority students. Both chapters emphasize the urgent need for further research on SES differences in relation to teacher–student interactions and their mediating roles in cognitive development. These chapters will be particularly helpful for researchers and practitioners in urban, cross-cultural, and multicultural education.

Why is it so difficult for adults to study a foreign language? What role do imitation and internal dialogue ("intrapersonal communication") play in second language acquisition? Everyone who has ever studied a foreign language in adulthood and was frustrated in the process can find inspiring answers in James P. Lantolf's chapter. By using a Vygotskian theoretical framework – including such concepts as imitation and play, inner speech and interiorization, and distinction between private and public speech – the author carried out a line of research with results and conclusions that can become a valuable resource for both theorists and practitioners in second language education.

The chapter by Carol D. Lee focuses on positive instructional outcomes of cultural modeling. She describes the fascinating results of a longitudinal study using African American Vernacular English in high school classrooms and provides detailed analysis of how more culturally compatible discourse can more successfully mediate cognitive development of African American students, stimulating their acquisition of scientific literary concepts. This chapter can be especially interesting for those who are looking for innovative ways of introducing "cultural funds of knowledge" to our classrooms, in general, and culturally compatible discourses (including foreign languages and dialects of English), in particular.

The cross-cultural analysis of perception of the Vygotskian heritage in the United States is the subject of the last chapter. Vladimir S. Ageyev provides an overview of the major cultural differences between Vygotsky's home country and the United States of America, analyzing the impact of those cultural differences on interpretation of Vygotskian ideas, and outlines some cultural biases and typical difficulties experienced by American graduate students in understanding Vygotskian theory. Ageyev argues for a more contextual, historically and culturally grounded interpretation of Vygotsky's work. This chapter can be helpful to those who teach Vygotsky-related courses for culturally diverse learners at the university level.

Reference

Stiegler, J., & Hiebert, J. (1999). *The teaching gap*. New York: Free Press.

PART I

CONCEPTS AND PARADIGMS

1

Psychological Tools and Mediated Learning

Alex Kozulin

What is the secret of Vygotsky's popularity? Why does a theory developed in Moscow a few years after the Russian Revolution capture the imagination of American educators at the beginning of the 21st century?

One possible explanation of this puzzling phenomenon is that Vygotsky's theory offers us answers to the questions that were not asked earlier. It is only now that we have started posing questions that make Vygotsky's "answers" relevant. Following this logic of explanation, instead of starting with a systematic exposition of Vygotskian theory, I would first focus on those contemporary questions that highlight the relevance of sociocultural theory.

Question 1: Multiculturalism. The issues of culture and learning have been inseparable for centuries for the simple reason that one of the main goals of learning is the transmission of culture from generation to generation. Nevertheless, the majority of educators were oblivious of this cultural element until confronted with it in the reality of the multicultural classroom. In a monocultural environment culture remains mostly invisible, and educators start paying attention to it only when two or more cultural patterns are empirically present in the same classroom at the same time. One may say that Vygotsky had a certain advantage in this respect because he worked in a period of great social upheaval that put different social and ethnic groups into the same educational focus. The issues of literacy, as well as ethnic and cultural diversity, were much more obvious for Vygotsky and his colleagues than for their Western contemporaries. Half a century later the same issues became a focal point in many Western classrooms.

Vygotsky's tentative answer to this challenge lies in his radical reorientation of learning theory from an individualistic to a sociocultural perspective. The key concept in this new orientation is that of psychological tools. Psychological tools are those symbolic artifacts – signs, symbols, texts, formulae, graphic organizers – that when internalized help individuals master their own natural psychological functions of perception, memory, attention, and so on (see Kozulin, 1998). Each culture has its own set of psychological tools and situations in which these tools are appropriated. Literacy in its different forms constitutes one of the most powerful of psychological tools.

The situation of the multicultural classroom can thus be operationalized as a copresence of different systems of psychological tools, and educational integration as a problem of acquisition by students – and sometimes also by teachers – of new systems of psychological tools. Literacy in this perspective ceases to be a homogeneous entity related to a student's ability to decode and comprehend standard written texts and appears as a diverse and heterogeneous phenomenon. Today one can speak about distributed literacy, in which a number of participants contribute to different aspects of one literacy action, or about scientific literacy, in which comprehension reaches beyond the everyday meaning of words. The formation of different literacies is intimately related to the appropriation of different psychological tools.

As contemporary education became aware of the challenge of the multicultural classroom, it also became aware of the need for cognitive education. Many of the students' problems apparently stem not from the poor presentation of content materials but from the lack of necessary cognitive strategies and metacognitive skills. Cognitive education programs aim at developing basic cognitive skills necessary for efficient study in all curricular areas or at fostering higher-level cognitive functions specific to a given curricular area, such as science, math, or literature. From a Vygotskian point of view the essence of cognitive education lies in providing students with new psychological tools that can shape either general or more domain-specific cognitive functions.

One can thus see how the questions regarding literacy and cognitive education that appeared on the Western educational agenda without the direct influence of Vygotsky's ideas acquire new meaning by meeting conceptual answers provided by sociocultural theory.

Question 2: Mediation. For a long time the predominant model of learning was that of acquisition (see Sfard, 1998). Children were perceived as containers that must be filled with knowledge and skills by teachers. The major disagreement among educators related to the degree of activity expected of the child. More traditional approaches portrayed the child as a rather passive recipient of prepackaged knowledge, whereas Piagetians and the proponents of discovery learning expected children to be independent agents of acquisition. In time it became clear that the acquisition model is wanting both theoretically and empirically. On the one hand, the child proved to be much more than a passive recipient of information; on the other hand, independent exploration often led to the acquisition of immature concepts and neglect of important school skills. A search for an alternative learning model moved to the fore such concepts as mediation, scaffolding, apprenticeship, and organization of learning activities.

Vygotskian theory stipulates that the development of the child's higher mental processes depends on the presence of mediating agents in the child's interaction with the environment. Vygotsky himself primarily emphasized symbolic tools–mediators appropriated by children in the context of particular sociocultural activities, the most important of which he considered to be formal education. Russian students of Vygotsky researched two additional types of mediation – mediation through another human being and mediation in a form of organized learning activity. Thus the acquisition model became transformed into a mediation model. Some mediational concepts such as scaffolding (see Wood, 1999) or apprenticeship (Rogoff, 1990) appeared as a result of direct assimilation of Vygotskian ideas; others such as Feuerstein's (1990) mediated learning experience have been developed independently and only later acquired new meaning in the context of sociocultural theory (Kozulin, 1998).

Question 3: Learning potential. The history of intelligence testing carries in itself an inherent paradox. On the one hand, one of the most important aspects of intelligence testing is its ability to predict the future performance of the child. On the other hand, the educational system that from the very beginning has been the major customer of psychometric testing aims at discovering and realizing children's learning potential, that is, their ability to change under the influence of instruction. The disparity between the stable psychometric properties of intelligence quotient (IQ) testing and the dynamic nature of a child's learning ability revealed itself in a number of IQ controversies. Gradually, alternative systems of dynamic assessment have emerged (Lidz, 1987; Sternberg & Grigorenko, 2002). What united all these systems was the introduction of the learning phase into the assessment situation. Instead of studying the child's individual performance, dynamic assessment focuses on the difference between performance before and that after the learning or assistance phase. Some of the dynamic assessment methods (e.g., Feuerstein, Rand, Hoffman, & Miller, 1979) emerged without the direct influence of Vygotskian ideas; others explicitly named Vygotsky's notion of the Zone of Proximal Development (ZPD) as their theoretical basis (Brown & Ferrara, 1985). The notion of ZPD gives three important insights to the issue of dynamic testing: (1) It focuses our attention on those psychological functions of the child that are emerging at a given moment but that have not yet been fully developed; (2) The concept of ZPD introduces assisted performance as a legitimate parameter of assessment procedure; (3) ZPD helps to conceptualize the difference between the level of actual performance and the learning potential of the child. Thus again the critique of IQ tests and the emergence of dynamic alternatives that occurred without direct influence of sociocultural theory

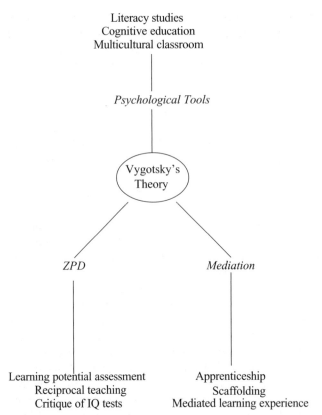

FIGURE 1.1 Vygotsky's theory and contemporary educational issues.

acquired new meaning in the context of the ZPD paradigm. Figure 1.1 presents the relationships between such Vygotskian concepts as psychological tools, mediation, and ZPD and those contemporary issues, such as cognitive education, learning potential assessment, and parent–child joint activity, that acquire new meaning through the encounter with the Vygotskian theoretical apparatus.

In the following I will focus on two major concepts of sociocultural theory, psychological tools and mediation, and attempt to show how these concepts can further contribute to the theory of learning and instruction.

AGENTS OF MEDIATION

Mediation serves as a key word in a considerable number of recent studies, some of them inspired by Vygotsky's theory and some developed independently (e.g., Feuerstein, 1990). One can distinguish two faces of mediation, one human, the other symbolic. Approaches focusing on the human mediator usually try to answer the question, What kind of involvement by the adult is effective in enhancing the child's performance? Those who focus on the symbolic aspect pose the question, What changes in the child's performance can be brought about by the introduction of symbolic tools–mediators?

THE HUMAN MEDIATOR

The role of the human mediator is defined in Vygotsky's (1978) theory through the notion that each psychological function appears twice in development, once in the form of actual interaction between people, and the second time as an inner internalized form of this function. Because of this, one of the central concerns of the sociocultural studies inspired by Vygotsky was to elucidate how the activities that start as an interaction between the child and the adult become internalized as the child's own psychological functions. In this respect the Wertsch and Stone (1985) study seems quite representative. The authors observed and recorded the interaction between a mother and her $2^1/_2$-year-old daughter during the course of the child's work on a puzzle. The child was to complete a "copy" puzzle in accordance with a "model" puzzle, while the mother was allowed to help her. At the beginning of the work the interaction between the child and the mother took the form of the child's asking where the piece should go and the mother's directing the child to the model. Toward the end of work the child's verbalization acquired the quality of self-direction, and the necessity to consult the model seemed to become appropriated by the child herself. In terms of Vygotsky's (1978, 1986) notion of the zone of proximal development (ZPD) what was accomplished was a transfer of the function of model use from the child's ZPD to the zone of the child's actual development.

Thus a true focus of the study was the transition of the function from the interpersonal to the intrapersonal plane rather than the properties of the mother's mediation, which was described in a contextual and concrete way (e.g., "directs the child to the model"). There are apparently a great number of different forms of adult mediation, from the adult's presence, which provides the child with a secure learning environment, to encouragement, challenge, and feedback (Schaffer, 1996). The main emphasis of the Wertsch and Stone (1985) study and other similar studies was, however, not on identifying mediation patterns but on establishing that (a) in the interactive situation children can indeed become involved in activities that are more complex than those they can master themselves and (b) joint activity results in the specific function's becoming appropriated by the child.

The examination of neo-Vygotskian studies confirms the impression that the parameters of human mediation turned out to be too numerous and context-dependent to allow for a simple classification. For example,

Tharp and Gallimore (1988) wrote about such forms of teacher mediation as modeling, contingency management (praise and critique), feedback, and, on the other level, cognitive structuring. Cognitive structuring belongs to a metacognitive level and includes strategies for the organization of students' work. It is clear that the parameters of teacher mediation mentioned belong to different levels and different aspects of interactive activity.

Even when the goal of mediated instruction is defined quite specifically, the forms of mediation remain open. For example, in their seminal study Palinscar and Brown (1984) proposed a reciprocal teaching framework for the development of literacy. Within this framework teachers and students took turns in reading and discussing the text. The teacher's goal was to use the interactive learning technique for developing students' questioning, summarizing, predicting, and clarifying strategies. Though the strategies themselves were defined quite precisely, the mediational means were less specific, including such disparate forms as strategy modeling, creation of awareness of the use of strategies, adjustment of presentation to the child's level of competence, and transfer of responsibility to students.

The difficulty of identifying different forms of mediation becomes particularly clear through Rogoff's (1995) analysis of mediation. Rogoff distinguished three aspects or strata of mediation: apprenticeship, guided participation, and appropriation. Apprenticeship provides a model of community activity that mediates sociocultural patterns to children or adult novices. Guided participation covers the interpersonal aspect of joint activity. Appropriation relates to changes occurring in the individuals because of their involvement in mediated activities. Though such a schema is useful for a general orientation, it cannot serve for the identification of specific mediational activities:

> The concept of guided participation is not an operational definition that one might use to identify some and not other interactions or arrangements. . . . The concept does not define when a particular situation is or is not guided participation, but rather provides a *perspective* on how to look at interpersonal engagements and arrangements. (Rogoff, 1995, pp. 146–147)

One possible way to analyze and classify different types of mediation is to distinguish between the *type* of mediation and the specific *technique* of mediation. For example, from the study of Bliss, Askew, and Macrae (1996) on scaffolding in science teaching one may conclude that whereas approval, encouragement, structuration, and organization of students' work are related to the *type* of mediation, more localized scaffolds such as the facilitation of the "first step" or provision of hints and slots are related to the *technique* of mediation. One significant finding of this study was, however, the low level of effective spontaneous mediation among teachers. The teachers either avoided the mediational approach altogether, using instead directive teaching strategies, or were unsuccessful in their mediational attempts. This poses a problem of a difference between home and school environments and the limitations imposed on the extension of the findings made about parental mediation at home to the classroom situation. Although the majority of parents apparently find the proper form of mediation for their children (Wood, 1999), this mediation is usually relevant only for everyday life activities. It remains to be shown in which way parental mediation is effective in promoting the child's classroom performance. The teachers' lack of spontaneous mediation in the classroom points to the necessity of providing them with systematic training in both the general types of mediation and specific techniques appropriate for a given age and subject matter.

Such mediational training of teachers was reported in the Lehrer and Shumow (1997) study that compared parental and teacher assistance to children solving math problems. Teacher assistance was aimed mostly at sense making and problem elaboration, whereas parental assistance tended to provide strategic control and problem definition. Parents more often resorted to direct intervention by telling children what to do. Teachers, on the other hand, tried to help students to make sense of the math problem and then encouraged them to solve the problem independently. To bridge the gap between teachers and parents, Shumow (1998) also developed a training program for parents. The training included written newsletter materials and counseling over the phone. Parents who participated in this program demonstrated a shift in their assistance toward greater problem elaboration and sense making.

The relevance of spontaneous parental mediation to classroom performance has been examined by Portes (1991). Fifth- and sixth-grade students were asked to perform a number of cognitive tasks (Block Design from WISC-R, classification of pictures and words, creativity tasks) while their mothers were allowed to help them. Portes identified three types of child interaction (questions and requests for help, agreement, and interruption) and nine types of mother interaction. The factor analytic study yielded one general factor, Maternal Verbal Guidance (MVG). The MVG represents the type of interaction that includes the mother's verbal prompts, cues, closed questions; mother and child elaboration during and after the task; and the child's questions relevant to problem solving. The MVG turned out to be a strong predictor of children's scholastic achievement in math, reading, and reference skills. The role of MGV was particularly strong in predicting math achievement, stronger than socioeconomic status (SES), race, and parental marital status. In the terms suggested earlier, Portes identified the core parental mediational *techniques* relevant to the problem-solving activity. These techniques apparently promote cognitive strategies that are effective in a wide range of formal learning situations. The significance of Portes's findings lies not only in a more specific identification of the mediational techniques, but also in the demonstration that not every type of parent–child interaction has a mediational effect.

Studies inspired by Vygotskian ideas of human mediation seem to be mostly data-driven. They start with empirical data on parent– or teacher–child interaction and attempt to identify the significant elements of human mediation. Studies inspired by Feuerstein's (1990; Feuerstein, Krasilovsky, & Rand, 1978) theory of mediated learning experience (MLE) are theory-driven. Feuerstein postulated that the quality of mediated learning experience can be achieved only if a number of MLE criteria are met. Among the most important of these criteria are intentionality and reciprocity of interaction, its transcendent character (i.e., having significance beyond a here-and-now situation), and the mediation of meaning. Studies that follow this paradigm focus on the presence of the specified MLE parameters in child–adult interaction and the consequences of the absence or insufficiency of MLE for the child's cognitive development and learning. With this objective in mind, a number of scales for measuring the presence of the major parameters of MLE were developed (Klein, 1988; Lidz, 1991).

Tzuriel (1997) demonstrated that the MLE scores of transcendence and regulation of behavior in the mother–child interaction were a good predictor of the second-grade children's cognitive performance in the Inferential Modifiability Test. Interestingly, the MLE score explained the child's cognitive posttest, but not the pretest, scores. Taking into account that the Inferential Modifiability Test is a dynamic test that has a learning phase between the pre- and posttest, it seems plausible that the quality of parental mediation influences the child's learning potential rather than direct performance level. In other words, children who receive more MLE through interaction with their parents become better learners. In Vygotskian terms that would mean that the quality of parental mediation influences the upper limits of the child's ZPD, rather than his or her zone of actual development.

Tzuriel (1996) also demonstrated that different parameters of mediation move to the fore, depending on the content of the joint mother–child activity. He contrasted free-play activity with more structured problem-solving activity. First of all, it was found that mothers tend to provide a greater overall amount of mediation in the free-play situation. Two parameters of MLE, mediation of meaning and mediation of the feeling of competence, turned out to be discriminating between these situations. Mothers apparently felt that the free-play situation is too "vague" and requires greater investment by them in order to define it properly for the child. In the problem-solving situation mothers apparently believed that the tasks themselves provide enough structure so that parental involvement is less important.

These results provide a useful clue to the differences between mediation at home and that in the classroom. The majority of home-based situations are not highly structured. Parents, therefore, feel obliged to provide extra mediation of meaning to make the situation clear to their children. In the classroom the activity is usually organized around highly structured learning materials. Many teachers apparently believe that the meaning embedded in these materials is sufficiently transparent to students and that the situation therefore does not warrant intensive mediation.

Studies on the human aspect of mediation confirmed the importance of mediated learning but at the same time revealed the episodic character of our understanding of this phenomenon. First of all, the common classification of mediational interactions is missing. This can be somewhat remedied by the already proposed distinction between the types of mediation and techniques of mediation. The predominance of certain types and techniques of mediation in both formal and informal learning settings should then be systematically investigated. Neo-Vygotskians might wish to take a cue from the Feuersteinian theory-driven studies and start investigating specific forms of mediation, such as transcendence (i.e., going beyond a here-and-now situation), in their relation to the development of the learning potential of the child. The students of MLE theory, on the other hand, might wish to reexamine critically their postulate of the three universal criteria of mediation (i.e., intentionality, transcendence, and meaning). They may ask themselves whether the MLE based on these criteria has a holistic character so that its effect depends on the overall amount of mediation or whether the adequate or inadequate amount of mediation associated with one specific criterion might acquire critical importance to the child's cognitive development.

SYMBOLIC MEDIATORS

Vygotsky's theory (Vygotsky, 1978, 1997; Vygotsky & Luria, 1930/1993) made an important distinction between experiences produced by the immediate contact of the individual with environmental stimuli and experiences shaped by interactions mediated by symbolic tools. Among the most ancient of these symbolic mediators Vygotsky (1978, p. 127) mentioned "casting lots, tying knots, and counting fingers." Casting lots appears in a situation when the uncertainty of decision caused by the presence of two equally strong opposing stimuli is resolved by an application of an artificial and arbitrary tool, a die. The individual links his or her decision to the "answer" given by a die, thus artificially resolving the situation that cannot be solved in a natural way. Tying knots exemplified the introduction of an elementary mnemonic device to ensure the retrieval of information from the memory. Finger counting demonstrates how an ever-present object (fingers) can serve as an external symbolic tool that organizes cognitive functions involved in elementary arithmetic operations.

Beyond these primitive tools lie the vast areas of higher-order symbolic mediators including different signs, symbols, writing, formulae, and graphic organizers. Cognitive development and learning, according to Vygotsky, essentially depend on the child's mastery of symbolic mediators, their appropriation and internalization in the form of inner psychological tools (Kozulin, 1998).

This general theoretical schema has produced a number of ramifications. One of them is the research on the understanding and use of symbols in early childhood (e.g., DeLoach, 1995). One important conclusion from this line of research is that one cannot take it for granted that children will detect a symbolic relation, no matter how obvious it appears to adults. The acquisition of symbolic relationships requires guided experience; it does not appear spontaneously. DeLoach observed that learning materials for young children are often designed in a way that presupposes that children have already mastered the symbolic relationships between object symbols and concepts. In reality these relationships do not emerge spontaneously but should be systematically formed.

Here we are touching upon an important issue of the relationships between symbolic and human aspects of mediation. Symbols may remain useless unless their meaning as cognitive tools is properly mediated to the child. The mere availability of signs or texts does not imply that they will be used by students as psychological tools. This fact becomes particularly clear in the studies on the outcome of literacy.

Writing in its different forms constitutes the major class of symbolic mediators. From the early studies of Vygotsky and Luria (1930/1993; Luria, 1976) the issue of the mediational role of literacy has been at the center of sociocultural debate. Vygotsky and Luria believed, and attempted to show in their pioneering field study in Central Asia, that the acquisition of literacy changes the entire system of the learner's cognitive processes. More recently the centrality of literacy and writing for the development of higher cognitive processes was reasserted by Olson (1994). There are, however, serious reasons to believe that literacy as such does not have an unequivocal influence on cognitive functioning. In order to pose a question properly, one should inquire about the type of literacy, the context in which it was acquired, and the type of tasks that require cognitive processes hypothetically influenced by literacy (Scribner & Cole, 1981; Scribner, 1997). Scribner and Cole demonstrated that forms of literacy acquired in the context of religious studies, home learning, and formal schooling all had different characteristics and a different impact on cognitive processing. For example, nonnative language literacy acquired in the context of religious studies aimed at memorization of holy texts turned out to influence the student's facility with memory tasks but failed to show any influence on other cognitive functions.

This finding returns us to the question of the appropriation of symbolic mediators. Such an appropriation is apparently dependent on the goal that a teacher or parent sets for the tool–mediator offered to the child.

We often tend to confuse literacy in a generic sense with a special type of analytic literacy that is supposed to be a goal of formal education. Not every type of literacy leads to the cognitive changes observed by Vygotsky and Luria (Luria, 1976). Moreover, even literacy acquired in the nominally formal educational setting does not necessarily lead to the cognitive changes unless this literacy is mediated to a student as a cognitive tool. Our study (Kozulin & Lurie, 1994) of new immigrant adults educated in Ethiopian schools demonstrated that their ability to read, write, and solve basic math problems in their native language had little relation to their ability to solve novel problems. Their initial cognitive task performance with Raven's Matrices and Block Design Test was much lower than would be expected when taking into account their educational level. The performance improved only after our subjects were systematically introduced to the symbolic systems relevant to the activity of problem solving. One may suspect that literacy and numeracy were taught to them as narrow technical skills with a limited goal of decoding, memorizing, and reproducing texts and performing basic calculations. Literacy and numeracy apparently remained in their minds as separate technical skills devoid of wider cognitive importance. The initial optimism of Vygotsky and Luria regarding the general transformatory power of symbolic mediators should thus be qualified. It is true that by their very nature symbolic mediators have the capacity to become cognitive tools. However, in order to realize this capacity the mediators should be appropriated under very special conditions that emphasize their meaning as cognitive tools.

The process of appropriation of psychological tools differs from the process of content learning. This difference reflects the fact that whereas content material often reproduces empirical realities with which students become acquainted in everyday life, psychological tools can be acquired only in the course of special learning activities. For example, a content knowledge that Rome is the capital of Italy corresponds to empirical reality and can be learned by the students both spontaneously in their everyday life or as a part of the school curriculum. On the other hand, a geographical map and its legend can be acquired only in the course of special learning activity. A map is a symbolic tool that helps students to find any geographical entity, for example, a capital of a certain country, even if both the country in question and its capital are unknown to them. For this reason the acquisition of psychological tools requires a different learning paradigm than the acquisition of empirical content knowledge. This learning paradigm presupposes (a) a deliberate, rather than spontaneous character of the learning process; (b) systemic acquisition of symbolic tools, because they themselves are systemically organized; (c) emphasis on the generalized nature of symbolic tools and their application.

If one compares these requirements with the universal criteria of Mediated Learning Experience defined by Feuerstein (1990) – intentionality, transcendence, and mediation of meaning – one will see a considerable overlap between them. This overlap is not surprising, because the role of MLE is to create cognitive prerequisites essential for successful direct learning. Many of these cognitive prerequisites are closely related to the use of symbolic tools. This is why it seems important to explore the relationships between the criteria of MLE interaction and conditions of psychological tool acquisition.

As mentioned, the acquisition of psychological tools must have the character of a deliberate action. If there is no intentionality of the teacher–mediator, psychological tools will not be appropriated by the students or will be perceived as another content item, rather than a tool. Sometimes, teachers fail to help students in identifying symbolic tools that are presented together with content material. As a result students receive tools together with content in a syncretic, undifferentiated manner and are unable to identify the instrumental part of the learning material.

The symbolic tool fulfills its role only if it is appropriated and internalized as a generalized instrument, that is, a psychological tool capable of organizing individual cognitive and learning functions in different contexts and in application to different tasks. That is why the inability to teach psychological tools in a transcendent manner inevitably leads to failure in their appropriation by students. Apparently this is exactly what happens when school-based instruction in reading, writing, and mathematics is carried out purely as content and skills training without mediation of the generalized instrumental function of these symbolic systems. As a result literacy and mathematical skills remain isolated and fail to influence the overall cognitive and problem-solving abilities of students (Kozulin & Lurie, 1994).

Mediation of meaning is an essential moment in the acquisition of psychological tools, because symbolic tools derive their meaning only from the cultural conventions that engendered them. Symbolic tools (e.g., letters, codes, mathematical signs) have no meaning whatsoever outside the cultural convention that infuses them with meaning and purpose. If this purpose is poorly mediated to learners, the proper understanding of the tools' instrumental function can be missing. For example, a foreign language is sometimes taught as a coding system that simply maps the correspondence between foreign words and the words in the native language of the learner. As a result the learner becomes severely handicapped in both comprehension and expression in the foreign language. If, on the contrary, the purpose of foreign language study is mediated as an ability to comprehend and formulate meaningful propositions, students become capable of grasping the instrumental role of the foreign sign system (see Wallace, Pandaram, & Modiroa, 1996; Kozulin & Garb, 2002).

MEDIATION: UNIVERSAL OR CULTURALLY SPECIFIC?

Though there is little doubt that certain forms of human mediation are universal and can be found in any culture, the questions as to what constitutes this universal core of mediation and which forms of mediation are culture-specific remain. It is also important to inquire whether the same aspects of mediation have identical meaning and importance in different cultures and for different social groups.

Feuerstein considered the first three criteria of MLE (intentionality, transcendence, and mediation of meaning) universal because they transcend not only culture but also the modality of mediation. According to Feuerstein and colleagues (1980, p. 23), the acquisition of MLE does not depend on either the content or the modality of interaction: "Using the example of instruction in a preliterate society, it is clear that mediation may take a nonverbal form. The mediator illustrates his actions to an interested observer with only limited verbal, and even less semantic, interaction occurring. In our experience, the changes that occur as a result of nonverbal mediation transcend both the content and the means by which the content is transmitted."

The subsequent research carried out within the MLE paradigm cast doubt upon this strong universalistic position. Both socioeconomic and ethnocultural factors proved to have influence on the amount and type of mediation. Tzuriel (1996) demonstrated that there is a strong correlation between the observed amount of MLE interactions and the SES of mothers: The higher the SES level the higher the MLE score. Three criteria of MLE, transcendence, mediation of meaning, and mediation of the feeling of competence, turned out to be particularly sensitive to the SES differences. For example, significant differences in the amount of mediation of transcendence (going beyond the here-and-now situation) were found not only between high- and low-SES mothers, but even between high- and medium-SES mothers. This indicates that certain aspects of human mediation are selectively emphasized in certain SES groups rather than others (see Portes and Vadeboncoeur, this volume).

The investigation of human mediation in the cross-cultural perspective also yielded results that favor culture-specificity rather than universality. In his study of mother–child interaction in immigrant families from Ethiopia, Tzuriel (1997) employed both traditionally oriented and Western-oriented interactional contexts. In the traditional context mothers interacted with their children while weaving, making pottery, and working on other handicrafts. The Western-oriented tasks included solving analogical problems. It was discovered that different aspects of mediation move to the fore, depending on the type of the task. For example, traditional activities elicited higher amounts of mediation of meaning and transcendence than Western tasks, but the amount of intentionality was lower in the traditional situations. When comparisons were made between mediational styles of Ethiopian and native Israeli mothers, it became clear that they emphasize different aspects of mediation. Intentionality and regulation of behavior were higher in Ethiopian mothers; mediation of the feeling of competence was higher in Israeli mothers. Moreover, whereas for the Israeli sample the amount of MLE exhibited during the mother–child interactions predicted the child's performance in the inferential reasoning test, this connection was absent for the Ethiopian sample. In other words, the aspects of MLE captured by the MLE observational scales were predictive for the ability to learn problem-solving tasks in Israeli children but not in Ethiopian children. One may thus question the ability of the MLE scales to capture the "same" forms of mediation in different cultural groups.

The sociocultural paradigm, though acknowledging the universality of some forms of mediation, such as guided participation of children in the activities of adults, focuses mostly on culture-specific interactions. In her study on guided participation Rogoff (1990) emphasized that the forms of human mediation directly depend on the sociocultural goals considered important by a given community. One may find useful the dichotomy between traditional societies in which children are directly involved in everyday work and other activities of adults and modern industrial societies that create environments, tasks, and activities attuned to what the community considers to be children's age-appropriate needs. In the traditional environments the child–adult interactions are usually less verbal and more contextual and are aimed at the successful integration of the child in traditional activities. In the modern environments the interactions are more verbal, more child-centered, and more "abstract" in the sense of fostering in the children those skills that have no immediate practical value but are perceived as prerequisites for their future integration into rapidly changing technological society. It is too early, however, to claim that we have a precise nomenclature of mediational patterns characteristic of these interactive environments. Rogoff's (1990, chapter 6) analysis of the research on parent–child interactions and the child's guided participation revealed a baffling variety of mediational styles. Even in the United States different communities display widely disparate styles of mediation from more tacit, observational, and topic-centered to more explicit, verbal, and concept-oriented.

The sociocultural theory suggests that the style of human mediation cannot be properly comprehended unless the role of available symbolic mediators is acknowledged. In the communities that use an elaborate system of mediators associated with literacy and numeracy a considerable amount of human mediation is directed toward the child's acquisition and appropriation of these tools–mediators. This cannot but leave an imprint of the mediational process. For example, the acquisition of higher-level mathematical and scientific symbolic systems (formulae, etc.) calls for a much greater amount of transcendence than the acquisition of a concrete manual operation.

One should, however, be aware that symbolic tools are always appropriated in terms of the goals of the given community. As a result the same system of symbolic mediators may become associated with a different system of mediational practices. Heath's (1983) study of literacy in different Appalachian communities demonstrated that nominally the same system of English literacy is embedded in a very different mediational system in the middle-class white families, working-class white families, and rural black families. Working-class white parents taught their children respect for the written word but did not involve text-based information in their everyday life. These children started well at school but failed later when they were expected to use literate skills in composing and interpreting complex texts. Black rural children were introduced by their parents to the creative and imaginative use of oral language, but the written word was not mediated to them. As a result these children experienced difficulties at the very first steps of the acquisition of school-based literacy and were rarely capable of realizing their creative verbal potential.

It would also be incorrect to think that the agency of literacy is necessarily a solitary individual. Though in technological society an individual is supposed to become autonomously literate (though the extensive use of computer spell-check qualifies even this assertion), this is not true in all communities. In their study of different forms of literacy in Morocco, Wagner, Messick, and Spratt (1986) present a case for distributed literacy. The agency of such distributed literacy is a group rather than an individual. Several individuals each possess only some aspects of literacy, and only by putting their efforts together can they function as a fully literate individual. Such findings have two implications for a study of mediation. First, they alert us to the issue of the mediation of literacy to children under conditions of distributed rather than individual literacy. Second, they pose a question of what kind of mediation takes place between the adult participants in the distributed literate action.

One may thus conclude that the search for both universal and culture-specific forms of mediation is only beginning. It is clear, however, that the social and cultural goals of a given community and the symbolic mediators available to its members will leave their imprint on the parameters and styles of mediation.

COGNITIVE EDUCATION AND PSYCHOLOGICAL TOOLS

The Instrumental Enrichment (IE) program (Feuerstein, Rand, Hoffman, & Miller, 1980) was first conceived as a method for developing learning potential in socioculturally disadvantaged adolescents, many of them members of ethnic minority groups. The authors of this program argued that both the low level of scholastic achievement and the low level of general cognitive performance of these students are products of the insufficient development or inefficient use of the cognitive functions that serve as prerequisites of effective thinking and learning. The source of these cognitive deficiencies was seen in the inadequate amount or type of mediated learning experience of the students. IE was thus designed as a remedial and enrichment program that would provide students with mediated learning experience; correct their deficient cognitive functions; teach them the necessary basic concepts, vocabulary, and operations; foster reflective reasoning; and turn these students from passive recipients of information into active learners. IE materials include 14 booklets of paper-and-pencil tasks that cover such areas as analytic perception, comparisons, categorization, orientation in space and time, and syllogisms. These booklets are called *instruments* because they help to "repair" a number of deficient cognitive functions.

As mentioned, the MLE theory served as an explicit theoretical foundation for the development of the IE. The concept of psychological tools and Vygotsky's sociocultural theory were absent in the original theoretical design of this program (Kozulin & Presseisen, 1995). It seems, however, that actually IE materials offer a fruitful synthesis of psychological tools and MLE paradigms. Moreover, the analysis of IE from the perspective of psychological tools may produce a set of principles suitable for the design of new cognitive intervention programs combining the MLE and psychological tools approaches.

The IE program uses materials that are content-free, activities with these materials are process-oriented, and each IE instrument and the IE battery as a whole are systemically organized. The content-free nature of IE materials helps the student to master them as tools directed primarily at his or her own cognitive processes. IE materials incorporate a large number of graphic–symbolic devices such as schematic representations, tables, charts, and graphs. All these devices facilitate the student's transition from direct interaction with material to interaction mediated by symbolic tools. Activities included in the IE program comprise coding and decoding, use of models and formulae, representation of one and the same problem in different modalities, generalization, and classification. All these activities in their essence are directed at appropriation and internalization of psychological tools and ultimately at the development of higher psychological functions dependent on these tools. The emphasis on process rather than product leads to the development of metacognitive awareness and control that are the constituent features of higher psychological functions.

One of the central characteristics of higher psychological functions based on psychological tools is their systemic nature. The IE program actively promotes this systemic organization. IE instruments are designed in a way that induces repeated integration of cognitive functions developed with the help of tasks located in different places within one instrument and within different instruments. The same cognitive principles reappear in different instruments in various modalities. One of the central goals of IE as a cognitive intervention program is to make symbolic psychological tools available to those students who because of their cultural difference, educational deprivation, or other circumstances never acquired these tools. IE provides an "artificial" or vicarious system of cognitive development, which under more favorable conditions unfolds in a "natural" way. When properly applied, the IE program seems to be an effective method for remediation of cognitive functions in culturally different, educationally deprived, and learning-disabled students (Ben-Hur, 1994; Kozulin, 2000).

COGNITIVE EDUCATION: CONTENT-BASED OR CONTENT-NEUTRAL?

Both the sociocultural theory and the MLE theory emphasize that cognition, learning, and instruction should not be considered in isolation. In both theoretical frameworks the development of students' cognitive functions is presented as an important goal of the educational process. Vygotsky (1978) spoke about instruction as a true motor of the child's cognitive development; Feuerstein (1990) emphasized that the instructional process can only be successful if it pays attention to cognitive prerequisites of learning. Both approaches generated applied programs aimed at the integration of the students' cognitive enrichment into the instructional process. These programs, however, differ in their treatment of the relationships between cognitive enrichment and content learning.

The goal of MLE-based educational intervention is to enhance the cognitive modifiability of students. This goal dictated the content-free nature of the IE program (Feuerstein et al., 1980). It was argued that the acquisition of the most basic cognitive functions and strategies, that is, the process of learning how to learn, does not require specific content materials: "When one deals with elementary cognitive functions that have not been established, for whatever reason, in the individual cognitive operations, then the issue of specificity is much less important" (Feuerstein, Hoffman, Egozi, & Ben Shachar, 1994, p. 32). In addition, Feuerstein presented a number of specific reasons for the content-free nature of the IE program. First is the resistance of students who perceive content material as information only and are reluctant to engage in a broader study of cognitive principles that might be embedded into this material. The second reason is the teachers' resistance to spending of time allocated to content material on thinking skills instruction. The third reason is that the content material has its own logic – mathematical, physical, literary, historical, and so on – that does not necessarily coincide with the logic of the enhancement of cognitive functions. Finally, there is the factor of failure previously experienced by students in their confrontation with specific content material. For all these reasons the Instrumental Enrichment program was designed as a content-free cognitive intervention program taught during specially allocated lesson time.

The fact that IE does not have a connection to a specific content area does not mean that it has no content. Tasks used in this program require some basic content knowledge, such as that of geometric figures. When students display the lack of particular knowledge necessary for the work with the program material, they obtain this knowledge during the IE lessons. This knowledge, however, is presented as a means rather than a goal. Mathematical, geographic, or linguistic information and rules are supplied with the general cognitive rather than specific disciplinary goal in mind. Once the general cognitive principles and strategies are developed during the IE lessons, they are bridged (i.e., transferred) to content subjects. The amount and quality of this bridging depend on the teacher's skill and initiative. Since the IE is primarily a cognitive enhancement program, its effectiveness was evaluated predominantly through cognitive measures. In this respect it seems to be quite effective in enhancing the students' problemsolving skills, especially as measured by nonverbal tests (Savell, Twohig, & Rachford, 1986; Kozulin, 2000). As to the effect of bridging to school subjects the results are not always consistent or easy to interpret. For example, Jensen (1990) pointed out that as scissors have two blades effective functioning requires both good cognitive skills and a knowledge base on which they can be applied. In the case of Jensen's study the IE was supposed to be taught as an adjunct to a strong academic curriculum so that the bridging could be done from the cognitive principles to rich content material. In reality, however, teachers participating in the program had little opportunity of offering any substantial and coherent body of academic knowledge to the target group of disadvantaged minority students. As a result the changes in the students' cognitive functioning had little repercussion in their content subject learning.

The attitude of sociocultural theory toward content learning is quite different. For Vygotsky (1986) content learning can be associated with two different conceptual processes: the formation of spontaneous, empirical concepts or the development of scientific concepts (see Karpov, this volume). The acquisition of everyday concepts does not add much to the student's cognitive development because these concepts are based on already existent cognitive mechanisms and just add empirically rich experience. Of course, sometimes the child's cognitive skills can be insufficient even for spontaneous concepts; in this case, cognitive intervention programs like IE may become quite useful. Vygotsky, however, was much more concerned with the necessity to lead the child beyond empirically rich but unsystematic and often contradictory spontaneous concepts into the realm of scholarly conceptualization that corresponds to systematic reasoning characteristic of sciences and humanities. Within this realm there is no opposition between cognitive mechanisms and content knowledge for the simple reason that content appears here in a conceptual form that defines not only the content but also the type of reasoning involved. Because sociocultural theory emphasizes the historical character of human cognition, the conceptual structure of disciplinary knowledge appears here as a veritable form of human thinking. In other words, there is no such entity as a pure thought applied at times to physical problems and at times to linguistic problems. The forms of reasoning in physics and in linguistics constitute the true forms of human thought corresponding to historically specific sociocultural activities such as physical or linguistic inquiry. Properly organized content learning would generate many of the general cognitive strategies that serve as a focus of cognitive education programs (cf. Fischer, 1990). The development of students' cognition is thus viewed in the sociocultural theory as an integral element of conceptual content learning.

This general paradigm was realized in a number of instructional programs (Davydov, 1988; Lompscher, 1984; Karpov & Bransford, 1995). The pivotal point of these programs lies in the formation of learning activity. The neo-Vygotskian theory distinguishes specially designed learning activity from learning in a generic sense. Learning in a generic sense is a part of many human activities, such as play, practical activity, and interpersonal interactions. Although an important component of these activities, learning, however, does not constitute their goal. What distinguishes learning as a special kind of activity is its focus on changes produced in the learner. The goal of learning activity is to make the individual a competent learner (see Zuckerman, this volume).

The formation of the prerequisites for learning activities should start as early as the kindergarten period:

Learning activity presupposes the development of theoretical thinking, the basis of which is a system of scientific concepts. For five year old children, however, logical–conceptual forms of cognition are not nearly as typical as visual–imaginative ones. Accordingly, at this age it is not yet a learning activity as such that should be developed, but rather its prerequisites. The most adequate foundation for the subsequent mastering of the system of scientific concepts is the generalized schematic notions which visually reflect the essential links and relationships of the concepts to be mastered. (Venger & Gorbov, 1993, p. 3).

One may notice a certain similarity between the emphasis on learning prerequisites in the Vygotskian regular preschool programs and Feuerstein's compensatory school-age programs. This similarity is not accidental, for the simple reason that one of the goals of Feuerstein's IE is to form in older children those functions that more advantaged children acquire at an earlier age. Thus IE in its compensatory function is similar to the development-generating function of Vygotskian preschool and first-grade programs.

Once the learning prerequisites are formed, the learning activity model can be fully implemented. This model dictates changes both in the learning material and in the classroom activities. The unit of learning material is no longer a separate mathematical problem or reading exercise, but a learning task that reflects the general principle of the formation or transformation of the subject matter of learning. The generality of such principles makes them similar to the tasks used in cognitive education programs, but they remain firmly linked to the disciplinary area. The classroom activity is also no longer a vehicle for simply conveying information from the teacher to students and back, but a means for actively constructing the students' theoretical understanding. The constructive nature of students' activities links the work of neo-Vygotskians with the constructivist paradigm in science teaching (Hatano, 1993). It should be remembered, however, that for neo-Vygotskians the construction of conceptual knowledge in students always appears as a guided construction, rather than independent exploration.

The insistence on theoretical rather than empirical understanding constitutes a distinctive feature of the neo-Vygotskian theory of content learning (Davydov, 1988; Hedegaard, 1990; Karpov & Bransford, 1995; see also Kozulin, 1990, chapter 7). Neo-Vygotskians argued that in empirical learning an essential distinction between everyday life experiences and scientific concepts is obliterated and the students fail to appreciate the distinctive logic of scientific inquiry. This view seems to be supported by the studies on science learning conducted from perspectives other than Vygotskian. Research on conceptual change indicated that the students' appreciation of the specificity of scientific approach and scientific language as distinct from the everyday one constitutes one of the major factors contributing to the acquisition of scientific concepts (Duit & Treagust, 1998).

The principles of theoretical learning were successfully applied in the primary and middle school instruction of mathematics, reading, science, and other subjects (Davydov, 1988; Davydov & Tzvetkovich, 1991; Hedegaard, 1990; Lompscher, 1984, 1997). The major result achieved by this approach was the formation in students of a generalized method of problem solving that transcended the external appearance of the individual problems. Students also learned such general forms of learning activity as creation and use of models, systematic manipulation with variables, identification of problems and separation of known and unknown, and metacognitive reflection strategies. Lompscher (1997) argued that these general features of theoretical learning cannot be achieved in a "pure form" without domain-specific instruction. All these features are in essence the outcomes of the well-organized learning activity that cannot be content-free. As long as content subjects retain their sociocultural meaning, the learning activity focused on them will retain its importance as a mechanism of cognitive enhancement.

CONCLUSION

Let us now review some of the lessons that can be derived from the encounter between the current educational problems and Vygotsky's theory.

The first lesson is that the process of learning is both individual and sociocultural, thus the importance of understanding not just individual but also social and cultural dimensions of the learning situation that are conceptualized by Vygotsky through the notions of psychological tools and mediation.

The second lesson is that neither of the notions mentioned is capable of shaping the situation of learning in isolation from the other. Symbolic tools have a rich educational potential, but they remain ineffective if there is no human mediator to facilitate their appropriation by the learner. By the same token, human mediation that does involve sophisticated symbolic tools would not help the learner to master more complex forms of reasoning and problem solving.

Thus, the third lesson is that cognitive education programs should be built as a combination of a system of symbolic tools with the didactic approaches based on the principles of mediated learning.

The fourth lesson is that such issues as the universality, sociocultural specificity, type, and technique of human mediation require further systematic investigation because our understanding of them is still very episodic.

The fifth lesson is that a boundary should be found between the basic cognitive functions that serve as a basis for any learning activity and the more specialized cognitive functions associated with conceptual learning in specific curricular areas. Apparently these basic functions become incorporated and transformed within the new conceptual system. The exploration of the process of such incorporation may lead us to a better design of content learning programs that include cognitive elements.

References

Ben-Hur, M. (Ed.) (1994). *On Feuerstein's instrumental enrichment.* Palatine, IL: IRI/Skylight.
Bliss, J., Askew, M., & Macrae, S. (1996). Effective teaching and learning: Scaffolding revisited. *Oxford Review of Education, 22*(1), 37–61.
Brown, A., & Ferrara, R. (1985). Diagnosing zones of proximal development. In J. Wertsch (Ed.), *Culture, communication, and cognition: Vygotskian perspectives* (pp. 273–305). New York: Cambridge University Press.
Davydov, V. V. (1988). Problems of developmental teaching. *Soviet Education, 30*(8), 15–97; *30*(9), 3–83; *30*(10), 3–77.

Davydov, V. V., & Tzvetkovich, Z. (1991). On the objective origin of the concept of fractions. *Focus on Learning Problems in Mathematics*, 3(1), 13–64.

DeLoach, J. (1995). Early understanding and use of symbols. *Current Directions in Psychological Science*, 4, 109–113.

Duit, R., & Treagust, D. (1998). Learning in science – from behaviorism toward social constructivism and beyond. In B. Fraser & K. Tobin (Eds.), *International Handbook of Science Education*, (pp. 3–25). Dordrecht: Kluwer.

Feuerstein, R. (1990). The theory of structural cognitive modifiability. In B. Presseisen (Ed.), *Learning and thinking styles: Classroom applications* (pp. 68–134). Washington, DC: National Education Association.

Feuerstein, R., Hoffman, M., Egozi, M., & Ben Shachar, N. (1994). Intervention programs for low performers. In M. Ben-Hur (Ed.), *On Feuerstein's Instrumental Enrichment* (pp. 3–50). Palatine, IL: IRI/Skylight.

Feuerstein, R., Krasilovsky, D., & Rand, Y. (1978). Modifiability during adolescence. In J. Anthony (Ed.), *The child and his family: Children and their parents in a changing world* (pp. 197–217). London: Wiley.

Feuerstein, R., Rand, Y., Hoffman, M., & Miller, R. (1979). *Dynamic assessment of retarded performer.* Baltimore, MD: University Park Press.

Feuerstein, R., Rand, Y., Hoffman, M., & Miller, R. (1980). *Instrumental Enrichment.* Baltimore, MD: University Park Press.

Fischer, R. (1990). *Teaching children to think.* Oxford: Basil Blackwell.

Hatano, G. (1993). Time to merge Vygotskian and constructivist conceptions of knowledge acquisition. In E. Forman, N. Minick, & C. Addison Stone (Eds.), *Contexts for learning* (pp. 153–166). New York: Oxford University Press.

Heath, S. B. (1983). *Ways with words.* Cambridge: Cambridge University Press.

Hedegaard, M. (1990). The zone of proximal development as a basis for instruction. In L. Moll (Ed.), *Vygotsky and education* (pp. 349–371). New York: Cambridge University Press.

Jensen, M. (1990). Change models and some evidence for phases and their plasticity in cognitive structures. *International Journal of Cognitive Education and Mediated Learning*, 1, 5–16.

Karpov, Y., & Bransford, J. (1995). Vygotsky and the doctrine of empirical and theoretical learning. *Educational Psychologist*, 30(2), 61–66.

Klein, P. (1988). Stability and change in interaction of Israeli mothers and infants. *Infant Behavior and Development*, 11, 55–70.

Kozulin, A. (1990). *Vygotsky's psychology: A biography of ideas.* Cambridge, MA: Harvard University Press.

Kozulin, A. (1998). *Psychological tools: A sociocultural approach to education.* Cambridge, MA: Harvard University Press.

Kozulin, A. (2000). Diversity of instrumental enrichment applications. In A. Kozulin and Y. Rand (Eds.), *Experience of mediated learning* (pp. 257–273). Oxford: Pergamon.

Kozulin, A., & Garb, E. (2002). Dynamic assessment of EFL text comprehension. *School Psychology International*, 23, 112–127.

Kozulin, A., & Lurie, L. (1994). Psychological tools and mediated learning: Cross-cultural aspects. Paper presented at the International Congress of Cross-Cultural Psychology, Pamplona, Spain.

Kozulin, A., & Presseisen, B. (1995). Mediated learning experience and psychological tools. *Educational Psychologist*, 30(2), 67–76.

Lehrer, R., & Shumow, L. (1997). Aligning the construction zones of parents and teachers for math reform. *Cognition and Instruction*, 15(1), 41–83.

Lidz, C. (1987). *Dynamic assessment*. New York: Guilford Press.

Lidz, C. (1991). *Practitioners guide to dynamic assessment*. New York: Guilford Press.

Lompscher, J. (1984). Problems and results of experimental research on the formation of theoretical thinking through instruction. In M. Hedegaard, P. Hakkarainen, & Y. Engestrom (Eds.), *Learning and teaching on scientific basis* (pp. 293–358). Aarus: Aarus University.

Lompscher, J. (1997). General effects without domain-specific effects? Paper presented at the 7th European Conference for Research on Learning and Instruction, Athens, Greece.

Luria, A. (1976). *Cognitive development*. Cambridge, MA: Harvard University Press.

Olson, D. (1994). *World on paper*. New York: Cambridge University Press.

Palinscar, A., & Brown, A. L. (1984). Reciprocal teaching of comprehension – fostering and monitoring activities. *Cognition and Instruction*, 1, 117–175.

Portes, P. (1991). Assessing children's cognitive environment through parent-child interactions. *Journal of Research and Development in Education*, 24, 30–37.

Rogoff, B. (1990). *Apprenticeship in thinking*. Oxford: Oxford University Press.

Rogoff, B. (1995). Observing sociocultural activity on three planes. In J. Wertsch, P. Del Rio, & A. Alvarez (Eds.), *Sociocultural studies of mind* (pp. 139–164). New York: Cambridge University Press.

Savell, J., Twohig, P., & Rachford, D. (1986). Empirical status of Feuerstein's Instrumental Enrichment. *Review of Educational Research*, 56, 381–409.

Schaffer, R. (1996). Joint involvement episodes as context for development. In H. Daniels (Ed.), *An Introduction to Vygotsky* (pp. 251–280). London: Routledge.

Scribner, S. (1997). *Mind and social practice*. New York: Cambridge University Press.

Scribner, S., & Cole, M. (1981). *Psychology of literacy*. Cambridge, MA: Harvard University Press.

Sfard, A. (1998). On two metaphors. *Educational Researcher*, 27, 4–13.

Shumow, L. (1998). Promoting parental attunement to children's math reasoning through parent education. *Journal of Applied Developmental Psychology*, 19(1), 109–127.

Sternberg, R., & Grigorenko, Y. (2002). *Dynamic testing*. New York: Cambridge University Press.

Tharp, R., & Gallimore, R. (1988). *Rousing minds to life*. New York: Cambridge University Press.

Tzuriel, D. (1996). Mediated learning experience in free-play versus structured situations among preschool children of low-, medium-, and high-SES. *Child Development and Care*, 126, 57–82.

Tzuriel, D. (1997). The relation between parent-child MLE interactions and children's cognitive modifiability. In A. Kozulin (Ed.), *The Ontogeny of cognitive modifiability* (pp. 157–180). Jerusalem: ICELP.

Venger, A., & Gorbov, S. (1993). Psychological foundations for the introductory course of mathematics for six year olds. *Focus on Learning Problems in Mathematics*, 15(1), 2–13.

Vygotsky, L. (1978). *Mind in society*. Cambridge, MA: Harvard University Press.

Vygotsky, L. (1986). *Thought and language* (rev. ed). Cambridge, MA: Harvard University Press.

Vygotsky, L. (1997). The history of the development of higher mental functions. In *The collected works of L. S. Vygotsky* (Vol. 4). New York: Plenum.

Vygotsky, L., & Luria, A. (1930/1993). *Studies on the history of behavior.* Hillsdale, NJ: Lawrence Erlbaum Associates.

Wagner, D., Messic, B., & Spratt, J. (1986). Studying literacy in Morocco. In B. Shieffelin, & P. Gilmore (Eds.), *The acquisition of literacy: Ethnographic perspectives* (pp. 233–260). Norwood, NJ: Ablex.

Wallace, B., Pandaram, S., & Modiroa, T. (1996). *Language in my world.* Kenvyn, South Africa: Juta Publishers.

Wertsch, J., & Stone, A. (1985). The concept of internalization in Vygotsky's account of the genesis of higher mental functions. In J. Wertsch (Ed.), *Culture, communication, and cognition: Vygotskian perspectives* (pp. 162–179). New York: Cambridge University Press.

Wood, D. (1999). Teaching the young child: Some relationships between social interaction, language, and thought. In P. Lloyd and C. Fernyhough (Eds.), *Lev Vygotsky: Critical assessments,* (vol. 3, pp. 259–275). London: Routledge.

2

The Zone of Proximal Development in Vygotsky's Analysis of Learning and Instruction

Seth Chaiklin

What kind of instruction is optimal for a particular child? Without doubt, this question is immediately comprehensible to any committed teacher in virtually any country in the world, and most teachers are likely to want concrete answers to the question, not only as a theoretical puzzle, but in relation to their immediate practices. If one were to look to scientific psychology and educational research for advice in relation to this practical problem, what would the answer(s) look like?

This simple question raises several profound problems. Normative and political issues about the goals of instruction and the resources available for realizing these goals must be resolved. A theory of learning that can explain how intellectual capabilities are developed is needed. If instruction is not viewed as an end in itself, then a theory about the relationship between specific subject matter instruction and its consequences for psychological development is also needed. This last problem was the main tension against which Vygotsky developed his well-known concept of *zone of proximal development*, so that the zone focused on the relation between instruction and development, while being relevant to many of these other problems. Vygotsky's concept of zone of proximal development is more precise and elaborated than its common reception or interpretation. The main purpose of this chapter is to provide a comprehensive introduction to and interpretation of this concept, along with comments about predominant contemporary interpretations. The chapter concludes with some perspectives and implications derived from the interpretation presented here.

Thanks to Jacob Klitmøller and Svend Brinkmann for their critical dialogue about the initial formulation of the analysis presented here, to Bert van Oers for his convincing me of the need to consider the issue of imitation more explicitly, and to Ray McDermott for subjective editing of the final version.

LOCATING THE ZONE OF PROXIMAL DEVELOPMENT

The term *zone of proximal development* is probably one of the most widely recognized and well-known ideas associated with Vygotsky's scientific production. The term now appears in most developmental and educational psychology textbooks, as well as some general psychology books. Within educational research, the concept is now used widely (or referred to) in studies about teaching and learning in many subject-matter areas, including reading, writing, mathematics, science, second-language learning (e.g., Dunn & Lantolf, 1998; Lantolf & Pavlenko, 1995), moral education (e.g., Tappan, 1998), and violin teaching (Gholson, 1998); with diverse kinds of pupils, including so-called disadvantaged, learning-disabled, retarded, and gifted students; with preschool children (e.g., Smith, 1993) and with adults (e.g., Kilgore, 1999); with information technologies and computer-mediated communication (e.g., Hung, 2001); with children's use of libraries (McKechnie, 1997); with discussions about teacher training (e.g., Jones, Rua, & Carter, 1998; Torres, 1996) and about nursing education (e.g., Spouse, 1998). The concept has also been picked up and used in serious and substantive ways in other academic disciplines and professional areas, including nursing (e.g., Holaday, LaMontagne, & Marciel, 1994), psychoanalysis (e.g., Wilson & Weinstein, 1996), psychotherapy (e.g., Leiman & Stiles, 2001), and occupational therapy (e.g., Exner, 1990; Lyons, 1984).

Although the term was already available in the 1962 translation of *Thought and Language,* it was primarily the appearance of chapter 6 in *Mind in Society* (1978) that marked a transition to sustained attention to the concept by an English-reading audience. At this moment in history, the concept, at least in a somewhat simplified form, is reasonably well known among educationally oriented researchers. Therefore, most readers of this chapter will have already encountered some or all of the standard phrases often used to explicate or define the concept, especially the definition from the aforementioned chapter: "*the distance between the actual developmental level as determined by independent problem solving and the level of potential development as determined through problem solving under adult guidance or in collaboration with more capable peers*" (Vygotsky, 1978, p. 86, emphasis in the original) or "what the child is able to do in collaboration today he will be able to do independently tomorrow" (Vygotsky, 1987, p. 211; see also, 1998b, p. 202).

Popularity has its price, however. Wertsch (1984) suggested that if this theoretical construct was not elaborated further, then there is a risk that "it will be used loosely and indiscriminately, thereby becoming so amorphous that it loses all explanatory power" (p. 7). Mercer and Fisher (1992) believe that "there is a danger that the term is used as little more than a fashionable alternative to Piagetian terminology or the concept of IQ for describing individual differences in attainment or potential" (p. 342). Palinscar (1998) suggests that in the context of research about the negotiated nature of teaching and learning it is "probably one of the most used and least understood constructs to appear in contemporary educational literature" (p. 370).

Just what does that famous phrase from page 86 mean? One rarely encounters other sources cited or discussed in relation to zone of proximal development beyond this 1978 text, with an occasional supplement from *Thinking and Speech* (1987). Is this the only or main definition? Is current knowledge about the zone of proximal development mostly reflective of attempts to interpret these textual fragments, possibly supplemented with a little general knowledge of Vygotsky's approach? Unless additional texts are considered, is there any reason to believe that one scholar has a better interpretation of those words than another?

Common Conceptions of the Zone of Proximal Development

The common conception of the zone of proximal development presupposes an interaction on a task between a more competent person and a less competent person, such that the less competent person becomes independently proficient at what was initially a jointly accomplished task. Within this general conception, three main aspects are often highlighted or emphasized (though not necessarily all three by a single researcher). For the sake of discussion, these three aspects together represent an 'ideal type' that will be called the *common interpretation* of the zone of proximal development. For ease of reference, the three aspects will be named *generality assumption* (i.e., applicable to learning all kinds of subject matter), *assistance assumption* (learning is dependent on interventions by a more competent other), and *potential assumption* (property of the learner that permits the best and easiest learning).

The first aspect focuses on the idea that a person is able to perform a certain number of tasks alone but in collaboration can perform a greater number of tasks. The "range of tasks" performed in collaboration is sometimes presented as the definition of zone of proximal development (e.g., Berk, 1997, p. 248), but this is surely mistaken. Even the classic definition refers to levels of development, not tasks. At best, the number (or kinds) of tasks must be taken as indicators to be interpreted in relation to a level of development. A related issue is what kinds of tasks involve a zone of proximal development. It is often assumed that the zone of proximal development is meant to be applied to any kind of learning task. "For any domain of skill, a ZPD can be created" (Tharp & Gallimore, 1998, p. 96), or in an "expanded" conception formulated by Wells (1999), zone of proximal development applies to "any situation in which, while participating in an activity, individuals are in the process of developing mastery of a practice or understanding a topic" (p. 333).

The second aspect emphasizes how an adult/teacher/more competent person should interact with a child. Sometimes this aspect is presented as the defining characteristic. "Arguably, the notion of the zone of proximal development is little more meaningful than that of a learning situation presented to a child, where adults and/or more advanced children directly or indirectly have a positive influence on the child" (Gillen, 2000, pp. 193–194).

The third aspect focuses on "properties of the learner," including notions of a learner's potential and/or readiness to learn. This aspect often seems to inspire the idea or expectation that it will be possible to accelerate greatly or facilitate a child's learning, if the zone can be identified properly. Here are two illustrations from recent textbook discussions: "It is within this zone that a person's potential for new learning is strongest" (Fabes & Martin, 2001, p. 42) or "Vygotsky's phrase for the individual's current potential for further intellectual development, a capacity not ordinarily measured by conventional intelligence tests" (LeFrancois, 2001, p. 587). Sometimes this aspect is interpreted to mean that teaching in the zone of proximal development should result in the easiest or most effortless form of learning for the child (e.g., "a student's zone of proximal development is the range of book readability levels that will challenge a student without causing frustration or loss of motivation," 1998 abstract in ERIC database).

Critique of the Common Conception

The common conception of the zone of proximal development supports or inspires a vision of educational perfection, in which the insightful (or lucky) teacher is able to help a child master, effortlessly and joyfully, whatever subject matter is on the day's program. With this kind of conception, a reader is likely to expect that a chapter about the zone of proximal development and instruction will explain (a) how to identify a child's zone of proximal development for each learning task, (b) how to teach in a way that will be sure to engage the zone of proximal development, which (c) in a smooth and joyful way will significantly accelerate learning. There are, however, some problems for this perfect vision.

Generality Assumption

If Vygotsky's intention was to use the concept for all kinds of learning, then why not name it the *zone of proximal learning*? Why does the term *development* appear in the concept? The use of the term is not coincidental. In several texts, Vygotsky analyzed how the relationship between learning and development was formulated within existing psychological traditions (1987, pp. 194–201; 1935b, see van der Veer & Valsiner, 1991, pp. 329–331 for a summary; 1935d, 1982b), concluding that there is a unity but not an identity between learning and inner developmental processes (Vygotsky, 1982d, p. 123). Vygotsky (1987) distinguishes instruction aimed "toward [the child's] full development from instruction in specialized, technical skills such as typing or riding a bicycle" (p. 212). In short, zone of proximal development is not concerned with the development of skill of any particular task, but must be related to development.

Assistance Assumption

Because a competent teacher is important for learning, the zone of proximal development notion is often used to focus on the importance of more competent assistance. However, when Vygotsky first introduces the zone of proximal development in *Thinking and Speech*, he considers it a well-known fact that "with collaboration, direction, or some kind of help the child is always able to do more and solve more difficult tasks that [*sic*] he can independently" (Vygotsky, 1987, p. 209). More important, in his view, is to explain why this happens. In other words, it is not the competence per se of the more knowledgeable person that is important; rather, it is to understand the meaning of that assistance in relation to a child's learning and development.

Potential Assumption

Vygotsky never assumed that learning related to the zone of proximal development is always enjoyable. He (1967, p. 16) gives an example: A child running a race may not be having pleasure, especially after losing, yet still this action can be part of the zone of proximal development. Similarly, as will be developed later, the potential is not a property of the child – as these formulations are sometimes interpreted – but simply an indication of the presence of certain maturing functions, which can be a target for meaningful, interventive action.

The preceding analysis is meant to raise doubts about common interpretations of Vygotsky's concept of zone of proximal development and justify the need to consider more concretely what Vygotsky meant by the concept. There are at least eight published texts in which Vygotsky used the expression *zone of proximal development* at least once (see Table 2.1 for a list of these texts, together with some of the published translations). Most of these texts have only brief comments about the concept; more extensive discussion is found in chapter 6 of *Thinking and Speech* and the chapter "Problem of Age." In other words, there is not an extensive corpus of material from which Vygotsky's true meaning, or official definition, or interpretation can be found (but see the bibliography in Rieber, 1999; it is likely that some of the unpublished, currently unavailable texts from 1933 and 1934 also discussed this concept). One could read most of the material listed in Table 2.1 in a few hours, especially because several of the texts have considerable overlap in their content. From that point of view, it should be easy to become an "expert" in Vygotsky's concept, with no need for an interpretative discussion.

TABLE 2.1. *Overview of Vygotsky's published texts in which the concept of* zone of proximal development *is discussed*

Date	Title	Event	Published Source
1933[1]	Play and its role in the mental development of the child	Stenographic transcript of lecture at A. I. Herzen Leningrad Pedagogical Institute	Vygotsky, 1966 Vygotsky, 1967 Vygotskij, 1982a Vygotskij, 1983a
March 17, 1933	The pedalogical analysis of the pedagogical process	Stenographic transcript of lecture at Epshtein Experimental Defectological Institute, Moscow	Vygotsky, 1935b (Summarized in van der Veer & Valsiner, 1991, pp. 329–331)
May 20, 1933	Development of everyday and scientific concepts in school children	Lecture at the scientific– methodological council, Leningrad Pedological Institute	Vygotsky, 1935e Vygotskij, 1982c
December 23, 1933	Dynamics of mental development of schoolchildren in connection with teaching	Stenographic transcript of lecture at Dept. of Defectology, Bubnov Pedagogical Institute, Leningrad	Vygotsky, 1935a (Detailed summary in van der Veer & Valsiner, 1991, pp. 336–341).
1934[2]	The problem of teaching and development during the school age	Manuscript	Vygotsky, 1935d Vygotskij, 1973b Vygotskij, 1982b Vygotskij, 1983b Vygotsky, 1985
1934	Teaching and development during the preschool age	Stenographic transcript of lecture at the All-Russian Conference on Preschool Education	Vygotsky, 1935c Vygotskij, 1973a Vygotskij, 1982d Wygotski, 1987b Vygotsky, 1995

Date	Title	Event	Published Source
1934[3]	The problem of age	Book chapter manuscript	Vygotsky, 1998 Wygotsky, 1987a
1934	*Thinking and speech* (Chapter 6: The development of scientific concepts)	Book chapter	Vygotsky, 1987

[1] This lecture is placed here because (a) it has a minimal discussion of ZPD, while (b) a 23 March lecture has the title "Problem of age: Play"; (c) was labeled "Concluding address to the seminar"; and (d) a lecture on the pedology of the preschool age was given on January 31 at same institute.

[2] Edited (shortened) version was published in Vygotsky (1956), and in translation Vygotski (1963), Wygotski (1987c).

[3] This text is listed in the *Collected Works* as being a stenographic record of a lecture from March 23, 1933 (Reiber, 1999, p. 297). This is a mistake. As noted in Vygotsky (1998, p. 329), this text is from a written chapter in the family archives. Valsiner and van der Veer (1993, p. 40), relying on the information reported in the *Collected Works,* reproduce this mistake.

It will be more productive, however, to focus on the conceptual problems that Vygotsky was trying to address when the zone of proximal development was introduced. The main interest then is to present an interpretation that can be more fully integrated with other theoretical concepts and arguments that Vygotsky was developing in relation to the zone of proximal development. Given that Vygotsky was the source of the arguments that are identified today as *zone of proximal development*, it seems worthwhile to allow his version to be presented from his own theoretical perspective, rather than filtering or refracting it through the lens of contemporary concerns and positions (Cazden, 1996, has a similar argument in relation to Vygotskian-inspired research on writing). This more comprehensive interpretation of Vygotsky's research program is not given here simply as a historical curiosity; the theoretical model deserves further investigation, criticism, and elaboration. As a first step, however, we should make sure to have a reasonable understanding of how the theoretical analysis is constructed and what it is trying to achieve.

ZONE OF PROXIMAL DEVELOPMENT IN VYGOTSKY'S THEORETICAL PERSPECTIVE

The zone of proximal development was introduced as a part of a general analysis of child development. It is not a main or central concept in Vygotsky's (1998b) theory of child development. Rather, its role is to point to an important place and moment in the process of child development. To understand this role, one must appreciate the theoretical perspective in which it appeared. That is, we need to understand what Vygotsky meant by *development* in general, if we are going to understand what he meant by *zone of proximal development* in particular. In this way, the reader can develop a generative understanding of the theoretical approach, which will be more valuable than a dictionary definition of the concept.

Vygotsky's Theory of Child Development

Vygotsky formulated several requirements or criteria that should be satisfied by a model of child development. First, the model must be explanatory, rather than descriptive. More specifically, the model should be organized by substantial principles that can explain development "as a single process of self-development" (Vygotsky, 1998b, p. 189). Second, the model should consider the *whole child*, as an integral person. Third, childhood should be divided into periods, such that each period is characterized in a principled and unified way. That is, the same abstract explanatory principles should be used to characterize each period (hence the unity), but the concrete manifestation of the abstract relations must be discovered and characterized for the particular content of each age period.

To meet these requirements, Vygotsky proposed that each period of childhood be characterized abstractly by a psychological structure, a set of integral relations among psychological functions (e.g., perception, voluntary memory, speech, thinking). This structure should reflect the whole child (i.e., as a person engaged in structured social relations with others) – not only as a description of the qualities of the child, but also as a description of the child's relationship to her environment. From a psychological point of view, this whole is described as an integrated structure of relationships among developed and developing higher psychological functions acquired through material interaction. This psychological description of a child focuses on interrelationships between functions, rather than considering individual psychological functions in isolation. For example, 2-year-old children tend to be directed more by reactions to what they can immediately perceive than by their willful formation of an imagined possibility (i.e., a thought). In this case, the functions of perception, thought, and will stand in a particular relation to each other, such that perception is dominant in relation to will and thought (Vygotsky, 1982d, p. 104). The psychological structure refers to the structural relationships among a set of psychological functions.

The focus on the whole precludes a methodological approach that considers specific functions without considering their relation to the whole. In this way, Vygotsky can realize his goal of "understanding development as a process that is characterized by a unity of material and mental aspects, a unity of the social and the personal during the child's ascent up the stages of development" (p. 190). These two unities (material–mental and social–personal) are alternative ways of expressing the same idea, and they are both unities because the child's psychological structure (i.e., the mental, the personal) is always reflecting a relation to the social and material. Vygotsky proposed to describe the development of children, from infancy to adolescence, as a series of relatively long stable periods (1 to 4 years), punctuated by shorter periods of crisis (see Mahn, this volume, for a comprehensive account of Vygotsky's model of age periods; also see Davydov, 1988, pp. 63–87). To explain the causal-dynamic of this development, one has to give an account of how and why there is a qualitative change in the psychological structure that is characteristic for each age period. The starting point for Vygotsky's explanation is the child's specific, but comprehensive, relationship to its environment, designated as the *social situation of development*. "The social situation of development represents the initial moment for all dynamic changes that occur in development during the given period"; therefore, to study the dynamics of any age, one must first explain the social situation of development (Vygotsky, 1998b, p. 198).

Each age period has a characteristic central *new-formation* in relation to which psychological functions develop (Vygotsky, 1998b, p. 197). This new-formation is organized in the social situation of development by a basic contradiction between the child's current capabilities (as manifested in the actually developed psychological functions), the child's needs and desires, and the demands and possibilities of the environment. In trying to overcome this contradiction (so that it can realize its activity), the child engages in different concrete tasks and specific interactions, which can result in the formation of new functions or the enrichment of existing functions. The central new-formation produced for a given age period is a consequence of the child's interactions in the social situation of development with relevant psychological functions that are not yet mature. (For a concrete analysis for the infant age period, cf. Vygotsky, 1998a, especially pp. 215–216; for a useful and related elaboration of Vygotsky's conception of development, cf. Schneuwly, 1994, pp. 282–284.)

Many (even most) of the child's specific actions in daily life do not need to be oriented to confronting this contradiction (sometimes called the *predominant activity*). However, the functions needed for a transition to a new age period (i.e., a structural change in the organization of functions) are formed and elaborated (in relation to the central new-formation) in those situations in which the child engages specifically in actions relevant to this contradiction. Each period has a leading activity that is the main source of development within a period (Vygotsky, 1967, pp. 15–16). The notion of "leading activity" is a way to identify the particular relations in the social situation of development that are likely to contribute to the development of the functions that lead to the structural reorganization of a child's psychological functions. (This general idea has been subsequently connected to the theory of activity and developed in more detail, e.g., El'konin, 1999.) The activity itself is not developing the child; rather, in order to realize the leading activity, the child engages in actions that serve to develop the psychological functions needed for that activity. The new-formation is a product, not a prerequisite, of an age period (Vygotsky, 1998b, p. 198).

It is important to recognize that these age periods are understood as historically and materially constructed – historically because the functions are constructed through the history of human practices, materially because the functions are developed as a consequence of tasks and interactions with others. The social situation of development provides a way to characterize the interaction between historically constructed forms of practice and the child's interests and actions (which reflect the current age period of the child). Rather than being a passive recipient of an objective environment, the child is selective about what is perceived and interesting. This relation changes with each specific age period, reflecting the structure of the psychological functions for that age. (See Lampert Shepel, 1995, pp. 429–431, for a related view.)

Changes in historical relations would incline a researcher to predict changes in psychological functions (see Bodrova and Leong, this volume, for a discussion of this question in relation to early childhood). It is important to recognize that these periods are not reflecting a biological necessity (because of genetic or other organic sources), even though the development of higher psychological functions (e.g., perception, voluntary memory, speech, thinking) is dependent on these natural conditions. When Vygotsky writes about "age," then it is understood as reflecting a psychological category and not only a temporal characteristic. Thus, in the statement "the actual level of development is determined by that age, that stage or phase within a given age that the child is experiencing at that time" (Vygotsky, 1998b, p. 199), one can understand "within a given age" to refer to the period of development. Similarly, none of the psychological functions is "pure" in the sense of a biologically given module or faculty. Rather they were formed, both historically in the phylogenetic development of human societies and individually in the ontogenetic development of persons within these societies.

The Zone of Proximal Development in Vygotsky's Theory of Child Development

We can now use this model of child development, as Vygotsky did, to introduce the idea of zone of proximal development. The zone of proximal development is used for two different purposes in the analysis of psychological development (i.e., transition from one age period to another). One purpose is to identify the kinds of maturing psychological functions (and the social interactions associated with them) needed for transition from one age period to the next. The other is to identify the child's current state in relation to developing these functions needed for that transition. Let us consider each use in turn.

For each age period, there are a group of psychological functions that are maturing in relation to the central new-formation and that will lead to the restructuring of the existing functions to the formation of a new structure. This new-formation results in a transition to the next age period. For clarity of reference, I will designate this tripartite constellation of present age, maturing functions, and next age as the *objective* zone of proximal development. This zone is 'objective' in the sense that it does not refer to any individual child but reflects the psychological functions that need to be formed during a given age period in order for the next age period to be formed.

The objective zone is not defined a priori but reflects the structural relationships that are historically constructed and objectively constituted in the historical period in which the child lives. One can say that the zone for a given age period is normative, in that it reflects the institutionalized demands and expectations that developed historically in a particular societal tradition of practice. For example, school-age children are expected to develop capabilities to reason with academic (i.e., scientific) concepts. Individuals who do not develop this capability can be said to have an intellectual structure different from that of most school-age children. Reasoning with concepts is a specific manifestation of the new-formations for this age, which Vygotsky suggests are *conscious awareness and volition*.[1]

All the major new mental functions that actively participate in school instruction are associated with the important new formations of this age, that is, with conscious awareness and volition. These are the features that distinguish all the higher mental functions that develop during this period. (Vygotsky, 1987, p. 213)

With different objective conditions (e.g., the lives of children working in English factories during the 19th century; see Marx 1990, chap. 10, sect. 3–6), the social situation of development would be different; thus one would need to characterize a different objective zone of proximal development for a given age period.

For a given objective zone of proximal development, it is possible to (attempt to) assess the current state of an individual child's development (in relation to the objective zone). According to Vygotsky's theory, the maturing functions are the source of changes in the internal structure of a

---

[1] The specific new functions for a given age (in this case, conscious awareness and volition) may be open to debate and analysis. For present purposes, we are concentrating on the conceptual from of Vygotsky's argument, and not whether the particular substantive claim in this case can be justified.

given age period. Assessment procedures should be aimed at identifying the current status of these maturing functions. Because these functions are inadequate for independent performance, it is necessary to identify them through dynamic, interactive procedures that provide indications for estimating the extent of their development (see Lidz and Gindis, this volume, for an extensive discussion of such procedures). This estimate can be understood in relative terms – that is, the current state of the maturing functions relative to the structural changes that characterize the next age period. One can refer to the extent to which a child's currently maturing functions are realizing the structure of the next age period as the *subjective* zone of proximal development. The subjective zone is called 'subjective' to indicate that one is speaking about the development of an individual person in relation to the objective, historically formed period of next development.

In sum, the main features of the analysis of zone of proximal development are (a) whole child, (b) internal structure (i.e., relationships between psychological functions), (c) development as a qualitative change in the structural relationships, (d) brought about by the child's actions in the social situation of development (reflecting what the child perceives and is interested in), where (e) each age period has a leading activity/contradiction that organizes the child's actions (within which subjective interests are operating) through which new functions develop. Zone of proximal development is a way to refer to both the functions that are developing ontogenetically for a given age period (objective) and a child's current state of development in relation to the functions that ideally need to be realized (subjective). In this respect, the zone of proximal development is both a theoretical and an empirical discovery.

IDENTIFYING (AND EXPLAINING) THE SUBJECTIVE ZONE OF PROXIMAL DEVELOPMENT: THE ROLE OF IMITATION

The main problem addressed here is "how does one identify or assess an individual child's zone of proximal development"? Several issues must be considered: (a) Why does one want to assess the zone of proximal development? (b) Why does the zone of proximal development exist? (c) What are the roles of imitation and collaboration? (d) What is the "size" of a subjective zone? These diverse aspects are unified by a general interest to understand the dynamics of development in relation to a psychology directed at practice. (The objective zone exists through the social situation of development.)

Why Do We Want to Assess the Zone of Proximal Development?

As a first step for understanding how Vygotsky formulated the subjective zone of proximal development, it is important and necessary to understand why one would want to make such an assessment. Remember that Vygotsky's interest is to develop a theoretical basis for appropriate pedagogical interventions, including principles for possible instructional grouping of children and identification of specific interventions for individual children. Interventions must be based on diagnostic procedures grounded in an explanatory understanding of a child's current state of development. In this view, it is not acceptable to have only (correlated) indicators or symptoms of psychological development; one must use a theoretical understanding of the processes by which a person develops. "A true diagnosis must provide an explanation, prediction, and scientific basis for practical prescription" (Vygotsky, 1998b, p. 205). A solution to the diagnostic problem is identical with having an explanatory theory of psychological development. From this perspective, one can understand why Vygotsky (1998b) links age level, practice, and diagnostics:

> The problem of age level is not only central to all of child psychology, but is also the key to all the problems of practice. This problem is directly and closely connected with the diagnostics of age-related development of the child. (p. 199)

In sum, if we understand the causal-dynamics of child development, then we should be able to develop procedures to assess a person's current state of development in a way that provides insight into what that person needs to develop. Vygotsky proposes that the zone of proximal development as a diagnostic principle "allows us to penetrate into the internal causal-dynamic and genetic connections that determine the process itself of mental development" (p. 203). To realize the ideal that Vygotsky proposes, one needs a theoretical explanation of why a subjective zone of proximal development exists and how it operates in order to assess an individual child's zone of proximal development (i.e., the subjective zone of proximal development).

Why Does the (Subjective) Zone of Proximal Development Exist?

To understand Vygotsky's explanation for the existence of the zone of proximal development, we have to consider his technical concept of imitation, around which his analysis is constructed. A person's ability to imitate, as conceived by Vygotsky, is the basis for a subjective zone of proximal development. (The objective zone exists through the social situation of development.) Imitation, as used here, is not a mindless copying of actions (1997a, p. 95; 1998b, p. 202). Rather Vygotsky wants to break from a copying view, to give a new meaning to *imitation* – reflecting a new theoretical position – in which imitation presupposes some understanding of the structural relations in a problem that is being solved (1987, p. 210).

A child is not able to imitate anything (1998b, p. 201; 1987, p. 209). "[I]mitation is possible only to the extent and in those forms in which it is accompanied by understanding" (Vygotsky, 1997a, p. 96). "It is well established that the child can imitate only what lies within the zone of his intellectual potential" (Vygotsky, 1987, p. 209). Imitation refers to "all kinds of activity of a certain type carried out by the child . . . in cooperation with adults or with another child" (1998b, p. 202) and includes "everything that the child cannot do independently, but which he can be taught or which he can do with direction or cooperation or with the help of leading questions" (1998b, p. 202).

The crucial assumption is that imitation is possible because (a) maturing psychological functions are still insufficient to support independent performance but (b) have developed sufficiently so that (c) a person can understand how to use the collaborative actions (e.g., leading questions, demonstrations) of another. The presence of these maturing functions is the reason the zone of proximal development exists. Alternatively, one can say that the zone of proximal development is defined as referring to those intellectual actions and mental functions that a child is able to use in interaction, when independent performance is inadequate.

Further Clarification of Imitation

Vygotsky probably believed that there was some likelihood that the term *imitation* would be misunderstood. He recognized that he was trying to give a new meaning to a term that had been used previously in other theoretical perspectives. For example, when he introduces this idea in *History of the Development of Higher Mental Functions* (1997a), he signals his intended reformulation ("which we might call by the generally accepted word *imitation*") and then immediately tries to prevent misunderstanding, "it may seem that in speaking of imitation . . . we are returning to the prejudices of which we have just spoken" (p. 95). Similarly, he sometimes refers to imitation "understood in a broad sense" (Vygotsky, 1987, p. 210) or "as defined above" (1998b, p. 202).

Vygotsky wanted to preclude these misunderstandings, because he considered imitation (as he was trying to define it) as "one of the basic paths of cultural development of the child" (1997a, p. 95). The term *imitation* in Vygotsky's texts should be read with an awareness that a special technical meaning is intended. Whether Vygotsky's concept of imitation is elaborated adequately is a different question and deserves further examination. For present purposes, let us try to understand what was intended with the concept.

We see here that Vygotsky used the term *imitation* to refer to situations in which a child is able to engage in interaction with more competent others around specific tasks that the child would otherwise not be able to perform alone, because of the presence of maturing psychological functions. "[T]he child can enter into imitation through intellectual actions more or less far beyond what he is capable of in independent mental and purposeful actions or intellectual operations" (1998b, p. 201). For example:

> If I am not able to play chess, I will not be able to play a match even if a chess master shows me how. If I know arithmetic, but run into difficulty with the solution of a complex problem, a demonstration will immediately lead to my own resolution of the problem. On the other hand, if I do not know higher mathematics, a demonstration of the resolution of a differential equation will not move my own thought in that direction by a single step. To imitate, there must be some possibility of moving from what I can do to what I cannot. (Vygotsky, 1987, p. 209)

Together with this attempt to shift the meaning of *imitation*, one can see a core idea of a subjective zone of proximal development in Vygotsky's thinking, formulated at least 2 years before its first recorded mention: "summarizing the new position of psychology in this area, we might say: *the circle of available imitation coincides with the circle of the actual development possibilities of the animal*" (Vygotsky, 1997a, p. 95). This critical assumption, for which Vygotsky (1998b) claims research support, is subsequently formulated in a stronger form: there is "a strict genetic pattern between what a child is able to imitate and his mental development" (p. 202).

Using Imitation to Assess the Zone of Proximal Development

We can now consider how the concept of imitation provides a theoretical justification for how to assess a child's (subjective) zone of proximal development. "The area of immature, but maturing processes makes up the child's zone of proximal development" (Vygotsky, 1998b, p. 202). For a given child, these maturing functions are more or less developed but unable to support independent performance. Independent performance cannot provide evidence of what maturing functions are present. If the child already had developed adequate mental functions, then independent performance would be possible. In an interaction situation (collaboration), the child can only imitate that for which the maturing functions are present. If the child had no capability to imitate, then this would be taken as an indication that relevant maturing mental functions were not present. In other words, the child is only able to take advantage of that assistance for which the child can understand the significance. So, one determines "what the child is capable of in intellectual imitation if we understand this term as defined above" (1998b, p. 202).

Successful (assisted) performance can be used as an indicator of the state of a maturing psychological function:

> Roughly speaking, by testing the limits of possible imitation, we test the limits of the intellect of the given animal. . . . If we want to learn how much a given intellect has matured for one function or another, we can test this by means of imitation. (Vygotsky, 1997a, p. 96)

In brief, we ask the child to solve problems that are beyond his mental age [as measured by independent performance] with some kind of cooperation and determine how far the potential for intellectual cooperation can be stretched for the given child and how far it goes beyond his mental age. (Vygotsky, 1998b, p. 202)

Purpose of Collaboration in Assessing and Characterizing the Size of the Zone of Proximal Development

Interaction or collaboration with a child is used to assess a child's (subjective) zone of proximal development, because it provides an opportunity for imitation, which is the way for identifying maturing psychological functions that are still inadequate for independent performance. This can be seen implicitly in the following:

By applying the principle of cooperation for establishing the zone of proximal development, we make it possible to study directly what determines most precisely the mental maturation that must be realized in the proximal and subsequent periods of his stage of development. (Vygotsky, 1998b, p. 203)

Vygotsky often uses the term *collaboration* in his discussion about assessing the zone of proximal development. The term should not be understood as a joint, coordinated effort to move forward, in which the more expert partner is always providing support at the moments when maturing functions are inadequate. Rather it appears that this term is being used to refer to any situation in which a child is being offered some interaction with another person that is related to a problem to be solved. The main focus for collaborative interventions is to find evidence for maturing psychological functions, with the assumption that the child could only take advantage of these interventions because the maturing function supports an ability to understand the significance of the support being offered.

Vygotsky does not seem to have any systematic principles, methods, or techniques that should guide how collaboration should be conducted by a person who is assessing a zone of proximal development – if one judges from his discussions in the texts being discussed here. Consider these examples of interventions for assessing the (subjective) zone of proximal development of a child. "We assist each child through demonstration, leading questions, and by introducing elements of the task's solution" (Vygotsky, 1987, p. 209). Here is the most comprehensive list I have been able to find, in which Vygotsky (1998b) proposes that after giving a problem to a child,

we show the child how such a problem must be solved and watch to see if he can do the problem by imitating the demonstration. Or we begin to solve the problem and ask the child to finish it. Or we propose that the child solve the problem that is beyond his mental age by cooperating with another, more developed child or, finally, we explain to the child the principle of solving the problem, ask leading questions, analyze the problem for him, etc. (p. 202)

I do not see any principled sequence in these types of interventions, and there is no discussion here (or elsewhere that I can find) about how to interpret responses to different interventions in relation to the zone of proximal development.

Interpreting the Results of Collaboration

Although Vygotsky does not give a detailed account of procedures to assess the zone of proximal development, he does indicate how one might (roughly) interpret the results of doing collaborative problem solving with a child, focusing on a (presumably) hypothetical example of two children whose mental age is measured (by standard intelligence testing procedures) to be 8 years (Vygotsky, 1998b, pp. 202–203; 1987, p. 209). After engaging in assisted problem solving (of unspecified problems) with the children, one determines that with assistance one child solves problems that correspond to the standards for a 12-year-old, and the other child solves problems that correspond to the standard for a 9-year-old. "With respect to maturing processes, one went four times further than the other" (1998b, p. 203).

Of greater interest is the use Vygotsky makes of these diagnostics in instructional experiments. If one assumes that it is possible, in an approximate fashion, to use a collaboration procedure and interpretation as described in the previous paragraph, then it should be possible to identify children who have "larger" and "smaller" zones of proximal development. It is important to note that this "size" refers to the extent to which a child can take advantage of collaboration to realize performance beyond what is specified by independent performance and relative to age norms. There is no reason to believe that this "size" is a fixed property of a child that remains constant across age periods.

With this procedure in hand, it was possible for Vygotsky to undertake experiments that explored the consequences of using the results of this procedure as a principle for grouping children for instructional purposes. In one article, which as far as I know is neither translated nor readily available, Vygotsky (1935a) describes a set of experiments in which children are tested and identified to have a high or low IQ as well as a large or small zone (as determined by the kind of procedure described in the previous paragraph). Subsequent school success is determined, and it appears that the size of the zone of proximal development was more predictive than IQ. That is, children with a larger zone of proximal development (i.e., more maturing functions currently available) had comparable intellectual development, regardless of IQ. Similarly, children with a smaller zone of proximal development had a comparable intellectual development, regardless of the initially measured IQ. In other words, the zone of proximal development gave a better indication for predicting or understanding future intellectual development than a measure of independent performance because it focuses on maturing functions. A greater number of maturing functions gives a child better opportunities to benefit from school instruction. A detailed summary of this article is found in van der Veer and Valsiner (1991, pp. 336–341).

Handling Some Theoretical Inelegancies

As a tentative summary, it appears that Vygotsky formulated a general theoretical logic for assessing the (subjective) zone of proximal development but only had an opportunity to work out specific procedures for making collaboration and interpreting the results in a rough or approximate manner. In presenting Vygotsky's concept of imitation and the way it is used to investigate the (subjective) zone of proximal development, I have tried to highlight this general theoretical logic, in particular, the ideas that the zone should be defined on the basis of an explanatory account of the nature of development and that assessment should be directed to these processes. Future work needs to consider whether to develop (or reject) this logic.

This distinction – between the theoretical logic and the specific proposals for realizing this logic – provides a useful way for handling some of the conceptual problems that arise in trying to frame the idea of zone of proximal development in terms of maturing functions, new-formations, and age periods, while relating it to the idea of mental age and independent performance, which is probably predicated on a different developmental theory.

In his published discussions, Vygotsky seems to accept uncritically that independent performance is, in fact, measuring fully developed psychological functions. Similarly, he refers to mental age, but how would this relate to the idea of an age period? What is the relationship between mental ages and the new-formations needed for transition to the next age period? The notion of imitation is tied to a Gestalt concept of structural insight – should that be dropped, revised, or supplemented? Much contemporary research has been done now on interactions in joint problem solving between an adult and a child. Does this work require revision and elaboration of Vygotsky's rather undifferentiated notion of collaboration? There are many more questions of this kind that could be raised. They are not likely to be solved semantically by refining definitions. More important is to focus on the framing of the problem (i.e., the theoretical structure of the general argument being formulated), in this case, having an explanation of development and a procedure for diagnosis motivated directly by that theory of development and not by symptoms of behavior. Future work should be focused on refining and elaborating that theoretical program (e.g., assessments of mental development should be directly related to the specific psychological functions that are developing; it is necessary to identify psychological functions needed for supporting the transition to the next age period), drawing on whatever additional understanding we have about processes of development and learning.

PERSPECTIVES AND IMPLICATIONS (IN LIEU OF A SUMMARY)

- In most general terms, the idea of zone of proximal development is meant to direct attention to the idea that instruction/teaching (*obuchenie*) should be focused on maturing psychological functions, rather than already existing functions, that are relevant for the general intellectual development to the next age period.
- The zone describes a structural relation, both in terms of the number, extent, and relations among maturing functions (subjective) and in relation to the functions needed for the next age period (objective). That is, the objective zone (i.e., what developments are going to lead to the next development) is the same for all the children, but individual children's subjective position in relation to this objective zone differ (1987, p. 209; 1986, p. 187; 1982b, pp. 116–119; for a summary of 1935a, see Van der Veer & Valsiner, 1991, pp. 338–339).
- The content and meaning of the zone change, depending on which age period is being considered. The general principle for understanding the dynamics of the structural change is the same, but one needs to examine the social situation for development, the existing psychological structure, and the next structure being formed in order to characterize the objective zone of proximal development for a given age period appropriately.
- The focus on the learning of academic or school concepts in relation to the zone of proximal development appears because this development is relevant in relation to school age, not because the zone of proximal development always involves development of academic concepts. Other age periods will have other foci.
- In relation to the school age, the theoretical function of Vygotsky's zone of proximal development research can be understood as a search for identifying a principled way for conceptualizing schooling in relation to the whole child and not just the child's performance on a single task (see Hedegaard, 1990, for a useful example).
- The zone of proximal development is not simply a way to refer to development through assistance by a more competent other. This assistance is meaningful only in relation to maturing functions needed for transition to the next age period.

- The zone is never located solely in the child, not even the subjective zone. The subjective zone is always an evaluation of a child's capabilities in relation to the theoretical model of the age period.

Implications in Relation to Contemporary Interpretations

- Some researchers have characterized Vygotsky's concept as "metaphorical" and/or "heuristical" (e.g., Daniels, 2001, p. 56; Kovalainen, Kumpulainen, & Vasama, 2001, p. 18; Lloyd & Fernyhough, 1999, p. 18; Valsiner, 1998, p. 68; Wells, 1999, p. 314), or rhetorical, descriptive, and not intended for systematic theoretical development (Valsiner, 1998, p. 69; Valsiner & van der Veer, 1993, p. 43). There does not seem to be any support for such assertions.
- Some researchers argue that the zone of proximal development is created in interaction between child and adult (e.g., Davydov, 1998, p. 29; Mercer & Fisher, 1992, p. 342; Sternberg & Grigorenko, 2002, pp. 37–38). These arguments deserve more analysis. According to the analysis presented here, the zone of proximal development refers to the maturing functions that are relevant to the next age period and that provide the means to perform in collaborative situations that could not be achieved independently. These functions are not created in interaction; rather interaction provides conditions for identifying their existence and the extent to which they have developed.

Many issues remain to be discussed:

- The historical context and methodological basis on which these ideas were developed
- Relations with Vygotsky's (1997a) theory of the development of psychological functions
- Relations with the scaffolding literature (see Stone, 1998, for a good discussion)
- Problems with Vygotsky's theoretical formulations
- Problems with many contemporary interpretations of the zone of proximal development
- Implications for theories of instruction and instructional design
- Implications for classroom teaching and diverse pupils

CONCLUDING COMMENT

One attraction of the idea of zone of proximal development in relation to educational practices is that it provides a distinctive perspective for conceptualizing the relation between human learning and development – a perspective that also has some fundamental differences with many of the currently predominant views about this relation. Despite slender textual material available from Vygotsky about the zone of proximal development, interpretations of the idea have been sufficient to stimulate a lot of research and reflection to clarify and elaborate the basic idea. This has yielded a diversity of interpretations and variations; such diversity is likely to continue in the coming decades, given the somewhat underspecified nature of the original formulation and the variety of practical situations in which the idea is being used. These variations and elaborations, together with their critical evaluation, are a necessary part of the scientific process needed to refine the zone of proximal development as a concept for understanding and developing educational practices. There is no reason to defend the infallibility or sufficiency of Vygotsky's arguments and achievements with the zone of proximal development concept. However, (a) Vygotsky was trying to raise a set of issues that have not been confronted adequately in the contemporary literature that refers to this concept; (b) many of the "resolutions" or "new developments" that diverse authors have proposed seem to be a dilution of these general theoretical issues, rather than a clarification or deepening; and (c) many of the arguments, criticisms, and concerns that have been raised are explicitly wrong or not pointed toward Vygotsky's theoretical perspective at all. Persons who want to use the zone of proximal development concept should, as a minimum, try to understand the particular theoretical and conceptual problems Vygotsky was trying to address when he formulated this concept.

Now that more of Vygotsky's texts are readily available, there is no excuse to continue to use limited or distorted interpretations of the concept. It seems more appropriate to use the term *zone of proximal development* to refer to the phenomenon that Vygotsky was writing about and find other terms (e.g., *assisted instruction, scaffolding*) to refer to practices such as teaching a specific subject matter concept, skill, and so forth. This is not to deny the meaningfulness of other investigations (e.g., joint problem solving, dynamic assessment of intellectual capabilities), only to indicate that there is no additional scientific value in referring to this as zone of proximal development unless one concurrently has a developmental theory to which these assessments can be related. It is precisely on this point that one can see, by way of contrast, how most work that refers to zone of proximal development does not have a such a developmental theory, even implicitly. This aspect deserves to be investigated more intensively.

References

Berk, L. (1997). *Child development* (4th ed.). Boston: Allyn & Bacon.

Cazden, C. B. (1996). Selective traditions: Readings of Vygotsky in writing pedagogy. In D. Hicks (Ed.), *Discourse, learning, and schooling* (pp. 165–185). Cambridge: Cambridge University Press.

Daniels, H. (2001). *Vygotsky and pedagogy*. London: RoutledgeFalmer.

Davydov, V. V. (1988). Problems of the child's mental developmental. *Soviet Education, 30*(8), 44–97.

Davydov, V. V. (1998). The concept of developmental teaching. *Journal of Russian and East European Psychology, 36*(4), 11–36.

Dunn, W. E., & Lantolf, J. P. (1998). Vygotsky's zone of proximal development and Krashen's "i + 1": Incommensurable constructs; incommensurable theories. *Language Learning, 48*, 411–442.

El'konin, D. B. (1999). Toward the problem of stages in the mental development of children. *Journal of Russian and East European Psychology, 37*(6), 11–30.

Exner, C. E. (1984). The zone of proximal development in in-hand manipulation skills of nondysfunctional 3- and 4-year-old children. *American Journal of Occupational Therapy, 38*, 446–451.

Fabes, R., & Martin, C. L. (2001). *Exploring development through childhood*. Boston: Allyn & Bacon.

Gholson, S. A. (1998). Proximal positioning: A strategy of practice in violin pedagogy. *Journal of Research in Music Education, 46*, 535–545.

Gillen, J. (2000). Versions of Vygotsky. *British Journal of Educational Studies, 48*, 183–198.

Hedegaard, M. (1990). The zone of proximal development as a basis for instruction. In L. Moll (Ed.), *Vygotsky and education: Instructional implications and applications of sociohistorical psychology* (pp. 349–371). Cambridge: Cambridge University Press.

Holaday, B., LaMontagne, L., & Marciel, J. (1994). Vygotsky's zone of proximal development: Implications for nurse assistance of children's learning. *Issues in Comprehensive Pediatric Nursing, 17*, 15–27.

Hung, D. W. L. (2001). Design principles for web-based learning: Implications for Vygotskian thought. *Educational Technology, 41*(3), 33–41

Jones, G. M., Rua, M. J., & Carter, G. (1998). Science teachers' conceptual growth within Vygotsky's zone of proximal development. *Journal of Research in Science Teaching, 35*, 967–985.

Kilgore, D. W. (1999). Understanding learning in social movements: A theory of collective learning. *International Journal of Lifelong Education, 18*, 191–202.

Kovalainen, M., Kumpulainen, K., & Vasama, K. (2001). Orchestrating classroom interaction in a community of inquiry: Modes of teacher participation. *Journal of Classroom Interaction, 36*(2), 17–28.

Lampert Shepel, E. N. (1995). Teacher self-identification in culture from Vygotsky's developmental perspective. *Anthropology & Education Quarterly, 26*, 425–442.

Lantolf, J. P., & Pavlenko, A. (1995). Sociocultural theory and second language acquisition. *Annual Review of Applied Linguistics, 15*, 108–124.

LeFrancois, G. (2001). *Of children: An introduction to child and adolescent development* (9th ed.). Belmont, CA: Wadsworth/Thomsen.

Leiman, M., & Stiles, W. B. (2001). Dialogical sequence analysis and the zone of proximal development as conceptual enhancements to the assimilation model: The case of Jan revisited. *Psychotherapy Research, 11*, 311–330.

Lloyd, P., & Fernyhough, C. (Eds.) (1999). *Lev Vygotsky: Critical assessments*. Vol. 3. *The zone of proximal development*. London: Routledge.

Lyons, B. G. (1984). Defining a child's zone of proximal development: Evaluation process for treatment planning. *American Journal of Occupational Therapy, 38,* 446–451.

McKechnie, L. (1997). Vygotsky's zone of proximal development – a useful theoretical approach for research concerning children, libraries, and information. *Journal of Youth Services in Libraries, 11,* 66–70.

Marx, K. (1990). *Capital* (Vol. 1, B. Fowkes, Trans.). Harmondsworth, England: Penguin.

Mercer, N., & Fisher, E. (1992). How do teachers help children to learn? An analysis of teacher's interventions in computer-based activities. *Learning and Instruction, 2,* 339–355.

Palinscar, A. S. (1998). Keeping the metaphor of scaffolding fresh – a response to C. Addison Stone's "The metaphor of scaffolding: Its utility for the field of learning disabilities." *Journal of Learning Disabilities, 31,* 370–373.

Rieber, R. W. (Ed.) (1999). *The collected works of L. S. Vygotsky.* Vol. 6. *Scientific legacy.* New York: Kluwer Academic/Plenum.

Schneuwly, B. (1994). Contradiction and development: Vygotsky and paedology. *European Journal of Psychology and Education, 9,* 281–291.

Smith, A. B. (1993). Early childhood educare: Seeking a theoretical framework in Vygotsky's work. *International Journal of Early Years Education, 1*(1), 47–61.

Spouse, J. (1998). Scaffolding student learning in clinical practice. *Nurse Education Today, 18,* 259–266.

Sternberg, R. J., & Grigorenko, E. L. (2002). *Dynamic testing: The nature and measurement of learning potential.* Cambridge: Cambridge University Press.

Stone, C. A. (1998). The metaphor of scaffolding: Its utility for the field of learning disabilities. *Journal of Learning Disabilities, 31,* 344–364.

Tappan, M. B. (1998). Moral education in the zone of proximal development. *Journal of Moral Education, 27,* 141–160.

Tharp, R., & Gallimore, R. (1998). A theory of teaching as assisted performance. In D. Faulkner, K. Littleton, & M. Woodhead (Eds.), *Learning relationships in the classroom* (pp. 93–109). London: Routledge.

Torres, M. N. (1996, October 21–24). Teacher-researchers in the "zone of proximal development": Insights for teacher education. Paper presented at the International Conference: A Cultural-Historical Approach to the Study of Education: Centenary of Lev S. Vygotsky, Moscow.

Valsiner, J. (1998). *The guided mind.* Cambridge, MA: Harvard University Press.

Valsiner, J., & van der Veer, R. (1993). The encoding of distance: The concept of the zone of proximal development and its interpretations. In R. R. Cocking & K. A. Renninger (Eds.), *The development and meaning of psychological distance* (pp. 35–62). Hillsdale, NJ: Erlbaum.

van der Veer, R., & Valsiner, J. (1991). *Understanding Vygotsky: A quest for synthesis.* Oxford: Blackwell.

Vygotski, L. S. (1963). Learning and mental development at school age (J. Simon, Trans.). In B. Simon & J. Simon (Eds.), *Educational psychology in the U.S.S.R.* (pp. 21–34). London: Routledge & Kegan Paul.

Vygotskij, L. S. (1973a). Apprendimento e sviluppo nell'età prescolare. In *Lo sviluppo psichico del bambino* (pp. 126–143). Roma: Riuniti.

Vygotskij, L. S. (1973b). Il problema dell' apprendimento e dello sviluppo intellettuale nell' età scolastica. In *Lo sviluppo psichico del bambino* (pp. 144–164). Roma: Riuniti.

Vygotskij, L. S. (1982a) . Legen og dens rolle i barnets psykiske udvikling [Play and its role in the child's psychological development] (N. Måge, Trans.). In *Om barnets psykiske udvikling: En artikelsamling* (pp. 50–71). Copenhagen: Nyt Nordisk Forlag Arnold Busck.

Vygotskij, L. S. (1982b). Spørgsmålet om undervisningen og den intellektuelle udvikling i skolealderen [The question about teaching and its intellectual development in the school age] (N. Måge, Trans.). In *Om barnets psykiske udvikling: En artikelsamling* (pp. 105–121). Copenhagen: Nyt Nordisk Forlag Arnold Busck.

Vygotskij, L. S. (1982c). Udvikling af dagligdags og videnskabelige begreper i skolealderen [Development of everyday and academic concepts in the school age] (N. Måge, Trans.). In *Om barnets psykiske udvikling: En artikelsamling* (pp. 125–149). Copenhagen: Nyt Nordisk Forlag Arnold Busck.

Vygotskij, L. S. (1982d). Undervisning og udvikling i førskolealderen [Teaching and development in the preschool age] (N. Måge, Trans.). In *Om barnets psykiske udvikling: En artikelsamling* (pp. 89–104). Copenhagen: Nyt Nordisk Forlag Arnold Busck.

Vygotskij, L. S. (1983a). Il giuoco e la sua funzione nello sviluppo psichico del bambino (R. Plantone, Trans.). In L. Mecacci (Ed.), *Vygotskij: Antologia di scritti* (pp. 227–253). Bologna: Il Mulino.

Vygotskij, L. S. (1983b). Il problema dell'istruzione e dello sviluppo mentale in età scolare. In L. Mecacci (Ed.), *Vygotskij: Antologia di scritti* (pp. 255–277). Bologna: Il Mulino.

Vygotsky, L. S. (1933, December 23). K voprosy o dinamike umstvennogo razvitie normal'nogo i nenormal'nogo rebenka. Unpublished stenographic transcript of lecture at the Bubnov Pedagogical Institute, Moscow.

Vygotsky, L. S. (1935a). Dinamika umstvennogo razvitiza shkol'nika v svjazi s obucheniem. In *Umstvennoie razvitie detei v protsesse obuchenia* (pp. 33–52). Moscow/Leningrad: Gosudarstvennoie Uchebno-pedagogicheskoie Izdatel'stvo.

Vygotsky, L. S. (1935b). O pedologicheskom analize pedagoheskogo processa. In *Umstvennoie razvitie detei v protsesse obuchenia* (pp. 116–134). Moscow/Leningrad: Gosudarstvennoie Uchebno-pedagogicheskoie Izdatel'stvo.

Vygotsky, L. S. (1935c). Obuchenie i razvitie v doshykol'nom vozraste. In *Umstvennoie razvitie detei v protsesse obuchenia* (pp. 20–32).Moscow/Leningrad: Gosudarstvennoie Uchebno-pedagogicheskoie Izdatel'stvo.

Vygotsky, L. S. (1935d). Problema obuchenia i umstvennoe razvitie v shkol'nom vozraste. In *Umstvennoie razvitie detei v protsesse obuchenia* (pp. 3–19). Moscow/Leningrad: Gosudarstvennoie Uchebno-pedagogicheskoie Izdatel'stvo.

Vygotsky, L. S. (1935e). Razvitie zhiteiskikh i nauchnykh ponyatii v shkol'nom vozraste. In *Umstvennoie razvitie detei v protsesse obuchenia* (pp. 96–115). Moscow/Leningrad: Gosudarstvennoie Uchebno-pedagogicheskoie Izdatel'stvo.

Vygotsky, L. S. (1935f). *Umstvennoie razvitie detei v protsesse obuchenia.* Moscow/ Leningrad: Gosudarstvennoie Uchebno-pedagogicheskoie Izdatel'stvo.

Vygotsky, L. S. (1956). Obuchenijia i umstvennoe razvitie v shkol'nom vozraste. In A. N. Leontiev & A. R. Luria (Eds.), *Izbrannye psikhologicheskie issledovanija* (pp. 438–452). Moscow: Izdatel'stov APN RSFSR.

Vygotsky, L. S. (1962). *Thought and language* (E. Hanfmann & G. Vakar, Eds. and Trans.). Cambridge, MA: MIT Press.

Vygotsky, L. S. (1966). Igra i ee rol' v psikhicheskom razvitti rebenka. *Voprosy Psikhologii,* No. 6, 62–76.

Vygotsky, L. S. (1967). Play and its role in the mental development of the child. *Soviet Psychology, 5*(3), 6–18.

Vygotsky, L. S. (1978). Interaction between learning and development (M. Lopez-Morillas, Trans.). In M. Cole, V. John-Steiner, S. Scribner, & E. Souberman (Eds.), *Mind in society: The development of higher psychological processes* (pp. 79–91). Cambridge, MA: Harvard University Press.

Vygotsky, L. S. (1985). La problème de l'enseignement et du développement mental à l'âge scolaire (C. Haus, Trans.). In B. Schneuwly & J.-P. Bronckart (Eds.), *Vygotsky aujourd'hui* (pp. 95–117). Neuchâtel: Delachaux & Niestlé.

Vygotsky, L. S. (1986). *Thought and language* (A. Kozulin, Trans.). Cambridge, MA: MIT Press.

Vygotsky, L. S. (1987). Thinking and speech (N. Minick, Trans.). In R. W. Rieber & A. S. Carton (Eds.), *The collected works of L. S. Vygotsky.* Vol. 1. *Problems of general psychology* (pp. 39–285). New York: Plenum Press.

Vygotsky, L. S. (1995). Apprentissage et développement à l'âge prescolaire. *Société française, 2/52*, 35–46.

Vygotsky, L. S. (1997a). *The collected works of L. S. Vygotsky.* Vol. 4. *The history of the development of higher mental functions* (M. Hall, Trans.; R. W. Rieber, Ed.). New York: Plenum Press.

Vygotsky, L. S. (1997b). The historical meaning of the crisis in psychology: A methodological investigation (R. van der Veer, Trans.). In R. W. Reiber & J. Wollock (Eds.), *The collected works of L. S. Vygotsky.* Vol. 3. *Problems of the theory and history of psychology* (pp. 233–343). New York: Plenum Press.

Vygotsky, L. S. (1998a). Infancy (M. Hall, Trans.). In R. W. Rieber (Ed.), *The collected works of L. S. Vygotsky.* Vol. 5. *Child psychology* (pp. 207–241). New York: Plenum Press.

Vygotsky, L. S. (1998b). The problem of age (M. Hall, Trans.). In R. W. Rieber (Ed.), *The collected works of L. S. Vygotsky.* Vol. 5. *Child psychology* (pp. 187–205). New York: Plenum Press.

Wells, G. (1999). *Dialogic inquiry: Towards a sociocultural practice and theory of education.* Cambridge: Cambridge University Press.

Wertsch, J. W. (1984). The zone of proximal development: Some conceptual issues. In B. Rogoff & J. V. Wertsch (Eds.), *New directions for child development.* No. 23. *Children's learning in the "zone of proximal development"* (pp. 7–18). San Francisco: Jossey-Bass.

Wilson, A., & Weinstein, L. (1996). The transference and the zone of proximal development. *Journal of the American Psychoanalytic Association, 44,* 167–200.

Wygotski, L. S. (1987a). Das Problem der Altersstufen. In J. Lompscher (Ed.), *Lew Wygotski: Ausgewählte Schriften*. Band 2. *Arbeiten zur psychischen Entwicklung der Persönlichkeit* (pp. 53–90). Köln: Pahl-Rugenstein Verlag.

Wygotski, L. S. (1987b). Unterricht und Entwicklung im Vorschulalter. In J. Lompscher (Ed.), *Lew Wygotski: Ausgewählte Schriften*. Band 2. *Arbeiten zur psychischen Entwicklung der Persönlichkeit* (pp. 255–270). Köln: Pahl-Rugenstein Verlag.

Wygotski, L. S. (1987c). Unterricht und geistige Entwicklung im Schulalter. In J. Lompscher (Ed.), *Lew Wygotski: Ausgewählte Schriften*: Band 2. *Arbeiten zur psychischen Entwicklung der Persönlichkeit* (pp. 287–306). Köln: Pahl-Rugenstein Verlag.

3

Vygotsky's Doctrine of Scientific Concepts

Its Role for Contemporary Education

Yuriy V. Karpov

Vygotsky's doctrine of scientific concepts as the content of school instruction is a direct elaboration of his general theoretical view of mediated learning as the major determinant of human development (see Kozulin, this volume). According to Vygotsky (1978, 1981, 1986), all specifically human mental processes (so-called higher mental processes) are mediated by psychological tools such as language, signs, and symbols. These tools are invented by human society, and they are acquired by children in the course of interpersonal communication with adults and more experienced peers. Having been acquired and internalized by children, these tools then function as mediators of the children's high mental processes.

Vygotsky viewed school instruction as the major avenue for mediated learning and, therefore, as the major contributor to children's development during the period of middle childhood. He emphasized, however, that such a development-generating effect of instruction would take place only if the process of instruction were organized in the proper way: "The only good kind of instruction is that which marches ahead of development and leads it; it must be aimed not so much at the ripe as at the ripening functions" (Vygotsky, 1986, p. 188). According to Vygotsky (1978, 1986), the major reason for the development-generating effect of properly organized school instruction relates to students' acquisition of "scientific concepts," which can be contrasted with "spontaneous concepts" of preschoolers.

Spontaneous concepts are the result of generalization of everyday personal experience in the absence of systematic instruction. Therefore, such concepts are unsystematic, not conscious, and often wrong. For example, a 3-year-old child, having observed a needle, a pin, and a coin sinking in water, reaches the wrong conclusion that "all small objects sink" and begins to use this concept for predicting the behavior of different objects in water (Zaporozhets, 1986, p. 207). Despite their "unscientific" nature, spontaneous concepts play an important role in children's learning as a foundation for the acquisition of scientific concepts. For example, "historical concepts can begin to develop only when the child's everyday [spontaneous, Y. K.] concept of the past is sufficiently differentiated" (Vygotsky, 1986, p. 194).

In contrast to spontaneous concepts, scientific concepts represent the generalization of the experience of humankind that is fixed in science, understood in the broadest sense of the term to include both natural and social sciences as well as the humanities. In the example given here, the scientific concept that would make it possible to predict the behavior of objects in water is Archimedes' law. Students are taught scientific concepts in the course of systematic instruction and acquire them consciously and according to a certain system. Once scientific concepts have been acquired, they transform students' everyday life knowledge: The students' spontaneous concepts become structured and conscious. Thus, the acquisition of scientific concepts creates "the zone of proximal development" of spontaneous concepts (see Chaiklin, this volume, for the analysis of Vygotsky's concept of the zone of proximal development).

The importance of the acquisition of scientific concepts is not limited to the fact that they "restructure and raise spontaneous concepts to a higher level" (Vygotsky, 1987, p. 220). Once acquired by students, scientific concepts begin to mediate their thinking and problem solving. That is why "instruction in scientific concepts plays a decisive role in the child's mental development" (Vygotsky, 1987, p. 220). Specifically, "reflective consciousness comes to the child through the portals of scientific concepts" (Vygotsky, 1986, p. 171). As a result, students' thinking becomes much more independent of their personal experience. They become "theorists" rather then "practitioners" and develop the ability to operate at the level of formal–logical thought.

In contrast to Piaget's (1970) and Dewey's (1902) constructivist notions (discussed later), Vygotsky held that children should not and cannot be required to understand the world by way of rediscovery of the principal explanatory laws already discovered by humankind. The development of human children is so special, in large part, because adults teach them these laws. That is why, according to Vygotsky, the acquisition of scientific concepts should arise from their presentation to school students in the form of precise verbal definitions (Vygotsky, 1986, p. 148).

Vygotsky himself clearly understood that "the difficulty with scientific concepts lies in their *verbalism*" (1986, p. 148). He pointed out that "scientific concepts ... just start their development, rather than finish it, at a moment when the child learns the term or word-meaning denoting the new concept" (Vygotsky, 1986, p. 159). Vygotsky, however, did not describe what the process of mastery of scientific concepts should be after the concepts have been presented to students. Neither did he support his theoretical doctrine of the role of scientific concepts in children's learning and development with strong experimental data. His ideas, nevertheless, provide a good theoretical basis for the analysis of what the content and process of school instruction should be to meet educational goals. Such an analysis is presented in the following sections.

THE ACQUISITION OF SCIENTIFIC KNOWLEDGE AS THE CONTENT OF SCHOOL INSTRUCTION

Very few contemporary educational researchers would advocate that school instruction be reduced to the acquisition of scientific concepts by students. One of the exceptions is Hirsch (1987), the author of the Cultural Literacy program. According to him, the acquisition of scientific concepts and other verbal cultural information, such as names, should be the major content of school learning. As Hirsch (1988) claimed, "Words refer to things; knowing a lot of words means knowing a lot of things" (p. 24). He has even developed a list of about 5,000 words that students should memorize at school. Thus, Hirsch takes a much more extreme stand than Vygotsky, who, as indicated, emphasized the importance of learning scientific concepts but not just verbal factual information, and who was far from proposing that concepts be learned through mindless memorization.

Although not fashionable among educational researchers, the idea of acquisition by students of scientific concepts as one of the educational goals implicitly underlies contemporary systems of school instruction in both the Unites States and Russia. Traditional classroom teachers often require students to memorize scientific rules, concepts, definitions, or theorems.

The acquisition of verbal scientific knowledge, however, has been shown not to lead to students' use of this knowledge for solving subject domain problems. Davydov (1990) has described the results of several studies with Russian students that illustrate this point. For example, having memorized the essential characteristics of mammals, birds, and fish, elementary school students, when classifying animals, proceeded from surface characteristics of the animals rather than from the memorized concepts (e.g., they associated the whale with the class of fish). In another study, sixth graders, having memorized the concept of a right-angled triangle, did not recognize as such a right-angled triangle when it was presented to them with the right angle at the top (they called it "an acute-angled triangle"). Similar results have been obtained in studies with American school students. For example, in one study, children's conceptual number knowledge was not shown to ensure their ability to do computational operations (Bruer, 1993).

The preceding discussion, however, is not meant to advocate the idea that teaching procedural knowledge (that is, subject-domain strategies and skills) rather than scientific concepts should be the major content of school instruction. Just the contrary, both American and Russian researchers hold that one of the shortcomings of the traditional system of school instruction in their countries is that it often leads to students' mastery of subject-domain procedures without the acquisition of the domain-relevant conceptual knowledge (Bruer, 1993; Davydov, 1990; Talyzina, 1981). In discussing the American traditional programs for teaching math, Bruer (1993) draws the following conclusion:

Many students don't know why the math procedures they learn in school work. Students leave school having the computational skills to solve standard problems but lacking the higher-order mathematical understanding that would allow them to apply their skills widely in novel situations. Too often, math instruction produces students who can manipulate number symbols but who don't understand what the symbols mean. (p. 81)

Other studies and observations have also shown that pure procedural knowledge, whether learned in math or in any other subject domain, tends to remain meaningless and nontransferable (Bruer, 1993; Davydov 1990; Hiebert & Wearne, 1985; Talyzina, 1981).

To summarize the previous discussion, neither the acquisition of scientific concepts nor the mastery of procedural knowledge in itself should be viewed as a desirable outcome of school instruction. That is why contemporary American psychologists came up with the idea of "marrying concepts to procedures" (Bruer, 1993, p. 95), that is, combining these two kinds of knowledge in the course of teaching.

A similar idea was formulated by Russian Vygotskians back in the 1930s (Leontiev, 1983) and has been elaborated by them in numerous studies since (Davydov, 1986, 1990; Galperin, 1957, 1969; Galperin, Zaporozhets, & Elkonin, 1963; Talyzina, 1981). They have enthusiastically accepted Vygotsky's doctrine of the role of scientific concepts as major mediators of students' thinking and problem solving in different subject domains. They, however, have emphasized that scientific concepts play such a mediational role only if they are supported by students' mastery of relevant procedures. As Leontiev (1983) indicated, "In order for a child to develop the highest generalization (that is, a concept), it is necessary to develop in him the system of psychological operations [procedures – Y.K.] that are relevant to this highest generalization" (p. 347).

The studies by Russian Vygotskians have demonstrated that the procedures that are the most relevant to subject-domain concepts are methods for scientific analysis in these subject domains. For example, the procedures that underlie Archimedes' law are the methods of calculating the density of different objects and comparing these densities with the density of water. Similarly, the procedures that underlie the concept of perpendicular lines are the methods of identifying within the given pair of lines those attributes that are necessary and sufficient for associating (or not associating) this pair of lines with the concept of perpendicular lines.

Having been acquired by students, the combination of conceptual and procedural knowledge was shown to be of a much higher quality than pure verbal scientific knowledge or meaningless nontransferable procedures, which, as indicated, are often the outcomes of traditional school instruction. The main features of such combined conceptual and procedural knowledge are a high level of mastery, broad transfer, and intentional use by students. Students are able to answer "why" questions, to substantiate the way in which they have solved a problem, and to defend the results obtained (Aidarova, 1978; Davydov, 1986; Elkonin & Davydov, 1966; Galperin, 1985; Talyzina, 1981).

Thus, the studies by Russian Vygotskians have supported Vygotsky's idea that scientific knowledge serves as a powerful mediator of students' subject-domain thinking and problem solving. This knowledge, however, cannot be reduced to the verbal definitions of scientific concepts but should include procedural knowledge relevant to these concepts as well.

THEORETICAL LEARNING AS THE AVENUE FOR THE ACQUISITION OF SCIENTIFIC KNOWLEDGE

For most educators and educational researchers, the question, How to teach?, is primary. Their answers to this question determine which instructional methods (discovery learning, cooperative learning, use of modern technology in teaching, etc.) they advocate. For Vygotsky and his Russian followers, the question How to teach? is secondary. Their answer to this question is determined by their answer to another question: What knowledge do we want the students to acquire? (Elkonin, 1989).

As indicated, Russian followers of Vygotsky have elaborated his views of the content of school instruction and have concluded that this content should be scientific knowledge (that is, a combination of scientific concepts and relevant procedures). Accordingly, they consider the process of students' learning to be properly organized only if it leads to the acquisition of such scientific knowledge.

What kind of learning will result in students' acquisition of scientific knowledge? To answer this question, Russian followers of Vygotsky have further elaborated his idea of the differences between spontaneous and scientific concepts. Their research has shown that the acquisition of spontaneous and scientific concepts is the result of fundamentally different types of learning (Davydov, 1986, 1990; Galperin, 1985; Talyzina, 1981). Following Davydov, we will refer to the type of learning that results in spontaneous concepts as *empirical learning* and to the type of learning that results in scientific concepts as *theoretical learning*.

Empirical learning is based on children's comparison of several different objects or events, picking out their common salient characteristics, and formulating, on this basis, a "general concept" about this class of objects or events. This strategy may work if the common salient characteristics of objects or events reflect their significant, essential characteristics (for example, the concept of red color can be developed by children in this way). However, this strategy will not work if the common characteristics of several representatives of a class of objects with which the child is dealing are not the common characteristics of all the objects of this class. This explains why the preschooler in the example given earlier, having observed a needle, a pin, and a coin sinking, wrongly concluded that "all small objects sink." Small size is a common salient characteristic of a needle, a pin, and a coin, but it is not the common characteristic of all the objects that sink. Moreover, even if the common characteristics of several objects with which the child is dealing do reflect the common characteristics of all the objects of this class, they still may not reflect the essential characteristics of these objects. A tail and fins are common, but not essential characteristics of fish. Therefore, the child's spontaneous concept of fish developed as the result of empirical learning would be a misconception.

Thus, empirical learning often leads to misconceptions. Given that both Russian and American school students have been shown to hold many such misconceptions (Davydov, 1990; DiSessa, 1982), it is reasonable to assume that the traditional system of school instruction often promotes empirical learning. Indeed, as indicated, under the traditional system of school instruction, students often are taught rote skills or verbal definitions of scientific concepts rather than true scientific knowledge (that is, combined conceptual and procedural knowledge in the given subject domain) (Bruer, 1993; Davydov, 1990). In both cases (whether students have mastered a rote skill or have learned the verbal definition of a scientific concept), the acquired knowledge cannot be flexibly applied for solving problems in the relevant subject domain: Rote skills are meaningless and nontransferable, and pure verbal knowledge is inert. That is why students, in fact, are forced to develop their own spontaneous concepts and relevant procedures with which to deal with the subject domain problems.

This explains why the elementary school students in the earlier example, having memorized the concepts of mammals and fish, when classifying animals, associated the whale with the class of fish. It could be reasonably assumed that, not being able to use the memorized definitions of these scientific concepts to solve the subject-domain problems, they involved themselves in the process of empirical learning. They compared "typical" fishes among themselves, picked out their common salient features, and formulated on this basis a spontaneous concept of fish, which turned out to be wrong. Probably, this misconception involved the shape of a body, fins, tail, and living in the water as the essential characteristics that are necessary and sufficient for belonging to the class of fish. In the same way, they developed a spontaneous wrong concept of mammals. Then, when asked to classify animals, they analyzed them by using the developed misconceptions as the basis for analysis, and that method resulted in their associating the whale with the class of fish.

Similarly, students' mastery of rote meaningless skills also results in spontaneous (and often wrong) concepts. For example, having mastered computational operations at the level of rote skills, students have difficulty figuring out which of these operations should be applied in solving a given word problem. In order to overcome such difficulty, they

look for a key word that reveals which operation to use. For example, "altogether" means add, "take away" means subtract, and "each" means multiply. Students pick an operation on the basis of the key word and apply it slavishly to every number in the problem, whether it makes sense or not. (Bruer, 1993, p. 102)

Thus, empirical learning reflects students' attempts to compensate for the deficiencies of the traditional system of school instruction by "discovering" for themselves the scientific knowledge that they have not been taught at school. These attempts, however, are mostly unsuccessful and lead to students' development of spontaneous rather than scientific concepts. That is why, having elaborated Vygotsky's idea of teaching scientific concepts as the content of school instruction, his Russian followers concluded that scientific knowledge should be directly taught to students rather than being discovered by them. The type of learning that meets this requirement has been called *theoretical learning*.

Theoretical learning is based on students' acquisition of methods for scientific analysis of objects or events in different subject domains. Each of these methods is aimed at selecting the essential characteristics of objects or events of a certain class and presenting these characteristics in the form of symbolic and graphic models. Teachers teach methods of scientific analysis, and students then master and internalize these methods in the course of using them. The methods then serve as cognitive tools that mediate the students' further problem solving.

A classical example of the use of the theoretical learning approach is the program of Pantina (1957), which was designed to teach 6-year-old children to write letters of the Russian alphabet. Rather than involving students in drill-and-practice learning (which is the way writing skills are taught in traditional classrooms), the instruction was built around teaching students a general meaningful procedure for copying any contour. The teacher explained that the essence of any letter (or, in general, of any contour) is represented by its *model*: a set of dots, each of which is placed in a position where a change occurs in the direction of the contour. Thus, in order to copy a letter, the students had first to construct its model, a process that involves the following steps: (a) analyzing the letter to be copied to determine where the direction of the contour changes, (b) placing dots in those positions where a change occurs in the direction of the contour, and (c) reproducing the same system of dots in another place on the page (i.e., constructing the model of the letter). Then, the students had to connect the marked dots, that is, to write the required letter. Initially, the students were taught to perform all of these steps at the visual-motor level, but as they mastered the procedure, its major parts started to occur at the visual-imagery level. They visually analyzed the letter to be copied, made a mental image of its model, and copied the letter promptly and surely.

The use of the program described has shown that both the course and the outcomes of the students' learning were very different from what can be observed in a "traditional" classroom (Pantina, 1957). The students' learning proceeded very fast and with very few errors. The mastered procedure was meaningful and broadly transferable; the students were able to use this procedure alone for copying any new contour, including letters of the Latin and Arabic alphabets, as well as unfamiliar pictures. Thus, the outcomes of the use of this program match the definition of scientific knowledge, which, as discussed in the previous section, should be the content of learning at school.

Similar outcomes (high level of mastery of acquired knowledge, its broad transfer, and its intentional use by students) were shown to be the results of the use of other theoretical learning programs. These programs have been used for more than 30 years to teach students of different ages (from 5-year-old children through college students) a variety of subjects, including elementary mathematics, algebra, geometry, physics, chemistry, biology, language, and history (Aidarova, 1978; Elkonin, 1976; Elkonin & Davydov, 1966; Galperin, 1977, 1985; Galperin & Talyzina, 1961; 1972; Salmina & Sokhina, 1975; Venger, 1986; Zhurova, 1978; and many others). Schmittau, an American researcher and one of the contributors to this volume, studied Russian elementary school students after they had been taught mathematics for 3 years under the theoretical learning approach. She revealed that they

evidenced mathematical understanding typically not found among U.S. high school and university students. . . . [She] found it refreshing to observe the degree to which . . . children . . . understood mathematics concepts at their most abstract level and were likewise able to generalize them to new and unfamiliar situations. (Schmittau, 1993, p. 35)

An even more important outcome of the systematic use of theoretical learning is that it has been shown to facilitate students' cognitive development. Particularly, theoretical learning develops students' ability to perform at the level of formal–logical thinking (Davydov, 1986, 1990; Talyzina, 1981). These developmental outcomes of theoretical learning are highly consistent with Vygotsky's (1986) predictions (discussed earlier) about the outcomes of properly organized instruction (for a more detailed analysis of developmental outcomes of different types of instruction, see Arievitch & Stetsenko, 2000).

Russian Vygotskians' ideas of the differences between empirical and theoretical learning and of the advantage of theoretical learning have directly influenced the work of several American educational psychologists (Howe, 1996; Panofsky, John-Steiner, & Blackwell, 1992; Schmittau, 1993). Moreover, these ideas are very close to the recent ideas of some non-Vygotskian-oriented American psychologists who have discussed different types of learning and transfer.

Thus, Bassok and Holyoak (1993) discuss bottom-up and top-down types of transfer. Bottom-up transfer is based on induction from examples: "By integrating information from multiple examples of a category, people can abstract the components shared by the examples. The features that remain relatively constant across examples are likely to be viewed as relevant" (p. 71). The disadvantage of this type of transfer, however, is that it "may lead to erroneous learning [misconceptions – Y. K.] if irrelevant features are constantly present in the examples" (Bassok & Holyoak, 1993, p. 72). In contrast to bottom-up transfer, top-down transfer occurs on the basis of students' knowledge of the "pragmatic relevance," that is, the knowledge of domain rules, laws, and principles, and it "will foster more flexible transfer to novel but related problems" (Bassok & Holyoak, 1993, p. 72). If such knowledge is missing, "the teacher (or the text) should provide direct instruction focusing the student's attention on the goal-relevant aspects" (Bassok & Holyoak, 1993, p. 73).

Similar views are expressed by some other American scholars. Detterman (1993), for example, emphasizes the advantage of providing the general rule to the students at the beginning of the instructional cycle, as opposed to expecting them to infer this rule from specific examples. Referring to the study of Biederman and Shiffrar (1987), Anderson, Reder, and Simon (1995) conclude that "20 minutes of abstract instruction [that is, teaching general rules – Y. K.] brought novices up to the levels of experts who had years of practice" (p. 8). A similar differentiation between a "mere generalization" (that "only correlates observables via actuarial techniques") and a "law of nature" (that "explains its subject matter") is provided in the literature in the philosophy of science (Hanson, 1970, p. 235).

However, it would be wrong to assert that the idea of the advantages of theoretical learning is dominant in American psychology. Many American psychologists advocate a very different perspective. Their position is analyzed in the next section.

DOES GUIDED DISCOVERY LEARNING LEAD TO THE ACQUISITION OF SCIENTIFIC KNOWLEDGE?

The ideas of empirical learning (or discovery learning, as it has been called in American psychological literature) were very popular among American educators in the 1960s and 1970s (for description and analysis, see Morine & Morine, 1973; Shulman & Keislar, 1966). The outcomes of the implementation of this approach in educational practices, however, turned out to be very consistent with the predictions of Russian Vygotskians described in the previous section. Spontaneous concepts that students "discovered" were often misconceptions (e.g., Brown & Campione, 1990). Summarizing the findings from the research on discovery learning, Anderson, Reder, and Simon (1995) point out that "there is very little positive evidence for discovery learning and it is often inferior" (p. 13).

Recently, however, the ideas of discovery learning have been reanimated by some influential American educational and cognitive psychologists (Brown & Campione, 1990, 1994; Brown, Campione, Reeve, Ferrara, & Palincsar, 1991; Chang-Wells & Wells, 1993; Cobb, Wood, & Yackel, 1993; Cobb, Yackel, & Wood, 1992; Cognition and Technology Group at Vanderbilt, 1990, 1992, 1994; Schoenfeld, 1985, 1992; Wells, Chang, & Maher, 1990). Although not advocating pure discovery learning because of its obvious shortcomings, they, at the same time, criticize the traditional school instruction. Its major deficiency, from their point of view, is that students do not achieve mastery of scientific knowledge because this knowledge is taught by the teacher rather than being discovered by the students themselves. Therefore, they "have argued in favor of a middle ground between didactic teaching and untrammeled discovery learning: That of *guided discovery*" (Brown & Campione, 1994, p. 230).

The guided discovery approach is heavily based on constructivist ideas of learning influenced by the works of Dewey (1902) and Piaget (1970). According to these ideas, scientific knowledge should not be taught to students but rather should be constructed by students themselves in the course of discussions, sharing their personal experiences, and carrying out some kind of research activity. A group of students, involved in guided discovery, is similar to a group of research collaborators solving a scientific problem (Cobb et al., 1992), whereas the role of the teacher is to guide and to orchestrate students' discovery processes (Brown & Campione, 1994).

Thus, in contrast to the position of Vygotskians, the adherents of guided discovery view the mastery of scientific knowledge by students as the outcome of the elaboration and refinement of their spontaneous concepts. Some of them clearly contrast Vygotsky's emphasis on "the importance of formal definitions and of the teacher's explicit explanations" with their own emphasis on "inquiry mathematics," which is "interactively constituted in the classroom" (Cobb et al., 1993, p. 100). To validate the Vygotskian position, it is necessary to test the validity of the theoretical assumptions of the advocates of guided discovery learning and to analyze the educational outcomes of the use of their instructional procedures.

The *theoretical assumptions* of the adherents of guided discovery learning are arguable. First, human progress, in general, occurs when every new generation appropriates the essence of knowledge accumulated by previous generations. Why, when dealing with particular students, should we require them to reinvent this knowledge, even if such reinvention is guided by the teacher? As Bruner (1966) noted, "culture . . . is not discovered; it is passed on or forgotten" (p. 101). Gagné (1966) expressed his position in this regard even more explicitly: "To expect a human being to engage in a trial-and-error procedure in discovering a concept appears to be a matter of asking him to behave like an ape" (p. 143).

Second, the criticism of the traditional system of school instruction that guided discovery advocates use to substantiate their approach seems to miss the point. As was demonstrated earlier, the shortcoming of traditional education is not that students are taught scientific knowledge rather than being involved in discovering this knowledge by themselves. Just the contrary, these students are actively involved in unsuccessful attempts to discover scientific knowledge because it has not been taught to them.

Third, guided discovery advocates often draw an analogy between a group of students involved in guided discovery and a group of scientists solving a scientific problem. This analogy has two weaknesses. First, the process of solving a scientific problem may take years, a period that is hardly acceptable in the case of school instruction. Second, research scientists possess methods of scientific research and analysis that were taught to them in special university courses or that they have developed during many years of research experience. School students are unlikely to possess these methods. Actually, as was shown earlier, the principal method of "scientific research" that they use in the situation in which they need to solve a problem in the absence of necessary scientific knowledge is empirical learning. Based on consideration of common salient features of phenomena rather than their essential characteristics, this learning often results in misconceptions.

Fourth, the process of elaborating and refining of spontaneous concepts into scientific concepts under guided discovery learning is inevitably a slow, step-by-step process. Even under the most favorable conditions, this process involves students' operating with their original spontaneous concepts (often, misconceptions) at the intermediate steps of learning. Probably, this is why the advocates of guided discovery seem to support enthusiastically students' rights to make errors in the course of learning: "As long as you're in my class it is okay to make a mistake" (Cobb et al., 1993, p. 98). Sometimes they even claim that "we especially want students to recognize that there is no right or wrong side in most decisions" (Heller & Gordon, 1992, p. 10). A theoretical concern that can be raised in this respect is that such a "relaxed" attitude toward scientific knowledge that is conveyed to the students will hardly contribute to their understanding of the value of acquiring this knowledge.

Finally, although students' learning under the discussed approach is supposed to be guided by the teacher, there is still a danger that this learning will result in misconceptions. As Brown and Campione (1994) observed, guided discovery is difficult to orchestrate. The procedures of guided discovery involve many unguided students' activities when, for example, they are working as a research group on a project. As Chang-Wells and Wells (1993) pointed out, "a great deal of the learning . . . takes place as students work together (more or less) collaboratively, without the involvement of the teacher" (p. 84). As was shown before, unguided learning activity often results in misconceptions. Moreover, some experimental data show that such activity of a group of peers may even result in their rejection of the correct concept in favor of an incorrect concept that one of them has formulated (Tudge, 1992).

Thus, the theoretical assumptions of the guided discovery approach are arguable. However, of much more importance to our discussion of this approach is the analysis of the educational outcomes resulting from the use of the guided discovery learning procedures.

The *educational outcomes* of the use of guided discovery learning as presented by its adherents seem to support the benefits of such learning. The reports indicate that students acquire and transfer knowledge better, their planning and monitoring activities improve, and their learning motivation is higher than under the traditional system of school instruction (Brown & Campione, 1994; Chang-Wells & Wells, 1993; Cobb et al., 1991; Cognition and Technology Group at Vanderbilt, 1994; Schoenfeld, 1992). However, as Anderson, Reder, and Simon (1995) point out, the problem with the evaluation by constructivists of the outcomes of their instructional methods "is a failure to specify precisely the competence being tested for and a reliance on subjective judgment instead" (p. 18). What follows is my analysis of two outcomes of the use of guided discovery learning procedures from the point of view of whether or not these procedures lead to students' acquisition of scientific knowledge. It is important to note that both examples are presented by advocates of guided discovery learning as proof of the advantages of this type of learning.

Heller and Gordon (1992), who worked on Brown and Campione's (1994) project, described a guided discovery lesson aimed at students' mastery of the concept of an animal. The major part of the lesson was spent on a rather long discussion, during which the children were exchanging their spontaneous concepts of an animal. Then, one of the children opened a dictionary and read aloud the scientific definition of an animal. The authors claimed that the lesson was a success because of the students' engaging in the discussion, keeping the discussion focused, asking for clarification when needed, and eliciting comments from their classmates. Two points, however, should be emphasized in regard to this example. First, the children took the ready-made scientific concept of an animal from a dictionary rather than discovering this concept by themselves via the elaboration of their spontaneous concepts. Second, there is no indication that the children's learning led to their mastery of the procedural knowledge relevant to the concept of an animal. For the given case, the procedural knowledge should be the method of identifying within the given object those attributes that are necessary and sufficient for associating (or not associating) this object with the concept of an animal.

The second example deals with the outcomes of the use of a Computer Supported Intentional Learning Environment (CSILE) instructional program (for a description, see Bruer, 1993, pp. 250–256). Heavily based on the constructivist ideas of guided discovery learning, CSILE also involves a broad use of modern computer technology, including students' exchange of e-mail messages and their collaborative generation of a curriculum-related database. According to Bruer (1993), the major outcome of the CSILE program is that the students' writing improves. Particularly, "when giving handwritten answers to the question 'What have I learned from doing this unit?' the CSILE students write well-constructed essays which contain some mature text conventions, whereas typically elementary students rely on straightforward knowledge telling" (p. 253). Since "better learning and better reasoning . . . lead to better writing" (Bruer, 1993, p. 251), Bruer interprets these data as proof of the success of the CSILE program.

To illustrate the benefits of the CSILE program, Bruer (1993) compares paragraphs from two "What I Learned About Primates" essays, one written by a CSILE student and the other by a non-CSILE student. I limit myself to quoting the three first and the three last sentences from each paragraph. A non-CSILE student wrote:

I know most about gorillas so that's what I'll start with. There are different types of gorillas. For instance, the mountain gorilla has much nicer, shinier fur than the lowland gorilla. . . . The silverback – the leader has exclusive breeding rights. The baby will sleep in the same night nest with their mother until the mother has another baby which will usually not happen until the first baby is about 4 or 5. A night nest is a big nest made of all kinds of big plants. (Bruer, 1993, p. 254)

A CSILE student wrote:

There is another primate which I want to talk about. I expressed great interest in learning about this one special gorilla. This gorilla's name is Koko. . . . I think that Koko is a warm and gentle gorilla who loves animals and people. I also want to say thank-you to Dr. Patterson who has taught Koko everything. I'm glad I did this project because I had fun doing it and I now feel that I know Koko myself. (Bruer, 1993, p. 254)

To support his view of the superiority of the paragraph by the CSILE student, Bruer (1993) points out that "independent judges consistently rate CSILE students' end-of-unit summaries higher than those of non-CSILE students on the quality of knowledge expressed and quality of organization and presentation" (pp. 253–254).

Bruer's evaluation of the quoted paragraphs seems arguable. First, the paragraphs do not make it possible to evaluate the students' procedural knowledge, that is, their ability to solve problems relevant to the discussed topic. Thus, the data presented can be used only for evaluation of their declarative knowledge. Second, even in regard to the quality of their declarative knowledge, Bruer's position is disputable. For the last 7 years, I have asked several hundreds of my graduate students (most of them have been highly experienced teachers) to evaluate the paragraphs quoted, and their responses have been consistently very different from Bruer's evaluation. They have indicated that, as opposed to the non-CSILE student's paragraph, the paragraph of the CSILE student was very egocentric, was immature, and did not match the topic of the essay. Whereas the non-CSILE student demonstrated his conceptual knowledge in the field by discussing the essential characteristics of gorillas, the CSILE student expressed her emotions in regard to Koko and presented some facts about this particular gorilla. Some of my graduate students even conjectured that the CSILE student was much younger than the non-CSILE student. Similar evaluations of the paragraphs discussed were given by my colleagues (psychologists, linguists, and educators) at the Graduate School of Education and Psychology of Touro College.

Thus, the examples of the educational outcomes of guided discovery learning discussed, as well as the theoretical concerns expressed earlier in regard to this approach, make it doubtful that guided discovery is the proper way to teach students scientific knowledge. This conclusion is consistent with a general statement of Anderson, Reder, and Simon (1995) that "constructivism advocates very inefficient learning and assessment procedures" (p. 1).

CONCLUSION

Vygotsky's doctrine of the acquisition of scientific concepts as the content of school instruction was not free of shortcomings. The most serious of them was Vygotsky's underestimation of the importance of acquisition of procedural knowledge by students. This doctrine, however, was used by his Russian followers as the theoretical basis for their analysis of what the content and process of school instruction should be to meet educational goals.

Having elaborated Vygotsky's ideas, Russian Vygotskians reached the conclusion that school instruction should be built around teaching students scientific knowledge that consists of methods of scientific analysis in different subject domains. It has been shown that traditional school instruction does not meet this requirement. Often, students in traditional classrooms are not taught scientific knowledge. Therefore, they, in fact, are forced to use empirical (discovery) learning to develop their spontaneous concepts to deal with subject-domain problems. As an alternative, Russian Vygotskians developed the theoretical learning approach built around their ideas in regard to the content and process of teaching. Instructional programs developed within this approach have been shown to result in students' mastery of meaningful and broadly transferable scientific knowledge, which they start to use for the analysis of subject-domain phenomena. Thus, under this approach, "the child as an independent learner is considered to be a result, rather than a premise of the learning process" (Kozulin, 1995, p. 121).

American guided discovery advocates support the opposite perspective in regard to traditional instruction and the ways to overcome its deficiencies. Heavily influenced by constructivist ideas, they claim that traditional school students do not master scientific knowledge because it has been taught rather than being discovered by the students themselves. Therefore, their programs promote empirical learning, which, from the point of view of Russian Vygotskians, aggravates rather than overcomes the shortcomings of traditional instruction. The examples of the educational outcomes of guided discovery learning that have been discussed in this chapter challenge the claim of guided discovery advocates that their programs lead to the acquisition of scientific knowledge.

As Prawat (1995) indicates, two previous reforms of American education built around constructivist principles have failed. On the basis of the preceding discussion, the guided discovery approach, which can be viewed as a part of the third wave of constructivist educational reform, does not look very promising either. These failures can be reasonably attributed to the shortcomings of constructivism as a theory of learning. In contrast, Vygotsky's doctrine of scientific concepts has been shown to be a powerful tool for the analysis of existing approaches to instruction and for the development of new approaches. This is one more illustration of the fact that Vygotsky's ideas, which were formulated back in the 1930s, are still surprisingly up to date.

References

Aidarova, L. I. (1978). *Psikhologicheskie problemy obucheniya mladshikh shkolnikov russkomu yazyku* [Psychological problems of teaching Russian language to elementary-school pupils]. Moscow: Prosveschenie.

Anderson, J. R., Reder, L. M., & Simon, H. A. (1995). *Applications and misapplications of cognitive psychology to mathematics education.* Available at: http://www.psy.cmu.edu/~mm4b/misapplied.html

Arievitch, I. M., & Stetsenko, A. (2000). The quality of cultural tools and cognitive development: Gal'perin's perspective and its implications. *Human Development, 43*, 69–92.

Bassok, M., & Holyoak, K. J. (1993). Pragmatic knowledge and conceptual structure: Determinants of transfer between quantitative domains. In D. K. Detterman & R. J. Sternberg (Eds.), *Transfer on trial: Intelligence, cognition, and instruction* (pp. 68–98). Norwood, NJ: Ablex.

Biederman, I., & Shiffrar, M. (1987). Sexing day-old chicks: A case study and expert systems analysis of a difficult perceptual learning task. *Journal of Experimental Psychology: Learning, Memory, and Cognition, 13,* 640–645.

Brown, A. L., & Campione, J. C. (1990). Communities of learning and thinking: Or a context by any other name. *Contributions to Human Development, 21,* 108–126.

Brown, A. L., & Campione, J. C. (1994). Guided discovery in a community of learners. In K. McGilly (Ed.), *Classroom lessons: Integrating cognitive theory and classroom practice* (pp. 229–270). Cambridge, MA: MIT Press.

Brown, A. L., Campione, J. C., Reeve, R. A., Ferrara, R. A., & Palincsar, A. S. (1991). Interactive learning and individual understanding: The case of reading and mathematics. In L. T. Landsman (Ed.), *Culture, schooling, and psychological development* (pp. 136–170). Hillsdale, NJ: Erlbaum.

Bruer, J. T. (1993). *Schools for thought: A science of learning in the classroom.* Cambridge, MA: MIT Press.

Bruner, J. S. (1966). Some elements of discovery. In L. S. Shulman & E. R. Keislar (Eds.), *Learning by discovery: A critical appraisal* (pp. 101–113). Chicago: Rand McNally.

Chang-Wells, G. L. M., & Wells, G. (1993). Dynamics of discourse: Literacy and the construction of knowledge. In E. A. Forman, N. Minick, & C. A. Stone (Eds.), *Contexts for learning: Sociocultural dynamics in children's development* (pp. 58–90). New York: Oxford University Press.

Cobb, P., Wood, T., & Yackel, E. (1993). Discourse, mathematical thinking, and classroom practice. In E. A. Forman, N. Minick, & C. A. Stone (Eds.), *Contexts for learning: Sociocultural dynamics in children's development* (pp. 91–120). New York: Oxford University Press.

Cobb, P., Wood, T., Yackel, E., Nicholls, J., Wheatley, G., Trigatti, B., & Perlwitz, M. Assessment of a problem-centered second grade mathematics project. *Journal for Research in Mathematics Education, 22,* 3–29.

Cobb, P., Yackel, E., & Wood, T. (1992). A constructivist alternative to the representational view of mind in mathematics education. *Journal for Research in Mathematics Education, 23,* 2–33.

Cognition and Technology Group at Vanderbilt. (1990). Anchored instruction and its relationship to situated cognition. *Educational Researcher, 19*(6), 2–10.

Cognition and Technology Group at Vanderbilt. (1992). The Jasper experiment: An exploration of issues in learning and instructional design. *Educational Technology Research and Development, 40,* 65–80.

Cognition and Technology Group at Vanderbilt. (1994). From visual word problems to learning communities: Changing conceptions of cognitive research. In K. McGilly (Ed.), *Classroom lessons: Integrating cognitive theory and classroom practice* (pp. 157–200). Cambridge, MA: MIT Press.

Davydov, V. V. (1986). *Problemy razvivayuschego obucheniya* [Problems of development-generating learning]. Moscow: Pedagogika.

Davydov, V. V. (1990). *Types of generalization in instruction.* Reston, VA: National Council of Teachers of Mathematics.

Detterman, D. K. (1993). The case for the prosecution: Transfer as an epiphenomenon. In D. K. Detterman & R. J. Sternberg (Eds.), *Transfer on trial: Intelligence, Cognition, and Instruction* (pp. 1–24). Norwood, NJ: Ablex.

Dewey, J. (1902). *The child and the curriculum.* Chicago: University of Chicago Press.

DiSessa, A. A. (1982). Unlearning Aristotelian physics: A study of knowledge-based learning. *Cognitive Science, 6,* 37–75.

Elkonin, D. B. (1976). *Kak uchit detei chitat* [How to teach children to read]. Moscow: Znanie.

Elkonin, D. B. (1989). *Izbrannye psikhologicheskie trudy* [Selected psychological works]. Moscow: Pedagogika.

Elkonin, D. B., & Davydov, V. V. (Eds.) (1966). *Vozrastnye vozmozhnosti usvoeniya znanii* [Age-dependent potentialities of acquiring knowledge]. Moscow: Prosveschenie.

Gagné, R. M. (1966). Varieties of learning and the concept of discovery. In L. S. Shulman & E. R. Keislar (Eds.), *Learning by discovery: A critical appraisal* (pp. 135–150). Chicago: Rand McNally.

Galperin, P. Y. (1957). Umstvennoe deistviye kak osnova formirovaniya mysli i obraza [Mental act as the basis for formation of thought and image]. *Voprosy Psikhologii, 6,* 58–69.

Galperin, P. Y. (1969). Stages in the development of mental acts. In M. Cole & I. Maltzman (Eds.), *A handbook of contemporary Soviet psychology* (pp. 34–61). New York: Basic Books.

Galperin, P. Y. (Ed.) (1977). *Upravlyaemoe formirovanie psikhicheskikh protsessov* [Guided formation of the mental processes]. Moscow: Izdatelstvo MGU.

Galperin, P. Y. (1985). *Metody obucheniya i umstvennoe razvitie rebenka* [Methods of instruction and the child's mental development]. Moscow: Izdatelstvo MGU.

Galperin, P. Y., & Talyzina, N. F. (1961). Formation of elementary geometrical concepts and their dependence on directed participation by the pupils. In N. O'Connor (Ed.), *Recent Soviet psychology* (pp. 247–272). New York: Liveright.

Galperin, P. Y., & Talyzina, N. F. (Eds.) (1972). *Upravlenie poznavatelnoi deyatelnostyu uchaschikhsya* [Guidance of cognitive activity of students]. Moscow: Izdatelstvo MGU.

Galperin, P. Y., Zaporozhets, A. V., & Elkonin, D. B. (1963). Problemy formirovaniya znanii i umenii u shkolnikov i novye metody obucheniya v shkole [The problems of formation of knowledge and skills in school-children and the new methods of instruction at school]. *Voprosy Psikhologii, 5,* 61–72.

Hanson, N. R. (1970). A picture theory of theory meaning. In R. G. Colodny (Ed.), *The nature and function of scientific theories* (pp. 233–273). Pittsburgh: University of Pittsburgh Press.

Heller, J. I., & Gordon, A. (1992). Lifelong learning. *Educator, 6*(1), 4–19.

Hiebert, J., & Wearne, D. (1985). A model of students' decimal computation procedures. *Cognition and Instruction, 2,* 175–205.

Hirsch, E. D. (1987). *Cultural literacy.* New York: Vintage Books.

Hirsch, E. D. (1988, July/August). A postscript by E. D. Hirsch. *Change,* 22–26.

Howe, A. C. (1996). Development of science concepts within a Vygotskian framework. *Science Education, 80*(1), 35–51.

Kozulin, A. (1995). The learning process: Vygotsky's theory in the mirror of its interpretations. *School Psychology International, 16,* 117–129.

Leontiev, A. N. (1983). Ovladenie uchaschimisya nauchnymi poniatiyami kak problema pedagogicheskoi psikhologii [Mastering scientific concepts by students as a problem of educational psychology]. In A. N. Leontiev, *Izbrannye psikhologicheskie proizvedeniya* (Tom 1, pp. 324–347). Moscow: Pedagogika.

Morine, H., & Morine, G. (1973). *Discovery: A challenge to teachers.* Englewood Cliffs, NJ: Prentice-Hall.

Panofsky, C. P., John-Steiner, V., & Blackwell, P. J. (1992). The development of scientific concepts and discourse. In L. C. Moll (Ed.), *Vygotsky and education: Instructional implications of sociohistorical psychology.* Cambridge: Cambridge University Press.

Pantina, N. S. (1957). Formirovanie dvigatelnogo navyka pisma v zavisimosti ot tipa orientirovki v zadanii [Formation of writing skills depending on the type of task orientation]. *Voprosy Psikhologii, 4,* 117–132.

Piaget, J. (1970). *Genetic epistemology.* New York: Columbia University Press.

Prawat, R. S. (1995). Misreading Dewey: Reform, projects, and the language game. *Educational Researcher, 24*(7), 13–22.

Salmina, N. G., & Sokhina, V. P. (1975). *Obuchenie matematike v nachalnoi shkole* [Teaching mathematics in elementary school]. Moscow: Pedagogika.

Schmittau, J. (1993). Vygotskian scientific concepts: Implications for mathematics education. *Focus on Learning Problems in Mathematics, 15*(2, 3), 29–39.

Schoenfeld, A. H. (1985). *Mathematical problem solving.* New York: Academic Press.

Schoenfeld, A. H. (1992). Learning to think mathematically: Problem solving, metacognition, and sense making in mathematics. In P. H. Grouws (Ed.), *Handbook of research on mathematics teaching: A project of the National Council of Teachers of Mathematics* (pp. 334–370). New York: MacMillan.

Shulman, L. S., & Keislar, E. R. (Eds.) (1966). *Learning by discovery: A critical appraisal.* Chicago: Rand McNally.

Talyzina, N. F. (1981). *The psychology of learning.* Moscow: Progress.

Tudge, J. (1992). Vygotsky, the zone of proximal development, and peer collaboration: Implications for classroom practice. In L. C. Moll (Ed.), *Vygotsky and education: Instructional implications and applications of sociohistorical psychology* (pp. 155–172). Cambridge: Cambridge University Press.

Venger, L. A. (Ed.) (1986). *Razvitie poznavatelnykh sposobnostei v protsesse doshkolnogo vospitaniya* [Development of cognitive abilities in the course of preschool education]. Moscow: Pedagogika.

Vygotsky, L. S. (1978). M. Cole, V. John-Steiner, S. Scribner & E. Souberman (Eds.), *Mind in society: The development of higher psychological processes.* Cambridge, MA: Harvard University Press.

Vygotsky, L. S. (1981). The genesis of higher mental functions. In J. V. Wertsch (Ed.), *The concept of activity in Soviet psychology* (pp. 144–188). Armonk, NY: Sharpe.

Vygotsky, L. S. (1986). *Thought and language.* Cambridge, MA: MIT Press.

Vygotsky, L. S. (1987). R. W. Rieber (Ed.), *The collected works of L. S. Vygotsky.* Vol. 1. *Problems of general psychology.* New York: Plenum.

Wells, G., Chang, G. L., & Maher, A. (1990). Creating classroom communities of literate thinkers. In S. Sharan (Ed.), *Cooperative learning: Theory and research* (pp. 95–121). New York: Praeger.

Zaporozhets, A. V. (1986). Razvitie myshleniya [The development of thinking]. In A. V. Zaporozhets, *Izbrannye psikhologicheskie trudy, Tom 1* (pp. 200–215). Moscow: Pedagogika.

Zhurova, L. E. (1978). *Obuchenie gramote v detskom sadu* [Teaching reading and writing at the kindergarten]. Moscow: Pedagogika.

4

Some Cognitive Tools of Literacy

Kieran Egan and Natalia Gajdamaschko

For the educator interested in such topics as how to engage children in becoming more fluently literate, Vygotsky has offered a crucially important insight. Before his work – and, of course, still commonly the case for those who have been unable to see its richer implications for education – approaches to education generally have tended to take one or more of three general approaches. We will sketch them very briefly and then indicate in what way Vygotsky's insight into the role of cognitive tools helps us to transcend the limitations of the three traditional approaches.

The main purpose of our chapter, however, is to explore some new implications of Vygotsky's insight, seeking to unfold it in ways that enable educators to discover new pathways to engage students in literacy successfully. We think, also, that this analysis of the cognitive tools that are constituents of literacy provides a novel expansion of Vygotsky's insight in ways directly applicable to education.

THREE TRADITIONAL CONCEPTIONS OF THE
EDUCATOR'S TASK

The first, and most ancient, conception of the educator's task is to engage the young learner in what today we call an apprenticeship relationship with an expert. The child would, consequently, learn by doing with an expert on hand to guide and correct the novice. This kind of learning has been perhaps the most common in human cultures across the world and was almost the exclusive mode of instruction in hunter–gatherer societies. And, for the teaching of certain kinds of skills, it remains of significant value to the educator.

The invention of writing transformed the educator's task. Increasingly, as literacy developed, significant amounts of knowledge were stored in coded form. Access to this store was attained only through becoming skilled in literacy. Consequently, all literate cultures invented some formal system of education into coding and decoding knowledge. The trouble with this task has been that at one level it seems it ought to be easy to teach the principles of the decoding system, and then all the stored knowledge would be available to the newly literate person. But it does not work so easily, partly because of the difficulty many people have in learning to become literate in even basic ways, and partly because of the complexity of what is stored in the codes of literate cultures. Not only does one have to teach the systems of coding and decoding, but one also has the harder task of trying to bring back to life the meanings inherent in those desiccated codes. The size of the problem was recognized early on; Plato said that anyone who writes something down and assumes that another will be able to understand exactly what the writer means is a fool.

The conception of education that derived from this accumulation of coded knowledge was one in which the task was to teach as much of certain privileged forms of knowledge as possible – privileged in the sense that they provided the learner with the fullest and truest account of the world. These accounts were systematically coded into forms of knowledge that came to be known as mathematics, history, science, literature, and so on. The mark of an educated person was her or his elaborate familiarity with these forms of knowledge. In this tradition, the mind was conceived largely as an epistemological organ; the educated mind was recognized as such because it contained a great deal of the most important knowledge.

The third conception of the educator's task grew out of the recognition that, somehow, just accumulating lots of important knowledge did not always produce a satisfactory kind of person. Something was missing, and the element that was missing was seen to be something to do with the fact that the mind's development was not exclusively an epistemological matter. During the past two centuries, it became increasingly recognized by many that the mind also seemed to have a distinctive form of development of its own. Jean-Jacques Rousseau forcefully expressed this idea.

Since Rousseau's time, attempts have been made to uncover and describe this underlying process of mental development, perhaps most spectacularly in the work of Jean Piaget. Increasingly the mind has come to be seen as a psychological organ, with its own schedules of development that are more or less independent of the particular forms of knowledge being learned. Educators were persuaded to see their task, then, as supporting the development of this internal developmental process, to further as far as possible this psychological conception of the mind's development.

The trouble for us today is that these different conceptions of the educator's task are not entirely compatible, and yet they all continue to have some claim on schools and on teachers' time and activities. Also, each of the conceptions by itself has problems. We do not intend to discuss these problems here (but see Lamm, 1976; Egan, 1997); they have been staples of polemics through the past century, with "traditionalist" educators pointing out the shortcomings of "progressivist" educators, and those concerned about "vocational" education deriding those "liberal" educators, and vice versa. Our concern, rather, is with an alternative conception of the educator's task that emerges from Vygotsky's work.

A COGNITIVE TOOLS APPROACH

Two difficulties educators have had with, for example, the Piagetian model of psychological development concern, first, just what is the model describing, and, second, how can it be integrated into the earlier epistemological conception of education. That is, first, are those detailed stages Piaget characterizes really descriptions of some spontaneous mental development, or are they rather artifacts of cultural contingencies and his research methods and assumptions, and so on. And, second, how does the Piagetian image of formal operations characterize an aim of education, and how can history and literature be accommodated to his stages? Much ingenuity has gone into answering these questions, but the results "at the chalk face" of schools have not sustained much confidence. The psychological conception of the educator's task has been consistently offered with the promise that if educators just attend to the new psychological theories about the mind, then a revolution in learning will take place. It is a century and a half since the beginnings of this progressivist–psychological promise, in the work of Herbert Spencer (1820–1903), and the revolution has stubbornly refused to occur. Indeed, maybe we should extend it to 200 years in the work of Johann Pestalozzi (1746–1827).

The alternative conception Vygotsky offers is to see the mind as being a psychosocial and cultural organ, and the cognitive tools we learn as providing the educator with a focus of attention that can make better sense of the task before us.

The psychological conception, exemplified by Piaget's work, and enormously influential still in education despite the decline in Piaget's reputation and increasingly radical criticisms of his work, still sees the educator's task as accommodating some model of psychological development. Vygotsky's crucial insight was to recognize that education should not be seen as "a superstructure built on the foundations of psychological functions, [rather] educational activity is seen as a process radically changing these very foundations" (Kozulin, 1998, p. 16).

Kozulin goes further in elaborating this conception by pointing out that through formal schooling people in developed and developing societies today "become exposed to a wide array of symbolic tools that not only become indispensable as cognitive tools but to a certain extent form the very 'reality' of the modern individual" (Kozulin, 1998, p. 17). So instead of the current assumption that we have some kind of independently developing psychological substructure to which educator's efforts must be made to conform, we may accept the liberating insight that the "Cultural devices of behavior do not appear simply as external habit; they comprise an inalienable part of personality itself, rooted in its new relations and creating their completely new system" (Vygotsky, 1997, p. 92). "Even now," Vygotsky continues, "many psychologists are inclined to consider the facts of cultural changes in our behavior from their natural aspect and think of them as facts of habit formation or as intellectual reactions directed toward a cultural content" (Vygotsky, 1997, p. 92).

Consider, for example, the case of written language. According to Vygotsky, most of the difficulties in teaching literacy arise from misunderstanding what written language is. He remarked that neither in theory nor in practice is written language being viewed as a "special system of symbols and signs the mastery of which signifies a critical turning point in the whole cultural development of the child" (Vygotsky, 1997, p. 132).

Instead, researchers commonly, and mistakenly, focus on written language as a phenomenon similar in nature to habit formation (such as dressing up or forming any other mechanical habit) that can be taught "naturally." We see such assumptions constantly asserted in, for example, the Whole Language (WL) movement. The WL classroom, we are told, is designed to conform with the way children naturally learn; it is like "homes where children are allowed and encouraged to be learners from the day they are born" (Peetboom, 1988, p. 246).

Relatedly, if asked how the child arrives at the conscious understanding of literacy, the answer is that the child "discovers" it. "The key to whole teaching and learning is the active involvement and enjoyment of children as they play with, manipulate and construct language through exposure to fun, enjoyable, rich, and meaningful literature" (Polette, 1990, p. 19). Children are viewed as accomplished learners when they arrive at school, and "the teacher should intrude only minimally into this process of discovery" (Altwerger, 1994, p. 40). Herbert Spencer's belief that the teacher should merely facilitate the child's own active discovery is a central tenet of WL: "Teaching is not 'teaching' at all. It is an act of guiding and appreciating" (Martin, 1990, p. 3).

In Vygotsky's words:

[T]he basic difficulty consists in overcoming the traditional prejudice closely linked with intellectualism, which still continues its cryptic dominance in child psychology. The basis of the intellectualistic view of the process of development is the assumption that development occurs like a logical operation. To the question as to how conscious use of speech develops in the child, the intellectualistic theory replies that the child discovers the meaning of speech. In attempts to substitute a simple logical operation for the complex process of development, not noting that such approach involves an enormous difficulty because it assumes as given that which requires explanation. (Vygotsky, 1997, p. 94)

So, Vygotsky concludes, "Where researches thus far saw either simple discovery or a simple process of the formation of a habit, the true study discloses a complex process of development" (Vygotsky, 1997, p. 95).

Approaching literacy from the Vygotskian perspective as a much more complex cultural phenomenon, we need to recognize that literacy will give a new set of cognitive tools to the child. It is not only the mechanics of writing to which a child is being introduced in school but the whole new system of cognitive psychological tools that literature has historically stored within itself.

Our purpose for the rest of this chapter is to try to elaborate Vygotsky's insight by considering some of the cognitive tools that are constituents of literacy. We will explore how they contribute to forming aspects of the "reality" of modern individuals and show how these cognitive tools provide a key to how best to educate students within this modern world.

There is a tendency to think of cognitive tools as discrete elements that might be deployed in thinking. Perhaps the unfortunate word *tools* encourages this kind of somewhat mechanistic tendency. But our concern is with forms of consciousness, or kinds of understanding, that are created by the deployment of such tools. The complex nature of the cognitive tools of literacy, if introduced properly in teaching, encourages not only development of logical operations but development of imagination, self-reflection, emotions, and awareness of the child's own thinking. So the kinds of categories that we will explore might initially seem rather odd, perhaps surprising. They are not, certainly, the usual kinds of topics one sees in psychological discussions of education. Nevertheless they are the categories we have arrived at by taking Vygotsky's arguments seriously and exploring their educational implications.

SOME COGNITIVE TOOLS OF LITERACY

The Limits of Reality and the Extremes of Experience

> The imagination of the adolescence is different from the play of the child in that it breaks the connection with real objects.
>
> (Vygotsky, 1998, p. 161)

If you tell a typical 5-year-old the story of Cinderella, you are not likely to be asked, What means of locomotion does the Fairy Godmother use? But if you tell a typical 10-year-old the equally fantastic story of Superman, you will need to explain his supernatural powers by reference to his birth on the planet Krypton and to the different molecular structure of our Sun from that of his home star, and so on. For the younger audience, magic is entirely unobjectionable as long as it moves the story along. One way to simplify what we see happening between age 5 and age 10 through such an example is to say that with literacy we begin to focus on what we ultimately call reality. It has been a part of the folklore of teaching that if you want to teach students about reality you must begin with what they already know, with what is familiar in their everyday environment, with "where they are at." This is a principle that derives from a focus on students' logicomathematical thinking. But if we also consider that their thinking is not limited by logicomathematical capacities but also has access to the range of cognitive tools that literacy provides to the imagination, we see something quite different from what this principle leads us to expect.

Consider for a moment, if you want to engage students' imaginations on a Friday afternoon, whether a unit on "the structure of your neighborhood" or one on "torture instruments through the ages" would do the job better. This is not a curriculum recommendation (!), but it exposes something that seems profoundly at odds with the recommendation that we begin with what the student already knows. The resolution, of course, is that the students do already know about pain and horror and cruelty. That is, if we consider the cognitive tools of their imaginative lives in what they "know," we can save the principle.

But we should reformulate that principle if it is to offer clearer guidance to teaching. The most casual observation of what engages adolescents' imaginations shows that materials that deal with the limits of reality and the extremes of experience are most engaging: the most courageous or cruelest acts, the most bizarre and strange natural phenomena, the most wonderful and terrible events. The *Guinness Book of Records* exploits this characteristic, most profitably for its publishers, as do TV shows, comics, films, books, and so on, that focus on the bizarre, the amazing, the extreme, the exotic. The initial exploration of the real world mirrors precisely this fascination with the wonders and extremes of reality (see, for example, Herodotus' *Histories*). This capacity for engaging the real world by such dramatic tools constitutes one of the powerful means students have to learn about reality.

So let us discard the logical principle that students' understanding moves along associations from the known to the unknown; clearly they can directly engage new knowledge that is affectively engaging and deals with some extreme or limit. In place of the logical principle we can try the reformulated one that we should note some exotic or extreme feature of any topic. This does not mean that every class must become an eye-popping extravaganza of the bizarre, but it does require the teacher to locate in the material something that is strange, wonderful, or extreme.

This principle is not intended to lead to empty sensationalism; it is designed rather to put students in touch with the boundaries, the limits, the context of the material they are dealing with. After all, attention to the limits and extremes is a perfectly sensible strategy for exploring the world being exposed by expanding literacy. We begin sensibly by locating the limits, setting clearly in place the context of our world. The principle of "starting where the student is" need not be mischievous as long as we remember that the student has an imagination, and "where the student's imagination is" can be in the valleys of the Moon as well as in his or her local neighborhood. We no less make sense of our neighborhood in terms of our imagination of the valleys of the Moon than we make sense of the valleys of the Moon in terms of our understanding of our neighborhoods. There is, that is, constant dialectical play between what we know and what we imagine. If our beginning principle focuses only on what we know in some simplistic logical sense, ignoring how that is enlightened by what we imagine, we will unnecessarily constrict our teaching, our curricula, and students' learning, and we will incidentally likely bore them mindless.

"What is substantially new in the development of fantasy during the transitional age is contained precisely in the fact that the imagination of an adolescent enters a close connection with thinking in concepts; it is intellectualized and included in the system of intellectual activity and begins to fulfill a completely new function in the new structure of the adolescent's personality" (Vygotsky, 1998, p. 154). It is this new and closer connection of imagination with thinking in concepts during adolescence that allows more freedom and new ways to deal with the extremes and limits of reality.

Transcendence Within Reality – the Heroic

> We can say that creative images produced by an adolescent's fantasy fulfill the same function that an artistic work fulfills for the adults. It is art for oneself. It is for oneself, in the mind, that poems and novels are produced, dramas and tragedies are acted out, and elegies and sonnets are composed.
> (Vygotsky, 1998, p. 165)

Adolescents are relatively powerless but grow increasingly aware that the society that hems them in and constrains them is one of which they are becoming a part. A common imaginative response to the constraints on their lives, such as the rules of parents, of schools, of authorities of all kinds, is to associate with those who seem best able to transcend, to overcome, the constraints that most irk the student. So a pop singer or basketball star might form the object of a "romantic association" because she or he might seem to embody the reckless disregard of conventions or the independence and strength the students lack or cannot express in their lives. The student associates with the confidence, self-reliance, persistence, ingenuity, strength, or whatever, of the heroic character and so shares the transcendence.

But it is not so much the heroic character with which the student associates, rather it is the transcendent quality the character embodies. It is not so much that we need to find heroic characters all the time, Sir Galahads or Florence Nightingales; we can locate transcendent qualities, such as courage, compassion, persistence, energy, power, or ingenuity, in almost anything in the world. It could be the tenacity of a weed on a rock face, the serene patience of a cat, or the endurance of standing stones in a gale; almost any feature of the world can be imbued with a transcendent quality if we conceive of it romantically. Associating with the transcendent involves the student in imaginatively inhabiting the object in some degree.

A principle that follows from this common observation is that we might plan to encourage students to see some transcendent quality in the material being studied with which she or he could romantically associate. The trick is to see how one can easily "heroize" anything: That discarded plastic cup, instead of being conceived simply as environmentally destructive litter, can be conceived, if only for a moment, as the product of immense ingenuity and the patient work of chemists over centuries; we can hold our fingers within millimeters of scalding liquids and not be burned or even feel discomfort. For a moment we can see it as an object of wonder. This capacity to highlight anything and hold it in a transcendent light is something we can turn on anything at any time. It is not exactly Wordsworth's "visionary gleam" but is perhaps a little sibling of it that the teacher can call upon to stimulate imaginative engagement with any material.

Image and Concept

> A real concept is an image of an objective thing in its complexity.
>
> (Vygotsky, 1997, p. 53)

Moving the cognitive tools of the literate imagination to the fore in thinking about education raises the question of the role of affective images in teaching. We have inherited ideas and practices of education that give pride of place to the disembedded concept and seem to have neglected or forgotten what all the most powerful communicative media in our cultural history make plain to us – that the affective image is crucial in communicating meaning and significance.

Certainly affective images are not necessary to all imaginative activity. We can define imagination as the capacity to think of things as other than they are, or of things as possibly being so (White, 1990), or even as "the subjunctive mood" (Sutton-Smith, 1988). But however we define imaginative activity, clearly significant to it are thinking and feeling using mental images. The kinds of images that are constituents of literacy are perhaps not so obviously new in our experience, but features of them are clearly distinct from those of childhood.

The images that seem to have most power are those we generate ourselves from words. Films, for example, rarely capture the emotional vividness and force of literature. This is to emphasize that we are not suggesting that there is a need for more visual illustration of materials, but rather that the teacher be more hospitable to the mental images evoked by any topic. In planning teaching, to draw a principle from this observation, we should not only dwell on the concepts that are important, but give at least equal time to reflecting on the images that are a part of them. It is the images that can vividly carry the concepts most richly to the students' understanding. The image can carry the imagination to inhabit in some sense the object of our study and inquiry. By such means mathematics and physics, history and auto mechanics are not conceived as external things that the student learns facts about but become a part of the student; students thus learn that they are mathematical, historical, mechanical creatures.

So, for example, in teaching poetry this principle will lead us to attend to images not only as things to be observed in the mind's eye and understood in the overall structure of the poem, but also as things the student can inhabit or get inside of, so to speak. Poetry, then, is not something we do, but something we are. Perhaps this principle is more urgent for the science or the mathematics teacher, by whom the image is more commonly neglected, but, even though images might be the focus of much poetry teaching, the affective power that can result from inhabiting them could probably be more frequently drawn upon. If teaching William Blake's "The Tiger," one can encourage the students to evoke as vividly as they can "the forests of the night" and then the "Tiger! Tiger! burning bright" within them. What are the students' forests of the night – the dread places of their imaginations? On a rereading, ask them to be the burning tiger, being violently constructed piece by piece; to feel the distant deeps that become the fire in their eyes, their massive pounding heart, the deadly terrors of their brain. On a further rereading, ask them to build an image of the maker of this deadly terror, twisting sinews in the awful factory with its inconceivable hammer, chains, furnace, and anvil; then after constructing this demonic horror perhaps turning to compose the Lamb. The images will likely not be precise quasi pictures, so much as intimations of power, terror, immensity in the fragmented, flashing images Blake uses to express a very particular kind of awe and wonder.

Vygotsky argues that "the false interpretation of fantasy consists in the fact that is it considered from one aspect alone, as a function connected with emotional life, with a life of drives and attitudes; the other aspect, related to intellectual life, remains in shadow" (Vygotsky, 1998, p. 153). Vygotsky was warning us about the possibility of making a mistake and disconnecting concept and image in education. He attributed this mistake to the traditional psychology point of view on how concepts develop: "From formal logic, traditional psychology adopted the idea of the concept as an abstract mental construct extremely remote from all the wealth of concrete reality" (Vygotsky, 1997, p. 53). In such a tradition, thinking about concepts is viewed as removed from concrete reality as a result of the process of generalizing and abstracting from concrete traits of reality. Highly abstract concepts become increasingly "poorer, scant and narrow" from the point of view of content.

Vygotsky argues that traditional psychology made a mistake in describing concept development in what he called a "mechanical way":

Not without the reason are such concepts frequently termed empty abstracts. Others have said that concepts arise in the process of castrating reality. Concrete, diverse phenomena must lose their traits one after the other in *course* that a concept might be formed. Actually what arises is a dry and empty abstraction in which the diverse, full-blooded reality is narrowed and impoverished by logical thought. This is the source of the celebrated word of Goethe: "Grey is every theory and eternally green is the golden tree of life."

This dry, empty, gray abstraction inevitably strives to reduce content to zero because the more general, the more empty the concept becomes. Impoverishing the content is done from fateful necessity, and for this reason, proceeding to develop the teaching of concepts on the grounds of formal logic, presented thinking in concepts as the system of thinking that was the poorest, scantiest, and emptiest. (Vygotsky, 1997, p. 53)

The true nature of concepts must be viewed in their inseparable connection to the image:

A real concept is an image of an objective thing in its complexity. Only when we recognize the thing in all its connection and relation, only when this diversity is synthesized in a word, in an integral image through the multitude of determinations, do we develop a concept. (Vygotsky, 1997, p. 53)

Idealism and Revolt

A new active persona enters the drama of development, a new, qualitatively unique factor – the personality of the adolescent himself.

(Vygotsky, 1998, p. 180)

Increasingly during adolescence, students recognize that the world that constrains them is also their inheritance. It is a period of adjustments, from powerlessness to growing independence and power. Inevitably students sometimes feel that the adult world is not according them appropriate independence and power; parents are unjustly restrictive, schools are excessively restraining, society at large treats them inconsiderately. Typically, students respond with revolt, even if only in the muted form of sulking reluctance to conform or quiet resistance. More visibly it takes the forms of flaunting styles of hair, clothing, music, and dancing that confront adult conventions and values.

It is the world's failure to live up to some ideal that justifies the revolt, in the student's eyes. The sense of the ideal world typically shifts unstably during these years, as do students' views of their ideal selves. We see them trying on roles: the serene lady, the rebel, the fashion plate or dandy, the hoyden, the macho, the tease, the socialite, the cool dude, the iceberg, the friendly innocent, and so on. These are reflections of roles played out more fantastically in the imagination – the waster of cities, the film star beloved of millions, the swashbuckling savior of nations, the preserver of the planet from polluters, and so on.

We routinely observe, and no doubt remember, this characteristic of adolescence. But how do we extract from it a principle for more imaginative teaching? It is a cliché that adolescents develop varied forms of revolt and begin to fashion ideals, and that these processes are connected. At the simplest level, material to be learned can be given a heightened "romantic" power of engagement by being shown in a context of revolt against unjust or inadequate and constraining conventions.

Even if it is just punctuation and paragraphing that we want to teach, we might see how they can be made more meaningful and engaging if we see them as revolts against constraining conventions in early manuscripts. So we might see their introduction by revolutionary figures like Hugh of Saint Victor (Illich, 1993), whose daring new ideas made texts easier to decipher and read. What this idea suggests in general is the desirability of reembedding knowledge we want students to learn in the emotional and imaginatively reconstructed reality of people's lives from which typical textbooks usually rip it. The idealism and readiness to associate with those who revolt against unjust constraints are other cognitive tools that are constituents of this curious tradition of literacy.

Details, Details

> Self-control and the principles and means of this control do not differ basically from control over the environment.... [T]he bare hand and the mind taken in themselves do not mean much – the deed is done with tools and auxiliary means.
>
> (Vygotsky, 1997, p. 218)

The cognitive tool we saw at work in the engagement with the extremes of reality represents one strategy newly literate students may choose to explore the world. It is reflected at the other end of the scale by another strategy that we see at work in students' collections or obsessive hobbies. By discovering everything about something, one can gain further intellectual security. The typical profile of a hobby or collection is that it gets seriously under way at about the time literacy becomes internalized – about age 7 or 8 in our culture – peaks at about age 11 or 12, and begins to lose energy at about age 15.

Students may collect almost anything; ornamental spoons, memorabilia of a favorite pop singer – records and tapes and CDs, tour T-shirts, pictures, and so on – hockey cards, dolls in national dresses, comic sets, beer bottle caps, the books of some author in a uniform edition, stones or shells, leaves, illustrations of costumes through the ages, or whatever. The object of the collecting instinct or the hobby seems arbitrary; what matter are the intellectual control of some feature of reality and the intellectual security it can provide.

This urge to master something in exhaustive detail is perhaps the most powerful learning drive that one sees in the typical adolescent. It is a drive exploited more by commercial interests than by educators, however, and seems largely ignored by educational research. But how can this observation lead to a principle for more imaginatively engaging teaching and learning? Obviously any material dealt with in schools can become a focus for detailed work. The trick here seems to be twofold. First, one of the other principles needs to be deployed to engage students with a particular topic; second, the teacher needs to focus on material within the topic that is exhaustible. Simply indicating material that might be studied in greater detail does not meet either of these two criteria. What is needed to meet the second criterion is material about which the student can learn everything, or at least learn securely what the scale of the topic is. Even if the students cannot learn everything, they can learn what would have to be known to exhaust the topic – as the collector of hockey cards may not have all of a set but knows additional further cards the whole set comprises.

Humanizing Knowledge

> We must not forget for a moment that both knowing the nature and knowing personality is done with the help of understanding other people, understanding those around us, understanding social experiences.
>
> (Vygotsky, 1997, p. 50)

As any journalist knows, information can be made more engaging if given a "human interest" angle. That is, knowledge seen through, or by means of, human emotions, intentions, hopes, fears, and so on, is not only more directly comprehensible but also more meaningful and engaging than if presented disembedded from its human source. Every teacher knows how the illustrative anecdote, particularly if it involves extremes of human endurance or foresight or ingenuity or compassion or suffering, grabs students' attention. Can we generalize from this widely recognized practice, seeing why it is so engaging of students' imaginations and develop a more widely applicable principle? The ability to see text not merely as an object but as a product of another human mind provides a further cognitive tool that are constituents of literacy.

The structure of typical textbooks with neatly organized and segmented knowledge tends to support the belief that the textbook or the encyclopedia exhibits the ideal form of knowledge. This bizarre idea is no doubt one of the more peculiar consequences of literacy. In the face of this seemingly unconscious assumption it is necessary to emphasize constantly in education that books do not contain knowledge. Books contain symbolic codes, which serve as external mnemonics for knowledge. Knowledge exists only in human minds, and in minds its meaning derives from the way it connects with our hopes, fears, and intentions, and with our imaginative lives.

In emphasizing the difference between inert symbolic codes in books and living knowledge in human minds, we want to draw attention to a point that is significant, and often neglected, about teaching. The goal is not to get the symbolic codes as they exist in books into the students' minds. We can of course do that – training students to be rather ineffective "copies" of books. Rather, the teaching task is to reconstitute the inert symbolic code into living human knowledge. The point that knowledge lives seems crucial. Knowledge in our minds is a function of the organization of our living organism; it is not some interchangeable code we can pick up, such as computer data.

The educational task, then, involves the resuscitation of knowledge from its suspended animation in symbolic codes. The task is to convert, reanimate, transmute the symbolic codes into living human knowledge in students' minds. This is the challenge whether the knowledge is about earthworms or is a literary text. The codes do not carry guarantees of meaning. The instrument best able to ensure the transformation from codes to living knowledge is the imagination. Students can most easily resuscitate knowledge if they learn it in the human context in which it was first generated or discovered.

Vygotsky views knowledge as a cognitive and semiotic tool that serves as a means of mediation for human activities. From this point of view, the emphasis on the mediator, without respect to the fact that knowledge is a tool for development and mastery of cultural behavior, leads to an inadequate approach to education. As Vygotsky reminds us constantly through his writing, knowledge should be viewed as serving two purposes – mediating human activity, on the one hand, and mediating development of higher psychological processes, on the other:

We must not forget for a moment that both knowing nature and knowing personality is done with the help of understanding other people, understanding those around us, understanding social experiences. Speech cannot be separated from understanding. This inseparability of speech and understanding is manifested identically in both the social use of language as a means of communication and in its individual use as a means of thinking. (Vygotsky, 1997, p. 50)

The Narrative Mind

Focus on the cognitive tools of imagination draws to the fore, as has been noted already, the emotions. The emotions in turn are not subject to neat categorization but seem to be expressible only in narratives. The main narrative we have for clearly conveying emotional meaning is the story: "Man is in his actions and practice, as well as in his fictions, essentially a story-telling animal" (MacIntyre, 1981, p. 201). Any event or action or information "becomes intelligible by finding its place in a narrative" (MacIntyre, 1981, p.196). As Barbara Hardy famously put it: "We dream in narrative, day-dream in narrative, remember, anticipate, hope, despair, believe, doubt, plan, revise, criticize, construct, gossip, learn, hate and live by narrative" (1968, p. 5). The focus on the imagination leads to the bold but entirely plausible claim that "the mind is . . . a narrative concern" (Sutton-Smith, 1988, p. 22).

Jerome Bruner's *Actual Minds, Possible Worlds* (1986) has helped popularize within educational research a conception of the mind that gives renewed prominence to the role of narrative in our ways of making sense of the world and of experience. The conception of the mind as, in whatever degree, "a narrative concern" is supported by a wealth of modern research, from Bartlett's celebrated studies on memory (1932), to Bransford's and associates' (Brunford & Johnson, 1972; Bransford & Mc_Currell, 1975) and Rumelhart's (1975) works in the 1970s to the recent and current large-scale focus on scripts, schemata, and narratives.

The capacity to think increasingly of the world and experience in narrative terms represents a further constitutive cognitive tool of literacy. Narrative provides us with one of the main tools for orienting our emotions to the contents of our narrative and consequently gives us the power to make increasingly complex meaning of our lives and of the world around us. The narratives that are constituents of literacy are different from the stories of our "oral" childhood in that they incorporate many of the cognitive tools we have mentioned earlier.

CONCLUSION

What we have tried to do, in a somewhat preliminary way, in this chapter is unfold some of the cognitive tools that are embedded in the larger cognitive tools of literacy, imagining literacy as, say, a screwdriver and the smaller scale tools as changeable heads. So we may see literate students' minds as routinely deploying such tools as a ready engagement with the limits of reality and the extremes of experience and a desire for a sense of transcendence within reality that finds one exemplar in the interest in the heroic, and a complex construction of mental images and concepts, and an emotional response to forms of idealism that lead to a tendency to revolt against conventions, and a desire to explore something in great detail exhaustively, and an easy engagement with knowledge by means of its human and emotional contexts, and a disposition to make sense of the world and experience in narrative terms.

Now, of course, these are qualities of our cognitive and emotional lives for which the word *tool* is hardly ideal. In what sense can we meaningfully talk of a desire as a tool? Well, what we see develop with literacy are certain set dispositions of minds, certain characteristic ways of engaging and being engaged by the world and experience. We do not have a very good vocabulary to talk about such characteristics of the mind. And what vocabulary we have has been largely formed in the context of views of the mind that are inhospitable to Vygotsky's ideas. We may call them *mediators* – things we learn that we then use to make richer sense. It may be that the metaphoric extension of the word *tool* is the least bad we can find. One of these mediators' most distinctive features, after all, is that they do for our minds something like what tools do for our bodies: They extend our powers.

References

Altwerger, Bess. (1994). In Art Levine, The great debate revisited. *Atlantic Monthly*, 38–44.

Bartlett, F. C. (1932). *Remembering*. Cambridge: Cambridge University Press.

Bransford, J. D., & Johnson, M. V. (1972). Contextual prerequisites for understanding: Some investigations of comprehension and recall. *Journal of Verbal Learning and Verbal Behavior*, 11, 522–531.

Bransford, J. D., & McCarrell, N. S. (1975). A sketch of a cognitive approach to comprehension: Some thoughts about understanding what it means to comprehend. In P. N. Johnson-Laird & P. C. Watson (Eds.), *Thinking: Readings in cognitive science*. Cambridge: Cambridge University Press.

Bruner, Jerome. (1986). *Actual minds, possible worlds*. Cambridge, MA: Harvard University Press.

Egan, Kieran. (1997). *The educated mind: How cognitive tools shape our understanding*. Chicago: University of Chicago Press.

Hardy, Barbara. (1968). Towards a poetics of fiction: An approach through narrative. *Novel*, 2, 5–14.

Illich, Ivan. (1993). *Hugh of St. Victor*. Cambridge: Cambridge University Press.

Kozulin, Alex (1998). *Psychological tools: A sociocultural approach to education*. Cambridge, MA: Harvard University Press.

Lamm, Zvi. (1976). *Conflicting Theories of Instruction*. Berkeley, CA: McCutcheon.

MacIntyre, Alasdair. (1981). *After virtue*. Notre Dame, IN: University of Notre Dame Press.

Martin, Bill, Jr. (1990). An overview of a humanistic language reading program. In N. Polette (Ed.), *Whole language in action* (pp. 223–228). O'Fallon, MO: Book Lures.

Peetoom, Adrian. (1988). Publisher's Afterword. In J. Bookwill & P. Whitman (Eds.), *Moving on: A whole language sourcebook for Grades three and four*. Toronto: Scholastic-TAB.

Polette, Nancy. (1990). *Whole language in action*. O'Fallan, MO: Book Lures.

Rumelhart, D. E. (1975). Notes on a schema for stories. In D. G. Bobrow & A. M. Collins (Eds.), *Representation and understanding* (pp. 117–131). New York: Academic Press.

Sutton-Smith, Brian. (1988). In search of the imagination. In K. Egan & D. Nadaner (Eds.), *Imagination and education* (pp. 3–29). New York: Teachers College Press; Milton Keynes: Open University Press.

Vygotsky, L. (1997). *The collected works of L. S. Vygotsky*. Vol. 4. *The history of the development of higher mental functions* (R. W. Reiber, M. J. Hall, & J. Glick, Eds.). New York: Plenum Press.

Vygotsky, L. (1998). *The collected works of L. S. Vygotsky*. Vol. 5. *Child psychology* (R. W. Reiber & M. J. Hall, Eds.). New York: Plenum Press.

White, Alan R. (1990). *The language of imagination*. Oxford: Blackwell.

5

Dynamic Assessment of the Evolving Cognitive Functions in Children

Carol S. Lidz and Boris Gindis

This chapter presents an application of Vygotsky's idea of the zone of proximal development (ZPD) as a basis for dynamic assessment (DA) of learning in children with typical and atypical development. After a discussion of the idea of ZPD and an overview of dynamic assessment, the chapter describes a specific DA procedure relevant for use with young children with two case studies of the application of this procedure.

Dynamic assessment is an approach to understanding individual differences and their implications for instruction that embeds intervention within the assessment procedure. The focus of most dynamic assessment procedures is on the processes rather than the products of learning. The dynamic, compared to static, nature of this approach reflects Vygotsky's observation that "it is only in movement that a body shows what it is" (Gauvain, 2001, p. 35). Moving pictures lead to very different impressions than still photographs.

DA was born of widespread dissatisfaction with traditional (product-oriented, static) means of psychological testing, as well as the social need to create psychological instruments that were culturally sensitive and responsive to the factors of socioeconomic and/or educational differences and deprivation as well as new language acquisition (Haywood & Tzuriel, 1992; Lidz, 1987; Lidz & Elliott, 2000). In this way DA has both psychoeducational and sociocultural significance.

VYGOTSKY'S CONCEPTUALIZATION OF THE ZPD AS A BASIS FOR DYNAMIC ASSESSMENT

Parents and teachers have frequently observed that with the appropriate help and in collaboration with a more experienced partner, a child is capable of more advanced performance than when functioning independently. It was Vygotsky, however, who elevated this otherwise trivial observation to the rank of the scientific paradigm known as zone of proximal development (ZPD). There is no more well-known, vigilantly scrutinized, yet still blurred notion in all of Vygotsky's scientific legacy than that of ZPD. Generally considered as a "space" where the evolving psychological functions of a child emerge during the process of joint or shared activities with a more competent partner, and where "everyday" concepts shift to "scientific" concepts, ZPD has practical implications in the two educational domains of assessment and instruction. Both of these aspects are discussed in this volume (see Chaiklin, this volume, for an in-depth analysis of ZPD as the theoretical background in relation to instruction). As one can learn from Chaiklin's discourse, the notion of ZPD in the domain of assessment has its own set of theoretical paradigms not identical to its application in the field of instruction. In this chapter ZPD is considered as the conceptualization of the approach to evaluation of students in educational and remedial contexts known as *dynamic assessment* (DA).

DA is a theory-driven approach; the following notions from Vygotsky's sociocultural theory provide the core of its theoretical base:

1. Cognitive, language, and social functioning in educational settings are not innate abilities or disabilities but are sociocultural formations resulting from the interactions of a child with culture. What is to be measured, therefore, is a child's evolving individual ability to master "psychological tools" (see Kozulin, this volume) that are in the process of development. This reflects Vygotsky's comment that "the area of immature, but maturing processes makes up the child's zone of proximal development" (Vygotsky, 1998, p. 202).

2. Assessment is not an isolated activity that is merely linked to intervention. Assessment, instruction, and remediation can be based on the same universal explanatory conceptualization of a child's development (typical and atypical) and within this model are therefore inseparable. "A true diagnosis must provide an explanation, prediction, and scientific basis for practical prescription" (Vygotsky, 1998, p. 205). Moreover, Vygotsky suggested that the means of assessment and the means of instruction (including remedial instruction) need to be age-specific, always attuned to the characteristics of development (Vygotsky, 1998, p. 199). Vygotsky made a clear distinction between what he called symptomatic and diagnostic assessment as follows:

    A symptomatic assessment focuses on behaviors and characteristics ... that are typical of children of a particular psychological type or developmental stage. In contrast, a diagnostic assessment relies on an explicit explanatory theory of psychological development in an attempt to penetrate the internal causal dynamic and genetic connections that define the process of mental development. (Vygotsky, in Minick, 1987, p. 135)

This distinction represents the difference between most of our norm-based, as well as developmentally based, procedures and those that attempt to reflect a theory, usually of intelligence. Even some of the current so-called theory-based procedures do not attempt to be explanatory, but merely correlational and descriptive. (Discrimination between theory and explanation is not straightforward; one person's theory may be another's explanation.) Clearly, what Vygotsky proposed was diagnostic explanation.

3. Vygotsky suggested that the "size" of the ZPD was determined by the child's ability to benefit from collaboration with an expert in order to advance the child's performance beyond what was already achieved by nonassisted performance. It is important to stress Chaiklin's observation in this volume that there is nothing in Vygotsky's texts that suggests that this "size" is a fixed property of the child that remains constant across age periods. DA should be able to describe the child's ever-changing ability to learn with assistance or guidance as well as to assess the individual "length" of ZPD.

4. Vygotsky insisted that assessment of the child's ability to learn through the method of collaborative activity was a better predictor of future cognitive functioning than a measure of independent performance through such measures as traditional tests of intelligence. His explanation was that the greater number of maturing (than already matured) functions gave the child better opportunities to benefit from school instruction (see van der Veer & Valsiner, 1991, pp. 336–341, for an elaboration and critique of this claim).

5. The ZPD should be measured in the context of what Vygotsky called either "shared/joint activity" (*sovmestnaya deajtelnost*) or "collaboration" (*sotrudnichestvo*), using these terms synonymously. He proposed "that an essential feature of learning is that it creates the zone of proximal development; that is, learning awakens a variety of developmental processes that are able to operate only when the child is interacting with people in his environment and in collaboration with his peers" (Vygotsky, 1978, p. 90).

6. Collaborative or assisted performance is viewed as an indicator of the status of the learner's maturing psychological functions: "In brief, we ask the child to solve problems that are beyond his mental age [as measured by independent performance] with some kind of cooperation and determine how far the potential for intellectual cooperation can be stretched for the given child and how far it goes beyond his mental age" (Vygotsky, 1998, p. 202). The main focus for collaborative interventions is to find evidence for maturing psychological functions. The assumption here is that the child can take advantage of these interventions because the maturing function creates an

ability to reap the utmost benefits from the support that is being offered. "By applying the principle of cooperation for establishing the zone of proximal development, we make it possible to study directly what determines most precisely the mental maturation that must be realized in the proximal and subsequent periods of his stage of development" (Vygotsky, 1998, p. 203).

7. Vygotsky turned to the psychological concept of imitation as a way of identifying maturing psychological functions that were still inadequate for independent performance. In Vygotsky's writings, *imitation* referred to "all kinds of activity of a certain type carried out by the child . . . in cooperation with adults or with another child" (1998, p. 202). In Vygotsky's words, "It is well established that the child can imitate only what lies within the zone of his intellectual potential" (Vygotsky, 1987, p. 209). He considered imitation as "one of the basic paths of cultural development of the child" (Vygotsky, 1997, p. 95). "The child can enter into imitation through intellectual actions more or less far beyond what he is capable of in independent mental and purposeful actions or intellectual operations" (Vygotsky, 1998, p. 201). In other words, imitation is possible because there are maturing psychological functions that are insufficient to support independent performance, yet are developed sufficiently to take advantage of collaborative actions. "Alternatively, one can say that the zone of proximal development is defined as referring to those intellectual actions and mental functions that a child is able to use in interaction, where independent performance is inadequate" (see Chaiklin, this volume).

Vygotsky's attitude toward standardized ("static") testing was somewhat inconsistent ("dialectical," as some of his passionate followers would say). On the one hand, Vygotsky seemed to accept uncritically two major concepts that have been challenged or rejected by contemporary science: "mental age" as a psychological construct and the validity of standardized tests as reliable measures of fully developed psychological functions through "independent performance." It was rather contradictory that the concept of "mental age" that was seemingly incompatible with Vygotsky' own theory of child development was casually used by him in a number of his works.

On the other hand, Vygotsky offered one of the most original and insightful critiques of standardized tests. His major objections to standardized tests were that they confused latent capacities with developed abilities; they mixed lower (natural) capability with higher (socially learned) expertise; they had low "ecological validity"; and they were only marginally relevant to educational processes. He suggested, as an alternative, the approach based on the notion of ZPD that is now called *DA*. He never, however, suggested the total abandonment of standardized tests; rather, he postulated the possibility of using both models of testing.

As presented by Kozulin (1998), there are two alternative sets of assumptions that underlie traditional standardized testing and dynamic assessment. The traditional testing paradigm includes the notions that (1) the manifest level of functioning reveals the child's inner abilities more or less accurately; (2) unaided performance is the best format for assessment; (3) the primary goals of testing are to predict future functioning and to classify the child according to level of abilities.

In contrast, DA includes the principles or assumptions that (1) cognitive processes are modifiable, and an important task of assessment is to ascertain their degree of modifiability, rather than to remain limited to estimation of the child's manifest level of functioning; (2) interactive assessment that includes a learning phase provides better insight into the child's learning capacities than unaided performance; (3) the primary goal of assessment is to suggest psychoeducational interventions aimed at the enhancement and realization of the child's latent abilities to learn.

Whereas standardized testing emphasizes products that result from currently existing skills, dynamic testing emphasizes the psychological processes involved in learning and taps more explicitly into evolving functions. Another major difference is the nature of the examiner–examinee relationship, which changes from neutral–impartial (static test) to teaching–assisting (dynamic test). During standardized testing, there is no feedback from the examiner to test-taker regarding the quality of performance. In DA this feedback is built-in, either explicitly or implicitly (Lidz, 1997). Ideally, dynamic testing is intertwined with instruction, and the examinee's learning ability is observed carefully while he or she is engaged in the process of learning. The goal of DA is to discover whether and how much the examinee will change under the influence of scaffolding activities (Tzuriel, 2001). As summarized by Lidz and Elliot (2000, p. 7). "The essential characteristics of DA are that they are interactive, open ended, and generate information about the responsiveness of the learner to intervention." As was observed by Lidz (1995), traditional standardized assessment follows the child's cognitive performance to the point of "failure" in independent functioning, whereas DA in the Vygotskian tradition leads the child to the point of achievement of success in joint or shared activity. DA begins where standardized testing ends.

TYPES AND FORMATS OF DYNAMIC ASSESSMENT

As of now, "there is a rather wide variety of procedures under the general umbrella of DA" (Lidz & Elliot, 2000, p. 6). DA itself is not limited to any single domain (e.g., psychology or speech pathology), content (e.g., math, history), activity (e.g., testing, teaching), or age. It is a "family" of different procedures that share a set of principles and formats. Sternberg and Grigorenko (2002, pp. 27–28) described the two most common formats of dynamic assessment as "sandwich" design and "cake" design. In the "sandwich" format of dynamic testing, the instruction is given all at once between the pretest and the posttest. In the "cake" format of dynamic testing, the instruction is given in graded layers after each test item in response to the examinee's solution of each test item. In the first format, examinees take a pretest, which is essentially equivalent to a static test. After they complete the pretest, they are given instruction in the skills or principles of problem solution involved in the pretest. After instruction, the examinees are tested again on a posttest. The posttest is typically an alternate form of the pretest (p. 27). The exact contents of the instruction as well as amount of instruction can be varied to suit the individual (or, in some cases, can be scripted and standardized).

In the second format, examinees are provided instruction item by item. An examinee is given an item to solve. If solved correctly, then the next item is presented. But if the examinee does not solve the item correctly, a graded series of hints follows. The hints are designed to make the solution successively more explicit. The examiner then determines how many and what kinds of hints the examinee needs in order to solve the item correctly. Prompting continues until the examinee is successful, or, if not, the assessor models the problem solution, at which time the next item is presented. (p. 27)

In Vygotsky's works, both types of formats are described, but in a very terse way. "We assist each child through demonstration, leading questions, and by introducing elements of the task's solution" (Vygotsky, 1987, p. 209). And, describing the action of the examiner:

We show the child how such a problem must be solved and watch to see if he can do the problem by imitating the demonstration. Or we begin to solve the problem and ask the child to finish it. Or we propose that the child solve the problem that is beyond his mental age by cooperating with another, more developed child or, finally, we explain to the child the principle of solving the problem, ask leading questions, analyze the problem for him, etc. (Vygotsky, 1998, p. 202)

Concern about the issue of how to provide assistance is far from idle. Because of the centrality of Vygotsky's assumption of the social origin of development of higher mental functions, it would be important to discriminate between those interactions that promote such development and those that do not, assuming that all interactions are not equal. Vygotsky emphasized the importance of language as a (if not the primary) mechanism of internalization of experiences but was not explicit regarding the details of how best to intervene during the course of the assessment. A number of writers have attempted to fill this gap. For example, Hogan and Pressley (1997) list a number of techniques that describe the various approaches to scaffolding by the chapter writers of their text. Others who have attempted to describe the type and nature of assistance provided during the scaffolding process included Tharp and Gallimore (1988) and Gauvain (2001).

The most comprehensive elaboration of components of interactions that facilitate the development of higher mental functions has been developed by Feuerstein and his collaborators (1980, 1997) under the idea of "mediated learning experiences." This includes the need to promote connections between ideas and events and to move the child beyond the perceptual elements of the situation (transcendence), the highlighting of perceptual characteristics of the activity that are important to notice (meaning), and the promotion of a strategic, planful approach to problem solving, based on awareness of basic principles of problem solution (task regulation).

As Kozulin and Presseisen noted (1995, p. 69): "The ultimate goal of mediated learning is to make the child sensitive to learning through direct exposure to stimuli and to develop in the child cognitive prerequisites for such direct learning." The specific outcomes of involvement in mediated learning experiences should also include development of higher mental functions in the child, including self-regulation, representational thinking, and strategic problem solving (Lidz, 1991).

DEVELOPMENT OF DYNAMIC ASSESSMENT IN RUSSIA
SINCE VYGOTSKY'S TIME

In different countries DA has been developed under different names (Lidz & Elliott, 2000). In Russia, there are assessment techniques that are derived from the concept of ZPD and are based on the basic principles of DA as known in the West. (A review and critical analysis of these methods may be found in Karpov, 1990; Gindis, 1992; Karpov & Gindis, 2000.) There are at least two approaches to DA in Russia that reflect different emphases in methodology and techniques. If the stress is on the "assessment," then it is *diagnistika obuchaemosti*, which may be translated as "diagnosis of learning aptitude" (Ivanova, 1976). If the methodological paradigm related to teaching and learning in ZPD is highlighted, then it is called *obuchayuchij experiment* (translated as "teaching/learning experiment") (Galperin, 1969).

There are several reasons to consider DA development in Russia in this chapter. First, whereas the history and the current state of DA in the West are relatively well known (see: Lidz, 1987, 1991; Lidz & Elliott, 2000; Sternberg & Grigorenko, 2002), the post-Vygotskian development of this domain in Russia is still in relative obscurity for the Western reader. This is rather a peculiar situation because, as pointed out by Sternberg and Grigorenko (2002, p. 37), DA was the only paradigm accepted in psychology and remedial education in the former Soviet Union. All standardized testing was prohibited by the state in 1936, and its slow return may be observed only since the early 1980s (Grigorenko, Ruzgis, & Sternberg, 1997; McCagg & Siegelbaum, 1989; Smith-Davis, 2000; Vlasova, 1984). Thus, in Soviet psychology, the nature of the responsiveness of children to prompts was the basis for differential diagnosis of children with organically based mental retardation and children who were educationally neglected or had temporary delays in cognitive functioning (Gindis, 1986, 1988, 1992). Second, the theoretical development of DA was undertaken, implicitly or explicitly, by a number of prominent Vygotskians in Russia such as Luria (1961), Elkonin (1977), Galperin (1969), Zaporozhets and Elkonin (1971), Lubovsky (1989), and Venger (1988). The fruitfulness of applying their conceptualizations and methods was convincingly demonstrated by Bodrova and Leong (1996 and this volume). Third, certain aspects of DA, such as emotional and motivational components, were particularly emphasized and elaborated in Russian research, whereas most Western developers of DA have been focusing on the cognitive aspects of this assessment procedure.

The best known method of assessing learning aptitude was developed by the Moscow psychologist Ivanova in the early 1970s. An example of Ivanova's diagnostic procedure includes classification of pictures with geometrical designs of different forms, sizes, and colors. The child is asked to sort these cards into groups on the basis of these attributes. In the process of performing this activity the child receives prescribed prompts from the examiner until the assignment is completed. Then another set of cards is offered for the same purpose, but this time without help. The "length" of ZPD (explicitly associated with learning aptitude) was determined through notation of the quality and quantity of the prompts that were needed and the child's ability to transfer the acquired cognitive skills to a new set of similar tasks (Ivanova, 1976). (Karpov [1990] observed that these qualitative and quantitative markers of ZPD may in fact reflect different psychological realities and that use of the "composite" indicator therefore may be misleading.)

The "teaching/learning experiment," also theoretically rooted in the concept of ZPD, was perfected in Russia as a measure of the level of internalization of problem solving cognitive strategies (Galperin, 1969). Children's transitions from one level of solving problems to the next is one of the most important characteristics of the process of internalization in their ZPD. In Russian neo-Vygotskian literature, the consecutive levels of internalization are described as visual-motor (actual manipulations with objects), visual-imagery (operations with visual images), and symbolic levels of internalization. In the course of normal development, children progress to increasingly higher levels of internalization of their problem-solving activity (Davydov, 1995). In the "teaching/ learning experiment" (see, for example, Karpov & Gindis, 2000) two characteristics of the child's learning during DA testing are considered as criteria in determining the cross-domain level of internalization of the child's problem-solving activity. These characteristics are (a) the highest initial level (symbolic, visual-imagery, or visual-motor) at which the child is able to understand the algorithm for a new problem-solving process and (b) the highest level at which the child is able to perform a new problem-solving process after planned and prescribed intervention. These characteristics are related to that child's cross-domain ability to learn and transfer new knowledge.

The most comprehensive attempt to create a theory-driven (Vygotsky's ZPD notion) DA in "diagnostic of learning aptitude" format was made by Lubovsky (1989, 1990) and his colleagues (Belopolskaya & Lubovsky, 1992). In many ways, their model is similar to the Campione and Brown (1987) method, but it was developed almost a decade earlier. Their similarities lie in the measurement and quantification of the amount of help that a child needs to perform a given task. In Lubovsky's works, however, one can find the elaborated procedures for observing a child's behavior, the detailed descriptions of gradually diminishing adult contribution to a joint or shared activity, and the attention to emotional and motivational aspects. It must be stressed that in Russia the emotional and motivational aspect of assessment was the center of attention both theoretically (Elkonin, 1977; Zaporozhets & Elkonin, 1971) and practically (Lebedinsky, 1985; Belopolskaya & Lubovsky, 1992). This is apparent in the study of the relationships between cognitively operational and personality–motivational aspects of the child's development and in Venger's (1988) notion of "sensory standards" (see Bodrova and Leong, this volume). Research on internal compared to external motivation issues of self-esteem and reaction to success and failure during a DA experimental situation found a prominent place among Russian followers of Vygotsky. Thus, Belopolskaya and Grebennikova (1997) in reviewing studies of dynamic assessment in Russia pointed out that researchers have differentiated children on the basis of (1) whether motivation was primarily internal or external, (2) whether the children demonstrated the need for moderate or strong stimulation, and (3) whether the children showed well-developed or underdeveloped self-esteem in the experimental situation. One of the most important findings that emerged from their work was the demonstration that a determining factor in task performance was the nature of the child's "emotional anticipation" of the process of task performance. According to these studies, task performance during DA starts with the appearance of emotional anticipation, which may facilitate or hinder the expression of intellectual abilities (Belopolskaya & Lubovsky, 1992). These and related studies demonstrated that investigating the affective–cognitive content of children's mental activity was useful in developing diagnostic instruments that more fully and accurately assess intellectual abilities and potential, providing more specific information regarding learning problems.

In the field of special education and early childhood intervention, Strebeleva (2000) and her associates at the Institute of Corrective Pedagogy in Moscow have created a number of nonverbal tests in a dynamic format designed for preschool children. The theoretical basis was derived from Vygotsky's notions of ZPD as collaboration (*sovmestnaya deyatelnost*) and imitation. The test (called Early Diagnostic Procedure – [EDP]) consists of 10 subtests. Each is presented in a classical test–teach–retest format and includes detailed instructions. Degree of exactness in imitation is measured by assigning points and is considered to reflect the "depth" of ZPD. According to Strebeleva, this method allows for differentiation between preschoolers who have organically based mental retardation (MR) and those who are educationally neglected and/or have temporary delays in psychological development. Strebeva's work is one of the first attempts to apply the concept of imitation as the basis of DA in differential diagnostic procedures for children with different degrees of developmental disorder. However, the EDP subtests are quite different in their difficulty of imitation and appear to address diverse cognitive functions (from elementary visual tracking to rather complex concepts of size, directionality, and object constancy). Nevertheless, the works of Strebeleva and her colleagues definitely warrant our attention, particularly in comparison with the DA procedure described in the next section.

As the reader can see, on the basis of Vygotsky's general conceptualizations, different approaches to DA that reflect the diverse cultural contexts of application may be developed. The method described later was developed in the late 1990s in the environment of North America's educational system and is unmistakably American. Nevertheless, the inner conceptual connections with Vygotsky's basic premises link it with the Russian experiences described. It is not only symbolic, but natural, that this method was successfully utilized to help children (see the case study later) who were adopted from orphanages in Russia by American families. As these children bridge two cultures, so DA based on Vygotsky's thinking leads to culture-specific and yet universal methods of assessment and remediation.

THE APPLICATION OF COGNITIVE FUNCTIONS SCALE

The Application of Cognitive Functions Scale (ACFS) (Lidz & Jepsen, 2000) is a dynamic assessment procedure developed for use with children functioning between the ages of 3 and 5 years. The six scales were designed to represent typical tasks tapping basic cognitive processes that represent foundations of learning and that characterize most preschool curricula in preschool programs throughout the United States. As it is a dynamic assessment procedure, each task is first administered without intervention, then followed immediately by intervention, and finally followed immediately by repetition of (or variation of) the pretest without intervention. The interventions provide mediation for the child through exposure to basic strategies and principles of task solution on materials that differ from the pretests and posttests. The intervention for each task represents instructional strategies relevant to that task.

The ACFS provides curriculum-based and descriptive information that responds to questions concerning the child's degree of mastery of each task, the child's approach to task solution, the child's interactions with the examiner as mediator, and the child's responsiveness to intervention. The interventions are scripted to provide standardized administration and to allow for scoring and monitoring of the child's progress over time. However, assessors may deviate from these scripts for further diagnostic exploration.

The six tasks of the ACFS include four core scales and two supplementary scales:

Core scales:

1. Classification: The child sorts multiattributed blocks into groups.
2. Auditory Memory: The child retells a short story.
3. Visual Memory: The child recalls a series of eight pictures and shares thoughts about how she or he will help herself or himself to remember the pictures.
4. Sequential Pattern Completion: The child completes a series of incomplete sequential patterns and justifies correct solutions with the reason for selection of the correct pattern piece.

Supplemental scales:

5. Verbal Planning: The child verbalizes a plan for a familiar cooking task.
6. Perspective Taking: The child teaches the assessor how to draw a picture from a model provided.

The interventions for each of these scales tap the components described by Feuerstein and his colleagues (e.g., 1997, 1980) as *Mediated Learning Experience*, as adapted and elaborated by Lidz (1991, 2002). The assessor offers intentional intervention, assuming a leading and guiding role that is sensitive and responsive to the child's responses and abilities and supplies scripted interventions that offer strategies and principles of task solution intended for generalization to the pretest–posttest tasks. These interventions include enhancement of the meaning of the task and accompanying materials, along with transcendence of the child's approach to task solution beyond the current situation.

A Behavior Observation Scale accompanies each task and is completed after each pretest and intervention phase of the subtests. The same Behavior Observation Scale is used across tasks, permitting comparison of the child's behavior across these varied domains. This scale captures the affective–motivational and metacognitive aspects of the child as learner. This scale is also available in a format independent of the scales described so that it can be completed by teachers and/or therapists to compare the child's behavior during the assessment and within the classroom and/or therapy situations. The seven dimensions rated on this scale are self-regulation, persistence, frustration tolerance, flexibility, motivation, interactivity, and responsivity. Each of these is rated on a scale of zero to two to reflect the degree to which it is in evidence during the designated segment of the assessment.

The ACFS yields scores to document the degree to which the child has mastered each of the tasks, summary scores for pretests and posttests, as well as change or gain scores between pretests and posttests, and the behavior scale ratings. These scores are useful for research and monitoring; however, the more significant value of the ACFS is the possibility of writing descriptive observations of the child in the process of performing each of the tasks independently and in interaction with a mediator.

A number of studies addressing issues of validity and reliability have been completed. One issue of construct validity for the ACFS as a dynamic assessment procedure is to document significant changes from pretest to posttest. This was documented by Lidz (2000) and Bensoussan (2002) with typically developing preschool children, as well as by Levy (1999) and Shurin (1998) in their studies of children with developmental delays and by Lidz (submitted) with young deaf children. The second issue of construct validity provides evidence that these changes can be attributed to the mediation or intervention. Studies with control groups by Benssousan (2002) and Malowitsky (2002) showed that only children exposed to mediation made significant pretest to posttest gains; those who received unmediated exposure to the same materials did not. Brooks (1997), using the Classification subtest, also demonstrated that only those children in the mediated group moved to the higher "grouping" level, beyond merely building with the blocks.

Issues of criterion validity include the ability of the ACFS to predict future cognitively related performance of the child; concurrent validity concerns the issue of correlation with other tests that purport to assess the same dimensions. This information is not yet available for the ACFS task scores. However, Shurin's (1998) study correlated the Behavior Observation Scale with the subtest task scores and found a moderately strong relationship between the total behavior ratings and the total ACFS scores of .65 ($p < .001$). Also, Aranov's (1999) study of children with developmental disabilities found significant relationships between the Behavior Observation Scale ratings by a visiting observer to the classroom (the researcher) and ratings by the children's classroom teacher and speech therapist.

Discriminant validity addresses the ability of the ACFS to differentiate between or among children with different levels of functioning or diagnostic categories. This information is provided by Levy (1999), who compared the ACFS performances of 22 children, half with disabilities and half without. Finally, issues of reliability concern the intratest integrity, as well as the very important (especially for dynamic assessment) need to rule out practice effects through test–retest administration with and without intervention. In Aranov's (1999) study, Cronbach alphas for the Behavior Observation Scale were .77 for the researcher and .81 for the speech therapist. Shurin's (1998) study showed that each component of the Behavior Observation Scale significantly correlated with the total score, with the exception of Interactivity, which was borderline ($p < .06$). In the studies by Benssousan (2002), Brooks (1997), and Malowitsky (2002), who each studied different ACFS subtests, there were no significant changes between the two administrations of the subtests for those children who did not experience mediation. That is, these studies provide supportive evidence for stability of unmediated subtests, as well as evidence against practice effects.

CASE STUDIES

The following are descriptions of the use of the ACFS with two children who were adopted from overseas orphanages and who currently live with their new families in the United States of America. In both cases, the children were administered standardized tests as well as the dynamic assessment; only the results of the latter are described. The first child, *Raymond*, was a 5-year 4-month-old boy who was adopted from Russia at the age of 2 years 9 months and had been diagnosed with pervasive developmental disability (PDD). The ACFS revealed two distinct characteristics of Raymond's current cognitive–language functioning and learning ability. First, Raymond presently possesses the cognitive skills needed to perform all of the tasks of this procedure. In fact, the examiner had to modify the Perspective Taking subtest and terminate administration of the Short Term Visual Memory subtest after the pretest because Raymond had reached the ceiling even before the teaching phase had been introduced. In two other activities (Classification and Sequential Pattern Completion) Raymond quickly attained a high level of performance on his own, and his functioning therefore did not show much improvement after the teaching intervention because of his high level of performance on the pretest. The testing demonstrated that Raymond had no difficulty with cognitive functioning per se. However, the dynamic assessment did reveal the extent and nature of Raymond's difficulties with the social–behavioral aspects of learning as well as with his self-regulation while engaged in mental activities. His responsiveness (the ability to be socially engaged) was inconsistent, and his interaction with the adult in a teaching role appeared defensive and resistant. His opposition to learning in a socially collaborative context reflected his noncognitive (emotional–motivational–behavioral) characteristics. Although he showed responsiveness to the interventions, he too often resorted to immature (and at times challenging) behavior during the intervention phases. His autistic-like behavior patterns blocked cooperation with a teaching authority and reduced his ability to benefit from scaffolding of the cognitive activity. In fact, he performed less effectively in the context of social collaboration with the examiner in a learning–teaching situation (dynamic assessment) than he did independently in the pretest phase of the ACFS or during standardized testing. This suggests that in order for learning to occur, Raymond would require considerably more time and intensity from a collaborative adult-led learning experience than expected for his typically developed peers. In fact, the dynamic assessment documented the depth of the challenge in addressing his learning needs and showed that, in spite of his high cognitive abilities, Raymond was not an easily modifiable child. The dynamic assessment also showed that Raymond's pragmatic language abilities to initiate, maintain, and terminate joint interactions were significantly impaired. It was difficult for Raymond to engage in goal-directed dialogue. His affective reaction to the intervention, motivation–interest in the material, and persistence on the task were well below age expectations. DA showed that such teaching methods as role playing and imitation from a model were neither easy nor engaging for him. Unfortunately, those are the major learning–teaching mechanisms for his age. Also, Raymond's tendency to become absorbed by the perceptual qualities of the objects at times interfered with his ability to profit from instruction. For example, during the storytelling activity (Short-Term Auditory Memory) the examiner explained more than once the purpose of using the materials as symbols, but Raymond appeared completely absorbed by the perceptual qualities of the materials and just played with them instead of using them as symbols for higher mental processing. During the ACFS activities, Raymond needed to be reminded frequently to focus his attention because he tended to look away and lose his train of thought. Finally, his difficulty with transitioning from one activity to another was evident during the dynamic assessment.

The second case, Stoyka, a 4-year 9-month-old girl, was adopted at the age of 3 years 10 months and was diagnosed with learning disability and language disorder. In contrast to Raymond, Stoyka performed more effectively in the context of social collaboration with the examiner in the learning–teaching situation than on her own in the pretest phase of the ACFS or during the standardized testing. However, the teaching effects were often minimal, and her gains were insignificant during the posttest phase. The dynamic assessment revealed that Stoyka was not an easily modifiable child, but for reasons that differed from those for Raymond. Her social strength evident during scaffolding activities was not effectively translated into performance gains. In other words, although she did show responsiveness to the interventions in a socially collaborative context, when left on her own, she tended to return to her initial levels of functioning. She thus had difficulty with storing and generalizing (transferring) her new learning experience. She showed particular difficulty with activities that either were based on or involved auditory memory, auditory association, or auditory–visual association, that is, that involved auditory processing. Stoyka's functioning was characterized by perseveration; that is, she repeated the same cognitive operations without apparent ability to switch to alternatives that were more appropriate to solving the problem. This was most evident when she was presented with problems that she failed to comprehend or did not know how to solve. At these times, she initially became perseverative and then became quite confused and disorganized, losing track of what she was doing. This suggests that appearance of perseveration and disorganization is likely a signal of her lack of task comprehension. Another observation was that the degree of structure of the activity seemed to be a key element relating to Stoyka's ability to succeed. The reduced structure of being asked to perform an activity independently, before provision of intervention, may have provoked the significant disorganization of her mental facilities, leaving her with insufficient guidelines regarding how to begin or to engage with the materials. Thus, the organization she has difficulty in providing from within must be provided externally until she develops more competence in task solution. Although it was difficult for Stoyka to create a pattern of performance independently, she was receptive to a suggested pattern, and her performance tended to improve significantly in response to the introduction of even minimal structure or provision of a model. Thus, her willingness to imitate and use the models presented to her provides important access for her to learning success.

These two cases demonstrate the contribution of dynamic assessment information to the understanding of children experiencing learning problems. With this information, it was possible to observe the different contributions of cognitive versus social–emotional factors to learner performance, as well as to elaborate the qualitative aspects of their functioning on a variety of tasks. Unique information about responsiveness to intervention and transfer of learning after intervention becomes available with this model of assessment.

CONCLUDING REMARKS

Dynamic assessment procedures are in a stage of rapid development, and research documenting their utility has been rapidly accumulating as well. Perhaps Luria's conviction that "the time has come when the high value given to psychometrics will come to an end" (1961, p. 14) was premature, but a high value ascribed to the dynamic approach to assessment seems on the horizon. However, the utility of dynamic assessment procedures does not require the demise of more traditional psychometric approaches. The full and meaningful diagnostic exploration of learners and the means of linking assessment with intervention requires a full repertory of assessment approaches. Dynamic assessment is unique in providing a basis for creating and exploring what Vygotsky has passed on to us as the ZPD.

References

Aranov, Z. (1999). Validity and reliability of the ACFS Behavior Observation Scale. *ERIC Document* TM 030602.

Belopolskaya, N. L., & Grebennikova, N. V. (1997). Neuropsychology and psychological diagnosis of abnormal development. In E. L. Grigorenko, P. M. Ruzgis, & R. J. Sternberg (Eds.), *Russian psychology: Past, present, and future* (pp. 155–179). Commack, NY: Nova Academic Press.

Belopolskay, N. L., & Lubovsky, V. I. (1992). Differentsial'no-psikhologicheskaia diagnostika deteei s intellektual'noi nedastatochnost'iu [Differential psychological diagnostics of children with cognitive deficiency]. *Psikhologichesky Zhurnal, 4*, 88–97.

Benssousan, Y. (2002). *The effectiveness of mediation on three subtests of the Application of Cognitive Functions Scale, a dynamic assessment procedure for young children.* Unpublished masters thesis, Touro College, New York.

Bodrova, E., & Leong, D. J. (1996). *Tools of the mind: The Vygotskian approach to early childhood education.* Columbus, OH: Merrill.

Brooks, N. D. (1997). *An exploratory study into the cognitive modifiability of pre-school children using dynamic assessment.* Unpublished masters thesis, University of Newcastle-Upon-Tyne, Newcastle, England.

Campione, J. C. & Brown, A. L. (1987). Linking dynamic assessment with school achievement. In C. S. Lidz (Ed.), *Dynamic assessment: An interactional approach to evaluating learning potential* (pp. 82–113). New York: Guilford.

Davydov, V. V. (1995). The influence of L.S. Vygotsky on education theory, research, and practice. *Educational Researcher, 24* (3), 12–21.

Elkonin, D. (1977). Toward the problem of stages in the mental development of the child. In M. Cole (Ed.), *Soviet developmental psychology.* White Plains, NY: M. E. Sharpe.

Feuerstein, R., & Gross, S. (1997). The learning potential assessment device. In Flanagan, D., Genshaft, J., & Harrison, P. (Eds.), *Contemporary intellectual assessment: Theories, tests, and issues.* New York: The Guilford Press.

Feuerstein, R., Rand, Y., Hoffman, N., & Miller, R. (1980). *Instrumental enrichment: An intervention program for cognitive modifiability.* Baltimore: University Park Press.

Galperin, P. Y. (1969). Stages in the development of mental acts. In M. Cole & I. Maltzman (Eds.), *A handbook of contemporary Soviet psychology* (pp. 34–61). New York: Basic Books.

Gauvain, M. (2001). *The social context of cognitive development.* New York: Guilford.

Gindis, B. (1986). Special education in the Soviet Union: Problems and perspectives. *Journal of Special Education, 20*(3), 375–383.

Gindis, B. (1988). Children with mental retardation in the Soviet Union. *Mental Retardation, 26*(6), 381–384.

Gindis, B. (1992). Successful theories and practices from Russia: Can they be adopted in the United States? *AAMR News & Notes, 5* (6), 2–4.

Grigorenko, E. L., Ruzgis, R. M., & Sternberg, R. J. (Eds.) (1997). *Russian psychology: Past, present, and future* (pp. 155–179). Commack, NY: Nova Academic Press.

Haywood, H. C., & Tzuriel, D. (1992). *Interactive assessment.* New York: Springer-Verlag.

Hogan, K., & Pressley, M. (Eds.) (1997). *Scaffolding student learning: Instructional approaches and issues*. Cambridge, MA: Brookline Books.

Ivanova, A. Y. (1976). *Obuchaemost kak printsip otsenki ymstvennogo pazvitia u detei* [Learning ability as an approach to the assessment of the child's intellectual development]. Moscow: Pedagogika, Moscow State University.

Karpov, Y. V. (1990). Obuchaemost kak characteristika umstvennogo razvitia [Learning aptitude as an indicator of cognitive development]. *Psikhologia, 14* (2), 3–16.

Karpov, Y. V., & Gindis, B. (2000). Dynamic assessment of the level of internalization of elementary school children's problem solving activity. In C. S. Lidz & J. G. Elliott (Eds.), *Dynamic Assessment: Prevailing models and applications* (pp. 133–154). Amsterdam: Elsevier Science.

Kozulin, A. (1998). *Psychological tools: A sociocultural approach to education*. Cambridge, MA: Harvard University Press.

Kozulin, A., & Presseisen, B. Z. (1995). Mediated learning experience and psychological tools: Vygotsky's and Feuerstein's perspectives in a study of student learning. *Educational Psychologist, 30*(2), 67–76.

Lebedinsky, V. V. (1985). *Narushchenia v psikhicheskom razvitii u detei* [Disorders in Children's Psychological Development]. Moscow: MGU Press.

Levy, C. (1999). The discriminant validity of the Application of Cognitive Functions Scale (ACFS): A performance comparison between typically developing and special needs preschool children. Unpublished masters thesis, Touro College, New York.

Lidz, C. S. (1987). Historical perspectives. In C. S. Lidz (Ed.), *Dynamic assessment: An interactional approach to evaluating learning potential* (pp. 3–34). New York: Guilford.

Lidz, C. S. (1991). *Practitioner's guide to dynamic assessment*. New York: Guilford.

Lidz, C. S. (1995). Dynamic assessment and the legacy of L. S. Vygotsky. *School Psychology International, 16*, 143–153.

Lidz, C. S. (1997). Dynamic assessment approaches. In D. P. Flanagan, J. L. Genshaft, & P. L. Harrison (Eds.), *Contemporary intellectual assessment: Theories, tests, and issues* (pp. 281–296). New York: Guilford.

Lidz, C. S. (2000). The Application of Cognitive Functions Scale (ACFS): An example of curriculum-based dynamic assessment. In C. S. Lidz & J. G. Elliott (Eds.), *Dynamic assessment: Prevailing models and applications* (pp. 407–439). Amsterdam: Elsevier Science.

Lidz, C. S. (2002). Mediated Learning Experience (MLE) as a basis for an alternative approach to assessment. *School Psychology International, 23*(1), 68–84.

Lidz, C. S. (2003). *Early childhood assessment*. New York: Wiley.

Lidz, C. S. (submitted). Successful application of a dynamic assessment procedure with young deaf students between the ages of four through eight.

Lidz, C., & Elliott, J. (Eds.) (2000). *Dynamic assessment: Prevailing models and applications*. Amsterdam: Elsevier Science.

Lidz, C. S., & Jepsen, R. H. (2000). *The Application of Cognitive Functions Scale*. Unpublished manuscript. (Author: zdilsc@aol.com)

Lubovsky, V. I. (1989). *Psikhologicheskie problemy diagnostiki anormalnogo razvitia detei* [Psychological issues in diagnosis of children with abnormal development]. Moscow: Pedagogika Press.

Lubovsky, V. I. (1990). *Psikhologicheskii Experiment v Differentcialnoi Diagnistike Um-stvennoi Otstalosti* [Psychological experiment in differential diagnosis of mental retardation in children]. *Defectology, 6*, 3–16.

Luria, A. R. (1961). An objective approach to the study of the abnormal child. *Journal of the American Orthopsychiatric Association, 31*, 1–16.

Malowitsky, M. (2002). *Investigation of the effectiveness of the mediation portion of two subtests of the Application of Cognitive Functions Scale, a dynamic assessment procedure for young children.* Unpublished masters thesis, Touro College, New York.

McCagg, W. O., & Siegelbaum, L. (Eds.) (1989). *The disabled in the Soviet Union.* Pittsburgh: University of Pittsburgh Press.

Minick, N. (1987). Implications of Vygotsky's theories for dynamic assessment. In C. S. Lidz (Ed.), *Dynamic assessment: An interactional approach to evaluating learning potential* (pp. 116–140). New York: Guilford.

Shurin, R. (1998). Validity and reliability of the Application of Cognitive Functions Scale with preschool children with disabilities. *ERIC Document* TM 030312.

Smith-Davis, J. (2000). People with disabilities in Russia: Progress and prospects. In: Keith, K. & Schalock, R. (Eds.), *Cross-cultural perspectives on quality of life.* Washington, DC: AAMR.

Sternberg, R. J., & Grigorenko, E. L. (2002). *Dynamic testing: The nature and measurement of learning potential.* New York: Cambridge University Press.

Strebeleva, E. A. (2000). *Rannyia diagnostika umstvennoi otstalosti* (Vol. 2, pp. 2–11) [Procedures for early diagnosis of mental retardation]. Moscow: Institute of Corrective Pedagogy, Almanah. Available at: www.ise.iip.net/almanah/2/st09.htm

Tharp, R. G. & Gallimore, R. (1988). *Rousing minds to life: Teaching, learning, and schooling in social context.* New York: Cambridge University Press.

Tzuriel, D. (2001). *Dynamic assessment of young children.* New York: Kluwer Academic/Plenum Publishers

van der Veer, R., & Valsiner, J. (1991). *Understanding Vygotsky: A quest for synthesis.* Oxford: Basil Blackwell.

Venger, L. A. (1988). The origin and development of cognitive abilities in preschool children. *International Journal of Behavioral Development, 11*(2), 147–153.

Vlasova, T. A. (1984). *Otbor detei v vspomogatelny shkolu* [Screening children for special schools]. Moscow: Pedagogika.

Vygotsky, L. S. (1978). *Mind in society: The development of higher psychological processes.* (M. Cole, V. John-Steiner, S. Scribner, & E. Souberman, Eds.). Cambridge, MA: Harvard University Press.

Vygotsky, L. S. (1987) *The collected works of L. S. Vygotsky.* Vol. 1. *Problems of General Psychology* (R. W. Rieber & A. S. Carton, Eds.; N. Minick, Trans.). New York: Plenum Press.

Vygotsky, L. S. (1997). *The collected works of L. S. Vygotsky.* Vol. 4. *The history of the development of higher mental functions* (M. Hall, Trans.; R. W. Rieber, Ed.). New York: Plenum Press.

Vygotsky, L. S. (1998) *The collected works of L. S. Vygotsky.* Vol. 5. *Child psychology.* (R. W. Rieber, Eds.). New York: Plenum Press.

Zaporozhets, A. V., & Elkonin, D. B. (Eds.) (1971). *The psychology of preschool children.* Cambridge, MA: MIT Press.

PART II

DEVELOPMENT AND LEARNING

6

Periods in Child Development

Vygotsky's Perspective

Holbrook Mahn

Smiles and coos of recognition; tentative first steps and first words; communicating and making sense of the world; anxious excitement on the first day of school; awareness of others; conceptual thinking; awareness of self; and the transition to young adulthood: As parents and teachers, we marvel at children's myriad journeys. At times, we experience frustration when we witness profound, often unsettling, changes in children's behavior and interactions with others. During these difficult times, such as the "terrible twos" or the "dreaded" adolescent years, children often seem to take on different personalities. How and why, we wonder, does this occur?

The same question fascinated Lev Vygotsky and was at the center of his theory of child development. He went further, asking what these times of crisis, or *critical periods* as he called them, demonstrate about the patterns and processes of children's mental and social functioning. The answers he developed are helpful today for educators trying to shape educational opportunities that meet the needs of all children. This chapter focuses on Vygotsky's analysis of the relationship between children's individual growth and development and the sociocultural situations into which they are born. At the center of his writings on child development is the relationship between "the line of natural development which is closely bound up with the processes of general organic growth and the maturation of the child [and] . . . the line of cultural improvement of the psychological functions, the working out of new methods of reasoning, the mastering of the cultural methods of behavior" (Vygotsky, 1994, p. 57).[1]

Vygotsky was particularly interested in the ways in which children make meaning of critical periods and navigate difficulties in social functioning

---

[1] Vygotsky's main work on child development is included in *Thinking and Speech* (1987); *Child Psychology* (1998), including "The Problem of Age," a central piece available for the first time in English; and the *Vygotsky Reader* (1994).

precipitated by the profound changes in their physical, mental, and social development. He analyzed children's perception, memory, attention, motivation, and emotions as they experience meaning in their sociocultural worlds. Qualitative leaps in the development of personality, identity, and awareness of self, as the child begins to think conceptually and to understand systems – social, linguistic, cultural, logical, and emotional – were of particular interest to him.

Vygotsky's work on the interdependence of individual and social processes in children's meaning-making provides an important foundation for developing teaching–learning environments that value the whole child and honor the different cultures, languages, prior experiences, and learning styles that children take to the classroom. His work helped the National Research Council conclude, "There is a good deal of evidence that learning is enhanced when teachers pay attention to the knowledge and beliefs that learners bring to a learning task, use this knowledge as a starting point for new instruction, and monitor students' changing conceptions as instruction proceeds" (1999, p. 11).

In a text he was preparing for teachers, Vygotsky focused on the concept of *meaning* to analyze the psychological development of children. Because he never completed the section on teaching approaches, this chapter focuses more on Vygotsky's theoretical analysis of children's meaning-making and why it is helpful to educators who are trying to design more effective and inclusive teaching practices. This analysis provides a theoretical and methodological background for other chapters in this volume that describe in more depth the practical applications that flow from his theory.

This chapter centers on Vygotsky's analysis of periods[2] of profound change in children's development: critical periods when they begin to walk and talk, when they start school, when they start to use conceptual thinking, and when they gain self-awareness during adolescence. Two themes are foremost in this examination of critical periods – children's meaning-making processes and the development of their social relations. Before discussing Vygotsky's analysis of critical periods it will be helpful to examine briefly the methodological approach and theoretical framework he used to develop his theory of child development. Because Vygotsky's approach is based on a system of logic different from that utilized in traditional Western science, it is sometimes difficult to understand and is variously interpreted. Understanding Vygotsky's methodological approach, therefore, is important for an appreciation of his theory of child development.

---

[2] Although there is not always consistency in Vygotsky's use of terminology, he tended to use the definitions of a fellow Soviet psychologist, Blonsky – *periods* and *stages* – to describe times of crisis in child development; however, he also used *period* to describe times of stability.

METHODOLOGICAL APPROACH

Vygotsky situated the process of learning and development in sociocultural environments. His dialectical approach has four central tenets: (1) that phenomena be examined as a part of a historical, developmental process from their origins to their terminus; (2) that change, a constant, is most clearly seen at times of qualitative transformation in phenomena; (3) that these transformations take place through the unification of contradictory, distinct processes; and (4) that these unifications or unities be analyzed through aspects that are irreducible and embody the essence of the whole.

Marx and Engels (1970) used this approach to develop their theory of historical materialism, on which Vygotsky relied heavily. They analyzed the development of human society from the primitive societies formed when humans first effectively marshaled natural forces to meet their basic needs to the complex social systems of their day. They focused on social revolutions – times of qualitative transformation in social relations – to understand the inner dynamics, the laws of motion, of social development. Marx and Engels placed human activity, shaped by language and consciousness, at the center of the origins of social formations. Vygotsky used their analysis of the origins and historical development of human society as a foundation for his examination of the development of consciousness. "The historical development of behavior was carried out as the organic part of the societal development of man, subject basically to all the patterns that determine the course of the historical development of humanity as a whole" (Vygotsky, 1998, p. 34). In line with historical materialism, Vygotsky's methodological approach focused on times of qualitative transformation in children's development – critical periods when fundamental change causes a restructuring of social relations.

Vygotsky examined these relations by using *meaning* as a unifying concept and using the unity of the personality formation and the "ensemble of social relations" in a child's environment to help understand children's meaning-making processes. He developed his approach to psychology by looking at the historical origin and development of the higher psychological functions of humans, which provide "the key to the understanding of their nature, composition, structure, form of activity, and at the same time the key to the whole problem of the psychology of man" (1997, p. 127).

Vygotsky's dialectical approach contrasts with evolutionary, linear approaches that analyze incremental growth but do not explain the creation of the new psychological structures that define the age levels. Linear approaches use formal logic to describe surface appearances of psychological development but do not reveal its internal essence – the process of motion, change, and development. Vygotsky felt that this essence was more apparent in critical periods than in stable periods in which the growth is slower, more incremental, and beneath the surface and thus harder to analyze. Vygotsky paraphrases Marx to underscore the need to discover the inner logic of development: "If the form of appearance and essence of things coincided directly, then all science would be superfluous" (1998, p. 54).[3] In psychology this discovery requires moving beyond describing and categorizing manifestations of mental activity to examining what lies behind these manifestations, what brings them into existence, and what determines their direction. His approach can be very useful for educators who want to examine the internal logic of change in cognitive growth and development (Newman, Griffin, & Cole, 1989).

A goal of educators who look to Vygotsky's analysis of child development is to make effective education available to all children by creating comfortable, stimulating, and engaging environments where teaching–learning is built on students' prior experiences, natural curiosity, and developmental processes. "Prior knowledge also includes the kind of knowledge that learners acquire because of their social roles, such as those connected with race, class, gender, and their cultural and ethnic affiliations" (National Research Council, 1999, p. 60). For Vygotsky, a key to meeting this goal was understanding the relationship between children's meaning-making processes and their sociocultural situations during critical periods in their development.

CRITICAL PERIODS

Vygotsky focused on developmental junctures of rapid, profound transformation in mental and social functioning. He believed that his analysis of such critical periods was a unique contribution to educational psychology and that his attempt "to interpret [critical periods] theoretically and include them in the general pattern of child development must be considered as almost the first such attempt" (1998, p. 191). He argued that the changes in individual processes and social relations during critical periods are so profound that they often lead to crises for the child. During these periods the internal patterns and logic of child development, including the transitions from one period to another, are more clearly revealed. The critical periods characterized by "abrupt and major shifts and displacements, changes, and discontinuities in the child's personality are concentrated in a relatively short time" during which "the child changes completely in the basic traits of his personality" (p. 191).[4]

---

[3] I have used *appearance* in place of *manifestation* as translated in Vygotsky (1998) as it conforms more accurately to the quotation from *Capital*, volume 3, "[A]ll science would be superfluous if the form of appearance of things and their essence directly coincided."

[4] Much of this chapter is based on the fifth volume of *The collected works of L. S. Vygotsky* (1998) and for the sake of readability, where there are a number of direct quotations from that work grouped together, page numbers only are indicated after the full citation.

Vygotsky discovered the internal essence of child development by analyzing the new mental formations that "determine the consciousness of the child, his relation to the environment, his internal and external life, the whole course of his development during the given period" (1998, p. 190). The unification of seemingly contradictory processes into qualitatively different forms is a central feature of the transformations in critical periods. Vygotsky studied the logic of the internal changes taking place in the child and used meaning-making to do so because "the crisis is most of all a turning point that is expressed in the fact that the child passes from one method of experiencing the environment to another" (1998, p. 295). Vygotsky argued that a close analysis of the origins, the character, and the forces giving direction to the development of *meaning-making* in the critical periods helps reveal the internal dynamics of stable and critical periods and the entire process of development.

Children vary in the onset, duration, and impact of critical periods, but they are all affected in a fundamental way – during this period a new mental formation, a *psychological structure* of the personality, is formed. Examples of these mental structures include language, verbal thinking, and thinking in concepts. These new formations become the driving force behind the transitions from one age level to the next and determine the character of the new age level. The dominant new formation also changes "in the transition from one stage to another, and the whole structure of the age is reconstructed. Each age has a unique and singular structure specific to it" (Vygotsky, 1998, p. 197). These new structures "basically determine the consciousness of the child, his relation to the environment, his internal and external life, the whole course of his development during the given period" (p. 190). The new formations precipitate "the reconstruction of the whole personality on a new base" (p. 197) and serve as the basic criterion for dividing child development into separate periods.

In critical periods, the tension between the dominant mental formation–structure and the emerging formations, which will govern development in the new period, comes to a head and the internal processes in both are laid bare. Particularly important in this transition are the qualitative changes in children's social relations and the ways that children make meaning of their interactions in and with their sociocultural environment. Understanding these changes can help parents and teachers construct effective parenting and teaching approaches. During critical periods a child can become "relatively difficult due to the fact that . . . the pedagogical system applied to the child does not keep up with the rapid changes in his personality" (Vygotsky, 1998, pp. 193–194).

Vygotsky approached development as a contradictory process characterized by longer periods of gradual growth interspersed with shorter periods of crisis and transition during which qualitative restructuring of mental functioning takes place.

The crisis of the newborn separates the embryonal period of development from infancy. The one-year crisis separates infancy from early childhood. The crisis at age three is a transition from early childhood to preschool age. The crisis at age seven is a link that joins preschool and school ages. Finally, the crisis at age thirteen coincides with the turning point in development at the transition from school age to puberty. (1998, p. 193)

Vygotsky ascribed three general features to these critical periods. First, they do not have clearly defined boundaries with stable periods on each side of them. "The crisis arises imperceptibly – it is difficult to determine its onset and termination" (p. 191), but there is a culminating point that clearly differentiates the critical period from the stable period in which it developed. Second, the rate of development slows during the critical period, and for school-age children, there is "a drop in the rate of success, a slacking of interest in school work, and a general decline in capacity for work" (p. 191). Whereas studies tend to focus on the child who experiences particular difficulties in these periods, Vygotsky emphasized that *every* child is affected. In describing the variation in the degree to which children are affected, Vygotsky (1998) recognized that "external conditions determine the concrete character of manifestation and passage of critical periods," but he also acknowledged that the "internal logic of the process of development itself is responsible for the critical, disruptive periods in the life of the child" (p. 192). The third feature Vygotsky identified is the dialectical character of development in the critical periods – during which "the child does not so much acquire as he loses some of what he had acquired earlier" (p. 192). However, Vygotsky asserted that "it would be a great mistake to assume that this is the whole significance of the critical ages. Development never ends its creative work, and during critical periods too, we observe constructive processes of development . . . consisting usually in the transition to a new and higher form" (p. 194).

Transitions

Key to the restructuring of mental functioning that takes place in these transitions is the unification of external and internal forces. Vygotsky (1998) examined the unity of personality[5] and environment to reveal the character, the motion, and the direction of development from critical to stable periods and from stable to critical. Stable periods in this process are marked by slow,

---

[5] Chaiklin (2001) describes two ways in which Vygotsky uses the concept "personality." One is "to refer to those human qualities of behaviour that result from cultural development as distinct from biological maturation. A second use is a more precise identification of the specific cultural development, which in Vygotsky's analysis was thinking with concepts, and a self-consciousness of this ability" (pp. 239–240).

evolutionary flow during which there are "no fundamental abrupt shifts and alterations that reconstruct the child's whole personality" (p. 190). They have more easily defined beginning and ending boundaries and tend to be longer than critical periods with a more gradual development of the child's personality in a "continuous construction of the new" (p. 192).

At any given age, there are both central and peripheral lines of development that are connected in differing degrees to the new formation that defines the critical period. Vygotsky argued that central processes become peripheral in the subsequent age period and those that had been peripheral become central in the following one. He used speech development to illustrate this point. During infancy the speech process may be peripheral, but it becomes central in early childhood and then peripheral once again in subsequent age periods. The key point in this determination is that the meaning and relative significance of the central and the peripheral lines of development change in the total structure of development.

FEATURES OF CRITICAL PERIODS

Vygotsky recognized that the onset of critical periods depends on historical and cultural development and cited as an example the prolonged period between sexual maturation and adulthood in modern society as compared with its shorter duration in early human social formations when childbearing began with puberty. Another example of historical and cultural influence is the variation in the age at which children begin school in different societies. Cultural norms, not physiological maturation, affect the onset of the critical period that is precipitated when a child enrolls in formal schooling. The qualitative transformation in the child's development is based on new social relations at school and the development of conceptual thinking and exposure to systems of knowledge in science, math, literacy, and language.

Vygotsky's approach to analyzing meaning-making and social relations in critical periods stood in sharp contrast to theories of child development in the early 1930s, some of which have echoes in educational psychology today. Vygotsky's emphasis on social interaction, especially between adults and children, differed from behaviorist theories in the West and particularly in the United States that sought to predict and control behavior on the basis of its observable manifestations. His emphasis on the relationship of the social and the individual also differed from the ideas of Piaget, who posited predetermined internal stages of development. Vygotsky (1998) in "The Problem of Age," the most complete elaboration of his theory of critical periods in child development, critiqued theories that used the concept of periods (Ratner, 1998).

Vygotsky argued that changes in the mental structures and functions reveal the essence of development – the dynamic relationship between the structures of the higher mental processing and the content of those structures – meaning-making. The interdependence of sociocultural contexts and individual physical and mental development on the one hand and the analysis of *meaning* and the ways it develops in human social interaction on the other are at the core of Vygotsky's theoretical framework. The analysis of this interdependence is central to his quest to understand the origins, structure, functioning, and internal pattern of the development of consciousness.

MAKING MEANING OF MEANING-MAKING

Vygotsky (1997) succinctly summarized his conception of meaning: "Meaning is not the sum of all the psychological operations which stand behind the word. Meaning is something more specific – *it is the internal structure of the sign operation.* It is what is lying between the thought and the word. Meaning is not equal to the word, nor equal to the thought. This disparity is revealed by the fact that their lines of development do not coincide" (p. 133, emphasis added). Vygotsky used the concept of meaning as an internal structure, resulting from the unification of thinking and speech, as the foundation for his investigation of the ways that the meaning of words mediates mental processes.

Vygotsky's analysis of meaning-making started with infants. Adults pull objects out of the undifferentiated, amorphous background of the infants' visual perception to focus attention on the objects. Adults simultaneously attribute intentionality to infants' gestures, which then become signs through which they act upon the objective world and communicate with those around them (Vygotsky, 1978). The change in the child's communicative ability creates a "dynamic change of the initial relation to the world" (Vygotsky, 1998, p. 231). Vygotsky analyzed how children, near the end of their first year, use a new formation – autonomous speech – to try to overcome the contradiction "between maximum sociability of the infant (the situation in which the infant finds himself) and minimum capability for interaction" (p. 216).

AUTONOMOUS SPEECH AND VERBAL THINKING

Autonomous speech, which provides the transition from an infant's babbling to communicative speech, has different laws of construction than regular speech. "[Autonomous] speech has another sound system, another sense aspect, other forms of communication, and other forms of connection" (Vygotsky, 1998, p. 252). Children create their own language, one that is dependent on the situation, since they are not able to use words for thinking when the visual stimulation is absent. Word use at this age level differs from later usage, which has more fixed and constant communicative meanings. Thinking is determined by the child's perception and affective – volitional tendencies, not through symbolization, as speech and thinking for the 1-year-old have independent paths of development.

Vygotsky recognized other important factors in children's development at the time that they turn 1 year old, including standing up and walking and increased affective outbursts; however, his emphasis was on the evolving changes in the child's consciousness for which "the study of speech is theoretically central to understanding all the other changes" (1998, p. 259). The formation of autonomous speech lays the foundation for a new relationship between speech and thinking, leading to the central new formation in the more stable and prolonged period of early childhood – the development of consciousness.

Vygotsky described two distinct but interrelated aspects of development that occur in early childhood: first, internal unification of speech and thinking as the child makes meaning through verbal thinking; and second, the external construction of perception in relationship to thinking – the transition from nonverbal perception to verbal perception, which is key in the move from visual thinking to verbal thinking. As speech becomes interwoven with visual perception, a level of interpretation is added, creating a "new synthesis in which visual impressions and processes of thinking are merged in a single alloy that can justifiably be called visual thinking" (1998, p. 88). My 2-year-old daughter, Emily, provided a wonderful illustration of this when she looked up at a half moon in the night sky and exclaimed, "Oh Daddy, it's broken!"

The function of perception becomes central in the mental structure in this age period, and its interrelationships with other functions constitute the new system of consciousness. These changes fundamentally alter the ways in which a child makes meaning because "the child, whose perception is directed by speech, *comprehends* the situation" (Vygotsky, 1998, p. 116). This comprehension results from children's using language to make meaning of their social reality. An important aspect of Vygotsky's theoretical framework and one that guides his analysis of the critical periods is the examination of the process through which the intertwining of speech and thinking results in *verbal thinking.*

Vygotsky's approach to verbal thinking differed from those that isolate language and thought from their contexts and ignore their distinct origins and processes of development. He started by analyzing the unification of speech and thinking, seeking a unity that is irreducible and that maintains the essence of the whole.

If you want to know how a unity developed, how it changes, how it affects the course of the child's development, it is important not to break down the unity into its component parts. Because when this is done, the essential properties of specifically this unity are lost. (1998, p. 294)

Vygotsky used the *meaning of the word*, the unity of speech and thinking, to analyze verbal thinking as it is irreducible and maintains the essence of the whole. Meaning, the internal structure of the sign operation, is a part of every word because without meaning it is not a word and "since all meaning of a word is a generalization, it is a product of the intellectual activity of the child. The meaning of a word is a unity of speech and thinking that can not be broken down further" (p. 294). The transformation in the way children make meaning through social interaction characterizes the stable period of early childhood and defines children's sociocultural situations of development.

SOCIAL RELATIONS

The interdependence of individual–internal and social–external processes in learning and development is the cornerstone of Vygotsky's theory and has been a focus of the interpretive work on his fundamental ideas (John-Steiner & Mahn, 1996; Wertsch, 1991). Much of this work focuses on Vygotsky's analysis of the role of social interaction in the development of higher psychological processes and, in particular, the ways in which culture shapes human mental development (Cole, 1996) and education (Moll, 1990; Wells & Claxton, 2002). However, less attention has been paid to his analysis of the ways in which individual development shapes the sociocultural environment. Changes in children's social situations of development result from and cause qualitative transformations in their perception, experience, appropriation, internalization, understanding, and memory of interaction in and with their environment.

Vygotsky viewed this interdependence "as a process that is characterized by a unity of material and mental aspects, a unity of the social and the personal" (1998, p. 190). This unity expresses "a completely original, exclusive, single, and unique relation, specific to the given age, between the child and reality, mainly the social reality that surrounds him. We call this relation the *social situation of development* at the given age" (p. 198). It is important to note that Vygotsky conceived of the social situation of development as a *relation*, not a context. He argued that "the child is a part of the social situation, and the relation of the child to the environment and the environment to the child occurs through the experience and activity of the child himself; the forces of the environment acquire a controlling significance because the child experiences them" (p. 294). The child's experience of social activity is essential to understanding the changes from one age period to the next because when the child's relation to the environment changes, "this means that the environment itself has changed, it means that the course of the child's development has changed and that a new period of development has started" (p. 292).

Vygotsky described the way the social situation of development influences the "reconstruction of the conscious personality [on the] base specific to the given age, [on] the forms of his social existence" (1998, p. 198). He added that to understand this reconstruction we must find "a path of reverse movement from the changed structure of the child's consciousness to a reconstruction of his existence. The child, having changed the structure of his personality, is already a different child whose social existence cannot but differ in a substantial way from the existence of the child of an earlier age" (p. 199). This change in the way that the child makes meaning of and internalizes interaction in a social environment should be an important consideration for educators interested in creating learner-centered teaching–learning environments.

Children's meaning-making changes dramatically during the critical periods because "the essence of every crisis is a reconstruction of the internal experience, a reconstruction that is rooted in the change of the basic factor that determines the relation of the child to the environment, specifically, in the change in needs and motives that control the behavior of the child" (Vygotsky, 1998, p. 296). The change in the needs and motives alters the internal experience, which in turn changes the relationship to the environment. The environment and its effect on the child are "completely different for a child at age one, three, seven, or twelve" (p. 293). Because these interrelated developments change children's mental functioning and their perception and experience of their sociocultural environment, their relationship to the environment changes. Vygotsky called this experience of *meaning* "one of the most complex problems of contemporary psychology and psychopathology of the personality" (p. 290). He used a Russian term – *perezhivanie* – to capture the process through which children make meaning of their social existence. This term refers to the way children perceive, emotionally experience, appropriate, internalize, and understand interactions in their environment. There is no adequate translation in English of the Russian *perezhivanie* and single- or two-word translations do not do justice to the concept. The translators of the article "The Problem of the Environment" in which Vygotsky (1994) explained *perezhivanie* write, "The Russian term [*perezhivanie*] serves to express the idea that one and the same objective situation may be interpreted, perceived, experienced or lived through by different children in different ways" (p. 354). Vygotsky also felt that the ways that social experience was appropriated and internalized were important aspects of *perezhivanie*.

CRITICAL PERIODS AND *PEREZHIVANIE*

"[T]he essential factors which explain the influence of environment on the psychological development of children and on the development of their conscious personalities, are made up of their *perezhivanie*" (Vygotsky, 1994, p. 339). The newborn's complete dependency on others to meet all physical and emotional needs defines the infant's relationship to the sociocultural situation into which she is born and characterizes this period of child development. "[T]he first contact of the child with reality (even in carrying out the most elementary biological functions) is wholly and completely socially mediated" (Vygotsky, 1998, p. 215). This mediation affects the functions of perception, memory, attention, and practical activity.Having described the dependent nature of the social interaction in this period, Vygotsky wrote that what remains is "to disclose what corresponds to the objective situation in the consciousness of the subject of development himself, that is, of the infant" (p. 215).

Social mediation helps shape these new formations in personality development since "the transfer inward of external social relations between people is the basis for the structure of the personality" (Vygotsky, 1998, p. 170). Vygotsky used *perezhivanie* – the "indivisible unity of personal characteristics and situational characteristics" (1994, p. 342) – to reveal the dialectical process in which the reconstructed personality shapes social relations and in which social relations shape the personality.

> *Perezhivanie* is a unity where, on the one hand, in an indivisible state, the environment is represented, i.e. that which is being experienced . . . and on the other hand, what is represented is how I, myself, am experiencing this, i.e., all the personal characteristics and all the environmental characteristics are represented in *perezhivanie*. (Vygotsky, 1994, p. 342)

To study this relationship Vygotsky examined children making meaning of social activity as a unity of the personal and the environment. His concept of environment extended beyond the physical context to include social and affective activity, products of cultural development such as speech and other symbol systems, and social systems and formations. Vygotsky defined the environment not just as the external circumstances of a child's life, but as a context that "included tools and cultural objects, as well as people" (National Research Council, 1999, p. 68). He felt that "the human environment is a social environment, that the child is a part of a living environment and that the environment is never external to the child" (Vygotsky, 1998, p. 293). The social environment is "transferred to a significant degree to within the child himself" (p. 295).

In describing the relationship between the individual and social activity, "not the situation in itself taken in its absolute indicators, but how the child experiences the situation" (p. 294), Vygotsky also describes affective processes – "how a child becomes aware of, interprets, [and] emotionally relates to a certain event" (1994, p. 341). Vygotsky (1999) stressed the role emotions play in the qualitative changes in social relations when children acquire language and when they go through adolescence. His uncompleted work on emotions, which only became available in English in 1999, has important implications for education (Mahn & John-Steiner, 2002).

SOCIAL RELATIONS AND THE 3-YEAR-OLD

The internalization of social relations is an important process in the critical period when the child turns 3 years old. After gaining an awareness of the objective environment through speech and social interaction, 3-year-olds become aware of their subjective environment – their relationship to others, their conscious contact with others to whom they become exposed through their ability to communicate. This awareness alters the way they perceive, experience, and appropriate their social interactions. As a part of this process they establish their independence, which often leads to "obstinacy, stubbornness, negativism, capriciousness, and self-will" (Vygotsky, 1998, p. 193).

A key to understanding these actions is realizing that the child is reacting to another individual not to the content of the interaction. A "No" at this stage is a general "No" directed toward everyone. "I" becomes the central axis, and "the personality of the child undergoes abrupt and unexpected changes" (p. 193). The child challenges the authority of the mother and father and thereby changes social relations. Becoming aware of others in relation to self characterizes the critical period of the 3-year-old as "the crisis occurs along the axis of a reconstruction of social interrelations of the child's personality and the people around him (p. 288). After the crisis at age 3, there is a prolonged stable period during which the child's speech develops with a concomitant development of consciousness. This establishes the foundation for the next critical period, when a child enters school.

DIFFERENTIATING THE INTERNAL AND EXTERNAL

In this critical period, the differentiation of internal and external life helps children understand themselves in relationship to others and aids them in the transition to schooling, in which they are introduced formally and systematically to conceptual thinking. "[T]he child begins to understand what it means when he says: 'I'm happy,' 'I'm unhappy,' 'I'm angry.' . . . He is developing an intellectual orientation in his own experiences. Precisely as a three-year-old child discovers his relation to other people, a seven-year-old discovers the fact of his own experiences" (Vygotsky, 1998, p. 291).

This discovery leads to what Vygotsky called the most essential trait of the crisis – "the beginning of the differentiation of the internal and external aspects of the child's personality" (p. 290). The childlike directness from the previous period, which results from a lack of differentiation of internal and external life, is lost, leading to frivolousness and clownishness when children enter school. Children become more independent and their relationships to others change. Children begin to compare and contrast as they build their classification systems of both objects and their self. The differentiation of the internal and external disrupts mental equilibrium, causing internal conflict and an instability of the will and mood. As a result children often have a difficult time making decisions. The profound changes in the child's development during this critical period are often mistakenly perceived by classroom teachers as willful, disruptive behavior.

During this period, children are also faced with the challenge of acquiring literacy in a school setting. Vygotsky's analysis of the ways in which children make meaning during this period provides a foundation for educators who place meaning-making at the center of teaching and learning literacy. His work has provided the foundation for key figures in writing and reading theory and research (Cazden, 1996; John-Steiner, Panofsky & Smith, 1994; Lee & Smagorinsky, 2000; Mahn & John-Steiner, forthcoming). His work is particularly important today, when literacy instruction has increasingly deviated from a focus on meaning-making to one that emphasizes skill building. Vygotsky stressed that for each child the acquisition of literacy is a novel process in which there are qualitative leaps as the child realizes that print communicates meaning. Vygotsky (1978) drew implications from his analysis: "Teaching should be organized in such a way that reading and writing are necessary for something . . . that writing must be relevant to life . . . [and] be *taught* naturally . . . that natural methods of teaching reading and writing involve appropriate operations on the child's environment . . . that children should be taught written language, not just the writing of letters" (pp. 117–119).

The representation of meaning through reading and writing lays the foundation for the two interrelated processes through which children's experiences of meaning grow and change – the development of higher mental functions and conceptual thinking. These processes develop in the stable school age period that follows the critical period when children start school and are central in the critical period through which adolescents pass at approximately age 13.

ADOLESCENCE

The transition to a new form of mental functioning is seen in adolescence when children take qualitative steps in the development of the "higher formations that are the foundation of the whole conscious existence of man" (Vygotsky, 1998, p. 149). The key to understanding these new formations is recognizing that the adolescent "masters for the first time the process of forming concepts, that he makes the transition to a new and higher form of intellectual activity – to thinking in concepts" (p. 38). For Vygotsky the most difficult problem in describing the critical period of adolescence was "understanding the development of personality and world view and their internal connection with the function of concept formation" (p. 147). School-age children are exposed to concepts about systems, but it is not until the critical period at about age 13 that a qualitative transformation takes place in the adolescent's thinking – "the function of *forming concepts* is the principal and central link in all the changes that occur in the psychology of the adolescent" (p. 81).

Vygotsky (1998) argued that the higher mental functions depend on new mechanisms that result not from the gradual, linear development of the elementary functions, but from "a qualitatively new mental formation [that] develops according to completely special laws subject to completely different patterns" (p. 34). This new formation results when the elementary functions, "processes that are more primitive, earlier, simpler, and independent of concepts in genetic, functional, and structural relations, are reconstructed on a new basis when influenced by thinking in concepts" (p. 81).

Vygotsky (1998) emphasized the role of speech and verbal thinking in the formation of the new psychological structures in the transformations *"from direct, innate, natural forms and methods of behavior to mediated, artificial mental functions that develop in the process of cultural development"* (p. 168). These new formations affect the development of children's perception and precipitate the shift from thinking in complexes to thinking in concepts and result in a radical change in "the nature of the participation of verbal thinking in the adolescent's perceptions" (p. 89). This change enables adolescents to create a more "systematic, ordered, categorical picture of reality" (p. 89), unlike younger children, who organize reality into complexes without understanding the systems of interconnections behind them (see Karpov, this volume). "We could say that both the child and the adolescent relate *in the same way* to what is perceived with a system of connections hidden behind words, but the system of connections itself in which what is perceived is included is *seriously different* for the child and the adolescent" (Vygotsky, 1998, p. 90).

A similar differentiation takes place with the function of fantasy for the child and the adolescent. For the child there is not a distinction between the subjective and objective imagination – the child makes no effort to hide fantasy play. The adolescent on the other hand, uses imagination in "the intimate realm of his experience, normally hidden from other people, and thus it becomes an exclusively subjective form of thinking, thinking exclusively for oneself. . . . An adolescent finds a means of expressing his rich inner emotional life and his impulses in fantasy" (Vygotsky, 1994, p. 284).

The adolescent, who thinks conceptually, discovers the "whole world of deep connections that underlie external, outward appearances, the world of complex interdependencies and relations within every sphere of activity and among its separate spheres" (Vygotsky, 1998, p. 42). The adolescent becomes aware of "self" as a conscious being in a complex social system. The awareness of one's self also helps adolescents understand that the actions of others in their social environment are likewise motivated by their own unique, internal worlds. The adolescent experiences a contradiction in this process – the adolescent's identity revolves around individual uniqueness at the same time that there is a need to belong.

Conceptual thinking helps the adolescent develop "consciousness of his personality and its unity on one hand, and the development of consciousness of [outward] reality and its unity on the other" (Vygotsky, 1998, p. 147). In addition to gaining a more profound understanding of reality and social relations, the adolescent begins to understand the complexity of "self" through the reflection and introspection resulting from conceptual thinking. This awareness of one's own internal mental processes through self-perception and reflection contributes to the fundamental change in the adolescent's perception and internalization of the experience of social interaction.

Perezhivanie undergoes a qualitative transformation when the adolescent thinks in concepts and perceives and understands social reality in its interconnectedness, as a system of systems. Vygotsky explains that in *perezhivanie* the "influence of environment on child development will, along with other types of influences, also have to be assessed by taking the degree of understanding, awareness, and insight of what is going on in the environment into account" (Vygotsky, 1994, p. 343). Understanding, awareness, and insight separate the adolescent's *perezhivanie* from the child's.

Along with the influence of the environment and social relations, the adolescent's perception, experience, and appropriation of the internal processes themselves shape the personality. "Together with the primary conditions of the individual cast of the personality (instincts, heredity) and secondary conditions of its formation (environment, acquired traits), there is a set of tertiary conditions (reflection, self-shaping)" (Vygotsky, 1998, p. 181). A consequence of the control that the adolescent begins to exercise over internal mental processes is that "practical activity becomes more and more mediated by speech" (p. 120). The adolescent becomes more reflective and introspective, and both "consciousness of self and [the] potential for controlling his actions develop" (p. 120). The adolescent conceptualizes activity and its consequences and, therefore, plans it in a way that a younger child cannot.

Pedagogical Implications

It is important in developing teaching approaches for adolescents to keep in mind the contradiction between the need to belong and the need to develop a unique personality. Providing opportunities for the co-construction of knowledge through dialogic inquiry helps establish the type of learning communities that recognize the process through which adolescents are passing (Wells, 1999). At the same time that adolescents are involved in dialogic co-construction of knowledge, they also need the time and space for individual reflection. The use of dialogue journals between teacher and student has been effective in creating opportunities for students to do this sort of reflection (Mahn, 1997; Mahn & John-Steiner, 2002).

To explore the unity between personality (individual–internal) and environment (social–external) in the development of consciousness of self,

Vygotsky used a dialectical approach, which examined phenomena as dynamic, contextual, complex entities in a constant state of change and situated the sociocultural development of the personality in humanity's historical development. This approach is particularly important in analyzing the critical period of adolescence, marked by self-awareness and the full development of consciousness.

CONCLUSION

Vygotsky's analysis of the role of *meaning* in the construction of consciousness provides the foundation for his main theoretical contributions – the development of higher psychological processes, the role of spontaneous and scientific concepts in the development of conceptual thinking, and learning and development through social interaction in the zone of proximal development – on which he relies for his work on critical periods in child-development. These theories may help guide educators who seek to understand learning–development in order to create efficacious teaching–learning environments. Vygotsky's theory of child development gives us "an approach that combines a high level of theoretical power, sophistication, and the possibility for scientific validation, with the possibility of actual implementation in real classroom settings by ordinary teachers" (Kerr, 2002).

Using Vygotsky's theoretical framework to understand the ways in which students experience classroom activities can help in constructing environments based on the needs of children, not those of politicians, policymakers, and publishing companies. This is particularly true when we are developing teaching approaches for students learning in a language other than their native one. These students face the challenge of learning in a situation in which their main device for making meaning, their native language, is not part of their new teaching–learning environment. The unity of the individual–internal and the social–external is severely disrupted at the very time when it is most needed as children experience a profound change in their social interactions. Their ability to grasp the concepts to which they are being introduced is sharply curtailed when those concepts are introduced in a language to which they are just gaining access. Using the students' native language to help them develop conceptual thinking at the same time that they are learning to speak their second language has been proved to help second language learners reach and surpass academic standards in both languages (Cummins, 2000; National Research Council, 1997; Thomas & Collier, 1997). Vygotsky's theoretical framework outlined in this chapter provides a strong argument for using bilingual education to the fullest extent possible.

Vygotsky's theoretical framework, which has been widely applied in education, had as a central component the analysis of transformations in children's personalities caused by changes in the relationship between individual and social forces. Vygotsky provides a solid foundation for building teaching–learning classrooms that honor cultural and linguistic diversity and that strive to educate and assess the whole child. Through his work, Vygotsky speaks to educators and parents across the decades and helps illuminate paths for educational reform.

References

Cazden, C. (1996). Selective traditions: Readings of Vygotsky in writing pedagogy. In D. Hicks (Ed.), *Discourse, learning and schooling* (pp. 165–185). New York: Cambridge University Press.

Chaiklin, S. (2001). The category of "personality" in cultural-historical psychology. In S. Chaiklin (Ed.), *The theory and practice of cultural-historical psychology* (pp. 238–259). Oakville, CT: Aarhus University Press.

Cole, M. (1996). *Cultural psychology: A once and future discipline.* Cambridge, MA: Harvard University Press.

Cummins, J. (2000). *Language, power, and pedagogy: Bilingual children in the crossfire (Bilingual education and bilingualism 23).* Clevedon, England: Multilingual Matters. Available at: http://www.iteachilearn.com/cummins/index.htm

John-Steiner, V., & Mahn, H. (1996). Sociocultural approaches to learning and development: A Vygotskian framework. *Educational Psychologist, 31*(3/4), 191–206.

John-Steiner, V., Panofsky, C. P., & Smith, L. W. (1994). *Sociocultural approaches to language and literacy: An interactionist perspective.* New York: Cambridge University Press.

Kerr, S. T. (2002). Why Vygotsky? The role of theoretical psychology in Russian education reform. Paper presented at the 1997 annual meeting of the American Association for the Advancement of Slavic Studies, Seattle. Available at: http://faculty.washington.edu/stkerr/whylsv.html

Lee, C., & Smagorinsky, P. (Eds.) (2000). *Vygotskian perspectives on literacy research: Constructing meaning through collaborative inquiry.* New York: Cambridge University Press.

Mahn, H. (1997). *Dialogue journals: Perspectives of second language learners in a Vygotskian theoretical framework.* Unpublished dissertation, University of New Mexico, Albuquerque.

Mahn, H., & John-Steiner, V. (2002). The gift of confidence: A Vygotskian view of emotions. In G. Wells & G. Claxton (Eds.), *Learning for life in the 21st century: Sociocultural perspectives on the future of education* (pp. 46–58). Cambridge, MA: Blackwell.

Mahn, H., & John-Steiner, V. (forthcoming). Vygotsky's contribution to literacy research. In R. Beach, J. L. Green, M. L. Kamil, & T. Shanahan (Eds.), *Multidisciplinary perspectives on literacy research* (2nd ed.). Urbana, IL: NCTE.

Marx, K., & Engels, F. (1970). *The German ideology.* New York: International Publishers.

Moll, L. C. (Ed.) (1990). *Vygotsky and education: Instructional implications of sociohistorical psychology.* New York: Cambridge University Press.

National Research Council. (1997). *Improving schooling for language-minority children: A research agenda*. Washington, DC: National Academy Press.

National Research Council. (1999). *How people learn: Brain, mind, experience, and school*. Washington, DC: National Academy Press.

Newman, D., Griffin, P., & Cole, M. (1989). *The construction zone: Working for cognitive change in schools*. New York: Cambridge University Press.

Ratner, C. (1998). Prologue. In R. Reiber (Ed.), *Child psychology: The collected works of L. S. Vygotsky*. Vol. 5. *Problems of the theory and history of psychology*, (pp. v–xv). New York: Plenum. Available at: http://www.humboldt1.com/~cr2/vygprol.htm

Thomas, W., & Collier, V. (1997, December). School effectiveness for language minority students. *NCBE Resource Collection Series*, No. 9. Available at: http://www.ncbe.gwu.edu/ncbepubs/resource/effectiveness/

Vygotsky, L. S. (1978). *Mind in society: The development of higher psychological processes*. Cambridge, MA: Harvard University Press.

Vygotsky, L. S. (1987). *The collected works of L. S. Vygotsky*. Vol. 1. *Problems of general psychology*. Including the volume *Thinking and Speech*. New York: Plenum.

Vygotsky, L. S. (1994). The problem of the environment. In R. van der Veer & J. Vlasiner (Eds.), *The Vygotsky reader* (pp. 338–354). Cambridge, MA: Blackwell.

Vygotsky, L. S. (1997). *The collected works of L. S. Vygotsky: Vol. 3. Problems of the theory and history of psychology*. New York: Plenum.

Vygotsky, L. S. (1998). *The collected works of L. S. Vygotsky*. Vol. 5. *Child psychology*. New York: Plenum.

Vygotsky, L. S. (1999). *The collected works of L. S. Vygotsky*. Vol. 6. *Scientific legacy*. New York: Plenum.

Wells, G. (1999). *Dialogic inquiry: Toward a sociocultural practice and theory of education*. New York: Cambridge University Press.

Wells, G., & Claxton, G. (Eds.) (2002). *Learning for life in the 21st century: Sociocultural perspectives on the future of education*. Cambridge, MA: Blackwell.

Wertsch, J. V. (1991). *Voices of the mind: A sociocultural approach to mediated action*. Cambridge, MA: Harvard University Press.

7

Development Through the Lifespan

A Neo-Vygotskian Approach

Yuriy V. Karpov

The problems of determinants and mechanisms of child development are the most important and difficult problems in child psychology. In contemporary Western psychology, there are detailed studies of the development of perception, memory, cognition, and other mental processes in each period of the child's life. But, what is almost always missing is an explanation of why the child transits from one period of development to the next. Even such a giant of child psychology as Jean Piaget could not give a satisfactory answer to this question. His explanation of the reasons for the child's transitions from one stage to the next was that these transitions "become necessary with development" (Piaget, 1971, p. 9). The weakness of such an explanation was formulated by Piaget (1971) himself: "This solution is difficult to prove. It is even difficult to express or to explain" (p. 9). Dissatisfaction of developmental and child psychologists with the absence of a powerful theory of child development reveals itself in the advocation by some of them of reductionist approaches, in which, as an example, developmental biology is suggested as a "metatheory for cognitive development" (Bjorklund, 1997, p. 144).

An innovative approach to the problems of determinants and mechanisms of child development was suggested by Vygotsky (1978, 1986, 1997, 1998). Because of the translation of practically all of Vygotsky's works into English, as well as the availability of numerous reviews of his theory by Western psychologists, English-reading psychologists are fairly familiar with his ideas. They, however, are much less familiar with the elaboration of Vygotsky's ideas by his Russian followers into a new theory of child development. I believe that this neo-Vygotskian theory presents the most comprehensive approach to the problems of determinants and mechanisms of child development. The goal of this chapter is to discuss this approach.

THE NEO-VYGOTSKIAN APPROACH: GENERAL THEORETICAL ASSUMPTIONS

To summarize briefly, Vygotsky's (1978, 1986, 1997, 1998) main ideas that underlie the neo-Vygotskian approach are as follows. Human mental processes, just like human labor, are mediated by tools. But, these are special, psychological tools such as language, signs, and symbols. Humans are not born with these tools, just as they are not born with tools of labor. These tools are invented by human society, and they are acquired by children in the course of interpersonal communication with adults or more experienced peers. Having been acquired and internalized, these psychological tools begin to mediate children's mental processes. Human mental processes mediated by tools were called by Vygotsky *higher mental processes*, to differentiate them from lower mental processes with which children are born, and which are specific for both young children and animals (see Kozulin, this volume, for more detailed analysis of Vygotsky's concepts of psychological tools and mediation).

Thus, human mental processes neither are developed in the course of children's independent activity (as constructivists would hold), nor "unfold" as a result of maturation (as nativists would hold), nor are inculcated into children by adults (as behaviorists would hold). The development of mental processes in each period of the child's life is determined by mediation in the context of the specific to the given period relationships between children and their social environment. These relationships were called by Vygotsky (1998) "the social situation of development" (p. 198).

In turn, new mental processes "that arise toward the end of a given age lead to a reconstruction of the whole structure of the child's consciousness and in this way change the whole system of relations to external reality and to himself...[which]...means that the social situation of development...must also change" (Vygotsky, 1998, p. 199). The change of the social situation of development results in the child's transition to the new period of development. Thus, children's development during each age period prepares them for the transition to the next period of development.

The model of development described made it possible for Vygotsky to give an innovative interpretation of different periods in children's development (for detailed analysis, see Mahn, this volume). However, the major shortcoming of this model was that the concept of the social situation of development, and, especially, the role of the child's activity as a component of the social situation of development, was not sufficiently elaborated by Vygotsky. To be sure, he was far from viewing children as passive recipients of psychological tools presented by adults in the course of interpersonal communication. After all, the "assumptions about human action...underlie the entire framework of Vygotsky's approach"

(Wertsch & Tulviste, 1992, p. 554). However, when turning his discussion to children's development at different stages, Vygotsky often limited this discussion to the analysis of their acquisition of verbal tools in the course of interpersonal communication (see, for example, Vygotsky's (1986) doctrine of acquisition of scientific concepts as instrumental in the development of school-age children). This analysis may lead to the position that "whatever is of major importance for the development of individual consciousness, is introduced into it through social consciousness" (Leontiev & Luria, 1968, p. 353) rather than being the result of children's activity oriented toward the external world. Such a position would undermine the theoretical view of both Vygotsky and his Russian followers of the child as a subject rather than an object of development.

The elaboration of Vygotsky's ideas by his colleagues and follow-ers (Elkonin, 1972, 1989; Leontiev, 1964, 1978, 1981; Zaporozhets, 1997; Zaporozhets & Elkonin, 1971) was aimed at overcoming the major shortcoming of his model of child development. The main assertion of their approach was that children's development occurs in the course of their activities oriented toward the external world. But, rather than be-ing independent activities, these are the children's joint activities with adults and peers. In the course of such activities, adults and more ca-pable peers supply children with psychological tools, which then me-diate the mental processes that serve these activities. As a result, the children's mental processes develop and transform into higher mental processes.

Another major outcome of mediation in the course of joint activities with adults and peers is the development of new motives in children (Leontiev, 1964; 1978). These motives "ripen" within children's current activities until they become strong enough to propel the children into participation in new activities.

Stressing the role of mediation in the course of joint activities with adults and peers as the major determinant of child development, Russian follow-ers of Vygotsky reinterpreted his understanding of different periods in children's development as well. For Vygotsky, as discussed, each period of development is characterized by the age-specific relationships between children and their social environment. For Russian neo-Vygotskians, each age period is characterized by children's *leading activity*, which is specific to this age period in the given culture (Leontiev, 1964, 1978; Elkonin, 1972, 1989; Zaporozhets, 1997; Zaporozhets & Elkonin, 1971). A certain activity is defined as *leading* for the given age period because mediation within this activity produces major developmental accomplishments in children, which provide the basis for their transition to the next period, to the next leading activity.

Thus, the neo-Vygotskian model of child development can be presented as follows (Fig. 7.1): In each period of development, children are involved

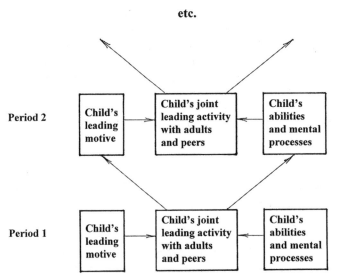

FIGURE 7.1 The neo-Vygotskian model of child development.

in the joint leading activity with adults and peers specific for this period in the given culture, which is driven by their leading motive. In the course of mediation within this activity, children develop the new leading motive, and new mental processes and abilities, which outgrow their current leading activity. This creates the basis for their transition to the new leading activity, which is specific to the next period of development.

The model of child development described was used by Russian neo-Vygotskians to analyze the development of children in industrialized societies. This analysis will be presented in the next section.

THE NEO-VYGOTSKIAN APPROACH TO THE ANALYSIS OF CHILDREN'S DEVELOPMENT IN INDUSTRIALIZED SOCIETIES

First Year of Life: Emotional Communication with Caregivers as the Leading Activity of Infants

In discussing the first year of life, Vygotsky (1998) emphasized infants' "biological helplessness" (p. 215), their inability to satisfy their vital needs by themselves, which results in their dependence on adults. This dependence "creates a completely unique character of the child's relations to reality (and to himself): These relations are always mediated by others" (Vygotsky, 1998, p. 216). As a result, adults become "the psychological center of every situation for the infant" (Vygotsky, 1998, p. 231), which creates the basis for adults' supplying infants with psychological tools. Once mastered, these tools transform the infants' mental processes. For example, the infants' mastery of an indicatory gesture as a tool to direct the behavior of others will become crucially important for the development of their self-regulation at the next stage of development.

Elaborating Vygotsky's ideas about infant–caregiver relationships as the basis for infants' development, Russian neo-Vygotskians characterized emotional communication with caregivers as the leading activity of infants during the first year of life. They have shown that the development of this activity proceeds through several stages (Lisina, 1986). During the first 4 weeks of life, infants do not demonstrate any emotional reaction to an adult. The primary caregivers take the initiative in establishing emotional contacts with infants, using the situations of feeding and changing the infants for talking to them, fondling them, and smiling at them. At the beginning of the fifth week, infants start to smile at an adult, but, what is important, only as a response to the adult's smiling at them. It is only at the age of 2 to 3 months that infants start to smile at an adult on their own initiative (so-called social smile) as well as to demonstrate a positive attitude toward the adult in other ways, such as vocalizing. Later on, this initial positive attitude toward any adult becomes the basis for the development of strong emotional bonds between the infant and the primary caregiver, which, starting with Bowlby (1969), has been called *attachment*.

On the basis of these observations, it has been concluded that infants' need in emotional communication with adults neither is unfolding by itself as a result of maturation, nor is an inevitable result of adults' fulfilment of infants' physiological needs. This need develops in infants only if adults take the initiative in the establishment of emotional relations, shifting the meaning of their contacts from pragmatic goals of gratification of physiological needs (including infants' need of sensory stimulation) to emotional communication as an end in itself. If adults fulfill young infants' physiological needs without initiating emotional contacts with them, these infants will not demonstrate a social smile and will subsequently manifest serious difficulties in developing attachment to other adults (Kistyakovskaya, 1970).

Russian neo-Vygotskians argue that the development of emotional relationships with caregivers plays the crucial role in infants' development. They state, first of all, that infants' positive attitude toward adults is transferred to everything that adults present to them or are doing in their presence. Thus, the initial interest of infants in language, in manipulation of objects, and in the external world in general appears as the result of infant–caregiver emotional relationships (Elkonin, 1989; Lisina, 1986; Rozengard-Pupko, 1948; Zaporozhets & Lisina, 1974). Figuratively speaking, infants become interested in the external world because it has been presented to them by loved adults.

For sure, the preceding statement of Russian neo-Vygotskians is too strong and can be disputed. It reflects their general disregard of the role of genetically predetermined maturation in child development, which will be discussed in the concluding section. Probably, a more balanced position in this regard would be that emotional communication with adults facilitates infants' interest in the external world rather than creates it.

The second important outcome of infant–adult emotional relationships as specified by Russian neo-Vygotskians is that these relationships lead to the infants' acceptance of adults as mediators of all their relations with the external world. This attitude toward adults becomes the basis for involving children in object-centered joint activity with adults by the end of the first year of life and beyond (Elkonin, 1972, 1989; Lisina, 1986; Zaporozhets & Lisina, 1974).

Thus, according to Russian neo-Vygotskians, the development of infants' emotional relationships with caregivers results by the end of the first year of life in the following outcomes: First, infants have developed an interest in the external world, which becomes much stronger than their interest in emotional communication with adults. Whereas young infants see a toy as just "the means of communication with an adult" (Elkonin, 1989, p. 277), older infants may even be irritated by an "idle caress" that has no relation to joint object-centered activity (Lisina, 1986, p. 53). Second, infants have "accepted" adults as mediators of all their relations with the external world. Accordingly, their emotional communication with adults has been replaced by so-called business-like communication (Zaporozhets & Lisina, 1974, p. 147), that is, communication in the context of joint object-centered activity. These outcomes lead to infants' transition to object-centered joint activity as their new leading activity.

Second and Third Years of Life: Object-Centered Joint Activity as the Leading Activity of Toddlers

Although infants are actively involved in manipulations of objects during the first year of life, Russian neo-Vygotskians emphasize the major difference between manipulations of objects during the first and second years (Elkonin, 1978, 1989; Lekhtman-Abramovich & Fradkina, 1949; Zaporozhets & Lisina, 1974). During the first year of life, infants manipulate objects in accordance with their physical characteristics: A ball rolls away if pushed, a rattle makes a sound if shaken, and so on. In order to make such "discoveries," an infant does not need an adult nearby: Physical characteristics of objects are surface, visible, and can be revealed in the course of independent explorations.

Of course, such manipulations of objects in accordance with their physical characteristics can be often observed during the second year of life. But Russian neo-Vygotskians give major importance to another type of children's object-centered activity during this period. This activity deals with children's manipulations of objects in accordance with their social meanings and includes, but is not limited to, children's play with toys. As opposed to physical characteristics of objects, their social meanings are not "written" (Elkonin, 1989, p. 48) on objects and, therefore, cannot be discovered by children independently. For example, children could discover by themselves that banging a spoon on the table will produce a sound, but they would not be able to discover without adults' mediation how to use a spoon for eating. Thus, child–adult joint activity is necessary for children's mastery of social objects.

Summarizing the results of the neo-Vygotskians' major studies (Elkonin, 1978, 1989; Lekhtman-Abramovich & Fradkina, 1949; Zaporozhets & Lisina, 1974), the development of child–adult object-centered activity can be presented as follows: At the age of around 10 to 11 months, infants start to imitate adults' actions with objects and toys in accordance with their social meanings (for example, feeding a doll with a spoon). Such imitations appear initially only in the course of joint activity, in which adults not only demonstrate appropriate actions but encourage infants to imitate them as well. As a result of such joint activity, during the second year of life, the number of children's nonspecific manipulations of objects (shaking, banging) decreases, and they imitate willingly the adults' actions even without encouragement. Children also become able to transfer acquired actions to new objects (for example, the action of feeding a doll with a spoon is transferred to using a spoon for feeding a toy dog, a toy horse, etc.).

The development of child–adult object-centered activity continues during the third year (Elkonin, 1978). The major accomplishment of this development is that children become capable of object substitutions (for example, they use a stick to represent a horse, a plastic cube to represent a piece of soap, and so on). These substitutions initially occur only after an adult has suggested using a certain object instead of a missing one and has named this object after the missing one.

Russian neo-Vygotskians (Elkonin, 1978, 1989; Lisina, 1985; Zaporozhets & Lisina, 1974) argue that child–adult object-centered activity is crucially important for the development of 1- to 3-year-old children, therefore, this activity is leading for this age period. First of all, this activity promotes the development of children's speech. Nonverbal means of communication (smiling, vocalizing, etc.) are good enough for serving the child's emotional communication with adults during the first year of life, but they are not appropriate for serving their joint object-centered activity. The need for communication with adults in the course of their joint object-centered activity leads to the development of the child's active speech, especially if adults are smart enough "not to understand" children's nonverbal means of communication, encouraging them to use words.

For Vygotsky (1978, 1986, 1998) and his Russian followers, the importance of acquisition of language is not limited to the child's mastery of the
main tool for social communication. They argue that acquisition of language plays the major role in the development of all mental processes of
children during the second and third years of life. For example, children's
self-regulation develops as a result of their appropriation of verbal directions used by caregivers to regulate their behavior and the use of these
directions for self-regulation. During the third year of life, children self-
regulate their activity by talking to themselves aloud while doing something (so-called egocentric or private speech), sometimes even imitating
the caregiver's voice (Luria, 1961). Step by step, egocentric speech becomes
internalized and turns into inner (nonvocal) speech, which later becomes
the tool for self-regulation.

The second major outcome of the child–adult object-centered activity
deals with the third-year child's object substitutions. For Vygotsky (1976)
and his Russian followers (Elkonin, 1978), the child's acting, for example,
with a stick as if it were a horse results in the child's separation of the
meaning of the word *horse* from a horse as an object. This "is a vital transitional stage to operating with meanings" (Vygotsky, 1976, p. 548). In other
words, object substitutions help children separate their thoughts from the
perceived objects and events, and that separation leads to the development
of symbolic thought. Although this idea was formulated by Vygotsky in
the 1930s and has been enthusiastically accepted by his followers, it still
lacks strong empirical support.

The third major outcome of the child–adult object-centered activity is
the shift of children's interests from the world of social objects to the world
of human relations (Elkonin, 1978, 1989; Leontiev, 1964). When playing,
for example, a mother–daughter game, a 2-year-old girl would imitate
concrete actions (i.e., using a spoon for feeding a doll). For a 3-year-old
girl who is playing the same game, the imitation of such actions may
be of secondary importance, whereas the imitation of mother–daughter
relationships (love, care, etc.) may have become the major aspect of the
game. As has been shown, such a shift in children's interests takes place
only if adults help children discover human relations that are hidden below actions with social objects (Elkonin, 1978; Lekhtman-Abramovich &
Fradkina, 1949; Slavina, 1948). A major step toward the accomplishment
of this goal would be the assigning by an adult of a play role to a child who
is involved in object-centered activity (i.e., "You, *like a mother*, are feeding
your daughter"; Elkonin, 1978, p. 186).

Thus, by the end of the third year, children's involvement in object-
centered joint activity results in the following outcomes: First, children have developed a strong interest in human relations and have already started to imitate these relations in the course of their play with
toys. Second, they have mastered language as the major tool for social

communication. Third, they have started to self-regulate their activity through the use of private speech. Fourth, they have developed the capacity for symbolic thought, a capacity that makes it possible for a child "to act independently of what he sees" (Vygotsky, 1978, p. 97). All these outcomes lead to children's transition to sociodramatic play as their new leading activity.

Three- to Six-Year-Olds: Sociodramatic Play as the Leading Activity During the Period of Early Childhood

The Vygotskian view on sociodramatic play is just the opposite of the common belief that play is children's free activity in which they do whatever they want, liberating themselves from any rules and social pressure. As indicated, Vygotsky (1976) and his Russian followers (Elkonin, 1978, 1989; Leontiev, 1964; Slavina, 1948; Usova, 1976; Zaporozhets, 1997) hold that by the age of 3 years children develop a strong interest in the world of human relations. The world of adults becomes very attractive to children, and they are looking forward to becoming a part of this world. In industrialized societies, however, children cannot fulfill this desire directly: They cannot be doctors or firefighters. That is why they enter the world of adults through imitating and exploring social relations in the course of sociodramatic play. Thus, the motive of sociodramatic play is "to act like an adult" (Elkonin, 1978, p. 150).

Although by definition sociodramatic play is children's joint activity, Russian neo-Vygotskians hold that adults should mediate children's play and that their major role is to present and explain different social roles to children. For example, to mediate children's play at a railway station, it is not enough to give them different toys (a model of the train, a model of a railway station, etc.). Adults should explain to them the social roles of different people at the station ("This is the station master – he is receiving a train; these are passengers – they are buying tickets; this is a conductor – he is checking the passengers' tickets"; etc.) (Elkonin, 1978). Without this, either children will not be able to play at all, or their sociodramatic play will be very immature and impoverished.

Russian neo-Vygotskians argue that the mediation of children's sociodramatic play by adults is especially important since play is the leading activity of children during this age period and, therefore, is crucial to their development. First of all, the neo-Vygotskians assert that the more children play, the more they become dissatisfied with such pseudopenetration into the world of adults. As Elkonin (1978) noted, the child "looks at himself from the point of view of the role he has taken . . . and discovers that he is not an adult yet" (p. 277). Thus, children come to realize that, in order to become adults, they should study at school but not play. As a result, by the age of 6 years, children develop a strong desire to study at school;

that is, they develop the learning motive as their new leading motive. The statement about the role of sociodramatic play in the development of children's learning motivation has been supported to some extent by psychologists' observations (Bozhovich, 1968). However, it remains a theoretical speculation of Russian neo-Vygotskians that is in need of strong empirical support.

Discussing the second contribution of sociodramatic play to children's development, Vygotsky (1976) and his followers (Elkonin, 1978; Leontiev, 1964) emphasize that children are not free in play. In the course of play, every child is supposed to act in accordance with his or her role even if this role is not very attractive to the child. All the children who participate in the play are very strictly controlling each other's behavior in terms of following the play roles. But each play role contains some implicit rules; as Elkonin (1978) noted, "the rule is hidden . . . under the role" (p. 248). Thus, in the course of play and mutual control, children learn to suppress their impulsivity and to follow rules, that is, develop the ability to self-regulate their behavior.

The next contribution of sociodramatic play to children's development deals with children's overcoming their "cognitive egocentrism," that is, inability to take into consideration the position of another person, to look at a certain event or object from different perspectives. When playing, children should treat their playmates not according to their real-life names and relations, but according to their play roles. They should also coordinate their play actions with the play actions of their playmates. Thus, in the course of sociodramatic play "the child's position towards the external world changes . . . and the ability to coordinate his point of view with other possible points of view develops" (Elkonin, 1978, p. 282).

Finally, in the course of sociodramatic play children use substitutes, that is, objects that stand for other objects. As discussed in the previous section, Vygotsky (1976) and his followers (Elkonin, 1978) speculate that object substitutions lead to the development of children's symbolic thought.

Thus, according to Russian neo-Vygotskians, by the end of the sixth year, children's involvement in sociodramatic play results in the following outcomes: First, they have developed the learning motive as their new leading motive. Second, they have developed the ability to self-regulate their behavior. Third, they have overcome their egocentric position in regard to other people and to the external world. Finally, their ability to be engaged in symbolic thought has further developed. Russian neo-Vygotskians (Bozhovich, 1968; Elkonin, 1978; Leontiev, 1964) consider these new characteristics and abilities of sixth-year-old children to be crucially important for their success at school. Thus, in the course of sociodramatic play, children develop prerequisites for learning at school, which becomes their new leading activity during the period of middle childhood.

The Period of Middle Childhood: Learning in Educational Settings as Children's Leading Activity

Vygotsky's (1978, 1986) view on the role of instruction in children's development is based on his general idea of mediation as the main determinant of development. He viewed school instruction as the major avenue for mediated learning and, therefore, as the major contributor to children's development during the period of middle childhood. He emphasized, however, that such a development-generating effect would take place only if the process of instruction were organized in the proper way: "The only good kind of instruction is that which marches ahead of development and leads it" (Vygotsky, 1986, p. 188).

According to Vygotsky (1978, 1986), the major reason for the development-generating effect of properly organized school instruction relates to students' acquisition of "scientific concepts," which can be contrasted with "spontaneous concepts" of preschoolers. *Spontaneous concepts* are the result of generalization and internalization of everyday personal experience. Therefore, they are unsystematic, empirical, not conscious, and often wrong. As opposed to this, *scientific concepts* represent the generalization of the experience of humankind that is fixed in science. These concepts are acquired by students consciously and according to a certain system. Once scientific concepts have been acquired and internalized, they mediate children's thinking and problem solving. That is why "instruction in scientific concepts plays a decisive role in the child's mental development" (Vygotsky, 1987, p. 220). Specifically, "reflective consciousness comes to the child through the portals of scientific concepts" (Vygotsky, 1986, p. 171). As a result, students' thinking becomes much more independent of their personal experience. They become "theorists" rather then "practitioners" and develop the ability to operate at the level of formal–logical thought.

Although, as it is commonly admitted, the contemporary system of school instruction has many shortcomings (see, e.g., Bruer, 1993), the general idea of Vygotsky about the development-generating outcome of school instruction has found strong empirical support in cross-cultural studies. The results of all these studies, starting with the classical study performed by Luria (1976) in the early 1930s and ending with the studies of contemporary researchers (see Segall, Dasen, Berry, & Poortinga, 1990, for a review), have shown that people in preliterate societies, who have not attended school, have very poor results when asked to perform at the level of formal–logical thought. Vygotsky and his Russian followers would attribute these results to those people's deficiency of formal–logical thought due to the lack of schooling. Some American scholars would not agree with this conclusion. Cole and Cole (1993), for example, argue that formal–logical thought is content-dependent; therefore, adults in preliterate societies are able to solve formal–logical problems other than those that were used in the cross-cultural studies mentioned. However, even those scholars who advocate the idea of content-dependency of formal–logical thought admit that "nonschooled individuals seem to prefer . . . to come to conclusions on the basis of experience rather than by relying on the information in the problem alone" (Rogoff & Chavajay, 1995, p. 863).

Following Vygotsky's understanding of the role of schooling in children's development, his Russian followers characterized learning in educational settings as the leading activity of children in industrialized societies during the period of middle childhood (Davydov, 1986, 1999; Elkonin, 1972, 1989; Leontiev, 1964). This was not, however, just a matter of applying a new label to what Vygotsky had already said; his ideas were elaborated substantially by his followers. First, they repudiated the vision of children as passive recipients of scientific knowledge presented by adults in the course of interpersonal communication (the position to which Vygotsky would never have subscribed, but to which his writings sometimes could lead). As Russian neo-Vygotskians hold, the acquisition of scientific knowledge is the outcome of students' special learning activity as organized and mediated by teachers (for detailed analysis, see Zuckerman, this volume). Second, the neo-Vygotskians argue that scientific knowledge that students should learn at school cannot be reduced to scientific concepts; it should also include procedural knowledge (that is, subject-domain strategies and skills) relevant to these concepts.

Elaborating their ideas in regard to properly organized learning, Russian neo-Vygotskians have analyzed different types of instruction and their developmental outcomes (Davydov, 1986, 1990, 1998; Galperin, 1989; Talyzina, 1981; for an overview see Arievitch & Stetsenko, 2000). The results of their studies have shown that instructional programs that are built around the ideas of the so-called theoretical learning approach have many advantages in comparison with traditional school instruction and other alternative approaches (for the analysis of the theoretical learning approach see Karpov, this volume, Vygotsky's doctrine of scientific concepts). One of the outcomes of the use of theoretical learning is that it facilitates the development of formal–logical thought in students. Thus, the use of theoretical learning has provided additional empirical support to the Vygotskian contention of the role of properly organized instruction in the development of formal–logical thought in children. These data are especially important in light of Vygotsky's (1998) idea that formal–logical thought is crucially important for children's transition to the next period of development, that is, the period of adolescence.

The Period of Adolescence: Interaction with Peers as the Leading Activity of Adolescents

Vygotsky (1998) argued that the change of adolescents' interests is "the key to the whole problem of the psychological development of the adolescent" (p. 3). This change has its roots in physiological maturation, especially in sexual maturation, but also "there is a reconstruction and formation of interests from the top, from the aspect of the maturing personality and the world view of the adolescent" (Vygotsky, 1998, p. 23). The development of adolescents' personality and worldview, according to Vygotsky, is the result of their transition to formal–logical thinking: As Vygotsky (1998) noted, "an adolescent appears before us primarily as a thinking being" (p. 30).

Because of this new ability to do formal–logical thinking "a whole world with its past and future, nature, history, and human life opens before the adolescent" (Vygotsky, 1998, p. 42). Formal–logical thinking also makes adolescents capable of self-analysis, the analysis of their feeling, and their place in the world, the existence of which they just "discovered."

As formal–logical thinking makes adolescents capable of self-analysis and of the analysis of their place in the world, the society, according to Vygotsky, provides adolescents with tools for such analysis and with the social norms from which their analysis proceeds. As he noted, "self-consciousness is social consciousness transferred within" (Vygotsky, 1998, p. 182).

Thus, Vygotsky (1998) developed a holistic model of adolescents' development, which integrates cognitive, social, emotional, and motivational aspects of this development. However, the role of physiological maturation (including sexual maturation), although declared by Vygotsky as the basis for the change in adolescents' motivation, was not elaborated by him well enough to become an integral component of his theoretical model.

From the point of view of Russian followers of Vygotsky, the major shortcoming of his model was that the role of adolescents' activity in their development was not demonstrated (Elkonin, 1972). This could lead to the wrong conclusion that adolescents are passive recipients of social norms and values rather than being active constructors of themselves and their relations with the world. Applying the concept of leading activity to the analysis of adolescence, Russian neo-Vygotskians suggested that interaction with peers is the leading activity during this period (Elkonin, 1972). Their studies and observations have demonstrated that in the course of this activity adolescents use social norms, models, and relations that exist among the adults in their society as standards for the behavior of their peers (Bozhovich, 1968; Dubrovina, 1987; Elkonin, 1989; Elkonin & Dragunova, 1967). As a result, they test, master, and internalize these social standards and start to use them for self-analysis. This leads to the development of their self-awareness (or personal identity, in Erikson's terms), which is the major accomplishment of this period that prepares adolescents for the transition to adulthood. Thus, adults continue to play an important role as mediators (although less direct) of adolescents' activity.

As was shown, Russian followers of Vygotsky added to his view of adolescence the idea of interaction with peers as the leading activity of adolescents, which results in the development of their personal identity. They, however, overlooked Vygotsky's idea of the role of physiological maturation in adolescents' development. Although maturation was not shown to determine adolescents' search for personal identity (Elkonin & Dragunova, 1967), the general disregard by Russian neo-Vygotskians of the role of maturation in adolescents' development seems arguable.

THE NEO-VYGOTSKIAN APPROACH TO CHILD DEVELOPMENT: ACCOMPLISHMENTS AND SHORTCOMINGS

Russian followers of Vygotsky have elaborated his theoretical ideas into a logical and internally consistent theory that integrates cognitive, motivational, and social aspects of child development. In this theory, mediation in the course of children's age-specific activity is considered to be the major determinant of their development. It is in the context of such leading activities that children develop new motives and abilities, which outgrow their current leading activity. This process results in children's transition to the new leading activity, which is specific to the next period of development. Thus, the neo-Vygotskian approach provides an answer to probably the most difficult question in child psychology: Why do children transit from one period of development to the next?

To be sure, the sequence of leading activities as described by Russian neo-Vygotskians is not "carved in stone." First of all, as they emphasize, children's leading activities are determined by their social environment (Leontiev, 1964). The leading activities described previously are those that are specific for children in industrialized societies. In preliterate societies, neither is sociodramatic play the leading activity during the period of early childhood (Elkonin, 1978), nor is learning in educational settings the leading activity during the period of middle childhood.

Moreover, even in industrialized societies, children may not be involved in a certain activity that, from the point of view of Russian neo-Vygotskians, is leading for the given period of development. It is interesting, however, that if this is the case, children's further development suffers. For example, contemporary American preschoolers are much more involved in watching TV and playing computer games than in doing sociodramatic play. From the point of view of Russian neo-Vygotskians, this should result in problems with these children's ability to self-regulate later on. It turns out that, indeed, the major complaint of American elementary school teachers is that "they have to 'sing, dance, or act like Big Bird' in order to teach" (Bodrova & Leong, 1996, p. 4).

Thus, the leading activities described by Russian neo-Vygotskians seem to be the most beneficial for children's development in industrialized societies. It is quite possible, however, that psychologists and educators may suggest another activity that could be even more beneficial for children's development than, for example, sociodramatic play. If this activity is also shown to "ripen" within the preceding leading activity of children and to result in their transition to the next period of development, it could be suggested to "replace" sociodramatic play as leading activity during the period of early childhood. Then, the efforts of adults and society in general should be directed to mediating this new type of leading activity rather than mediating children's sociodramatic play.

In general, the neo-Vygotskian model of child development seems to have found strong experimental support in the studies of contemporary Russian and Western scholars, which I did not discuss in detail because of space limits. However, as I have indicated, some of the contentions of Russian neo-Vygotskians remain at the level of theoretical speculation or can be disputed. Their most disputable contention seems to be the disregard of the role of genetically predetermined physiological maturation in children's development. Maturation is considered by Russian neo-Vygotskians to be only a prerequisite for development that does not determine either the general characteristics of children's development or the individual differences in their development (Zaporozhets, 1997; Zaporozhets & Elkonin, 1971). This position can hardly be justified in light of well-known findings of contemporary Western psychologists about the role of genetically predetermined maturation in child development (Buss & Plomin, 1975; Plomin & DeFries, 1980; and others).

Thus, it would seem advisable to include maturational factors in the neo-Vygotskian model of child development. This suggestion, however, has nothing to do with the ideas of "adding nature to nurture" and of calculating the proportional contribution of heredity and environment to children's development, to which many contemporary scholars are inclined (see, e.g., Scarr, 1992). Rather, as Tomasello (1999) indicates, human development should be analyzed in terms of complex interactions between cultural and maturational factors, which differ in each life period. Thus, in respect to the neo-Vygotskian model of child development, it seems promising to analyze how maturational factors contribute to children's leading activity in each period of life (for example, how children's temperament influences their participation in sociodramatic play). Such an analysis would enrich the neo-Vygotskian model of child development with maturational factors without losing its emphasis on the role of mediation in the course of children's joint activity with adults and peers as the major determinant of their development.

References

Arievitch, I. M., & Stetsenko, A. (2000). The quality of cultural tools and cognitive development: Gal'perin's perspective and its implications. *Human Development, 43*, 69–92.

Bjorklund, D. F. (1997). In search of a metatheory for cognitive development (or, Piaget is dead and I don't feel so good myself). *Child Development, 68*(1), 144–148.

Bodrova, E., & Leong, D. J. (1996). *Tools of the mind: The Vygotskian approach to early childhood education*. Englewood Cliffs, NJ: Prentice-Hall.

Bowlby, J. (1969). *Attachment and loss*: Vol. 1. *Attachment*. New York: Basic Books.

Bozhovich, L. I. (1968). *Lichnost i ee formirovanie v detskom vozraste* [Personality and its development in childhood]. Moscow: Prosveschenie.

Bruer, J. T. (1993). *Schools for thought: A science of learning in the classroom*. Cambridge, MA: MIT Press.

Buss, A. H., & Plomin, R. (1975). *A temperament theory of personality development*. New York: Wiley.

Cole, M., & Cole, S. (1993). *The development of children*. New York: Scientific American Books.

Davydov, V. V. (1986). *Problemy razvivayuschego obucheniya* [Problems of development-generating learning]. Moscow: Pedagogika.

Davydov, V. V. (1990). *Types of generalization in instruction*. Reston, VA: National Council of Teachers of Mathematics.

Davydov, V. V. (1998). The concept of developmental teaching. *Journal of Russian and East European Psychology, 36*(4), 11–36.

Davydov, V. V. (1999). What is real learning activity? In M. Hedegaard & J. Lompscher (Eds.), *Learning activity and development* (pp. 123–138). Aarhus, Denmark: Aarhus University Press.

Dubrovina, I. V. (1987). *Formirovanie lichnosti v perekhodnyi period ot podrostcovogo k iunoshkeskomu vozrastu* [Development of personality during the transitional period from adolescence to adulthood]. Moscow: Pedagogika.

Elkonin, D. B. (1972). Toward the problem of stages in the mental development of the child. *Soviet Psychology, 10* , 225–251.

Elkonin, D. B. (1978). *Psikhologiya igry* [Psychology of play]. Moscow: Pedagogika.

Elkonin, D. B. (1989). *Izbrannye psikhologicheskie trudy* [Selected psychological works]. Moscow: Pedagogika.

Elkonin, D. B., & Dragunova, T. V. (Eds.) (1967). *Vozrastnye i individualnye osobennosti mladshikh podrostkov* [Age-dependent and individual characteristics of young adolescents]. Moscow: Prosveschenie.

Galperin, P. Y. (1989). Organization of mental activity and the effectiveness of learning. *Soviet Psychology, 27*(3), 65–82.

Kistyakovskaya, M. U. (1970). *Razvitie dvizheniay u detei pervogo goda zhizni* [The development of motor skills in infants]. Moscow: Pedagogika.

Lekhtman-Abramovich, R. Ya., & Fradkina, F. I. (1949). *Etapy razvitiya igry i deistviy s predmetami v rannem vozraste* [Stages of development of play and manipulation of objects in early childhood]. Moscow: Medgiz.

Leontiev, A. N. (1964). *Problems of mental development*. Washington, DC: US Joint Publication Research Service.

Leontiev, A. N. (1978). *Activity, consciousness, and personality.* Englewood Cliffs, NJ: Prentice-Hall.

Leontiev, A. N. (1981). The problem of activity in psychology. In J. V. Wertsch (Ed.), *The concept of activity in Soviet psychology* (pp. 37–71). Armonk, NY: Sharpe.

Leontiev, A. N., & Luria, A. R. (1968). The psychological ideas of L. S. Vygotskii. In B. B. Wolman (Ed.), *Historical roots of contemporary psychology* (pp. 338–367). New York: Harper & Row.

Lisina, M. I. (Ed.) (1985). *Obschenie i rech: Razvitie rechi u detei v obschenii so vzroslymi* [Communication and speech: The development of children's speech in the course of communication with adults]. Moscow: Pedagogika.

Lisina, M. I. (1986). *Problemy ontogeneza obscheniya* [Problems of the ontogenesis of communication]. Moscow: Pedagogika.

Luria, A. R. (1961). *The role of speech in the regulation of normal and abnormal behavior.* Oxford: Pergamon Press.

Luria, A. R. (1976). *Cognitive development: Its cultural and social foundations.* Cambridge, MA: Harvard University Press.

Piaget, J. (1971). The theory of stages in cognitive development. In D. R. Green, M. P. Ford, & G. B. Flamer (Eds.), *Measurement and Piaget* (pp. 1–11). New York: McGraw-Hill.

Plomin, R., & DeFries, J. C. (1980). Genetics and intelligence: Recent data. *Intelligence, 4,* 15–24.

Rogoff, B., & Chavajay, P. (1995). What's become of research on the cultural basis of cognitive development? *American Psychologist, 50*(10), 859–877.

Rozengard-Pupko, G. L. (1948). *Rech i razvitie vospriyatiya v rannem vozraste* [Language and the development of perception in early age]. Moscow: AMN Publisher.

Scarr, S. (1992). Developmental theories for the 1990s: Development and individual differences. *Child Development, 63,* 1–19.

Segall, M. H., Dasen, P. R., Berry, J. W., & Poortinga, Y. (1990). *Human behavior in global perspective.* New York: Pergamon.

Slavina, L. S. (1948). O razvitii motivov igrovoi deayatelnosti v doshkolnom vozraste [On the development of play motives at preschool age]. *Izvestiya APN RSFSR, 14,* 11–29.

Talyzina, N. F. (1981). *The psychology of learning.* Moscow: Progress.

Tomasello, M. (1999). *The cultural origins of human cognition.* Cambridge, MA: Harvard University Press.

Usova, A. P. (1976). *Rol igry v vospitanii detei* [The role of play in children's upbringing]. Moscow: Pedagogika.

Vygotsky, L. S. (1976). Play and its role in the mental development of the child. In J. S. Bruner, A. Jolly, & K. Sylva (Eds.), *Play: Its role in development and evolution* (pp. 537–554). New York: Basic Books.

Vygotsky, L. S. (1978). M. Cole, V. John-Steiner, S. Scribner & E. Souberman (Eds.), *Mind in society: The development of higher psychological processes.* Cambridge, MA: Harvard University Press.

Vygotsky, L. S. (1986). *Thought and language.* Cambridge, MA: MIT Press.

Vygotsky, L. S. (1987). R. W. Rieber (Ed.), *The collected works of L. S. Vygotsky:* Vol. 1: *Problems of general psychology.* New York: Plenum.

Vygotsky, L. S. (1997). R. W. Rieber (Ed.), *The collected works of L. S. Vygotsky*: Vol. 4: *The history of the development of higher mental functions*. New York: Plenum.

Vygotsky, L. S. (1998). R. W. Rieber (Ed.), *The collected works of L. S. Vygotsky*, Vol. 5: *Child psychology*. New York: Plenum.

Wertsch, J. V., & Tulviste, P. (1992). L. S. Vygotsky and contemporary developmental psychology. *Developmental Psychology, 28*(4), 548–557.

Zaporozhets, A. V. (1997). Principal problems in the ontogeny of the mind. *Journal of Russian and East European Psychology, 35*(1), 53–94.

Zaporozhets, A. V., & Elkonin, D. B. (Eds.) (1971). *The psychology of preschool children*. Cambridge, MA: MIT Press.

Zaporozhets, A. V., & Lisina, M. I. (Eds.). (1974). *Razvitie obscheniya u doshkolnikov* [The development of communication in preschoolers]. Moscow: Pedagogika.

8

Learning and Development of Preschool Children from the Vygotskian Perspective

Elena Bodrova and Deborah J. Leong

Although Vygotsky's interest in the issues of learning and development was not limited to any specific age, it seems that many of his best known ideas are often discussed in the context of the development of younger children. It makes our job as authors who venture to present the Vygotskian perspective on this subject both easy and challenging. The easy part is to review these well-known ideas, including the relationship between teaching/learning and development, the role of make-believe play, and the evolution of oral speech from public to private. The challenging part is to look beyond these familiar themes and to present an integral picture of preschool age from Vygotsky's perspective and in the broader context of the cultural–historical perspective. Considering that Vygotsky's own writing on this subject is sometimes fragmented and presents more of a series of brilliant insights than a complete theory, we believe that adding the work of post-Vygotskians will enrich the readers' theoretical understanding and at the same time provide a necessary connection to possible practical applications.

DEFINITION OF PRESCHOOL AGE

When describing Vygotsky's approach to the issues of learning and development of preschool children, one should be aware of the meaning of the term *preschool age* in Vygotsky's times. Meaning literally "prior to entering school," this term was used to describe a child up to the time he or she reached the age of 7 or even 8 years. In this sense, the upper boundaries of the "preschool age" can be roughly equivalent to the end of "early childhood" – the term used in the Western literature to cover the entire period from birth to age 8. As for the lower boundaries, in Russia, children begin to be referred to commonly as "preschoolers" when they reach the age of 3 years. This "everyday" definition of what *preschool* means is consistent with Vygotsky's own references to the youngest children as "infants," to toddlers as "children of early age," and finally to children who are yet older as "preschoolers." Therefore, for the purposes of this chapter we will primarily focus on how Vygotsky's theory describes learning and development for this entire age group. Looking at subsequent elaboration of Vygotsky's ideas of early development and learning in the works of his students and colleagues, we can see that the meaning of the term *preschool* had changed. As a result of changes in social practices such as the beginning of formal schooling at an earlier age, the term *preschoolers* is used by post-Vygotskians to describe only those children between the ages 3 and 6.

Preschool age for Vygotsky is more than just a chronological concept. As are other ages (e.g., infancy and early age), it is defined in terms of the systemic changes that take place in the structure of child's mental processes and in terms of its major developmental accomplishments (or "neoformations" if translated literally) that emerge as a result of a child's growing up in a unique "social situation of development" (Vygotsky, 1984). Other references to preschool age as a distinct period in child development can be found in Vygotsky's works on the critical periods in child development (ibid.). In his theory of critical periods, Vygotsky places preschool between the crisis of 3 years of age on one end and the crisis of 7 years of age on the other (see Mahn, this volume, for in-depth description of Vygotsky's theory of critical periods).

Describing child development during preschool years, Vygotsky follows several major themes. The first is the formation of child's mind as a dynamic system of mental functions with new higher mental functions emerging and changing already existing lower mental functions. The preschool age is the period when this formation goes through its initial stages, when children's use of language continues to transform their perception and begins to transform their attention, memory, imagination, and thinking. The second theme is the view of child development as the child's growing mastery of his or her behavior. In this respect, preschool years culminate in the child's overcoming the dependence on the environmental stimuli and becoming capable of intentional behavior through the use of self-regulatory private speech and participation in make-believe play. The third theme is the idea that child development is a holistic process with emotions and cognition acting in unity and affecting each other. This third theme is not elaborated in Vygotsky's writing at the same level of detail as the first two and sometimes makes critics place Vygotsky's theory in the category of "cognitive." However, in describing development of preschool children, Vygotsky indicated that his views of mental development go beyond "thought and language" to include such issues as integration of emotions and cognition at the end of the preschool years and a complex interplay of emotional and cognitive components in make-believe play. Finally, the last theme is the theme that is central to Vygotsky's view on child development – the idea that the social situation of development is the

"basic source" of development. This idea determines Vygotsky's approach
to the transition from preschool to school age, including the issue of school
readiness, since the social situation of development

represents the initial moment for all dynamic changes that occur in development
during the given period. It determines wholly and completely the forms and the
path along which the child will acquire ever newer personality characteristics,
drawing them from the social reality as from the basic source of development, the
path along which the social becomes the individual. (Vygotsky, 1998, p. 198)

PSYCHOLOGICAL CHARACTERISTICS OF PRESCHOOL AGE

Acquisition of Cultural Tools and Emergence of Higher Mental Functions

During preschool years, important changes take place in the very structure
of mental processes. Whereas most behaviors are still governed by "natural" or "lower" mental functions, the first signs of future higher mental
functions emerge – first in play and later in other contexts. These first signs
are displayed in behavior that is deliberate and purposeful rather than im-
pulsive, self-regulated rather than reactive, and mediated by language or
other symbolic cultural tools. Of all mental functions, perception becomes
the first to be transformed from a set of diffuse and disorganized sensa-
tions into the system of stable representations with culturally determined
meanings. Other mental functions, such as attention, memory, and imagination, only start their process of transformation during the preschool age
and acquire their deliberate and mediated forms during primary school
years.

The beginning of preschool age is the time when child's mental functions
first become organized in a uniquely human and systemic way. Designating
memory as the dominant mental function of preschool age that will be
later replaced by thinking in school-aged children, Vygotsky notes that
for younger children "thinking is remembering," whereas for the older
ones "remembering is thinking" (Vygotsky, 1998). Before the preschool
years, the child's cognitive functioning is dominated by perception and
other mental functions, such as memory, attention, and thinking, are not
yet separated from it. In this sense, Vygotsky's description of cognitive
functioning of toddlers is similar to that of authors (such as Piaget) who
refer to this period as the period of sensori-motor thinking.

The systemic organization of the preschooler's mind is the outgrowth
of the processes that take place during the previous – early – age and
is primarily associated with children's mastery of speech. As they use
speech to communicate to others, toddlers form and then refine their first
generalizations – the development that Vygotsky considered critical in

integrating thought and language. These first generalizations refer primarily to immediately perceived objects and help young children build a constant picture of the world around them. As children start using words in addition to manipulating physical objects, their thought becomes liberated from the limitations of what is immediately perceived, and consequently perception loses its dominant position in children's minds. Ability to store and retrieve the images of the past, now greatly enhanced by children's use of language, makes it possible to use past experience in a variety of situations – from communication to problem solving – thus placing memory in the center of the cognitive functioning of preschoolers.

The nature of first generalizations reflects general changes in the structure of the child's mental functions. In his study of concept development (Vygotsky, 1987), Vygotsky traces the evolution of the content behind generalizations used by children of different ages. He describes the very first generalizations – typically appearing at the end of infancy and beginning of toddlerhood – as *syncrets* that are based on the child's general and undifferentiated emotional perception of an object or an action. As toddlers acquire larger vocabularies and larger repertoires of practical actions, their generalizations become tied to their perception – the dominant mental function of the period immediately preceding preschool age. Preschoolers develop more elaborate generalizations, which transcend the limits of perceived characteristics of the objects to include characteristics that can be inferred (such as their function or relation to other objects). These inferences are often based on children's past experience, emphasizing the important role memory plays in the mental functioning of preschoolers. However, even these, more advanced, generalizations are not yet true concepts: Concept formation according to Vygotsky requires the child's ability to use words or other signs in a specific instrumental function (Vygotsky, 1987).

The ability to use words in their instrumental function develops during primary school years and can be largely attributed to the specific social situation of development that children of this age enter – formal schooling. Acquisition of specific cultural competencies such as literacy brings about a major change in children's use of words and other cultural tools. However, certain preparatory processes must occur during the preschool years to allow this major change to take place. One of these processes is children's use of words and other signs (such as gestures) in a symbolic way. Vygotsky notes that younger preschoolers are not yet able to separate an object from the word that labels this object. It takes several years of increasingly complex make-believe play for children to become able to think of the words (and other symbols) independently of the objects they denote.

Describing development of speech during preschool years, Vygotsky focused primarily on children's use of oral language, while recognizing children's drawing as an emergent form of written speech. Preschool age is the period when children's use of oral language undergoes the most dramatic change. According to Vygotsky, it is during preschool years, that children start using their speech not only for communicating to others but also for communicating to themselves, and a new form of speech – private speech[1] – emerges. Unlike Piaget, who associated this phenomenon with children's egocentrism and considered it a sign of immature thinking, Vygotsky viewed private speech as a step on the continuum from public (social) speech to inner speech and eventually to verbal thinking (Vygotsky, 1987). From this perspective, private speech becomes not a sign of immaturity but instead a sign of progressive development of cognitive processes.

Vygotsky described two major changes that occur in the use of private speech during preschool years. First, the function of private speech changes. Children start using private speech to accompany their practical actions. At this point, it is closely intertwined with social speech, which is directed to other people and which, Vygotsky believes, serves as a precursor to private speech. Later, private speech becomes exclusively self-directed and changes its function to organize children's own behavior. At the same time, the syntax of private speech changes as well. From complete sentences typical for social speech, a child's utterances change into abbreviated phrases and single words unsuited for the purposes of communication to other people but sufficient for communicating to oneself. Vygotsky uses these two metamorphoses of private speech to illustrate what he believed to be the universal path of the acquisition of cultural tools: They are first used externally in interactions with other people and then internalized and used by an individual to master his or her own mental functions. The onset of private speech marks an important point in the development of children's thinking: the beginning of verbal thought. At the same time it signals an important development in self-regulation: Starting with regulation of their practical actions, children expand their use of private speech to use it to regulate a variety of their mental processes.

Development of Self-Regulation

The concept of self-regulation plays a prominent role in Vygotsky's view of the preschool years, constituting one of the most critical advances in child development that happens at this time. According to Vygotsky, what changes in preschool years is the relationship between child's intentions and their subsequent implementation in actions. Younger preschoolers act spontaneously, paying no attention to the possible consequences of their

---

[1] Vygotsky used the term *egocentric speech* to describe audible self-directed speech; however, in the Western literature, this phenomenon is commonly referred to as *private speech* (see, e.g., Berk & Winsler, 1995).

actions. By the end of preschool age, children acquire the ability to plan the actions before executing them. Whether they discuss the play scenario with their peers, choose paints for their art project, or decide on the final appearance of their block structure – in all these situations children are guided by a mental image of the future actions (Vygotsky, 1956). Vygotsky writes about the development of self-regulation in preschoolers in two contexts – in relation to the development of private speech and in relation to the development of make-believe play. Private speech provides children with the tool: The same words that adults used to use to regulate children's behavior can be now used by children themselves for the purposes of self-regulation. Make-believe play provides a unique context that supports the use of self-regulation through a system of roles and corresponding rules. Play also keeps preschoolers willing to forgo their immediate wishes in favor of following the rules by allowing them to fulfill their greater desires in a symbolic form.

Make-Believe Play as a Leading Activity

Vygotsky's interest in make-believe play grew out of his earlier studies in psychology of art as well as his work on the theory of development of higher mental functions (Elkonin, 1978). In play, Vygotsky saw one of the earliest contexts in which children learn to use objects and actions in their symbolic function. Since mastery of cultural signs and symbols constitutes the core of the development of higher mental functions, play was considered by Vygotsky to be the leading activity of modern day preschoolers, the activity that creates their zone of proximal development (Vygotsky, 1977). Vygotsky noted, however, that in a different social context such as nonliterate societies of hunters and gatherers, play carries a different function – children's practice in and preparation for grown-up activities – and may not involve a symbolic component at all.

When describing the use of symbols as a defining feature, Vygotsky limited the scope of play to the dramatic or make-believe play typical of preschoolers and children of primary school age. Thus, Vygotsky's definition of play does not include many kinds of other activities such as movement activities, object manipulations, and explorations that were (and still are) referred to as *play* by educators as well as noneducators. "Real" play, according to Vygotsky, has three major features: Children create an imaginary situation, take on and act out roles, and follow a set of rules determined by specific roles (Vygotsky, 1978).

Each of these features plays an important role in formation of a child's mind, in development of higher mental functions. Role-playing in an imaginary situation requires children to carry on two types of actions – external and internal. In play, these internal actions – "operations on the meanings" – are still dependent on the external operations on the objects. However, the very emergence of the internal actions signals the beginning of a child's transition from the earlier forms of thought processes – sensorimotor and visual–representational – to more advanced symbolic thought. Thus, make-believe play prepares the foundation for two higher mental functions – thinking and imagination. Another way make-believe play contributes to the development of higher mental functions is by promoting intentional behavior. It becomes possible because of the inherent relationship that exists between roles children play and rules they need to follow when playing these roles. For preschoolers, play becomes the first activity in which children are driven not by the need for instant gratification, prevalent at this age, but by the need to suppress their immediate impulses. Finally, in play, the first signs of generalized emotions appear; that means that the emotions are now associated with a broad category of people and situations rather than a specific event. For example, when a child cries when playing "patient," he does it because he knows that all children do it when they are given a shot. In another situation, when a child takes on a specific role of a doctor or a firefighter, she does it to fulfill a universal wish "to act like an adult."

Integration of Emotions and Cognition

Vygotsky describes the integration of emotions and cognition as one of the developmental accomplishments of preschool age, sometimes even referring to it as the main developmental accomplishment (Vygotsky, 1998). In younger children, emotions follow actions, presenting children with positive or negative feedback about the action and its results. In preschoolers, emotions start appearing before the action, providing a special kind of anticipation of the possible consequences of this action. When children develop this emotional anticipation, they become able to imagine what will happen if they do a certain thing, how it will make them feel, and how it will make other people feel. As a result, the cognitive actions of perception, imagination, thinking, and reflection acquire an emotional component – cognition becomes emotional. On the other hand, emotions no longer appear as a reaction after the fact but acquire planning and regulatory functions – emotions themselves become thoughtful.

Vygotsky draws an analogy between the development of generalized perception in toddlers and the development of generalized emotions in children who are in transition from preschool to school age. Similarly to the way that the integration of perception and speech helps younger children to organize their external environment in a meaningful way, integration of emotions and cognition now helps children organize and then master their internal processes. On the cognitive side, children become aware of their emotions; their emotions become meaningful. At the same time, on the emotional side, children develop generalized emotions.

Vygotsky compares the relationship between generalized emotions and singular emotions to the relationship between concepts and singular images, referring to the "emotional logic" that begins to regulate behavior of school-age children. The emergence of generalized emotions makes it possible for a child to function in a complex social environment of a classroom, thus becoming one of the indicators of school readiness.

Transition to School and the Issue of School Readiness

Vygotsky's view on school readiness stems from his theory of child development driven by changes in social situations in which the child participates. Therefore, the issue of school readiness has two aspects. The first one is the social situation itself, which comprises societal practices of schooling and expectations associated with the role of a student. The second aspect is child's awareness of these expectations and ability to meet them. To gain this awareness, a child actually has to participate in school activities and to enter specific social interactions with teachers and other students. Therefore, Vygotsky views school readiness as being formed during the first months of schooling and not before school entry. However, certain accomplishments of preschool age make it easier for children to develop this readiness. Among these accomplishments are mastery of some mental tools, development of self-regulation, and integration of emotions and cognition. With these prerequisites in place, a preschool child could make the necessary transition from learning that "follows child's own agenda" to learning that "follows the school agenda" (Vygotsky, 1956).

SUBSEQUENT STUDIES OF PRESCHOOL AGE IN CULTURAL–HISTORICAL TRADITION

In the years after Vygotsky's death, many of his colleagues and students continued study of child development, following major themes outlined earlier in this chapter. These studies resulted in further elaboration of theoretical concepts and principles introduced by Vygotsky as well as in the development of practical applications of these principles. In regard to the processes of learning and development of preschool-age children, important contributions to cultural–historical theory were made in the areas of play, cognitive development, and emotional development.

Importance of Make-Believe Play for the Development of Preschool Children

Although Vygotsky himself used the term *leading activity* in describing make-believe play, he used it more as a metaphor than as a theoretical construct. The Vygotskian idea that a leading activity may be used as an indicator of a specific age was later extended and refined in the work of Alexei Leont'ev and Daniel Elkonin, who described leading activities throughout childhood and identified their role in producing the main developmental accomplishments of each age period (Leont'ev, 1978). In Elkonin's theory of periods in child development, play is placed on the continuum of leading activities following object-oriented activity of toddlers and followed by learning activity of primary grade children (Elkonin, 1977). In a thorough analysis of play, Elkonin identified the essential characteristics that make play the leading activity of preschoolers, emphasizing the importance of play for cognitive development and for development of self-regulation. According to Elkonin, the center of make-believe play is the role that a child acts out. Since children act out not the exact actions of their role models but rather synopses of these actions, they, in fact, generate a model of reality – something that requires symbolic generalization. Elkonin concludes that in make-believe play, children learn to use symbols in two different ways: when they use objects in their symbolic function and when they act out a symbolic representation of relationships that exist between their role models. In both instances, the use of symbols first is supported by toys and props and later can be communicated to play partners by means of words and gestures. Elkonin sees this evolution of play as a reflection of the universal path of cognitive development: from object-oriented actions accompanied by private speech to thinking aloud with no objects involved to mental actions proper (Elkonin, 1978).

The power of play to support development of intentional, self-regulatory behavior was attributed by Elkonin to the fact that the roles children play are mostly the roles of adults (doctors, drivers, chefs, etc.) engaged in socially desirable behavior. By imitating this behavior in play, children learn to adjust their actions to meet the norms associated with the behavior of role models, thus practicing planning, self-monitoring, and reflection essential for intentional behavior (Elkonin, 1978). Thus, Elkonin enriched Vygotsky's idea that play creates a child's zone of proximal development with concrete details about the mechanisms involved in elevating a preschool child to the level where he is "a head above himself" (Vygotsky, 1978, p. 74).

Acquisition of Cultural Tools and Cognitive Development of Preschoolers

Major contributions of post-Vygotskians to this area of study are associated with the search for the cultural tools specific for this age period and for the mechanisms of their acquisition. In Vygotsky's own view, the majority of cultural tools are language-based. This view was challenged in the works of Zaporozhets and his group (see, e.g., Venger, 1988, 1996;

Zaporozhets, 1970; Zaporozhets & Elkonin, 1974), who proved that the major principles of cultural–historical theory could be applied to acquisition of nonverbal cultural tools. Moreover, their studies of perception and visual–representational thinking demonstrated the great relevance of these tools to cognitive development of preschoolers.

As Vygotsky identifies perception as the dominant mental function of children before their preschool years, he writes about this period in rather general terms, referring to perception as being "mediated" by language. However, he does not specify how perception becomes mediated and whether this mediation involves use of cultural tools other than language. Building on Vygotsky's idea that mediated perception is one of the first mental processes to be "enculturated," Alexander Zaporozhets and Leonid Venger have studied the nature of this mediation in young children. Vygotsky attributed emergence of mediated perception to children's use of speech, not specifying how this mediation occurs. Zaporozhets and Venger proposed the concept of *sensory standards* to describe specific mental tools responsible for elevating perception from the level of a natural mental function to the level of a higher mental function. They defined *sensory standards* as "representations corresponding to socially elaborated patterns of sensory characteristics of objects" (Venger, 1988, p. 148). Among the first standards to be acquired by young children are the colors of the spectrum, simple geometric shapes, and basic tastes. Experimental studies of how children acquire these sensory standards and what effect they have on their ability to discriminate perceptually between objects confirmed Vygotsky's idea that this process can start as early as the toddler years. First sensory standards are usually acquired in isolation and not as a culturally determined system. However, preschoolers can be taught these standards in a more systematic fashion in the meaningful context of what Venger called "productive activities" (block building, drawing, cooking, crafts, etc.). Research conducted by Venger and his colleagues demonstrated that with proper instruction, all preschoolers could achieve the level of mastery in regard to these standards (e.g., in art and music) that had been traditionally reserved for "gifted" children only (Venger, 1986). By identifying the new class of productive activities tied to critical advances in child development, Venger challenged Vygotsky's claim (also supported by Leont'ev and Elkonin) that make-believe play is the only leading activity of preschool age.

Elaborating on the idea of nonlinguistic cultural tools, Venger broadened the notion of sensory standards to include more abstract forms of nonverbal representation referred to as *models*. Examples of models include a variety of phenomena from schematic drawings typically produced by young children to block structures that vaguely resemble real buildings to children's use of play props that have little in common with the real objects they are supposed to represent. All these examples demonstrate that most activities preferred by young children and considered "developmentally appropriate" by parents and educators alike share one common feature – children are modeling real relationships between people or between objects by creating their schematic external representations. Abbreviated and sometimes inexact characteristics of these models do not reflect a child's inability or unwillingness to generate a more accurate depiction but rather the child's focus on the most essential properties of the object they represent or the role they play, sometimes at the cost of ignoring the nonessential ones. According to Venger, ability to generate these models, understand them, and use them makes it possible for young children to develop general cognitive competencies and constitutes one of the major developmental accomplishments of preschool age. Employing the methodology of the "instructional experiment" used by many Vygotskians, Venger introduced elements of modeling actions in a variety of preschool activities such as block building, retelling of stories, music lessons, and make-believe play. The analysis of cognitive gains made by children in the course of this experimental instruction proved that these gains were not limited to the contexts in which the initial instruction took place but affected the children's performance on a variety of assessment tasks (Venger, 1986). These results support the idea that the use of models has a general impact on the cognitive development of young children, moving them in the direction of mediated cognition, characteristic of the higher mental functions. Thus, external representations reflecting children's mental models of the objects and situations appear to be among the first mental tools acquired by young children.

Emotional Development of Preschoolers

Although Vygotsky placed great importance on the idea of the integration of emotions and cognition, he had time to provide only a brief outline of this principle. This strand of Vygotsky's work was carried on by Alexander Zaporozhets and his research team, who focused on the development of "higher emotional processes" in preschool-aged children. The definition of these higher emotional processes is consistent with Vygotsky's definition of higher mental functions that Vygotsky himself applied primarily to cognitive processes (Vygotsky, 1978). Similarly to other higher mental functions, higher emotional processes are built on the foundation of more primitive affective reactions that eventually become transformed by these more advanced social emotions. Higher emotional processes are shaped by the social interactions children participate in and reflect cultural norms and expectations. As a result, a child begins to experience emotions that are uniquely human (e.g., pride and compassion) and are not directly related to the basic affective reactions common to humans and animals (e.g., fear and joy).

Zaporozhets studied the development of higher emotions in preschoolers from the perspective of the activity theory (Leont'ev, 1978), thus adding new dimensions to this topic such as the relationship between emotions and motivation and the relationship between emotions and personal meaning (Zaporozhets & Neverovich, 1986). Research done in this paradigm proved that the integration of emotions and cognition could in fact be observed in children by the end of preschool age, especially if these children have been engaged in activities with specific content and structure. Examples of such activities include acting out certain stories and fairy tales, engaging in sociodramatic play, and working on joint projects, especially the ones that require cooperation between partners and ability to empathize with these partners (Zaporozhets & Neverovich, 1986). A child cannot successfully participate in these activities without having to foresee distant results of his or her own actions, which often depend on emotional reactions of the partners (real as well as imaginary) and their subsequent actions. Depending on how these expected results are perceived emotionally, the child might make adjustments in what he or she planned to do – the mechanism that Zaporozhets called "emotional correction of behavior." As the activities become more complex, the mechanism of emotional correction involves more cognitive components reflecting the child's growing understanding of the situation and of other people, as well as a growing awareness of his or her own behavior.

The changing relationship between cognitive processing of information by toddlers and preschoolers and their emotional experiences was demonstrated not only in children's changing overt behavior but also in the corresponding changes in the patterns of their brain activity. In a series of studies (see, e.g., Khrizman, Eremeeva, Loskutova, & Stetsenko, 1986), children of various ages repeatedly listened to stories that contained scary or exciting episodes (e.g., "Little Red Riding Hood"). Their brain activity was recorded along with several physiological indicators commonly associated with emotional reactions (pulse rate, muscle tone, etc.). It was found that toddlers and younger preschoolers exhibited significant changes in brain activity as well as in the physiological processes that coincided with the most emotionally charged episodes – such as when the wolf ate the grandma. This pattern remained stable with subsequent readings of the story. By contrast, older preschoolers changed their pattern of response during the second reading of the story, exhibiting all signs of emotion during an earlier episode – when Little Red Riding Hood decided to take a path through the woods in spite of what her mother told her to do. Not only were the older children able to predict the consequences of the story character's actions, they were also experiencing emotions consistent with these predictions (Zaporozhets & Neverovich, 1986).

On the basis of these findings, Zaporozhets concluded that the major ideas of the cultural–historical theory – the idea of the internalization of mental processes and the idea of their cultural mediation – could be applied to emotional development similarly to the way they were applied by Vygotsky to cognitive development.

Transition to School and the Issue of School Readiness

Interest in the Vygotskian perspective on school readiness as not acquired completely before the onset of schooling has grown especially high during the last 25 years. It could be attributed to two major factors. First, the changes in educational practices in Russia led to lowering of the age required for school entry from 7 to 6 years, causing renewed attention of educators to the issue of children being ready for school and schools being ready for children. The second factor is the progress in the studies of learning activity carried out by Daniel Elkonin, Vasily Davydov, and their collaborators (Davydov, 1990). This work resulted in an in-depth analysis of the structure and the components of learning activity as well as an analysis of instructional practices that facilitate its development (for a discussion of specific issues regarding learning activity see Zuckerman, this volume).

Affected by these new developments in the cultural–historical tradition, the understanding of school readiness by the post-Vygotskians has evolved significantly to include the child's readiness to engage in the learning activity. According to this definition, to become a successful student, a child does not need to master a requisite set of skills or to acquire specific knowledge. Instead, the child has to develop general underlying social and cognitive competencies that will allow him or her to become a deliberate, self-regulated learner capable of establishing adequate social relationships with other participants in the teaching/learning process that takes place in the school. The list of these competencies includes many of those discussed earlier in this chapter (e.g., ability to regulate one's own behavior and ability to use age-appropriate cultural tools in solving a variety of cognitive problems). In addition, success in school learning will depend on the child's ability to adopt a specific position of a "student" characterized by such attributes as interest in the very process of learning, willingness to play by the school rules, and readiness to follow the teacher's directions.

Theoretical as well as applied studies done by post-Vygotskians demonstrate that it is possible to design a preschool/kindergarten curriculum that provides the foundations for future learning activity without attempting to impose it prematurely on young children (e.g., Venger, 1986). This and similar curricula, however, cannot guarantee that every first grader will be ready and willing to engage in learning activity. As a result, the issues of school readiness assessment and special interventions arise. Both the assessment and the interventions developed from the perspective of learning activity differ radically from the ones commonly used in the West (as well as in those of Russian schools that adopted alternative educational philosophies). Instead of focusing on discrete skills and knowledge (e.g., letters and numbers), a kindergartner is assessed on his or her ability to follow multistep directions (oral or presented as graphic schemas), draw a mirror image of a sample picture, answer a series of questions about fictitious children who attend school or preschool, etc. (see, e.g., Bugrimenko, Venger, Polivanova, & Sushkova, 1992; Venger & Kholmovskaya, 1978). Many of the tasks are administered repeatedly with different degrees of adult assistance (see Gindis, chapter 10, this volume, for a discussion of assessment methodology). Assessment results are interpreted in the terms of the child's perception of the task he or she has worked on (e.g., as a learning task, as a game, as a topic for conversation with an adult). Whereas some children might need individual interventions, most work on assisting children in making the transition from kindergarten to school is done by a classroom teacher, first as a special "introductory" class in the beginning of the first grade and then in various formats for the rest of the year (Bugrimenko et al., 1992; Zuckerman & Polivanova, 1996).

This approach to assessing and promoting school readiness appears to hold potential for addressing the problems facing educators in the West. As the demands for higher accountability make preschools and kindergartens look more and more like elementary classrooms, a Vygotskian-based perspective on school readiness presents a promising answer to the question of what is and what is not developmentally appropriate in early childhood education.

APPLYING VYGOTSKY'S IDEAS IN THE AMERICAN EARLY CHILDHOOD CLASSROOM

Implementing Vygotsky: Accomplishments and Challenges

As we mentioned earlier, many of theoretical and practical contributions to the cultural–historical theory were made by post-Vygotskians, especially when we consider the topic of child development in preschool age. Unfortunately, most of these works are virtually unfamiliar to the Western audience. As a result, the general perception of the Vygotskian approach continues that it is a philosophy that may provide educators with inspiration and maybe general guidance but is not very helpful in designing practical solutions to classroom problems. In this role, the Vygotskian approach produced a strong following in the West as many theorists proposed changes in educational practice based on such ideas as the zone of proximal development, socially shared learning, and the importance of private speech and make-believe play (e.g., Berk & Winsler, 1995). However, most attempts to replicate some of the original instructional methods developed by the post-Vygotskians did not succeed at all or ended up in reducing an integrated system of instruction to a collection of isolated teacher tricks, as is the case with the "Elkonin boxes" widely used in the remedial reading programs.

In our own experience of implementing Vygotskian ideas in an early childhood classroom in the Unites States, we found that this implementation cannot take the route of importing instructional practices designed in another country, even if they proved to be successful when applied in their original context. An alternative is to design new practices that are based on the same theoretical and methodological principles but address the unique needs of an American classroom. An example of Scaffolded Writing demonstrates the possibilities of this approach.

Scaffolded Writing

The Scaffolded Writing method was developed as a response to a dilemma facing early childhood teachers: how to help emergent writers to acquire specific literacy skills while preserving the genuine sociolinguistic context of their writing. Research shows that in order for the emergent writing to have the beneficial effects on the early literacy development, it has to become a fairly extended and engaging activity initiated by children and involving their self-generated messages (see, e.g., Morrow, 1997; Snow, Burns, & Griffin, 1998). At the same time, young children need teachers' assistance in mastering the conventions of writing and in making the transition from idiosyncratic symbols to phonetically consistent representation. Existing approaches to this issue usually involve either providing formal instruction in writing that may not be appropriate for young children or withholding instructional assistance until children are considered "ready to learn" about the writing conventions. Neither approach seems to promote the kind of children's writing that is most beneficial for their literacy development. In our attempt to solve this dilemma we proposed to maintain the child-initiated context of writing but assist the children by equipping them with appropriate mental tools (Bodrova & Leong, 1995, 1998).

During Scaffolded Writing sessions, a teacher helps a child plan his or her own message by drawing a line to stand for each word the child says. The child then repeats the message, pointing to each line as he or she says the word. Finally, the child writes on the lines, attempting to represent each word with some letters or symbols (see Fig. 8.1 for an example of Scaffolded Writing with the teacher drawing the lines and the child writing on them). During the first several sessions, the child may require some assistance and prompting from the teacher. As the child's understanding of the concept of a word grows, the child becomes able to carry on the whole process independently, including drawing the lines and writing words on these lines. Thus an activity that starts as shared by the child and the teacher later changes to the child's own individual activity carried out in the context that

FIGURE 8.1 An example of a 5-year-old child's teacher-assisted use of Scaffolded Writing. The message read, "My favorite holiday is Halloween. I like Jack-o-lanterns they scare kids."

is authentic for writing (see Fig. 8.2 for an example of Scaffolded Writing used in a journal entry with the child planning her message with the lines and then writing on them and Fig. 8.3 for an example of Scaffolded Writing used by a child describing her play plan).

In the Scaffolded Writing procedure, a line that is drawn to represent each word in an oral message serves as an external mediator for this word. The lines separated by spaces represent the existence of individual words, and their sequence in a sentence, thus creating a visual model of this sentence similar to the models we discussed earlier in relation to the work of Venger and his colleagues. An additional tool used is private speech, which seems to support writing children use in at least three ways. First, when a child talks to herself when writing, talking helps her remember more words from her initial message. Second, as a child repeats a word while drawing a line, she practices voice-to-print correspondence, which reinforces the emergent concept of a word. Finally, with lines reminding her of other words of the message, the child can concentrate on repeating any word as many times as may be necessary to produce phonemic representations.

FIGURE 8.2 An example of a 5-year-old child's independent use of Scaffolded Writing. The message reads, "My boyfriends has to get used to me. He is afraid of me because I love him."

The use of Scaffolded Writing improves children's learning by helping children perform at the highest level of the zone of proximal development as they start to write independently and by contributing to the formation of more advanced mental processes and concepts involved in writing (e.g., the alphabetic principle, ability to map a spoken message into a written one, and knowledge of the conventions of print). When using this method, children write in a more advanced manner as compared to their ability to write before its introduction (see Fig. 8.4 for an example of typical writing of a 5-year-old child immediately before the introduction of Scaffolded Writing). After having used Scaffolded Writing for some time, children internalize the procedure of planning (modeling) the sentence so that they gradually give up first the teacher assistance and

FIGURE 8.3 An example of a 4-year-old child's independent use of Scaffolded Writing. The message reads, "I am going to Art and play with my friend Sara. She is my best friend."

eventually the lines themselves as the quality of their writing improves (Bodrova & Leong, 1998; Bodrova & Leong, 2001). The example of Scaffolded Writing demonstrates how better understanding of the concepts and methods contributed by the contemporary Vygotskians to the field of early childhood education might have a significant impact on classroom practices.

Research done in Vygotsky's tradition not only deepens our understanding of child development during preschool years but also has important implications for the educational practice. These implications can be summarized in one term coined by Alexander Zaporozhets – amplification of child development. The idea of amplification focuses on the role of education in child development, emphasizing that properly designed education does not stifle development of preschool children but instead promotes it (Zaporozhets, 1986), thus presenting a logical extension of Vygotsky's

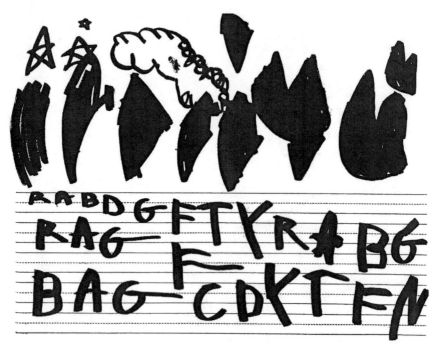

FIGURE 8.4 An example of a 5-year-old child's writing immediately before the introduction of Scaffolded Writing. The child said her message read, "I like diamonds, stars, snakes, and I like hearts. I learn a lot about snakes." When asked to read the same message later, the child could not remember what she had written.

principle of instruction leading child development. Years of research from the cultural–historical perspective produce concrete guidelines on how this education should be designed and what effect it has on the child's development in preschool years.

References

Berk, L. E., & Winsler, A. (1995). *Scaffolding children's learning: Vygotsky and Early Childhood Education* (Vol. 7). Washington, DC: NAEYC.

Bodrova, E., & Leong, D. J. (1995). Scaffolding the writing process: The Vygotskian approach. *Colorado Reading Council Journal, 6*, 27–29.

Bodrova, E., & Leong, D. J. (1998). Scaffolding emergent writing in the zone of proximal development. *Literacy Teaching and Learning, 3*(2), 1–18.

Bodrova, E., & Leong, D. J. (2001). *The Tools of the Mind project: A case study of implementing the Vygotskian approach in American early childhood and primary classrooms.* Geneva: International Bureau of Education, UNESCO.

Bugrimenko, E. A., Venger, A. L., Polivanova, K. N., & Sushkova, E. Y. (1992). *Gotovnost' detej k shkole: Diagnostika psychicheskogo razvitija i korrektsija ego neblago-prijatnykh variantov* [School readiness: assessment and interventions]. Tomsk: Peleng.

Davydov, V. V. (1990). *Types of generalization in instruction.* Reston, VA: National Council of Teachers of Mathematics.

Elkonin, D. (1977). Toward the problem of stages in the mental development of the child. In M. Cole (Ed.), *Soviet developmental psychology* (pp. 538–563). White Plains, NY: M. E. Sharpe.

Elkonin, D. (1978). *Psychologija igry* [The psychology of play]. Moscow: Pedagogika.

Khrizman, T. P., Eremeeva, V. D., Loskutova, T. D., & Stetsenko, S. A. (1986). Nejrophisiologicheskoje issledovanije emotsional'nykh protsessov u detej [Neurophisiological study of emotional processes in children]. In A. V. Zaporozhets & Y. Z. Neverovich (Eds.), *Razvitije social'nykh emotsij u detej doshkol'nogo vozrasta: Psychologicheskije issledovanija* [Development of social emotions in preschool children: Psychological studies] (pp. 204–205). Moscow: Pedagogika.

Leont'ev, A. (1978). *Activity, consciousness, and personality.* Englewood Cliffs, NJ: Prentice-Hall.

Morrow, L. M. (1997). *Literacy development in the early years: Helping children read and write* (3rd ed.). Needham Heights, MA: Allyn & Bacon.

Snow, C. E., Burns, S. M., & Griffin, P. (Eds.) (1998). *Preventing reading difficulties in young children.* Washington, DC: National Academy Press.

Venger, L. A. (Ed.) (1986). *Razvitije poznavatel'nykh sposobnostej v processe doshkol'nogo vospitanija* [Development of cognitive abilities in the process of preschool education]. Moscow: Pedagogika.

Venger, L. A. (1988). The origin and development of cognitive abilities in preschool children. *International Journal of Behavioral Development, 11*(2), 147–153.

Venger, L. A. (Ed.) (1996). *Slovo i znak v reshenii poznavatel'nykh zadach doshkol'nikami* Word and image in the preschoolers' cognitive problem solving. Moscow: INTOR.

Venger, L. A., & Kholmovskaya, V. V. (Eds.). (1978). *Diagnostika umstvennogo razvitija doshkol'nikov* [Assessment of cognitive development of preschool children]. Moscow: Pedagogika.

Vygotsky, L. S. (1956). Obuchenije i razvitije v doshkol'nom vozraste [Learning and development in preschool children]. *Izbrannye Psychologicheskije Trudy* [Selected psychological studies]. Moscow: RSFSR Academy of Pedagogical Sciences.

Vygotsky, L. S. (1977). Play and its role in the mental development of the child. In M. Cole (Ed.), *Soviet developmental psychology.* White Plains, NY: M. E. Sharpe.

Vygotsky, L. (1978). *Mind in society: The development of higher mental processes.* Cambridge, MA: Harvard University Press.

Vygotsky, L. S. (1982). Emotsii i ikh razvitije v detskom vozraste [Emotions and emotional development of children]. In V. V. Davydov (Ed.), *Sobranije Sochinenij* [Selected works], Vol. 2 (pp. 416–436). Moscow: Pedagogika.

Vygotsky, L. S. (1984). Voprosy detskoy (vozrastnoy) psychologii [Issues in child (developmental) psychology]. In D. B. Elkonin (Ed.), *Sobranije Sochinenij* [Selected works], Vol. 4 (pp. 244–385). Moscow: Pedagogika.

Vygotsky, L. (1987). *Thinking and Speech* (N. Minick, Trans.) (Vol. 1). New York: Plenum Press.

Vygotsky, L. (1998). *Child Psychology* (M. J. Hall, Trans.) New York: Plenum Press.

Zaporozhets, A. V. (1970). The development of perception in the preschool child. In *Cognitive development in children: Five monographs of the Society for Research in Child Development*. Chicago, IL: University of Chicago Press.

Zaporozhets, A. (1986). *Izbrannye psychologicheskie trudy* [Selected works]. Moscow: Pedagogika.

Zaporozhets, A. V., & Elkonin, D. B. (Eds.) (1974). *The psychology of preschool children*. Cambridge: MIT Press.

Zaporozhets, A. V., & Neverovich, Y. Z. (Eds.). (1986). *Razvitije social'nykh emotsij u detej doshkol'nogo vozrasta: Psychologicheskije issledovanija* [Development of social emotions in preschool children: Psychological studies]. Moscow: Pedagogika.

Zuckerman, G. A., & Polivanova, N. K. (1996). *Vvedenije v shkol'nuju zhizn'* [Introduction to school life]. Tomsk: Peleng.

9

The Learning Activity in the First Years of Schooling
The Developmental Path Toward Reflection

Galina Zuckerman

The notion *learning activity* in its broad meaning comprises the educational practices that treat the student as not only a performer of a teacher's instructions but, more important, as the agent of cognitive actions that are distributed between the teacher and the student. With the emphasis on activity of the learner, the term *learning activity* refers to a diverse set of educational practices that are consistent with constructivist theories. The educational philosopher John Dewey and the developmental psychologists Lev Vygotsky, Jean Piaget, and Jerome Bruner, among others, propose that children actively construct knowledge, and that this knowledge is constructed in a social context. Accordingly, it is the student who sets the goals, searches for the means and methods to achieve them, and engages in self-control and self-evaluation of the achievements that result.

The term and the concept of *learning activity*, in its narrow sense, were developed in the late 1950s by Daniil Elkonin (1904–1984). A student and associate of Lev Vygotsky, this prominent Russian developmental and educational psychologist strongly influenced several generations of educators and researchers in his country. Elkonin and his immediate associate Vassily Davydov (1930–1998) worked out an innovative theory of education along with the associated educational practices that both embody and exemplify the theory. This system of education helps the child to become the agent of self-change aimed at transcending the limits of one's own experience, knowledge, skills, and abilities and at acquiring methods for

Preparation of this chapter was generously supported by the Fulbright fellowship from the Council for the International Exchange of Scholars. The author is grateful to the Wisconsin Center for Educational Research (WCER), the University of Wisconsin–Madison, for the friendly support during her stay in WCER as a Fulbright Scholar. I am especially grateful to Professor Leona Schauble (UW–Madison) for her deep conceptual suggestions and meticulous editing of my manuscript.

self-learning (Davydov, 1988; Elkonin, 1988). Elkonin started the experimental construction and verification of this educational practice in 1958 in a single Moscow school. Now his approach has developed into an influential educational system adopted by about 10% of the schools in Russia and by many educators around the world (Amano, 1999; Carpay & Van Oers, 1999; Hedegaard, 1990; Lompscher, 2000). This chapter deals with the psychological foundations of the theory of learning activity. These foundations are based upon Vygotsky's cultural historical theory, particularly his idea that education leads development.

In current psychological and educational discourse, the notion of *learning activity* is often misused to include any kind of activities incorporated in classroom lessons; this is not the meaning of the term featured in this chapter. As Michael Cole explains, "It is very difficult to find real learning activity in a school setting, at least the normal school settings that occupy millions of Russian and American children daily" (Davydov & Markova, 1982, p. 50). When educators construct learning activity in classrooms, they open new developmental possibilities for their students. Instead of traditional laboratory experiments, the basic research method for investigating learning activity is the *design experiment*, in which the experimenter actively participates in curriculum building, teacher education, long-term observations and interventions in the classrooms, and monitoring of developmental changes in both students and their teachers. The design experiment as a research method "presents a methodological headache for traditional psychology, allergic as it is to multiply-confounded experiments" (Brown, 1992, p. 166). At the same time it is a fruitful, though extremely labor-consuming tool for supporting and studying education, development, and their relations.

LEARNING ACTIVITY CONSTRUCTS THE ORIENTING BASIS FOR FUTURE ACTION

Learning is an inevitable part of any activity: Whatever one does or experiences, he or she inevitably acquires new impressions and attitudes, intentions and meanings, information and vocabulary, skills and abilities, pieces of wisdom and mental schemes. Children are specially blessed with the capacity to learn. In our first 5 years of life, we pick up more than in all the remaining years of existence. To illustrate, compare the difference in motor development between (a) a beginner athlete and a world champion and, on the other hand, (b) a newborn baby and a 5-year-old child. The two cases differ in at least two aspects. First, during the initial 5 years of life, children acquire more motor skills and capacities than do athletes during 5 years of hard training. Moreover, the skills gained by the child are more fundamental, not only for training in sports, but also for many other fields of human motor activity. Second, most of the skills gained by children are the side products of other activities. Children run, jump, and play ball not for the cognizant, deliberate purpose of developing skills, but chiefly for the pure fun of body adventure.

From ancient times, school has been a specific social institution that transforms preschool learning – originally entwined with the broad repertoire of the child's activities – into an isolated activity. School emerges when it becomes impossible to teach children new skills through direct imitation of adults' actions in the process of everyday joint practices. In other words, formal school education insulates instruction from real-life practice. Theories of situated learning and cognition (Lave & Wenger, 1990) criticized this insulation by arguing that learning is normally a function of the activity, context, and culture in which it occurs (i.e., it is situated). These claims of the situated learning theories throw suspicion on many classroom activities, which often involve knowledge that is abstract and out of context.

The disadvantages of such decontextualized education are well known. When learned out of authentic contexts, action loses its motivational impetus, and as a consequence, the learning becomes boring and meaningless. Educators must seek to develop new motives of learning activity beyond immediate utility, for example, cognitive interest, the pleasure of inquiry into the unknown, and the joy of self-perfection. Yet, in spite of these challenges, there are psychological advantages of at least partially separating instruction from everyday practice. To understand them better, let us distinguish between two components of any human action – mental and manual, verbal and nonverbal, conscious and unconscious, perceptive and mnemonic: *performance* and *orientation*. A famous Russian child psychologist, Piotr Galperin (1902–1988), who was the student of Vygotsky and a close colleague and friend of Elkonin, introduced the notion of *orienting basis of an action* (OBA). *OBA* refers to the whole set of orienting elements that guide the person along in the performance of an action and that therefore determine its quality. OBA is a sort of a "cognitive map," providing the learner with the information necessary for the performance of a new action and for self-correction. When performing a new action, the learner must take into account such orienting conditions as the projected results, means and objects of the action, and sequence of its operations (Galperin, 1992).

The younger the child, the less separated are the performance and the orientation. For example, an infant typically does not first examine a new gadget in detail before turning on all its knobs and buttons. Young children learn through acting. Adults, at least those who become good learners, first examine and then act. School is the place where learning is deliberately cut off from practical acting to help students consciously build the orienting basis of actions.

There are three important dimensions that can be used to classify OBA with respect to their developmental status:

- Whether the OBA is provided by the teacher or constructed by the student
- Whether the OBA is complete and sufficient to generate unerring action or incomplete, hence associated with trial and error or step-by-step correction and modification of the initial OBA during the process of acting
- Whether the OBA is general, thus providing for the unerring solution of a wide class of similar tasks, or partial, failing to support transfer of the particular method into a new area

Learning activity is the self-propelled activity of the student who is building a general and complete OBA in the cultural practices traditionally chosen for schooling new generations: mathematics, arts, languages, natural sciences, and so on. For educators, the challenge is to construct such activity when most students entering school are eager to act on the spot, manifesting little or no observable propensity for preliminary orientation in their future actions.

LEARNING ACTIVITY: A NEW VISION OF AGE-APPROPRIATE DEVELOPMENTAL TASKS

Purposeful increase and amplification of one's repertoire of competencies and abilities are among the most traditional goals of formal education. Centuries and nations differ dramatically in their ways to raise and answer the perpetual questions of school education: What should they develop and boost in younger children? What should they carry out from school?

Explicating Vygotsky's insight of education as the major by vehicle for child development, Elkonin (1972) came up with an unexpected and pointed question: What is the norm of development? The norm is usually regarded as the statistically average performance observed in a particular age group in a particular sphere of expertise. This statistical notion of the norm obscures the effect of education on the level of each child's achievements by the very procedure of defining the developmental norms for each age group. Meanwhile, "most existing theories of development capture just one possible version of development – the version that is bound to deficient cognitive tools employed in the currently dominating type of instruction" (Arievitch & Stetsenko, 2000, p. 69).

A vicious circle is easily formed around the statistical concept of the norm. The product of an educational system is perceived as a norm of "natural" development, is consequently never challenged, and is accepted finally as an invariant. Nobody asks the obvious question, Could it be different? Instead, children are considered to be "naturally" able or unable to arrive to a certain developmental level at a certain age. The education that supports safe arrival at this level of development is the one considered to be age-appropriate. A child who is scheduled to reach this level of development at a certain time and does not fail to do it is labeled *ready*.

It is distressingly difficult to break this vicious circle if one presumes the statistical approach to identifying norms of development. Yet, there exists an alternative vision of the norm – as a model or ideal. For example, it is considered a norm never to lie, though many of us relate minor inaccuracies or avoid saying the whole truth at least once a day. Elkonin proposed that the vision of *the norm as the highest potential level of achievement* is a more *general* sense of norm than the statistical sense. Moreover, it is a sense more appropriate to the Vygotskian view of the pivotal role of education in development. *The development of a child will reach its highest potential level when education releases and promotes these possibilities.* In this view, both "education" and "development" are regarded as interdependent – even more essential, as artificial – variables constructed in the interactions of adults and children. In short, education and development are made, fashioned, or designed, rather than naturally occurring.

In the Vygotskian perspective, the potential level of achievement that can be attained with the help of a more knowledgeable partner (e.g., a teacher) is often associated with a concept of the *zone of proximal development*. This concept was revised within the theory of learning activity.

LEARNING ACTIVITY: A NEW VISION OF THE ZONE OF PROXIMAL DEVELOPMENT

The zone of proximal development (ZPD) is often defined as an individual range of learning potential. This potential ability exceeds the actual ability of the individual, when learning is facilitated by someone with greater expertise (Wertsch, 1991). With help from a knowledgeable partner, a child can perform on a higher level than when acting without assistance. The concept of ZPD is elaborated by Seth Chaiklin in this volume; therefore, I will highlight only one aspect, namely, the multidimensional landscape of developmental potential, where choosing one possibility means rejecting others (Waddington, 1957).

At each point of development each child has multiple, as yet unactualized potentials for further accomplishments. Some of these would become manifest if supported, but that support would also curb, restrain, or undermine alternative trajectories of potential development. To understand better the ambivalent nature of educational support, which always simultaneously both promotes and restrains, one has to overcome the common notion of development as a linear pathway from point *A* (the developmental level already achieved) to point *B* (the potentially accessible level of development). In a developmental landscape designed by a Vygotskian, the educational system is the factor that chooses the pathway for future development of a child and cultural tools that cut the particular developmental trajectories. Such a nonlinear and multidimensional vision of the developmental potential leads us to an immediate educational consequence. Different educational systems send the students in diverging directions by facilitating particular developmental potentials, while ignoring and/or curbing others. To illustrate, the traditional elementary school, which was initially constructed by the emerging industrial society to prepare most students for the factory and the field, canalized development in a direction completely unaligned with the mission of the elementary school at the turn of the 20th century, when the major developmental task for junior schoolchildren is to prepare for life-span education and self-learning.

Let us identify the developmental trajectories promoted and curbed by the traditional elementary school system. Its top products are deep motivation for conscientious labor, working self-discipline, propensity to follow work already started zealously, inclination for exacting work as planned, and abilities and skills for following instructions presented as texts, signs, and symbols. At the same time, traditional schooling hinders the development of critical attitudes toward rules and models, and the capacity for creatively transforming existing rules and ways of action and modifying them on one's own initiative.

In spite of the restrictions imposed by the traditional school on child development, very few children, conventionally called *gifted*, manifest outstanding capacities for creativity, intellectual initiative, and critical thinking. Elkonin hypothesized that the "spontaneous" abilities usually attributed only to gifted 6- to 12-year-old students in traditional schools can be developed in the majority of elementary school children under another system of education. His daring hypothesis was verified by the evidence from 30-year-long experiments conducted by Elkonin, Davydov, and their collaborators. The practical outcome of their work was a new system for school education designed to equip students with *learning activity*.

LEARNING ACTIVITY AS THE SCAFFOLD FOR DEVELOPMENT OF REFLECTIVE ABILITIES

What intellectual possibilities of elementary schoolchildren are hindered by the traditional type of education? What kind of human potentials might be met by a new type of education? Half a century ago Elkonin and Davydov gave a brief answer to these questions. It is reflection as a basic human ability (a) to consider the goals, motives, methods, and means of one's own and other people's actions and thoughts (the mental facet of this ability is sometimes called *metacognition*); (b) to take other people's point of view, that is, view matters from perspectives other than one's own; and (c) to understand oneself; study one's own strong points and limitations in order to find ways to excel or to accept shortcomings. Introspection is one part of this remarkable human potency; the power for self-changing and for transcending one's limitations is another element of the human capacity for reflection.

Of course, this is a definition of highly developed reflection, which is achieved neither in elementary school age nor in adolescence. In fact, few adults manifest highly developed reflective abilities. The problem is whether the primary components of intellectual, social, and personal reflection can be developed in elementary school children with due support of education. One might ask why it should be developed in such an early age, when most children are not expected to show a predisposition for reflection. The solution of this problem is Elkonin's approach to the potential of elementary school children. When children are assisted in those discoveries that "the gifted" seem to make spontaneously (primarily, reflective ways of acting essential for the independent building of the general and complete OBA), the majority of this age cohort appropriates reflection. When education does not channel students along the reflective ways of acting and thinking, this invaluable capacity remains a characteristic of the privileged minority, as indeed happens in our imperfect reality.

The claim that the learning activity leads the development of elementary schoolchildren toward reflective abilities does not represent what occurs naturally. Rather, this state of affairs is the product of intentions declared by those educators who consider it essential to stretch the ZPD of elementary school children toward reflective intelligence. Choosing the developmental trajectory (the choice made by adult society for children) always means concurrently rejecting other developmental scenarios. Therefore, we must explicitly identify which abilities are developed through the learning activity and which are not.

The learning activity purposefully and systematically develops reflection as a capacity to discriminate between the known and unknown and, when one hypothesizes on an unknown, to reason on one's own actions and those of one's partners. The ability to inquire into the unknown and to request indispensable information; the habit of criticizing one's own and others' opinions and actions, declining to accept unsubstantiated evidence; and the propensity to look for proofs and for diverse points of view – these are the behavioral manifestations of the development of reflective abilities in elementary school children.

The learning activity does not develop the initially nonreflective abilities, such as trustfulness, empathy, mimetic behavior, and spontaneous flight of the imagination. The development of these talents will proceed independently of the learning activity. These talents are promoted by other activities, which are enriched by the learning activity but not substituted by it. When constructing the learning environment, designing the curriculum, and planning the lesson, the educator must balance various activities. Building only the learning activity will result in lopsided child development.

Sparks of reflections are already observed in the actions and thoughts of preschoolers, yet reflection as a general behavioral attitude is hardly likely before systematic schooling. It is impossible even in elementary school age if education does not consistently support its development. In this case, harmful habits of intellectual work would be cultivated, such as taking the opinion of an authority as a final truth, without seeking proof, and maintaining a black-and-white attitude toward different opinions. Later such habits of mind will limit students' access to self-learning. It is extremely difficult to subdue such habits in middle school; it is much easier to lead elementary school children directly toward reflective habits of mind. Further, we will define the educational support required to make elementary school children systematically reflective.

THE CONTENT OF LEARNING ACTIVITY

Thinking and learning are always an interplay of general and subject-specific skills and knowledge. To equip students with the means for acquiring socially valued human practices and at the same time with the ability for orienting himself or herself independently in new spheres of expertise, the theory of learning activity introduces an innovative and powerful tool. The introduction to every new class of tasks should begin with the discovery by students of the most *general method* of solving these tasks (Davydov, 1990). Children discover this method through hands-on activities and experiments with the subject under study and then express their discoveries in a *model* or a *scheme* that represents the *general concept*. The subject is further explored by concretizing and enriching the initial general concept with every new fact that crops up. The system of concepts describing the whole field of knowledge is deduced from the initial most generic "embryonic" concept. Students move from the generic to the particular when they encounter contradictions between a new fact and the knowledge set down in the model. It is the resolution of these contradictions that enriches the initial concept (Davydov, 1988).

The metaphor for this initial, most general concept is the *initial cell* or *embryo*, which contains the whole future system of concepts in its most primeval forms, just as the seed is the promise of the future tree. The initial cell metaphor helps explain the movement from the generic to the particular. The tree is a well-structured and highly developed system, whereas the embryo appears unsophisticated yet already contains in a latent form the future sensual richness and integrity of complex organization. The Vygotskian would add that although the embryo would naturally grow into the tree, the initial concept would develop into the system of concepts only if and when the teacher scaffolded each educational step.

How can educators benefit from introducing students to a new field of knowledge through the most general concepts? First, each new unit is built systematically on students' prior knowledge. Second, any concrete facts are viewed by learners through this concept as particular manifestations of the general law, or as contradictions inspiring the transformation of the previous concepts.

Curriculum builders meticulously choose the general, initial concept, taking into consideration two epistemological assumptions: (1) The concept as a mental scheme of action is an uttered (verbally or schematically) remake of this action; (2) signs, schemes, and symbols serve as the mediators between the action and its mental scheme:

The models or schemas of the "hidden" rational structure of the objects and their essential relations, once they are internalized by children, become a key part of children's orientation in a broad subject domain. As new powerful cognitive tools, these models . . . qualitatively change the child's whole way of viewing things, thinking about things, and operating with things in a given domain. In fact they advance the child's cognitive development to a new, unusually high level. (Arievitch & Stetsenko, 2000, p. 86)

Modeling is recognized as the central action of the learning activity because it helps students hold together and consider simultaneously the objects and ideas about the nature and origin of these objects (Davydov, 1988; Lehrer & Schauble, 2000). The Vygotskian concept of models and other forms of mediation as central mechanisms for human development is elucidated in greater detail by Alex Kozulin in this volume.

From this point of view, instruction about any object should revolve around considering general methods for producing it rather than simply listing its essential properties. Similar approaches to the vexing educational problem of deciding what themes or concepts should be selected for organizing a curriculum, determining appropriate starting points for teaching, and deciding on how units should be sequenced thereafter are often referred to in U.S. education as the problem of identifying the "Big, or Deep Ideas" in a discipline (Steen, 1990; Schifter & Fosnot, 1993). Big Ideas are the core organizing principles of the particular field of knowledge; they integrate the themes and interdisciplinary units of learning. A single *Big Idea* may often carry through several different grade levels to be explored from multiple viewpoints at varying depths. When Big Ideas are rephrased as open-ended, guiding questions, they become the fundamental query that navigates the search for understanding. Routinely articulated, they sustain the underlying purpose of the students' work. Big Ideas put the focus on learning, activate the curriculum, and make all students investigators. In this way Big Ideas facilitate long-lasting meaning after less significant concepts are forgotten.

Initially these Big Ideas or general concepts surface in the classroom discourse as a result of students' discovery, guided by the teacher. How can individual students appropriate these concepts? How can these concepts become instrumental as the mental tools for thinking about the subject under study and for further learning? To answer these questions, let us revisit Vygotsky's concept of internalization of initially joint action distributed between the teacher and students.

FROM COOPERATIVE TO INDIVIDUALIZED FORMS OF THE LEARNING ACTIVITY

Independent, Yet Not Alone

Explaining the genesis of human capacities, Vygotsky emphasizes the role of child–adult cooperation, in which the child has both the need and the opportunity to attempt new cultural practices.

Every function in the child's cultural development appears twice: first, on the social level, and later on the individual level; first, between people (interpsychological), and then inside the child (intrapsychological). This applies equally to voluntary attention, to logical memory, and to the formulation of concepts. All the higher functions originate as actual relations between human individuals. (Vygotsky, 1978, p. 57)

These relations, or cooperative actions are defined as interpsychological or intermental, because they do not belong completely to any participating individual. They are also *nonadditive*: They cannot be reduced to a sum of operations performed by all of the participants (The idea of the nonadditive nature of joint action will be further expounded later, in a discussion of peer cooperation.) Vygotsky points out that each human ability is born *not within an individual*, but in the interpsychological *space of human interaction*.

It is easy to oversimplify this vision of human abilities evolving *from without to within*, from an initially cooperative action to an individual one. An adult presents a model of a new action, and a child imitates this model. After a series of exercises assisted by the adult, the child can perform this action alone, without any help. This gradual increase of skillfulness is often interpreted as growing independence or, in Vygotskian terms, as a child's success at internalizing adult's models. This interpretation is based on several implicit speculations: (a) Education is perceived as pouring knowledge from its holder to one lacking it; (b) the terms *individual* (intrapsychological) and *independent* are used as synonyms; and (c) *independence* is defined as the ability to imitate the adult's models without the help of an expert. However, when imitation of the adult's models is the only mechanism of learning, there is no place for the child's initiative. Let us observe a small boy who is examining a new gadget and pestering his parents with questions: "How?" "Why?" "What if?" This child initiates learning cooperation with the adult to get help with those actions that are not yet learned and can be performed only together with the adult. So the child's independence is an attribute of interpsychological action.

The source of the child's independence in interpsychological action cannot be reduced to mastering the means and methods of action. We assume that long before children become independent in practicing instruments, symbols, notions, or ideas, they acquire *independence in initiative at interacting with the adult*. They start using interaction instrumentally, intentionally building their own learning environment. There are two components of independence: (1) *interpsychological independence,* manifested in the ability of a learner to initiate help from an expert, and (2) *intrapsychological independence,* manifested in the ability of the learner to accomplish the task without any help. Let us emphasize that *interpsychological independence appears earlier in child development than intrapsychological independence.*

The ability to do something independently, alone, without somebody's help is also often mystified. From the sociocultural perspective, there is no such thing as an individual action. By their origin, all autonomous human actions are performed in the presence of partners who may be invisible and unheard by an external observer. That means that the progress from interaction to individual (individualized) action does not exclude the partner and the very process of interaction. Internalization is understood as the transition from physical to mental partnership. From this point of view, the popular metaphor of scaffolding is rather misleading. Consider the tendency of a child to initiate interaction with an adult when this interaction is essential for solving a task. We cannot treat the interaction only as a supplementary and transient element of psychological development, a sort of scaffold for a future individual capacity that will be deconstructed as soon as an individual capacity is molded. Rather, the child's ability to initiate and maintain different forms of interaction is valuable in itself. It is one of the major developmental outputs of learning in the social context.

These general ideas derived from Bakhtin (1981) and Vygotsky are the framework for designing the learning activity. First, the means and methods of interaction with partners (both teachers and other learners) become as important a consideration for teaching as the curriculum content (concepts and skills). Second, the teacher must pay utmost attention to facilitating existing forms of learning initiative (students' queries, doubts, suggestions, and hypotheses), along with generating new ones.

The Content and the Form of Interaction

A child's initiative has two focuses. Any joint action is, aimed first at the *content* of a task, second, at *the partner* involved in the task together with the child. A learner accomplishes a complex task of constructing a new meaningful concept by identifying the invariants of the content in the whole class of similar tasks. An example is recognizing a letter not only in a printed text, but also as the same sign made from sticks or drawn in the dust. The learning child spends as much effort to identify a type of partnership in an empirical diversity of interactions. The invariants of interaction recognized as a pattern will be further referred to as a *form of interaction*. This form is determined by (a) the mode of distributing functions among the partners, (b) the formula for inviting the partner to interact, (c) mutual expectations of the partners.

By separating the content and the form of interaction, we can discriminate between two often-confused products of internalization, or *psychological innovations*. These include innovations related to learning new skills or concepts and those related to mastering new kinds of human relations, new forms of interaction. Psychological innovations of the first type ensure the success of individualized activity. Psychological innovations of the second type provide the capability to establish a certain kind of interrelation with other people, that is, to become capable of independently creating interpsychological conditions for self-learning (Zuckerman, 1997).

Recognizing the difference between the content and the form of interaction, we can avoid a few methodological dead ends of psychology. For example, in a classical diagnostic experiment, psychologists usually ignore the fact that the interacting child is not a tabula rasa with respect to an adult's expectations. Because of the work of Piaget and his followers, we now know a lot about how children view the *content* of joint activity, but are we also conscious of how children view the *forms* of their interaction with adults (Siegal, 1991)? Students entering any particular situation of education or assessment have already stored a good deal of experience, enabling them to initiate various forms of interaction with adults independently. By setting children to a task or giving them a problem to solve, the adult always invites them to interact, and children are perfectly aware of that. In this invitation, children perceive certain expectations of the adult. Some children anticipate that adults want them to come up with original ideas; others believe that their conformity and diligence are primarily expected; a third group of children may accept the task as an invitation to play and/or establish personal contacts. A basic methodological consequence follows: We fall into a trap set by our own experimental design if we suppose that it is possible to interpret a child's actions in any educational or testing situation as if these anticipations are not at play. Whenever the adult fails to define the expected form of interaction, children choose it themselves. And if the adult has neither the means nor the intention to devise the form of interaction beforehand, it is impossible to distinguish a poor solution to the problem that has been posed from an excellent answer to some other question that has not been asked. To resolve this dilemma one needs clear-cut criteria for distinguishing between different shared activities in which learning takes place.

A Classification of Basic Forms of Child–Adult Interaction

Table 9.1 helps to discern the learning activity from other forms of child's activities. Elkonin's theory of stages of child development (Elkonin, 1972) serves as the basis for the proposed classification.

Recall that the term *learning activity* used in this paradigm is not a synonym for *learning*. Learning takes place in any activity, in most cases as its side effect. Learning as a principal goal of activity, aimed at acquiring subject-specific concepts and general methods of problem solving, is referred as a learning activity per se. To become the agents of learning activity, students have to become able to initiate and maintain learning interactions that compose an adequate environment for mastering specific content of the learning activity. When children enter a classroom for the first time in their life, they do not become the agents of the learning activity automatically, though they take into the classroom all the rich experience of preschool activities. At school, the children are faced with previously unknown ideas, both fascinating and mysterious: number, word, motion, shape, and so forth. At first, students are helpless in implementing these ideas and need assistance and support. However, children are by no means helpless in organizing interaction. On their very first school-day, children are already active and full of initiative in applying already mastered preschool forms of interaction: playing, manipulating things, communicating, and others. Not all of these, however, fit the content of learning activity, although children are completely unaware of that. If students are not specially taught new forms of *learning* cooperation, they will maintain habitual preschool forms of interaction. Moreover, the form of interaction affects its content: A playing, learning, and communicating child constructs different meanings while working on the same task. For this reason, an adult has to be alert and sensitive to a child's intuitive choice of the form of interaction. People of any age, when communicating emotionally, mainly discuss personal matters, and the subject under study is usually lost. Playing is directed at the process itself, so that the final result is usually disregarded or devaluated. Imitation-directed cooperation does not require reflection. Therefore, a student who is engaged primarily in imitating a teacher's models often misses their reflective aspects. Meanwhile, imitation as a form of student–teacher interaction is often confused with learning cooperation. Therefore, we next compare these two forms of interaction in more detail.

The Difference Between Imitation and Learning Cooperation

When inviting an adult into joint action, a child shows what kind of help and participation she or he expects from the partner. For instance, a child approaches an adult with a typical appeal: "I cannot fix it. . . . It does not

TABLE 9.1. *Basic Traits of Child–Adult Cooperative Activities and Their Developmental Effects*

Features of the Activity	The Activity Leading the Development of a Child Toward the Socioculturally Determined Aims			
	Unmediated Personal Emotional Communication	Tool-Manipulative Activity	Play	Learning Activity
1. Content	Another person as a source of love, understanding, and acceptance	Ways of using the tools and signs	Social norms and meanings of human relationships	General methods of solving problems
2. Mode of interaction	Symbiotic fusion	Imitation, action by model and instruction	Imaginative, symbolic imitation	Quest for the method of joint action without a pattern
3. Pattern of initiative invitation of the partner to cooperate	Manifestation of benevolence (mainly nonverbal)	Request for model, control, and evaluation	Alternation of play and communication concerning the rules of interaction	Query for the lacking knowledge
4. Child's expectations of the adult partner	Compassion, support, kind attention, and unconditional acceptance	Demonstration of models, step-by-step help, control, and evaluation	Designing the general project and free improvisation within already agreed rules	Help in verifying students' hypotheses, indicating the contradictions
5. Developmental results of mastery of the content of the leading activity	Basic trust in people, oneself, and the world	Speech, actions with tools and signs	Imagination, symbolic function	Metacognition

6. Developmental results of mastery of the form of the leading activity	Need in another person, capacity to trust people, openness to new experience	Capacity for imitation	Capacity for coordinating actions, taking into account the play role of the partner	Ability for self-learning
7. With age-specific innovation completely developed, we observe	Trust in oneself and others, resistance to emotional stresses, empathy	Capacity to learn by models and instructions	Capacity to act in mental space, to create; social skills of cooperation with adults and peers	Knowledge of the limits of one's own capacities and ability to transcend these limits and independently set and solve new problems
8. With age-specific innovation underdeveloped, we observe	Incapacity to love and trust, disbelief in oneself	Helplessness when mastering new tools, difficulties in acquiring new skills, poor self-organization	Poor imagination, problems when dealing with nonstandard situations, social egocentric behavior	Lack of ability for self-learning, predominant rationality
9. With age-specific innovation overdeveloped, we observe	Dependence on emotional support and evaluation by other people, requirement for overprotection, lack of interest in any content, except interpersonal communication	Need of instructions, lack of one's own position, uncritical and reproductive approach, difficulties in analyzing models	Escape into imagination, lack of sense of reality, loss of product-oriented motivation, self-will in choosing activities	Disdain of performing components of the action, loss of interest after the general method of acting is discovered

work. . . . Help me." These requests suggest that a child has already done a significant amount of reflection about the problem. He or she has tried to reach the goal, has met some obstacle, has recognized it as an obstacle, and now indicates it to an adult. The adult's expected task is to accomplish the reflection needed to identify the reason for child's failure, to find a way out, to model a successful action, and to encourage a child to take a new risk. Toddlers practice this form of cooperation even before they become really verbal, as when they need an adult's help with a "disobedient" zipper or drawer. An adult often initiates the same form of cooperation to learn new skills from an expert (e.g., computer users typically make many such appeals to specialists).

Quite a different type of help is requested by a student who addresses a teacher not with a global cry for help, but with a specific inquiry (for examples see Zuckerman, Chudinova, & Khavkin, 1998). "I know what I do not know. I have some assumptions about the unknown. I expect my teacher to help me to verify my conjectures." That is the formula for the student's initiative in learning interaction with a teacher. *Directed inquiry and discovery* is one of the names for the learning cooperation described, which is initiated by the learner who is searching for missing pieces of information or the tools to validate a hypothesis. The ability for self-*learning* is the name for the intrapsychological product of learning cooperation.

The ideal student who has mastered learning cooperation is not the child who gives correct answers and repeats what the teacher has said, but the learner who is able to question conventional opinions, to develop his or her own point of view, and to disagree with generally accepted beliefs. That is why the new wine of the learning activity cannot be poured into the old bottle of imitative cooperation, and first graders must be taught not only the new content, but also new methods of learning cooperation starting from the very first days of their school life (Tsukerman, Elizarova, Frumina, & Chudinova, 1995; Zuckerman, 1994a).

Cooperation with Peers as the Necessary Condition for Development of Reflective Abilities

Until now, we discussed teacher–student interaction as a prerequisite for initiating the child to the learning activity. Keeping in mind that ZPD is built through the interaction of a child with a knowledgeable partner, we might conclude that teacher–student interaction is both necessary and sufficient for child development. Is it, indeed?

General concepts necessitate reflection, whereas everyday concepts do not. One cannot adequately work with a general concept without considering the limits of its application, and one cannot acquire a general concept without consciously examining the boundary of one's own knowledge and understanding (Davydov, 1988). Everyday concepts and relevant skills can be acquired by imitating models. An essential condition for this type of learning is that an expert must present these models to a novice. However, the more knowledgeable partner both induces and limits the acquisition of general concepts (Slobodchikov & Tsukerman, 1992). At the very beginning of dealing with general concepts, when learning cooperation has not yet been established, students tend inevitably to slip into preschool forms of cooperation, especially imitation. Note that imitation does not include hypotheses and questions about the unknown or contradictory realities. The result is that the burden of reflection is shifted toward the adult. It was experimentally proved that to teach students to reflect on their methods and the causes of their failures and errors, the teacher must address a group of peers, rather than an individual child (Zuckerman, 1994b). In their initial interpsychological form, reflective actions with general concepts are distributed not between a child and an adult, but between an adult and a group of peers solving problems together (Rubtsov & Guzman, 1984).

Peer cooperation when mastering general concepts is constructed as the joint work of children on tasks that provoke different viewpoints or positions. That is why such cooperation is called *positional*. These tasks are usually aimed at resolving contradictions of students' opinions and/or cognitive conflicts (Perret-Clermont, 1980; Doise & Mugny, 1981). The overt exposition of the contradiction helps the participating students take different perspectives on the subject of discussion and to *decentrate* from their primary point of view and develop a new more sophisticated approach (Zuckerman, 1994b). At the first steps of teaching students to cooperate when solving these contradictory tasks, the teacher can assign participants to the roles corresponding to the different positions. When such a group attacks a task, each of its members, by playing a particular role, will probably work out his or her own point of view and then coordinate it with that of the others. The focus of learning cooperation is the moving borderline between children's knowledge and ignorance at each step of their studies. Learning cooperation with peers can be presented as a specific materialization of such a frontier, when the action or the suggestion of one student helps other partners to reflect on their own actions and beliefs.

The teacher organizes the learning interaction with peers in two complementary modes: (a) whole-class discussions and (b) small-group discussions. The latter is recognized as a hothouse, where the social skills of learning interaction germinate, grow, and mature in the most protected, unthreatening environment. A group of peers can reflectively draw their teacher into cooperation by suggesting the task, function, and role of the adult in the common work as an adviser and coordinator of children's points of view. Addressing the teacher in a reflective format, the students seek missing information, demonstrate that already mastered methods are not adequate for new problem tasks, and request that the teacher equip them with new methods. Or they suggest their own version of the problem solution and ask the teacher to help justify their hypotheses.

Educators have arrived at the necessity and profit of peer cooperation, collaboration, or communities of inquirers–learners from diverse theoretical perspectives, pursuing different practical goals. Yet in each of these cases, educators all recognize the importance of the joint work of a group of children in which an adult does not participate directly as a powerful educational tool to raise students to more meaningful, less infantile forms of learning from experts (Brown & Campione, 1994; Rogoff, 1994; Slavin, 1995; Wells, 1999). This experimental evidence on expanding independence of learners opposes one of the prevailing interpretations of Vygotskian doctrine. It is not only cooperation with a more advanced partner, but also cooperation with inexpert partners that contributes to the development of student's initiative in learning cooperation (Zuckerman, 1994b). The often-quoted words of Vygotsky about more capable peers as a resource of development have been refuted by research in cooperative learning (Forman & McPhail, 1993; Tudge, 1992). Wells (1999, p. 324) claims that

in tackling a difficult task as a group, although no member has expertise beyond his or her peers, the group as a whole, by working at the problem together, is able to construct a solution that none could have achieved alone. In other words, each is "forced to rise above himself" and, by building on the contributions of its individual members, the group collectively constructs an outcome that no single member envisaged at the outset of the collaboration.

The cooperation of equally inexperienced partners becomes the crucial proof of the *nonadditive nature of human interaction*, when the group result exceeds the sum of operations performed by all the participants. The result of cooperation of an expert and a novice is too often reduced to the input of the expert.

The novice who is willing to be taught and ready to plunge into new forms of cooperation with the teacher becomes the learner able to initiate learning cooperation with experts. This transfer manifests "the happy end" in the development of learning independence at the elementary school age. We suggest that the ability for self-learning or learning independence of elementary school children is present only in its interpsychological form, as the ability to teach oneself with the help of an expert. Further accomplishment toward learning independence proceeds in adolescence. For middle school students, the opportunity to work in the position of a teacher for a young student (learning cooperation in diverse age groups) is an efficient and rewarding route toward consummating their learning independence on the intrapsychological level.

THE DANGERS OF REFLECTION

> Thus conscience does make cowards of us all.
>
> (*Hamlet*, act 3, scene 1, line 83)

> For in much wisdom is much grief:
> And he that increaseth knowledge increaseth sorrow
>
> (Ecclesiastes, chapter 1, verse 18)

Both wise Ecclesiastes and Shakespeare through his hero, the most reflective celebrity of European literature, make one and the same claim: The ability for reflection is both human bondage and invaluable gift. Without reflection, we would never perceive pangs of conscience, permanent dissatisfaction and disagreement with oneself, uncertainty, and the problem of choice. Developing reflection is as dangerous as experimenting in nuclear physics and genetic engineering, with an outcome just as uncertain. For the conscience of an educator, developing reflection in children and adolescents is as painfully inevitable and unsolvable an issue as the everlasting, "To be or not to be?" To develop reflection in children or not? If yes, to what extent, and how to determine the critical permissible level? This set of questions primarily relates to moral values. Once the personal choice is made, it is time to pursue scientific research on the age potentials and limitations of development of reflective abilities: to elucidate ways to evoke and strengthen reflection, the methods to assess it, and, foremost, the means to confine reflection within safe limits.

CONCLUSION

"This student does not help me: he completely agrees with me." Twenty-five centuries ago, the great Chinese philosopher Confucius (552/551–479 b.c.) captured a dilemma of schooling that remains current today – how to develop educated, knowledgeable students who have mastered the cultural values of the past, yet are capable of overcoming the confines of cultural traditions by going beyond generally accepted solutions and frameworks to solve novel problems. In bygone years, these ambitions were considered appropriate only for the education of an intellectual elite; today they are important for everyone. Making these goals accessible to the majority has been the focus of 30 years of practical education according to the Elkonin–Davydov system, elaborated and developed within the Vygotskian paradigm.

What really distinguishes an authentic learner is not profound and extensive knowledge, nor a brilliant display of what one has learned. It is the ability and incentive to seek and find knowledge independently, to transcend the limits of one's own erudition and of established, stereotyped beliefs. Asking questions, formulating one's learning goal – such is the starting point of true learning, which has to begin no later than the first day of schooling. Only in this case will the majority of children, rather than only the elite group, become true learners.

The learning activity is aimed at mastering general concepts and reflection as an essential component of actions with these concepts. To be an agent of learning interaction means to be capable of independently (on one's own initiative) going beyond the limits of already achieved levels of knowledge, skills, understanding, and capacity for finding ways of acting in new situations. At initial stages of education, the primeval learning initiative takes the form of questions – hypotheses in which the child pinpoints contradictions between the ways of action she or he already knows and new problems that require new ways of acting. At the very onset of education, it is the teacher who structures the conditions for the child's actions and also designs situations that elicit the child's question–hypothesis. Later on, at a higher level of learning independence, the students themselves reveal the propensity to change the conditions for their action and to seek new ways of acting.

Children's learning initiative may be distinguished from nonlearning ones by the form in which experts are addressed. *The formula of the nonlearning activity* is, "I do not know. I cannot do it. Show me how." Thus, the child who recognizes the limits of his or her capacities leaves to the adult both the right and the obligation to be the agent of their joint activities – to discover the reasons for the child's difficulties, find the way to overcome them, and provide a model. *The formula of the learning activity* is altogether different: "I will be able to do it if/when I learn the following." In the latter case, the student recognizes and openly states the limits of his or her capacities and transcends these limits by suggesting a hypothesis about the missing method or bit of knowledge.

When the content of interaction presumes reflection (as in the case of the learning activity), the role of the teacher becomes ambivalent: A dominating pattern for sharing responsibilities with the expert could curb the child's capacity for mastering reflective actions. The child expects the expert to set goals, plans, and controls and to evaluate his or her zealous efforts to follow the expert's instructions and models. Therefore, the interaction with inexpert equals is necessary to release and develop reflective capacities in children. The class or the group of students, in fact, a collective agent of the learning activity, advances a whole cluster of possible hypotheses, evoking a learning discussion directed at verifying each hypothesis and seeking a new method of acting.

At present, we recognize three conditions that are necessary to draw forth the student's initiative in formulating a hypothesis:

1. A special *way of introducing the subject matter*: through the most general notions, which potentially include a conceptual system describing the given *subject matter*. By providing the student with a

general concept, educators seem to lift children up to a summit from which they can make out the possible routes for their further movements in investigating the subject. Outlining the potential prospects of the forthcoming learning gives the student greater freedom and initiative in setting educational goals.

2. A special nonimitative *way of interacting with an adult*. A student acting as the learner does not anticipate ready solutions or models from the teacher. The child is capable of initiating cooperation with the teacher, of pointing out what assistance the student needs when she or he has already formulated his/her hypothesis and does not as yet know how to verify it.

3. A special positional way of *interacting with the peers* ensured by joint work, which helps distribute the various points of view on the problem under discussion among the participants and helps coordinate the viewpoints produced by the group. The pattern of positional learning cooperation should stem from the context of the learning activity. That is why one of the conditions of educating learners is working out a system of problems that cannot, in principle, be solved individually and require a diversity of opinions in the class.

During the initial 2 or 3 years that children spend in school, learning activity exists only in its interpsychological form. It means that the class as a community of learners can generate all the components of the learning activity, from setting the goal to controlling and evaluating the final results, while the individual students do not as yet operate the learning activity as a whole. It is the task of the elementary school to build a community of learners that embraces all the children in the class. In middle school this initially joint learning activity becomes individualized, shaping the students who desire and dare to seek life-span expansion of their knowledge, skills, and abilities.

References

Amano, K. (1999). Improvement of schoolchildren's reading and writing ability through the formation of linguistic awareness. In Y. Engeström, R. Miettinen, & R.-L. Punamäki (Eds.), *Perspectives on activity theory* (pp. 183–205). Cambridge: Cambridge University Press.

Arievitch, I. M., & Stetsenko, A. (2000). The quality of cultural tools and cognitive development: Gal'perin's perspective and its implication. *Human Development, 43*, 69–92.

Bakhtin, M. M. (1981). *The dialogic imagination: Four essays by M.M. Bakhtin* (M. Holquist, Ed.). Austin: University of Texas Press.

Brown, A. L. (1992). Design experiments: Theoretical and methodological challenges in creating complex interventions in classroom settings. *Journal of the Learning Sciences, 2*, 141–178.

Brown, A. L., & Campione, J. C. (1994). Guided discovery in a community of learners. In K. McGilly (Ed.), *Classroom lessons: Integrating cognitive theory and classroom practice* (pp. 229–270). Cambridge, MA: MIT Press.

Carpay, J., & Van Oers, B. (1999). Didactic models and the problem of intertextuality and polyphony. In Y. Engeström, R. Miettinen, & R.-L. Punamäki (Eds.), *Perspectives on activity theory* (pp. 298–313). Cambridge: Cambridge University Press.

Davydov, V. V. (1988). *Problems of developmental teaching: The experience of theoretical and experimental psychological research.* [Published as a series of papers: The basic concepts of contemporary psychology. *Soviet Education, 30*(8), 15–43; Problems of the child's mental development. *Soviet Education, 30*(8), 44–97; Learning activity in the younger school age period. *Soviet Education, 30*(9), 3–47; The mental development of younger schoolchildren in the process of learning activity. *Soviet Education, 30*(9), 48–83 and (10), 3–36.]

Davydov, V. V. (1990). *Types of generalization in instruction: Logical and psychological problems in the structuring of school curricula.* Reston, VA: National Council of Teachers of Mathematics.

Davydov, V. V., & Markova, A. K. (1982/83). A concept of educational activity for schoolchildren. *Soviet Psychology, 21*(2), 50–76.

Doise, W., & Mugny, G. (1984). *The social development of the intellect.* Oxford: Pergamon Press.

Donaldson, M. C. (1978). *Children's mind.* New York: Norton.

Elkonin, D. B. (1972). Toward the problem of stages of the mental development of the child. *Soviet Psychology, 10*(3), 225–251.

Elkonin, D. B. (1988). How to teach children to read. In J. A. Downing (Ed.), Cognitive psychology and reading in the USSR. *Advances in Psychology, 49*, 387–426.

Forman, E. A., & McPhail, J. (1993). Vygotskian perspectives on children's collaborative problem-solving activities. In E. A. Forman, N. Minick, & C.A. Stone (Eds.), *Contexts for Learning* (pp. 213–229). New York : Oxford University Press.

Gal'perin, P. Y. (1992). Stage-by-stage formation as a method of psychological intervention. *Journal of Russian and East European Psychology, 30* (4), 60–80.

Hedegaard, M. (1990). How instruction influences children's concepts of evolution. *Mind, Culture, and Activity, 3,* 11–24.

Lave, J., & Wenger, E. (1990). *Situated learning: Legitimate peripheral participation.* Cambridge: Cambridge University Press.

Lehrer, R., & Schauble, L. (2000). Modeling in mathematics and science. In R. Glaser (Ed.), *Advances in instructional psychology.* Vol. 5. *Educational design and cognitive science* (pp. 101–159). Mahwah, NJ: Lawrence Erlbaum Associates.

Lompsher, J. (2000). Use of theory of developmental education in German school (to the 70th birthday of V. V. Davydov). *Voprosy Psikhologii, 4,* 97–106.

Perret-Clermont, A-N. (1980). *Social interaction and cognitive development in children.* London, New York: Academic Press.

Rogoff, B. (1994). Developing understanding of the idea of communities of learners. *Mind, Culture, and Activity, 1* (4): 209–229.

Rubtsov, V. V. (1981). The role of cooperation in the development of intelligence. *Soviet Psychology, 19*(4), 41–62.

Rubtsov, V. V., & Guzman, R.Y. (1984–1985). Psychological characteristics of the methods pupils use to organize joint activity in dealing with a school task. *Soviet Psychology, 23*(2), 65–84.

Schifter, D., & Fosnot, C.T. (1993). *Reconstructing mathematics education: Stories of teachers meeting the challenge of reform.* New York: Teachers College Press.

Siegal, M. (1991). *Knowing children: Experiments in conversation and cognition.* Howe, London: Lawrence Erlbaum Associates.

Slavin, R. E. (1995). *Cooperative learning: Theory, research, and practice.* Boston: Allyn & Bacon.

Slobodchikov, V. I., & Tsukerman, G. A. (1992). The genesis of reflective consciousness at early school age. *Journal of Russian and East European Psychology, 30*(1), 6–27.

Steen, L. A. (1990). Pattern. In L. A. Steen (Ed.), *On the shoulders of giants: New approaches to numeracy* (pp. 1–10). Washington, DC: National Academy Press.

Tsukerman, G. A., Elizarova, N. B., Frumina, M. I., & Chudinova, E. V. (1995). Learning cooperation in school lessons. *Journal of Russian and East European Psychology, 33*(1), 65–81.

Tudge, J. R. H. (1992). Processes and consequence of peer collaboration: A Vygotskian analysis. *Child Development, 63*, 1364–1379.

Vygotsky, L. S. (1963). Learning and mental development at school age. In B. Simon, & J. Simon (Eds.), *Educational Psychology in the U.S.S.R* (pp. 21–34).

Vygotsky, L. S. (1978). *Mind in society: The development of higher psychological processes* (M. Cole, V. John-Steiner, S. Scribner, & Souberman, Eds.) Cambridge, MA: Harvard University Press.

Waddington, C.H. (1957). *The strategy of the genes: A discussion of some aspects of theoretical biology.* New York: Macmillan.

Wells, G. (1999). *Dialogic inquiry: Towards a sociocultural practice and theory of education.* New York: Cambridge University Press.

Wertsch, J. V. (1991). *Voices of the mind: A sociocultural approach to mediated action.* Cambridge, MA: Harvard University Press.

Zuckerman, G.A. (1994a). A pilot study of a ten-day course in cooperative learning for Russian first-graders. *Elementary School Journal, 94*, 405–420.

Zuckerman, G.A. (1994b). The child's initiative in building up cooperation: the key to problems of children's independence. In J. J. F. ter Laak, P. G. Heymans, & A. Podol'skij (Eds.), *Developmental tasks: Towards a cultural analysis of human development* (pp. 125–140). Dordrecht: Kluwer Academic.

Zuckerman, G. (1997). The transition from preschool to school activity: A Vygotskian perspective. *Tijdschrift voor Ontwikkelingspsychologie, 23*, 205–229.

Zuckerman, G., Chudinova, E., & Khavkin, E. (1998). Inquiry as a pivotal element of knowledge acquisition within Vygotskian paradigm: Building a science curriculum for the elementary school. *Cognition and Instruction, 16*, 201–233.

10

Remediation Through Education

Sociocultural Theory and Children with Special Needs

Boris Gindis

In spite of the fact that the field of remedial (special) education and school psychology was the source and testing ground for many of Vygotsky's innovative ideas, this domain itself has remained in the shadow of his scientific heritage in the West. The publication of the second volume of Vygotsky's collected works, *The Fundamentals of Defectology* (Vygotsky, 1993), has created a knowledge base for the theoretical elaboration and practical implications of Vygotsky's ideas within the North American system of special education. In order for this volume to be of the utmost help, the following should be considered:

1. *Defectology* is the term that reflects the area of Vygotsky's research and practice that is relevant to contemporary special education and school psychology. The term itself sounds rather degrading. As once noted by McCagg (1989, p. 40), this term would not survive a scientific discussion in the Western world today because it carries too many negative connotations regarding individuals with a disability. Ironically, the negative undertone of the term itself is in no way present in the inspiring and positive attitude of Vygotsky writings. The word *defectologia* (or *defectology* in the English transliteration) literally means the study of defect. In Russia, for more than a century this term has referred to the study of children with disabilities and the methods used for their evaluation, education, and upbringing. To be technically precise, in the Russia of Vygotsky's time this term covered individuals who had the following disabilities: those with impaired hearing and deafness (*surdo-pedagogica*); the visually impaired and blind (*tiflo-pedagogica*); children with mental retardation (*oligophreno-pedagogica*); and speech- and language-impaired children (*logopedia*) (Petrovsky & Yaroshevsky, 1998, p. 364). Roughly, defectology covers the so-called low-incidence domain of special education in North America, embracing children with serious

organic or sensory impairment and severe developmental delays. As one can see, defectology does not include psychopathology, learning disability, or emotional disturbance as known in North America. Indeed, in Vygotsky's time and until the 1990s in post-Soviet Russia, the notions of learning disability, emotional disturbance, and behavioral disorder as educational classifications were not recognized. At the time, educational ideology influenced the formation of a specific nomenclature of handicapping conditions. It was based almost entirely on organic impairment of the central nervous system and severe sensory deficiency. Children with nonorganic, relatively mild learning disability were outside the realm of Russian defectology until very recently (Gindis, 1986; Sutton, 1988; Suddaby, 1988; Daniels & Lunt, 1993; Smith-Davis, 2000; Malofeev, 2001). That is why the attempt to explain the term *defectology* as a combination of "learning disability and abnormal child psychology," as done by the publisher of the second volume of Vygotsky's *Collected Works* (Vygotsky, 1993) or L. Berk and A. Winsler (1995), is not accurate (see more about the confusion in terminology in Gindis, 1994). Considering the fact that emotionally disturbed and learning-disabled students account for more than half of the special education population in the United States of America (Schulte, Osborn, & Erchul, 1998), the issue of the congruency of the Vygotskian defectology to contemporary special education in North America needs to be taken into consideration.

2. When trying to apply Vygotsky's ideas to contemporary special education, we have to realize that it may be difficult for special education professionals to understand Vygotsky's texts. This difficulty may be caused by many factors, including the differences in psychological and general humanistic traditions in American and Russian science (van der veer & Valsiner, 1991), the innovative nature of Vygotsky's writing, his nonacademic and sometimes unsystematic and contradictory ways of expressing ideas, his passionate argumentation with authors who are completely forgotten today, and obsolete terminological relics that sound harsh to our ears. No doubt Vygotsky belongs to the cohort of the so-called romantic scientists (as it was defined by his most prominent colleague, Alexander Luria, 1979) and his "romanticism" determined the style of his discourse. Vygotsky's writing is not an academic text in the traditional sense, but rather an inspirational humanistic appeal (in the very broad, almost biblical sense) to reconstruct social and cultural reality. In order to comprehend and fully appreciate his conceptualization in the field of special education, readers must understand the historical background of the development of his ideas and Vygotsky's dialectical mode of thinking (for more elaboration, see Kozulin, 1986, 1990; Van der Veer & Valsiner, 1991; Yaroshevsky, 1993). By no means does

The Fundamentals of Defectology contain a complete theoretical system, ready for application and free of contradictions or blind spots. It is an approach rather than a paradigm, a blueprint for further elaboration rather than a tested model.

3. There is one more factor to consider: The translated tome (Vygotsky, 1993) reflects the contents of volume 5 of the original Russian publication (Vygotsky, 1983). Since it was published, several important, previously unpublished papers relevant to special education and school psychology written by Vygotsky (in some cases in collaboration with A. Luria, B. Warshava, and other colleagues) have appeared in the Russian language. In 1995, in Moscow, the most complete collection of Vygotsky's writings on special education, school psychology (*pedology*) and related matters was published under the title *Problemy Defectologii* (Problems of defectology) (Vygotsky, 1995), increasing his legacy in the field of special education. In this chapter, I have made an attempt to incorporate writings by Vygotsky that are previously unknown in the West.

It is my goal to demonstrate that in spite of some obvious lack of congruence between the fields of Vygotsky's defectology and contemporary North American special education, Vygotsky's theoretical and methodological findings could serve as a powerful source of professional inspiration for current and coming generations of special education professionals. There are two perfectly compatible ways of applying Vygotsky's theories to contemporary special education: his general cultural–historical theory (known in the West as *cultural-historical activity theory* [CHAT]) and his special theory (less known outside Russia), which Vygotsky himself called the "theory of disontogenesis" (meaning the "theory of distorted development"). I will briefly outline the major tenets of Vygotsky's writings relevant to special education, discuss the remedial methodologies developed on this theoretical basis, and point to possible directions in advancing Vygotsky's legacy in remediation through education of children with special needs.

HANDICAP AS A SOCIAL AND CULTURAL PHENOMENON

Understanding the nature of a disability and the means of its remediation is the core of any system of special education. The uniqueness of Vygotsky's approach lies in his perception of disability as a sociocultural developmental phenomenon. Breaking away from the common assumption that disability is mainly biological in nature, Vygotsky's insight was that the principal problem of a disability is not the sensory or neurological impairment itself but its social implications: "Any physical handicap . . . not only alters the child's relationship with the world, but above all affects his interaction with people. Any organic defect is revealed as a social abnormality in behavior. It goes without saying that blindness and deafness per se are biological factors; however, teachers must deal not so much with these biological factors by themselves, but rather with their social consequences" (Vygotsky, 1983, p. 102). On the basis of a comprehensive review of many anthropological and historical studies, including reports by individuals with impaired sensorimotor functioning, Vygotsky argued that a disability is perceived as an "abnormality" only when and if it is introduced into the social context. Human eyes, ears, or limbs are not just physical facilities. Impairment of any of these functions " . . . leads to a restructuring of social relationships and to a displacement of all the systems of behavior" (Vygotsky, 1983, p. 63). Vygotsky observed that a handicap is psychologically different in diverse cultural and social environments: "The blindness of an American farmer's daughter, of a Ukrainian landowner's son, of a German duchess, of a Russian peasant, of a Swedish proletarian – these are all psychologically entirely different facts" (Vygotsky, 1983, p. 70).

Within the context of his paradigm of the social nature of disability, Vygotsky introduced the concepts of the primary disability and secondary disability and discussed the issue of their interaction. A *primary disability* is an organic impairment. A *secondary disability* refers to distortions of higher psychological functions due to social factors. A biological impairment prevents a child from mastering social–cultural means and ways and acquiring knowledge at a proper rate and in a socially acceptable form. It is the child's social milieu, however, that modifies his or her course of development and leads to distortions and delays. From this point of view, many symptoms such as behavioral infantilism or primitivism of emotional reactions in individuals with mental retardation are considered to be secondary handicapping conditions because they are acquired in the process of social interaction. If untreated, these conditions may effectively exacerbate the primary disability, as observed by Haywood (1989, p. 10): "The experience of being retarded makes one more so." Thus, a social–cultural reaction to a subtle neurological difficulty in mastering reading and writing skills often leads to what Gerald Cole described as a "learned learning disability" (Cole, 1987, p. 71). Expectations, attitudes, and the spiritual atmosphere created by society influence the access of a child with a disability to sociocultural knowledge, experiences, and opportunity to participate in shared or joint activities with peers. That is why Vygotsky so passionately insisted on changing negative societal attitudes toward individuals with disabilities. The search for positive capacities and qualitative characteristics in the upbringing (nurturing) of children with disabilities is the trademark of Vygotsky's approach. He called for the identification of a disability in a child from the perspective of strengths, not weaknesses. He described this approach as "positive differentiation." He contrasted it to what he sarcastically labeled as an "arithmetical concept of handicap" (Vygotsky, 1993, p. 30), that is, viewing of a child with disability as the sum of his or her negative characteristics. He suggested, for example, that special education teachers identify the levels of overall independence and need for support rather than levels of feeblemindedness in children with mental retardation (Vygotsky, 1995, p. 114). It is worthwhile noting that 60 years later, the American Association on Mental Retardation (AAMR) employed this exact approach in their newest manual on terminology and classification (AAMR, 1992).

In the essay "Defect and Compensation," Vygotsky (1993, pp. 52–64) wrote about the "two-sided nature" of a handicap: the underdevelopment or absence of the functions related to an organic defect and formation of an adaptive–compensatory mechanism. He stated that the most efficient compensation for the loss or weakness of natural functions could be achieved through the development of the higher psychological functions. Paradoxically, whereas what may be impaired are the natural processes (visual, auditory, kinesthetic), the objects of rehabilitation are the cultural processes of abstract reasoning, logical memory, voluntary attention, and goal-directed behavior. Vygotsky pointed to the limitations of traditional sensorimotor training. He said that pure biological compensation (e.g., superior hearing in the individuals who are blind) has been the exception rather than the rule, whereas the domain of higher psychological functions has no limit. "Training sharpness of hearing in a blind person has natural limitations; compensation through the mightiness of the mind (imagination, reasoning, memorization, etc.) has virtually no limits" (Vygotsky, 1983, p. 212). Vygotsky wrote that the usefulness of compensatory strategies (timeliness and appropriateness of the remedial methodology used) may be relatively free of the severity or type of the child's disability. "Cultural development is the main area for compensation of deficiency when further organic development is impossible; in this respect, the path of cultural development is unlimited" (Vygotsky, 1993, p. 169). One of the most outstanding confirmations of this rather bold statement was the accomplishment of a Russian special educator and psychologist, A. Meshcheriakov, working within Vygotsky's paradigm, with deaf–mute–blind children (Meshcheriakov, 1979; Chulkov, Lubovsky, & Martsinovskaia, 1990).

HANDICAP IN THE DEVELOPMENTAL PROSPECTIVE

Vygotsky emphasized the dynamic nature of disability and argued that constant change in the structure and content of a disability takes place during development and under the influence of education and remediation. He insisted that his basic principles of child development are fully applicable to children with disabilities. According to Vygotsky, these principles include internalization of external cultural activities into internal psychological processes. Development in handicapped children as well as in their nondisabled peers is not a straight path of quantitative growth and accumulation. It is a series of qualitative, dialectic transformations; a complex process of integration and disintegration, gains and losses. The essence and uniqueness of human development reside in its mediation by physical (material) instruments and social signs–language (for more elaboration, see Kozulin, this volume).

Expanding his ideas further, Vygotsky discusses two classes of psychological functions. They are *lower* or natural, that is, the biological predisposition of the child's development, and *higher* or cultural, specifically human functions that appear gradually in the course of the transformation of natural functions through mediated activity and psychological tools. For an extensive review and critique of this conceptualization, see Bruner (1987), Kozulin (1990), and van der Veer and Valsiner (1991). According to Vygotsky's view, progressive divergence in social and natural development leads to social deprivation as society's response to the child's organic impairment. This, in turn, adversely affects the whole developmental process and leads to the emergence of delays and deficiencies, the so-called secondary handicapping conditions, as well as compensatory ways of coping. These ideas constitute the essence of Vygotsky's theory of disontogenesis (Bein, Vlasova, Levina, Morozova, & Shif, 1993). Elaborating on his paradigms of the natural and cultural lines of development, Vygotsky clearly differentiated development of children with neurological (organically based) or severe sensory or physical impairment from that of those who were intact neurologically, physically, and sensorially but who had endured severe cultural deprivation and educational neglect. Using the unfortunate terminology of his time, Vygotsky called the first group *defectives* and the second group *primitives* (using Feuerstein's [1997] apt definition, the latest category is retarded performers rather than retarded individuals). Both groups may achieve similar results academically, on psychological tests or in the domain of adaptive behavior and social skills, but the nature of their needs and the remedies to be used differ. Under the rubric *child–primitive*, in fact, Vygotsky described a psychological profile of students who today constitute a significant proportion of children with learning disability due to early childhood sociocultural deprivation, institutionalization, or harmful environmental conditions (war, poverty, displacement). For these students learning disability means inability to use age-appropriate psychological tools such as cognitive language (language as a means of reasoning, a tool of literacy) and to benefit from a mainstreamed educational environment. As a result of turbulent revolutionary times, thousands of "child-primitives" were roaming Russia when Vygotsky started his career as a defectologist. For him and his collaborators, evaluation and remediation of these children became a significant part of their research and practical everyday work. In the West, similar problems appeared about a half-century later with an influx of immigrants from the third world, child victims of regional conflicts, and, recently, internationally adopted post-institutionalized children (Gindis, 1998).

HANDICAP AS A QUALITATIVELY SPECIFIC WAY OF DEVELOPMENT

Vygotsky observed that traditionally, a child with a disability had been considered to be an either underdeveloped or developmentally delayed (e.g., in the case of mental retardation) individual or a child lacking a sensory organ (in the case of sensory impairment). In other words, the difference between a child with a disability and his or her nondisabled peers was considered to be only quantitative. Vygotsky disagreed. He insisted that the development of individuals with disabilities is not a slowed or missing variation of normal development: "A child whose development is impeded by a defect is not simply a child less developed than his peers but is a child who has developed differently" (Vygotsky, 1993, p. 30). The development of a child with a disability has major qualitative differences in the means and ways of his or her internalization of culture. As mentioned earlier, in Vygotsky's view, the core of a disabled child's development is the divergence between his or her natural and social paths of development. Vygotsky pointed to two major differences in the development of a child with a disability in comparison with that of his typically developing peers. They are the formation of compensatory strategies (mechanisms) and the emergence of social complications due to the disability (*secondary defect* in his terminology). No effective remediation is possible without an understanding of these qualitative differences. Vygotsky suggested that in the future, science would be able to create a disability-specific profile of the discrepancy between the "natural" and "social" courses of development as the most important characteristic in the psychological growth of the child with a particular disability. As the milestones of this profile, he listed the dynamic and forms of socialization, appropriation of psychological tools, and formation and use of compensatory strategies (Vygotsky, 1993, pp. 110–122). Compensatory strategies are by no means mechanical substitutions of impaired functions. Rather they are the product of the child's individuality, personal experiences, and what Vygotsky called "the social situation of development" (see Mahn and Karpov, chapter 7, this volume). Compensatory strategies are aimed at mastering psychological tools and using them to acquire cultural forms of behavior. When the direct way of acquiring psychological tools is blocked (e.g., in the case of blindness), compensatory strategies offer an indirect path to the same goal of cultural development. Creation of disability-specific compensatory strategies was Vygotsky's vision of the future of remedial education.

The notion of a "disability-specific psychoeducational profile" has been elaborated by a number of Vygotsky's followers in Russia. One such approach is offered by A. Venger (1994), who suggested considering three strata or components in disability. The first is composed of different, individual characteristics of the child, of which his or her disability is one such characteristic. The second layer consists of those individual characteristics that are disability-specific and disability-dependent. The third stratum describes how individual and disability-specific distinctiveness determine the child's social interaction. Venger stresses that the content of social and cultural interaction influences not only the third stratum but the two previous strata as well, creating a reciprocal and dynamic process. Another approach was suggested by Lubovsky (1989) and later elaborated by Belopolskaya and Lubovsky (1992). The base of this model is the relationship between the primary and secondary deficits, as spelled out in Vygotsky's theory of disontogenesis. The authors point to a complex and dialectic interrelationship between primary and secondary disabilities. The same primary defect (organic impairment) may lead to different secondary disabilities, and different primary defects may cause the same secondary disability. Lubovsky suggested a rather elaborate and complex schema of a disability profile (in relation to mentally retarded students) that includes cognitive, emotional, and motivational components. Lubovsky made an interesting and productive attempt to connect his profile with an assessment called "the teaching/learning experiment" that is one of the forms of dynamic assessment (for a more detailed discussion of Lubovsky's experiments, see Lidz and Gindis, this volume).

HANDICAP AND PSYCHOEDUCATIONAL ASSESSMENT

The assessment of children with handicapping conditions has been a socially and politically sensitive and emotionally charged issue for a long time. Dissatisfaction with the existing arsenal of evaluation tools and procedures has spurred the search for more useful alternatives (Haywood & Tzuriel, 1992). One of the most promising options is called *dynamic assessment*, Vygotsky is rightfully considered the "founding father" of this approach (Minick, 1987; Lidz, 1995).

Vygotsky noted that standardized intelligence tests inappropriately equalize natural and cultural processes. They are, therefore, unable to differentiate impaired functioning that can be due to cultural deprivation, the result of organic damage, or a combination of both. In the essay "The Difficult Child," Vygotsky (1993, pp. 139–149) described the case of a bilingual Tatar girl (a nation within the Russian Federation – B.G.) who was diagnosed as having mental retardation. In fact, her poor performance on standardized tests was due to her social and cultural deprivation and related to her limited mastery of both Russian and her native language. Vygotsky showed that, as a result, she had not attained the level of acculturation expected at her age. Her overall development was inhibited, and, according to an intelligence test, she appeared to have mental retardation. The most appropriate evaluation tool in this case should have been an assessment that, as Vygotsky pointed out, would concentrate on mental processing and certain qualitative metacognitive indicators. Examples are the cognitive strategies employed by the child, the type and character of mistakes, the ability to benefit from the help provided by the examiner, and emotional reactions to success and failure (Vygotsky, 1995, p. 114).

Although Vygotsky had no chance to elaborate on specific assessment operations, his notion of a "zone of proximal development" has formed the foundation of a group of testing procedures now commonly recognized as dynamic assessment (DA). This is an interactive procedure that follows a test–intervene–teach–retest format, focusing on the cognitive processes and metacognitive characteristics of a child. Through an analysis of a child's pretest and posttest performance after test-embedded teaching intervention, an evaluator can derive important information about the child's cognitive modifiability, his or her responsiveness to an adult's mediation, and his or her amenability to instruction and guidance. Therefore, the DA provides information not readily available through standardized testing that is crucial for effective remediation, the ultimate goal of the assessment (Haywood, Brown, & Wingenfeld, 1990). In the last two decades, we have witnessed an accelerating shift from standardized testing of children with handicapping conditions to dynamic assessment of their learning potential. A group of prominent researchers in different countries (see Lidz & Elliot, 2000) are productively developing different aspects of DA in its application to individuals with different disabilities. Nevertheless, as of now, DA is still mostly a procedure that is supplementary to traditional assessment in the domain of special education. To the best of this writer's knowledge, Russia and Israel are the only countries where different forms of dynamic assessment are the mainstreamed conventional procedures in special education and school psychology. One can find well-elaborated, elegant, and effective dynamic assessment procedures for children of different ages and diverse handicapping conditions in works by R. Feuerstein and associates (1980, 1997), D. Tzuriel (2001), A. Ivanova (1976), V. Lubovsky (1990), and E. Strebeleva (2000). (For more discussion of this subject, see Lidz and Gindis, this volume.)

REHABILITATION, COMPENSATION, AND REMEDIATION FROM A SOCIOCULTURAL PERSPECTIVE

In Vygotsky's view, the specificity of remedial education lies in addressing the secondary disability, that is, in countering the negative social consequences of the primary disability. Vygotsky believed that physical and mental impairment could be overcome by creating alternative but essentially equivalent roads for cultural development. Through acquiring the psychological tools, a disabled child transforms his or her natural abilities into higher mental abilities, as do his or her nondisabled peers.

The concept of the internalization of psychological tools has particular importance for remediation. Specifically, in Vygotsky's defectology, this notion lies in the dialectic relationship between means (sign, psychological tool) and content (meaning). Disability prevents the child from acquiring psychological tools similar to those of his or her nondisabled peers. A child with disability requires different methods of teaching and learning for his or her appropriation of psychological tools. The sociocultural meaning, however, remains the same and is to be delivered via alternative means (modified signs, specialized psychological tools). Vygotsky wrote, "Different symbolic systems correspond to one and the same content of education.... Meaning is more important than the sign. Let us change signs but retain meaning" (Vygotsky, 1983, p. 54). In Vygotsky's analysis, the essence of any remedial educational program is in the process of substituting signs while retaining the meaning of the internalization.

The issue of specificity of psychological tools for remediation was the center of Vygotsky's attention. He pointed out that humankind has already developed different means (e.g., Braille, sign language, lip-reading, and finger-spelling) to accommodate the unique means of acculturation of a child with a disability by acquiring different symbolic systems (psychological tools). Continuing to develop specific psychological tools to address special needs was the crux of Vygotsky's message. This appeal was made well before the era of sophisticated electronic gadgets and computers! Since Vygotsky's time, many psychological tools designed for remediation have been put into practice. One well-known contemporary system of psychological tools designed specifically for cognitive remediation is Feuerstein's Instrumental Enrichment procedure. It includes 14 different booklets of paper-and-pencil activities (called *instruments*) related to such cognitive operations and skills as comparison, categorization, spatial orientation, and syllogistic reasoning (Feuerstein, Rand, Hoffman, & Miller, 1980).

The process of appropriation of psychological tools is determined by the nature of the disability and correlated modifications of teaching methods. For example, the concept of spontaneous and scientific notions in developing higher forms of reasoning (see Karpov, chapter 3, this volume) has its specificity in the domain of educational remediation. Everyday (spontaneous) concepts appear as a result of the child's thinking about his or her immediate experience. Usually these concepts are unsystematic and contextual. "Scientific" concepts (not necessarily science-related) are the result of specialized learning activity based on formal logic and are decontextual. In the course of typical development there are a particular dialectical dynamic and interaction between these two kinds of notions, as analyzed by Vygotsky (1987, pp. 167–240). In the case of children with handicapping conditions (in particular, those with severe sensory impairments), this relationship is atypical. Spontaneous notions are limited and may be distorted (e.g., in the case of deaf–blind–mute children). In this situation, the meaning and value of scientific notions are increased tremendously, and the teaching methodology must be modified significantly in comparison with teaching those for whom spontaneous concepts are ordinary facts of their daily lives. Scientific concept formation is disability-specific, as shown in the works of Rubinstein (1979), Akhutina (1997), and Lurie and Kozulin (1998).

One of the most impressive accomplishments in this respect is the methodology developed by the Russian psychologist Alexander Meshcheryakov for blind–deaf–mute children (Meshcheryakov, 1979; Chulkov et al., 1990). It is based on Vygotsky's statement that "the development of scientific concepts begins with verbal definition" (Vygotsky, 1987, p. 168). Meshcheryakov introduced the notion of *primary gesture* (as an alternative psychological tool for a child who cannot speak, see, and hear). The *primary gesture* originates from the movements that make up the shared–joint activity of the handicapped child and his/her teacher. At first, it may just reproduce physical activity (e.g., to move the hands upwards from knees to waist as part of a "putting on trousers" movement). Later, the primary gesture is simplified and decontextualized by acquiring symbolic meaning (the same abbreviated gesture now means "We are going outside"). Finally, it is linked to a dactylic language that makes it possible "to form generalized images that reflect the facts of real life correctly and in depth" (Meshcheryakov, 1979, p. 189).

Similarly, the concept of mediated learning has its specificity in the field of remedial education. Nonmediated learning (that is, immediate interaction with the environment through independent observation, trials, contacts, probing, and testing) is limited and distorted for a disabled child. Therefore, mediated learning that is done through an adult who selects, modifies, and interprets environmental stimuli has a special implication for a disabled child. (Do "remediation" and "mediation" have a deeper connection than simply similar graphic representation?) Remediation as well as development of higher psychological function in a disabled child depend upon the quality and quantity of mediating activity personalized in a teacher and in the structure and organization of the learning environment. The general principles of mediation are the same for disabled and nonhandicapped students. A human mediator makes learning intentional (turning it into a learning activity; see Zuckerman, this volume), teaching strategies and principles entrenched in learning material rather than just facts and notions, and providing transfer of these cognitive strategies and principles to new material and new situations in different content areas and subjects. Since not every act of learning is developmental in nature (that is, one that leads to the development of cognitive and emotional faculties), not every act of learning is remedial in nature. To become remedial, learning activity has to transform and advance the learner's psychological functions. As stated by Kozulin and Presseisen (1995, p. 74), a remedial "learning task, when properly constructed, always reflects the general principle of the formation and transformation of the learning subject."

The unity of psychological tools and mediating learning experience plays an exceptional role in remedial education. As observed by Kozulin (this volume), symbolic tools have a rich educational potential, but they remain ineffective if there is no human mediator to facilitate their appropriation by the learner. By the same token, human mediation that does not involve sophisticated symbolic tools would not help the learner to master more complex forms of reasoning and problem solving. It is the unity of psychological tools and teaching based on "mediated learning" that makes remediation effectual.

"INTEGRATION BASED ON POSITIVE DIFFERENTIATION" AS THE FUTURE DESIGN FOR SPECIAL EDUCATION

As Kozulin (this volume, p. 15) noted, Vygotsky often offered answers to questions posed well after his time. One amazing piece of evidence is Vygotsky's writing on the subject of inclusion, an issue that was not even on the agenda of his contemporaries! It is difficult to explain the passion with which Vygotsky expressed his thoughts on this subject. The whole idea of inclusion was outside the mindset of both professionals in the field and the public at large (McCagg, 1989). A reader of volume 2 of his *Collected Works* (Vygotsky, 1993) may be somewhat confused that Vygotsky was equally critical of what he called the "unlawful segregation" of the disabled and the lack of differentiated educational environments for children with special needs. Vygotsky worked several years to develop his vision for the future model of special education that can be called, using his own words, "integration based on positive differentiation" (Vygotsky, 1995, pp. 114, 167).

There is a philosophical and practical distinction between the concepts of mainstreaming and inclusion in contemporary special education in North America. Unfortunately, the translators of volume 2 of Vygotsky's texts (Vygotsky, 1993) use both terms interchangeably, confusing a practitioner in the field who may wonder what was actually meant. The concept of *mainstreaming* is part of a traditional pattern of special education service delivery. It means the selective placement of special education students in general education classes based on their demonstrated ability to function on the same level as the majority of students in that classroom. Usually, mainstreaming is a procedure for declassification of a child with handicapping conditions when his or her disability has been compensated or remediated to the extent that it does not prevent the child from benefiting from a regular (mainstreamed) curriculum (Stainback, Stainback, & Forest, 1989).

Inclusion as an educational concept negates special education (with the exception of a small number of cases of severe sensory–physical–mental disability) as a segregated placement. The proponents of this approach believe that a child with a handicap belongs in general education with support services delivered to the child rather than moving the child to the services. Generally, advocates of inclusion accept the necessity of a partial or temporal partition from a general education class if the need arises. However, within the inclusion movement there is a radical trend called *full inclusion* that insists that all students, regardless of the severity of the handicapping condition, be placed in a regular classroom or program full-time, with all services delivered to the child in that setting (Fuchs & Fuchs, 1994).

It is true that in the early stages of his career as a researcher and an educational administrator, Vygotsky did call for "normalization through inclusion" of all children with disabilities, sometimes to the extreme. Vygotsky argued against what he called "social prejudices against the handicapped" (Vygotsky, 1993, pp. 65–76). This appeal found a deaf ear in Russia (McCagg, 1989) but was fully appreciated by a broad audience in the United States of America half a century later (Newman & Holzman, 1993). Many aspects of his earlier writing had a lot in common with what is now called the *full inclusion model* or *regular classroom initiative*, as described in Lipsky and Gartner (1996). Vygotsky's criticism of the "negative model of special education" as a combination of lowered expectations, a watered-down curriculum, and social isolation sounds very much up to date and is enthusiastically cited by the proponents of full inclusion (Fuchs & Fuchs, 1994).

On the other hand, in his later works Vygotsky expressed the firm conviction that only a truly differentiated learning environment can fully develop the higher psychological functions and overall personality of a child with a disability. Special education should be provided in a specially designed setting where the entire staff is able to serve the individual needs of a child with a disability exclusively. It should be a special system that employs its own specific methodologies because students with disabilities require modified and alternative educational methods of teaching. Students with disabilities need specially trained teachers, a differentiated curriculum, special technological auxiliary means, and simply more time to learn. How realistically can these demands be met in a regular classroom situation? These arguments are used by the proponents of the current (segregated) system of special education in contemporary Russia (Knox & Stevens, 1993; Belopolskaya & Grebennikova, 1997; Smith-Davis, 2000) and the opponents of "full inclusion" in the United States (Kauffman & Hallahan, 1995).

This obvious contradiction in Vygotsky's position is inherent in the controversy over the very notion of inclusion: how to address special needs in a general school environment, how to integrate specialized and generalized teaching methodologies, how to escape separation in a "closed society" and attend to exceptional individual demands at the same time (for more on this topic see Kauffman & Hallahan, 1995). Summarizing Vygotsky's view on this matter, one can observe that in the process of developing his approach, Vygotsky moved from an understanding of inclusion as a predominantly geographical (being in the same classroom) and temporal (being in the same classroom at the same time) concept to an essentially sociocultural concept of integration. It is important to see that although he suggested physical separation in specialized day or boarding schools, real integration in his view is achieved through similar curriculum content (by providing extra time, adapting specific methods of teaching, and providing additional adult assistance) and the appropriation of culturally meaningful psychological tools. He continued to insist on geographical and temporal proximity in what he called "political and social activity" (see, for example, Vygotsky, 1995, pp. 462–467). This is similar to what we now identify as social mainstreaming. These "nonacademic activities," such as assemblies, gym, lunchtime, playground, music, and art, provide an opportunity for social learning not only for children with handicapping conditions but also for their nondisabled peers (Kauffman & Hallahan, 1995). Vygotsky's main premise was that a child with a disability must be accommodated with experiences and opportunities that are as close as possible to the mainstreamed situation, but not at the expense of "positive differentiation." This should be based on a child's potential rather than on his or her current limitations. It was his firm belief that the future of remedial education lies in employing its specific methods to achieve mainstreamed social and cultural goals. Vygotsky's idea of integration of children with disabilities into the social and cultural life of their communities as a condition of effective rehabilitation and compensation was never realized in his native country, Russia (Lubovsky, 1996; Smith-Davis, 2000) but was enthusiastically embraced in North America in the last quarter of the 20th century.

SOCIOCULTURAL THEORY AND THE PRACTICE IN CONTEMPORARY SPECIAL EDUCATION

Vygotsky's ideas have influenced, directly and indirectly, at least two domains of contemporary remedial education worldwide. One includes the curricula and methods of teaching in the disability-specific domains. A detailed discussion of this influence is definitely beyond the scope of this chapter; interested readers can find a comprehensive account of the Vygotsky-inspired arsenal of innovative remedial methods in the education of deaf students in Knox and Kozulin (1989), Jamieson (1994), Berk and Winsler (1995), and Zaittseva, Pursglove, and Gregory (1999). Vygotsky's theory-based method of raising multiply handicapped children (e.g., mute–deaf–blind), developed in Russia by Meshcharyakov and his colleagues, received laudatory reviews worldwide (Bakhurst & Padden, 1991). The specific textbooks, modified curricula, and adapted teaching material developed by the Institute of Corrective Pedagogy in Moscow (formerly the famous Institute of Defectology, founded by Vygotsky in 1926) for mentally retarded pupils are examples of effective specialized "psychological tools" presented via mediational techniques (Vlasova, 1984; Vlasova, Lubovsky, & Tsypina, 1984; Lebedinski, 1985; Strebeleva, 2000; Almanah ICP, 2000–2002: electronic version is available at *www.ise.iip.net/almanah*).

The second domain is a wide range of remedial methodologies that are directed to "high incidence" disabilities (e.g., reading disability) and are based on or inspired by Vygotsky's ideas. Some of these remedial systems explicitly claim Vygotsky's or neo-Vygotskian theories as the basis or major source. *The Reading Enhancement Program* developed in Canada by J. P. Das and his colleagues (Das & Kendrick, 1997) may serve as an example. This remedial technology is based on the PASS theory (Das, Naglieri, & Kirby, 1994) (the acronym *PASS* stands for planning, attention, simultaneous, successive). The program employs two key Vygotskian concepts: appropriation of psychological tools and social–cultural mediation. It consists of two parts, the global cognitive process training unit, which provides students with a guided opportunity to internalize cognitive strategies, and the bridge unit, which offers training in specific strategies relevant to reading and writing. Das and his collaborators presented the PASS theory as an intermediate-level conceptualization that connects Vygotsky's theory with remedial practice. (For a more detailed review of this remedial methodology, see Gindis, 1996.)

Other remedial techniques were empirically based findings or "best practices" that, at a certain point in their development, were reconceptualized from Vygotsky's or neo-Vygotskian theoretical perspectives. Two characteristic models are the *Reading Recovery* methodology (Clay & Cazden, 1990) and the *Instructional Conversation* method in its application in special education settings (Rueda, Goldenberg, & Gallimore, 1992; Echevarria & McDonough, 1993). Both approaches undertook the practicable development of such Vygotskian concepts as mediation internalization of symbolic systems, and cognitive education as specially organized learning activities.

A distinct group of cognitive remediation methods with the most operational, detailed, and thoroughly approbated techniques were developed in Israel by Feuerstein and his collaborators (Feuerstein et al., 1980; 1997). It is known that, historically, *Mediated Learning Experience (MLE)* theory and *Instrumental Enrichment (IE)* practice emerged independently from Vygotsky's theory (Presseisen & Kozulin, 1994). Recently, Kozulin and his collaborators have started a challenging endeavor to integrate MLE and IE with Vygotsky's and neo-Vygotskian theoretical paradigms in order to create a broader base for comprehensive remedial cognitive programs (Kozulin, 1998).

One of the most representative applications of Vygotskian theory in the practice of special education is *Bright Start: Cognitive Curriculum for Young Children* (Haywood, Brooks, & Burns, 1992). Although the theoretical basis of *Bright Start* includes components of different paradigms (e.g., Haywood's transactional conceptualization, Piaget's concrete operational stage, and Feuerstein's MLE), Vygotsky's influence is the most pronounced. Indeed, the mediation of psychological tools in the context of the zone of proximal development is the essence and major distinguishing feature of the program. Moreover, although different theories contributed to the creation of *Bright Start*, understanding and practical implementation are more efficiently accomplished from a Vygotskian perspective (H. C. Haywood, personal communication, January 2002). Let us consider this methodology more closely.

Bright Start is a program of cognitive education and remediation for preschool and primary grade children. This methodology is designed for use with children who may have pervasive developmental disorders as well as those at high risk of learning failure in the primary grades as a result of severe deprivation and educational neglect in early childhood (e.g., internationally adopted postinstitutionalized children). The specific goals of *Bright Start* include enhancing the development of basic cognitive processes and thinking skills, developing task-intrinsic motivation, and increasing learning effectiveness and readiness for school leaning. The most distinctive characteristics of *Bright Start* are the "mediational teaching style" and a "cognitive-mediational behavior management system" (Haywood, 1993). *Mediational teaching style* consists of methods of mediating the children's basic thinking skills, generalizing meanings of the children's own experiences, and managing their metacognitive processes. Thus, during structured activities, teachers try to elicit evidence of systematic thinking ("Give me a reason why we should look carefully at this picture before describing it"), use process-oriented questioning ("Why do you think it is better to count this way?"), and accept the children's responses while challenging their answers and requiring justification ("That is a correct answer, but can you tell me why it is correct?"). As one can see, the type of questions asked in process-oriented lessons differs from the type of questions asked in content-oriented lessons. By using a mediational teaching style the teachers facilitate the children's understanding of the generalized meaning of their experiences, efficient strategies of gathering information and its elaboration, systematic thinking processes, and accurate communication strategies. *Cognitive-mediational behavior management* refers to applying the mediation principles to behavior problems that arise either in organized teaching sessions or in spontaneous social interactions among children. The teacher might encourage children to think again about a reaction before they actually respond, think about reasons or motives for behavior (theirs and others), suggest alternative responses, weigh advantages, and disadvantages and mentally represent reactions of others to their choices.

Seven cognitive instructional units, used with children in small groups, constitute the core of the program:

1. Self-Regulation: The teacher presents activities that deal with cues that help monitor fast and slow body movements. The teacher might present a picture (or a rhythm on a small drum) and ask the children to walk slowly or quickly in response to the picture (or the rhythm). Later on, the teacher presents symbols and abstract cues that tell children how to self-regulate their behavior. After each activity, the teacher tries to elicit meaningful examples of the cognitive principle learned based on the children's experiences.

2. Number Concepts: The teacher introduces basic number concepts – amounts, numbers, ordinal relations, and conservation. Starting with one-to-one correspondence, children learn concepts that help them respond to events in a quantitative way.

3. Comparison: The teacher introduces the concept of similarities and differences in a systematic way. Children learn to define and make comparisons based on characteristics such as size, shape, and color.

4. Role Taking: This activity develops the ability to take different perspectives, first on the physical, then on the social level. Children learn to consider other people's feelings and viewpoints.

5. Classification: The process develops the function of classifying across three dimensions – color, size, and shape – then progresses into representational classification.

6. Sequence and Pattern: Children learn to identify items within classes according to their serial position. The lessons focus on number and pattern progression and finding of patterns in groups of stimuli.

7. Letter–Shape Concepts: Children learn to identify and classify objects and events according to certain prominent characteristics. This will be crucial to learning of the letters of the alphabet.

As one can see, the educational units address fundamental aspects of preschool children's cognitive functioning and are psychological tools in the most genuine Vygotskian sense. Each lesson of these units is taught in small groups (from two to six children) or individually for a period of 20 to 40 minutes daily. There is an optional follow-up component performed by parents at home; it is based on the special Parents' Manual. The effectiveness of Bright Start as a remedial program has been evaluated repeatedly in different countries since the early 1990s. The overall outcome of these studies is highly positive, showing significant effects on cognitive development itself, self-regulation of motor behavior and metacognitive operations, intrinsic motivation, and subsequent school achievement.

The quality and quantity of mediation are the key factors in the success of the program (Tzuriel, Kaniel, Kanner, & Haywood, 1999; Tzuriel, 2001).

CONCLUSION

Lev S. Vygotsky formulated a theoretical framework for a comprehensive, inclusive, and humanistic practice of special education. The timeliness and fruitfulness of many of Vygotsky's theoretical concepts in the domain of special education have been substantiated by empirical data accumulated over half a century since his death. Scientific validation and actual implementation of others are still pending. Future development of Vygotsky's theory and practice in special education may include the following:

1. Developing further the theory of disontegenesis, including the dialectic relationship between primary and secondary handicapping conditions, a disability-specific "zone of proximal development," and the concept of inclusion, and studying the internalization of external cultural activities into internal processes via psychological tools and mediated learning in relation to high- and low-incidence disabilities.
2. Creating disability-specific psychoeducational profiles of different handicapping conditions along with constructing disability-specific sets of psychological tools and disability-specific mediation techniques.
3. Perfecting the dynamic assessment of children with handicapping conditions and effectively connecting it with remedial methodologies.

Vygotsky's appeal to consider psychoeducational assessment and methods of teaching as a united social–cultural process is finding acceptance with thousands of professionals throughout the world. His formulation of a remedial process, integration to the fullest extent possible in social–cultural interaction, provision of appropriate and effective "psychological tools," and ensuring of scaffolded (mediated) learning experience creates a new perspective for socialization, acculturation, and development of children with special needs. Vygotsky's socially, culturally, and developmentally oriented theory has the potential to unify, restructure, and promote special and remedial education as a science, profession, and social institution. Vygotsky's scientific legacy maps a course to follow for special education in the 21st century.

References

AAMR (1992). *Mental retardation: Definition, classification, and systems of supports* (9th ed.). Washington, DC: American Association on Mental Retardation.

Akhutina, T. V. (1997). The remediation of executive functions in children with cognitive disorders: The Vygotsky-Luria neuropsychological approach. *Journal of Intellectual Disability Research, 41*(pt. 2), 144–151.

ALMANAH (2000-2002). Moscow: Institute of Corrective Pedagogy. Available at: www.ise.iip.net/almanah

Bakhurst, D., & Padden, C. (1991). The Meshcheryakov experiment: Soviet work on the education of blind/deaf children. *Learning and Instruction, 1*, 201–215.

Bein, E. S., Vlasova, T. A., Levina, R. E., Morozova, N. G., & Shif, Z. I. (1993). Afterword. In *The collected works of L. S. Vygotsky*. Vol. 2. *The fundamentals of defectology (abnormal psychology and learning disabilities)*, pp. 302–314. (Jane E. Knox and Carol B. Stevens, Trans.) (R. W. Rieber and A. S. Carton, Eds.). New York: Plenum Press.

Belopolskaya, N. L., & Grebennikova, N. V. (1997). Neuropsychology and psychological diagnosis of abnormal development. In E. L. Grigorenko, P. M. Ruzgis, & R. J. Sternberg (Eds.), *Russian psychology: Past, present, and future* (pp. 155–179). Commack, NY: Nova Academic Press.

Belopolskaya, N. L., & Lubovsky, V. I. (1992). Differentsial'no-psikhologicheskaia diagnostika deteei s intellektual'noi nedastatochnost'iu [Differential psychological diagnostics of children with cognitive deficiency]. *Psikhologichesky Zhurnal, 4*, 98–97.

Berk, L. & Winsler, A. (1995). *Scaffolding children's learning: Vygotsky and early childhood education*. Washington, DC: National Association for the Young Children.

Bruner, J. (1987). Prologue to the English edition. In R. W. Rieber and A. S. Carton, (Eds.), *The collected works of L. S. Vygotsky*. Vol. 1. *Problems of general psychology*, pp. 1–16 (Norris Minick, Trans.). Editors of the English translation: New York: Plenum Press.

Chulkov, V. N., Lubovsky, V. I., & Martsinovskaia, E. N. (Eds.) (1990). *Differentsirovannyi podkhod pri obuchennii i vospitan slepoglukhikry detei* [Differentiative approaches to the teaching and upbringing of deaf-blind children]. Moscow: Academia Pedagogicheskikh Nauk.

Clay, M. M., & Cazden, C. B. (1990). A Vygotskian interpretation of reading recovery. In L. Moll (Ed.), *Vygotsky and education: Instructional implications and application of social-historical psychology* (pp. 206–222). London: Cambridge University Press.

Cole, G. (1987). *The learning mystique: A critical look at "learning disabilities."* New York: Fawcett Columbine.

Daniels, H., & Lunt, I. (1993). Vygotskian theory and special education practice in Russia. *Educational Studies, 19*(1), 79–89.

Das, J. P., & Kendrick, M. (1997). PASS Reading Enhancement Program: A short manual for teachers. *Journal of Cognitive Education, 5*(3), 193–208.

Das, J. P., Naglieri, J. A., & Kirby, J. R. (1994). *Assessment of cognitive processes: The PASS theory of intelligence*. Boston: Allyn & Bacon.

Echevarria, J., & McDonough, R. (1993). Instructional conversations in special education setting: Issues and accommodations. Educational Practice Report: 7. National Center for Research on Cultural Diversity and Second Language Learning. Washington, DC. Available at: http://www.ncbe.gwu.edu

Feuerstein, R., & Gross, S. (1997). The learning potential assessment device. In D. Flanagan, Genshaft, J., & Harrison, P. (Eds.), *Contemporary intellectual assessment: Theories, tests, and issues.* New York: Guilford Press.

Feuerstein, R., Rand, Y., Hoffman, N., & Miller, R. (1980). *Instrumental enrichment: An intervention program for cognitive modifiability.* Baltimore: University Park Press.

Fuchs, D., & Fuchs, L. (1994). Inclusive school movement and the radicalization of special education reform. *Exceptional Children, 60,* 294–309.

Gindis, B. (1986). Special education in the Soviet Union: Problems and perspectives. *The Journal of Special Education, 20*(3), 375–383.

Gindis, B. (1994). Vygotsky's defectology. *American Journal on Mental Retardation, 100*(2), 214–216

Gindis, B. (1996). Assessment of cognitive processes: The PASS theory of intelligence. *School Psychology International, 17*(3), 305–308.

Gindis, B. (1998). Navigating uncharted waters: School psychologists working with internationally adopted post-institutionalized children. Communiqué (National Association of School Psychologists) September (Part l) 27(1), 6–9 and October (Part ll) 27(2), pp. 20–23.

Haywood, H. C. (1989). Multidimensional treatment of mental retardation (Edgar A. Doll Award Address). *Psychology in Mental Retardation and Developmental Disabilities, 15*(1), 1–10.

Haywood, H. C. (1993). A mediational teaching style. *International Journal of Cognitive Education and Mediated Learning, 3*(1), 27–38.

Haywood, H. C., Brooks, P. H., & Burns, S. (1992). *Bright start: Cognitive curriculum for young children.* Watertown, MA: Charles Bridge.

Haywood, H. C., Brown, A., & Wingenfeld, S. (1990). Dynamic approaches to psychoeducational assessment. *School Psychology Review, 19*(4), 411–422.

Haywood, H. C., & Tzuriel, D. (1992). *Interactive assessment.* New York: Springer-Verlag.

Ivanova, A. Y. (1976). *Obuchaemost kak printsip otsenki ymstvennogo pazvitia u detei* [Learning Aptitude as a Diagnostic Method in Cognitive Development of Children]. Moscow: Pedagogika.

Jamieson, J. R. (1994). Teaching as transaction: Vygotskian perspective on deafness and mother-child interaction. *Exceptional Children, 60,* 434–449.

Kauffman, J. M., & Hallahan, D. P. (1995). *The illusion of full inclusion.* Austin, TX: Pro-Ed.

Knox, J., & Kozulin, A. (1989). The Vygotskian tradition in Soviet psychological study of deaf children. In W. O. McCagg & L. Siegelbaum (Eds.), *The disabled in the soviet union,* pp. 88–99. Pittsburgh: University of Pittsburgh Press.

Knox, J., & Stevens, C. (1993). Vygotsky and Soviet Russian defectology: An introduction. In R. W. Rieber & A. S. Carton (Eds.), *The collected works of L. S. Vygotsky.* Vol. 2: *The Fundamentals of Defectology (abnormal psychology and learning disabilities),* pp. 1–28. New York: Plenum Press.

Kozulin, A. (1990). *Vygotsky's psychology: A biography of ideas.* Cambridge, MA: Harvard University Press.

Kozulin, A. (1986). Vygotsky in context. In L. S. Vygotsky, *Thought and language* (rev. ed.). Cambridge, MA: MIT Press.

Kozulin, A. (1998). *Psychological tools: A sociocultural approach to education.* Cambridge, MA: Harvard University Press.

Kozulin, A., & Presseisen, B. (1995). Mediated learning experience and psychological tools: Vygotsky's and Feuerstein's perspectives in a study of student learning. *Educational Psychologist, 30*(2), 67–75.

Lebedinsky, V. V. (1985). *Narushchenia v psikhicheskom razvitii u detei* [Disorders in children's psychological development]. Moscow: MGU Press.

Lidz, C. (1995). Dynamic assessment and the legacy of L. S. Vygotsky. *School psychology international, 16*(2), 143–153.

Lidz, C., & Elliott, J. (Eds.) (2000). *Dynamic assessment: Prevailing models and applications.* Oxford: Elsevier Science.

Lipsky, D., & Gartner, A. (1996). Inclusion, school restructuring, and the remaking of american society. *Harvard Educational Review, 66*, 762–796.

Lubovsky, V. I. (1989). *Psikhologicheskie problemy diagnostiki anormalnogo razvitia detei* [Psychological issues in diagnostic of children with abnormal development]. Moscow: Pedagogika Press.

Lubovsky, V. I. (1990). Psikhologicheskii Experiment v Differentcialnoi Diagnistike Umstvennoi Otstalosti [Psychological experiment in differential diagnosis of mental retardation in children]. *Defectology, 6*, 3–16.

Lubovsky, V. I. (1996). L. S. Vygotsky i Spetcialnaya Psikhologia. [L. S. Vygotsky and special psychology]. *Voprosy Psikhologii, 6*, 118–125.

Luria, A. R. (1979). *The making of mind: A personal account of Soviet psychology.* Cambridge, MA: Harvard University Press.

Lurie, L., & Kozulin, A. (1998). The instrumental enrichment cognitive intervention program with deaf Ethiopian immigrant children in Israel. In A. Weisel (Ed.), *Issues unresolved: New perspectives on language and deaf education* (pp. 161–170). Washington, DC: Gallaudet University Press.

McCagg, W. O. (1989). The Origins of Defectology. In W. O. McCagg & L. Siegelbaum (Eds.), *The disabled in the Soviet Union*, pp. 1–18. Pittsburgh: University of Pittsburgh Press.

Malofeev, N. N. (2001). Specialnoe Obuchenie v Rossii I Zagranistei [Special Education in Russia and Abroad]. Moscow: Institute of Corrective Pedagogy, Pechatnyi Dvor. Available at: www.ise.iip.net/almanah

Meshcheryakov, A. (1979). *Awakening to life: Forming behavior and mind in deaf-blind children* (K. Judelson, Trans.). Moscow: Progress.

Minick, N. (1987). Implication of Vygotsky's theories for dynamic assessment. In C. Lidz (Ed.), *Dynamic assessment: An interactional approach to evaluating learning potential*, pp. 116–140. New York: Guilford.

Newman, F., & Holzman, L. (1993). *Lev Vygotsky: Revolutionary scientist.* London, New York: Routledge.

Petrovsky, A., & Yaroshevsky, M. (1998). *Kratki Psickologicheskii Slovar* [Brief psychological encyclopedia]. Rostov-na-Dony, Russia: Fenix.

Presseisen, B., & Kozulin A. (1994). Mediated learning: The contribution of Vygotsky and Feuerstein in theory and practice. In M. Ben-Hur (Ed.), *On Feuerstein's instrumental enrichment*, pp. 51–82. Palatine, IL: IRI/Skylight.

Rubinshtein, S. Y. (1979). *Psikhologia umstvenno otstalogo shkolnika* [Psychology of a mentally retarded student]. Moscow: Prosvecshenie Press.

Rueda, R., Goldenberg, C., & Gallimore, R. (1992). Rating instructional conversations: A guide. Educational Practice Report: 4. National Center for Research on Cultural Diversity and Second Language Learning. Washington, DC. Available at: http://www.ncbe.gwu.edu

Schulte, A., Osborn, S., & Erchul, W. (1998). Effective special education: A United States dilemma. *School Psychology Review, 27*(1), 66–77.

Smith-Davis, J. (2000). People with disabilities in Russia: Progress and prospects. In Keith, K., & Schalock, R. (Eds.), *Cross-cultural perspectives on quality of life*, pp. 126–134. Washington, DC: AAMR.

Stainback, S., Stainback, W., & Forest, M. (1989). *Educating all students in the mainstream of regular education*. Baltimore: Brookes.

Strebeleva, E. A. (2000). *Rannyia diagnostika umstvennoi otstalosti* [Procedures for early diagnostic of mental retardation] (Vol. 2, pp. 2–11). Moscow: Institute of Corrective Pedagogy, Almanah, Available at: www.ise.iip.net/almanah/2/st09.htm

Suddaby, A. (1998). Children with learning difficulties. In J. Riordan (Ed.), *Soviet education: The gifted and the handicapped*. London: Routledge.

Sutton, A. (1988). Special education for handicapped pupils. In J. Riordan (Ed.), *Soviet education: The gifted and the handicapped*. London: Routledge.

Tzuriel, D. (2001). *Dynamic assessment of young children*. New York: Kluwer Academic/Plenum Publishers.

Tzuriel, D., Kaniel, S., Kanner, A., & Haywood, H. C. (1999). The effectiveness of Bright Start Program in kindergarten on transfer abilities and academic achievements. *Early Childhood Research Quarterly, 14*, 111–141.

van der Veer, R., & Valsiner, J. (1991). *Understanding Vygotsky: A quest for synthesis*. Oxford: Basil Blackwell.

Venger, A. L. (1994). Structura Psychologicheskogo Syndroma [Structure of psychological syndrome]. *Voprosy Psichologii, 4*, 82–92.

Vlasova, T. A. (1984). *Otbor detei v vspomogatelny shkolu* [Screening children for special schools]. Moscow: Pedagogika.

Vlasova, T. A., Lubovsky, V. I., & Tsypina, N. A. (Eds.) (1984). *Deti s zaderzkoi psikhicheskogo razvitia* [Children with delayed mental development]. Moscow: APN RSFSR.

Vygotsky, L. S. (1983). *Sobraniye Sochinenii* [Collected works] (Vol. 5). Moscow: Pedagogika.

Vygotsky, L. S. (1987). *The collected works of L. S. Vygotsky*. Vol. 1. *Problems of general psychology* (Norris Minick, Trans.) (R. W. Rieber & A. S. Carton. Eds.). New York: Plenum Press.

Vygotsky, L. S. (1993). *The collected works of L. S. Vygotsky*. Vol. 2: *The fundamentals of defectology (abnormal psychology and learning disabilities)* (Jane E. Knox and Carol B. Stevens, Trans.) (R. W. Rieber & A. S. Carton, Eds.). New York: Plenum Press.

Vygotsky, L. S. (1995). *Problemy Defectologii* [Problems of defectology] Moscow: Prosvecshenie Press.

Yaroshevsky, M. G. (1993). *L. S. Vygotsky: V Poiskach Novoi Psichologii*. [Vygotsky: In search for the new psychology]. St. Petersburg, Russia: Publishing House of International Foundation for History of Science.

Zaitseva, G., Pursglove, M., & Gregory, S. (1999). Vygotsky, sign language, and the education of deaf pupils. *The Journal of Deaf Studies and Deaf Education, 4*(1), 9–15.

PART III

SOCIOCULTURAL THEORY APPLICATION IN THE CLASSROOM

11

Cultural–Historical Theory and Mathematics Education

Jean Schmittau

Mathematics education in the United States is currently undergoing an attempt at reform. In this chapter an alternative in the form of a Vygotskian-based approach to mathematics pedagogy is explored. While embracing teaching methods similar to those advocated within the reform movement, the Vygotskian-based curriculum, in its genetic analysis of mathematics concepts, their derivation from measurement, and representation by schematic modeling, differs substantively from both historical and current U.S. reform efforts. The teaching and curricular similarities and differences of reform practices and Vygotskian-based pedagogy reflect their respective grounding in divergent theoretical perspectives – the former in constructivism and the latter in cultural–historical theory. Here the cultural–historical approach is addressed, and some of the effects of these two pedagogical approaches on the adequacy of mathematical understanding is explored. It is necessary, however, to begin with a summary consideration of the antecedents of the current reform effort.

Mathematics education throughout the past century has come under the dominance of several learning paradigms. First was the early period of behaviorist pedagogy, succeeded by the formalism of the "new math," then the rapid reversion to "basics," and finally the emergence of constructivism, which continues to maintain its pedagogical hegemony to the present day. It is curious that throughout these periods of changing pedagogical approaches, all grounded in different philosophies of mathematics (Schmittau, 1991), a single practice persisted unchallenged. This was the practice of building children's understanding of the real number system, which Davydov (1990) asserts is the dominant subject matter of school mathematics, on the activity of counting.

The continuance of this practice is partly the result of a certain ambivalence with respect to concept development that has characterized the history of mathematics education in the United States. Behaviorism, after all, was not concerned with concept development, and the "back to basics" movement that reverted to it characteristically focused on procedural rather than conceptual competence. The "vulgar formalism" (Browder & MacLane, 1979, p. 344; cited in Hanna, 1983, p. 88) of the "new math" virtually reduced mathematics to a syntactic system, and formalist mathematics, in which the "new math" was grounded, actually generates the real numbers from the positive integers through an axiomatic system. So it is obvious why formalism not only failed to question, but actually ratified an approach to number centered on the counting numbers. The final and present period in mathematics education, unlike previous periods in which procedural competence or logical deduction was emphasized, is marked by an awareness of the importance of concepts. When clinical interviewing, a research method of choice by the mid-1980s, revealed that the direct transmission of mathematical understanding from teacher to student was not occurring despite clear explanations of mathematical content, the notion that students must "construct their own knowledge" took center stage in mathematics education. It is perhaps significant that it did so in the absence of any competing paradigm. The pendulum swing from the transmission model with its grounding in behaviorism (with some surviving formalist contaminants) was, to all appearances, extreme. Yet constructivism, as did its pedagogical predecessors, continues to ground number in counting. The fact that children typically enter school with some more or less valid knowledge of counting is doubtless a consequence of the fact that we live in a world of "stuff," most of it eminently countable. And since constructivism posits that children must construct their own concepts, what better basis could there be on which to build future mathematical understanding than children's own spontaneous counting concepts?

Unlike the mathematics teacher, the science teacher realizes that it is dangerous to assume that children's spontaneous concepts constitute an adequate basis on which to develop further understandings. When she asks these same children why a cork floats in a tub of water and a nail sinks, she may hear that it is because the nail is long and thin and the cork is more round. Now disconfirming evidence is called for, and the teacher may place a wooden matchstick and a steel ball bearing in the water, clearly challenging the children's naïve concepts by the fact that the match floats and the bearing sinks. At this point, however, the children are still very far from an understanding of density, which is a concept that cannot be grasped empirically but requires a theoretical mode of thinking for its appropriation (cf. Davydov, 1990). It is one of the concepts Vygotsky called *scientific* to distinguish them from the spontaneous concepts children form through their interactions within their everyday environment. Scientific concepts (which are not limited to the field of science) require pedagogical mediation for their appropriation. It is important to mention that only scientific concepts were considered to be true concepts by Vygotsky (Kozulin, 1990), and that virtually all mathematics concepts fit this designation (Schmittau, 1993a).

The difficulty of trying to ground children's mathematical development in their spontaneous notions of number emanating from counting, rather than reorienting them (as the science teacher must) to a more adequate theoretical development of the concept, is illustrated by Davydov (1991). He cites the fact that since number becomes identified for children with the action of counting, which only generates the positive integers, and formalist mathematics generates real numbers from these as well, a rational number (and hence a fraction) is defined as a quotient of two integers a/b such that $b \neq 0$. (This allows, for example, for 2/3, and 5/4, while properly excluding 2/0 from the realm of number.) Fractions, of course, did not evolve in this manner any more than language evolved from the rules of grammar (cf. Riegel, 1979; Schmittau, 1993b). This is a formalist definition and is in keeping with the axiomatic integer genesis of real number within that paradigm. However, since such a designation makes very little sense to children, educators divide circles into sectors and illustrate fractions from the ratios formed, thereby providing a visual interpretation of a formal definition. That this visual representation leads to less than an accurate grasp of the concept of fraction is the subject of meticulous scrutiny by Davydov, who indicts this approach on a number of counts, not the least of which is that it separates fractions from their historical origin in measurement.

Historically fractions clearly were not developed as quotients of integers. The axiomatization and formalization of mathematics that occurred in the 19th and early 20th centuries represented an attempt to reestablish mathematics on a foundation that was rigorously deductive. Hence, formalism may appropriately be viewed as a cognitive reflection – occurring very late in mathematics history – on a body of knowledge that actually developed in a very different way over a period of several thousand years. The fallacy of the "new math" was the assumption that formalist notions could be directly learned by students, who could skip the development of concepts as they had actually occurred, and instead learn mathematics by beginning at the end, so to speak, of the history of mathematical development. The primary reason for the failure of the "new math" was that ordinary students could not learn mathematics in this way. Rigorous deduction and formal logic were not the paths of conceptual genesis.

Further, it is significant that the formalist reestablishment of the category of real number as an emanation of the positive integers (or counting numbers) has the character of a generative metonymy. In his provocative book *Women, Fire, and Dangerous Things: What Categories Reveal About the Mind*, Lakoff (1987) discusses the manner in which the real numbers constitute a generative category, that is, one characterized by its generation from a member or subgroup of members according to rules. Lakoff observes that the set of single-digit numbers generates all the counting numbers through the rules of positionality in our base 10 numeration system. The rational numbers are then defined as quotients of these, and the irrationals as infinite nonrepeating decimals composed of the digits 0 through 9. Lakoff further notes that generative categories tend toward metonymy, as the generative subcategory becomes representative of the category as a whole.

Our research (Schmittau, 1994) indicates that this development of the real numbers as a generative category is not confined to formalism, but occurs whenever the counting numbers are taken as primary, that is, when the concept of number is allowed to develop from the action of counting. Consequently the entire category of real numbers may be interpreted by students in terms of the counting numbers, and the smaller the representatives, the better. There are, moreover, other far-reaching consequences of the acceptance of the counting numbers as a basis for the development of the concept of number. Since fractions and irrational numbers cannot be generated through counting, not only do many students – and even adults – fail to see fractions and irrationals as numbers (Skemp, 1987; Schmittau, 1994), but they may inadequately conceptualize the so-called fundamental operations (i.e., addition, subtraction, multiplication, and division) on these numbers as well. By way of illustration, we shall focus on one of these, the operation (or more properly the *action*) of multiplication.

Conventional pedagogical practice in the United States (by which we shall mean common textbook approaches that in practice become the basis for curriculum) define multiplication as repeated addition. Hence, 5×4 means $5 + 5 + 5 + 5$. This is, of course, an extension of the generative metonymic, since one can repeat an action such as adding 5 to itself only an integral (but not a fractional or irrational) number of times. Textbooks sometimes present other "models" of multiplication, such as arrays in which circles, squares, or other symbols appear in equal groups. It is generally unclear whether these constitute the same notion – that is, one is just repeatedly adding the same number of objects in each group – or whether they represent disparate concepts (in which case one might well wonder why they are both called *multiplication*). Increasingly, rectangular models are finding their way into textbooks as well and often prove helpful in providing meaning to the operation, but again absent the requisite conceptual connections, it is unclear whether in and of themselves they will be sufficient to transform the learning of multiplication from instrumental (a collection of rules) to relational (an integrated system of knowledge) (Skemp, 1978).

A VYGOTSKIAN LEARNING PARADIGM FOR NUMBER AND MULTIPLICATION

However, in the curriculum developed and researched by V. V. Davydov and his colleagues in Russia for more than 40 years and grounded in

Vygotskian cultural–historical psychology, a very different approach to the genesis of both number and fundamental actions such as multiplication is taken. Number is developed out of the action of measurement rather than counting.

Generation of Number from Measurement

Preparatory activities for the development of measurement in Davydov's curriculum reflect the essence of mathematics as the science of quantity and relation. The first-grade course (Davydov, Gorbov, Mikulina, & Saveleva, 1999) begins with the comparison of two quantities (length, area, volume, or weight), which differ sufficiently to permit a visual determination of their equality or inequality without placing them in spatial proximity. In the case of weights, merely hefting them in the hands is sufficient to determine which is greater. Next children are presented with quantities that do not differ so significantly and therefore require alignment to effect a determination as to which is greater. They may be asked to compare the length of a pencil and a pen, for example, or the area of a textbook and a notebook, or the volume of liquid in two identically shaped containers. Two weights may be so close that a balance is necessary to make a determination about which of them is greater. No sooner have students mastered these requisite alignments than they are confronted with a task requiring them to compare quantities that cannot be aligned. They might be asked to compare the height of a bookcase and the length of the teacher's desk, the area of the classroom door and that of the overhead projector screen, or the volume of liquid in two containers having very different shapes. Now the children must find an intermediary, such as a piece of rope to compare the lengths, or a third container into which to pour the original liquids to determine which of them has greater volume.

Once children have become comfortable with these methods, they will then be confronted with the task of comparing two long line segments with only an intermediary unit such as a short strip of paper to use for this purpose. They must now lay off the strip on each of the segments as many times as required: That is, they must *measure* each one. The measure is then expressed as a ratio of the length of the original segment to the length of the unit. For example, if the length of the original segment is designated A and the length of the strip of paper is designated U, then A/U is the required measure. This measure may be a whole number or a fraction, or even an irrational number. Measurements resulting in fractions (or irrationals) are not encountered in the first grade, of course, but occur later in the child's education and significantly do not require a reconceptualization of number when they do occur. In curricula where number develops from the action of counting, however, successive reconceptualizations of both the concept of number and the various operations performed on numbers are required each time a new type of number is introduced. Thus the genesis of number from measure gives greater coherence to the category of real number and spares the student such successive conceptual upheavals, which as Skemp (1987) attests and our own research (Schmittau, 1994) shows, are rarely accomplished.

Progressive Task Difficulty

The first-grade curriculum of Davydov not only is grounded in cultural–historical theory, following the anthropological and historical development of mathematics and framing significant moments in this development in ways psychologically accessible to children, but accomplishes this through a stream of progressively more difficult problems, without demarcation into chapters or sections. The teaching methods employed greatly resemble those advocated by constructivism, but with very different theoretical foundations. Vygotsky and Luria (1993) carried out an extensive investigation of the development of primates, traditional peoples, and children and concluded that cognitive development occurs only when members of these groups are confronted with a problem for which previous solution methods are inadequate. Hence, the progressively more difficult problems of comparison of quantity in the first-grade curriculum described above reflect this view. No sooner do children master one solution method than they are confronted with a problem for which this method is no longer adequate.

The following classroom episode described by Lee (2002) is illustrative. The first graders have just learned that if $A > B$, they can conclude that $B < A$ without reverting to concrete objects. The teacher cuts a paper plate into three parts labeled A, B, and C (with areas $A > B > C$) and places them into an envelope out of sight of the students. She then presents the task: If $A > B$, then B __ C. All children write $B < C$ and cite their previous conclusion from $A > B$ (viz., $B < A$) as the reason. They have drawn a false conclusion based on syntactic similarity. The teacher points out that C does not appear in the initial inequality, but the children are unmoved. They see their error when presented with the plate pieces, but the teacher's attempts to elicit a correct conclusion without such concrete aids are unsuccessful. So the teacher tries another approach.

She asks the children to compare the height of classmates Mike (T) and Sue (C), eliciting $T > C$. She then inquires as to how T compares with the height of an unknown first grader, Ellen (E). Mike promptly writes $T > E$, explaining that this must be true since he is the tallest first grader! Having made an obviously ineffective choice of students, the teacher then asks the children to compare Mike's height with the height B of another child, Bobby, whom they do not know. A flurry of questions about Bobby's grade, age, and so on, ensues, to which the teacher responds that she either does not know or cannot tell. The children finally agree that the correct answer is T ? B, since they do not know Bobby and cannot conclude anything about the relationship between the heights of the two boys. And the fact that $T > C$ was of no importance to their argument.

Clearly Davydov's curriculum is anything but didactic. At this writing, we have completed the implementation of the first 3 years of his program in a school setting in the Northeast (to our knowledge a first in the United States), and we have found the problem solving–inquiry focus challenging for both students and teacher. It has typically taken our American children a year to develop the intense focus and sustained concentration required consistently and productively to engage with the problems, which appear to continuously expand their zones of proximal development (Vygotsky, 1934/1986). The problems themselves are very interesting to the children, but the challenge is unrelenting, and there is never a day when they can simply "kick back" and do "fun stuff" or drill on "facts." After Vygotsky, for whom learning leads development, Davydov's program, in both curriculum and teaching methodology, has as its intended goal not only a deep understanding of mathematics but cognitive development itself.

Genetic Analysis of Concepts

In his *Types of Generalization in Instruction: Logical and Psychological Problems in the Structuring of School Curricula*, Davydov (1990) explains this orientation toward cognitive development. He cites a study of Krutetskii in which students unfamiliar with the square of a sum were presented with the basic example $(a + b)^2$ and taught its meaning. They were then presented with another square of a sum, $(C + D + E)(E + C + D)$, whose surface features were very different from those of the original example. Many students, whom Krutetskii identified as average, had to be given intermediate examples such as $(3x - 6y)^2$ and 51^2 before they were able to discern the conceptual structure of $(C + D + E)(E + C + D)$ as the square of a sum (i.e., $[(C + D) + E][(C + D) + E]$, which, if $C + D = K$, is $(K + E)^2$). A few students immediately grasped the *theoretical essence* of the first example $(a + b)^2$ and easily discerned it in $(C + D + E)(E + C + D)$, which was judged to be the most syntactically different example in the series (there were eight examples in all). Rather than labeling these students "gifted," Davydov noted that their mental activity was qualitatively different from that of the less capable students.

Confronting a specific problem they primarily tried to discover its "essence," to distinguish the main lines by abstracting themselves from its particular features – from its concrete form . . . striving to delineate the internal connections among its conditions (this is peculiar to theoretical generalization). (Davydov, 1990, p. 133)

Davydov observed that theoretical generalization is necessary for the appropriation of Vygotskian scientific concepts and set about the task of attempting to develop in ordinary students this ability, which is generally evidenced by only the most capable. Hence, his curriculum is a rich synergy of content and method designed not only to enable students to grasp mathematics at a deep conceptual level, but to develop their ability to think theoretically.

Before such a curriculum can be created, however, there must be an epistemological analysis of the concepts in question that encompasses both historical and conceptual analyses. This often entails a lengthy and arduous process, but a necessary one, since symbolic forms of thought (typical of mathematics) "absorb" the genesis of a concept, making it "necessary to trace all of the *historically* available methods of solving the same problems in order to see the initial forms behind the abbreviated curtailed thought processes [represented symbolically], to find the laws and rules for this curtailment and then to detail the complete structure of the thought processes being analyzed" (Davydov, 1990, p. 322). This genetic analysis is reflected in the development of number from measure in Davydov's curriculum, since historically it became necessary to admit the results of measure, such as irrational numbers, into the system of real numbers (otherwise such common quantities as the diagonal of a unit square or the circumference of a circle could not be designated numerically). This was not accomplished without upheaval, since the Greeks had relegated irrationals to the category of "magnitudes" while admitting only integers as numbers. By developing the real numbers through measurement, this historically Herculean cognitive restructuring by students is avoided.

The approach to multiplication in Davydov's curriculum also reflects the understanding gained from a genetic analysis of the concept. The first-grade curriculum actually lays the groundwork for multiplication by presenting children with many tasks that require them both to build and to measure quantities. And they use a schematic form to designate these actions. For example, the designation

$$U \xrightarrow{\;|||\;} A$$

indicates that three units have been used to build or measure quantity A. The symbol $U \xrightarrow{\;|||\;} ?$ indicates that the student must *build* a quantity using four units. The unit is specified and may be one or more line segments, squares, or other shapes, which then must be combined to build the quantity. Alternately, the symbol $U \xrightarrow{\;?\;} A$ indicates that the student must *measure* quantity A using unit U, and thereby determine the value of the ?. The students do many varieties of such problems. Then they are confronted in the second grade with a situation in which they must do a measurement of a very large quantity with a very small unit, and the process is thus a deliberately tedious one (Davydov, 1992).

For example, following Davydov (1992), children may be told to pretend that they are working for the local animal shelter and must give each kitten a very small paper cup of water poured from a large pitcher. They need to know how many kittens will receive water. The process is tedious, and there are other larger glasses on the table, but no mention is made of them. Eventually a child will suggest that we find out how many little paper cups of water one of the larger glasses will hold and then determine how many of the larger glasses we can fill from the pitcher. For example, a glass may hold five of the paper cups, and the pitcher may hold six glasses. Now the situation must be schematized a bit differently. Since we found it too tedious to do a straightforward measure of the volume of the pitcher with the unit paper cup, we cannot represent our measure as we did previously, by designating the number of units U in quantity A. Now our schematic must represent the *change in unit* from a smaller unit U (here the little paper cup) to a larger unit G (the glass) with which we then measured the volume of water. The children therefore indicate this action as follows:

Multiplication is now defined as a method for taking an indirect measurement by means of a change in unit (from a smaller to a larger unit) (Davydov, 1992). This reflects Lebesgue's (1960; cited in Davydov, 1992) stress on multiplication as a change in the system of units. One can see how the need for such a process as multiplication arose historically as the numerosity of quantities increased with cultural complexity. Here multiplication is not reduced to addition, which is a different action (of composition rather than of measurement).

It is important to note the use made of mathematical models or schematics, such as the building, measurement, and multiplication models, in Davydov's curriculum, which preserve in representational form the mathematical action that constitutes the essence of the concept in question. In my research in Russia with Davydov and his colleagues, I saw the power of such models in classrooms where I observed Davydov's program being taught and have now observed it even more extensively in our implementation of the program here in the United States. A particularly powerful (albeit deceptively simple) schematic is the part–whole model from which first graders write three equations derived from their actions with quantities before numbers are introduced. This model suggests putting together or taking apart a set of objects or quantities.

$$A = B + C$$
$$A - B = C$$
$$A - C = B$$

Since this schematic represents the essence of actions of composing and decomposing quantities, adding and subtracting are not perceived as formally separated operations, but as complementary actions. The whole (A) must be found from composing the parts (B and C); a part must be the difference between the whole and the remaining part(s). Children have no difficulty with missing addend problems as a result. Children in the United States, however, typically find missing addend problems such as the following difficult: "John has 14 baseball cards. Eric gave him 6 cards. How many cards did John have originally?" The sentence representing this problem appears to indicate addition: $? + 6 = 14$. However, it is necessary to *subtract* 6 from 14 to obtain the solution. No such confusion arises if the preceding schematic is employed to analyze and represent such a problem, as 14 is the whole, 6 is one part, and the other part is found by subtraction.

Now that we have completed the implementation of the first 3 years (these years constitute the 3 years of Russian elementary school) of Davydov's curriculum in a U.S. setting, our research has confirmed the effects of these models firsthand. The power to analyze situations such models afford children cannot be overstated. Neither can their ability to connect the conceptual content of mathematics at very deep and important levels. The function of a model is, after all, either to render hidden features visible or to render particular (or essential) features salient. Hence, appropriately constructed models might be expected to give students the ability to grasp conceptual structure at its most abstract level, thereby enabling them to ascend from the abstract to the concrete, as Hegel, whose influence on Vygotsky was considerable, advocated. In addition, these schematics allow conceptual *connections* (the sine qua non of learning) between mathematical actions previously viewed as separate operations. Finally, they provide students with the *tools of analysis* required for problem solving.

Although with the publication of the National Council of Teachers of Mathematics (NCTM, 1989, 2000) standards, the U.S. curriculum has shifted in recent years from procedural and algorithmic dominance to more work with concrete materials, it lacks the critical intermediate work with schematic models, the genetic analysis, and the emphasis on conceptual *essence* that are so central to Davydov's curriculum.

A CROSS-CULTURAL STUDY OF THE CONCEPTUAL STRUCTURE OF MULTIPLICATION

How does the understanding of students who experience a curriculum designed in such a way as to foster the development of a generative metonymic structure for the categories of real number and multiplication differ from that of students instructed in Davydov's curriculum, which develops the concepts of number and multiplication very differently?

A comparative study conducted with 40 secondary and university students in the United States and 24 elementary and secondary students in Russia addressed this question (Schmittau, 1994). The U.S. university students represented a diversity of course majors and varying backgrounds in mathematics (high school geometry through calculus, statistics, and linear algebra). The secondary student component consisted almost entirely of high school students, 90% of these rated "very good" or high-achieving in mathematics by teachers and mathematics grades. The Russian students consisted of fourth and fifth graders and a cohort of ninth- and tenth-grade students, all of whom had experienced Davydov's curriculum during their elementary years, the first 3 years of Russian schooling. After these 3 years, the older students had experienced a variety of mostly traditional approaches to the teaching of mathematics. The Russian elementary students were rated either good or average by their teachers, and all Russian secondary students were rated average.

Our investigation of conceptual structure took into account the fact that commonly held assumptions in psychology predicating the structure of conceptual categories on genus and differentia have given way in recent years to massive evidence of family resemblance and comparison-to-exemplar structures (Lakoff, 1987). Rosch (1973) was the first to establish evidence of such category organization. She found that when subjects were asked to rate instances of fruit on a scale of 1 to 7 for degree of membership in the category, a prototypic instance emerged to which all other instances were compared. An apple, for example, might receive a rating of 1, designating it as an exemplary member of the category "fruit," and an olive might receive a 7, indicating that the subject did not regard it as a good example of a fruit or perhaps did not consider it to be a fruit at all. The rating for "fig" might fall somewhere between these two instances. Rosch determined that the characteristics of the apple, especially that it was juicy and sweet, were believed by subjects to be essential to fruit. Hence, they judged all other instances of the category on this basis, and the apple functioned as a prototype for the category. Her work has been widely replicated, and evidence of prototypicality has been confirmed even in such highly structured domains as science and mathematics. Armstrong, Gleitman, and Gleitman (1983), for example, extended Rosch's work to the categories of odd and even numbers and found prototype effects for both.

Subjects in our study were assigned the task of rating instances of multiplication (on a scale of 1 to 7) for degree of membership in the category. The instances to be rated included integers, fractions, irrationals, monomial and binomial products, and a product of length and width yielding rectangular area. Upon completion of the rating task, subjects were asked the question "What is multiplication?" This question emanates from the Vygotskian *method of concept definition* (Luria, 1981, p. 56), in which subjects are asked, "What is – ?" with respect to the concept of interest. After this, subjects were asked with respect to each instance of multiplication appearing on the rating task, "In what sense do you consider this (particular instance of integer, irrational, or binomial multiplication, for example) to be multiplication?" A flexible clinical interview format was employed in probing subjects' responses. This third measure was a variant of the Vygotskian *comparison and differentiation* method (Luria, 1981, p. 58), in which the designated instance and the subject's own meaning for multiplication are juxtaposed.

Results on the rating task indicated that for the American students multiplication possessed a prototypic structure. Every U.S. student assigned the positive integer instance 4×3 a rating of 1 but rated other instances as considerably less representative of multiplication, thereby indicating the exemplariness of the cardinal instance. Triangulation of the data yielded confirmation from the second measure. In response to the question "What is multiplication?" all the U.S. subjects stated that it was repeated addition. Finally, on the third measure, in more than 90% of the cases in which students gave evidence that an instance of multiplication had any meaning for them, this meaning was linked to the exemplar or prototypic instance. For example, after the cardinal instance 4×3, the monomial product ab received the most favorable ratings. Twenty-three of the U.S. students found it meaningful, and all substituted small positive integers for a and b, thereby establishing linkage to the positive integer prototype for multiplication. Only one student noted that a and b could represent any real numbers, and that the substitution of positive integers did not resolve whatever conceptual difficulties existed for the multiplication of other types of real numbers (fractions, for example). The results were similar for the instance of binomial multiplication $(2x + y)(x + 3y)$; only 12 of the U.S. students reported that binomial multiplication had any meaning for them at all. Of those for whom it did, all illustrated its meaning by substituting small whole numbers for x and y. The most popular choices among the university students were 1 and 2, which yielded a product of 4×7 and effected a reduction to the counting number prototype. In effect, these subjects deformed the generalized algebraic product into their limited understanding of binomial multiplication predicated on cardinality.

Another disturbing finding was that half of the U.S. university students and two-thirds of the secondary students indicated that they did not see the area of a rectangle as multiplication. These subjects were unable to draw a grid in a rectangle that would illustrate how its area is a product of length and width. They could not go beyond the simple substitution of small whole numbers for b and h in the formula $A = bh$ (area = base × height), whereby they again effected a reduction to the cardinal number prototype. Moreover, they accomplished this merely by substitution of counting numbers into the formula, which they were able to do in order to produce a value for A without perceiving any apparent connection to a rectangle at all. They also gave evidence of considerable confusion between area and perimeter.

By way of contrast, the Russian students did not give evidence of prototypicality on the ratings task. The younger students actually rated the rectangular area instance $A = bh$ as more exemplary of the category than 4×3, and many commented that this counting number instance was too easy and, therefore, uninteresting to them. Nor did they characterize the meaning of multiplication as repeated addition; rather the essential change in the system of units was reflected in their conceptualization of area. None of the Russian students confused area with perimeter, and even the youngest students were very explicit about the conceptual transitions necessary to establish rectangular area as multiplication. All were explicit about the change of unit, from a small square to a row of such squares, which then must be repeated to form the rectangle. This is the essence of rectangular area, and it emanates directly from the conceptual essence of multiplication. None of the U.S. students had this understanding. The protocols of virtually all of the Russian students, however, even the youngest, consistently identified first the change in quantity from the base b (or height h) of the rectangle to the area of a rectangular strip having dimensions $b \times 1$ (or $h \times 1$). They also explicitly noted the change in unit from a single unit square within the rectangle to a rectangular strip of such squares (Fig. 11.1).

Similarly, *every* Russian student, including beginning fourth graders who had never been introduced to binomial multiplication, was able to obtain the product of two binomials and explain in what sense it represented multiplication. Unlike the U.S. students, they did not reduce either the monomial or the binomial factors to small whole numbers in order to understand the action to be performed as multiplication. Instead, they expressed this understanding at a higher level of generalization, that of algebraic abstraction. Only later, when requested to do so, did they substitute specific numbers to obtain a product. This typifies the ascent from the abstract to the concrete advocated by Hegel. Unlike the U.S. university students who substituted the smallest whole numbers they could think of for x and y, the Russian children, when asked to illustrate their abstract understandings with a concrete solution, chose numbers such as 64, 206, and 103.9 as factors. These children evidenced a confidence not found in the

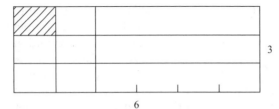

FIGURE 11.1a Model of area by a Russian student illustrating change in unit from a single square to a rectangular strip of such squares.

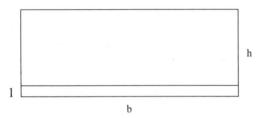

FIGURE 11.1b Model of area by a Russian student illustrating transition from linear dimension b to a rectangular strip of dimensions $b \times 1$.

American subjects, whose age and subject matter background advantages might have been expected to result in the generalized understandings actually shown by the Russian children who were uninstructed in binomial multiplication. Some of the Russian students explained binomial products by drawing a rectangular model with dimensions $2x + y$ and $x + 3y$, then showing a strip of dimensions $2x + y$ by 1 repeating $x + 3y$ times. (Fig. 11.2).

The U.S. students who converted fractions to decimals reported that they mentally removed the decimal points (thereby effecting a reduction to the positive integer prototype), multiplied the resulting integers, and then invoked the "rule" to reposition the decimal point in the product. None knew how or why the "rule" worked. A fifth-grade Russian student made a similar transition from fractions to decimals, writing:

$$\frac{2}{3} = \frac{20}{30} = .6 \quad \text{and} \quad \frac{4}{5} = \frac{40}{50} = .8 \quad \text{Then} \quad 0.6 \times 0.8 = .48$$

In contrast to his U.S. counterparts, this child, when questioned about how he saw this as multiplication, explained without hesitation, ".08 repeats 6 times."

The product of irrationals (Π and $\sqrt{2}$) had meaning for only one secondary and two U.S. university students, who explained it correctly by successive approximation of two nonrepeating decimals. For many students, however, the multiplicative difficulties were compounded by the added failure to understand the irrational numbers themselves. Some regarded

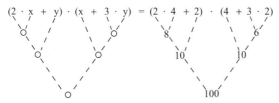

FIGURE 11.2a Model of binomial multiplication by a Russian fourth-grade student.

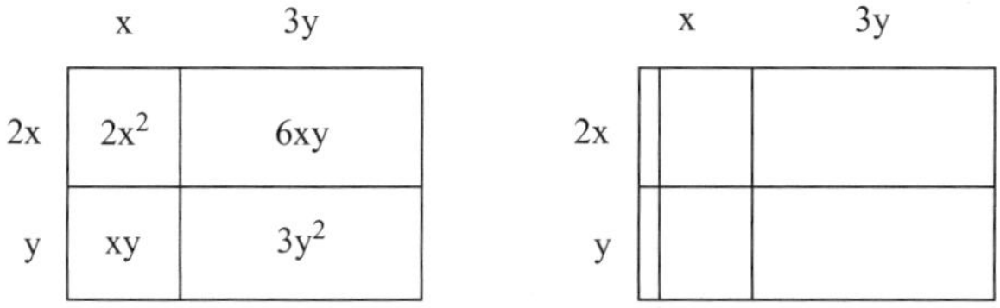

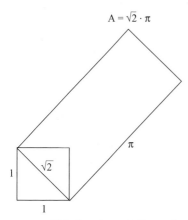

FIGURE 11.2b Model of binomial multiplication by a Russian student showing repetition of a rectangular strip of dimensions $2x + y$ by 1.

$$A = \sqrt{2} \cdot \pi$$

FIGURE 11.3 Russian ninth-grade student's model of $\sqrt{2} \cdot \Pi$ as the area of a rectangle.

Π and $\sqrt{2}$ as "mere symbols" to be consigned to a calculator for solution; others insisted that 2 does not have a square root. The older Russian students used successive decimal approximation as well as area models for this problem. One sketched $\sqrt{2} \cdot \Pi$ as the area of a circle having radius $\sqrt[4]{2}$; another marked off $\sqrt{2}$ as the diagonal of a unit square, then drew a rectangle using this as one side and Π as the other. The area she identified as $\sqrt{2} \cdot \Pi$ (Fig. 11.3). Those who used successive approximation were challenged to explain how 1.4 (an approximation for $\sqrt{2}$) could repeat 3.14 (an approximation for Π) times. Their immediate explanation was that first 314 was multiplied by 14 (or repeated 14 times), and then the required divisions by 10 and 100 were performed, resulting in the relocation of the decimal point. The Russian students never mentioned "rules"; they spoke of "actions" instead, and the meaning of such actions was consistent throughout a variety of algorithmic reformulations (cf. Schmittau, 1993b, for a more extensive discussion of grounding mathematical meaning in action).

Davydov's curriculum maintains students' mathematical actions at Leontiev's (1983) level of goal-directed action, whereas the "rules" U.S. students referred to occur at the operational level where actions have become routinized. The algorithm for multiplication of decimals is one example. Fortunately, constructivist influences are focusing more attention on goal-directed action in U.S. classrooms, but difficulty in linking conceptualization to the algorithm often occurs, with computation consigned to a calculator. Dependency on a calculator for the simplest computations has fueled the current "back to basics" movement in the United States. Ironically, while constructivism rails appropriately against mindless drill on algorithms, it promotes calculator usage, which is the ultimate mechanization of human action, "transmitting to the machine those elements that begin to be formalized in human activity itself" (Tikhomirov, 1981, p. 275). From a Vygotskian perspective, the algorithm is an important cultural–historical product, and great pains are taken in Davydov's curriculum to trace its historical and conceptual links to fundamental mathematical actions, of which the algorithm is a symbolic trace. As a result, our children who have completed 3 years of Davydov's curriculum here in the northeastern United States not only have a deep conceptual understanding of the mathematics involved, but are accurately multiplying three-digit numbers and dividing three-digit numbers into six- and seven-digit numbers. The conceptual versus procedural debate in the United States reflects a false dichotomy; an algorithm is a *symbolic trace of the meaningful mathematical actions* required to solve a problem. We move to manipulation of the symbols (such as numerals) when cultural factors bring about an increase in complexity whereby action on objects becomes tedious and consequently prone to error.

The dysfunctional manner in which American students reduced conceptually complex structures to cardinal instances reflected the fact that this category was for them structured around the counting number prototype. We originally anticipated that this category, developed pedagogically in the form of a generative metonymy, might have a formalistic structure, but we found no evidence that any student had succeeded in apprehending it as a generative metonymy with formalist connections among the instances. (None, for example, defined a fraction as a quotient of two integers a/b, such that $b \neq 0$.) Perhaps this, together with the difficulties encountered by students during the "new math" era, reflects the human need to traverse individually a cognitive path similar to that taken by the culture as a whole in the original development of these concepts (Vygotsky & Luria, 1993). Clearly, the cultural-historical development followed by Davydov's curriculum resulted in far greater conceptual coherence for the category of multiplication for real numbers.

MULTIPLICATION AS A VYGOTSKIAN SCIENTIFIC CONCEPT

There is, however, one final and extremely important consideration. Davydov (1990) extended Vygotsky's research into spontaneous and scientific concepts, finding a primary distinction in their manner of formation. The process of empirical abstraction, of identifying similarities and differences at the level of appearances, is sufficient only for the formation of spontaneous concepts. What can be empirically abstracted concerning a phenomenon such as the diurnal cycle, for example, is the "fact" of the Sun's revolution about the Earth. The rotation of the Earth on its axis, the real cause of the Sun's "rising" in the east and "setting" in the west, cannot be apprehended at the phenomenological level (Lektorsky, 1984; Kozulin, 1990), but requires the development of a theoretical mode of thought (Davydov, 1990). This is the case for mathematical concepts as well, but Davydov observes that because pedagogy has for the most part advanced no further than the level of Lockean empiricism, such empirical methods as comparison and contrast are reinforced throughout schooling.

What our combination of Rosch's and Vygotsky's research methods detected in the U.S. subjects were the results of attempts at formation of a scientific concept through the cognitively dysfunctional means of empirical abstraction. Prototypic organization, a common occurrence in generative metonymic categories (Lakoff, 1987), develops empirically on the basis of representativeness of features and is extended through a comparison-to-exemplar process. We may consider the construction of the category "fruit" investigated by Rosch (1973). One who has appropriated the scientific concept as "that which contains the seeds" has apprehended a theoretical essence that is not apparent among a variety of surface features. Such an individual might be expected to approach pertinent new botanical knowledge in a fundamentally different way than those to whom a fruit is quintessentially an apple.

In the case of mathematics the consequences of empirical abstraction are more devastating, however. Once a premature cognitive commitment (Langer, 1989) has been made to a cardinal structure, one cannot determine empirically by a process of comparison of their differential features what multiplication might mean for various types of numbers, such as fractions, irrationals, and their algebraic formulations (Schmittau, 1993b). The result is not a true scientific concept but a pseudoconceptual generalization, the Vygotskian designation for many of the so-called alternate conceptualizations or misconceptions found in the data of U.S. subjects, but conspicuously absent in the protocols of the Russian students. We saw no evidence, for example, of such common misconceptions as "multiplication makes bigger," the apparent result of conceptualizing multiplication within the framework of cardinality. Because the Russian children apprehended the theoretical essence of multiplication, the concept retained its constancy of meaning across contexts and, hence, could confidently be extended into new ones.

The pedagogical experiences of the Russian students, however, were the result of an extensive historical, conceptual, and psychological analysis on the part of Davydov and his colleagues. The generation of the real numbers through actions of measuring (rather than their derivative formation as "quotients," for example, of numbers that arise through actions of counting) avoids the scholastic repetition of the historical development of the concept of real number, in which 2,000 years were required to unite the products of counting and the products of measuring into one conceptual system. It is here that considerations of Davydov's work and its theoretical basis have the potential to open up new perspectives in our own reform process. In addition to providing a prototype of pedagogy informed by Vygotskian psychology, they have much to contribute to considerations of epistemological and psychological foundations for curriculum and instruction.

THE EXTENSION OF MULTIPLICATION TO EXPONENTIATION: ANOTHER GENERATIVE METONYMY

It is significant that the generative metonomy is not confined to multiplication in American mathematics pedagogy. When multiplication is extended to exponentiation, for example, the basis of this extension is again the counting numbers. Typically the textbook and classroom treatment of this subject begins with the definition of an exponent as repeated multiplication. That is, x^3 is defined as $x \cdot x \cdot x$, or the repeated multiplication of x by itself. Consequently $5^4 = 5 \times 5 \times 5 \times 5$, which is analogous to the definition of multiplication as repeated addition. Hence, as multiplication was defined as a simple extension of addition, rather than a separate mathematical action or operation, we now have exponentiation as a simple extension of multiplication, and another category that is developed as a generative metonymy. However, just as with multiplication, students must encounter and be able to understand exponents that are fractional or irrational, and the generative metonymic approach is not sufficient to account for these since it is predicated on counting numbers.

We researched the understanding of university students with respect to this category and found so little understanding of this concept among students who were not mathematics majors that often they told us that an exponent was a little number in the upper-right-hand corner next to another number or letter, but they did not know what this little number meant. We presented a "fantasy" problem of plant growth, which was not designed to mimic botanical reality, but to explore the concept of exponentiation from a cultural–historical perspective rather than as the generative metonymic category it has become. The plant is first noticed (on day 1) and found to be 3 cm in height. It is measured at the same time on successive days and found to have heights of 9, 27, and 81 cm, respectively. Students are asked to assume this pattern is representative and to give the heights on several days previous to the first day on which the plant was observed. This yields heights of 1, 1/3, 1/9, and so on, and generates the nonpositive integer exponents for powers of 3 (3^0, 3^{-1}, 3^{-2}, etc.). Then students are asked the plant's height 12 hours before it was first measured. Even students who have nearly completed master's degrees in mathematics find this surprisingly difficult. They want to say that the height is $3^{1/2}$, which they "know" (i.e., have been told and accepted) is $\sqrt{3}$, but find this difficult to establish.

This problem follows the cultural–historical development of exponents and logarithms, which involved mathematicians in the juxtaposition of arithmetic and geometric sequences similar to those that constitute the domain and range of the plant growth function. In solving the problem, which approaches the development of exponents through the analysis of an exponential *function*, a student is constantly working back and forth across these two sequences, the arithmetic representing time and the geometric, growth. Such a development is consistent with cultural–historical theory, provides greater conceptual coherence for the category, and prevents its development as a generative metonymy emanating from the positive integers.

CONCLUSION

I have noted several differences between constructivism and cultural–historical theory, especially as these pertain to mathematics pedagogy. There is another important difference. From a Vygotskian perspective, the scientific concept has been constructed historically by the culture, a product of "universal generic thought" (Davydov, 1990, p. 311). In order to allow its appropriation by the individual, such a concept must be subjected to genetic and psychological analyses and pedagogically mediated. A student has very little chance of "constructing" the scientific concept of multiplication independently. Further, "within the theoretical learning approach, 'the child as an independent learner is considered to be a result, rather than a premise of the learning process'" (Kozulin, 1995, p. 121; cited in Karpov & Haywood, 1998, p. 33). This explains the underlying difference beneath the surface similarities in classroom teaching from a constructivist and a cultural–historical perspective. Because the problem solving done within the curricular structure in Davydov's program is designed to develop the cognitive abilities of theoretical generalization, the approach to the subject matter is fundamentally different, although in both cases the teacher may function as a facilitator and the instruction is in neither case didactic.

It is scarcely possible to close this discussion without commenting on currently popular attempts within mathematics education to frame Vygotsky as a "social constructivist." In light of all that has been said here, it would appear that such attempts not only are ill conceived, but, in fact, miss the mark by a wide margin. At the very least, they obscure the deep theoretical and pedagogical differences between constructivism and cultural–historical theory that are reflected both in the construction of curricula and in the actual processes of teaching and learning mathematics.

References

Armstrong, S. L., Gleitman, L. R., & Gleitman, H. (1983). What some concepts might not be. *Cognition, 13,* 263–308.

Browder, F. E., & MacLane, S. (1979). The relevance of mathematics. In L. Steen (Ed.), *Mathematics today: Twelve informal essays.* New York: Springer-Verlag.

Davydov, V. V. (1990). *Types of generalization in instruction: Logical and psychological problems in the structuring of school curricula.* Reston, VA: National Council of Teachers of Mathematics.

Davydov, V. V. (1991). On the objective origin of the concept of fractions. *Focus on Learning Problems in Mathematics, 13*(1), 13–64.

Davydov, V. V. (1992). The psychological analysis of multiplication procedures. *Focus on Learning Problems in Mathematics, 14*(1), 3–67.

Davydov, V. V., Gorbov, S. F., Mikulina, G. G., & Saveleva, O. V. (1999). *Mathematics: Class 1.* Binghamton: State University of New York.

Hanna, G. (1983). *Rigorous proof in mathematics education.* Toronto: Ontario Institute for Studies in Education.

Karpov, Y. V., & Haywood, H. C. (1998). Two ways to elaborate Vygotsky's concept of mediation. *American Psychologist, 53*(1), 27–36.

Kozulin, A. (1990). *Vygotsky's psychology: A biography of ideas.* Cambridge, MA: Harvard University Press.

Kozulin, A. (1995). The learning process: Vygotsky's theory in the mirror of its interpretations. *School Psychology International, 16,* 117–129.

Lakoff, G. (1987). *Women, fire, and dangerous things: What categories reveal about the mind.* Chicago: University of Chicago Press.

Langer, E. J. (1989). *Mindfulness.* New York: Addison-Wesley.

Lebesgue, H. L. (1960). *Ob izmerenii velichin, per.s frants* [On the measurement of quantities]. Moscow: Uchpedgiz.

Lee, J. (2002). *An analysis of difficulties encountered in teaching Davydov's mathematics curriculum to students in a U.S. setting and measures found to be effective in addressing them.* Doctoral dissertation, State University of New York at Binghamton.

Lektorsky, V. A. (1984). *Subject object cognition.* Moscow: Progress Publishers.

Leontiev, A. N. (1981). The problem of activity in psychology. In J. V. Wertsch (Ed.), *The concept of activity in Soviet psychology* (pp. 37–71). Armonk, NY: M. E. Sharpe.

Luria, A. R. (1981). *Language and cognition.* New York: John Wiley.

National Council of Teachers of Mathematics (1989). *Curriculum and evaluation standards for school mathematics.* Reston, VA: Author.

National Council of Teachers of Mathematics (2000). *Principles and standards for school mathematics.* Reston, VA: Author.

Riegel, K. (1979). *Foundations of dialectical psychology.* New York: Academic Press.

Rosch, E. (1973). On the internal structure of perceptual and semantic categories. In T. E. Moore (Ed.), *Cognitive development and the acquisition of language.* New York: Academic Press.

Schmittau, J. (1991). Mathematics education in the 1990s: Can it afford to ignore its historical and philosophical foundations? *Educational Theory, 41,* 121–133.

Schmittau, J. (1993a). Vygotskian scientific concepts: Implications for mathematics education. *Focus on Learning Problems in Mathematics, 15*(2–3), 29–39.

Schmittau, J. (1993b). Connecting mathematical knowledge: A dialectical perspective. *Journal of Mathematical Behavior, 12,* 179–201.

Schmittau, J. (1994, April). Scientific concepts and pedagogical mediation: A comparative analysis of category structure in Russian and U.S. students. Paper presented at the Annual meeting of the American Educational Research Association, New Orleans.

Skemp, R. (1978). Relational understanding and instrumental understanding. *The Arithmetic Teacher, 26*(3), 9–15.

Skemp, R. (1987). *The psychology of learning mathematics.* Hillsdale, NJ: Erlbaum.

Tikhomirov, L. S. (1981). The psychological consequences of computerization. In J. V. Wertsch (Ed.), *The concept of activity in Soviet psychology* (pp. 256–278). Armonk, NY: M. E. Sharpe.

Vygotsky, L. S. (1986). *Thought and language.* Cambridge, MA: MIT Press.

Vygotsky, L. S., & Luria, A. R. (1993). *Studies on the history of behavior: Ape, primitive, and child.* Hillsdale, NJ: Erlbaum.

12

Sociocultural Theory and the Practice of Teaching Historical Concepts

Jacques Haenen, Hubert Schrijnemakers,
and Job Stufkens

> Learning awakens a variety of internal developmental processes that are able
> to operate only when the child is interacting with people in his environment
> and in cooperation with peers.
>
> (Vygotsky, 1978, p. 90)

In our teacher education courses, we discuss with the trainee teachers
educationally relevant topics from the field of learning theory. One of these
topics is the acquisition of historical concepts. Through practical experiences and classroom assignments, the trainee teachers become aware of
some of the problems involved in the teaching of concepts. Often, they plan
to teach concepts in a straightforward matter-of-fact manner using a transmission model of teaching. As teacher educators, we challenge this idea
in order to replace this approach with more effective models. So, with our
trainee teachers we discuss how secondary education students can achieve
a deeper understanding of concepts. Two basic elements of helping trainee
teachers teach for understanding are (1) methods to create powerful learning environments and (2) methods to present the historical subject matter
in terms of a meaningful whole.

This approach is influenced by a Vygotskian sociocultural theory of
teaching and learning. In this perspective the creation of a learning environment can be conceived of as a shared problem space, inviting the students
to participate in a process of negotiation and co-construction of knowledge. Lev Vygotsky, the founder of the sociocultural theory, developed a
new framework for conceptualizing these educational dialogues, through
which students acquire new modes of handling knowledge and solving
problems. Piotr Galperin (1982) extended this framework in the light of its
educational implications. Galperin placed the students' conceptual change
at the heart of education and emphasized the contribution to the teaching–
learning process of both the teacher and the students' peers. In this chapter,
the focus is on the school-based implementation of a Vygotsky–Galperian

learning–teaching context and the way trainee teachers learn to operate effectively in such a context for teaching history. First, we provide a theoretical overview, including background on conceptual change, relevant Vygotskian terms, and the contribution of Galperin's mental action theory in elaborating Vygotsky. Then, we illustrate how we have used this framework to teach historical concepts, both in our classroom research and in our teacher education courses at Utrecht University.

CONCEPTUAL CHANGE

Teaching historical concepts is often associated with fostering conceptual change. Conceptual change within the context of education can be achieved to the extent that the induced learning experiences correspond with the level of the students' prior knowledge. Conceptual change implies the presence of prior knowledge in the students' minds. This point seems obvious, but it is often overlooked. This is not surprising. As teacher educators and history teachers, we know from our own classroom experiences how difficult it is to pinpoint the level of the students' prior knowledge and use it as a foundation for further learning.

The relevance of prior knowledge as the basis for all education has been clearly put forward by Ausubel (1968, p. IV), who simply stated that "the most important single factor influencing learning is what the learner already knows. Ascertain this and teach him accordingly." This assumption has not been challenged and still forms the basis of current research (cf. Alexander, 1996), although its formulation has changed slightly over the years. In *How People Learn*, Bransford and associates (2000) summarize: "There is a good deal of evidence that learning is enhanced when teachers pay attention to the knowledge and beliefs that learners bring to a learning task" (p. 11).

However, what are still a matter of discussion are how prior knowledge should be made educationally profitable and how this knowledge base should be accessed, especially when it concerns the teaching and learning of concepts. Students enter secondary education with a huge number of concepts representing a complicated and genuine ability to think and reason, which mirrors students' daily experiences. These practice-based concepts are often simple word meanings at a very basic level of generalization. For example, to Grade 7 students the concept *history* is still not very specified. In general, they consider history as "all that happened in the past." In the course of secondary education this phrasing needs to be enriched into a more sophisticated conceptualization of history as "the past as far as we know it from the sources we have," or even more specified as "an interpretation of the past based on sources used by the author informing us about it." And if we also ask these students to describe what it is like to live in a democracy, they tend to call a nation a democracy if it holds elections. They understand the notion that elections lead to the supremacy of the majority opinion (the winner takes all), because they often take votes about issues and proposals in their own classrooms. This practical experience-based notion needs to be enriched in history classes with a basic democratic idea such as "The majority takes care of the interests of the minorities, who never stand a chance to win elections."

In secondary education, the level of practice-based thinking, associated with such concepts as history and democracy, should be raised to a higher conceptual level. As outlined in the next section, we achieve this change by imposing on students a series of assignments that invite them to work with these concepts. This approach in turn gives rise to the appearance of new concepts, which have to be incorporated into the students' thinking. This process of concept formation usually requires the reconceptualization of students' existing body of prior knowledge. As we will see further on, this reconceptualization of word meanings and concepts and its role in teaching are a major point in Vygotsky's sociocultural theory. However, research indicates it is not an easy process.

Research in science education has shown that students' prior knowledge is highly resistant to change. Research on conceptual change has become prominent in the field of science domains, especially as it is currently being studied from the constructivist view of learning. In science education, particular emphasis has been put on introducing cognitive conflicts and anomalies as an instructional approach to fostering conceptual change (Limón, 2001). However, the use of conflicting information does not always lead to the desired results. Vosniadou (1999) has reviewed its effectiveness. According to her, students often fail to spot the inconsistencies or simply start combining them superficially. These students do not really understand the meaning of such inconsistencies. Being confronted with conflicting issues does not change the semantic level of their concepts. They tend to merge the diverse information into a loose and unstructured whole. In fact, this constitutes what could be called, with Vygotsky (1987, p. 135), a "syncretic image," whose principal property is that it draws together the complex relationships between the inconsistencies. A Grade 11 student's synthetic conception of heat and temperature can serve as an example of such a syncretic image in secondary education. Harrison and colleagues (1999) found that students consistently fail to distinguish between these two basic physics concepts, viewing them as equivalent entities. During instruction, the syncretic image of both concepts may not necessarily change in the desired manner. However, Harrison and coworkers (1999) showed the variety of learning activities that may adequately restructure the students' conceptions. One of the implications of their study is that in secondary education much more time needs to be spent on such basic physics concepts; otherwise, the students' intuitive conceptions may remain intact. In our own research, we drew the same conclusion, as basic historical concepts are at stake. Although reasoning in the humanities differs from reasoning in the sciences, we see comparable results when teaching historical concepts at school. The content of these concepts is frequently of a rather schematic nature, and, without special arrangements, this condition will remain the same even after deliberate teaching.

Of particular interest to history teaching is Mason's (2001) qualitative study on the role of anomalous data in relation to topics such as the construction of the Giza pyramids in Egypt. She asked eighth graders (aged about 14) to consider anomalous information conflicting with the dominant theory, which indicates that the Egyptians built the Giza pyramids as the burial places of pharaohs in about 2700–2500 B.C. A recently proposed alternative theory suggests an alignment between the pyramids and Orion's belt, leading to the conclusion that the pyramids might have been built by a much earlier civilization than the Egyptian and not at all meant to be tombs. In her instructional strategy, Mason introduced the conflicting information along with the alternative theory and its supporting data. This is more than is being done in traditional conceptual change research, which has usually merely introduced anomalous data in order to promote a new understanding of students' own conceptions. The instructional context established by Mason appeared to be more effective in regard to conceptual change, because her secondary school students were given an alternative theory explaining why the anomalous data contradicted the leading theory.

Although Mason (2001, pp. 473, 477) mentions this finding only in passing, it is important, because it is in accordance with the sociocultural view on teaching and learning. By the teacher's introducing opposite and contrasting information at the start and discussing its relevance in relation to the dominant theory, students will be stimulated to become aware of an alternative way of thinking. This approach, however, demands skillful teaching and discussion techniques of teachers, because they have to deal with students' emerging questions and answers. The teacher's role becomes more explicit in guiding the students' thinking processes. This prominent role for the teacher is in accordance with the sociocultural view on teaching and learning. It could be said that this view integrates a student-centered approach with a form of deliberate teaching, at least as it has been proposed by the Russian psychologist Piotr Galperin (1902–1988).

DEVELOPMENTAL TEACHING

According to Galperin (1982), learning will be more effective if, from the very beginning of the teaching–learning process, the students are aware of the different aspects of the learning task. On the basis of this awareness, students develop their independent learning processes through their own activities. This development results from the teacher's guidance, because he or she is instrumental in presenting the learning task and the knowledge and skills to be learned. First, for these to be learned, they are called to the students' attention and outlined within their horizon of problems to be solved. Students receive an advance organizer of the action and its goal. This provides the initial requirements to stimulate motivation and to maintain it during the subsequent teaching–learning process. According to Galperin, this method requires that the learning content be presented as a meaningful whole right from the start of the teaching–learning process (see later how this should be done in practice). This sense of the whole will enhance the students' personal involvement in the learning process that follows. Presenting knowledge as a meaningful whole implies presenting it as some kind of "tomorrow's knowledge." First, students have to understand and accept the affective, motivational, and cognitive value of the to-be-acquired knowledge before the focus shifts to the actual appropriation and ability to use it. As we will see, this can be considered as one of the practical consequences of Vygotsky's concept of "developmental teaching" and its maxim that education "is only useful when it moves ahead of development" (Vygotsky, 1987, p. 212). Galperin has lent momentum to Vygotsky's adage by outlining what the first steps in instruction have to be like. He proposed concrete student activities revealing the relevant and substantial aspects of the learning task and providing the means for a systematic orientation toward it (cf. Arievitch & Stetsenko, 2000). By doing so, Galperin helps the students to retrieve and elaborate new information and experience the boundaries of currently held – and perhaps to be changed – concepts. In our research over the past several years, we have examined students' own learning activities instrumental to these processes of conceptual change.

TWO TYPES OF CONCEPTS

In order to get hold of such activities, we point to Vygotsky, who elaborated on the principal psychological differences between the students' personal concepts ("everyday concepts") and the concepts to be learned at school. Vygotsky (1994, p. 359) calls the latter "academic concepts," because they are formed during the students' learning of academic knowledge at school. In principle, these academic concepts are part of a systematic, scientific domain of knowledge. In the context of school learning, academic concepts are called *scientific*, not because their contents are scientific, but because they are systematically learned. The historical notion of democracy described earlier would be an example of an academic or scientific concept.

According to Vygotsky, the development processes of everyday concepts and academic concepts are different. Everyday concepts originate in the child's own life experiences, whereas academic concepts develop during the teaching–learning process. However, the two types are united "into a single system of concepts formed during the course of the child's mental development" (Vygotsky, 1994, p. 365). The formation of academic concepts influences the already existing concepts and triggers a change in their structure. With this interpretation of the two types of concepts, Vygotsky (1978) took issue with the traditionally held view (at that time proposed by Jean Piaget in 1924) that there is an antagonistic relationship between teaching–learning and development (Stetsenko & Arievitch, 2002). Vygotsky, on the contrary, considered the processes of teaching–learning as intertwined with learning's leading development.

For Vygotsky, the child's development is structured through, embedded in, and mediated in and by relationships with peers and adults. Psychological functions and the means mediating development are viewed as emerging from the child's social interaction with adults, peers, and objects. Before these functions become an integral part of the personality, they manifest themselves in the "outer" world as interaction between the child and the people around him or her. They emerge in the social context and are gradually absorbed and transformed "inwardly." Vygotsky views social interaction as analytically prior to individual functioning, or, as he puts it, "It is through others that we develop into ourselves" (Vygotsky, 1981, p. 161).

ZONE OF PROXIMAL DEVELOPMENT

Vygotsky (p. 163) formulated the idea of the zone of proximal development in his often cited "general genetic law of cultural development," stating that a psychological function appears twice: first on the social plane, and then on the psychological plane. As a consequence, to put it in current terminology, psychological functions are basically "socially distributed." Traditionally, these functions (attention, memory, cognition) were treated as being properties of the individual mind. This conception of "individuality" has lain the foundation for much educational practice. In our times – and Vygotsky was instrumental in this – this conception has been totally changed. In recent educational psychology, psychological functions are conceived as encapsulated and distributed in a community of learners. This turning away from a predominantly individualized to a contextualized and social approach to education has entered the mainstream of educational psychology (cf. Davydov, 1995; Forman, Minick, & Stone, 1993; Kozulin, 1998; Mercer, 1995; Rogoff, 1998; Salomon & Perkins, 1998; Wells, 1999; Wertsch, 1998).

In order to elaborate the social dimension of psychological functioning concretely, Vygotsky developed his well-known notion of a zone of proximal development (ZPD). He placed the interaction with adults and more competent peers at the very heart of this zone, providing "the foundation

upon which, in an ideal world, the education of children would be organized" (Cole, 1996, p. 111). Therefore, the formative role of education is significant in Vygotsky's ZPD. It is in this very zone that teachers can lay their
hands on the actual learning processes going on in the students' minds, in
Vygotsky's words: "Learning awakens a variety of internal developmental
processes that are able to operate only when the child is interacting with
people in his environment and in cooperation with peers" (Vygotsky, 1978,
p. 90).

Vygotsky did not follow up his "new look" on learning in relation to its
educational implications, but continued to use cross-sectional and cross-
cultural comparative methods to diagnose mental development. It is at this
point that Piotr Galperin (1969, 1982, 1989, 1992) added to Vygotsky's new
approach by exploring a new educational program within a Vygotskian
framework. He tried to fill a gap and outlined some steps in the teaching–
learning processes that take place in "Vygotsky's zone." For this purpose,
Galperin developed his model of the formation of mental actions (Haenen,
1996, 2001).

In the early 1950s, Galperin with some coworkers (among them V. V.
Davydov and N. F. Talyzina) began to study the mental actions and concepts (elementary arithmetical and geometrical concepts) that have to
be learned in the classroom. They studied the qualitative changes the
teaching–learning process has to go through in order to achieve the status
of mature mental actions. On the basis of both empirical and theoretical
knowledge, Galperin distinguishes the steps an action passes through before becoming a fully fledged mental action. Depending on the action to
be learned, the specific learning task, and the learners' prior knowledge,
the steps can be shortened, combined, or even skipped. Also, the sequence
of the steps can be altered. So Galperin's stepwise approach is a working model or blueprint outlining the teaching–learning process and the
instructional interventions of the teacher in supporting and guiding the
learners.

THE FORMATION OF MENTAL ACTIONS

Galperin capitalizes on insightful learning integrated into activity. He sees
the appropriation of knowledge and skills from the point of view of the students' actions. The teaching–learning process aims at the qualitative and
gradual improvement of the students' repertoire of actions. Within the
framework of activity theory, actions are conceived as conscious attempts
to change objects according to some intended result (Galperin, 1992). Action has to be very broadly conceived. It refers to the sawing of a branch,
the decoration of a room, the doing of a sum, the using of a concept, and so
on. The examples show that an action can be simultaneously executed on
several levels of abstraction. So Galperin classifies each concrete form of an

action into four basic levels of abstraction: the materialized, the perceptual, the verbal, and the mental levels. At the *materialized* level, the action is performed with the aid of physical objects or their material representations – models, pictures, diagrams, displays. At the *perceptual* level, the action is based on the information stored in images and performed without the actual hands-on manipulation of the physical objects or their representations (e.g., refurbishing one's own room by looking around and "moving" the furniture mentally). At the *verbal* level, the action is performed "speaking aloud"; at this level the external objects are no longer needed. At the *mental* level, the action is exclusively performed internally ("in the mind"), and both external objects and audible speech are no longer necessary (cf. Haenen, 2001).

According to Galperin, these fundamental levels of abstraction are of identical importance and each should have its place in a teaching–learning process, especially when new learning actions have to be appropriated. When the actions pass through all these levels, there is, according to Galperin, a reasonable guarantee that a fully fledged mental action will be formed. The reason for this is twofold and can be subsumed under the labels of *generalization* and *abbreviation*. First, passing through all the levels requires that several different representations of the materials involved have to be used in order to draw the students' attention to both the essential and the inessential properties of the objects of an action. This contributes to the *generalization* of an action representing the degree to which those properties of the object of an action that are constant and essential to its performance are isolated and distinguished from the inessential and variable ones. This ensures that the students become fully familiar with the distinctive features of the learning task. Second, as an action develops through the four basic levels, the number of operations originally part of an action is reduced and the action becomes abbreviated. Initially, at the materialized level, an action is executed in its most extended form. Then, some of its operations are joined or telescoped, as it were. Thus, the *abbreviation* of an action contributes to the mastery of an action and the ease and speed with which an action will be carried out.

To summarize, Galperin developed an idea about how to form mental actions based on four levels of abstraction. Apart from theorizing, he conducted research into how to implement his approach in real classroom contexts (Arievitch & Stetsenko, 2000; Arievitch & van der Veer, 1995; Fariñas León, 2001; Haenen, 1996, 2001; Karpov & Haywood, 1998). Galperin and his coworkers designed experimental curricula for such educational subjects as handwriting, elementary arithmetic, elementary grammar of the Russian language, and geometrical concepts. In addition, Galperin's approach has provided the learning–psychological basis for our curriculum project on historical concepts. Our study is a part of wider research into factors playing a role in knowledge restructuring in history learning

(Haenen & Schrijnemakers, 2000; Schrijnemakers, 2001; Van Drie & Van Boxtel, 2003).

THE PRACTICAL IMPLICATIONS OF GALPERIN'S APPROACH

Discussing with our trainee teachers the implications of Galperin's innovative approach for their own lessons, we formulated three practical solutions for the teaching of historical concepts:

- Orientation to the task
- Use of models
- Educational dialogue

These practical solutions integrate the four levels of abstraction. They allow students to become familiar with a historical concept by elaborating its content at the materialized and perceptual level (through the use of models) and at the verbal level (through the educational dialogue). But, before working with the concept at these levels, there is the importance of orientation to the task. Already at the very beginning of the teaching–learning process, Galperin provides the students with the means to orient themselves systematically to the subject to be studied. As a result, the students reach a higher degree of independence from the teacher in the course of their education. This lays a robust foundation for the second and third aspects of our approach to the teaching of historical concept, that is, the use of models and the educational dialogue. We are making extensive use of models in order to visualize the processes of thinking and reasoning and to make tangible to the students which products of their thinking efforts are available in the process of acquiring new concepts. These results should be compared and discussed in cooperative learning sessions (Cohen, 1994), because individual learning is supported by educational dialogue, or – as the original Russian terms used by Galperin may be translated – by communicated and dialogical thinking (Haenen, 1996, 2001; Wertsch, 1991).

Those are the practical approaches to the teaching of historical concepts we discuss with the trainee teachers participating in our courses. However, we need to supplement these with additional educational literature to make trainee teachers sensitive to and knowledgeable about the issues under discussion. In the Netherlands, after receiving a university degree in the teaching subject, one needs to take a 1-year full-time teacher education course to qualify as a teacher. In this teacher education course, special attention is paid to the translation of subject matter content for students at the secondary school level and its different grades. In addition to the subject matter theory, used as a basis for how to proceed in translating the subject content, we offer a basic grounding in relevant educational, developmental, and learning psychology. All of these ways of thinking have to be integrated within the teacher in such a way that together they form a suitable knowledge base for daily reference in the classroom (Korthagen & Kessels, 1999).

Thus, we try to pursue a fitting alternation between the practical and theoretical components of the course. We avoid being general and theoretical and present the theoretical themes through brief practical assignments in the trainee teachers' own classrooms. The results of these assignments are discussed during group meetings at the university. In reporting their practical experiences, the trainee teachers are expected to reflect on the relevant theories, such as those found in Woolfolk (2001). Woolfolk (pp. 278–286) provides a good basis for our trainee teachers from which to start thinking in terms of a student-centered approach to concept learning. She gives an introduction to the traditionally held theory on concepts as categories and describes, among others, Bruner's model (Bruner, Goodnow, & Austin, 1956). This model is of particular interest, because it emphasizes the importance of active and inductive learning. Joyce and coworkers (2000) have given this model a practical elaboration for use in teacher education courses (cf. Haenen & Schrijnemakers, 2000). In addition, it gives room to the teachers in their guidance of the process of knowledge restructuring in the learning of historical concepts. So on the basis of this literature we enter into discussions with the trainee teachers about the teacher's role in student learning, one of the central themes of sociocultural theory. Starting from the study of concepts as categories, we pursue a line of thinking, giving the trainee teachers guidelines as to how to teach concepts in today's classrooms.

CONCEPTS AS CATEGORIES

The study of concepts as categories is a very well-developed domain within learning theory. Concepts are the building blocks of human thought; they reduce the complexity of the environment and enable us to respond to it efficiently. The learning of concepts consists essentially of a process of abstraction, because a concept refers to the essential common features of a class of objects. At first sight it may be a class of rather arbitrary objects (e.g., castles may look quite different). However, when carefully compared, they have features in common. Because of these common features of objects, a concept is helpful in identifying regularities in the environment. In order to expand this notion of a concept into the direction of the teaching and learning of concepts and to improve the quality of instruction for concept learning, we distinguish five elements in any concept (Bruner et al., 1956):

1. A *name* is given to a category or class of experiences, objects, events, or processes; think of such names as *citizen, federation, treaty, castle,* and *slave.*

2. *Examples* (positive or negative) refer to the instances in which the concept may or may not be used. Windsor Castle and the Gravensteen in Ghent are positive examples of a castle, whereas Versailles is not a castle, but a palace. Nineteenth-century laborers may have had a hard life, but generally they were not slaves.

3. *Attributes* are the common and essential features leading us to the decision to subsume examples within the same category. The functions of castles are to defend and to shelter. Form, construction materials, and the presence of towers, steeples, or belfries are not essential attributes, however determinant they may be to the image of a particular castle. A slave could be sold or killed, because he was a possession. Consequently, knowing a concept also means being able to distinguish essential attributes from nonessential ones.

4. The *value* range of attributes: The examples of a concept are not standardized. Castles were built in many centuries, and they all look quite different. Nevertheless, we call them all castles. However, American castle-like buildings constructed in the 20th century can hardly be called castles, because they lack any defensive functions. A serf was neither a free man nor a slave. We speak of the acceptable variation of a given attribute as its value range.

5. A *rule* specifies the essential attributes and the connection between them. For example, a guild is an association of people sharing an interest in a craft, business, or profession. Within the teaching–learning process, a rule is a provisional working definition or statement that has to be elaborated further in the course of the students' gradual grasping and understanding of the concept elements.

The five elements of a concept mentioned can be further illustrated by outlining Joyce and associates' (2000) proposal of how to teach concepts in the classroom. First, the teacher leads the students through an exercise, giving them the opportunity to describe a concept in terms of the essential and nonessential attributes and to list positive and negative examples. The students consider different concepts and think and talk about their elements. For this purpose, a form may be used as a students' exercise page (see Table 12.1). In this form, particular blanks are designated to fill in the details about the elements of a concept. We also use this form as a preparation tool for the trainee teachers' lessons in which concepts are discussed and conveyed to the students.

The rule or working definition in the form is provisional. Many questions can and have to be asked in order to make the usually somewhat abstract character of a rule more tangible. Here lies the practical relevance of the use of such a student's exercise form. The listing of the elements and the weighting of what has to be considered as positive or negative give rise to a working definition leading on to new questions. And as the proverb

TABLE 12.1. *Sample Form – Analyzing the Elements of the Concept Decolonization*

Name of the Concept	Decolonization	
	positive (= matches the rule)	negative (= does not match the rule)
Examples	Algerian independence	The Dutch Revolt
	Mahatma Gandhi's political actions	War between India and Pakistan
	Proclamation of the Republic of Indonesia	Abdication of the shah of Iran
Features	No national sovereignty	No relation between motherland and colony
	Before a colony, dominated by the motherland	
Values	In the 20th century	Before the 20th century
Rule (= working definition)	Decolonization = Territories that were colonies before becoming independent states in the 20th century	

says, A good question is half the answer. In discussing questions such as "Is the American Revolution an example of decolonization?" the students experience the boundaries of a concept and have the opportunity to specify the concept further. In working along these lines the trainee teachers begin to understand better how the students' concept formation can be nourished and how a lesson plan can be made for this purpose.

The next section of this chapter shows the application of conceptual change based on the sociocultural theory in the context of school learning and teaching. In secondary education, this implies that the teacher organizes the structure of a lesson in such a way that the students feel themselves invited to think about and discuss the concepts to be learned. Instead of conveying to the students the definition of the concept under study, the teacher prepares a series of assignments inducing the process of the students' working with the concept's content.

STARTING A LESSON ON IMPERIALISM

As part of our research we videotaped a teacher in Grade 7, working with 12-year-old students, which in the Dutch educational system is the first grade of secondary education. This teacher deals with the history of the Roman Empire and starts a particular lesson with the following sentences introducing the first assignment:

TEACHER: What are we going to do this lesson? We will have ample opportunity to dwell extensively on the concept of imperialism. That is an awkward concept. In your study book something has been written about this concept. Who can take me to these particular sentences in your study book and read them aloud?

[The student Lennart raises his hand and gets a turn to read aloud a few sentences out of the textbook.]

TEACHER: Thank you, Lennart, that is very good. You found these sentences halfway on the page, but probably you agree with me that these sentences are not easy to understand directly and do not say much about such an awkward concept. There is a lot more to say and to know about it.

Now, I want you to take your notebook and, on your own, start making a concept map. You know how to construct it: place *imperialism* in the center and around it write words that, according to you, are connected with it. You may find it helpful to use your textbook, but you may also try to think of what you yourself already know about it. So, in your opinion, what is relevant to the concept of imperialism? What is it all about? Start to work on this assignment by yourselves, not together yet.

[The students silently start working on the concept map. After a short time the teacher asks for the students' attention:]

TEACHER: I want to go back to the sentences read aloud to you by Lennart. Lennart has just said that the essence of imperialism is that one nation controls another. How can you control a nation?

STUDENT 1: By keeping the people in revolt, in order to prevent them from leaving; so, to keep them as slaves.

[Obviously, this student has no clear concept of imperialism. He even says something ("By keeping the people in revolt") that is actually contrary to the meaning of imperialism, because he wrongly uses the word revolt. But, from his words it can be concluded that he has, nevertheless, a vague, still unfocused idea of the concept of imperialism. The teacher makes small corrections:]

TEACHER: To keep in revolt? Maybe you have in mind; to oppress?

STUDENT 1: Yes, to oppress, to exert power over them.

TEACHER: How could someone have power over them?

STUDENT 2: By placing soldiers along the border.

[This student also has a vague notion about imperialism. This time, the teacher does not make corrections, but builds on the student's answer:]

TEACHER: Yes, by placing soldiers along the border.

STUDENT 3: Wage a war.

TEACHER: Wage a war. Yes, I think it is far from strange what you are considering, because your first idea, of course, is something military. However, there are a lot of other ways to control a nation. But before you all tell me what possible ways there are, I have something else for you.

[The teacher gives a second assignment, requiring the students to read a supporting text.]

I have chosen a text telling you how the Romans used to control the nations and regions conquered by them. First, read the text by yourself, and subsequently work in pairs in order to make a diagram in which you put down the examples of imperialism found by you in the text. But, first, have a look at the blackboard. I have already put the empty diagram. Also, you will notice the four kinds of themes you will find in the text. I listed the themes at the left side. These are the Roman religion, judicial system, education, and architecture.

STUDENT 4: What is a judicial system?

[This question of one of the students gives the teacher an unplanned opportunity to try to elicit from the students' prior knowledge, however vague it might still be, the concept of judicial system.]

TEACHER: Judicial system! Who can tell what a judicial system is about? That also is not an easy concept! Jasper?

JASPER: That is what a judge does starting a lawsuit. It is in order to maintain the law.

[The student Jasper mentions in this case his everyday concept of judicial system. The teacher does not interrupt by reacting to the mistaken aspect of the answer, for instance, by saying something like "That is only partly correct" or (more positively) "That is a positive start for an answer," but he accepts Jasper's answer to continue the discussion:]

TEACHER: Try to clarify it by giving an example. When do we need to take someone to court?

STUDENT 4: When there is some kind of disagreement, for example, when there is a fight between two persons, who is guilty and how the row has started.

[The teacher does not aim at a fully fledged definition of the concept of judicial system, either passed on to the students by him or formed by the students themselves. On the contrary, he feels satisfied that the students work with a prescientific notion of that particular concept without knowing its essence.]

TEACHER: Yes, you are right, when there is a row between two persons or two groups of persons, somehow a solution has to be found. In that case, justice has to be done. Thank you, Jasper, correctly answered.

[After this clarification of the concept of judicial system, the teacher proceeds with his enumeration of the categories of Romans' imperialist strategies to be used by the students to analyze the text.]

TEACHER: Besides religion and judicial system, there are also education and architecture. These are all ways by which the Romans tried to control a nation. So, apart from military means, there are other means as well. That is called *romanizing*.

Now, I will hand out the text. First, read the text in silence by your-selves. Then, in pairs, try to fill in the diagram with the appropriate examples. And, if you have written this in your notebooks, try to imagine what the opposite of that particular example will be. Add that to the diagram in your notebooks. Or, in other words, what do you consider not to be imperialist?

THE SERIES OF ASSIGNMENTS

Summarizing the series of assignments, we see that the students have to do the first assignment on their own. From the transcription of the videotaped lesson, we learn that this first assignment is meant to give the student an orientation to the concept. After a short discussion with the whole class, the teacher gives a text to the students to be used as a starting text for the next assignment, that is, in pairs to think of positive and negative examples of the concept *imperialism*.

These assignments are aimed at stimulating a broad range of learning activities such as

- Activating prior knowledge
- Making a map of concepts related to the concept being studied, and thus exploring the connection and range of concepts and their relationships
- Independently thinking of positive and negative examples of the con-cept under discussion
- Putting these examples into a diagram
- Exchanging the results with other students

In terms of sociocultural theory, all these assignments function as scaf-folds for the students' understanding by mutual exchange, negotiation, and co-construction of the concept's essence. The teacher's role is prepar-ing and organizing the series of assignments and can be characterized as coaching and guiding the process of the students' gradual grasping of the concept's content. The teacher is no longer the "sage on the stage," but a valuable coach during the students' acquisition of knowledge.

In order to process knowledge along these lines and to visualize and imagine positive and negative examples of the concept to be learned, the student should have some notion of the concept, however vague and non-specific it may be. According to Vygotsky, this notion functions as an ev-eryday concept, and its existence forms the basis for the acquisition of academic concepts (van der Veer & Valsiner, 1991, p. 274). In relation to historical concepts, the following example may be illustrative. Young chil-dren of preschool age have a fairly clear idea of the concept *king*. Disguising themselves in pretend play, 4-year-olds usually know that a king wears a crown and often some kind of a long robe. In elementary education, and also beyond it, for example, by watching television or by inference from other sources, students learn to combine the concept *king* with splendor, magnificence, and power: "The king is in charge." An everyday concept of that kind has to be present, when, in secondary education, the differences among monarchy, oligarchy, and democracy will crop up in a discussion, and, in later years, the differences between absolute and constitutional monarchy. During secondary education, there is no further reference to the religious–magical aspect of kingship. In the Netherlands the position of the monarchy is at present being debated, because a large part of the population adheres to a strong, but irrational, relationship of "God, the Netherlands, and the House of Orange." The Dutch people consider the Orange family as chosen by God to lead the nation through hard times, such as the 16th-century revolt against Spain, the assault on the United Provinces by France and England in 1672, and the German occupation in 1940–1945. There is an irrational belief in the monarchy (especially the Protestant monarchy) that makes people support it in spite of the pleas for modernization of the Dutch governmental system. Nevertheless, religious aspects of the monarchy such as the ceremonies at the Byzantine Court or the healing of the sick by the French king (cf. Bloch, 1924/1983) are never referred to in the classroom. Therefore, the religious–magical background of kingship never figures in the social debate about the monarchy. The concept *king* is neither completely understood in school nor in society. One could even ask whether a concept ever could be. This forms a serious obstacle to the definition of this concept, because an important feature remains neglected. Thus, the concept *king* will not be completely understood or finished after formal teaching in secondary education. This holds true for any educational and professional level: A definition of kingship will always remain a working definition to be developed further and adjusted as one becomes more and more knowledgeable and familiar with the concept. Even for the scholar of constitutional law, the working definition will be the starting point for further study.

The 12-year-old students in our research are restricted to their everyday knowledge of the concept, partly enriched by elementary education. But in secondary education, this concept has to be developed further toward a more sophisticated concept, more fit for thinking and reasoning on the aspects of democracy. This process requires continuing education, and it has to be the teacher's task to situate the development of that particular concept in the zone of the students' proximal development. Researchers such as Piotr Galperin have shown us which kinds of learning activities suit the demands of that zone.

THE PRACTICE OF INITIAL TEACHER EDUCATION

The teacher's task is twofold. First, in the history lesson, the teacher stimulates the students to connect their knowledge, partly acquired beyond secondary education, with the academic concepts to be learned formally at school. And, second, the teacher has to prevent an academic concept from remaining an empty shell for the student, that is, a concept that is not experienced or understood and can only be learned by rote. Experience teaches us that such undigested knowledge is of no use to students and rapidly evaporates. Teachers must learn how to guide their students in sequences of assignments aiming at using everyday knowledge as a means to absorb and "own" academic concepts. In our teacher education courses, we devote ample discussion time to these tasks of the history teacher. Basic to these tasks is a learning-psychological starting point, combined with our interpretation of historical consciousness.

Our learning-psychological starting point is inspired by a Vygotsky–Galperian approach to the orchestration of teaching–learning processes. We have translated this into a series of assignments to be practiced in class so as to make the students familiar with the content of historical concepts. This is a gradual and step-by-step process. In practical terms, it means a genuinely student-centered teaching approach, with teaching–learning processes based on the students' own learning activities. The teacher helps the students to find, retrieve, process, and elaborate new information by a sequence of short exercises, discussions, explanations, and questions. Performing these learning activities, the students experience the boundaries and range of a concept and are forced to specify it further.

Such a student-centered approach is an explicit aspect of our teacher educations courses. In experiencing these approaches firsthand, the trainee teachers become aware of the necessity of using everyday concepts as a basis for building academic concepts and preventing these concepts from remaining empty shells or undigested knowledge. For this demands of trainee teachers an inquiring attitude toward their students. However, secondary students are not usually accustomed to such a pervasive teacher attitude demanding that they perform learning activities that turn them into productive co-constructors of the historical knowledge to be learned. Additionally, we should mention that these kinds of student activities are not described and prescribed in the history teaching methods used by the trainee teachers at their practice schools. So, during the institute meetings, we discuss with them their lesson preparation plans, focusing on the mediating student activities related to the everyday concepts. For example, during such meetings the trainee teachers introduced for discussion the following assignments prepared for their forthcoming lessons:

- Could you give an example of a medieval town in Holland? How do you know it is medieval?
- Could you tell us a myth and a legend? What distinction do you make in telling us?
- Please make a full sentence using the concept *modernization*.

- What is the opposite of an army of mercenaries? (to introduce the concept of *conscription*).
- Please, tell me in your own words, what is meant by *industrialization*.
- Did any relatives of yours tell you about the resistance to the German occupation during the Second World War?

TRAINEE TEACHERS' RESPONSIVENESS

As teacher educators, we discuss with the whole group of trainee teachers what kind of responses can be expected during that lesson and how to react and continue. Next, we look for additional possibilities in order to make the assignments and their formulations even more student-centered, for instance, by having the students draw up concept maps, make diagrams, look for patterns, and work collaboratively. Because all of the trainee teachers take in their preparations, objectives, and expectations for a particular lesson, we have ample material for discussion. Often, we do a simulation in which we play out a lesson part: The group plays the roles of that specific grade, and one of them presents her lesson. So these trainee teachers become well prepared to give that lesson in vivo. We ask them to report the results of teaching the lesson in the schools on the discussion pages of the electronic course environment (we use Blackboard). In reporting their practical experiences, they are expected to reflect in such a way that their colleagues can react from their own individual experiences.

In this way we discover that trainee teachers often experience in their lessons that their students have only a very limited or partial idea of the concepts they have to learn, and that they act on these concepts starting from their own individual level. This results in unexpected student answers and additional questions, which demand a kind of not-yet-acquired responsiveness of the trainee teachers. Often, this leads to a trainee teacher's expression of dissatisfaction with the teaching method and with the results of a lesson. As teacher educators, we should be very attentive to intent in such signals and make them educationally productive in our courses. If such feelings do not crop up after that particular lesson, they often do after the assessments using paper and pencil tests. Then, it surfaces that the students do not correctly understand the lesson content and that a lot of additional teacher work has to be done. But now, the trainee teacher understands that "telling isn't teaching." Gradually, along these lines, we teach the trainee teachers to determine the level of the concepts they want their students to attain in a single lesson or lesson period and act accordingly.

This process of the gradual formation of historical concepts also follows from the requirements issuing from the complexity of historical concepts (Husbands, 1996; Pendry, Husbands, Arthur, & Davidson, 1998). It is part of historical consciousness that these concepts are never definitively definable. Historical concepts are ill definable, and this turns history into a "discussion without an end" (Geyl, 1955). Historians are continuously rein-terpreting the past, a process that leads to the shifting content of history education. Each generation newly writes its own history and constructs its historical images differently. As part of their historical consciousness, students have to be well aware of this aspect of historical knowledge. It is our conviction that such an educational objective can only be achieved by a student-centered approach. To get at the historical concepts, history teaching to a large extent has to rely on the students' own construction abilities. This means that the history teacher must create a "construction zone" to give the students ample opportunities to come to grips (under the teacher's guidance) with their own historical concepts. This is more easily said than done; it asks for skillful and subtle teaching activities and it should be quite systematically practiced. Piotr Galperin has given us the tools to orchestrate these kinds of classroom practices, in which the students' learning activities receive central place.

References

Alexander, P. A. (1996). The past, the present and future of knowledge research: A reexamination of the role of knowledge in learning and instruction. *Educational Psychologist, 31*, 89–92.

Arievitch, I. M., & Stetsenko, A. (2000). The quality of cultural tools and cognitive development: Galperin's perspective and its implications. *Human Development, 40*, 69–92.

Arievitch, I., & Van der Veer, R. (1995). Furthering the internalization debate: Galperin's contribution. *Human Development, 38*, 113–126.

Ausubel, D. P. (1968). *Educational psychology: A cognitive vie.* New York: Holt, Rinehart & Winston.

Bloch, M. (1924/1983). *Les rois thaumaturges. Etude sur le caractère surnaturel attribué à la puissance royale, particulièrement en France et en Angleterre.* Réédition. Paris: Gallimard.

Bransford, J. D., Brown, A. L., & Cocking, R. R. (Eds.) (2000). *How people learn. Brain, mind, experience, and school.* Washington, DC: National Academic Press.

Bruner, J., Goodnow, J., & Austin, G. (1956). *A Study of Thinking.* New York: John Wiley.

Cohen, E. G. (1994). Restructuring the classroom: Conditions for productive small groups. *Review of Educational Research, 64*, 1–35.

Cole, M. (1996). *Cultural psychology: A once and future discipline.* Cambridge, MA: Harvard University Press.

Davydov, V. V. (1995). The influence of L. S. Vygotsky on education theory, research, and practice. *Educational Researcher, 24*(3), 12–21.

Fariñas León, G. (2001), Toward a hermeneutical reconstruction of Galperin's theory of learning. In S. Chaiklin (Ed.), *The theory and practice of cultural-historical psychology* (pp. 260–282). Aarhus: Aarhus University Press.

Forman, E. A., Minick, N., & Stone, C. A. (Eds.) (1993). *Contexts for learning: Sociocultural dynamics in children's development.* Oxford: Oxford University Press.

Galperin, P. I. (1969). Stages in the development of mental acts. In M. Cole & I. Maltzman (Eds.), *A handbook of contemporary Soviet psychology* (pp. 249–273). New York: Basic Books.

Galperin, P. I. (1982). Intellectual capabilities among older preschool children: On the problem of training and development. In W. W. Hartup (Ed.), *Review of child develoment research* (Vol. 6, pp. 526–546). Chicago: University of Chicago Press.

Galperin, P. I. (1989). Organization of mental activity and the effectiveness of learning. *Soviet Psychology, 27*(2), 65–82.

Galperin, P. I. (1992). The problem of activity in Soviet psychology. *Journal of Russian and East European Psychology, 30*(4), 37–59.

Geyl, P. C. A. (1955). *Use and abuse in history.* New Haven, CT: Yale University Press.

Haenen, J. (1996). *Piotr Galperin: Psychologist in Vygotsky's footsteps.* Commack, NY: Nova Science Publishers.

Haenen, J. (2000). Gal'perian instruction in the ZPD. *Human Development, 43*, 93–98.

Haenen, J. (2001). Outlining the teaching-learning process: Piotr Galperin's contribution. *Learning and Instruction, 11*, 157–160.

Haenen, J., & Schrijnemakers, H. M. G. (2000). Suffrage, feudal, democracry, treaty... history's building blocks: learning to teach historical concepts. *Teaching History*, Issue 98, February, 22–29.

Halldén, O. (1998). Personalization in historical descriptions and explanations. *Learning and Instruction, 8*, 131–139.

Harrison, A. G., Grayson, D. J., & Treagust, D. F. (1999). Investigating a Grade 11 student's evolving conceptions of heat and temperature. *Journal of Research in Science Teaching, 36*(1), 55–87.

Husbands, C. (1996). *What is history teaching? Language, ideas, and meaning in learning about the past.* Buckingham, England: Open University Press.

Joyce, B., Weil, M., & Showers, B. (2000). *Models of teaching.* Boston: Allyn & Bacon.

Karpov, Y. V., & Haywood, H. C. (1998). Two ways to elaborate Vygotsky's concept of mediation: Implications for instruction. *American Psychologist, 53*(1), 27–36.

Korthagen, A. J. F., & Kessels, J. P. A. M. (1999). Linking theory and practice: Changing the pedagogy of teacher education. *Educational Researcher, 28*(4), 4–17.

Kozulin, A. (1998). *Psychological tools: A sociocultural approach to education.* Cambridge, MA: Harvard University Press.

Limón, M. (2001). On the cognitive conflict as an instructional strategy for conceptual change: A critical appraisal. *Learning and Instruction, 11*, 357–380.

Mason, L. (2001). Responses to anomalous data on controversial topics and theory change. *Learning and Instruction, 11*, 453–483.

Mercer, N. (1995). *The guided construction of knowledge: Talk amongst teachers and learners.* Clevedon, England: Multilingual Matters.

Pendry, A., Husbands, C., Arthur, J., & Davison, J. (1998). *History teachers in the making: Professional learning.* Buckingham, England: Open University Press.

Rogoff, B. (1998). Cognition as a collaborative process. In D. Kuhn & R. S. Siegler (Eds.), *Handbook of Child Development* (5th ed., Vol. 2, pp. 679–744). New York: John Wiley & Sons.

Salomon, G., & Perkins, D. N. (1998). Individual and social aspects of learning. In P. D. Pearson & A. Iran-Nejad (Eds.), *Review of research in education* (Vol. 23, pp. 1–24). Washington, DC: AERA.

Schrijnemakers, H. M. G. (2001). Wat weten ze nog van geschiedenis? [What do they still know about history?] *Kleio, 42*(6), 26–30.

Stetsenko, A., & I. M. Arievitch (2002). Teaching, learning and development: Contributions from post-Vygotskian research. In G. Wells & G. Claxton (Eds.), *Learning for life in the 21st century: Sociocultural perspectives on the future of education* (pp. 84–96). London: Blackwell.

van der Veer, R., & Valsiner, J. (1991). *Understanding Vygotsky: A quest for synthesis.* Oxford: Blackwell.

Van Drie, J., & Van Boxtel, C. (2003). Using concept mapping in history lessons. *Teaching History.* Issue 110, March 27–31.

Vosniadou, S. (1999). Conceptual change research: state of the art and future directions. In W. Schnotz, S. Vosniadou, & M. Carretero (Eds.), *New perspectives on conceptual change* (pp. 3–13). Amsterdam: Pergamon.

Vygotsky, L. S. (1978). Interaction between learning and development. In M. Cole, V. John-Steiner, S. Scribner, & E. Souberman (Eds.), *Mind in society. The development of higher psychological processes* (pp. 79–91). Cambridge, MA: Harvard University Press.

Vygotsky, L. S. (1981). The genesis of higher mental functions. In J. V. Wertsch (Ed.), *The concept of activity in Soviet psychology* (pp. 144–188). Armonk, NY: M. E. Sharpe.

Vygotsky, L. S. (1987). Thinking and speech. In R. W. Rieber & A. S. Carton (Eds.)., *The collected works of L. S. Vygotsky.* Vol. 1. *Problems of general psychology* (pp. 39–285). New York: Plenum Press.

Vygotsky, L. S. (1994). The development of academic concepts in school aged children. In R. van der Veer & J. Valsiner (Eds.), *The Vygotsky reader* (pp. 355–370). Oxford: Blackwell.

Wells, G. (1999). *Dialogic inquiry: Towards a sociocultural practice and theory of education.* Cambridge: Cambridge University Press.

Wertsch, J. V. (1991). *Voices of the mind: A sociocultural approach to mediated action.* London: Harvester Wheatsheaf.

Wertsch, J. V. (1998). *Mind as action.* Oxford: Oxford University Press.

Woolfolk, A. (2001). *Educational psychology.* Boston: Allyn & Bacon.

13

Formation of Learning Activity and Theoretical Thinking in Science Teaching

Hartmut Giest and Joachim Lompscher

PROBLEMS OF SCIENCE CLASSROOMS

One of the main tasks of schools today consists of preparing students for lifelong learning. That means, first of all, enabling students to learn and think independently and efficiently. It is well known that learning tasks and demands in science education present substantial difficulties for the majority of students (Solomon & Aikenhead, 1994; Yager, 1996; Wiser & Amin, 2001; Vosniadou, Ioannides, Dimitrakopovlov, & Papademetriov, 2001; Mikkilä-Erdmann, 2001). International comparisons (e.g., by the Third International Mathematics and Science Study [TIMSS] and the Programme for International Student Assessment [PISA]) have shown large problems concerning application tasks, problem solving, and scientific argumentation, whereas reproductive tasks and skills were better mastered. Science education suffers – among other shortcomings – from the dominant orientation toward isolated, nonsituated facts, which are seldom applied to real-life situations. This approach leads to difficulties in understanding and a loss of sense and motivation in many students.

In this context, many important questions arise, among others: What can teachers do to maximize the effective construction of adequate science knowledge by students? How can teachers maximize the opportunities for students to construct new schemata, new ways of thinking about the world (Adey & Shayer, 1994; Demetriou, Shayer, & Efklides, 1992)? The problem and the questions are not new. And there exist different approaches and answers. The present predominant "theory-oriented programs" that focus on cognition are either Piagetian in nature (e.g., Lawson, 1982; Rowell & Dawson, 1983; Shayer & Wylam, 1981) or based on some form of an information processing model of cognition (e.g., Larkin, McDermott, Simon, & Simon, 1980). The "theory of conceptual change" (Posner, Strike, Hewson, & Gertzog, 1982; Chi, Slotta, & de Leeuw, 1994; Carey & Spelke, 1994) lies between these two.

One main problem of learning science consists in the need for conceptual change. If the learner really acquires science concepts adequately, her or his preinstructional conceptual structures have to be fundamentally restructured. Science classrooms fail to enable students to master conceptual change and to reach a theoretical level of scientific thinking. This situation seems to be the root of the recent crisis in science education (Black & Atkin, 1996). Whereas in the 1970s many investigations of students' preinstructional concepts (often misconceptions) in various science domains were conducted, in the 1980s and early 1990s conceptual change approaches which were based on more or less radical constructivist epistemological positions, moved to the foreground (Duit, 1999a, 1999b).

The constructivist approach has given many benefits to science classrooms and facilitated the understanding of learning processes in students. But currently some severe problems and limits of this approach are being discussed. Radical constructivism tends to overemphasize the individuals' conceptions and development, reduce cognitive development to the content level, often overlook that learning science content has to be embedded in learning environments that support the acquisition of these rational issues (Pintrich, Marx, & Boyle, 1993), overemphasize the sudden insights facilitated especially by cognitive conflict (Vosniadou & Ioannides, 1998; Limón, 2001), and overlook that a theory of science learning has to include not only individual cognitive development but also the situational and cultural factors facilitating it.

The main problem of the constructivist approach we see consists in the fact that the learners' construction processes are interpreted predominantly as activity developing from "inside," based on the existing cognitive structures, which mostly depend on the operation modes matured so far. The question of how conceptual change really takes place has not been clearly answered (Caravita, 2001). It seems that sudden insights facilitated by cognitive conflicts cause changes in the cognitive structure and promote conceptual change in students. Teachers' more or less direct influence on the students' activity in the classroom seems to be impossible or not helpful in this approach. Teachers only moderate students' learning, rather than helping to shape it.

We see a second important limitation of the radical constructivist approach. If learning depends most on what the learner already knows, a productive cognitive conflict will occur only when the student encounters a problem with more or less familiar and meaningful terms. That often means the problem stems from everyday life. So, the difficulty arises of how conceptual change will occur (in the direction of a paradigmatical change of thinking), if knowledge acquisition is seen only in terms of its immediate usefulness in everyday contexts. Certain scientific concepts and methods may be formed this way, but the learners' perspective remains an everyday one (empirical thinking, which is discussed later). The necessary change of perspectives – toward what is characteristic of a scientific approach that enables people to apply scientific knowledge (e.g., laws and rules) to a wide range of different everyday life situations – does not take place. Thus, the central task of instruction consists of teachers' creating conditions for the emergence and development of a new kind of activity in students corresponding with what is characteristic for science, both in domain-specific and in more general respects, including special motives and attitudes, goals and actions. That means, from our perspective, that a systematic formation of learning activity is needed.

THE ACTIVITY-THEORETICAL APPROACH AND ITS EDUCATIONAL APPLICATION

Theoretical Prerequisites

Activity theory was elaborated in the framework of cultural–historical theory by Leontiev (1978) and many others (see, e.g., Chaiklin, Hedegaard, & Jensen, 1999; Engeström, Miettinen, & Punamäki, 1999; Lektorsky, 1990; Lompscher, 2002) and was applied to learning activity by Galperin (1992), Davydov (1988, 1996), Engeström (1990), and others. It has great potential for solving the task discussed (for further details see also the chapters by Chaiklin, Zuckerman, and Karpov, this volume).

Activity is understood as the fundamental interaction between humans and the world – humans behave actively toward the world (fragments of it), change it (them), and change themselves in this process. Humans as active subjects make fragments of the world objects of their activity and at the same time are affected by the world (fragments of it). The cultural–historical process of societal development is the main basis of individual psychological development, which depends mainly on the concrete conditions, opportunities, and qualities of activity. *Learning activity* is a special kind of human activity developed in the course of societal development as an important aspect of human culture that has to be appropriated by individuals in order to be used, then, for concrete learning goals that depend on learning motives, objects, and conditions. Learning processes and outcomes are essentially determined by prior knowledge and interest, on the one hand, and by already acquired learning means (actions, strategies, but also material means, such as models, schemata, books, computers, as essential artifacts of cultural–historical development) available to be applied to new learning tasks, on the other hand.

The crucial point here is that learning activity cannot be reduced to the acquisition (or "construction") of domain-specific knowledge. It is a process of acquiring the domain-specific activity itself in all its complexity as a product of cultural–historical development – according to the level of the learners' psychological prerequisites (the zones of actual performance as well as of proximal development) (Vygotsky, 1998). A major task for the teacher, therefore, consists of creating conditions under which the learning activity makes sense for the students and may be formed according to the learning object (e. g., science), of organizing the students' learning activity as interaction and cooperation, of giving the necessary learning means or leading the process of finding and further developing them. This is much more than the position of an observer, mentor, coach, attendant, or the like – the teacher has to guide learners in such a way that they experience learning as a meaningful, necessary activity that makes them increasingly competent and independent.

Instruction has to be organized in such a way that students really can become subjects of their own activity (instead of being more or less passive objects of educational arrangements and teachers' actions). That means learners must become more or less conscious of the goals, course, and results of the activity and become actively engaged with the learning material, analyzing this material, solving problems in that context, drawing their own conclusions – not under pressure but through their own initiative. This is possible only if students acquire the necessary means and develop attitudes directed toward the essence of the learning material and the learning process itself. These means must include, first of all, their own learning actions directed toward understanding and applying the material to be learned with regard to the specific subject matter or content (Hedegaard & Lompscher, 1999; Hedegaard, 2001; Lompscher, 1989a, 1999a, 1999b, 1999c; Giest, 1998, 2001). Active learning begins when people (1) want to learn and (2) know what they want to know and be able to do. Learning activity develops as a unity of learning motives, learning goals, and learning actions – but this is not the result of a spontaneous process under accidental conditions: As part of the societal culture, learning activity has to be appropriated by learners and formed through instruction.

Among the developmental effects of learning activity we especially stress *theoretical thinking* because of its high importance to the quality of knowledge and competences to be acquired. Theoretical thinking is a level or quality of thinking characterized by the ability (and motivation!) to reveal the essence, the substantial features, and the relationships of an object (cf. Davydov, 1988). It is distinguished from *empirical thinking,* which is more directed toward superficial features and relationships of phenomena.[1] These two levels or qualities are interrelated and necessary

---

[1] This discrimination was elaborated in gnoseology, especially in dialectical logic, used by Vygotsky and Rubinstein in the psychological analysis of the problem of generalization and concept formation, for example, with the discrimination between everyday and scientific concepts, and especially further elaborated and applied to learning and teaching by one of Vygotsky's outstanding followers, Davydov, and his coworkers.

aspects of thinking. But a lack of theoretical thinking has strong (negative) consequences for the acquisition of scientific concepts and methods. Many problems we find in today's science classrooms are strongly related to students' lacking ability to discriminate between and interrelate empirical and theoretical concepts and respective levels of domain-specific thinking by way of conscious mental actions.

There are several similarities and correspondences between the activity-theoretical approach and the constructivist one: orientation toward independent acting and thinking, reflection and metacognition, social cooperation, role of prior knowledge, and cognitive conflict. But there are also principal differences concerning the understanding of the role of teacher and teaching, the societal essence of activity, acquisition, and development.

The main difference between the activity-theoretical and the constructivist approaches – without detailing different versions – may be seen in the fact that the former implements concrete and differentiated ways of promoting the learners' activity and development. That means, first of all,

1. Orientation toward the concrete learning activity relevant for a certain object domain in the course of which the necessary and adequate motives and personal meanings emerge and the psychic development as a whole is taking place[2]
2. Orientation toward the availability of learning means as products of cultural–historical development that help acquire the corresponding activity as the main condition for the learners' cultural development
3. Orientation toward the systematic formation of that activity with such substantial features as theoretical thinking and cognitive motivation in the process of ascending from the abstract to the concrete (discussed later).

Developmental Teaching

There are a wide range of positions concerning the *relationship between psychological development and teaching or instruction* – from denying teaching a substantial role in development to overemphasizing that role – with different positions between these extremes, such as models of direct and indirect instruction (Bliss, 1996; Weinert & de Corte, 1996; and others), of combining instruction and construction (Pravat 1999; Oers, 1998; Mandl, 1997), of guided participation (Newman, Griffin, & Cole, 1998; Rogoff, 1995;

---

[2] This does not mean that psychic development is taking place in learning development only. Other kinds of activity have specific potentials and shape specific conditions for psychic development as well.

Rojas-Drummond, Hernandez, Vélez, & Villagrán, 1998; and others). The activity-theoretical approach claims not only that development takes place under conditions of teaching, but that it organizes the concrete learning activity and its formation. Davydov (1988, 1996) used the term *developmental teaching* in this respect. We use the same term (Giest, 2001), though our concept differs somewhat from Davydov's.

From our point of view, teaching has to use the dialectical relationship between different developmental zones (sensu Vygotsky). In a *first phase*, the teacher creates conditions for a high degree of self-regulated and discovery learning in the students' *zone of actual performance*, applying what was learned and acquired so far. She or he tries to stimulate the emergence of problem situations (cognitive conflicts) corresponding to main tasks, goals, and contents of the teaching–learning process. In such problem situations, learning goals emerge, when the learners' efforts are not directed only toward solving but also toward reflecting on their own prerequisites in relation to the demands of the situation, in order to find out what is *not known* or *cannot be performed yet* and what can be done well and why. Such (conscious) learning goals as an orientation toward the unknown are prerequisites and are the motivational basis for powerful effects in the further process of learning activity.

The *second phase* is more characterized by direct instruction and systematic learning in the *zone of proximal development*. The teacher's task now is to help students reach their own learning goals by stimulating their learning activity (creating the orientation basis for new learning actions; making available necessary learning means; guiding their adequate application, including the possibility of making mistakes and correcting them; forming the whole learning activity necessary for the acquisition of new pieces or domains of subject matter and/or more general aspects of culture; organizing cooperation and discourse among the students and with the teacher). The central point here is to help children acquire what is necessary to know and what must be performed in order to solve the problems and reach the learning goals.

In the *third phase of developmental teaching* (when the zone of proximal development becomes a new zone of actual performance), students solve problems by themselves, work on projects, and the like. Self-regulated and discovery learning are the foreground again and a new phase of indirect teaching starts, but on a higher level. Thus a new zone of proximal development opens.

It is clear that this approach puts high demands on the teachers' psychological and educational competence concerning the differentiated analysis of the real developmental state, including its potentials and permanent changes; the determination of tasks, problems, means, and so on, according to that developmental process; and the creation of suitable conditions for the formation of efficient and increasingly independent learning activity.

Ascending from the Abstract to the Concrete

In order really to understand the world, to acquire and apply relevant knowledge and skills, and to become able to act in an adequate and competent way, the learner must have the opportunity to incorporate the material to be learned into existing knowledge and skill systems. The problem is that, as a rule, such systems are not available at the beginning but emerge and develop only in the process of acquisition of the applicable knowledge and skills. This contradiction and the learning difficulties caused by it can be overcome by ascending from the abstract to the concrete.

Relatively early in a learning process *starting abstractions* based on the learners' own practical and mental actions are generated. They contain the most essential and constitutive features and relationships of a learning domain and serve as a framework and cognitive tool for further analysis and acquisition of the learning objects in the process of ascending to the concrete (as a second step in the learning process). Here the concept *concrete* means that the object has been cognitively processed more or less deeply (on a theoretical level) and has been understood and incorporated into a network of relationships (a theory). Starting abstractions emerge, when the learners actively operate on the object and try to change and transform specific aspects of it. In such situations, learners have the opportunity to distinguish features that are essential and necessary for a certain object (these remain stable in varying forms of the same object) from other features that may change in different phenomena of the same essence.

Starting abstractions that are appropriate for transcending the phenomena given and can serve as cognitive tools for further penetrating a learning domain must not be presented by the teacher, but have to be formed *by the learners themselves* through their own practical and cognitive activity (of course, under the teacher's guidance). That means that the process does not start with these abstractions, but with special actions on particular objects and situations. These are also "concrete," but they have not yet been cognitively processed and understood. Thus, the whole cognitive cycle moves from the concrete not yet understood, via the abstract containing a limited number of essential and constitutive features and relationships for a certain object or domain (and therefore easier to be understood and stored in memory than a number of isolated facts, as often is the case in beginning phases of introduction to a new domain), to an increasingly differentiated and deep understanding of the *concrete complexity of phenomena and processes* in a given domain. In this way, students can achieve (among other results) systematic and flexible knowledge as well as theoretical thinking and cognitive motivation through their own activity and cooperation.

Mostly, instruction is organized "the other way around": Concrete phenomena are shown and compared with each other, in order to find out which features of the objects correspond and which are different. The generalization based on such comparisons, as a rule, leads to formal or empirical abstractions not containing the really essential features and relationships, because it lacks a criterion for distinguishing the general and the essential. Such a criterion is available in the process of actively changing the object under study, as explained earlier. In this process theoretical generalization and corresponding abstraction take place.

The conception of ascending from the abstract to the concrete was elaborated in the framework of gnoseology and dialectical logic based on the analysis of the historical development of science and applied to psychological and didactic problems (Davydov, 1988, 1996; Hedegaard, Hakkarainen, & Engeström, 1984; Lompscher, 1989b). This teaching strategy gives a general orientation to be concretely elaborated in each case related to the theoretical and factual content of subject matter. The success of its implementation to a large degree depends on the teachers' active participation in the elaboration process (and then in the process of implementation itself and reflection on it). That means, above all, that the teachers themselves have to acquire the strategy, find ways and methods of putting it into practice, and be motivated to work correspondingly. We are conscious of the fact that our description of the activity-theoretical approach and its educational application is short and abstract itself. In the next section we give selected examples from some of our empirical investigations in order to make clear how this theory works and which practical results it produces.

EMPIRICAL RESEARCH

Disciplinary Classrooms

Operationalization of the Theoretical Approach

At first, we analyzed the basic theories, concepts, and models of science relevant to comprehension of the learning objects in elementary and middle grade classrooms. This analysis included the corresponding modes of scientific operations and methods. On the basis of an analysis of the students' prior knowledge, interests, and everyday concepts, we generated a hypothesis concerning their zone of proximal development. In line with the dominant goal of our investigation, we focused on cognitive and motivational aspects of learning and development, especially learning motives, learning goals, learning actions and tasks, modes of action regulation, and other aspects. A condition that received particular consideration was that the teachers' activity was not to dominate the students' activity. The teacher had to create learning environments that enabled students to shape their own development by way of learning activity.

On the basis of these considerations we constructed experimental courses. The independent variables in the investigations were (1) choice, order, and structure of the learning object (aspects of motivation and knowledge); (2) learning actions (hypothetically) necessary for the acquisition of the learning object (aspect of action); and (3) systematic formation of the learning activity (aspect of formation). The formation experiments (about 30 lessons or more) were conducted with a pre–posttest design with experimental and control classes. The tasks contained characteristic requirements of the respective scientific domain (science, mathematics, geography, history, native and foreign language) concerning, first of all, components of theoretical thinking and learning motives as well as knowledge qualities. We generally chose the beginning phases of subject matter teaching or a new segment of a subject, because in such introduction phases the formation of learning motives, goals, and actions is especially important to further progress in the respective domain and general development as a learner. In what follows we illustrate the design and organization of the formation of learning activity in science education.

FINDING STARTING ABSTRACTIONS. If children are to learn to explain natural phenomena, they have to trace them to their essence. Various phenomena in nature can be traced to particularities of movement of matter. In a philosophical sense, movement means change. Changes in nature are called *natural processes*. They take place under defined conditions and cause further changes, further natural processes. A necessary condition is *energy*, which is transmitted during a natural process. In a very elementary form, these considerations should enable students to develop more dynamic knowledge of nature. They should understand that nature has developed and continues to develop.

The starting abstraction of our primary science course in grade 4 (10-year-olds) contained the following statements (Irmscher, 1982): (a) Changes in nature are permanently proceeding; (b) changes in nature indicate natural processes; (c) natural processes run under specific conditions and produce further effects, that is, further natural processes; (d) the existence of energy is a necessary condition for all natural processes; (e) there are different energy forms (e.g., movement energy, thermal energy, light energy, electrical energy), which are tied to specific energy straps; (f) energy may be transferred to different natural processes; (g) often, energy transmission is connected with energy conversion. These statements have to be discovered by the students through special learning activity (described later).

The formation of theoretical thinking (directed to conceptual change in the sense of changing the paradigm of thinking) is a long-term process. Therefore, it does not make sense to reduce it to a single classroom experiment. So, the recognition and understanding of the essence of natural phenomena were picked up in grade 5 (introduction into biology and physics). In the physics experiment (Giest, 1985) we concretized the concept natural process and elaborated the *concept of physical process*, which is characterized by changing physical quantities but invariability of the substance. A major problem in physics education are the difficulties of the learners with mental discrimination and connection of the visible level of phenomena with the level of physical explanation, which is characterized by high abstraction. We argued that a possible way to overcome these difficulties might be the presentation of the abstract explanatory level in the form of a graphic model. In physics there are two basic abstractions (the particle–spatial discontinuum; the field–spatial continuum). These can be used as starting abstractions in order to acquire knowledge about physical processes. The two basic models that correspond to these abstractions are the particle and the field model. Because of its relevance to physics and high potential for graphic presentation, important not only in grade 5, we chose the *particle model* as the basic idea of the instructional course. The main aspects here were the construction of bodies (solids) from particles and primary importance of energy as the condition for changing bodies (solids) in the framework of a physical process. The *starting abstraction* was characterized by the following statements: (a) Bodies are made of particles, which are invisible; (b) the way bodies are constructed from particles is changing during a physical process (the particles themselves are unchanging in the physical process); (c) energy is an essential condition for changes in the construction of bodies. The starting abstraction connected two sides: the observable changes of the bodies and the invisible changes in the construction of the bodies from particles that can be described with the help of the particle model. Phenomena on the "body level" justify the statements that were derived from the model (on the "particle level"). These statements in turn can be consulted for the explanation of the observable phenomena.

ASCENDING TO THE CONCRETE. In grade 4 the elaboration of the starting abstraction took place as a process of actively dealing with natural phenomena that led the children to a deeper understanding of the emergence of wind, the water cycle, nutrition, and growth of plants, animals, and humans, tracing them back to their essence. Ascending to the concrete in the physics course, the concepts and statements on the "particle level" were the basis for the explanation of various phenomena of thermodynamics (diffusion, volume change with temperature change, aggregate states and their change, heat conduction, and others). In the process of ascending to the concrete, the particle model became concretized (changes of the distance between the particles, the kinetic and potential energy of the particles, and the kind of movement).

MODELING THE LEARNING OBJECT. Fourth graders are hardly able to work with starting abstractions without specific educational support directed to the formation and acquisition of the corresponding learning actions at a mental, internalized level (discussed later). A stepwise elaboration of the starting abstraction is required and sensory structures are necessary in order to allow students to deal with the abstract learning object via concrete materialized actions. In this process, the teacher gradually developed a *learning model* together with the children (cf. Figure 13.1).

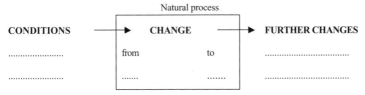

FIGURE 13.1 Learning model: natural process.

Adequate models were also worked out in the other courses on the basis of this learning model. Choosing the physics course as an example, we will show how this was done.

At first the students were confronted with a paradoxical phenomenon. Everyday experience leads us to the explanation that by pouring one volume-part of a liquid into a glass twice we will get two volume-parts of mixture. And even if we take two different liquids we do not expect another result. But after pouring one part of water and one part of alcohol (each 100 ml) into a glass students recognized that the resulting quantity of liquid was not, as expected, 200 ml, but 180 ml. So, the problem – What happened to the missing 20 ml of water and alcohol? – arose. Children discussed different possibilities, and they repeated the experiment, but each time the same result occurred.

Students could not find a way to solve the problem. So, the teacher showed them two glasses, one containing sand and one peas. He then asked the children what they expected to happen if the sand and the peas were mixed. After this they tried it out and confirmed their expectations. This way the children (supported by the experiment) found the answer and solved the problem: We could imagine the two liquids as being constructed from particles of different size. So the small ones could move into the space between the bigger ones, and this process would lead to a possible explanation of the phenomenon: Water and alcohol (like each body) are built from particles and these particles are of different sizes or are at different distances from one another.

In analogous learning situations all the starting abstractions were generated stepwise together with the respective graphic model (learning model). These learning models represented the corresponding starting abstractions and gave sensory support to the learners. It was in principle beneficial that now the considerations were already theoretically oriented (could be carried out on the basis of the starting abstractions worked out and modeled so far). This made it easier for the students to think scientifically and acquire the corresponding learning activity adequately, using the models in the classroom more and more independently.

MODELING THE LEARNING ACTIONS. The acquisition of a learning object is tied to the acquisition of adequate learning actions, which are the main means of learning activity. We concentrated on learning actions that allowed students to cope with large classes of learning tasks within the respective domain. Solving scientific problems (finding answers to a question concerning nature) is appropriate for this goal and ensures an adequate acquisition of the learning object. *Problem solving* as a complex mental action and method includes other important science methods (observation, experimentation, modeling). These are powerful means to reach the learning goal of our courses of study and are of principal importance for theoretical thinking. Children need scaffolding in the form of learning models for the acquisition of learning actions, such as problem solving, as well. The learning model is used as an orientation basis for the acquisition of the learning action and as sensory scaffolding during actions.

PROVOKING COGNITIVE CONFLICTS. Learning was arranged as a process of problem solving evoked by statements that contradict everyday experience (Heraklit: "Nobody can enter the same river twice") or by use of contradictory experiences ("In the morning the grass was wet, although there was no rain at night") or paradoxes, and the like (discussed earlier). This way of proceeding was characteristic of the whole learning path of ascending from the abstract to the concrete.

STEPWISE FORMATION OF MENTAL ACTIONS. The acquisition of learning actions was organized according to the concept of stepwise formation (Galperin, 1992; see also Haenen, 2001). Materialization of thinking in a visible form is a powerful tool for acquisition of the learning object and for successful learning in general. In the physics course, it was necessary to connect the observations on the visible level of the physical body with the explanation on the level of the particle model. To give an example: Starting from everyday experience (if we try to mix water and syrup we must always stir to get a good mixture), the teacher asked what would happen if we did not stir. Students planned an experiment and carefully poured water and syrup into a glass and observed for several hours and days what happened. They observed that if we wait long enough, water and syrup mix. This observation was stated and drawn using the corresponding learning model. The question of what energy might be driving the process arose. Another experiment was planned and executed. Students compared the process of mixing under different heat (energy) conditions. This way they found out that it is heat that causes the mixing. Mechanical energy (stirring) or heat energy causes the mixing of water and syrup. But why? Guided by the learning model students looked for analogies on the particle level that might explain the observations on the body level. Before the natural process started, particles of water and syrup are separate. After the process they are mixed. So, the particles must have moved. The two energies (mechanical and heat) must be connected with the movement of the particles. Additionally guided by a corresponding drawing that showed the mixing of particles, the students developed an explanation: We *observed* that water and syrup were mixed (without stirring), and we *explain* this (using the particle model) by the movement of the particles caused by energy (the particles' movement energy). Further conclusions were drawn: The movement energy of particles must correspond to the temperature of a body, and so on.

Selected Results of the Formation Experiment

In order to test the learning results of our classroom experiments, we were interested in whether the students were able to have a generalized concept of the natural process, to analyze concrete natural processes with the help of that abstract and generalized concept (that means they had to be able to put it in concrete terms), and to solve problem tasks. Only 5% to 10% were unable to do so. In individual investigations, we analyzed the solution of a problem whose content was the subject of instruction in both control and experimental classes. Here, too, the experimental classes outperformed the control classes significantly. Of the students in the experimental classes 86% could generate an adequate question, whereas only 60% of the control class children could; 77% of the experimental class students – versus 46% of the control class children – generated an assumption independently or with little help; 43% succeeded in planning an experiment independently, versus 25% in the control classes. The children of our experimental classes developed more interest in problem-solving tasks (versus receptive and reproductive ones) and in means and methods of knowledge acquisition (versus mere results) when compared with children in control classes (Scheibe, 1989). Böhme (1989) conducted small group experiments based on the same science course with low-performance students and achieved learning results corresponding to the average performance of students in classroom experiments.

As one result of the physics course in grade 5, half of the experimental class students were able to move mentally between the two levels (observations of physical processes *and* "explanations"[3] on the basis of the particle model), which was a tremendous problem even for 6th, 8th, or 10th graders.

The intellectual potential of the children is higher than expected in traditional curricula, but this potential can only be realized by alternative classroom instruction. In special investigations, we compared *direct instruction* and tendencies of *indirect instruction* with *developmental teaching* (Giest, 2001). Direct instruction had little influence on cognitive development: The dominant orientation in teaching (without giving space for the students' own activity) restrains learning. But only trusting students' self-regulated learning without guiding them into efficient learning activities does not

---

[3] From the point of view of scientists in the domain of physics, it is a description on a model level, not a real explanation.

lead to better results. Developmental teaching (discussed earlier) clearly reached a higher level of concept formation and theoretical thinking. For example, a class inclusion task with the concept *plant* was solved by 68% of the students, whereas in classrooms with the other instructional models the solution rate was two to four times lower.

Up to this point, our research had been directed to disciplinary learning and disciplinary classrooms. Starting abstractions were formed for the acquisition of disciplinary knowledge and the formation of (disciplinary) scientific thinking. This is no longer viable since humankind's problems are growing more and more complex. In order to solve them it is not enough to approach them solely from the point of view of a single discipline. Disciplinary thinking has to be complemented by inter- or transdisciplinary thinking that includes skills in dialectical thinking. Thinking dialectically means thinking in units of contradictions and in mental systems. This point has not been satisfactorily resolved in our research on ascending from the abstract to the concrete and in developmental instruction reported to date.

Because of the limitations of disciplinary science, instruction has to be complemented by transdisciplinary instruction, including not only different sciences but also arts as a different kind of acquisition (Huber, 2001). This might be another step to overcoming the crisis of science education, which is mainly a crisis of meaningfulness in the view of students. Transdisciplinary instruction has to put humankind's problems and their solution at the center and has to ask whether and how disciplinary science can contribute to the solution of such complex problems. And a further point: Modern society is characterized by the need for lifelong learning, in order to enable citizens to cope with a steadily (exponentially) growing knowledge base. Self-directed learning associated with modern media might be a solution to such problems of modern society. Therefore, we now focus our research on *system education* and *distance learning* by means of *modern media*.

Transdisciplinary Classroom, Distance Learning, and Hypermedia

FINDING STARTING ABSTRACTIONS. One of the complex problems mentioned earlier is related to the necessity to change the present relationship between humans and nature. So far, both sides form a contradiction: Nature rules over humans, or vice versa. The environmental problems of our world may be solved only if an alliance between humans and nature is created. Our research is aimed at categorical thinking in the form of *interdisciplinary concept pairs* such as part–whole, inside–outside, order–chaos, and determining–being determined as a special kind of starting abstraction (Giest & Walgenbach, 2002).

ASCENDING TO THE CONCRETE. We developed an educational course subdivided into several successive learning modules in different activity fields: Starting from experience with water (representing here fluid in general), the starting abstraction (concept pairs) is generated. In a second module, water (fluid, flowing matter) is examined and discovered as *both the subject of art and the means in artistic activity* by separating content and form. By putting a page *of paper* on top of the *water surface*, pressing it down lightly, and then lifting it up, the form of the water is caught in a picture. By separating content (water) and form, it is possible to examine the different forms not only of flowing water. The forms captured on paper represent forms of moved liquid in general. And, at the same time, new perspectives are opened on the basic problem of art. Forms are special subjects of art, and the artist deals with forms to create new meaning, new knowledge, new perspectives on reality. The third module invites the learner to leave the forms and to move to a more abstract dimension of the problem: Now the genesis of motion forms of water is investigated by methods of science. The concrete flowing water is reduced to particles in movement. This way *laws of the particles' movement* can be recognized. Their behavior is dependent on three factors: the form of disturbance, the flowing speed, and the viscosity of the fluid. Using the Reynolds number, the relationships between these parameters can be *expressed quantitatively*. The lower the Reynolds number the more order can be observed; the higher, the more chaotic it is. The ideal Karmanic turbulent path is situated exactly on the border between order and chaos.

The fourth module offers experience with fluid, flowing matter in the form of *points as subjects of mathematical* relationships freed from content. The main objectives are to recognize and analyze mathematical (algebraic, geometrical) analogies to flow. By experience with mathematical equations (structures of numbers) and dot sets (a typical order of dots found in fractal images) it is possible to analyze the interrelation between order and chaos or determining and being determined at the level of mathematical abstraction, modern mathematical, and scientific theories such as fractal geometry and chaos theory. In the last (fifth, etc.) modules, the learner is invited to discover *possible worlds in virtual reality*; to rediscover sensitivity, sensitive chaos, in it; and to establish relations to a given reality. He or she has to look for analogies between the world of abstract possibilities analyzed earlier and the given reality – sensitive chaos in "cultivated" nature, different forms of relationships created between order and chaos, and so on. At the end of the course the learner is invited to develop an example of a concrete utopian ecological system and to implement it practically or to participate in practical implementation of such a project existing elsewhere.

What has been discussed so far is a completely different approach to the development of inter- and transdisciplinary system education, compared, for instance, with the usual environmental projects, which start with a complex real-world problem. The approach presented here chooses a selected or constructed paradoxical situation (with the character of a *miniature)* as the starting point of learning. It represents the whole complexity, but on

FIGURE 13.2 Vortex street: a special kind of learning model (at the same time abstract and concrete).

a small scale. In order to deal with that complexity it is necessary to use powerful cognitive (conceptual) means. Basic categories in the form of concept pairs are such means. At the beginning, these categories are abstract and have little concrete content. But in the process of ascending from the abstract to the concrete, the categories become increasingly complex and concrete.

MODELING THE LEARNING OBJECT. In order to recognize and use categories in thinking, a special learning object is needed. It must provide the opportunity to start thinking dialectically by containing or presenting both contrasting sides of a dialectical contradiction in a sensorily perceptible form (sensitive scaffolding). For this aim we chose Karman's "vortex street," a system of spirals in a fluid with different increasing sizes (see Figure 13.2). It serves as a *learning model* because it represents not only itself, but (as a prototype) a much wider learning object.

The learning model used here is not simply an illustration or application of a learning object, but a heuristic means that may enable the learner to develop theoretical (dialectical) thinking and to acquire new (theoretical) knowledge. For instance in the first learning module (discussed earlier) the learner is confronted with the *vortex street* as a fascinating "gestalt" that can be discovered and observed in the water of a river, but also in other flowing matter, in air or gas. Each learner can produce it by using a basin with liquid (e.g., water). This way one can imagine and experience that behind the visible forms of moved water certain dialectical contradictions are hidden and may be discovered, for instance, between *order* (laminar currents) and *chaos* (turbulence) or between *determining* (I can determine the water) and *being determined* (at the same time I am determined by the water).

PROVOKING COGNITIVE CONFLICTS. With the help of the vortex street, the learner can start deep experiences in categorical thinking. It is not a simple instance of a natural phenomenon, but a very productive *heuristic means* for the production of knowledge using and concretizing the concept pairs mentioned. The vortex street is a "case which has the value of thousand cases and contains them all" (Goethe, cited in Riedl, 1995; see also Bortoft, 1996). It is a provocation for the learner's thinking: She or he cannot think in the same way as in everyday life – either it is order or it is chaos. Order and chaos are in interaction with one another; both sides are complementarily or dialectically interrelated. This experience may drive the learner toward a *more theoretical level* of thinking – a need for penetrating the paradoxical situation and understanding its substance will emerge.

FORMATION OF MENTAL ACTIONS. It has to be mentioned here that the course we report on was developed for secondary level education.[4] In order to use our approach of such complex, systemic education in a given educational setting, we developed a *hypermedia module* (a complex web-based program). On the one hand, we did this with respect to the educational requirement of self-directed learning, which is strongly connected with information and communication technology–based distance learning; on the other hand, computer use is essential for the learning object (e. g., fractal geometry and chaos theory).

The program construction follows the principles of formation of learning activity described earlier but pays more attention to self-regulated and self-directed learning, in our eyes, a prerequisite for successful distance learning.

- The program offers a structure of successive learning areas that constitute learning steps, but learners have the opportunity to decide whether to follow them (each is constructed in a way that allows successful and meaningful learning within a learning step). Depending on the learning prerequisites, learners can start with a module of their choice.
- The program offers learning goals, learning tasks, and learning actions, but the learners have to decide whether to use and integrate them into their own activity.
- The program offers learning assistance in many ways (information, direct help, interactive programs to study a special theme or problem, integrated links to relevant Internet sites).
- The program purposefully encourages the learner to leave it and to turn off the computer to learn together with peers in cooperative work and to work directly in nature.

In a formation experiment on distance learning, after brief instruction, university students received a compact disc (CD) with the program and

---

[4] We also developed and evaluated a similar course for primary school students (see *http://www.uni-potsdam.de/u/grundschule/sach_giest/delfin/index.htm*) but there are currently no data available.

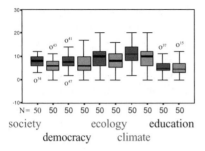

society   ecology   education
        democracy   climate

FIGURE 13.3 Pole differences in pre- and posttests.

studied only with the help of this program at home or in the university's Computer Investment Program pools.

SELECTED RESULTS. In order to investigate changes in students' cognitive orientation[5] we asked them to rate the poles of antinomical concept pairs on a 6-point scale (6, highest relevance; 1, lowest relevance) concerning different complex subjects (systems): *society, democracy, ecology, climate, education*. The concept pairs (conceptual poles) that the students had to rate were *order versus chaos; determining versus being determined; self-determination versus outside determination; freedom versus responsibility*. Figure 13.3 gives an overview.

Without specifying the details here, we can conclude that concerning the various systems or the concepts representing these systems, students' thinking in antinomies decreased; the differences between the systems became smaller (concerning the rating of antinomical concept pairs). The knowledge did not remain abstract but became applicable to everyday life. We can interpret these findings as an indication for transdisciplinary thinking and for crossing of the boundaries of domain-specific knowledge on a high level of theoretical thinking. Further investigations are necessary in order to show the applicability of this approach aimed at promotion of theoretical thinking in different contexts and different developmental stages.

CONCLUSIONS

In this chapter, we have described several phases of our research concerning science teaching and learning. The investigations had different goals, content, and forms of realization but were united by the concept of learning activity and its formation (here with a stress on theoretical thinking as one – but not the only – aspect of the students' psychological development). This concept, elaborated in the general framework of cultural–historical

[5] For details see Giest and Walgenbach (2002).

theory, shows efficient ways and conditions of promoting cognitive development through learning and instruction (as shown by other authors as well) and opens broad perspectives for further theoretical and empirical research.

The implementation of this approach depends on concrete cultural and regional conditions and individual differences among students, including their educational background. For example, the material, financial, and technical allocations of schools and universities vary considerably among and within countries. The growing and increasingly efficient use of new media for educational purposes is one of today's most important challenges. Scientific research has to create necessary preconditions for relevant changes in this direction. But, at the same time, society, politics, economy, and educational systems have to do their job in this regard as well. There is yet a lot to do!

The instructional strategies directed toward the formation of learning activity and the promotion of independent, critical thinking and acting, discussed in this chapter, may provide powerful guidance under different conditions (e.g., with and without new media and technology) because they focus on principal aspects of development through activity and result in the formation of motives and competencies necessary for coping with today's and tomorrow's challenges.

References

Adey, P. S., & Shayer, M. (1994). *Really raising standards: Cognitive intervention and academic achievement.* London: Routledge.

Black, P., & Atkin, J. M. (Eds.) (1996). *Changing the subject: Innovation in science, mathematics and technology education.* London: Routledge in association with OECD.

Bliss, J. (1996). Piaget und Vygotsky: Ihre Bedeutung für das Lehren und Lernen der Naturwissenschaften [Piaget and Vygotsky: Their meaning for instruction and learning of science]. *Zeitschrift für Didaktik der Naturwissenschaften, 2*(3), 3–16.

Böhme, B. (1989). *Besonderheiten leistungsschwacher Schüler 4. Klassen bei der Ausbildung von Lernhandlungen zum selbständigen Erkennen von Ursache-Wirkung-Zusammenhängen* [Peculiarities of 4th grade low performance students in the formation of learning actions for independent recognizing causal relations]. EdD dissertation, Akademie der Pädagogischen Wissensch afteh [Academy of Pedagogical Sciences].

Bortoft, H. (1996). *The wholeness of nature: Goethe's way toward a science of conscious participation in nature.* New York: Lindisfarne Press.

Caravita, S. (2001). A re-framed conceptual change theory? *Learning and Instruction, 11*(4–5), 421–429.

Carey, S., & Spelke, E. S. (1994). Domain specific knowledge and conceptual change. In L. A. Hirschfeld & S. A. Gelman (Eds.), *Mapping the mind: Domain specifity in cognition and culture* (pp. 169–200). Cambridge: Cambridge University Press.

Chaiklin, S., Hedegaard, M., & Jensen, U. J. (Eds.) (1999). *Activity theory and social practice.* Aarhus: Aarhus University Press.

Chi, M. T. H., Slotta, J. D. & de Leeuw, N. (1994). From things to processes: A theory of conceptual change for learning science concepts. *Learning and Instruction, 4*(1), 27–44.

Davydov, V. V. (1988). Problems of developmental teaching. *Soviet Education, 8*, 15–97; *9*, 3–83; *10*, 3–77.

Davydov, V. V. (1996): *Teorija razvivajuscego obucenija* [Theory of developmental teaching]. Moscow: Intor.

Davydov, V. V. (1999). What is real learning activity? In M. Hedegaard & J. Lompscher (Eds.), *Learning activity and development* (pp. 123–138). Aarhus: Aarhus University Press.

Demetriou, A., Shayer, M., & Efklides, A. (Eds.) (1992). *Neo-Piagetian theories of cognitive development*. London: Routledge.

Duit, R. (1999a). Conceptual change approaches in science education. In M. Carretero, W. Schnotz, & S. Vosniadou (Eds.), *New perspectives on conceptual change*, (pp. 263–282). Amsterdam: Pergamon.

Duit, R. (1999b). Towards inclusive views of conceptual change. Paper presented on the Second International Conference of the European Science Education Research Association (E.S.E.R.A.) Research in Science Education: Past, Present, and Future, August 31–September 4, 1999, Kiel, Germany. Available at: http://www.ipn.uni-kiel.de/projekte/esera/book/s201-dui.pdf

Engeström, Y. (1990). *Learning, working and imaging: Twelve studies in activity theory.* Helsinki: Orienta-Konsultit Oy.

Engeström, Y., Miettinen, R., & Punamäki, R.-L. (Eds.) (1999). *Perspectives on activity theory*. Cambridge: Cambridge University Press.

Galperin, P. Y. (1992). Stage-by-stage formation as a method of psychological investigation. *Journal of Russian and East European Psychology, 30*(4), 60–80.

Giest, H. (1985). *Einführung der Schüler in die Physik nach der Lehrstrategie des Aufsteigens vom Abstrakten zum Konkreten* [Introduction of students to physics based on the teaching strategy of ascending from the abstract to the concrete]. EdD dissertation. Berlin. Akademie der Pädagogischen Wissenschaften.

Giest, H. (1998). Von den Tücken der empirischen Unterrichtsforschung [On the malice of empirical instructional research]. In H. Brügelmann, M. Fölling-Albers, & S. Richter (Hrsg.), *Jahrbuch Grundschule: Fragen der Praxis – Befunde der Forschung* (pp. 56–66). Seelze: Friedrich.

Giest, H. (2001). Instruction and learning in elementary school. In M. Hedegaard (Ed.), *Learning in classrooms* (pp. 59–76). Aarhus: Aarhus University Press.

Giest, H. & Walgenbach, W. (2002). System-learning – a new challenge to education – bridging special field to transdisciplinary learning. In B. Zeltserman (Ed.), *Obrazovanije 21 veka: dostizhenija i perspektivij. Mezhdunarodnij sbornik teoreticheskikh, metodicheskikh i prakticheskikh rabot po problemam obrazovanija* [Education in the 21st century: Results and perspectives. International anthology of theoretical, didactical and practical work on problems of education] (pp. 21–37). Riga: Pedagogiskais centrs "Eksperiments."

Haenen, J. (2001). Outlining the teaching-learning process: Piotr Gal'perin's contribution. *Learning and Instruction, 11*(2), 157–170.

Hedegaard, M. (Ed.) (2001). *Learning in classrooms*. Aarhus: Aarhus University Press.

Hedegaard, M., Hakkarainen, P., & Engeström, Y. (Eds.) (1984). *Learning and teaching on a scientific basis*. Aarhus: Aarhus Universitet, Psykologisk Institut.

Hedegaard, M., & Lompscher, J. (Eds.) (1999). *Learning activity and development.* Aarhus: Aarhus University Press.

Huber, L. (2001). Stichwort: Fachliches Lernen [Headword: Domain-specific learning]. *Zeitschrift für Erziehungswissenschaft, 3*(1), 307-331.

Irmscher, K. (1982). *Ausbildung der Lerntätigkeit im 4. Schuljahr nach der Konzeption des Aufsteigens vom Abstrakten zum Konkreten bei der Einführung in die Naturwissenschaften unter besonderer Beachtung des biologischen Aspekts* [Formation of learning activity in grade 4 based on the conception of ascending from the abstract to the concrete at the introduction into science education under special consideration of the biological aspect]. EdD dissertation, Berlin. Akademie der Pädagoglschen Wissenschaften.

Larkin, J., McDermott, J., Simon, D., & Simon, H. (1980). Expert and novice performance in solving physics problems. *Science, 208,* 1335–1342.

Lawson, A. (1982). The reality of general cognitive operations. *Science Education, 66*(2), 229–241.

Lektorsky, V. A. (Ed.) (1990). *Activity: Theories, methodology and problems.* Orlando, FL: Deutsch Press.

Leontiev, N. A. (1978). *Activity, consciousness and personality.* Englewood Cliffs, NJ: Prentice-Hall.

Limón, M. (2001). On the cognitive conflict as an instructional strategy for conceptual change: A critical appraisal. *Learning and Instruction, 11*(4–5), 357–380.

Lompscher, J. (1989a). Formation of learning activity in pupils. In H. Mandl, E. de Corte, N. Bennett, & H. F. Friedrich (Eds.), *Learning and instruction: European research in an international context* (Vol. 2.2, pp. 47–66). Oxford: Pergamon Press.

Lompscher, J. (Ed.) (1989b). Psychologische Analysen der Lerntätigkeit [Psychological analyses of learning activity]. Berlin: Volk und Wissen.

Lompscher, J. (1999a). Learning activity and its formation: Ascending from the abstract to the concrete. In M. Hedegaard & J. Lompscher (Eds.), *Learning activity and development* (pp. 139–166). Aarhus: Aarhus University Press.

Lompscher, J. (1999b). Activity formation as an alternative strategy of instruction. In Y. Engeström, R. Miettinen, & R.-L. Punamäki (Eds.), *Perspectives on activity theory* (pp. 264–281). Cambridge: Cambridge University Press.

Lompscher, J. (1999c): Lern- und Lehrforschung aus kulturhistorischer Sicht [Research on learning and instruction from a cultural–historical point of view]. In H. Giest & G. Scheerer-Neumann (Eds.), *Jahrbuch Grundschulforschung* (Vol. 2, pp. 12–34). Weinheim: Beltz, Deutscher Studienverlag.

Lompscher, J. (2002). The category of activity – a principal constituent of cultural–historical psychology. In D. Robbins & A. Stetsenko (Eds.), *Vygotsky's psychology: Voices from the past and present.* New York: Nova Science Press.

Mandl, H. (1997). How should we learn to really learn? *Life Long Learning in Europe, 4,* 195–199.

Mikkilä-Erdmann, M. (2001). Improving conceptual change concerning photosynthesis through text design. *Learning and Instruction, 11*(3), 241–257.

Newman, D., Griffin, P., & Cole, M. (1998). *The construction zone: Working for cognitive change in school.* Cambridge: Cambridge University Press.

Oers, B. V. (1998). From context to contextualizing. *Learning and Instruction, 8* (6), 473–488.

Pintrich, P. R., Marx, R. W., & Boyle, R. A. (1993). Beyond cold conceptual change: The role of motivational beliefs and classroom contextual factors in the process of conceptual change. *Review of Educational Research, 6,* 167–199.

Posner, G. J., Strike, K. A., Hewson, P. W., & Gertzog, W. A. (1982). Accomodation of a scientific conception: Toward a theory of conceptual change. *Science Education, 66,* 211–277.

Pravat, R. S. (1999). Dewey, Peirce, and the learning paradox. *American Educational Research Journal, 36*(1), 47–76.

Riedl, R. (1995). Goethe and the path of discovery: An anniversary. Available at: www.kla.univie.ac.at/Journal.

Rogoff, B. (1995). Observing sociocultural activity on three planes: Participatory appropriation, guided participation, and apprenticeship. In J. V. Wertsch, P. del Rio, & A. Alvarez (Eds.), *Sociocultural studies of mind* (pp. 139–164). Cambridge: Cambridge University Press.

Rojas-Drummond, S., Hernández, G., Vélez, M., & Villagrán, G. (1998). Cooperative learning and the appropriation of procedural knowledge by primary school children. *Learning and Instruction, 8*(1), 37–62.

Rowell, J. A., & Dawson, C. J. (1983). Laboratory counter examples and the growth of understanding in science. *European Journal of Science Education, 5*(2), 203–216.

Scheibe, I. P. (1989). Entwicklung kognitiver Lernmotive [Development of cognitive learning motives]. In J. Lompscher (Ed.), *Psychologische Analysen der Lerntätigkeit* (pp. 182–230). Berlin: Volk und Wissen.

Shayer, M., & Wylam, H. (1981). The development of the concepts of heat and temperature in 10-13 year olds. *Journal of Research in Science Teaching, 18*(5), 419–434.

Solomon, J., & Aikenhead, G. (Eds.) (1994). *STS Education: International perspectives on reform.* New York, London: Teachers College Press.

Vosniadou, S., & Ioannides, C. (1998). From conceptual change to science education: A psychological point of view. *International Journal of Science Education, 20,* 1213–1230.

Vosniadou, S., Ioannides, A., Dimitrakopoulou, A., & Papademetriou, E. (2001). Designing learning environments to promote conceptual change in science. *Learning and Instruction, 11*(4–5), 381–420.

Weinert, F. E., & de Corte, E. (1996). Translating research into practice. In E. de Corte & F. E. Weinert (Eds.), *International encyclopedia of developmental and instructional psychology* (pp. 43–50). Oxford: Elsevier Science.

Wiser, M., & Amin, T. (2001). "Is heat hot?" Inducing conceptual change by integrating everyday and scientific perspectives on thermal phenomena. *Learning and Instruction 11*(4–5), 331–356.

Yager, R., E. (Ed.) (1996). *Science, technology, society: A reform in science education.* Albany: State University of New York Press.

14

How Literature Discussion Shapes Thinking

ZPDs for Teaching/Learning Habits of the Heart and Mind

Suzanne M. Miller

Within the last few decades literature has been broadly recognized in many disciplines as a major way of knowing, a distinct narrative mode of understanding that can contribute to a keen and critical mind. By stimulating attention to dilemmas, alternative human possibilities, and the many-sidedness of the human situation, literature provides "the varying perspectives that can be constructed to make experience comprehensible" (Bruner, 1986, p. 37). Theoretical conceptions of the act of reading literature have also changed during the last century from New Critical approaches for *getting* static meaning out of a text to constructivist approaches requiring readers' active *making* of meaning (Bartholomae & Petrosky, 1986; Rosenblatt, 1978). Literature learning, in this view, involves creating and elaborating responses and interpretations within the constraints and resources of the text and classroom conversations – as a means of learning to enter into larger cultural conversations about interpretations and possible meanings (Applebee, 1996).

Research evidence, however, suggests that literature learning as taught in the secondary school has not generally supported such constructivist ways of knowing and thinking. In many classroom contexts, interactions about literature cut off students from their own responses and reflection – even teachers who believe they are holding "discussions" insist on their own "correct" textual interpretation (e.g., Applebee, 1996; Marshall, Smagorinsky, & Smith, 1995; Nystrand & Gamoran, 1991). Research in such classrooms reveals what students learn: that their responses and interpretations play no role in school literature reading, that they should *not* draw on their social knowledge about human experience to make sense of literary texts (Hynds, 1989). Such a stance toward literary texts marginalizes students as passive consumers of teacher-made interpretations (e.g., Friere, 1998; Scholes, 1985).

In contrast, engaging in open-forum classroom discussions in which multiple perspectives on texts are invited can provide students with opportunities to examine individual interpretations in conversation with others (e.g., Bridges, 1979). In the sociocultural approach to mind, thinking originates in such collaborative dialogues, which are internalized as "inner speech," enabling children to do later in "verbal thought" what they could at first only do in talk with supportive adults or more knowledgeable peers (Vygotsky, 1986; 1978; Wertsch, 1991). Vygotsky applied this idea to literature teaching in his *Psychology of Art* (1971), where he argues that the effects of literature excite the individual reader aesthetically, but that the teacher must aim, further, to form reflective consciousness through "intelligent social activity" that extends the "narrow sphere of individual perception."

In the ethnographic research I have conducted over the past decade, I have examined the influence of open-forum class discussion on students' thinking over time. This work traces how teacher mediation for students in open-forum discussion of texts can create a zone of proximal development – an assistive social space – through which students learn with the teacher and other students both how to make meaning from literary texts and how to reflect on possible meanings. Using a framework integrated from Vygotsky's sociocultural psychology (1986, 1978), narrative theory (Bruner, 1986; Polkinghorne, 1995), and sociolinguistics (Bakhtin, 1981; 1986; Gee, 1996; Hymes, 1974), in this chapter I synthesize findings from these studies of how constructivist literature study – particularly open-forum discussion – shapes students' knowing and thinking. This research provides evidence, as Vygotsky argued (1978, 1986), that what begins as purposeful social interaction in discussion moves inward to become students' psychological tools (see also Kozulin, 1998). These tools of the mind appropriated by students vary with the interactional context but include, for instance, new social languages (Bakhtin, 1981) and specific meaning-making strategies. Literature discussion plays, I argue, a central role in developing students' self-conscious reflection.

In the following sections, I first provide a short historical overview of the theoretical and research bases for approaching the literature curriculum as conversation (Applebee, 1996), focusing on the perceived problems and tensions of the teacher's role. I then turn to a series of ethnographic classroom studies that provide evidence that (1) students develop specific habits of mind when teachers play a mediational role in literature discussions; (2) students learn qualitatively different habits of the mind and heart in contexts in which teachers mediate discussion of texts from multiple cultural and critical perspectives; and (3) students carry these ways of thinking into meaning-making contexts in other school subjects.

RESEARCH ON CLASSROOM TALK

Research on the nature of classroom interaction in Western schools (e.g., Hoetker & Ahlbrand, 1969; Barnes, Britton, & Rosen, 1969; Cazden, 1988) highlights a century-long persistence of classroom recitation as the major way of talking. In response to this pervasive evaluative genre of school discourse, which inhibits student thinking, James Britton (1970) and his colleagues (Barnes et al., 1969) in the United Kingdom argued the need in schools for exploratory talk as a central *means* of learning and of developing higher psychological functions. Grounding their work in Vygosky's educational theory, they focused on the power of purposeful talk as a mediational means to help students make knowledge their own. In this language across the curriculum (LAC) movement in the 1970s, literacy was reconstrued as sense-making activity – as reading, writing, and *talking* to respond to the world and make sense of it. "Talking to learn" through collaborative exploration in discussion served as the key to developing student understanding and thinking (Barnes et al., 1969; Barnes, 1976; Barnes & Todd, 1977; Britton, 1970; Wells, 1986).

However, since traditional teacher talk focused almost solely on questioning and evaluating correct responses, the LAC movement was faced with the "problem" of the teacher. The group, including many teacher–researchers, engaged in extensive inquiry on student small-group discussion outside classrooms, to examine the potential of students to make meaning without the traditionally intrusive teacher role (e.g., Barnes & Todd, 1977; Britton, 1970; Edwards & Westgate, 1987). LAC researchers documented students' abilities in these small groups collaboratively to use cognitive strategies, to explore connections between personal knowledge and the text, and to create their own understanding jointly through language. Similar findings in the United States have demonstrated elementary students' capacities to use their own language to explore problems of meaning, for example, in book groups (Eeds & Wells, 1989) and book clubs (McMahon & Raphael, 1997). In a statewide assessment in Connecticut (Fall, Webb, & Chudowsky, 2000) even a 10-minute discussion in three-student groups had a substantial influence on students' understanding of a story according to measurements on a language arts test – as compared to those without benefit of discussion. This work is largely grounded in the notion that students pursue understanding *interdependently*, at times acting as and other times learning from more knowledgeable peers (Vygotsky, 1978).

Evidence suggests, though, that such peer-led talk in many instances has not resulted in students' equal rights of constructing knowledge (e.g., Lewis, 1997) or productive conversations (e.g., Alvermann, 1996). The limitation of students' social and cognitive strategies in small student groups has led educators to suggest the additional need for teacher-supported discussion (e.g., Barnes & Todd, 1977). The teacher's role in such classroom discussion has persisted as a problematic issue in literacy research (Miller, 1997), though. What is not clear is *how* practicing teachers initiate changes in conventional roles, discourses (Gee, 1996), and speech genres (Bakhtin, 1986) to create open-forum discussions that engage and transform students.

STUDIES OF TEACHER-MEDIATED TEXT DISCUSSION

In the ethnographic case studies discussed in what follows, I selected innovative secondary-school English teachers (i.e., those teaching students ages 13–18) through a process of progressive focusing in each study. To begin, I observed teachers who were recommended by colleagues as using open-forum discussion in their classrooms: This was an essential stage, since what teachers mediate and students learn in such discussion contexts was the phenomenon of interest. In general, each case study involved weekly audiotaped observations in the classrooms over the course of a school year, transcriptions of semistructured interviews of teachers and focal students, descriptive field notes, class artifacts, and, sometimes, student writing. Throughout each study I continued annotation and recursive analysis of emerging data (LeCompte & Preissle, 1993), triangulating different data types and sources to identify salient themes or categories relevant to student engagement in thinking for each focal student. These were taken to students and teachers for verification or confirmation, including stimulated recall sessions with discussion transcripts. Through descriptive–narrative accounts tracing the developing thinking for each focal student and each class, I created pattern explanations of how supported opportunities for thoughtful discussion develop students' thinking.

Because of space limitations, each study cannot be reported on in detail (see specific reports for complete accounts). Instead, I focus on key issues that emerged within and across studies, emphasizing the findings that contribute to our understanding of how teacher-mediated literature discussion can create a zone of proximal development that shapes students' habits of mind.

THE NEED TO TRANSFORM CLASSROOM CONTEXT — ROLES, PURPOSES, EPISTEMOLOGIES

Vygotsky argues (1978) that the zone of proximal development (ZPD) can be determined by comparing what a student can do alone and what she can do during "problem solving under adult guidance or in collaboration with more capable peers" (p. 86) (see also Chaiklin, this volume). In classrooms, then, "functions which have not yet matured" can become the focus of instruction only in the context of collaborative problem solving. To create such an activity context, teachers need to transform much that has been traditional in schools: the roles they and their students play, the purposes for their talking, and the stance toward knowing and understanding. In the Critical Thinking/Discussion study (Miller, 1988; 1990; 1992), I examined three urban-school contexts for whole-class discussion of brief versions of challenging philosophical and narrative texts, largely Western classics (e.g., short excerpts from Kafka, Bacon, Pascal). Though all of the texts were not literary, many were narrative, and the professional development project the teachers engaged in approached these texts in classes across the curriculum as open to interpretation, asking students to draw on prior knowledge to make meaning. An overview of selected findings from these classrooms provides insight into why two of the teachers successfully transformed their classroom social contexts for open-forum discussion, while one could not.

"Trying to Understand Together" in Linda's Class

Many students in Linda Mitchell's ninth-grade class found open-forum discussion unfamiliar and at first did not actively participate: Her student Jack told me that he quietly observed in early discussions, to see "what was normal." To transform typical classroom talk, Linda said, she tried to send consistent "messages" to students that as a group they all would be "working together." Rearranging the desks into an "almost perfect circle" where they all sat facing to see and hear each other, she physically signaled distribution to students of authority to interpret the text. She focused on changing her singular role as the knowledge expert by changing her usual verbal behavior: Besides asking authentic questions about what puzzled her in the reading, she listened to students more than she talked, allowed students to determine their own turns for speaking, and changed to informal nonevaluative language ("I'm kinda' confused"), to become a facilitative participant and encourage students to take on new active roles for themselves.

For students in early discussions who tended to "dispute" about who was "right," Linda provided strategies for helping students consider differences reflectively. For instance, she modeled probing strategies for responding to alternative perspectives, asking students to clarify what they said: "So are you saying . . . ?" She allowed long pauses (often more than 20 seconds), reminding students of the need for "thinking time." Often she focused on enforcing group-developed ground rules ("Julie didn't finish yet") and provided strategies to help students learn discussion behavior – "to listen, respond, and collaborate." Linda persistently reminded them to "listen to others," supplying metaphors for collaboration ("meaning will build and grow"), demonstrating useful, concrete strategies: For example, it is evident on videotape that students look at each speaker, as Linda had suggested. During discussion she looked thoughtfully around the circle, reading students' behavior to see how she could help (e.g., "David's been waiting" or "Did you want to ask Rose a question?"). In interviews students pointed to their "ground rules," developed together in an initial discussion and enforced by Linda or students, as creating a "safe" atmosphere and a "serious purpose" (David) for discussion. As different points of view emerged, students discovered what for many was the surprise and lure of discussion: "People do have a lot of different opinions," Nicole marveled; "you would think they would have an opinion like yours."

As social changes began to occur through negotiation in the talking itself, students were cognitively transforming, as well, developing a more reflective stance toward meaning. They began to adopt Linda's socially useful language strategies for trying to understand: They kept the talk open to possibilities by stating claims tentatively ("Maybe not, maybe it's . . ."), owning their ideas ("I think that what he's saying is . . ."), suggesting alternatives ("Could it mean that . . . ?"), and asking, as Linda often did, for clarification that invited others to explain, for example, "You're saying [that behavior] helps, but it doesn't solve the problem?"

Over time, with Linda's help at points when they needed it, the students saw themselves change from their "debating" attitude. They began "talking *with* each other" rather than "talking *at* each other," Jack explained, which is "something that two people not in a discussion do." Students I interviewed repeatedly pointed out that "how we learned to listen" and "talk with" each other were shaped by their purpose of "trying to understand together."

The "Text Written in Stone" in Rita's Class

At first it seemed that Rita Wilson introduced discussion similarly to her class, telling students that the purpose was for them to provide proof for their beliefs and opinions about texts. However, the quantitative profile of thinking and discussion for the class – including indicators for students' providing evidence, explanation, questions, and collaborating – declined after the initial discussion. Rita's response to student questions in discussions illustrated a tension in her discussion goals. In an early discussion of a text by Francis Bacon, for example, when a student posed the initial question "What is revenge?" Rita responded:

You mean, what is revenge according to him? To Bacon? When is the only time it's allowed? To him. Wait. Why don't we find that spot and figure it out because it's a good question (two-second pause). What is it then? When does he allow it?

In the subsequent six turns, students searched for the place in the text that tells when Bacon allowed revenge and asked Rita for "hints" about where to look, and Rita told them where. When they found the right answers, students were not sure what they had accomplished: One asked, "Do we have an opening question?" and Rita went to write on the board to explain.

In six instances (two or three turns each) of students' speaking to each other in that discussion, Rita intervened to answer, explain, repeat, or change the subject. By answering and transforming students' questions, heading off their interaction, and focusing mainly on finding text answers to her questions, Rita worked against her stated purpose of having students generate alternatives and weigh the evidence for them. She communicated that teacher and student roles would not change, and student attempts to ask questions and collaborate virtually disappeared in subsequent discussions.

Her discussion behavior revealed tension from conflicting attitudes about the teacher's discussion role: "To become an authority figure shuts the whole thing down," but "to play, to accomplish that [new] role is very difficult." In interviews she expressed anger about a student who asked questions to introduce new topics: "He is trying to be the teacher." Over time, as Rita maintained a physical position of authority, often standing at the chalkboard to explain, her behavior seemed to derive from strong beliefs about texts.

When students in discussion of a music video did not see "*the* meaning of the song" that Rita saw, she told them, "You are just not thinking critically enough to see some of the similarities." She did not support her interpretations but increasingly added them to conclude discussions: for example, "What Schopenauer is trying to tell you...." Because of these lessons that she could see in both written and visual texts, Rita eventually told students: that "makes me think a little more critically than you." On the basis of her gradually revealed view that text meaning is, she said, "written in stone," to be read each time the same, Rita understandably had concluded that it was students' failure to interpret and think critically that led them to alternative interpretations: "They want to talk, but not think."

Rita's 11th graders felt that, as her student Andrea put it, discussion went "downhill" over time. Andrea, who was at first excited by discussion and actively participated, eventually fell silent, as many did. She and other students became increasingly passive, waiting, as Michael put it, "to see if we had the right answer." Andrea perceived a problem: Ms. Wilson "brings us to a conclusion... she has a better background, but it throws us off." All five of the students I interviewed said that compared to other classes, the social "atmosphere" was not good for discussion. Jeremy, whom Rita called a "bright student," stopped participating. He concluded that Ms. Wilson was like "most teachers," who "give you class work and say, 'Okay, the answers are in the book,' not letting the student really think about the answers. So students never really use critical thinking." Taken together, these two cases, Rita's and Linda's discussions, illustrate the importance of teachers' explicit and implicit messages about text meanings, student and teacher roles, ways of knowing, and purposes for talking in discussion. Rita's conflicting messages undermined her explicit invitation to discussion: Students saw that they were not authorized to ask questions or give their own responses or interpretations in the class. In contrast, Linda's consistent messages that the purpose for talking was a problem-solving activity – making sense of a perplexing text together – created new reciprocal roles in an engaging social space. The successful teacher initiated the social context for discussion, and the resulting mediated conversation created a zone of proximal development – allowing students to do together with assistance what they could not do on their own.

TEACHERS AS MEDIATORS: SUPPORTING WAYS OF TALKING AND THINKING

Teachers who mediated discussion successfully listened well, providing support carefully when it was needed – after waiting to see whether other students might provide a next step or move. These teachers showed continual respect for students' emerging new abilities, allowing room for students to take responsibility for posing and pursuing questions.

Supporting Interpretive Questioning

Over time, the way of questioning and reading that Linda Mitchell demonstrated and encouraged during discussion influenced how students learned to discuss. She asked what she called "legitimate questions," ones she did not think she "knew the answer for," in a manner that suggested the text needed to be responded to and puzzled over: She began one discussion with, "I wondered about why the fourth reason was different and I thought we could talk about that." Questioning the text in this way and publicly sharing even vaguely formed responses became the habitual approach for students in the class.

Linda also mediated specific interpretive strategies for trying to understand together by asking questions that structured a movement back and forth *from* students' own experiences and responses *to* the written text. The manner of her mediation of these routines for meaning-making is evident in the sequences of her questions during the first class discussion. Linda responded to encourage movement from personal response back to the text in 30% of her 20 turns, an emphatic signal to students to look at what they were composing through the frame of the text. Within this one discussion two students began to return to the text *on their own* to question meaning. Over time, discussions became more textual as students took on this useful strategy that Linda fostered.

These students felt their developing sense of interpretive authority most sharply when they pursued student-generated questions together. In the 16th discussion of the year, for example (of an excerpt from Euclid's *The Elements*), Ivan was keenly perplexed about what Euclid meant by "A point is that which has no parts." Even before Linda could ask her prepared opening question, Ivan said, "I don't understand this; can someone explain this to me?!" This authentic question prompted students to go spontaneously to the chalkboard for the first time to draw their explanations. Ivan's question produced a quickening of the talk: The group examined their ways of understanding "point" and other concepts – "angle," "next to," and "straight line" – in a closely textual discussion that many, including the teacher, felt was their best. Students asked more questions of the text and each other than ever before as they saw "so many complications," Laura said, that they had never considered when they had memorized similar definitions for their first geometry test. Much as Dewey (1933) argues, perplexity spurred their reflection.

The results of coded discussions showed that the number of student substantive and probing questions and text-base comments rose in discussion of this "difficult" mathematics text and then was sustained at a generally higher level for the last three discussions. Over the course of the year all indicators for collaborative thinking increased, including student–student collaboration and student-initiated questioning, interpretations, explanations, and evidence.

Supporting Evaluative Questioning

In this same study, in contrast to Linda's discussion focus on interpreting the text, another teacher, Pat Baker, structured questions that provided strategies for an evaluative stance toward text meaning. She explicitly tutored students in evaluative question-finding by asking them to "focus in on some of the stuff I just read" – say what the author might mean. Then, she asked students to consider, "Do you agree with that?" For example, she began discussion of Pascal's *Pensées* with "What is Pascal saying?" After students made a few interpretive observations, she asked, "Do you agree?" Rather than working only within the text to interpret it, the question suggests, students evaluate – they analyze whether they are with or against the author.

Pat approached evaluation of text justifications with a similar strategy, another questioning structure, which provided her with a solution to the problem that she had early on identified – developing her discussion role, that is, how to help students "to clarify without the teacher doing all the clarification." Her questioning routines supplied her with the answer. For instance, she asked of the text written by Galileo, "How does he try to prove his point?" When Tannis said, "He uses examples," Pat followed with this sequence of questions: "What is his example? [students provided one] . . . Show us where you have that [students looked at the printed example] . . . So is he proving his point or disproving it?" This structured movement helped students learn to move between claims and examples to evaluate justification – Pat's own approach to meaning-making. At points of need she supported what she called students' "working on a process" of questioning and evaluating justifications for beliefs.

After 6 months of discussion in Pat's class, a student for the first time took up Pat's repeated request for students to pose the opening question for discussion. The dramatic text by Thucydides was a conversation between Athenian and Melian leaders. Jane tentatively asked, "Do you feel the Melians were right [to fight the more powerful Athenians and die], or do you feel they should have given up?" After 43 seconds of silence (an eternity in classroom time), Pat nudged students to respond to Jane's "excellent question"– an evaluative one that called for questioning the values operating in the text.

Terry immediately responded, "I think they should have given in!" When students in an alarmed chorus asked, "Why?!" she answered that it was "a chance for survival." Pat probed students' unelaborated claims until a specific problem of the text became focused, when Jane said the Melians were fighting for a "just cause," and Terry scoffed at this version of the world as a "fairy tale." In the face of the opposing perspective to which Terry gave voice, students searched for ways to persuade her in long stretches of collaboration without the teacher's help. To illustrate, the following sequence occurred at the end of discussion, after Terry argued that the Melians should give up because the Athenians were "stronger":

(1) STUDENT: But they [Melians] are still going to fight [as Athenian conscripts]!

(2) TERRY: I think that's foolish. That's foolish.

(3) JANE: When it is one-against-one you should fight, but when it's a larger amount against a large, larger amount they should give up? (A reference to Terry's earlier comment that she would fight a bully for her lunch money)

(4) TERRY: I'm just taking into consideration all the people's lives that are going to be lost. And all the people's lives that are going to be saved (students speak all at once).

(5) TANNIS: On page 98, in the last paragraph where it says it was "a hard fight." Okay, you don't know. (2-second pause) For the ones that got killed, yeah, some of them got killed, yeah. But the ones that started the fight [Athenians], their men got killed, too. So they are saying life was taken and they was fighting for a good reason.

(6) DON: Terry (2-second pause), they were going to have to fight anyway. Why fight on a side that you really don't want to, instead of fighting for something that you do want to?

(7) TERRY: They didn't want to fight period. They didn't even want to fight for this (students all speak at once)

(8) JANE: Terry, that's what everyone is trying to tell you. So why not fight for something you want to protect, rather than go over there

and fight and help these people? (an idea supported earlier – help Athenians conquer other peoples)

(9) TANNIS: For something you don't believe in (4 seconds).

(10) JANE: Do you understand that?

(11) TERRY: Yeah . . . (students speak at once)

(18) ANDRE: (speaking for the first time, loud, above the rest) On page 96, the third paragraph, that sum it up right there. It say, "If your subjects will risk so much to be free of you, how can you expect us to submit to you?' We're still free. Shouldn't we try everything to avoid losing that?' " . . . Anything can happen in a war.

In this excerpt, students test the power of an array of justifications and reasoning for their claims: framing a contrast to question Terry's reasoning (3); translating words of the text as a drama of self-defense (5); posing questions of motivating choices in the text (6); recasting Terry's objection as an argument for fighting "to protect" (8) – and in other previous sequences numerous examples, analogies, explanations.

Right after Andre's text evidence (18) Terry said, "Okay, I agree, I agree with that." Students broke into applause, but then, immediately, asked, "Why?" – a question the teacher had frequently asked her students. Terry summed up the class arguments that persuaded her. It was "our best discussion all year," both Jane and Terry later told me, spurred on by "my one little opposition." In this discussion students saw for the first time what they could do together. They felt their community form around raising their own questions and pursuing them collaboratively – the essence of critical thinking (Dewey, 1933).

The results of discussion coding in Pat's class illustrate the dramatic changes that occurred in this class that at the beginning Pat said "just won't discuss." The proportion of student turns taken in each discussion changed from a low of 58% to a high of 88% in this turning point discussion, the 19th of the year. The proportion of student–student collaborative turns made similar changes, to a high of 76% of student turns, and was sustained at this new higher level for the last coded discussion. Student-initiated substantive questions, probing questions, explanation, and text-based comments increased in this discussion and continued to rise. The greatest amount of providing evidence also occurred. These gains were accompanied by decreases in Pat's questions. For example, she asked about one-third as many probing questions as students did in this turning point discussion.

Pat's students were quite aware of what had happened in the class and of these changes themselves. Jane saw Miss Baker as "giving us things we're missing," but Sam explained how, then, she began to "let it go and see if it can go by itself." As discussions changed and students initiated and sustained their own inquiry, Pat was able to begin, as Sam suggested, to "slowly break away." Asking questions was a sign, Terry said, of "really thinking": She explained, "At first it was hard," but "as time went on, we started making up our own questions," and by the end, "we led" discussion, in a process that gives "students more ability to think for themselves. . . . It is like we are in control." Pat's student Sam told me that after class he had "discussions" in his mind, so that it was "hard to concentrate in gym class." These and other comments suggest that the dialogue of critical thinking was moving inward.

In these two case studies, the teachers successfully transformed classroom ways of talking by constructing a classroom epistemology in which texts were open to multiple interpretations and ways of knowing. Teachers mediated class discussions in these contexts, creating a zone of proximal development in discussion by providing the mediational means at the points of need for interpreting written and oral texts together. Over time students appropriated socially useful assistance from teachers and other students to solve perceived problems of meaning. In two classes the change to new intellectual dispositions was evident in students' conscious use of the mediated social and cognitive strategies.

INSTRUCTIONAL ASSISTANCE FOR STUDENTS WITH MANY NEEDS — SHARON'S CLASSES

In the Literature Discussion Study[1] (Miller, 1991a; 1991b; 1999) I worked with a teacher who carefully "read" the needs of her students to figure out how to assist their performance. Sharon Legge mediated students' narrative modes of thinking in multiple activities, but particularly through text discussions. She saw that to engage students in the "at-risk program," she needed to provide more instructional assistance than in her college-bound class. As students in both classes resisted and then took up her invitation to share their thinking and feeling responses to literature, she provided narrative strategies at points of need, including heuristics to help students (1) notice narrative gaps, (2) pose narrative dilemmas, and (3) speculate on possible intentions behind human actions by drawing on their own lived experience.

Sharon created varying forms of assistance to meet the needs of her seniors who were at-risk of not graduating. She used writing as a tool for generating response, giving students time "to just jot down what they think about something and read it back" as a means of starting discussion. When students had difficulties understanding first-person narratives, Sharon read the texts aloud, functioning as a "fellow reader," stopping often to ask the class to respond and speculate about possible interpretations; in short, she externalized the internal dialogue of reading. Her

---

[1] This work was sponsored by the National Council of Teachers of English Research Foundation Grant-in-Aid Program.

close attention to what students needed was at the center of her effective teaching – both an intellectual *and* an emotional attentiveness (see DiPardo and Potter, this volume).

Teacher-Mediated Discussion in the Narrative Mode

Students in the at-risk class, who had failed in other literature classes, were not accustomed to drawing on their life experience in school. During discussion Sharon drew on her connection-making strategies, improvising stories of her own experiences – of a relative's losing her memory, Sharon's refusal to go to her brother's funeral viewing, an acquaintance's being illegally jailed – and in the process demonstrated how she used what she knew from her own and others' experiences as a tool to make sense of texts.

The questioning procedures she provided also supported students' making personal connections. In one questioning structure, for example, Sharon moved from talking about one part of the text to ask, "Can you connect that to your experience?" and, then, in response to students' experiences, "So what do you make of the text, based on that connection?" For instance, as the character Adam in *I Am the Cheese* tried to figure out his past, the doctor asked him about his earliest memory. At this point Sharon asked students the same question. Students shared their memory stories for 21 turns and Sharon said, "What's a common thread about the memories we have?" Mark summed up, "They're bad." Kate said, "Scary." Then Sharon asked students to take their stories back "to the painful experiences Adam has in the story" to understand his feelings better. Sharon was asking students to use their own "storied experiences" as "a basis for understanding new action episodes by means of analogy" (Polkinghorne, 1995, p. 11), the central move of narrative reflection in literature and in life. This repeated sequence of Sharon's questioning helped students successfully draw on personal social knowledge to inform their understanding of narrative text.

These students soon began to appropriate this strategy. For instance, when students talked of how Holden was rebuffed by a boy he had been nice to, Cara spontaneously drew on her own experience, providing a long storied explanation of how "that usually happens," how "people seem to forget" what you do for them, even "best friends." Sharon asked students to connect this knowledge back to the text: "What do you suppose Holden's experience in that area has been?" Students then seemed to feel Holden's loneliness. Cara said, "He's gotten nothing back from anybody." This ability to see the social, psychological dimensions of texts in ways similar to viewing events from their own lives has been shown to be an important strategy for making inferences about character actions, motives, and goals, a strategy that is often excluded from school approaches to texts (Hynds, 1989). In literature, readers always need to "supply what is meant from what is not said" (Iser, 1978, p. 168), interpretive gaps even college undergraduates have difficulty bridging on their own (Earthman, 1992). Sharon's instructional assistance for inquiring into the gaps supported the dialectic of narrative reflection (Bruner, 1986).

Student-Initiated Narrative Reflection

Increasingly these students felt the usefulness of elaborating responses to develop their own understanding and persuade others and began to appropriate the strategies, "interiorizing" them, Vygotsky (1978) would say. The discussions provide evidence that students were consciously engaging in the kind of dialogic reading and narrative reflection that Sharon had been supporting all year. In many sequences they raised problems in the text for consideration, made connections to their lives to try to understand, suggested explanations that would fill the gaps in plot and character, and returned to the text for further consideration.

A fairly typical sample of conversation from the end of the school year shows how students initiated the learned narrative strategies as tools for making sense and reflecting on narrative significance. As students read their written responses to the film *Stand by Me*, Janet suddenly posed a question in response to another student's interpretation: "Why did it take a stranger's death to make Gordie realize that his brother was gone? . . . Why did it make him grow up so fast?" Janet was clearly perplexed, even agitated, as she spoke, and students responded by speculating on reasons, drawing on the text and their own experiences. They suggested that Gordie had not been able to say good-bye to his brother and then that the brother's death was just too shocking and unfamiliar, as were the recent deaths of their own classmates. Sharon listened as her students puzzled over these genuine questions. Here is a sample of how these students had learned to make narrative sense together (underlined parts spoken simultaneously):

(1) JANET: When I heard that Bill Spear died, I mean I didn't know him, I knew he went to this school, he was my age, it didn't affect me in the sense of that I grew up.

(2) MARK: But when Sammy Kelly [another classmate] died, it was just like, when you're a teenager, <u>and</u> –

(3) JANET: <u>I was</u> emotionally attached to Sammy!

(4) MARK: Like when you're a teenager you don't think there's any chance you're dying until you're old, and then Sam died –

(5) JANET: It's hard, there's a lot of people, there've been four or five people that died since I've been in school here.

(6) TERRY: Yeah, but you're older, they [the boys in the film] were a lot younger. They were just getting out of elementary schools. They're not used to really dealing with it.

(7) KATE: They needed something visual to make them realize death.

(8) TERRY: When you're in high school and you're a senior, I mean, you've probably had grandmothers or a friend or somebody who died, at least you have that realization then.

(9) JOYCE: When you're younger, you think no one dies.

(10) TERRY: We have that maturity to deal with it, more than you have when you're younger.

The strategies for narrative reflection students used on their own here were the ones that Sharon had been providing all year at points of student need. It seems clear here that students used the strategies seamlessly – as tools of the mind ready for use. At first Janet (1) made a connection in a personal story of their classmate Bill's death to suggest a different possible world where death does not cause growth and awareness. Then, from their repertoire of stories, Mark introduced the story of how Sam's death shattered a belief they shared as teenagers (2, 4). With this connection, an experience Janet had felt more keenly (3), she began to remember consciously (5) a different story of the possibility that another's death might profoundly change the living. Terry (6) continued this narrative potentiality by relating it to the boys in the text, pointing out how differences in life experience made Janet's experience with Bill Spear less helpful in understanding Gordie, a much younger boy. Kate (7) persuaded further by speculating on another possible reason for Gordie's realization: the physical–visual incarnation of death shocked him into an internal change. Terry (8) entered in to finish working out the differences in perspective between them, as seniors, and the 12-year-old boys in the film: She enlarged Mark's comment to suggest additional experiences teenagers their age might have had. This collaboration illustrates live narrative reflection – students' moving from interpretations of their experiences to reason out the puzzling perceptions and beliefs of the characters. As they shuttled back and forth between personal experiences and the text, they used their connections to consider together how the boys in the movie are both like them, in trying to deal with death, and, unlike them, "a lot younger." As they filled the textual gaps with connections to their own lived experiences, they developed personal relationships with the text and each other. Such recurring instances of students' attention and desire to understand impelled their aesthetic and narrative reflection.

In discussions such as this *Stand by Me* excerpt, students were engaged in narrative reflection that "gives us explanatory knowledge of why a person acted as he or she did; it makes another's action as well as our own, understandable" (Polkinghorn, 1995). In the whole stretch of discussion, they sustained their narrative reflection *interdependently* to understand the significance of a shared experience for the problem they posed and pursued. Greene (1995) argues that the kind of question Janet asked about what it means to understand death "can be refined only by sensitive inquiry, by dialogue, by connectedness" (p. 102). Brett, who was headed to the navy after graduation, was conscious of how the dialogue had become part of his thinking: "Discussions in Ms. L.'s class always have meaning.... We always talk about what we are reading so everybody gets these questions.... We ask questions of ourselves and if they sound good we ask them aloud. We learn from everybody else's experiences as well as our own when we take part." As students appropriated tools for their own inquiry, they were learning to use narrative as "an instrument of mind on behalf of meaning making" (Bruner, 1986, p. 41).

MEDIATING CULTURAL CRITIQUE IN LITERATURE DISCUSSIONS

On one level, the mediated strategies for making sense of texts in the previous studies were varied. From another view, however, many of these sense-making strategies required students to work primarily with the text to interpret it, rather than questioning the text to critique its assumptions. An important question thus arises, Which habits of mind do teachers mediate through literature discussion? (Miller, 1996a). Sociocultural theorists who focus specifically on social uses of language as markers of identities and group membership suggest that the worldviews of texts must be part of what we teach. For example, Gee (1996) suggests that to develop powerful literacy students need to learn to critique the dominant or mainstream cultural discourse, with its worldview, through the lens of a secondary discourse. This notion is congruent with Bakhtin's formulation that only through "interanimation" of different social languages can one engage in critical thinking by becoming conscious of such languages as perspectives and actively "choosing one's orientation among them" (Bakhtin, 1981). In current literature scholarship, many (e.g., Scholes, 1985) argue that students need to learn how to question and historically contextualize texts to gain textual power through consciousness of embedded cultural values. In only one context that I studied – three integrated English–social studies classes taught by the same pair of teachers[2] – did teachers consistently provoke and support this kind of critical thinking about narratives.

Assisting Critical-Narrative Thinking

The long-term problem for the integrated English–social studies class – composing a coherent personal vision of the American Dream – served as a guiding inquiry for students (Miller, 1996b, 1996d, 1998b). Several

---

[2] This work was sponsored by the National Research Center for Literature Teaching and Learning, U.S. Department of Education.

"ongoing conversations" characterized the talk and activity of the class as they pursued this problem. Kira called it "the back and forth" of the class, which included the recursive movement between the private and public (e.g., from private journals to public discussion to private journals), between fiction and nonfiction texts (e.g., *The Jungle* and the Statue of Liberty inscription), and among social–cultural perspectives (e.g., early Europeans and Native Americans).

In the Native American/Immigrant Experience theme, for example, students all read Hawthorne's *The Scarlet Letter* and individually read Native American fiction, autobiography, and biography, which they reported on and discussed with the whole class. Films included the fictional *Thunderheart* and *Avalon* and a documentary on Geronimo. Students individually researched, wrote, and reported on family immigration histories and also wrote poems about the Native American experience. By using stories of the lived experiences of individuals or groups, whether autobiographical or fictional, the teachers aimed to have students understand the "effects of [historical] events on people's lives." As one student described it, "We talk about the little struggles of people, rather than only the big struggles of countries."

Sharon, the English teacher described earlier, later in her career collaborated with Ron, a social studies teacher in this class; together they aimed to create an "ongoing dialogue of history and stories and events." As students "entered into" lived experiences in reading literature and dramatizing history (e.g., the Columbus Trial and labor history newscasts), Sharon and Ron supported activities and provided instructional tools. Sharon again used the narrative reflection strategies that had been successful in the at-risk class – such as guiding students to connect their own experiences to the text to make sense of narrative gaps. In addition, new conversational strategies emerged for helping students reflect on their own and others' assumptions and values – including raising alternative cultural perspectives, questioning the author's values, and seeking missing voices. A key heuristic mediated and learned in the class was a series of questions central to critique of power and social relations: "Who is the speaker?" "What is the speaker's agenda?" "What voices are left out?" This sequence became the basis for a critical-narrative text stance, which specifically asked students to make sense of stories, but also to question perspectives and stories and to generate alternative cultural perspectives or stories not presented by a text (or a discussion). Students were well aware that Sharon and Ron provided them with what their student Nick called "major tools for understanding" both texts and social issues. As Maria saw it, "We're kind of taught *how* to think, which is not taught *what* to think. . . . You have to catch everything, you have to put it all together . . . everything connects to something else." During the school year students in all three classes learned to use these teacher-mediated tools consciously to engage in cultural critique with emphasis on how cultural, social, historical perspectives shape values and interests.

Interiorizing Critical-Narrative Thinking

In discussions throughout the year students were raising questions about events and intentions, generating opposing interpretations, looking through others' perspectives, bringing to bear all that they knew (from television news, from personal experience), moving between lived experience and authoritative discourse (of textbooks, laws, public statements), seeking out what was problematic or limited in stories and claims. By the end of the year, Kim told a story to exemplify her ability to consider multiple perspectives. It was a conversation she had had with her mother as they were passing a wealthy neighborhood bordered by a trailer park. "My mother said, 'Imagine what it is like to live in those beautiful houses and have to look out and see a trailer park!' I said, 'Imagine what it is like to live in the trailer park and have to look out and see those beautiful houses, knowing you can't have one?'" Kim told me this story as evidence of how looking through multiple perspectives and questioning single perspective in the class had changed her thinking. Here she proposes a missing story of lived experience in her mother's comment. Kim's explanation is consistent with Friere's notion that in learning to read texts critically students also learn to read the world (1998).

As students experienced the power of literature as a way of knowing, some argued that this kind of narrative understanding was essential to understanding history and the world. For instance, Kim saw the events in the literature they read as in a sense "real" and said that only through such stories could she know "what to do with" the "bundle of facts" from history textbooks. During one discussion after students in groups had compared the history textbook version of topics that they had researched on their own from multiple primary sources, students were struck by how much was left out. They considered the problem together. The following short collaboration in a whole-class format began with reference to something Andre had said earlier about history textbooks' being "factual":

(1) KRIS: This is for Andre. Just wondering, if you were in a concentration camp and someone was writing about that in a history book, wouldn't you want the story of the people in there to be in the book?

(2) ANDRE: What is a fact? It should just tell what happened.

(3) MARK: Facts can also be quotes from people.

(4) KRIS: [to Mark] But he says if it's not in there [textbook], go read another book.

(5) PAM: If there's 9 million people in the population and you want everyone's point of view, that's what you guys are saying. If a text just had facts it would be thin.

(6) MARCOS: We could make a book with all facts, but what would be the point of reading that book?

(7) LORI: It's like, you know there was a Russian Revolution, but you don't know what it was about.

Kris (1), who had written in her journal that reading the Native American stories had "set a fire" inside her, asks the class to look through the eyes of someone in a concentration camp to understand the importance of people's stories' being represented in history. Despite her passion for this topic, she addresses Andre thoughtfully, with an explicit appeal to looking through others' eyes to understand the private human consequences in these public events. Andre (2) names a problem that has been implicit in much of their talk about the nature of "facts" – what are they? – and Mark (3) contends that what people have to say, their stories, would count as "facts" – a redefinition to include subjectivities in the factual. Pam's (5) individualist stance is evident as she reduces the problem to an apolitical one of just too many views (9 million!) and limited space. Marcos (6) and Lori (7) take up her "just facts" idea and collaborate briefly on the idea that history needs to include people's stories in order to understand "the point" or "to know what it was about." In this conversation and in many others, students were seriously reflecting on the problem of what counts as knowing. Not only did Chris, Pam, Marcos, and Lori problematize "facts," they collaboratively argued the need for narrative knowing.

Their argument echoes Bruner (1986): We need narratives to "constitute the psychological and cultural reality in which the participants in history actually live," to understand the "life stuff" of history (p. 43), and, I think they would add, to hear a play of multiple stories on that history. These kinds of conversations were not happenstance, but carefully prepared for in the talk and activity of the class. The interdisciplinary social context evolved into a democratic classroom culture in which multiple perspectives became valued. With the teachers' assistance, students learned how literature provides understanding of the human consequences of public events, and how history provides the sociocultural public context for personal experience and action.

The role of literature in imagining change was also made clear in the class. Literature, Bruner (1986) has argued, functions to "open us to dilemmas, to the hypothetical, to the range of possible worlds that a text can refer to.... Literature subjunctivizes, makes strange, renders the obvious less so, the unknowable less so as well.... Literature, in this spirit, is an instrument of freedom" (Bruner, 1986, p. 159). Literature as "an instrument of freedom" gained power in the class when the teachers, and then students, situated texts within their social–historical contexts and by, narrative analogy (Polkinghorne, 1995), within larger contexts of human intention and action.

Through this focus, students learned strategies for cultural critique and learned about the power of collective action and commitment. In their final discussion of the book *The Scarlet Letter*, a lengthy collaboration prompted by a student's question illustrates the point. When Dick asked about the scarlet letter, "Was that like a physical thing, or was it like mental? ...I don't understand," students examined the text and the context, eventually connecting this symbol to other historical symbols of resisting tyranny. Alice connected it to the "Star of David" Jews were forced to wear by Nazis. Ron identified Alice's comment as "historical thinking" and asked students for other examples. Students collaborated to provide an example in Denmark of the people's wearing Jewish symbols in collective action against the Nazis. Cara (44) provided a similar example of a whole town's resistance to oppression from neo-Nazis in the United States. This conversation demonstrated how the mutual orchestration of cultural stories and histories provided the means of constructing the idea of democratic action through conversation on a canonical text. In the end, Ron proposed that such resistance helps to redefine power away from uniforms and authoritative discourse and toward a social life based in dialogue and joint action. Ron and Sharon's dialogic pedagogy (Miller, 1993) offers a conversational vision of schooling through which it is possible not only to teach and learn critical-narrative thinking, but also to promote the possibility of such social "habits of the heart" (Bellah, Madsen, Sullivan, Swindler, & Tipton, 1985).

THE ROLE OF LITERATURE IN LEARNING ACROSS THE CURRICULUM

Potentially, the habits of the heart and mind learned in literature discussion could play a role in student learning and meaning-making in other disciplinary contexts. To examine this possibility, in a 4-year longitudinal ethnography[3] (e.g., Miller 1994; 1996c; 1998c), I examined what role teacher-mediated open-forum discussion in English classes played over time in developing students' thinking. Of particular interest was how 10 students moving from class to class and teacher to teacher made sense of the reading, writing, and talking they encountered in classes during their high school years; what thinking they engaged in; and whether they used ways of thinking developed in literature classes in their other school experiences.

---

[3] This work was sponsored by the National Research Center for Literature Teaching and Learning, U.S. Department of Education.

Dialogic Habits of Mind

As in previously described classrooms, the focal students in these case studies did develop new habits of mind through open-forum literature discussions. Over the first year students internalized the teacher-mediated discussion heuristics, initiating a kind of dialogic reading and reflection (Gadamer, 1967) that shuttled between text and self, response and reflection, private and public understandings. In particular, students learned to extend and question initial responses for themselves in ways that became socially valued in the class: For example, in the collaborative group and then alone in writing, they connected text and personal experience; questioned the text and each other; evaluated possible interpretations; identified difficult passages and generated plausible explanations; moved back and forth from the landscape of actions to speculation about human intentions and consciousness; and created imagery, metaphor, dramatization to generate understanding. There is much evidence of students' initiating movement among perspectives to create reasoned positions in discussion and writing about literature. Evidence from discussion-based literature classes suggests that students' discussion experiences shaped their dialogic thinking, characterized by both self-reflexive strategies and the intellectual disposition to use them. Most students used these dialogic thinking strategies learned in one English class in their subsequent ones.

Use of Strategies Learned in Literature in Other Classes

But learning these mediated strategies for reflecting about literary texts did not assure use of these strategies in other classroom contexts. As the 10 students moved into their science, social studies, and mathematics classes, differences in students' *inclination* to respond to, elaborate, question, and monitor understanding of the content of class lessons were not related to specific disciplines, but to *students' interpretations* of the purposes for and the nature of class talk and activity. During extensive interviewing over 4 years, students distinguished classes on the basis of which social contexts invited or required active engagement in thinking. Students reported how they "read" the class talk and activity as instructional "texts" that were open or closed to influence by students, what Bakhtin (1981) would call univocal – not modifiable by others – or dialogic – an invitation to thinking and producing meaning (Wertsch, 1991).

Some of the observed social studies, math, and science classes invited a dialogue of alternative possibilities as a means of creating understanding. For example, in chemistry class students worked in pairs on ill-formed problems, and Saul introduced questioning strategies from literature discussions as the means of generating and speculating on alternative possibilities and then evaluating them. In Anya's Global Studies class students acted out simulations, dramatizing the clash of Chinese landowners and traders, to create a dialogue for understanding the lived experience of those alternative perspectives; in this class students also did research on a country, and each became an expert dramatizing that point of view in discussions around global concerns, such as environmental issues. In these instances, the play of perspectives was treated as important to understanding the dynamic whole, opening students to multiple possibilities for the topic, constituting a narrative stance toward understanding, rather than linear analysis toward one fixed idea.

Students also used a general mode of narrative thinking to understand problems in classes they felt allowed such reflection. In math, Cara wrote her "Math Biography," in which she told the story of what math had been like for her and then continued that story in her mathematics journal, to include her feelings; she became aware of her different ways of thinking about math by exploring responses to assignments and class events, by exploring possibilities for the graphics calculators, by examining ways of studying, by considering her uses of strategies. The emphasis on her lived experience and feelings, on developing strategies, on the stimulation problems can provoke invited Cara to see math for the first time, she said, as a motivated sense-making activity done by "people . . . not just computers." This context engaged Cara differently than earlier mathematics classes had: It focused on her process of coming to know.

Another student, Grady, engaged in an ongoing conversation with a social studies teacher (whom he called Mr. V.). Among other strategies, we have evidence of Grady's overtly and covertly composing what Mr. V. called "learnings," a heuristic he explicitly taught for connecting historical stories of motivated action with modern parallels. Sometimes Grady used literary parallels, which Mr. V. accepted as valid personal connections. For instance, in a social studies discussion of how society judges terrible crimes, Grady provided the story of the murders in Steinbeck's *Of Mice and Men*, read the previous year in English class, as a means of examining how judgments about crimes can change as one considers the circumstances in context, through a human perspective of the lived consciousness of experience. This narrative strategy for understanding human action by examining the landscape of inner intention was, of course, central to English class discussions. Grady identified Mr. V. as the first social studies teacher to engage him to "see a bigger picture" of "history as a living thing." All of these teachers were constructing knowledge jointly with students in order for them to understand deeply and personally; conversational strategies for meaning learned in literature discussion became relevant and useful in such classroom contexts, regardless of discipline.

In some instances, though, the teacher's view of disciplinary knowledge made the strategies inappropriate or irrelevant. In contrast to the apprenticeship with Mr. V., Grady remembered the frustration and the lack of respect he had felt 4 years earlier in eighth grade, when his social studies teacher passed over his question – "What did it feel like to live through the Civil War?" – in order to finish a review of definitions of words in a chronological outline. Grady compared this teacher to a "priest, always saying the gospel the same," who, when asked a question, always gave back a "textbook answer." Students regarded the textbook in such classes as a source of fixed knowledge that was treated as not open to questioning or speculation. In another example, Cara's tendency to make meaning with stories emerged in her science class when she shared brief personal experiences with physical forces, as when the stone wall in front of her house repeatedly fell down. The teacher discouraged her talk and in our interview asked us, "Can you get her to stop telling personal anecdotes? She slows us down." This gap in perceptions between what Cara and her science teacher found relevant can be traced to different views of knowledge as fixed in texts *or* created by knowers. In these and other cases, the students were relating their existing knowledge, experience, and meaning-making strategies to the class content. Over time, such instances decreased, as students learned a narrower view of relevance. Todd, for instance, at first voiced his keen interest in questions of fairness and human relations in science and social studies classes, but over time he learned this was "Stuff off the subject, so I don't usually ask."

In dialogic classes students used organic metaphors for describing the classroom interaction and thoughtfulness ("We ask a question, like a seed and think about it together, like fertilizer, until it blooms"). In contrast, students perceived themselves mechanically in monologic contexts: one student said he was a "vacuum cleaner that sucks up some facts that will be on the test." Students concluded that thinking was not required in such classes, and they were keenly aware of which classes provided authentic invitations for reflection on course content.

Episodes from these and many other classes revealed that students most often used strategies when they felt they were in a dialogue with a human being who played with ideas and engaged them in conversations about problems – that is, in Vygotsky's terms, classes in which teachers engaged students in talk and activity to create a zone of proximal development (ZPD) for learning. These teachers created an atmosphere in which the recursive, dialogic process of problem posing and solving included curiosity and visualizations, feelings and mistakes, questioning and pursuing of possible answers. Teachers in these classes seemed to be acting out disciplinary thinking, each in her or his own dialectic of creative and critical thinking. The consistent message students read in the purposes for these classes was inventive, strategic, and collaborative sense-making that engaged the class in authentic disciplinary practice and in exploration of meaning as connected with everyday knowledge – what Brown, Collins and Duguid (1989, p. 38) call "cognitive apprenticeship." I want especially to emphasize the importance to students of the social and relational aspects of the teaching in these classes and the context it generated by calling it a *social–cognitive apprenticeship*. All of the focal students perceived such collaborative teaching as warmly inviting their sense-making and thinking.

CONCLUSIONS AND IMPLICATIONS

In all, this series of studies illustrates that in teacher-mediated open-forum discussion in which a problem of understanding is jointly pursued, the context becomes a supportive social space in which mutual assistance creates new ways of talking and thinking about text – that is, such discussion creates a zone of proximal development. Successful teachers both constructed these ZPDs through their approaches to literature and interactions *and* drew on their own ways of reading to mediate students' meaning-making. At points when students needed support – when, they were puzzled or did not elaborate or justify – teachers used their conversational turns to provide sequences of supports and questions as strategies. Each teacher's essential role was supporting students' responses to the text and each other, guiding attention, and providing instructional assistance for students' questioning, monitoring, and elaborating. Generally these strategies provided a structure for students to move from their initial responses toward more reasoned ones in a dialectical procedure that shuttled between text and self, interpretations and evaluations, personal response and public responsibilities to justify. Over time the dialogic strategies moved inward to become part of students' repertoires for meaning-making. In varying ways each teacher mediated specific habits of mind by lending her "structuring consciousness" (Vygotsky, 1978) to enable students to think in increasingly complex ways about texts, knowledge, and the world.

A few important factors in creating these open-forum discussions as ZPDs emerged across studies and warrant emphasis. First, the personal and relational aspects of teaching in the zone cannot be overstated. All of the many students whom I interviewed pointed to their teachers as deeply respectful of them as human beings who were capable of tackling challenging problems with support; in short, teaching in the ZPD requires personal–emotional relations with students, not simply cognitive attention (see also DiPardo & Potter and Ageyev, this volume). Second, associated with this issue, the students *over time* began to refer to themselves as a group – as a "we" – working together on what perplexed them. This reenvisioning of a class of individuals as a collective, as a learning community, came about *through* discussion and, sometimes, happened only through the teacher's persistent efforts to transform roles and purposes for talking. Third, turning points occurred in discussions in *all* cases when students felt empowered and perplexed enough to pose their own burning questions to the class. This finding also supports Dewey's argument (1933) that it is puzzlement that prompts reflection. Finally, the use of multiple cultural texts and stories, in itself, did not prompt critical-narrative thinking in Sharon's and Ron's classes. Diversifying the literature curriculum with voices of many cultures is important, but lasting contribution to students' thinking and democratic orientations result from the way the teachers treated students, authority, controversy – particularly their openness to cultural critique (see Miller, 1998a; Miller & Trzyna, 2000, for more on this issue).

Whether students used the varied ways of talking and thinking learned in these literature classes in other school contexts depended on whether those contexts opened social spaces for constructing knowledge through dialectical activity. Vygotsky's sociocultural approach to mind and Bahktin's dialogicality, taken together, provide an explanatory framework that contributes to our understanding of what inclines students consciously to think and make meaning in classroom contexts. This framework further explains how specific forms of discourse in open-forum literature discussion define specific text stances and literacy practices – potentially opening dialogic spaces for critical-narrative reflection and cultural critique or closing off such habits of heart and mind.

There are several implications of this work for teacher development. If teacher educators want to encourage the kinds of classroom conversations described here, we need to engage preservice and practicing teachers in open-forum discussions of texts in literature and pedagogy classes. Given the potentially powerful influence of teachers' strategies on students' literacy learning, those teachers need to learn new roles as mediators through their own *mediated opportunities* (1) to reflect on their existing reading strategies for making sense of diverse texts; (2) to learn to expand their repertoires, to include strategies for narrative and critical thinking and cultural critique; and (3) to engage in and support discussions aimed at developing multiple, powerful literacy strategies for reading texts and the world. As a profession we need to rethink our ways of talking about literature and preparing teachers for multicultural education – that is, *if* we want teachers and their students to learn how to enter into larger cultural conversations with critical habits of mind and social habits of heart.

References

Alvermann, D. E. (1996). Peer-led discussions: Whose interests are served? *Journal of Adolescent & Adult Literacy, 39*, 282–289.

Applebee, A. N. (1996). *Curriculum as conversation: Transforming traditions of teaching and learning*. Chicago: University of Chicago Press.

Bahktin, M. (1981). *The dialogic imagination* (C. Emerson & M. Helquist, Trans.). Austin: University of Texas Press.

Bakhtin, M. M. (1986). *Speech genres and other late essays* (C. Emerson & M. Holquist, Eds.) (V. W. McGee, Trans.). Austin: University of Texas Press.

Barnes, D. (1976). *From communication to curriculum.* Harmondsworth, England: Penguin.

Barnes, D., Britton, J., & Rosen, H. (1969). *Language, the learner, and the school.* Harmondsworth, England: Penguin.

Barnes, D., & Todd, F. (1977). *Communication and learning in small groups.* London: Routledge and Kegan Paul.

Bartholomae, D., & Petrosky, A. (1986). *Facts, artifacts, counterfacts.* Portsmouth, NH: Boynton/Cook.

Bellah, R., Madsen, R., Sullivan, W., Swindler, A., & Tipton, S. (1985). *Habits of the heart: Individualism and commitment in American life.* New York: Harper & Row.

Bridges, D. (1979). *Education, democracy and discussion.* Winsor, England: NFER.

Britton, J. (1970). *Language and learning: The importance of speech in children's development.* Penguin.

Brown, J. S., Collins, A., & Duguid, P. (1989). Situated cognition and the culture of learning. *Educational Researcher, 18*(1), 32–42.

Bruner, J. (1986). *Actual minds, possible worlds.* Cambridge, MA: Harvard University Press.

Cazden. C. B. (1988). *Classroom discourse: The language of teaching and learning.* Portsmouth, NH: Heinemann.

Dewey, J. (1933). *How we think: A restatement of the relation of reflective thinking to educative process.* Boston: D.C. Heath.

Dewey, J. (1934). *Art as experience.* New York: G. P. Putnam's Sons.

Earthman, E. A. (1992). Creating the virtual work: Readers' processes in understanding literary texts. *Research in the Teaching of English, 26,* 351–384.

Edwards, A. D., & Westgate, D. P. G. (1987). *Investigating classroom talk.* London: Falmer.

Eeds, M., & Wells, D. (1989). Grand conversations: An exploration of meaning construction in literature study groups. *Research in the Teaching of English, 23*(10), 4–29.

Fall, R., Webb, N. M., & Chudowsky, N. (2000). Group discussion and large-scale language arts assessment: Effects on students' comprehension. *American Educational Research Journal, 37*(4), 911–941.

Friere, P. (1998). *Pedagogy of hope.* Lanham, MD: Rowman & Littlefield.

Gadamer, H. (1976). *Philosophical hermeneutics* (D. Linge, Ed. and Trans.). Berkeley: University of California Press.

Gee, J. (1996). *Social linguistics and literacies: Ideologies in discourses.* London: Taylor and Francis.

Greene, M. (1995). *Releasing the imagination: Essays on education, the arts, and social change.* San Francisco: Jossey-Bass.

Hoetker, J., & Ahlbrand, W. (1969). The persistence of recitation. *American Educational Research Journal, 6,* 145–167.

Hymes, D. (1974). *Foundations in sociolinguistics.* Philadelphia: University of Pennsylvania Press.

Hynds, S. (1989). Bringing life to literature and literature to life: Social constructs and contexts of four adolescent readers. *Research in the Teaching of English, 23,* 30–61.

Iser, W. (1978). *The act of reading*. London: Routledge and Kegan Paul.

Kozulin, A. (1998). *Psychological tools: A sociocultural approach to education*. Cambridge, MA: Harvard University Press.

LeCompte, M. D. & Preissle, J. (1993). *Ethnography and qualitative design in educational research*. Academic Press.

Lewis, C. (1997). The social drama of literature discussions in a fifth/sixth-grade classroom. *Research in the Teaching of English, 31*, 163–204.

Lotman, Y. M. (1988). Text within a text. *Soviet Psychology, 26*(3), 32–51.

McMahon, S. I., & Raphael, T. E. (Eds.) (1997). *The book club connection: Literacy learning and classroom talk*. New York: Teachers College Press.

Marshall, J. D., Smagorinsky, P., & Smith, M. W. (1995). The language of interpretation: Patterns of discourse in discussions of literature. *NCTE Research Report No. 27*, Urbana, IL: National Council of Teachers of English.

Miller, S. M. (1988). *Collaborative learning in secondary-school discussion of expository texts* (University Microfilms No. 89-05, 229). Doctoral dissertation, University of Pittsburgh.

Miller, S. M. (1990). Critical thinking in classroom discussion of texts: An ethnographic perspective. Paper presented at the Annual Meeting of the American Educational Research Association, Boston.

Miller, S. M. (1991a, March). Planning for spontaneity: Supporting the language of thinking. *English Journal, 80* (3), 51–56.

Miller, S. M. (1991b, May). Room to talk: Opening possibilities with the "at risk." *English Leadership Quarterly, 13*(2), 10–11.

Miller, S. M. (1992). Trying to understand together: Restructuring classroom talk about texts. In J. L. Collins (Ed.), *Restructuring the English classroom* (pp. 45–59). Portsmouth, NH: Boynton/Cook.

Miller, S. M. (1993). Why a dialogic pedagogy? Making space for possible worlds. In S. Miller & B. McCaskill (Eds.), *Multicultural literature and literacies: Making space for difference*. Albany: State University of New York Press.

Miller, S. M. (1994, September). Vygotsky and education: The sociocultural genesis of dialogic thinking in classroom contexts for open-forum literature discussions. In *Selected Papers of the International Conference on L. S. Vygotsky and the Contemporary Human Sciences*. Moscow, Russia. Available at: http://rantzj.hanover.edu/vygotsky/miller.html

Miller, S. M. (1996a, February). Open-forum text discussion as a zone of proximal development: Shaping which habits of mind? Presentation at the NCTE Research Assembly's 1996 Vygotsky Centennial: Vygotskian Perspectives on Literacy Research, Chicago.

Miller, S. M. (1996b, October 21–24). Vygotsky's zone of proximal development in a transformative pedagogy: Scaffolding multicultural discourse in integrated literature-history classes. In Conference Proceedings of the International Conference, In Celebration of L. S. Vygotsky, 1986–1996: A Cultural-Historical Approach to the Study of Education, Moscow.

Miller, S. M. (1996c). How literature learning shapes thinking in high school classes. In The *Final Report of the National Research Center on Literature Teaching and Learning* (Grant No. R117G10015), Office of Educational Research and Improvement, U.S. Department of Education.

Miller, S. M. (1996d). Making the paths: Constructing critical-narrative discourse in literature-history classes. Research Monograph Series. Albany: Center for English Learning and Achievement.

Miller, S. M. (1997). Language, democracy and teachers' conceptions of "discussion": What we know from literacy research. *Theory and Research in Social Education, 25*(2), 196–206.

Miller, S. M. (1998a, Spring). Missing links between self and society: What no literature discussion means for multicultural literacy. *Language and Literacy Spectrum, 8*, 16–29.

Miller, S. M. (1998b, Winter). Entering into multicultural conversations in English-history classes. *Arizona English Bulletin, 40*(2), 10–26.

Miller, S. M. (1998c, Fall). How literature learning shapes thinking in the secondary school. *English Quarterly 30*(1–2), 38–66.

Miller, S. M., & Legge, S. (1999, August). Supporting possible worlds: Transforming literature teaching and learning through conversations in the narrative mode. *Research in the Teaching of English,* pp. 10–64.

Miller, S. M., & Trzyna, G. D. (2000). "They don't want to hear it": Ways of talking and habits of the heart in the multicultural literature classroom. In C. Cornbleth (Ed.), *Curriculum politics, policy, practice: Cases in context.* Albany, NY: SUNY Press.

Nystrand, M., & Gamoran, A. (1991). Instructional discourse, student engagement, and literature achievement. *Research in the Teaching of English, 25*(3), 261–290.

Polkinghorne, D. E. (1995). Narrative configuration in qualitative analysis. In J. A. Hatch & R. Wisniewski (Eds.), *Life history and narrative.* London: Falmer Press.

Rosenblatt, L. M. (1978). *The reader, the text, the poem.* Carbondale: Southern Illinois University Press.

Scholes, R. (1985). *Textual Power: Literary Theory and the Teaching of English.* New Haven, CT: Yale University Press.

Vygotsky, L. S. (1971). *The psychology of art.* Cambridge, MA: MIT Press.

Vygotsky, L. S. (1978). *Mind in Society* (M. Cole, V. John-Steiner, S. Scribner, & E. Sauberman, Eds.). Cambridge, MA: Harvard University Press.

Vygotsky, L. S. (1986). *Thought and language* (rev. ed.). Cambridge, MA: MIT Press.

Wells, G. (1986). *The meaning makers: Children learning language and using language to learn.* Portsmouth, NH: Heinemann.

Wertsch, J. V. (1991). *Voices of the Mind.* Cambridge, MA: Harvard University Press.

15

Beyond Cognition

A Vygotskian Perspective on Emotionality and Teachers'
Professional Lives

Anne DiPardo and Christine Potter

> The emotions are not "a state within a state." They cannot be understood
> outside the dynamic of human life. It is within this context that the emotional
> processes acquire their meaning and sense.
>
> (Vygotsky, 1987, p. 333)

That teaching is emotionally charged work is hardly news to those who
face its rigors and rewards on a daily basis. At its best, teaching offers
exhilaration – the high of watching a class come alive, a reluctant student suddenly motivated, of generating fresh strategies with a group of
trusted colleagues. But frustration and sorrow can be constant compan-
ions as well – the stress of too much work, too little relational and material
support, students who present ever-larger challenges. These more negative emotions have tended to become increasingly prevalent of late, as a
wave of top-down school reform has carried the dispiriting implication
that something is wrong with teachers' efforts that calls for external fixes
and vigilant monitoring (Hargreaves, 1998, 2000). Now more than ever,
recruiting and retaining sufficient numbers of able teachers demand attention to the affective aspects of their jobs. Borrowing from the language of
best-selling books, we might say that educators must continually find the
passion, energy, and courage to sustain their work (Fried, 1995; Graves,
2001; Palmer, 1998).

Invoking a neo-Vygotskian theoretic framework, Roland Tharp and
Ronald Gallimore have argued that school reformers too often underestimate the relation between optimal learning conditions for students and
similarly supportive working conditions for their teachers (Gallimore &
Tharp, 1990; Tharp & Gallimore, 1988; Tharp, 1993): That is, anytime we
want students to adopt a new practice, we must first ensure that such

The authors thank Jim Marshall and Melanie Sperling for their helpful feedback and
suggestions.

practices are integrated into the system as a whole, characterizing as well the ways teachers approach their daily tasks (see also Clift, Veal, Holland, Johnson, & McCarthy, 1995; Little, 1993; Maeroff, 1993; Sarason, 1996). Whereas it is widely recognized that students need both caring sensitivity and intellectual challenge, school reformers, theorists, and researchers alike have been slower to recognize that the same can be said of teachers' work and on-the-job learning. Even as burgeoning qualitative studies of teachers and classrooms are providing countless portraits of the at-once cognitive and affective nature of teaching and learning, seldom is this integration explicitly identified or conceptually framed. Our theorizing has tended to ignore the role of emotion in informing thought and action, reflecting a strong cultural tendency to deny the dialectic between cool reason and unruly feeling (Nietzsche, 1971; Oatley, 1992). And so it is that we have appropriated the cognitive aspects of Vygotsky's theory, largely sidestepping his conception of the central role of emotionality in mental development and "the dynamic of human life" (1987, p. 333).

VYGOTSKY ON EMOTIONS

Although Vygotsky stopped short of providing extensive insight into the emotional aspects of teaching and learning, his work repeatedly suggested a marked interest in issues of affect (Minick, Stone, & Forman, 1993). His doctoral thesis, belatedly published as *The Psychology of Art*, included a provocative chapter exploring the role of emotional catharsis in literary appreciation (1971; see also Kozulin, 1990). Readers of *Thought and Language* may recall his occasional nods to the dynamic relationships among emotion, thought, and motivation: "Thought," he wrote, "is engendered by motivation, i.e., by our desires and needs, our interests and emotions. Behind every thought there is an affective-volitional tendency, which holds the answer to the last 'why' in the analysis of thinking" (1986, p. 252). He condemned the tendency to separate intellect and affect into distinct fields of study, believing that this separation had created the false illusion that thinking is somehow segregated from the fullness of life and from the needs and interests of the thinker. Vygotsky noted that such misleading binaries had legislated against close attention to emotion's role in stimulating thought, as well as to "the influence of thought on affect and volition" (1986, p. 10).

Vygotsky provided a somewhat fuller discussion of the relationship between thought and emotion in a lecture delivered in 1932, "Emotions and Their Development in Childhood" (published in *The Collected Works*, 1987), in which he critiqued then-prevalent conceptions of emotionality and explored promising scholarly directions. In suggesting the need for further theory building and research, Vygotsky displayed his trademark interest in the progression of human development, seen as encompassing a complex interrelationship among what are commonly regarded as separate functions, and an ongoing dialectic between self and world (Vygotsky, 1987; see also Bruner, 1987; and Luria, 1987). He began with a ringing critique of Charles Darwin's conception of emotions, as remnants of our origins in lower species that continue to dwindle in a process of evolutionary adaptation (Darwin, 1998). "This gives rise to the concept that the man of the future will be without emotion," Vygotsky wryly observed, quickly adding that such a position is rendered absurd by both "our immediate psychological experience" and mounting experimental evidence (1987, p. 326). The influential James–Lange theory had acknowledged the persistence of human emotions (James, 1950); Vygotsky, however, took issue with its central tenet – that affective response is primarily physiological, associated with "the most primitive levels of mankind's historical development" (p. 328). According to James and Lange, emotions arise as interpretations of physiological events; hence one cries not because one is sad, but rather one feels sad because tears *prompt* an emotional response. Vygotsky maintained that in regarding emotionality as a separate function, James and Lange not only "stripped the emotions from consciousness," but also provided "the anatomical and physiological foundation" for a mistaken view of human development:

The emotions are torn from the unified whole, from the rest of man's mental life. . . . James himself emphasized this point, arguing that the organ of human thought is the brain, while the emotions are associated with the vegetative internal organs. Thus, the substratum of the emotions was transferred from the center to the periphery. Moreover, the theories of James and Lange made it even more difficult to pose the question of the development of emotional life. . . . James' theory excluded any potential for imagining the genesis of human emotions, despite the emergence of new emotions in man's historical life. (p. 328)

For Vygotsky, William James's later attempts to distinguish certain higher emotions such as aesthetic appreciation and altruistic care only made matters worse, positing a further binary of "lower" emotions associated with "biologically ancient internal organs" (p. 332), and loftier, more spiritual leanings (James, 1950; see Denzin, 1984, pp. 16–21, for an overview of critiques of the James–Lange theory).

Reviewing contemporary physiological and psychological research, Vygotsky saw ample evidence that emotional response did not reside in the "organs of the periphery," but, rather, at what he regarded as "the center" – the human brain (p. 332). For Vygotsky, this intimate connection between mind and emotion was neither neatly bounded nor static; "emotional processes," he observed, "are not settled but nomadic" (p. 334). Drawing on contemporary empirical work, Vygotsky suggested that as does thought, the emotions transition from the external to the internal, playing a central role in such functions as motivation, planning, and action.

That is, we might imagine emotions as appearing, as Vygotsky said of thought, first "on the social plane, and then on the psychological plane" (1978, p. 163). As with all internalized processes, emotions do not exist as "a state within a state," but interact with other processes in a social–cognitive process of development (1987, p. 333; see also Bruner, 1987). The emotions develop in concert with the whole of a person's cognitive and social life, continually constructed through social interaction and progressively internalized.

Vygotsky's interest in the relation between thought and speech takes on new meaning where we understand both to be saturated with emotional as well as rational sense; the affective aspect of his theory remains seldom acknowledged by educators in the United States, however, let alone extensively applied to problems of teaching and learning. Occasional efforts to extend this dimension of Vygotsky's thought have typically involved aligning his somewhat sporadic attention with compatible conceptions more specifically addressing issues of affect. Mark Tappan (1998), for instance, has perceived a strong affinity between Vygotsky's notion of socially assisted learning and Nel Noddings's care theory (1984, 1992, 1995), which emphasizes the importance of nurturing students' individual interests and need and modeling an "ethic of care" – for self, for family and community, and for the global ecosystem (1992, p. 21). Tappan maintains that Vygotsky's emphasis on the relational nature of effective teaching and learning suggests a close connection to Noddings's more fully articulated interest in the moral and affective aspects of instructional scaffolding; the process of coaxing Vygotskian "buds" into the "fruits" of development (1978, p. 86) can therefore be seen as entailing not only intellectual coaching, but also issues of motivation, trust, and rapport. "At its core," concludes Tappan, Vygotsky's sociocultural psychology endorses "a caring, relational, dialogical process as the key to good learning" (p. 32).

Noting his own dissatisfaction with theories that address cognition apart from affect, the developmental psychologist Joseph Glick has encouraged a reconsideration of Vygotsky's work in juxtaposition to his contemporary Heinz Werner, a Gestalt psychologist who remains relatively unknown to educational researchers. Born in Vienna in 1890, Werner pursued psychological research at the University of Hamburg, emigrating to the States at the dawn of the Nazi era, eventually continuing his work at Clark University until his death in 1964. Like Vygotsky, Werner was a developmentalist who adopted an "organic" (p. 40) perspective informed by a systemic, dynamic conception of human growth and development, involving the interaction not only of multiple motor and perceptual functions, but also of self and world.

Werner's most widely read work, *Comparative Psychology of Mental Development* (1948), explored what he saw as important similarities in the thinking of small children, psychotics, and so-called primitive peoples.[1] Drawing from experimental studies, case study records, and anecdotal evidence, Werner argued that the thinking of all three groups tends toward what he called "syncretism" (p. 53) – that is, diffuse and undifferentiated patterns of perception that render thought, emotion, and action virtually indistinguishable. For Werner, early human development exists in a kind of primordial soup of indistinctive perceptions; affect permeates this mix, often strongly influencing what is perceived or understood. Werner saw all development as governed by what he came to call the "orthogenetic principle" – that is, a progression toward increasing differentiation and hierarchical organization (Werner & Kaplan, 1963, p. 7). Thus for most people living in the industrialized world, particular emotions are readily distinguishable, and empirical data and logical abstraction tend to take a lead role in governing perception and decision making.

On the other hand, Werner suggested, these earlier "childlike" or "primitive" tendencies are always with us, albeit largely unlearned or veiled much of the time. Werner believed that these tendencies remain particularly strong in writers (and especially poets), whose metaphoric language retains what he termed the *physiognomic* quality of associating objects with their felt or perceived qualities. Werner observed that whereas many take for granted a linear progression toward higher mental activities, reality is a good bit messier, as new functions emerge from earlier ones, and the dynamic of development is marked by both progression to new patterns and regression to older ones (see also Flavell, 1966; Wapner, 2000). In his foreword to *Comparative Psychology of Mental Development* (1948), Gordon Allport surmised that Werner's unspoken but central point was that we all retain certain "childlike" or "primitive" tendencies: "While tactfully confining himself to children, primitives, and psychotics," Allport observed of Werner, "the author tells us in a sly way more than a little about our own mental lives" (1948, p. xii).

For Glick, Werner's dynamic language of "vectorial," connected forces bears certain similarities to the Vygotsky of *Thought and Language,* who indulged in "talk of expressive, affect laden, ineffabilities" (1983, p. 47). Although Glick argues that Werner's theories more fully integrated the role of emotionality in learning and development (see also Franklin, 2000), he notes that this body of work has largely dropped from view – an absence

---

[1] According to Werner's former student Margery Franklin (1997, 2000), Werner did not intend to invoke the term's pejorative connotations; rather, he had in mind human origins, an existence in closer proximity to the rhythms and forces of nature. In this Werner appears to foreshadow the later work of the philosopher Susanne Langer (1942), who explored the power of symbolic meanings carried in such vehicles as ritual, music, dance, and metaphor, arguing that the industrialized world is out of touch with these foundational and profoundly emotional sources of meaning.

Glick attributes to Werner's often elusive, impossible-to-summarize language and his failure to provide empirically useful frames to guide investigations of particular psychological functions (1983, 1992). Kozulin (1990) observes that whereas both Vygotsky and Werner were attentive to the social and cultural contexts in which learning occurs, Werner appeared less interested in that which most preoccupies educators and developmental psychologists – that is, the particular mechanisms by which mental processes come to be reorganized and advanced (p. 118).

For Vygotsky, who perceived an "intimate connection between the emotional reactions and the rest of the human mind" (1987, p. 332), these "mental processes" decidedly involved both emotion and thought. Where Vygotsky's conception of "thought" is mistakenly understood as both cognitive and social but somehow void of emotion, it makes particular sense to look for fitting supplements in the work of theorists such as Werner or Noddings, both of whom placed emotions more squarely at the center of human development.[2] Although these conceptual compatibilities are useful and meaningful, it is important that we meanwhile acknowledge the whole of the Vygotskian theory we seek to extend and elaborate, acknowledging his own explicit (if intermittent) interest in issues of affect.

Jerome Bruner has described the pervasive tendency to draw "heavy conceptual boundaries between thought, action, and emotion," a set of distinctions that forces us "to construct conceptual bridges to connect what should never have been put asunder" (1986, p. 106). These very terms are abstractions that obscure their "structural interdependence," argues Bruner; "to isolate each is like studying the planes of a crystal separately, losing sight of the crystal that gives them being" (p. 118). One might argue that a certain crystalline quality pervades Vygotsky's conception of human development, a quality obscured by our tendency to take up only those aspects of his thought most compatible with our own preoccupations and cultural norms.

RECENT PERSPECTIVES ON EMOTION AND TEACHING

Popular attention to teachers' professional lives has long been preoccupied with competence and expertise, most recently manifest in proposals for tests of teacher knowledge and for linking of pay to indices of student achievement. Such proposals are causing distress, eliciting strong responses, and attracting new attention to the ways that affect permeates the lives of teachers. But teaching has always been emotional work, and a

---

[2] One might add Piaget here as well: "We must agree that at no level, at no stage, even in the adult, can we find a behavior or a state which is purely cognitive without affect," he noted, "nor a purely affective state without a cognitive element included" (Piaget, 1962, p. 130; quoted in Derry & Murphy, 1986, p. 29).

number of observers have acknowledged this over the years; in addition to Noddings's care theory (1984, 1992, 1995), one thinks of Sergiovanni's characterizations of compassionate school communities (1994), or of Clandinin and Connelly's depictions of emotional attentiveness in teachers' relationships and development (1995). In his book *The Tact of Teaching*, Max van Manen (1991, p. 146) describes the "thinking attentiveness" and "caring orientation to others" that characterize the work of effective teachers; what Christopher Clark calls *Thoughtful Teaching* (1995) is similarly informed by an integrated vision of the academic, emotional, and ethical dimensions of teaching. School change theorists are also turning their attention to the affective fallout of attempts to alter practice and policy, addressing troublesome emotions such as grief and anxiety, as well as the need for hopefulness and trust (Evans, 1996; Fullan, 1991; 1993; 1999; Hargreaves, 1997, 1998, 2000). If, as Vygotsky suggested, emotions are socially constructed and, as they "go inward," play a key role in shaping motivation and thought (1987), then it makes sense to attend closely to the affective aspects of teachers' workplaces, and to the ways that emotions inform what are commonly seen as the purely academic aspects of their labors.

Related to this new emphasis on emotionality are heightened concerns around teacher stress, estimated to prompt the departure of nearly 50% of new teachers within their first decade in the classroom (Beer & Beer, 1992), this in an era of growing teacher shortages. Research in this area has traditionally cast teacher stress in individual terms, as a person's coping resources are exhausted (Dunham, 1984), and feelings of anger, frustration, and depression take root (Rudow, 1999). Even research addressing the importance of environment in spawning teacher stress has tended to focus on individuals' responses as the site of potential difficulties (Cedoline, 1982; Greenberg, 1984), particularly when teachers perceive a loss of control over their work (Czubaj, 1996; Swick & Hanley, 1985). Accordingly, practical advice to teachers has tended to focus on personal strategies for alleviating feelings of stress, including relaxation techniques, adequate sleep, and improvement of classroom management skills (Bradshaw, 1991; Cedoline, 1982). Only more recently has attention turned to the stress provoked by ambitious school change initiatives. As Little (1996) has suggested, even teachers who are initially enthusiastic about such initiatives often report feelings of discouragement within a few years, as the hard work of change takes an inexorable toll, and the distance between imagined ideals and present realities remains. This tendency to up the ante on teachers' work (with or without their assent) has come to bear the Marxist term *intensification,* first applied to educational labor by Michael Apple (1988). Linking the problem of intensification to a growing incidence of teacher burnout, Peter Woods (1999, p. 188) observes that "There is more for teachers to do, including a proliferation of administrative and assessment tasks. There is less time to do it in, less time for re-skilling and for leisure and sociability." This recent work promises to complicate conversations concerning "stress" and "burnout" by highlighting the importance of working conditions in contributing to teachers' feelings of psychological exhaustion and discouragement. What remains to be seen is whether such conversations will eventually push districts beyond isolated workshops bent on improving teachers' coping strategies, and toward more thoroughgoing efforts to transform workplaces and workloads.

In her provocatively titled *Feeling Power*, Megan Boler (1999) casts a critical eye on the common tendency to discourage the expression of emotions that might be regarded as challenging or problematic. Boler's feminist argument that emotions are neither individual nor private, but rather "representative of a socially and collaboratively constructed psychic terrain" (p. xxi), is evocative of Vygotskian perspectives on the social–cultural construction of meaning, a process encompassing both emotion and thought (Vygotsky, 1986, 1987). Boler's central interests, however, rest in the political ramifications of such constructions. Surveying a long history of school-based attempts to control students' and teachers' emotions (from the "social efficiency" and "mental hygiene" movements of the early 20th century to more recent proposals to assess students' "emotional intelligence" [Goleman, 1995]), Boler concludes that "the social control of emotions is thus reflected in the combination of moral and scientific discourses that function to govern individuals" (p. 53). Following in the tradition of Hochschild's classic *The Managed Heart* (1983), Boler explores the "emotional labor" of teaching, particularly when teachers' work is closely monitored from above and expectations of complacency and cooperation remain cultural fixtures. Too often, she concludes, the work of teachers is constructed in ways that constrain affective freedom and the collective action strong emotion can inspire.

Andy Hargreaves's influential work on emotionality in teachers' professional lives (1997, 1998, 2000) also highlights the socially constructed and political aspects of affect. Hargreaves frames his work primarily in sociological theory, drawing particularly on Norman Denzin's classic *On Understanding Emotions* (1984). Teaching, argues Hargreaves, is what Denzin would term an *emotional practice*, embedded in meaningful contexts, provoking changes in consciousness and physiology, and "giving emotional culmination to thoughts, feelings, and actions" (1984, p. 89; quoted in Hargreaves, 2000, p. 1). These emotional practices are significantly shaped by the degree of emotional understanding (or misunderstanding) that teachers encounter in relations with colleagues, parents, and administrators. Such practices, understandings, and their relevant contexts together constitute what Hargreaves calls *emotional geographies*, defined as "the spatial and experiential patterns of closeness and/or distance in human interactions and relationships that help create, configure and color the feelings and emotions we experience about ourselves, our world and each other" (2000, p. 6). These geographies can be marked by reciprocity and care, but they can also be plagued by misunderstandings or denials, facilitating the construction of negative emotions such as shame and guilt (see also Scheff & Retzinger, 1991; Scheff, 1994; and DiPardo, 2000).

Acknowledging the heightened and often negative emotionality provoked by recent school reform initiatives, Hargreaves argues (1998, 2000) that what may seem at first glance purely cognitive aspects of teachers' work – planning curricula, carrying out the daily work of instruction, discussing their work with colleagues, parents, or administrators – is in fact saturated with emotional meanings and influences. In other words, what we usually think of as the intellectual aspects of teaching cannot ultimately be separated from the emotional charge that attends them; nor can emotions be meaningfully considered apart from the social, political, and material dimensions of teachers' professional lives.

In this, Hargreaves echoes not only more recent philosophic perspectives on emotionality (Boler, 1999; Nussbaum, 2001), but also a long line of psychological research documenting the relationship between emotions and problem solving (Isen, Daubman, & Nowicki, 1998; Oatley & Jenkins, 1998), creativity (Hjort & Laver, 1997), and belief systems (Calhoun, 1984), as well as burgeoning neurological evidence that emotion is indispensable to rationality (Damasio, 1994; 1999). "Reason may not be as pure as most of us think it is or wish it were," writes Antonio Damasio; "emotions and feelings may not be intruders in the bastion of reason at all: they may be enmeshed in its networks, for worse *and* for better" (1994, p. xii). Even well before a diverse body of empirical evidence began to document this meshing, educators have from time to time sensed its reality. Nearly a half-century ago, Arthur Jersild suggested in a study of teachers' emotional lives that "much of what is called thinking is actually governed by undisclosed feelings" (Jersild, 1955, p. 86; see also Salzberger-Wittenbert, Henry, & Osborne, 1983). This fusion is particularly key to work as fraught with ambiguity and human complexity as teaching; "where there's uncertainty, emotions come into play," writes the psychologist Keith Oatley, noting that emotions promote "cognitive properties adapted to imperfect knowledge, to possibilities of goal conflicts, and to coordinating action with other people" (1992, p. 165). Our emotions are inevitably aroused in situations in which matters of importance slip beyond ease of control and are therefore markers of both our vulnerabilities and our deepest commitments (Nussbaum, 2001).

The public discourse concerning school reform seldom acknowledges the pervasive presence of emotionality, casting issues and people in binary terms – that is, those who care about learners as whole people and those committed to academic excellence, the sentimental types versus the hard-headed taskmasters. In an essay provocatively titled "In Praise of the Cognitive Emotions," Israel Scheffler acknowledges that his eponymous notion "may well evoke emotions of perplexity or incredulity":

For cognition and emotion, as everyone knows, are hostile worlds apart. Cognition is sober inspection; it is the scientist's calm apprehension of fact after fact in his relentless pursuit of Truth. Emotion, on the other hand, is commotion – an unruly inner turbulence fatal to such pursuit but finding its own constructive outlets in aesthetic experience and moral or religious commitment. Strongly entrenched, this opposition of cognition and emotion must nevertheless be challenged, for it distorts everything it touches: mechanizing science, it sentimentalizes art, while portraying ethics and religion as twin swamps of feeling and unreasoned commitment. Education, meanwhile – that is to say, the development of mind and attitudes in the young – is split into two grotesque parts: unfeeling knowledge and mindless arousal. (1991, p. 3)

As we have seen, Vygotsky too took pointed exception to the tendency to regard cognition and emotion as "hostile worlds apart," insisting that affect cannot be understood as a "state within a state," but only within the systemic context of human thought and action, and within the social–cultural environments from which we draw the raw material of our inner lives (Vygotsky, 1987, p. 333). In most quarters, however, Scheffler's words continue to ring all too true. While educators remind us of the importance of care, passion, and morale, would-be reformers remain single-mindedly fixed on measurable academic outcomes, seemingly unaware of the human costs many of their favored strategies inevitably entail (Hargreaves, 1998, 2000; Miller, 2002). As change initiatives chisel away at teachers' sense of agency and efficacy, the research community notes the toll on spirit and resolve, at long last naming emotions as a crucial aspect of both student learning and teachers' work. Given our accustomed terms of reference, it is hard to escape the sense of Cartesian polarity that permeates our language of head and heart. As emotionality is rendered a hot new topic, we are in danger of missing the larger implication of so much recent work, so clearly presaged by Vygotsky – that is, the recurrent suggestion that reconsidering the role of emotionality in the teaching–learning process means understanding its central place in the whole of human life.

Given our Western tendency to separate emotion from rationality and to focus single-mindedly on the latter, it is unsurprising that U.S. educators have been primarily attracted to the cognitive aspects of Vygotskian theory, ignoring the emotional aspects of the "social" in social constructivism (Brand, 1991) and the notion that thought is fundamentally "engendered by motivation" (Vygotsky, 1986, p. 252). Some have argued that Vygotskian internalization is political as well as intellectual, situated among competing agendas and institutional histories (Palinscar, Brown, & Campione, 1993; Wertsch, 1991). We would argue that the process is also profoundly and inextricably emotional – that is, if all learning is imbued with emotional meanings and influences, all teaching is, too. Teachers must be learners, after all, as they negotiate the multiple demands of their work-days, restlessly seeking more effective and satisfying paths. In so doing, they draw not only on distributed cognitions, but also on the distributed emotions that are scattered across the terrain of workplace and profession, key elements in the social constructions that continually go inward, eventually to constitute thoughts and feelings that are both "ours" and profoundly shared.

As our accustomed analytic language tends to fall short of this sense of dynamism and integration, the narrative mode would seem well suited to capturing the at-once affective and cognitive complexities of teachers' workdays, filled with uncertainties, thorny situations, and hard dilemmas demanding immediate resolution (Bruner, 1986; Carter, 1993). And yet even here, as we will see in the two narratives that follow, many of us have persistent difficulty escaping the pervasive tendency to drift into a language of false binaries, separating self from context, mind from body, and emotion from intellect.

FEELING, THINKING, AND TEACHING: A NARRATIVE TURN

We embark here on a bit of a detour, turning from reflection on others' ideas to a reconsideration of our own lived experience. As we have pondered recent efforts to reintegrate what has been generally torn asunder, we have been moved to think anew about stories the two of us have constructed over the past few years. One describes Chris's firsthand experience with stress and burnout in her seventh year in the classroom; the other, that of a middle-aged teacher of at-risk youth whom Anne followed through a process of professional loss and renewal. Only after long reading, reflection, and conversation have we come to see how our past constructions of these stories have signaled our own tendency to distinguish what is ultimately indistinguishable, to place issues of curriculum and instruction to one side and affect to the other. Jerome Bruner (1986) has argued that our narrative constructions (and reconstructions) provide important clues to our stances and subjectivities; dealing in human vicissitudes and multiple possibilities, our attempts at story-making not only communicate information about chains of events, but represent the holistic sense we ultimately make of them (see also Connelly & Clandinin, 1990; Polkinghorne, 1988). In revisiting these two narratives here, we explore ways that sociocultural theory might inform and enrich their construction, and that such narratives might in turn inform and enrich theory.

Chris: Isolation and the Problem of "Burnout"

Chris's teaching career began and ended in a small town in the rural Midwest; enrollment in the K–12 school was 400, and Chris was the only

English teacher for grades 10–12. Socioeconomic class divisions tended to be keenly felt among Chris's mostly European-American students, some of whom were growing up on prosperous farms, others in rural poverty. Whether her students' plans included going on to college or managing a local gas station, Chris wanted to ensure that each found her classes engaging, challenging, and meaningful. Students who had seldom completed extended writing would turn in essay after essay for Chris's close perusal, exploring issues that lifted them well beyond the norms and preoccupations of this often insular setting – including responses to literary works, lengthy research papers, and persuasive essays that were later sent to real-world audiences. In this place where students and their families were tightly defined by income and time in residence, many of Chris's students had grown accustomed to unchallenging work and low expectations. Intent on opening new doors, Chris was pleased to have these students in her courses over consecutive years, time to gain their trust and push the limits of the possible. Whenever someone asked about her long-term plans, Chris always said that she saw herself putting in several decades of dedicated work here, retiring one distant day from this very district.

She had initially been hired just a few days before the start of the new year, entering her classroom to find scant materials and virtually no curriculum. Chris would soon double the school's language arts offerings, adding courses in literature and writing designed to capture the interests of both reluctant and accelerated students; in all, she taught five writing-intensive courses every day as well as supervising a study hall. She was also responsible for a number of extracurricular activities – directing a fall play and spring musical, coaching volleyball and the speech team, sponsoring the honor society and senior class, as well as serving on several demanding school committees. For a time, these extra activities seemed a natural extension of Chris's love of teaching and connection to her students. When she was unable to keep up, she tended to assume there was something wrong with her time management strategies or energy level. Determined to give her students her best efforts (and stretch to do better still), Chris reacted to the strain by putting in longer hours, arriving at school by 7:30 A.M. and often staying long into the night to respond to student writing and put the finishing touches on the next day's plans. Because the tax base was relatively low in this rural district, so too were teachers' salaries, and Chris felt fortunate to secure summer employment – scrubbing, waxing, and polishing every nook and cranny of the very school building where she spent the balance of the year.

Over time, Chris would struggle to meet the demands of her work with a gathering sense of personal inadequacy. As she watched her less passionate colleagues move through the days and weeks with seeming ease, she was increasingly troubled by her own lack of time and sagging spirits. Surely she just needed to work harder, she thought, to be more organized, to become a tougher and more self-reliant kind of person; surely the fact that it all seemed so overwhelmingly hard was a sign of weakness in her own personality and work habits. She began to experience frequent headaches, bouts of fatigue, and feelings of failure, symptoms she would recognize only later as classic signs of stress (Bradshaw, 1991). She tried various management strategies – daily walks, singing in her church choir, taking Sunday afternoons off – but she was slowly realizing that there would be no easy fixes. During the initial weeks of Chris's seventh year in the classroom, she reached a point of crisis.

That year had begun much as the previous 6 years had, as Chris felt the familiar rush of late-August excitement, reentering her classroom with renewed energy and optimism. Even before the required preterm preparation days, Chris had been hard at work – organizing files and bulletin boards, developing new reading and writing activities, and eagerly awaiting the arrival of her students. This early-year honeymoon generally carried Chris to Halloween, but this time would prove radically different, as an abrupt crash occurred with clarity and speed. Three weeks into the new year, Chris found herself facing each day with deepening sadness and suddenly finding little pleasure in her work with students. She had experienced mild periods of depression since embarking on her teaching career, times of low energy and dampened enthusiasm, but this was markedly more profound. It was the timing that alarmed her most of all, this September stagnation an intensified version of a listlessness that generally occurred only in late spring. She began imagining the once-unimaginable: becoming a teacher who no longer cared about her students' progress and well-being, the kind who settled for too many filler periods devoted to "free reading" or video viewing. It was a prospect that seemed even more frightening than her deepening sadness. By mid-October, less than 2 months into the new school year, Chris decided to leave teaching.

At the time, Chris fully believed that she alone was responsible for the loss of her old intensity and commitment – in the usual metaphoric shorthand, that she had failed to "manage her stress," and, though once "on fire," had unfortunately "burned out." Our prevalent metaphors tend to be revealing windows onto cultural norms and assumptions (Lakoff & Johnson, 1983), and the seldom-interrogated rhetoric of teacher "burnout" represents a provocative case in point. When teachers like Chris fail to tend their own fires – failing, that is, to "manage" their professional stress – they face the personal embarrassment of careers engulfed. For Chris's former administrators and colleagues, this "burnout" problem was hers, and the problem was wholly emotional.

Only as Chris entered graduate school two years later did she question her tendency to frame this experience as a personal failure, a lapse in her private store of "emotional intelligence" (Goleman, 1995). Chris came to see that just as she was not guided solely by intellect when she was thriving as a teacher, neither could her professional crisis be dismissed as exclusively affective. Her job had provided too much to do, to think about, and to feel, strands that could not ultimately be teased apart. Nor could Chris continue to underestimate the shaping power of her workplace context, with its norms of isolation, chronic understaffing, and teachers' prevailing feelings of disempowerment (for environmental perspectives on teacher stress, see Kelchtermans & Strittmatter, 1999; Maslach & Leiter, 1999). Although Chris would continue to interrogate her own tendency to take on too much and request too little, she began to appreciate teachers' need for integrated support encompassing the emotional, pedagogic, and political aspects of their work.

As Chris explored the scholarly literature on teacher stress, she particularly noted the significance of strong collegial networks and administrative support. Because her school had offered few opportunities for cross-disciplinary teaching and most departments were staffed by solitary instructors, the burden of developing curricula tended to fall exclusively on individuals. Chris's long search for pedagogic collaboration had repeatedly come up dry, as she found her colleagues too busy or too philosophically divergent to allow for substantive joint work. As Chris grappled with her decision to leave teaching, she approached several colleagues to ask for support and guidance, people with whom she had enjoyed cordial if somewhat distant relationships. Although Chris's colleagues expressed sympathy, they understandably felt more comfortable with the energetic young teacher they had long known her to be, and she went away from these encounters even more convinced that responsibility for her malaise rested solely on her shoulders. It would be several years before she encountered research suggesting that close collegial relationships tend to prepare workers to cope effectively with job stress, whereas norms of isolation often lead to the emotional distance Chris observed in her fellow teachers (Ross & Altmaier, 1994). This tradition of autonomy took a political toll as well, as Chris and her colleagues lobbied as solitary individuals for resources and improved working conditions, their lack of agency setting the stage for still greater stress among those most committed to their students and work (Czubaj, 1996; Ross & Altmaier, 1994). Although school administrators were appreciative of Chris's efforts and sympathetic as she struggled with her decision to leave teaching, they did little to alleviate these consistent problems of overwork, isolation, and insufficient material support (for an examination of the role of administrative support in alleviating teacher stress, see Russell, Altmaier, & Van Velzen, 1987).

As Chris began reading Vygotsky (1978, 1986), she thought immediately of her students' learning and development, of the kinds of close, scaffolded support she had longed to provide to each of them through her hectic days of teaching. Recalling Tharp and Gallimore's neo-Vygotskian argument for pervasive norms of assisted learning – scaffolding that might support the work of school administrators, teachers, and students alike (Gallimore & Tharp, 1990; Tharp & Gallimore, 1988; Tharp, 1993) – we might say that there was something drastically wrong with Chris's workplace activity setting (Cole, 1985; Leontiev, 1981), something that negatively impacted not only her morale and sense of efficacy, but ultimately her students' learning as well. Chris's story serves to underscore the need to move from an individual, behavioristic view of teacher stress to a social–cultural conception that acknowledges the importance of workplace traditions, conditions, and norms. Although accepting that teachers may respond in more- and less-wholesome ways to stressful situations (see Russell et al., 1987), Chris began to grasp the folly of placing all responsibility for "managing" stress on individual teachers, or of taking up issues of stress apart from the pedagogic, political, and material aspects of their workplaces. As teacher stress appears to be increasing along with national interest in education reform, research and practice alike might be usefully informed by a neo-Vygotskian conception of the nature and root causes of such disturbances, encouraging integrated attention to teachers' thoughts and emotions and to the relationship between teachers' well-being and their students' learning. In attending closely to the workplace contexts that produce teachers' interlinked emotions, thoughts, and actions, such a conception might shed new light on how these contexts sometimes undermine teachers' best efforts – or, as in our second narrative, can provide substantive resources and support.

Max: Vital Company and Mindful Practice

Anne first met a science teacher pseudonymously named "Max" while gathering data for an ethnographic study of teacher collaboration at four midwestern public schools (DiPardo, 1999). Framed in Vygotskian conceptual terms, the project had set out to explore how highly collaborative teachers inform one another's thinking and practice. But soon after she began fieldwork at the Self-Directed Learning Center (SDLC), a small school for at-risk youth, Anne realized that a good bit more was involved here than "thinking" and "practice." In often intense daily meetings, the SDLC's dozen teachers strategized about particular students, developed innovative programs and classes, laughed, and veered into heated but ultimately friendly arguments. As one of Max's colleagues liked to say, these gatherings often looked and sounded like "one big dinner table," albeit with added doses of urgency, wackiness, and drama. "We have it all," he observed, "joy, tragedy, comedy."

As much as he relished his close work with like-minded colleagues, Max consistently challenged himself to work with those who presented the biggest differences. This made for friction, fresh angles of vision, and some highly unusual interdisciplinary courses, with names like *Artometry* (combining art and geometry), *Rivers* (art, writing, and science on a nearby riverbank), and *Food and Feet* (conversations about nutrition while strolling among local eateries). In the magazine production workshop class that Anne followed, Max and his language arts colleague Bill struggled to spark excitement in a group of students with generally weak writing skills and erratic engagement. The school was concurrently in the midst of preparation for an accreditation review, which involved long after-school meetings full of generative, contentious conversation culminating in consensus only now and then. Then in mid-October, one of the SDLC's students died in an evening of drug experimentation, and the school was thrown into a wave of grief and deepening exhaustion.

Somewhere in the midst of all this, Anne added this quotation to her literature review, referencing efforts to elaborate and expand Vygotskian conceptions of sites for teaching and learning:

> To say that social interaction and cognition develop as part of an integral system in connection with motivation, affect, and values does not merely imply the need for an addendum to earlier theoretical formulations. A fundamental reconceptualization of mind and its development in social practice is implied . . . this reconceptualization has profound theoretical, methodological, and pragmatic implications that we are only just beginning to understand and address. (Minick et al., 1993, pp. 6–7)

Suffice it to say that Anne too was just beginning to understand that this is more than "an addendum," as the drama of the moment subsumed her tentative attempts to make sense of this blur of events. Here was a group of teachers tending to multiple urgencies – working in collaboration with local substance abuse counselors to prevent a domino effect among the school's grieving students, mustering energy to meet their self-study deadline, and struggling to resurrect a sense of purposeful academic focus among their students as well as themselves.

Even in better times, Max's language-arts colleague Bill seemed in many ways his polar opposite. Whereas Max was tough and demanding, Bill was ostensibly open-hearted and kind, and while Max moved through these months with sturdy resiliency, Bill found himself drifting toward depression and inertia. Max noted that there was a downside to his own "high tolerance for pain," a tendency to be seen as "not as sensitized," even "a little callused." Soon after Bill joined the school's staff, he had gone to Max to ask for help in coping with the emotional rigors of this place and these young people. Max had searched unsuccessfully for something useful to say, his response bearing certain surface similarities to the responses of Chris's colleagues. "I don't have a way of offering a whole lot of support," he would later explain to Anne. "That's not in my repertoire, and so sometimes I feel like I should be doing more than I had inside me. I mean I couldn't really do any more, so I didn't" (DiPardo, 1999).

Anne would hear the old saw about two heads being better that one countless times as she collected data across sites and talked to teachers, students, and administrators. But beginning with Max and his colleagues at the SDLC, she began to see that substantive partnerships inevitably involve more than shared cognition. Max and Bill's work – and their students' learning – would be unimaginable without a profound investment that was at once thinking and feeling. Because their students' lives were so full of risks and uncertainties, these teachers' work was, too, their collaboration serving to address the pedagogic and emotional rigors of managing high-stakes ambiguity. These teachers presented a pool of diverse resources, as each individual turned to others for missing pieces and fresh ideas.

In this regard it was perhaps a bit too tempting to cast Max and Bill in tidy binaries: this science teacher as tough-minded thinker, this language arts teacher as open-hearted caretaker. It is a binary that pervades discussion of educational issues, reflecting a quintessential opposition that has organized so much of Western thought, often posited as Enlightenment rationality versus Romantic feeling (Wertsch, 2000). These are powerful and time-honored polarities; various cultures tend to organize their discourse about emotions in distinctive ways (Wierzbicka, 1999), and this polarization was certainly a reflection of cultural biases shared by researcher and participants alike. Max and Bill tended to cast themselves as sides of a coin, and Anne's narrative largely allowed the opposition to stand – casting Max as a thinking resource, Bill as an emotional one. As Anne would describe it (DiPardo, 1996; 1999), their collaboration had introduced a generative tension into their shared work, even as their individual emphases represented distinctive strengths and vulnerabilities.

Max's professional life would take unexpected and challenging new turns in the months and years to come. As Anne's book about Max and Bill's classroom moved into print, their school was under increasing attack from a district administration intent on conserving funds and moving toward more standardized curricula. During this time Anne had a number of conversations with school board members and district administrators in which she tried to describe the mix of care and curricular creativity that characterized the collaborative work of the school's faculty. She found that although no one needed convincing that this group of teachers showed concern for their students, administrators and board members appeared to regard this as quite separate from the school's academic charge. Juxtaposed with the school's affective strengths they perceived important deficits – in the school's ever-shifting interdisciplinary curriculum, in the troubled students who perennially dropped in and out, even in the staff's penchant for energetic argument. Amid waves of protest from former and present students and parents, the SDLC was closed, to be replaced with a program that would rely heavily on worksheet packets purchased from a local general equivalency diploma (GED) program.

For Max, one of the school's great treasures had rested in the very penchant for disagreement that district officials found so untenable. Max would go on to a larger, better-supported school in another district, rediscovering the exhilaration of those moments of intense focus on students. But his new school is several times larger, and he notes a bit more caution among the staff, less opportunity to talk as an entire faculty about their daily struggles and satisfactions. This also means less time to build the foundations of common purpose and mutual trust that had given the SDLC staff license to disagree and argue – a process that Max occasionally found draining and futile, but more often exciting and vital. The open, usually productive discord that marked the SDLC is indeed rare in school workplaces, where harmony tends to be valued above the generative but risky play of divergent perspectives (Evans, 1996).

Vygotsky tended to highlight the importance of intellectual and social harmony in collaboration, prompting a number of efforts to expand social–cultural theory to encompass these more contentious aspects of productive teaching and learning. Although such efforts have on occasion incorporated Piagetian (Piaget, 1970; see Damon, 1984; and DiPardo & Freedman, 1988) or Bakhtinian (Bakhtin, 1981; see Wertsch, 1991) perspectives, a particularly appropriate frame for Max's work can be found in the works of John Dewey (Dewey, 1966; see also Glassman, 2001). Several teachers at the SDLC explicitly referenced *Democracy in Education* in characterizing the school as a kind of societal microcosm, marked by a sense of community and belonging, but also challenged by daily conversations across boundaries of difference. Invoking both Vygotsky and Dewey, we could say that these conversations – which Max described as sometimes trying, but more often productive and "exhilarating" – were at once infused with intellectual and emotional energies.

In the essay "Affective Thought" (1984), Dewey critiqued the same philosophic tendencies that organized Anne's narrative about Max and his colleague Bill – that is, this penchant for assigning the "feeling" function to people preoccupied with the arts and humanities, the "thinking" function to scientists like Max, with everyday practical action cast as another matter entirely. For Dewey – and indeed for Max – these separations simply give way on closer examination. In *How We Think* (1933), he would go on to counter the prevalent assumption that emotion and imagination are somehow unnecessary to the work of so-called informational and intellectual subjects such as the sciences (see also Polanyi, 1958). "Human beings are not normally divided into two parts, the one emotional, the other coldly intellectual," Dewey observed:

The split does, indeed, often get established, but that is always because of false methods of education. Natively and normally the personality works as a whole. There is no integration of character and mind unless there is fusion of the intellectual and the emotional, of meaning and value, of fact and imaginative running beyond fact into the realm of desired possibilities. (1933, p. 278)

Although Max tends to describe his work in terms of thought and action, this emotional charge becomes increasingly obvious on extended observation – in his tendency to lighten discouraging moments with wry asides; in his understated movement among states of excitement, discouragement, and frustration; and perhaps most of all in the intensely watchful gaze he fixes upon students. Our usual vocabulary of care tends to conjure rather different images, of teachers full of tender regard, reaching out with ostensible compassion and gentleness. Max's sort of care is challenging and goal-oriented, always moving toward the next step, focusing on the emotions of the moment only as they inform the development of strategies and solutions.

Max's work also brings to mind van Manen's characterization of "tactful teaching," in which developing "the feeling for the right action" arises from "a certain thinking attentiveness" (1991, p. 146). Max's thinking about his work – work performed in such close company that the Vygotskian relation between the interpsychic and intrapsychic is rendered particularly apparent (Vygotsky, 1978, p. 57) – is persistently marked by efforts to understand past efforts better and to plan thoughtfully for the future. His challenge – like ours here – is continually to renarrativize (Polkinghorne, 1988; Sarbin, 1986), to work toward more satisfying and productive ways of imagining the lives of his students as well as his own life as a teacher. Such habits of narrative reflection are at once cognitive and affective, marked by concern for students, love of subject matter, and thoroughgoing knowledge of both content and pedagogy (Miller, 1999).

For Max, then, the emotional charge around his work is inseparable from the central challenge of serving students, providing what Vygotsky called the "affective–volitional" basis of thought (1986, p. 252). Although he agrees that the affective dimension of teaching must be acknowledged and honored, Max finds something vaguely dissatisfying about well-meaning efforts to talk about emotionality in the abstract, in special workshops, or as items on meeting agendas ("Someone tell us one good thing that happened this week"). When Anne pressed him to describe what he was thinking and feeling in one of those intensely focused conversations with students, he spoke of a heightened sense of alertness, of a sense akin to watching himself from a slight distance, observing the interaction, feeling his way to the next step. He described himself as unusually still and calm at such times, his mind uncluttered and intently focused. Max's description bears an affinity to Csikszentmihalyi's notion of "flow" experiences (1991), in which concentration is so intense that one scarcely notices the passing of time; it also calls to mind Noddings's argument that caring is characterized by "engrossment" in the needs of the cared for, and a strong desire to provide assistance that she terms "motivational displacement" (1984, 1992, pp. 15–16). The two concepts provide a more satisfying frame when taken together rather than invoked separately, as Max's watchful gaze entails both mental concentration and deep concern for students.

As we have seen, however, the pervasive tendency is to cast intellectual and emotional engagement as distinct elements – sometimes with important political consequences, as when teachers like Max must struggle to explain the nature of their work to skeptics. As soon as the SDLC faculty's concern for students' welfare began to be named as a distinct strand of their work, it was readily dismissed as not at all central to the school's academic mission – as something nice and mildly commendable, but hardly crucial. Similarly, the staff's penchant for hammering out strategies through contentious, often charged conversations was interpreted as an indication that they were relationally "dysfunctional" and "unable to collaborate." The fact that these various elements were of a piece – teachers' concerns for students' overall welfare *and* their academic progress, collaboration, *and* contention – was overlooked, with decisive political consequences.

We could use better language to describe Max's and the SDLC's sort of care – indeed, to describe the full range of ways in which teachers negotiate the varied emotions of their work and manage the affective toll a strong investment in teaching exacts. As Hargreaves suggests (2000), we need fine-grained descriptions of particular "emotional geographies" with their idiosyncratic opportunities and constraints – in social–cultural terms, the activity settings (Cole, 1985; Leontiev, 1981) wherein teachers interact with students, administrators, parents, and one another. Whereas individual teachers must be seen as existing in dynamic relationship with their contexts – that is, being shaped by their school settings as well as shaping those settings – Max's case also suggests the need to acknowledge the varied ways that particular teachers approach their work. Such a conceptual frame would acknowledge the strong emotional investment of all committed teachers, whether they speak predominantly in the language of intellect or feeling, and whether they come away from trying times with Max's indefatigable desire to go on – or, as in the case of his colleague Bill, with a decision to join Chris and too many others in leaving the profession.

EMOTIONS AND THE DYNAMIC OF TEACHERS' LIVES

Chris and Max are in many ways a study in contrasts, their stories suggesting the benefits of collaboration and the risks of isolation, a work life among polite-but-distant colleagues versus hourly interaction with contentious intimates, and the overarching need for support tailored to particular contexts and needs. These narratives are marked by quiet similarities, too, as both Chris and Max approached their work with passionate commitment – putting in long hours, caring about students as people as well as learners, persistently searching for activities to engage and challenge even the most reluctant. In ways that neither could ultimately tease apart, they acted, thought, and felt a great deal. Teachers so invested in their work are arguably the most vulnerable to frustration and exhaustion when they find themselves facing hard challenges and insufficient support – especially now, as so many are describing a waning sense of agency, an intensification of their daily responsibilities, and often misguided efforts to render schools more accountable.

It is hard to imagine a life in teaching truly devoid of emotional charge. Dickens's Gradgrind comes to mind, embodying the familiar head-heart dichotomy, and the strong Western tendency, often traced to Plato (Brand, 1989; Oatley, 1992) and later to Descartes (Damasio, 1994), to celebrate the head and distrust the heart. And yet one somehow senses that by novel's end comeuppance will be had, the heart given its due, hearts and minds put in a rightful relation. We know this only in part because we know Dickens; we know it, too, because we recognize that teaching is human work, and that both teachers and students are indelibly emotional creatures.

The choice is not whether to feel or not; what emerges in the extended Vygotskian framework sketched here, as well as in more recent neurological and psychological work, is that emotions are inevitably present in any teaching–learning event. As key strands in the "web of meaning" (Vygotsky, 1986, p. 182), our emotions are intimately connected to our thoughts and actions and shaped in important ways by the institutional, cultural, and historic contexts in which we live and labor. We act on the basis of socially constructed thoughts and emotions, which, "gone inward," become what we tend to regard as our private sensibilities and understandings. If the setting in which such construction occurs is disturbed or unbalanced, our thoughts, emotions, and actions will bear the requisite marks. In this conception, positive emotions become much more than a side issue labeled teacher "morale" or well-managed "stress"; rather, positive affect is of the essence, crucial to good thinking and effective action for teachers and students alike. As Vygotsky's attention to affect has been largely ignored, so too has this aspect of his foresight. Even as emotionality edges toward preeminence in neurology, psychology, philosophy, and sociology, neo-Vygotskians have left this aspect of classroom life largely undertheorized, lagging behind the provocative interdisciplinary focus fast developing elsewhere in scholarship on teachers' emotionality (Boler, 1999; Hargreaves, 1997, 1998, 2000).

We clearly need a more developed and politically viable theoretic base in order to argue for enhanced attention to emotion in teacher education, in teacher development, and in empirical research on teaching and learning. Certainly the expanded Vygotskian theory that we have traced comprises a start, especially as we acknowledge the many ways that Vygotsky presaged more recent cross-disciplinary work exploring the rich connections among affect, cognition, and action. We would further argue that by aligning Vygotskian theory with widely noted educational conceptions of emotionality, we can give new credibility and political clout to efforts to raise issues of affect, while also further developing the social–cultural conception of teaching we have begun to sketch here. Following Tappan (1998), we see a fruitful affinity between Noddings's conceptions of care (1984, 1992, 1995) and Vygotsky's view of assisted learning in the zone of proximal development (ZPD) (1978). We would add to this enriched theoretic base a recognition of recent work on narrative ways of knowing, with its emphasis on constructing subjective, holistic meanings out of the complex vicissitudes of human experience (Bruner, 1986; Polkinghorne, 1988); on habits of reflection that encompass concern for students as well as love of one's subject (Miller, 1999; Gudmundsdottir, 1995); and on the need for collegial receptivity and support (Clandinin & Connelly, 1995).

Work on narrative ways of knowing serves to enrich Vygotskian conceptions of teachers' professional lives in several ways. First, it provides a framework that can help us better understand how intellectual and emotional understandings are internalized and developed – that is, through a process of narrativizing experience and continually revisiting and refining these narratives that they might reflect more robust conceptions of teaching and learning (Clandinin & Connelly, 1995). Second, this work provides many concrete examples of the relationship between teacher reflection and student learning (DiPardo, 2000; Miller, 1999; Vinz, 1996) long argued by neo-Vygotskians (Gallimore & Tharp, 1990; Tharp & Gallimore, 1988; Tharp, 1993). Finally, when narrative theory has informed empirical research on teaching and learning, we have seen countless portraits that align nicely – albeit implicitly – with Vygotsky's belief the emotions "cannot be understood outside the dynamic of human life," the contexts in which "the emotional processes acquire their meaning and sense" (1987, p. 333). As these politically charged times make attention to teachers' emotions increasingly crucial (Hargreaves, 1997; 1998; 2000), it is important that we heed Vygotsky's caution and refrain from rendering affect the focus of decontextualized, reductionist study. The best research on teachers' narrative ways of knowing encompasses an understanding long held by imaginative writers: that whereas emotion is as central to narrative power as it is to human life, it cannot be treated apart from the fabric of relationships and circumstance that ultimately allow readers to forge connection and construct understandings (Eliot, 1971; Spark, 2000; Tolstoy, 1971). Emotion, as Vygotsky emphasized, cannot be usefully imagined as a "state within a state"; in educational research, as in fictional narratives, emotions are best explored as integral threads in the larger web.

If, as Bruner (1986) has suggested, there are essentially two ways of knowing that exist side by side – the "narrative" and the "paradigmatic" – then it makes sense to balance our understandings by pursuing both, while taking care to avoid the common cultural tendency to privilege the latter over the former. Vygotsky's conception of the relations among emotion, thought, and human activity provides a paradigmatic though admittedly sketchy framework; narratives of classroom life, meanwhile, give these ideas concrete realization, moving us to see our own contexts and activities anew, in what qualitative researchers have called *reader* or *user generalizability* (McCutcheon, 1981; Merriam, 1997; Walker, 1980). Taken together, these bodies of work can provide more satisfying and politically viable ways of conceptualizing teachers' professional lives, as we endeavor to articulate the concrete universals that can be deduced from carefully drawn narratives.

If we acknowledge that teaching is politically charged work involving both emotional and intellectual investments and challenges, we must also recognize that threats to teachers' professional well-being undermine the very core of their labors. Amid all the talk of late about ways to intensify and evaluate teachers' work, their need for sustenance and renewal is too often given short shrift. The affective aspect of teachers' professional lives tends to be filed away in separate categories – "morale," "stress," even "emotional intelligence" – and made gist for facile workshops or administrative quick fixes. An expanded neo-Vygotskian conception of the work of teachers can enrich the efforts of researchers, policymakers, teacher educators, and administrators to provide enhanced understanding and better support structures that encompass their emotional as well as intellectual needs. These neo-Vygotskian conceptions have moved our understandings of teaching and learning forward in multiple ways, beyond the narrowly individualistic and behavioristic, toward an appreciation of the constitutive role of social interaction and the shaping power of the cultural, institutional, and historic contexts in which such interactions occur. We see the role of emotionality as an untapped vein in this generative and still-developing theoretic base, representing a conceptual challenge that holds key implications for research, policy, and practice. Ensuring the vitality of our nation's teachers demands these still-richer theoretic conceptions – conceptions that might empower our efforts to understand and support teachers like Max and Chris, as they in turn strive to understand and support students who are (as we all are) at once feeling and thinking beings.

References

Allport, G. (1948). Foreword. In H. W. Werner, *Comparative psychology of mental development* (pp. ix–xii). Chicago: Follett.

Apple, M. (1988). *Teachers and texts: A political economy of class and gender relations in education*. New York: Routledge.

Bakhtin, M. M. (1981). *The dialogic imagination: Four essays by M. M. Bakhtin* (M. Holquist, Ed. and C. Emerson and M. Holquist, Trans.). Austin: University of Texas Press.

Beer, J., & Beer, J. (1992). Burnout and stress, depression and self-esteem of teachers. *Psychological Reports, 71*, 1331–1336.

Boler, M. (1999). *Feeling power: Emotions and education*. New York: Routledge.

Bradshaw, R. (1991). Stress management for teachers: A practical approach. *The Clearing House, 65*, 43–47.

Brand, A. (1989). *The psychology of writing: The affective experience*. Westport, CT: Greenwood.

Brand, A. (1991). Social cognition, emotions, and the psychology of writing. *Journal of Advanced Composition, 11*(2), 395–407.

Bruner, J. (1986). *Actual minds, possible worlds*. Cambridge, MA: Harvard University Press.

Bruner, J. (1987). Prologue to the English edition. In R. Rieber & A. Carton (Eds.), *The collected works of L. S. Vygotsky* (N. Minick, Trans.) (Vol. 1, pp. 1–16). New York: Plenum Press.

Calhoun, C. (1984). Cognitive emotions. In Calhoun, C. & Solomon, R. (Eds.), *What is an emotion? Classic readings in philosophical psychology* (pp. 327–342). New York: Oxford University Press.

Carter, K. (1993). The place of story in the study of teaching and teacher education. *Educational Researcher, 22*(1), 5–12.

Cedoline, A. J. (1982). *Job burnout in public education: Symptoms, causes, and survival skills*. New York: Teachers College Press.

Clandinin, D. J., & Connelly, F. M. (1995). *Teachers' professional knowledge landscapes*. New York: Teachers College Press.

Clark, C. (1995). *Thoughtful teaching*. New York: Teachers College Press.

Clift, R., Veal, M., Holland, P., Johnson, M., & McCarthy, J. (1995). *Collaborative leadership and shared decision making: Teachers, principals, and university professors*. New York: Teachers College Press.

Cole, M. (1985). The zone of proximal development: Where culture and cognition create each other. In J. V. Wertsch (Ed.), *Culture, communication, and cognition: Vygotskian perspectives* (pp. 146–161). New York: Cambridge University Press.

Connelly, M., & Clandinin, J. (1990). Stories of experience and narrative inquiry. *Educational Researcher, 19*(5), 2–14.

Csikszentmihalyi, M. (1991). *Flow: The psychology of optimal experience*. New York: HarperCollins.

Czubaj, C. (1996). Maintaining teacher motivation. *Education, 116*, 372–378.

Damasio, A. (1994). *Descartes' error: Emotion, reason, and the human brain*. New York: Avon.

Damasio, A. (1999). *The feeling of what happens: Body and emotion in the making of consciousness*. New York: Harcourt Brace.

Damon, W. (1984). Peer education: The untapped potential. *Journal of Applied Psychology, 5*, 331–343.

Darwin, C. (1998). The expression of the emotions in man and animals. Excerpted In J. Jenkins, K. Oatley, & N. Stein (Eds.), *Human emotions: A reader* (pp. 288–297). Malden, MA: Blackwell.

Denzin, N. (1984). *On understanding emotion*. San Francisco: Jossey-Bass.

Derry, S., & Murphy, D. (1986). Designing systems that train learning ability: From theory to practice. *Review of Educational Research, 56*(1), 1–39.

Dewey, J. (1933). *How we think: A restatement of the relation of reflective thinking to the educative process.* New York: D. C. Heath.

Dewey, J. (1966). *Democracy and education.* New York: Free Press.

Dewey, J. (1984). Affective thought. In J. Boydston (Ed.), *John Dewey: The later works,* (Vol. 2, pp. 104–110). Carbondale: Southern Illinois University Press.

Dickens, C. (1961). *Hard times.* New York: New American Library.

DiPardo, A., & Freedman, S. W. (1988). Peer response groups in the writing classroom: Theoretic foundations and new directions. *Review of Educational Research, 58*(2), 119–149.

DiPardo, A. (1996). Seeking alternatives: The wisdom of collaborative teaching. *English Educations 28*(2), 109–126.

DiPardo, A. (1999). *Teaching in common: Challenges to joint work in classrooms and schools.* New York: Teachers College Press.

DiPardo, A. (2000). What a little hate literature will do: "Cultural issues" and the emotional aspect of school change. *Anthropology & Education Quarterly, 31*(3), 306–332.

Duhnam, J. (1984). *Stress in teaching.* New York: Nichols.

Eliot, T. S. (1971). Hamlet and his problems. Reprinted in H. Adams (ed.), *Critical theory since Plato* (pp. 788–790). New York: Harcourt Brace Jovanovich.

Evans, R. (1996). *The human side of school change: Reform resistance, and the real-life problems of reform.* San Francisco: Jossey-Bass.

Flavell, J. (1966). Heinz Werner on the nature of development. In S. Wapner & B. Kaplan (Eds.), *Heinz Werner, 1890–1964: Papers in memoriam* (pp. 17–31). Worcester, MA: Clark University Press.

Franklin, M. (1997). Constructing a developmental psychology: Heinz Werner's vision. *Contemporary Psychology, 42*(6), 481–485.

Franklin, M. (2000). Considerations for a psychology of experience: Heinz Werner's contribution. *Journal of Adult Development, 7*(1), 31–39.

Fried, R. (1996). *The passionate teacher: A practical guide.* Boston: Beacon.

Fullan, M. (1991). *The new meaning of educational change.* New York, Toronto: Teachers College Press/OISE Press.

Fullan, M. (1993). *Change forces: Probing the depths of educational reform.* London: Falmer.

Fullan, M. (1999). *Change forces: The sequel.* London: Falmer.

Gallimore, R., & Tharp, R. (1990). Teaching mind in society: Teaching, schooling, and literate discourse. In L. Moll (Ed.), *Vygotsky and education: Instructional implications and applications of sociohistorical psychology.* New York: Cambridge University Press.

Glassman, M. (2001). Dewey and Vygotsky: Society, experience, and inquiry in educational practice. *Educational Researcher, 30*(4), 3–14.

Glick, J. (1983). Piaget, Vygotsky and Werner. In S. Wapner & B. Kaplan (Eds.), *Towards a holistic developmental psychology* (pp. 35–52). Hillsdale, NJ: Erlbaum.

Glick, J. (1992). Werner's relevance for contemporary developmental psychology. *Developmental Psychology, 28*(4), 558–565.

Goleman, D. (1995). *Emotional intelligence: Why it can matter more than IQ.* New York: Bantam.

Graves, D. (2001). *The energy to teach.* Portsmouth, NH: Heinemann.

Greenberg, S. (1984). *Stress and the teaching profession*. Baltimore: Paul H. Brookes.

Gudmundsdottir, S. (1995). The narrative nature of pedagogical content knowledge. In H. McEwan & K. Egan (Eds.), *Narrative in teaching, learning and research* (pp. 24–38). New York: Teachers College Press.

Hargreaves, A. (1997). Introduction. In A. Hargreaves (Ed.), *Rethinking educational change with heart and mind: 1997 ASCD Yearbook* (pp. vii–xv). Alexandria, VA: ASCD.

Hargreaves, A. (1998). The emotional politics of teacher development. Keynote speech presented at the American Educational Research Association Annual Meeting, San Diego.

Hargreaves, A. (2000). Emotional geographies of teaching. Paper presented at the American Educational Research Association Annual Meeting, New Orleans.

Hjort, M., & Laver, S. (Eds.) (1997). *Emotion and the Arts*. New York: Oxford University Press.

Hochschild, A. (1983). *The managed heart: The commercialization of human feeling*. Berkeley: University of California Press.

Isen, A. M., Daubman, K. A., & Nowicki, G. P. (1998). Positive affect facilitates creative problem solving. In J. Jenkins, K. Oatley, & N. Stein (Eds.), *Human emotions: A reader* (pp. 288–297). Malden, MA: Blackwell.

James, W. (1950). *The principles of psychology*. New York: Dover.

Jersild, A. T. (1955). *When teachers face themselves*. New York: Teachers College Press.

Kelchtermans, G., & Strittmatter, A. (1999). Beyond individual burnout: A perspective for improved schools. In R. Vandenberghe and M. Huberman (Eds.), *Understanding and preventing teacher burnout: A sourcebook of international research and practice* (pp. 304–314). Cambridge: Cambridge University Press.

Kozulin, A. (1990). *Vygotsky's psychology: A biography of ideas*. Cambridge, MA: Harvard University Press.

Lakoff, G., & Johnson, M. (1983). *Metaphors we live by*. Chicago: University of Chicago Press.

Langer, S. K. (1942). *Philosophy in a new key: A study in the symbolism of reason, rite, and art*. Cambridge, MA: Harvard University Press.

Leontiev, A. N. (1981). The problem of activity in psychology. In J. V. Wertsch (Ed.), *The concept of activity in Soviet psychology* (pp. 37–71). Armonk, NY: Sharpe.

Little, J. W. (1993). Teachers' professional development in a climate of educational reform. *Educational Evaluation and Policy Analysis, 15*, 129–151.

Little, J. W. (1996). The emotional contours and career trajectories of (disappointed) reform enthusiasts. *Cambridge Journal of Education, 26*(3), 345–359.

Luria, A. R. (1987). Afterword to the Russian edition. In R. Rieber & A. Carton (Eds.), *The collected works of L. S. Vygotsky* (N. Minick, Trans.) (Vol. 1, pp. 359–373). New York: Plenum Press.

McCutcheon, G. (1981). On the interpretation of classroom observation. *Educational Researcher, 10*, 5–10.

Maeroff, G. I. (1993). *Team building for school change: Equipping teachers for new roles*. New York: Teachers College Press.

Maslach, C., & Leiter, M. (1999). Teacher burnout: A research agenda. In R. Vandenberghe & M. Huberman (Eds.), *Understanding and preventing teacher* burnout: *A sourcebook of international research and practice* (pp. 295–303). Cambridge: Cambridge University Press.

Merriam, S. (1997). *Qualitative research and case study applications in education*. San Francisco: Jossey-Bass.

Miller, S. (1999). Supporting possible worlds: Transforming literature teaching and learning through conversations in the narrative mode. *Research in the Teaching of English, 34*(1), 1064.

Miller, S. (2002). Conversations from the commissions: Reflective teaching in the panic of high-stakes testing. *English Education, 34*(2), 164–168.

Minick, N., & Stone, C. A., & Forman, E. A. (1993). Introduction: Integration of individual, social, and institutional processes in accounts of children's learning and development. In E. A. Forman, N. Minick, & C. A. Stone (Eds.), *Contexts for learning: Sociocultural dynamics in children's development* (pp. 3–16). New York: Oxford University Press.

Nietzsche, F. (1971). The birth of tragedy from the spirit of music. Excerpt reprinted in H. Adams (Ed.), *Critical theory since Plato* (pp. 636–641). New York: Harcourt Brace Jovanovich.

Noddings, N. (1984). *Caring: A feminine approach to ethics and moral education*. Berkeley: University of California Press.

Noddings, N. (1992). *The challenge to care in schools: An alternative approach to education*. New York: Teachers College Press.

Noddings, N. (1995). Care and moral education. In W. Kohli (Ed.), *Critical conversations in philosophy of education* (pp. 137–148). New York: Routledge.

Nussbaum, M. (2001). *Upheavals of thought: The intelligence of emotions*. Cambridge: Cambridge University Press.

Oatley, K. (1992). *Best laid schemes: The psychology of emotions*. Cambridge: Cambridge University Press.

Oatley, K. & Jenkins, J. (1998). *Understanding emotions*. Malden, MA: Blackwell.

Palincsar, A. S., Brown, A. L., & Campione, J. C. (1993). First-grade dialogues for knowledge acquisition and use. In E. A. Forman, N. Minick, & C. A. Stone (Eds.), *Contexts for learning: Sociocultural dynamics in children's development* (pp. 43–57). New York: Oxford University Press.

Palmer, P. J. (1998). *The courage to teach: Exploring the inner landscape of a teacher's life*. San Francisco: Jossey-Bass.

Piaget, J. (1962). The relation of affectivity to intelligence in the mental development of the child. *Bulletin of Menninger Clinic, 26*, 129–137.

Piaget, J. (1970). Piaget's theory. In P. H. Mussen (Ed.), *Carmichael's manual of child psychology* (3rd ed., Vol. 1, pp. 703–732). New York: Wiley.

Polanyi, M. (1958). *Personal knowledge: Towards a post-critical philosophy*. Chicago: University of Chicago Press.

Polkinghorne, D. (1988). *Narrative knowing and the human sciences*. Albany: State University of New York.

Ross, R., & Altmaier, E. (1994). *Intervention in occupational stress: A handbook of counseling for stress at work*. Thousand Oaks, CA: Sage.

Rudow, B. (1999). Stress and burnout in the teaching profession: European studies, issues, and research perspectives. In R. Vandenberghe & A. Michael Huberman

(Eds.), *Understanding and preventing teacher burnout: A sourcebook of international research and practice*. Cambridge: Cambridge University Press.

Russell, D., Altmaier, E., & Van Velzen, D. (1987). Job-related stress, social support, and burnout among classroom teachers. *Journal of Applied Psychology, 72*(2), 269–274.

Salzberger-Wittenbert, I., Henry, G., & Osborne, E. (1983). *The emotional experience of learning and teaching*. London: Routledge & Kegan Paul.

Sarason, S. B. (1996). *Revisiting "The culture of the school and the problem of change."* New York: Teachers College Press.

Sarbin, T. R. (Ed.) (1986). *Narrative psychology: The storied nature of human conduct*. New York: Praeger.

Scheff, T. (1994). *Bloody revenge: Emotions, nationalism, and war*. Boulder, CO: Westview.

Scheff, T., & Retzinger, S. (1991). *Emotion and violence: Shame and rage in destructive conflicts*. Lexington, MA: Lexington Books.

Scheffler, I. (1991). *In praise of the cognitive emotions and other essays in the philosophy of education*. New York: Routledge.

Sergiovanni, T. (1994). *Building community in schools*. San Francisco: Jossey-Bass.

Spark, D. (2000). Handling emotion in fiction writing. *Writer's Chronicle, 33*(3), 5–13.

Swick, K., & Hanley, P. (1985). *Stress and the classroom teacher*. Washington, DC: National Education Association.

Tappan, M. B. (1998). Sociocultural psychology and caring pedagogy: Exploring Vygotsky's "Hidden Curriculum." *Educational Psychologist, 33*(1), 23–33.

Tharp, R. (1993). Institutional and social context of educational practice and reform. In E. Forman, N. Minick, & C. A. Stone (Eds.), *Contexts for learning: Sociocultural dynamics in children's development* (pp. 269–282). New York: Oxford University Press.

Tharp, R., & Gallimore, R. (1988). *Rousing minds to life: Teaching, learning, and schooling in social context*. New York: Cambridge University Press.

Tolstoy, L. (1971). What is art? Excerpted in H. Adams (Ed.), *Critical theory since Plato* (pp. 708–710). New York: Harcourt Brace Jovanovich.

van Manen, M. (1991). *The tact of teaching: The meaning of pedagogical thoughtfulness*. Albany, NY: SUNY Press.

Vinz, R. (1996). *Composing a teaching life*. Portsmouth, NH: Boynton/Cook-Heinemann.

Vygotsky, L. (1971). *The psychology of art*. Boston: MIT Press.

Vygotsky, L. (1978). *Mind in society*. Cambridge, MA: Harvard University Press.

Vygotsky, L. (1986). *Thought and language*. Cambridge, MA: MIT Press.

Vygotsky, L. (1987). Lecture 4: Emotions and their development in childhood. In R. Rieber & A. Carton (Eds.), *The collected works of L. S. Vygotsky* (N. Minick, Trans.) (Vol. 1, pp. 325–358). New York: Plenum Press.

Walker, R. (1980). The conduct of educational case studies: Ethics, theory and procedures. In W. B. Dockerell & D. Hamilton (Eds.), *Rethinking educational research* (pp. 30–63). London: Hodder & Stoughton.

Wapner, S. (2000). Person-in-environment transitions: Developmental analysis. *Journal of Adult Development, 7*(1), 7–22.

Werner, H. (1948). *Comparative psychology of mental development*. Chicago: Follett.

Werner, H., & Kaplan, B. (1963). *Symbol formation: An organismic-developmental approach to language and the expression of thought*. New York: John Wiley & Sons.

Wertsch, J. (1991). *Voices of the mind: A sociocultural approach to mediated action*. Cambridge, MA: Harvard University Press.

Wertsch, J. (2000). Vygotsky's two minds on the nature of meaning. In C. D. Lee & P. Smagorinsky (Eds.), *Vygotskian perspectives on literacy research* (pp. 19–30). Cambridge: Cambridge University Press.

Wierzbicka, A. (1999). *Emotions across languages and cultures: Diversity and universals*. Cambridge: Cambridge University Press.

Woods, P. (1999). Intensification and stress in teaching. In R. Vandenberghe & M. Huberman (Eds.), *Understanding and preventing teacher burnout: A sourcebook of international research and practice* (pp. 115–138). Cambridge: Cambridge University Press.

PART IV

DIVERSE LEARNERS AND CONTEXTS OF EDUCATION

16

Intrapersonal Communication and Internalization in the Second Language Classroom

James P. Lantolf

This chapter considers an aspect of sociocultural research that has not been fully explored with regard to second language learning – the process through which learners develop the repertoire of symbolic artifacts they use when engaging in communicative activities (verbal and visual) in the second language. I will argue that the key to this development resides in *internalization*, a process closely affiliated with private speech. Carroll (2001, pp. 16–17) points out that the process of acquisition is "not directly observable" and can only be inferred "on the basis of other observable events such as the utterances that learners produce, the interpretation they assign to utterances they hear or read, the time it takes to interpret an utterance, their judgements of the acceptability of utterances, etc." The specific goal of this chapter is to argue that it is possible to observe, at least in part, the process of language learning through analysis of the intrapersonal communication (private speech) produced by learners in concrete objective circumstances of the language classroom.

Unlike most theories of language acquisition, in particular that espoused by Chomsky's innatist theory, the sociocultural perspective recognizes that humans are not completely at the mercy of their biology; rather it sees humans as agents who regulate their brains rather than the other way around. As Vygotsky put it: "*I only want to say . . . that without man[1] [sic] (=operator) as a whole the activity of his apparatus (brain) cannot be explained, that man controls his brain and not the brain the man* (Yaroshevsky, 1989, p. 230). To be sure, Vygotsky recognized that biology constrains mental processing in important ways, but from this it does not follow that biology, and only biology, controls our mental activity. Indeed, as Vygotsky argued (1987), higher mental functions arise as a consequence of humans' gaining control over their biologically endowed brains through culturally specified

---

[1] Alex Kozulin (personal communication, January 2002) points out that the original Russian, *chelovek*, should be rendered in English as "human being" and not as "man."

medational means. Thus, there is a tension, or as Vygotsky characterized it, "a drama," between our natural inheritance and our sociocultural inheritance, and it is in this drama that we develop.

INTRAPERSONAL COMMUNICATION AND PRIVATE SPEECH

The cornerstone of Vygotsky's theory is his conception that the human mind, unlike other minds, is mediated by symbolic artifacts (see especially chapters 1 and 2 in Vygotsky, 1999), which means that the external world is never directly apprehended but recast and deferred (Frawley, 1997, p. 96). The links between us and our world are formed through what Vygotsky, by analogy with Marx's thinking about physical tools, called "psychological tools." The most important of these psychological tools, or signs, is human language.

Internalization

Sign-based mediation first is intermental and then becomes intramental as children learn to regulate the mediational tools of their culture and, with this, their own social and mental activity. The process of moving from the inter- to the intramental domain takes place through internalization, or, as some translate the Russian original, *interiorization*. According to Kozulin (1990, p. 116), "the essential element in the formation of higher mental functions is the process of internalization." Frawley (1997, pp. 94–95) notes that the original Russian term, *vrashchivanie*, frequently translated into English as "interiorization," means "ingrowing." In Frawley's words, "The dynamic and developmental character of the notion is lost by the English nominal translation." The Russian term, according to Frawley, very much implies the emergence of "active, nurturing transformation of externals into personally meaningful experience" (p. 95). As A. R. Luria (1979, p. 45) writes, "It is through this interiorization of historically determined and culturally organized ways of operating on information that the social nature of people comes to be their psychological nature as well."[2]

Internalization represents Vygotsky's attempt to overcome the Cartesian mind–world dualism. According to Galperin (1967, pp. 28–29), through internalization what is originally an external and nonmental form of activity becomes mental; thus, the process "opens up the possibility of bridging this gap" (between the nonmental and the mental). It is important to emphasize

---

[2] Internalization is a concept that is not without its controversies. Unfortunately, space does not permit even a brief discussion of the debates that continue around this concept. The interested reader should consult works such as Newman, Griffen, and Cole (1989); Wertsch (1998); Arievitch and van der Veer (1995); Arievitch and Stetsenko (2000); and Matusov (1998).

that internalization does not mean that something literally is "'within the individual' or 'in the brain,'" but instead "refers to the subject's ability to perform a certain action [concrete or ideal] without the immediately present problem situation 'in the mind'" (Stetsenko, 1999, p. 245) and with an understanding that is derived from, but independent of, "someone else's thoughts or understandings" (Ball, 2000, p. 250–251). Thus, on this view, mental activity is carried out "on the basis of mental representations, that is, independently of the physical presence of things" (Stetsenko, 1999, p. 245). With regard to second-language (L2) learning, internalization is the process through which learners construct a mental representation of what was at one point physically present (acoustic or visual) in external form. This representation, in turn, enables them to free themselves from the sensory properties of a specific concrete situation. Again, to cite Stetsenko, the formation of intrapersonal processes

is explained as the transition from a material *object-dependent* activity (such as the actual counting of physical objects by pointing at them with a finger in the initial stages of acquiring the counting operation) to a material *object-independent* activity (when a child comes to be able to count the objects without necessarily touching them or even seeing them). (1999, pp. 245–255)

Private Speech

Internalization as a concrete phenomenon is marked by the "abbreviation of interactive social speech into audible speech to oneself, or *private speech* and ultimately silent speech for oneself, or *inner speech*. Social dialogue condenses into a private dialogue for thinking" (Frawley, 1997, p. 95). Private speech is potentially understandable to someone "eavesdropping." Inner speech, on the other hand, if it were somehow to be audibly projected, because of its formal and semantic condensation, would be "incomprehensible to a listener" (Dance, 1994, p. 200).

Vocate (1994) argues that, as with social talk, self-talk is dialogic, but instead of an "I" who is talking to a "You," private speech entails an "I" that makes choices on what to talk about and a "Me" that interprets and critiques these choices. The selection and interpretation process is common in a variety of human social activities, including intentional instruction, in which concepts are frequently restructured by the teacher in ways that will make sense to the student and thus facilitate internalization. The student, of course, as Vocate (p. 12) notes, must be open-minded and willing to deal with the new material. A similar process also occurs through intrapersonal communication, but in this case, instead of interaction between teacher and student, the interaction is between the I and the Me. This means that people are capable of mediating their own learning on the intrapersonal level, but they do it in ways that reflect their interpersonal experiences (i.e., those activities valued and promoted by their particular community) (see Tulviste, 1991).

Daniel Dennett (1998, p. 292), not an adherent of sociocultural theory, nevertheless argues for a perspective on self-directed speech that parallels Vygotsky's:

> We refine our resources by incessant rehearsal and tinkering, turning our brains (and all associated peripheral gear we acquire) into a huge structured network of competencies. In our own case, the principle components of this technology for brain manipulation are words, and no evidence yet unearthed shows that any other animal is capable of doing anything like what we do with our words.

Clark (1998, p.178), also a mainstream cognitive scientist, notes that our public language is ideally suited to be co-opted for intrapersonal functions, because, as with social communication, we lay open to inspection, critique, and modification ideas, concepts, and problems. In intrapersonal communication we talk ourselves into development (Yingling, 1994).

Once private speech becomes inner speech, of course, its form and specific content are no longer observable to a third party. Vygotsky theorized, however, that because of the genetic link between private and inner speech (that is, private speech, itself derived from social speech, is the precursor to inner speech), mental development can be studied, at least in part, through analysis of private speech (Vygotsky, 1987; Luria, 1982).

Imitation

Fundamental to internalization is *imitation* (Vygotsky, 1987, p. 210). Largely because of the behaviorist legacy, many developmental and cognitive psychologists continue to understand imitation as essentially a copying process. Before the rise of behaviorism, especially in its North American variety, imitation was considered to be "a critically important developmental activity because it is the chief means by which in early childhood human beings are related to as other than, and in advance of, who they are"; it "is aimed at the future and not at copying the past. It is development because something new is created out of saying or doing 'the same thing'" (Newman & Holzman, 1993, p. 151). Tomasello (1999) argues that imitation, unlike exposure, stimulus enhancement, mimicking, and emulation, is a uniquely human form of cultural transmission. In imitative learning, "the goal or intention of the demonstrator is a central part of what they [children] perceive, and indeed the goal is understood as something separate from the various behavioral means that may be used to accomplish it" (Tomasello, 1999, p. 30).

According to James Mark Baldwin, North American predecessor of Vygotsky, internalization and imitation are the key processes through which social control carried out by others "gradually becomes reconstructed by the person oneself" (Valsiner, 2000, p. 32). Baldwin distinguishes two types of imitation – *imitative suggestion* and *persistent imitation*. The former entails movement of the organism increasingly closer to a particular model from one trial to the next and can, under given circumstances, result in a "faithful replication of the model"; in fact, "going beyond the model is not possible" (Valsiner, 2000, p. 30). The latter concept is "reconstruction of the model in new ways" (Valsiner, 2000, p. 30). Persistent imitation anticipates the future and as such involves "feed-forward" (instead of feedback), which enables the organism to preadapt to "future encounters with the world" (Valsinar & van der Veer, 2000, p. 153).

Lightbown and Spada (1993), no doubt influenced by the behaviorists' construal of the term, define *imitation* with reference to language learning as "word for word repetition of all or part of someone else's utterance" (p. 2) and note that although children do indeed imitate what they hear around them, it occurs in less than 10% of the cases. Importantly, however, they point out that "children's imitation is selective and based on what they are currently learning" (p. 3). From Lightbown and Spada's perspective then, imitation is the equivalent of parroting, or in Tomasello's terms, mimicking.

At the core of both Vygotsky's and Tomasello's understanding of imitation, however, is its transformative potential, a feature missing from the behaviorist-based interpretations. This is a crucial point, because, for one thing, repetition does not in itself imply agency and intentionality, whereas imitation does. Many phenomena in nature repeat in the clear absence of agency and intentionality; for example, waves breaking on a beach, the Earth orbiting around the Sun, the change in seasons (personal communication, Steve Thorne, October 2001). Thus, the distinction between repetition and imitation is basic to an understanding of the process through which human mental capacity is formed in the transition from external to internal activity.

To be sure, "in human life, there are situations in which precise copying of the models is crucial, and others in which the models need to be creatively transcended" (Valsinser, 2000, p. 30). For example, in sites such as traditional educational institutions where learning is assumed to entail the exact replication of information presented by some authority, or expert, imitation that fails to result in transformation is normally valued over imitation that is creative. In such cases, imitation no longer emerges as a creative way to "express oneself" (ibid.).[3]

---

[3] Shor (1996, p. 11) discusses the imposition of the traditional syllabus in schools and universities as the carrying out of an "epistemic illusion" in which "what has been socially and historically constructed by a specific culture becomes presented to students as undebatable and unchangeable, always there, timeless" as if it were a natural rather than a cultural creation. As such, it is to be repeated, not transformed.

Imitation is not limited to child development but occurs among adults as well. This is not surprising, given the principle of *continuous access* (Frawley & Lantolf, 1985), which sees development as a dynamic process in which earlier ways of knowing are maintained rather than surrendered as in linear models of cognitive growth. However, as the data to be considered here illustrate, children tend to exhibit a higher degree of persistent (transformative) imitation than do adults, at least in the educational setting.

The following examples, borrowed from Lightbown and Spada (1993), illustrate the imitative process, as Vygotsky interprets it, among children as they interact with adults. In (1) and (2) we see evidence of imitative suggestion reminiscent of the pattern drill activity of traditional language classrooms. The difference, of course, is that the process is constructive and not replicative, as is the intent of pattern drills.

(1) CINDY (24 months, 16 days) *is playing with a stuffed rabbit*
    PATSY (adult): What does this rabbit like to eat?
    CINDY: (uninterpretable speech) eat the carrots.
        (*she then gets another stuffed rabbit.*)
    CINDY: He (*uninterpretable speech*) eat carrots. The other one eat carrots. They both eat carrots.
(2) Cindy now at 25 months (*playing with several dolls, one of which she calls a "tiger"*)
    CINDY: Doll go to sleep
    PATSY: Does the doll want to go to sleep?
    CINDY: (*not answering Patsy, but talking to dolls in 'motherly' tones*) Okay, I take you. Come on, Doll . . . (XXX). Go to sleep with the tiger (XXX) go to sleep. Doll wants to go to sleep.
    PATSY: Does the tiger want to go to sleep?
    CINDY: Tiger wants to go to sleep. The doll wants to go to sleep. He go to sleep (Lightbown & Spada, 1993, p. 4).

In (3) and (4) are examples of persistent transformative imitation:

(3) DAVID (3 years, 11 months)
    MOTHER: Get undressed (*after many repetitions*)
    DAVID: I'm getting undressed.
        I'm getting *on* dressed. (*italics in original*)
        I'm getting on dressed.
        I'm getting *off* dressed. (*italics in original*)
(4) At a 12th birthday party, adults propose several toasts with grape juice, as in the following utterance:
    FATHER: I'd like to propose a toast
Following a period of time during which no toasting was going on, David (5 years, 1 month) utters:
    DAVID: I'd like to propose a piece of bread.

The adults, not realizing that David was serious, began to laugh, "which sent David slinking from the table" (Lightbown & Spada, 1993, p. 6).

According to Lightbown & Spada (p. 7), utterances such as those illustrated in (3) and (4) cannot be accounted for on the basis of imitation, "since the forms created by the child were never produced by adults." From the perspective argued for here, however, the novel forms produced by the children represent persistent imitation, as defined by Baldwin.

Language Play

Closely linked to imitation is the notion of play and, in particular, for our purposes, language play. Play, as Vygotsky argues, is not an "accidental whim, a pastime, but an important vital necessity" (1997, p. 88). Play, or game (in Russian, the words are the same), according to Vygotsky, entails imitation and is linked with future activity. Play for Vygotsky is more than having fun, although to be sure, this is an important feature of play; it is about opening up a zone of proximal development in which children behave beyond their current level of ability (1978).[4] Vygotsky also notes that play and work are not "polar opposites" but in fact "possess absolutely the same psychological nature. This underscores the fact that games are the natural form of work in children, a form of [leading] activity which is inherent to the child, as preparation for his life in the future" (1997, p. 93).

It turns out that in addition to playing with physical objects and with each other, children engage in play with symbolic artifacts, most especially language. Kuczaj (1983) documents three distinct types of language play produced by young children: social play (interactional play); social contact play (play that is not interactional but that occurs in the presence of other children), and solitary play (which occurs when the child is alone, as when in the crib) (see also Weir, 1962). According to Kuczaj (1983, p. 199), language play is directed toward three goals: control, enjoyment, and mastery.

Since play, in the position I am arguing for here, opens up a zone of proximal development (ZPD), one might expect that as speakers gain proficiency and ability in the language (L1 or L2) the frequency of language play would decline. This is because if the ZPD is where the present and future interface, as the distance between the two domains narrows, there is less to learn (see Lantolf, 1997, and de Guerrero, 1999, for support of this claim). Cook (2000, p. 204), taking a slightly, but not radically different theoretical perspective, argues that "play can take place at all levels of language proficiency" and regardless of whether an L1 or an L2 is involved, but nevertheless agrees that "language play is no longer

---

[4] Carruthers (1998, p. 115) argues that the appearance of pretend play in the human species was crucial in the development of the uniquely human ability to engage in visual and sensory forms of imagination.

seen as a trivial and optional extra but as the source of language knowledge, use, and activity" (p. 204).

PRIVATE SPEECH AND L2 LEARNING

Children

To my knowledge, before the present study, there have only been four previous studies of private speech in L2 learning: Heath (1985), De Courcy (1993), Saville-Troike (1988), and Ohta (2001). Although these studies present interesting and important data and, in fact, argue that private speech plays a role in language learning, they do not take as explicit a position as I am advocating here – that private speech as internalization, is, in fact, language learning in "flight," as Vygotsky (1978) was fond of saying when discussing the formation of higher forms of consciousness. I will consider data from three of the four studies, which provide support for my theoretical claim. For present purposes I will overlook Heath's interesting study for two reasons: Unlike in the other studies, the focus is not on classroom learners, and it is concerned with the learning of narrative rather than specific formal features of the L2.

De Courcy's (1993) study dealt with 12- to 15-year-old middle-school French- immersion children in Australia. According to De Courcy, her original research focus had been on what students said aloud, but at about the third month of the course, she noted that learners were producing private speech. Unfortunately, she does not present any specific examples of self-directed speech, but she does report on her student interviews regarding the phenomenon. She writes, "What had previously seemed (to the ear) to be rows of students listening attentively, but passively to what the teacher was saying was transformed into a group of students participating actively, but silently, in the lesson" (p. 176). She noticed, for example, that when one student answered the teacher's questions publicly, other students answered privately. She also observed that some students practiced their responses privately before making them public. Interviews with the students revealed four reasons for their use of private speech: (1) positively reinforcing one's answer; (2) saving face, by avoiding calling out a possible incorrect answer; as one student put it, "You say it in your mind because you're afraid to say it out loud because it might be wrong"; (3) making sense of the question asked by the teacher; (4) getting practice in using the language (p. 176). When asked by the researcher why he talked to himself, one student responded, "So that I'm not doing it for the teacher, I'm doing it for myself, so I'm learning" (p. 177). One particularly interesting response was that of a Grade 8 student, who remarked: "Sometimes I know an answer and I'll say it in my head . . . but somebody that is really good . . . will yell it out before you've had a chance and then the teacher thinks that you're not participating because you're not answering any questions, but you are" (p. 177).

Saville-Troike's study focused on nine children between the ages of 3 and 8 years old in an English-speaking North American classroom setting. The native languages of the children were Chinese, Korean, and Japanese. Saville-Troike made audio and video recordings of the children over a 6-month period. She found that when many, though not all, of the children realized that others in their environment did not speak their native language and that they themselves had difficulties communicating in English, they withdrew into a (socially) "silent period" in which they avoided linguistic interaction with users of the L2. The criteria Saville-Troike (1988, p. 573) developed for identifying utterances as private speech were lack of eye contact while speaking, apparent lack of expectation of response, and reduced volume of utterance. During this so-called silent period, which lasted from 1 to 23 weeks, depending on the child, children engaged in language-focused private speech in English. Interestingly, when the children struggled with nonlanguage issues, such as math, their private speech emerged in their L1 (p. 586).

In their language-focused private speech, the children practiced English sounds, meaning, and grammar. Saville-Troike categorizes the private speech patterns uncovered as follows: repetition of others' utterances, recall and practice, creation of novel forms, expansion and substitution practice, and rehearsal for interpersonal communication.[5] Similar patterns are reported by Weir (1962) and Kuczaj (1983) in the language play of young L1 children. Following are a few examples of language-focused private speech provided by Saville-Troike.

Example (5) is taken from a 3-year-old child and example (6) is from a 4-year-old.

(5) Three years old
A. PEER: I want you to ride the bike
   CHILD: Bike
B. TEACHER: I need you to walk ?
   CHILD: Walk ? Walk ? Walk ? Walk ?

---

[5] A total of nine children were the original focus of her study, but three of these failed to produce private speech during the period of the study. Saville-Troike characterizes these children as socially – rather than internally – oriented in their learning, since their preferred learning strategies appeared to be interpersonal from the beginning. These children, when communicating with English speakers, used "all means, verbal and nonverbal, at their disposal" (p. 586). In light of the theoretical argument I am trying to construct, however, the fact that the three children did not produce audible private speech does not necessarily mean they did not generate subvocal private speech. It merely means that they failed to produce overt private speech during Saville-Troike's recording sessions.

(6) Four years old
A. TEACHER: You need to be down here and waiting too.
   CHILD: Waiting too.
B. TEACHER: What's happened there? *[sic]*
   CHILD: What's happened there? (Saville-Troike, 1988, p. 578)

Examples (5) and (6A) evidence Slobin's learning principle – pay attention to the ends of utterances (Saville-Troike 1988, p. 578). The repetition in (6B), however, entails the teacher's entire utterance. According to Saville-Troike, these imitative utterances were produced with reduced volume, and lack of eye contact with an interlocutor and did not anticipate a response. What is more, in all four examples the children imitate their interlocutors' intonation contour. This is especially clear in (5B).

The examples that follow in (7) are particularly interesting in light of the interactionist hypothesis on second language acquisition (see Long, 1996), which maintains that learners acquire a second language when engaged in negotiated interaction with other, usually more proficient speakers of the language. Although this may certainly be the case, (7) shows that learners also attend to the second language when "eavesdropping" on the interpersonal communication of others. The child here produced the utterances while playing alone with his back to a group of three other children. Eavesdropping on others' interactions may allow learners to free up processing capacity, since they attend to form without paying close attention to meaning. Clearly, of course, a single protocol does not make a strong case, but it is suggestive and worth further investigation.

(7) Four years old
   PEER: Hey, look.
   CHILD: Hey, look.
   PEER: What are you doing ?
   CHILD: What are you doing ? (Saville-Troike, 1988, p. 579)

In examples (8) and (9) the child experiments with English morphology:

(8) Three years old
   TEACHER: Let's go outside
   CHILD: Out. Outside
(9) Four years old
   CHILD: Walking, walking, walk. Walking, walking, walk. (Chanted while walking)
   CHILD: Quick. Quick, quick. Quickly. Quick.
   CHILD: Bathroom. Bath (Saville-Troike, 1988, p. 584)

In (8) the child responds to the teacher's suggestion that the children go outside, not with a communicative turn, but by decomposing of the compound word *outside*. In (9) the child manipulates participles and verbs, adjectives and adverbs, and compounds. We are not told whether these utterances arose immediately after the child heard utterances containing the structures produced by someone else, or whether, as L1 research has shown (Kuczaj, 1983), the child more or less spontaneously produced the utterances from something he had attended to and stored away to experiment with at a later time.

The utterances in (10) are, indeed, produced "quite apart from any visible or audible stimulus"; moreover, the child did not likely know the meaning of what he had said (p. 582).

(10) Four years old
CHILD: Whose.
Babe. Hi, babe.
Don't bother me. (*twice*)
Yucky.
Don't bother me (*three times*) (Saville-Troike, 1988, p. 583)

How is it possible for children to imitate utterances they do not fully understand? In my view, even though the child in (10) may not have understood the full meaning and illocutionary intent of the utterances, at some level, he had to be able to detect the utterances he had apparently heard someone else produce; otherwise, the utterances would have been perceived as noise and not noticed at all. Thus, some features of the utterances had to be within the child's ZPD; precisely what these features were, of course, we have no way of knowing.

In example (11) the child makes what in adult speech would be an inappropriate substitution in the teacher's utterance:

(11) Four years old
TEACHER: You guys go brush your teeth. And wipe your hands on the towel.
CHILD 2: Wipe your hand. Wipe your teeth. (Saville-Troike, 1988, p. 584)

The child responds to the teacher's utterance with what from a conversational perspective has to be considered as an inappropriate move; the child's utterance, however, is not intended as an interpersonal turn, but as an imitation of the teacher's language. It results in a transformation, or as some might put it, an overgeneralization, as the child produces what appears to be a violation of a cooccurrence constraint on *wipe*. Of course, under some circumstances, it would be appropriate to say "wipe your teeth," as when one perhaps has a bit of lettuce stuck on a tooth. The resulting pattern is reminiscent of the L1 child's imitations in (3) and (4).

Even clearer examples of transformative, persistent imitation, which occurs in the absence of any immediate other-generated patterns, are illustrated in (12). Here the child combines snippets of speech that he most likely had heard in his environment and had stored in his English repertoire in order to build new meanings. (N.B.: Translations are provided by Saville-Troike.):

(12) Four years old
    A. CHILD: Mine is let's go (i.e., 'I will leave')
    B. CHILD: My it's go house in (i.e., 'I am going into the house')
        (Saville-Troike, 1988, p. 585)

As a final example, in (13) we see a 5-and-a-half-year-old practicing English auxiliaries, including contraction, as well as the insertion of objects into verbal predicates:

(13) Five and a half years old
    CHILD: I finished
        I have finished
        I am finished.
        I'm finished
    CHILD: I want
        I paper. Paper. Paper.
        I want paper (Saville-Troike, 1988, p. 585)

Adult Foreign Language Learners

As Vygotsky recognized, because adults have a more developed consciousness than children, they understand the difference between private and social setting, consequently, adults generally do not converse with themselves in public venues as readily as children. Nevertheless, Ohta (2001), as well as a project completed at Penn State with a learner of Spanish (discussed later), have uncovered fairly robust samples of adult private speech in classroom settings.

Japanese as a Foreign Language

Ohta (2001), using a similar data-collection procedure to Saville-Troike's collected a corpus of private speech produced by six first-year and four second-year university students of Japanese as a foreign language. Ohta recorded the students from a minimum of four to a maximum of seven times throughout the course of one academic semester (approximately 15 weeks). She noted a wide range in the frequency of private speech produced by the learners, as one student produced on average only 2 private speech utterances per session and another generated a robust average of approximately 52 such utterances per class. Ohta detected three different patterns in the private speech of her learners: repetition of others' utterances, manipulation of patterns produced by others, and vicarious response, in which a learner responded privately to a question or problem posed by the teacher to some other student. By far the most frequent pattern noted by Ohta was repetition, particularly of lexical items. This was followed by vicarious response, a pattern not reported in Saville-Troike's study; pattern manipulation, a relatively robust pattern among Saville-Troike's children, occurred much less often in Ohta's data. In the interest of space, I will consider only two samples from Ohta's study.

The first example entails repetition of the pattern for adjectival negation in Japanese. The learner, Candace (C), is attending to an interaction between the teacher (T) and another student, Hyun (H). According to Ohta (2001, p. 58), Japanese has two ways of marking negation on adjectivals – one for adjectives and one for adjectival nouns. The former is negated by affixing –*ku* to the adjective stem and then adding the negator *nai* or *arimasen*, the latter is formed by affixing *ja* (or *dewa*) to the adjectival noun accompanied by the negative form *nai* or *arimsen*.

(14) T: *Kon shuumatsu hima desu ka ? Hyun-san*
    Huyn, are you free this weekend ?
 H: *Um (..) iie (.) um (.) uh:: (.) hima- (.) hima: (.) hima nai,*
    Um (.) no (.) um (.) uh:: (.) free- (.) free: (.) free-NEG *(incorrect negator)*
 T: *Hima ja ˆarimasen*
    You're not free *(correction negation)*
 H: *Oh ja arimasen (overlapping with teacher)*
    Oh not free
 C: *himaˆ ja arimasen*
    not free *(whispered and overlapping H)*
 T: *Hima ja arimasen (.) ii desu ne (.) Eh :to ja S-san kon shuumatsu hima desu ka ?*
    You're not free (.) well done (.) Uh so S, are you free this weekend?
    (Ohta, 2001, p. 59)

According to Ohta, C, although not directly engaged in the interaction between T and H, nevertheless participates in the exchange from the periphery. She repeats softly to herself the correct form of the negative adjectival noun. Most importantly, C uses this form "correctly in peer interaction, as well as when, in subsequent teacher-fronted practice, she covertly corrects classmates who use the wrong form" (Ohta, 2001, p. 59).

In (15), we note a brief, but compelling, example of Candace's manipulating the adjective *warui* "bad."

(15) C: *waru- waruku (.) waru::ku (.) ku warui::* (Ohta, 2001, p. 64)

In a series of breakdowns and buildups reminiscent of the language play documented by Kuzcaj and Weir for L1 children and by Saville-Troike for L2 children, the student silently experimented with the adjective without any immediate external stimulation from the teacher or other students. She first expanded the stem to form the adverbial *waruku* and then preposed the suffix; finally, she produced the nonpast adjective form *warui*.

An English as a Second Language Learner

Over the course of a 2-week period, we carried out daily recordings of an adult English as a second language (ESL) learner enrolled in an intensive literacy class at Penn State University. The student was a 37-year-old female native speaker of Korean. She began studying English in Korea at the age of 14 and continued to study the language through high school. At the time the recordings were made she had been living in the United States for approximately 6 months.[6] A total of approximately 10 hours of recordings was made using a Sharp Mini-disc recorder and microphone attached to the student's clothing. The criteria used to determine whether an utterance should be classified as private or social speech were those used in Saville-Troike's and in Otha's studies.

During all of the recording sessions, the ESL learner focused her attention exclusively on vocabulary, as illustrated in (16). In all of the protocols, T is the teacher and L the learner in question.

(16) T: Argue (*loudly*)
    L: Argue means ... (*with rising intonation and with sufficient volume to be social*)
    T: Disagree.
    L: Disagree (*falling intonation, somewhat softly*) Yeah. (*very softly*).
    T: Thank you (*apparently addressing another student who had done something for the teacher*). And it means using words, you disagree using your words, not fight.
    L: Argue (*very softly*).

The learner uses ellipsis with rising intonation as a way of requesting a definition of the word *argue* from the teacher. The teacher first provides a synonym, which L repeats softly, telling herself that she understands, which is how I interpret her use of falling intonation accompanied by "Yeah." The teacher then offers a definition, after which L repeats "argue." I interpret this as an attempt to keep the item within the focus of her attention while she mulls over its meaning (see Frawley, 1997, on the role of private speech and focus).

---

[6] I would like to acknowledge Yvonne Cranmer and Eun Ju Kim, who collected and transcribed the private speech data discussed here.

The next example is related to learning a new word. After completion of a reading passage, the instructor is explaining vocabulary items to the students in the class. Specifically, the teacher provides synonyms for *significant*.

(17) T: Important or notable.
  L: Ah, notable (*rising intonation*). Notable (*rising intonation*). Mm (*very softly*)

The teacher seems to think that "significant" is unfamiliar to the students and therefore provides two synonyms, on the assumption that they are likely to know these words. Yet, this was not the case for L, who indeed encountered something new; it just was not what the teacher assumed it would be. *Important* is a fairly common word in English, whereas *notable* is less so, and although L's performance could represent an example of Slobin's "Pay attention to the ends of utterances" principle, I think something more is happening here. L most likely knows what *important* means but does not know *notable*, as indicated by her use of rising intonation. She may or may not know *significant* and perhaps even discovered its meaning as a result of the teacher's linking it to *important*.

The Korean student also produced private speech that focused on morphology, as in (18), which occurs after the students had completed the course evaluations.

(18) T: Were you taking a nap, a little sleep ? (*directed at another student*)
  L: nap, I take nap . . . ing

L experiments with *nap*, which the teacher defines as "a little sleep." In her attempt to imitate the teacher, L substitutes the teacher's *you* with the first-person singular *I*. However, she uses the present form of the verb rather than what would be the expected past progressive "I was taking a nap," or perhaps "I was napping." The pause after the second instance of *nap* is interesting. It could signal that the learner was struggling to reproduce an appropriate version of the utterance but was confused between the two alternatives and ended up producing what looks like a hybrid "*I take napping." I propose this as an example of persistent imitation in adult private speech.

An Adult Learner of Spanish

The final set of examples is taken from a longer study by Lantolf and Yañez-Prieto (2003), which reports on the private speech of an adult classroom learner of Spanish as a foreign language. The data that I will focus on here illustrates two aspects of private speech not documented in previous research – use of L1 and metacommentary. At one point, the student (L), who was participating in a university intermediate-level Spanish composition class, encountered problems with the passive construction. S relies on repetition in English as a way of telling herself which Spanish preposition is required in the passive construction. The episode begins in (19), when L simultaneously and privately repeats the appropriate preposition as she works with her partner (C) to construct a sentence jointly.

(19) C: (*addressing the teacher*) And we wanna say *las montañas están cubiertas . . . *por nieve ?*
'the mountains are covered by/with snow?'
L: *De, de* (*simultaneously providing along with the instructor, but in a low voice, the correct preposition*)

C appears to confuse the construction in which the past participle *cubiertas* functions as an adjective with the passive construction. He does not recognize that the verb in this case is *estar* (to be),[7] which occurs with descriptive adjectives, and not *ser* "to be," required in the passive construction. Learners have a difficult time distinguishing real passive constructions (formed with the copula *ser* + past participle + *por* (by) + agent) from adjectival constructions (formed by the copula *estar* + past participle functioning as an adjective + *de* (by/with) + noun). L clearly seems to understand the construction. However, she then overgeneralizes the preposition from the adjectival construction to constructions with the passive, as in (20), in which the instructor (T) unsuccessfully prompts L to respond with the appropriate preposition.

(20) T: *Mi pintura favorita . . .* 'My favorite painting . . .'
L: *Fue pintada *de Monet ?* 'Was painted *of Monet ?'
T: *Fue pintada . . . ?* 'Was painted . . . ?'
L: **De Monet ?* '*Of Monet ?'
T: *Por . . .* 'By" . . .
L: *Por, no de* (*privately, while overlapping T's correction*) 'By, not of'
T: *Mi pintura favorita fue pintada por Monet.* 'My favorite painting was painted by Monet.'
L: (*while T moves on to work with other students*) **From, from, from**

L immediately repeats the correct preposition *por* silently to herself and then tells herself in Spanish that *de* in the passive construction is incorrect, "*no de.*" In L's whispered repetition of the English preposition at the conclusion of the exchange she is telling herself that Spanish *de* means "from" in English, as of course it does in some cases, but not in any of the constructions at issue. Thus, L has formulated a way of distinguishing the two prepositions. The problem is that in Spanish *de* also has the English

---

[7] Spanish has two copula verbs – *ser* and *estar*. The former derives from Latin *essere* "to be" and the latter from Latin *stare* "to stand." Determining which of the two forms is appropriate in a given construction is notoriously difficult for English speakers.

equivalent *of*, as well as *with* or even *by*, as in (19). Instructing herself that *de* can be rendered as *by* in English, at least on some occasions, would, no doubt, have complicated matters for L, since she would then be faced with two L2 forms with the same meaning. It makes matters less complicated to assign different meanings to different forms (avoidance of synonymy), as Anderson's (1984) "one-to-one principle" proposes. Another English equivalent of *de*, frequently occurring at the early stages of instruction, is *from*, as in *De dónde es Ud. ?* 'Where are you from ?' Thus, it is not surprising that L selects this option as a way of keeping things straight, as it were. The problem, unfortunately, is that what L has attempted to internalize is likely to lead to a problem if she wants to say something like "The road is covered with snow," which she would likely render as *El camino está cubierto con/por nieve.*

Example (21) contains a vicarious response but at the same time displays an interesting use of the learner's L1. T is working with the entire class on an exercise in which students are to convert active sentences into *se*-passive constructions (roughly equivalent to English "one does something").

(25) T: Más autos fueron vendidos el año pasado. 'More cars were sold
last year'
C1: *Se vende más autos.* 'One sells more cars'
T: *Se* what ? 'One what ?'
C2: *Se vendieron.* 'One sold'
L: *Vendieron* . . . I knew it !

L realizes from the outset that what C1 says is incorrect and waits for the correct response to emerge from some other student; that happens when C2 responds to T's leading question. Almost simultaneously, L quietly utters the correct verb form and then tells herself that she was correct. This is an important episode, because L's evaluative metacomment "I knew it" gives us a glimpse into her beliefs about what she thinks she knows about the language. If L really "knew it," she most likely would not have produced any private speech at all and might have even responded publicly to T's prompt. Thus, I believe that L was not really sure that she knew the correct form and needed confirmation (i. e., feedback) from an external source. Once C2 provided this confirmation, L told herself that her assumption had been accurate.

CONCLUSION

It seems clear that children and adults rely on similar processes to internalize the properties of a language. Learners actively engage in the imitative process as they undertake to learn a first or a second language. It also appears that learners are active in determining which aspects of the language to focus on, paying attention to those properties of the language that are within their ZPD. This becomes particularly clear in the case of the adult Japanese and English language learners, who exhibited instances of private speech in which they attended to features of the relevant L2 that were often at variance with the intent of the teacher's instructional activity. This is a very important area for future research to explore more fully. For one thing, it is likely to help teachers understand how and why learners react as they do to their pedagogical efforts at the microlevel. From a theoretical perspective, a close analysis of learners' private speech ought to inform our understanding of which features available in their environments learners attend to, and it should also provide information on how learners operate on these features as they attempt to internalize them.

Although there are similarities in the language-focused private speech of children and adults, there are also important differences. Adults, at least those in classroom settings, seem to be less likely than children to engage in persistent imitation. A possible explanation for this difference is that adults, especially those enrolled in university courses, have spent a great deal of their lives in the educational environment, which in most cases values "correct answers" over freewheeling experimentation.

A particularly powerful factor working against experimentation in the adult classroom is the pervasiveness of the native-speaker model. Adults have been saturated with the idea that they are expected to produce the right answer and failure to do so often results in some form of discipline, such as a lower exam or course grade. As Bakhtin argued with regard to "authoritative discourse," perhaps the dominant mode of talk in the institutional setting we call school, such discourse "demands that we acknowledge it, that we make it our own; it binds us, quite independent of any power it might have to persuade us internally; we encounter it with its authority fused to it"; "it demands our unconditional allegiance" and "allows no play with its borders, no gradual and flexible transitions, no spontaneously creative stylizing variants on it" (cited in Wertsch, 1991, p. 78). On this account, then, because of their history with authoritative language, adults are less likely, even in private, to experiment with a language in the freewheeling way attested among children. Children in the educational setting are still being inculcated into the culture of "correct answers," and therefore they still have some elbow room for experimentation. Moreover, in the case of Saville-Troike's study, the classroom was not uniquely focused on language learning but was subject-matter-oriented; that meant that the children were not expected to have the right answer in their L2. It remains for future research to determine whether adult L2 learners outside the classroom setting manifest a greater degree of experimentation in their imitative patterns than do their institutionalized counterparts.

Other important differences between child and adult private speech are the presence of metalinguistic comments in the L1 as well as overt comparison between the L1 and the L2. Neither of these features was noted in

Saville-Troike's study. Although the experimental behavior that is manifest among children in language play clearly shows that they are able to
manipulate language as a metalinguistic object (Cazden, 1976, p. 603), adult
classroom foreign language learners generally have more enhanced metalinguistic awareness than do children. Vygotsky's discussion of native and
foreign language learning nicely characterizes the distinction. According
to Vygotsky (1987, p. 221), native and foreign language learning "move in
opposite directions." The child uses the grammatical and phonetic features
of the native language with ease but does so without conscious awareness.
On the other hand, the school child intentionally sets out to learn the foreign language and is very much aware of its grammatical and phonetic
properties, but, unlike with the native language, is unable to use the language easily until much later in the learning process. Through schooled
instruction (i.e., learning to read and write) the child's native language becomes visible and she develops "mastery" (i.e., intentional and conscious
use) of its grammatical and phonological properties. The problem for foreign language learners, however, not directly addressed by Vygotsky, is
that they must ultimately develop the ability to use the language freely
and spontaneously without conscious awareness; or, in terms of activity
theory, the language must be used at the level of operation as a tool for
realizing specific concrete activities.

Assuming that Vygotsky is correct, it is not surprising that when language is maintained in focus as more an object of study and analysis than
a means to an end, as is usually the case in university classrooms, adults
would produce private speech that contains metalinguistic language. It is
therefore important to uncover the kinds of properties that characterize
the private speech of learners whose exclusive or primary experience with
a foreign or second language is in a content-based or immersion format. In
the case of so-called natural learners of second languages in which explicit
tutoring is unavailable, we might expect to observe imitation and play
but not metatalk. Of course, this is an empirical question that can only be
answered through additional research.

Another intriguing difference emerged with regard to use of the L1
in the private speech of the ESL and Spanish foreign language learners.
Whereas the Spanish learner produced intrapersonal communication in
her L1, English, and even carried out an overt comparison of the L1 and
L2, the Korean ESL learner produced no overt speech in her L1. The study
by Frawley and Lantolf (1985) also failed to uncover any use of the L1 in
the private speech of ESL speakers as they struggled to relate a picture
story. The function of private speech in this case was different (i.e., task
completion as opposed to internalization); nevertheless it is striking that
the L1 was not overtly accessed by any of the speakers. Two possible explanations suggest themselves: The English learners were more proficient
in their L2 and therefore had the ability to regulate themselves through

this language, or the material circumstances in which individuals function influence which language emerges in private speech. In the present study, as well as in Frawley and Lantolf's study, the dominant social language used in the general community was English, and therefore speakers might have felt compelled to rely on this language for self-regulation. Some indirect support for this possibility comes from Swain and Lapkin's (1998) study of L1 English, French-immersion learners in Toronto, an Anglo-dominant community. In collaboratively completing a puzzle task, some of the learners relied on English, their native language, as the metalanguage for organizing their joint activity, even though they clearly had the requisite proficiency in French. Clearly, this intriguing topic needs to be explored further.

Finally, an important difference between Saville-Troike's study and the two adult studies is that the former, unlike the latter, was able to document, at least, sporadically, the children's transfer of structures worked on in private to their social speech. Saville-Troike, for instance, reports that one of her children privately practiced talking about the weather in English for about a week and then decided one day to respond socially to the teacher that it was "cold" and importantly, according to Saville-Troike, did so with confidence. Future research must establish a firm connection between private and social speech, if the theoretical argument on the relevance of private speech for internalization made here is to be sustained.

References

Anderson, R. (1984). The one-to-one principle of interlanguage construction. *Language Learning, 34*, 77–95.

Arievitch, I., & Stetsenko, A. (2000). The quality of cultural tools and cognitive development: Gal'perin's perspective and its implications. *Human Development, 43*, 69–92.

Arievitch, I., & van der Veer, R. (1995). Furthering the internalization debate: Gal'perin's contribution. *Human Development, 38*, 113–126.

Ball, A. F. (2000). Teachers' developing philosophies on literacy and their use in urban schools: A Vygotskian perspective on internal activity and teacher change. In C. D. Lee & P. Smagorinsky (Eds.), *Vygotskian perspectives on literacy research: Constructing meaning through collaborative inquiry*. Cambridge: Cambridge University Press.

Carroll, S. E. (2001). *Input and evidence: The raw material of second language acquisition.* Amsterdam: John Benjamins.

Carruthers, P. (1998). Thinking in language? Evaluation and a modularist possibility. In P. Carruthers & J. Boucher (Eds.), *Language and thought: Interdisciplinary themes* (pp. 94–119). Cambridge: Cambridge University Press.

Cazden, C. (1976). Play with language and meta-linguistic awareness: One dimension of language experience. In L. Bruner, A. Jolly, & K. Sylva (Eds.), *Play: Its role in development and evolution* (pp. 603–608). New York: Basic Books.

Clark, A. (1998). Magic words: How language augments human computation. In P. Carruthers & J. Boucher (Eds.), *Language and thought: Interdisciplinary themes.* Cambridge: Cambridge University Press.

Cook, G. 2000. *Language play, language learning.* Oxford: Oxford University Press.

Dance, F. E. X. (1994). Hearing voices. In D. R. Vocate (Ed.), *Intrapersonal communication: Different voices, different minds.* Hillsdale, NJ: Erlbaum.

De Courcy, M. (1993). Making sense of the Australian French immersion classroom. *Multilingual Matters, 14,* 173–186.

de Guerrero, M. C. M. 1999. Inner speech as mental rehearsal: The case of advanced L2 learners. *Issues in Applied Linguistics, 10,* 27–55.

Dennett, D. (1998). Reflections on language and mind. In P. Carruthers & J. Boucher (Eds.), *Language and thought: interdisciplinary themes.* Cambridge: Cambridge University Press.

Frawley, W. J. (1997). *Vygotsky and cognitive science: Language and the unification of the social and computational mind.* Cambridge: Harvard University Press.

Frawley, J., & Lantolf, J. P. (1985). Second language discourse: A Vygotskyan perspective. *Applied Linguistics, 6,* 19–44.

Gal'perin, P. Y. (1967). On the notion of internalization. *Soviet Psychology, 5,* 28–33.

Heath, S. B. (1985). Narrative play in second-language learning. In L. Galda & A. D. Pellegrini (Eds.), *Play language and stories.* Norwood, NJ: Ablex.

Kozuliln, A. (1990). *Vygotsky's psychology: A biography of ideas.* Cambridge, MA: Harvard University Press.

Kuczaj. S. A., II. (1983). *Crib speech and language play.* New York: Springer Verlag.

Lantolf, J. P. (1997). Language play and the acquisition of L2 Spanish. In W. R. Glass & A-T. Perez-Leroux (Eds.), *Contemporary perspectives on the acquisition of Spanish.* Vol. 2. *Production, processing and comprehension* (pp. 3–35). Somerville, MA: Cascadilla Press.

Lantolf, J. P., & Yañez-Prieto, M. C. (2003). Talking yourself into Spanish: Private speech and second language learning. *Hispania, 86,* 98–110.

Lightbown, P., & Spada, N. (1993). *How languages are learned.* Oxford: Oxford University Press.

Long, M. H. (1996). The role of the linguistic environment in second language acquisition. In W. C. Ritchie & T. K. Bhatia (Eds.), *Handbook of second language acquisition.* San Diego, CA: Academic Press.

Luria, A. R. (1979). *The making of mind: A personal account of Soviet psychology.* Cambridge, MA: Harvard University Press.

Matusov, E. (1998). When solo activity is not privileged: Participation and internalization models of development. *Human Development, 41,* 326–349.

Newman, D., Griffin, P., & Cole, M. (1989). *The construction zone: Working for cognitive change in school.* Cambridge: Cambridge University Press.

Newman, F., & Holzman, L. (1993). *Lev Vygotsky: Revolutionary scientist.* London: Routledge.

Ohta, A. S. (2001). *Second language acquisition processes in the classroom: Learning Japanese.* Mahwah, NJ: Lawrence Erlbaum.

Saville-Troike, M. (1988). Private speech: Evidence for second language learning strategies during the "silent period." *Journal of Child Language, 15,* 567–590.

Shor, I. (1996). *When students have power: negotiating authority in critical pedagogy.* Chicago: University of Chicago Press.

Stetsenko, A. P. (1999). Social interaction, cultural tools and the zone of proximal development: in search of a synthesis. In S. Chaiklin, M. Hedegaard, & U. J. Jensen (Eds.), *Activity theory and social practice: Cultural historical approaches* (pp. 235–252). Aarhus: Aarhus University Press.

Swain, M., & Lapkin, S. 1998. Interaction and second language learning: Two adolescent French immersion students working together. *The Modern Language Journal, 82,* 320–337.

Tomasello. M. 1999. *The cultural origins of human cognition.* Cambridge, MA: Harvard University Press.

Tulviste, P. (1991). *The cultural-historical development of verbal thinking.* Commack, NY: Nova Science.

Valsiner, J. (2000). *Culture and human development: An introduction.* London: Sage.

Valsiner, J., & van der Veer, R. (2000). *The social mind: Construction of the idea.* Cambridge: Cambridge University Press.

Vocate, D. R. (1994). Self-talk and inner speech: Understanding the uniquely human aspects of intrapersonal communication. In D. R. Vocate (Ed.), *Intrapersonal communication: Different voices, different minds.* Hillsdale, NJ: Erlbaum.

Vygotsky, L. S. (1978). *Mind in society: The development of higher psychological processes.* Cambridge, MA: Harvard University Press.

Vygotsky, L. S. (1987). *The collected works.* Vol. 1. *Problems of general psychology: Including thinking and speech.* New York: Plenum.

Vygotsky, L. S. (1997). *Educational psychology.* Boca Raton, FL: St. Lucie Press.

Vygotsky, L. S. (1999). *The collected works.* Vol. 6. *Scientific legacy.* New York: Plenum.

Weir, R. (1962). *Language in the crib.* The Hague: Mouton.

Wertsch, J. V. (1991). *Voices of the mind: A sociocultural approach to mediated action.* Cambridge, MA: Harvard University Press.

Wertsch, J. V. (1998). *Mind as action.* Oxford: Oxford University Press.

Yaroshevsky, M. (1989). *Lev Vygotsky.* Moscow: Progress Press.

Yingling, J. (1994). Childhood: talking the mind into existence. In D. R. Vocate (Ed.), *Intrapersonal communication: Different voices, different minds.* Hillsdale, NJ: Erlbaum.

17

Mediation in Cognitive Socialization

The Influence of Socioeconomic Status

Pedro R. Portes and Jennifer A. Vadeboncoeur

Social activities and adult–child interactions[1] form the basis for cognitive socialization. The extent to which everyday activities differ by socioeconomic status (SES), and the extent to which they are employed differently, becomes a contentious topic when different outcomes in social and academic competence are linked. Socialization results in attitudes, values, and cognitive and linguistic skills that children use as they grow and ultimately become means or tools for development. Children develop competencies through various patterns of adult–child and other social interactions. Often what is seen as important and valuable for socialization varies across communities. Only some of the literature on adult–child interaction addresses elements of SES differentiated activity settings – for example, family structures, scripts, values, and task demands – that are historically embedded. This chapter focuses on a cultural–historical analysis of research linking SES to variations in adult–child interaction.

Although the scope of the chapter limits the extent to which these topics may be explored,[2] a sample of research is examined and framed within the structure provided by *Cultural–Historical Activity Theory* (CHAT),[3] along with examples of adult–child interaction research approached from a CHAT perspective. CHAT is characterized by a developmental and social analysis of human action that is mediated generally by different cultural

---

[1] We are using "adult–child" interaction to reflect dyads between parents and their children, as well as significant adults and children.

[2] Although issues related to methodological differences between studies are important, we are unable to provide more than a cursory discussion here.

[3] We have chosen to use the term *Cultural–Historical Activity Theory* (CHAT) as a general paradigm that can extend the work of Vygotsky, Leont'ev, and Luria. Emphases on mediated activity, dynamic developmental analyses, as well as the role of activity settings in the co-construction of mind are the focus. We use only aspects of activity theory that recognize the role of action, labor, and activity setting variables in relation to access to mediated learning and development.

tools. To understand differences in individual development, variations in the latter must be considered across activity settings, as well as the way a person responds in terms of shared values, expectations, and practices. The CHAT framework is particularly instrumental because in understanding any relationship, such as that of SES and development, a dynamic, historical analysis is required not only of individuals, but also of activity settings in which individuals interact.

The purpose of this chapter is to integrate the literature regarding adult–child interaction, linking factors related to SES to differences in socialization. The first section outlines theoretical and research questions regarding the influence of SES on adult–child interaction patterns. The second section provides a sample of both mainstream and CHAT adult–child interaction studies with connections to SES differences in mediation. The third section focuses on the historical construction of socioeconomic status, along with SES differences and cultural capital. A model that articulates the dynamic relationship between individuals and society, through participation in activity settings over time, is sketched. In the last section, areas of future research that are particularly significant in terms of advancing both CHAT theory and research regarding adult–child socialization with respect to SES are identified.

THEORETICAL AND RESEARCH QUESTIONS IN UNDERSTANDING THE INFLUENCE OF SOCIOECONOMIC STATUS

Adult–child socialization patterns form the basis for different values, expectations, scripts, and task demands that impact a child's development across a variety of social contexts. In current American mainstream psychology, a typical research study might hypothesize that SES differences in student outcomes such as achievement or alienation are mediated by motivational contexts (Murdok, 1999). Participants are measured on a variety of instruments, and both direct and indirect effects are modeled and found significant. The findings confirm that low SES is a risk factor for alienation (low engagement and disciplinary problems), associated with less efficacy, and perceptions of unfairness, low support, and appraisals by teachers. Unfortunately, research based on such "mediated" models fails to specify the co-construction of attitudes and behavior that might precede the snapshot described. This type of study provides different pieces of a much larger puzzle that may be made more explicit by sociocultural questions such as the following:

- What exactly is being socialized differently by group membership in different SES groups (for example, a worldview or an attitude about what kind of life a child might want for the future)?

- What is being co-constructed developmentally that might account for predictable variations in development (for example, an enduring belief or skill)?
- Is a person's development to be explained by antecedent interaction patterns with particular activity settings over time, in terms of both availability and level of participation, or mainly by the continuity of those patterns (for example, what surfaces when we compare interaction patterns in the home and at school and the degree to which they are congruent)?
- To what extent is socialization homogeneous within an SES group (in other words, what is the nature of the time lag between parent socialization, or participation in activities today, and the actions a child will take tomorrow)?
- Why does a person's development vary from that of peers with similar background, access, and interaction patterns (for example, how do individuals construct different psychological realities under similar conditions)?

As different as these questions are, they serve to test the mettle of any theoretical approach. It is increasingly clear that parental values drive socialization practices that, in turn, influence actual participation and become more SES-differentiated over time. Parental values and expectations help to mediate teacher relationships and possibly delay peer influences, all of which are associated with the child's motivation, attitudes, and goals. A closer look may reveal that these are not individual outcomes but, rather, co-constructed patterns of activity based on socially shared cognitions or expectations. Activity settings, as a unit of analysis, require attention to objective features such as those often quantified and qualified by researchers (e.g., the HOME Inventory, Caldwell, & Bradley, 1984). They also require attention to subjective features from the individual's standpoint. For example, some scholars note how curricula and participation structures in school settings favor interaction patterns of the dominant middle-SES culture in the United States (Fine, 1989; Oakes, 1985). The effects of various settings on human development are significant and numerous; a theory is thus needed to help us identify both (1) what is being socialized through activities across settings and how and (2) the child's perspective and concomitant cognitive and behavioral actions.

Central for this discussion is the description by Valsiner (1989) of the definition of the cultural–historical study of mind. For Valsiner (1989), "The 'historical' portion of the label cultural–historical refers specifically to the developmental nature of all psychological phenomena," along with the recognition that historical thinking implies a connection not just with the past, but with the present and future as well (p. 60). For a historical analysis, attention must be directed at the social relations that both persons and groups have constructed and in which they participate. In addition, the forms of activity associated with labor, as well as the resultant material conditions of the surrounding context, serve to situate development. The *cultural* portion of the term refers to the dialectical nature of instrumental human activity, in particular, the way in which people act upon their social contexts aided by cultural tools. Action is thus dialectical and shapes the environment, while it transforms human development across various fields and contexts. Cultural tools may be seen as extending along a continuum constrained by social institutions and economic conditions on one end, and moving to the other where individuals transform them through mediated action(s).

In addition, certain elements need clarification before the literature on adult–child interaction is examined. For example, individual consciousness and development are not actually individual, but rather shared and constructed socially. The "boundary" between the external and the internal is not as clear-cut as traditional psychological approaches have presumed (Zinchenko, 2001). In adult–child interaction, the learning history of the child is co-constructed within the zone of proximal development. Internalization is mediated by cultural tools, such as sign systems and concepts, that are afforded to the child through social interactions, only later to be internalized and transformed for their own use. Linguistic and cognitive skills, values, expectations, and, indeed, future methods of interaction are at the core of the outcome of adult–child interactions, articulated within a specific context as cultural capital.

ADULT–CHILD INTERACTION RESEARCH

Research on adult–child interactions has been of increasing theoretical interest in cognitive-developmental research ever since the pioneering work by Baldwin, Kalhorn, and Breese (1945) and others that extended this research genre. A central concern in these studies has been the role of cognitive socialization practices and their relevance in understanding differences in areas of academic and social competence. Interaction differences have been associated with cultural factors such as socioeconomic status and ethnicity in relation to children's intellectual and socioemotional development and task outcomes (e.g., Hess & Shipman, 1965). A relevant question concerns the extent to which these forms are situated or dependent on the task employed, the context, or both. Although cultural differences in either performance or interaction are generally confounded with SES and factors related to literacy acquisition (e.g., Sigel, Anderson, & Shapiro, 1966), this research area is of strategic value in uncovering aspects of culture that are often related to cognition and instruction, as well as group differences in associated outcomes (Laosa, 1981; Portes, 1988).

Mainstream Adult–Child Interaction Research

Most microgenetic research on adult–child interactions involves infants and toddlers; that focus anchors generalizations about adult–child interaction patterns to early development of children related to affect and sensori motor measures (Piaget, 1954). Adult–child interactions that support joint attention begin with simple face-to-face events and move to interactional events that include objects, such as toys (Isabella & Belsky, 1991; Stern, 1985). Existing research on correlations of adult–child interactions with SES show some differences in terms of scripts, values, and frequency of talk (Hart & Risley, 1992; Heath, 1983), although there are also studies that show that SES is unrelated to certain types of adult–child interaction, such as joint attention (Saxon & Reilly, 1999).

Several studies have examined parental teaching practices with preschoolers since the 1960's, when research on conceptualization styles (Kagan, Moss, & Sigel, 1963) and parental teaching strategies (Hess & Shipman, 1965; Laosa, 1981) advanced the field. Others have also examined preschoolers' interactions with adults and peers with similar goals. For example, Henderson (1991) examined adult and 3- to 6-year-old child interactions during exploration activities and found agreement on common purposes. In general, research on adult–child interactions for school-age students has focused on school performance. A study conducted by Carlson, Sroufe, Collins, Jimerson, Weinfield, Hennighausen, Egeland, Hyson, Anderson, and Meyer (1999) concluded that problem-solving support provided in adult–child interactions during toddler and preschool years predicted early adolescent school adjustment "even after academic achievement and socioemotional functioning in middle childhood were taken into account" (p. 87).

Microgenetic studies of adult–child interaction have contributed to the development of models, such as the distancing model (Sigel, Stinson, & Flaugher, 1991). This model provides children with challenging questions that allow them to distance themselves from the task at hand, in order to practice representational skills. Interestingly, there is also a body of research highlighting the power of the child to direct the sequence of events in adult–child interaction (e. g., Kucznski & Kochanska, 1990; Lytton, 1990), in addition to evidence for cycles of mutual and reciprocal influence (Patterson, 1982).

Adult–Child Interaction Research Related to Cultural–Historical Activity Theory

Until recently, Vygotsky's work and the role of mediated action have been absent from this literature. Yet, constructs such as scaffolding (Wood, Bruner, & Ross, 1976) and assisted performance (Tharp & Gallimore, 1988) share many concepts found in adult–child interaction studies. This line of research is important because it serves to unpack some of the aggregated factors inherent in SES and culture (Dunham, Kidwell, & Portes, 1995). Some studies have examined interaction characteristics of assistance or scaffolding through analyses of adult–child interactions with children of varying ages (e.g., Diaz, Neal, & Amaya-Williams, 1991; Portes, 1988; Wertsch, Minick, & Arns, 1984). The metacognitive guidance provided by parents, as more capable peers, has generally been the main focus of this literature, along with various aspects of the theory (e.g., the zone of proximal development). Means of assistance – such as questioning, contingency management, feedback, and cognitive restructuring – appear to be distributed differently across both SES and culture. The same patterns of assistance may have different consequences, depending on how children's minds are socialized initially, how grades are earned in school, and which goals of the activity are identified by both parents and teachers.

Other examples of adult–child interactions from this approach are highlighted in the discussion that follows. For example, Valsiner (1984) looked at the interactions of mother and young child during mealtime routines. With school-age children, Rogoff and Gardner (1984) studied 32 mothers and 6- to 9-year-old child dyads performing memory tasks such as sorting grocery items and other objects and found that successful instruction involved the child in the solution. Wertsch and associates (1984) examined model construction in 12 adult–child dyads and found differences in mother versus teacher regulation. When Radziszewska and Rogoff (1991) studied 32 dyads (adult or peer with 9-year-old children), they found that adult guidance, as compared to peer guidance, was more effective when planning errands. Gauvin and Rogoff (1989) constituted dyads with trained peers, untrained peers, and parents; they found the latter more effective in planning activities. The field of adult–child interaction studies has advanced various interactive models that include not only cognitive domains, but also pertinent domains such as parental and community values as determinants of social practices.

Only a few studies with school-age children have explored the link between interaction style and cognitive performance (e.g., Portes, Zady, & Dunham, 1998; Tzuriel, 1996). One advantage of working with preschool and school-age children is that the association between observed interaction characteristics and school performance in various content areas can be examined. Some microgenetic studies of adult–child interaction have contributed to the development of models, such as the carrier wave model (Dunham, Kidwell, & Portes, 1995) and reciprocal teaching (Palincsar & Brown, 1984). In general, these research studies support a modest relationship between certain adult–child interaction characteristics and children's intellectual performance.

Cultural context variations have not been examined directly with respect to adult–child interaction style in ways that control for SES differences until recently. For example, Portes and colleagues (1998) studied whether children's aptitudes in science were advanced when cognitive supports were made available through interactions with more capable individuals. The sample included 32 seventh graders and their mothers, from a convenience sample of 98 volunteer dyads. There were 16 students with low science achievement, identified as having a mean score of 36.4 on the California Test for Basic Skills (CTBS), 10 girls and 6 boys. In addition, there were 16 students with high science achievement, identified as having a mean score of 83.6 on the CTBS, 9 girls and 7 boys. Balancing the sample with respect to SES was difficult: There were few students with low SES and high achievement. In addition, the average education levels for the parents were 12 to 15 years for the students with low achievement and 13 to 16 years for the students with high achievement.

The study had three phases. First, the students' attitudes toward science were measured on a questionnaire. Next, both the student and his or her mother were interviewed about their interests in science, science assistance in the home, and the student's locus of control for success in science. Finally, the dyads were asked to complete three increasingly difficult science tasks. An overall interaction pattern was identified by positive reinforcement, encouragement, and agreement, with reciprocal interruptions by both mother and child. This was labeled a *cooperative problem solving* (CPS) factor. This interaction pattern, which was associated with middle-class parents, was significantly correlated with the child's intellectual performance in these tasks, and with general school achievement.

Recent research has also explored the question of universality in the ways adults assist intellectual development. Portes, Cuentas, and Zady (2000) examined the question of whether "cultural continuity" in assisting child performance exists across social contexts. The work identified critical problems in research linking family socialization to individual development. The main finding suggests that different avenues for cognitive socialization exist, particularly in the area of formal or scientific concepts. Interaction patterns related to a specific set of task constraints vary with ethnocultural context, even when literacy, SES, and gender are controlled. Effective cognitive socialization practices in one context may not be necessarily considered effective in another, insofar as a particular goal, attribute, or type of (sociocognitive) performance is of concern to the participants and researcher.

Mainstream and Cultural–Historical Activity Theory Cross-Cultural Studies

Mainstream cross-cultural studies that examine socialization practices in various countries tend to underdetermine the role of the cultural context in providing the basis for both affordances and constraints available for use and transformation by the research participants (e.g., see volume edited by Roopnarine & Carter, 1992). Some cross-cultural research contrasting schooled and unschooled children on various conceptual tasks reflects both direct connections to CHAT and indirect ones (e.g., Cole, Gay, & Glick, 1968; Saxe, 1994). The literature on cultural differences in children's development is mostly concerned with the cognitive consequences of schooling, a macrocultural factor. For example, Vygotsky (1978) and his collaborators were among the first to examine the cognitive consequences of different cultural–historical contexts on cognition, a tradition subsequently followed by Scribner and Cole (1981) and others.

Research focusing on cultural and cross-cultural differences in adult–child interaction and cognitive socialization is problematic for several reasons. One of the main problems in studying crucial cultural differences with unschooled subjects is the gap between the psychological reality created by the researchers and the psychological reality of individuals in their everyday lives. As Cole (1996) notes, the ambiguous significance of the data has limited the advancement of theory. Although studying schooled subjects in different ethnocultures may approximate psychological realities, so far little is known about differences in interaction patterns and their relation to individual development. In addition, a range of methods, personnel, ages, backgrounds, and research goals make systematic comparisons nearly impossible (e.g., Conroy, Hess, Azuma, & Kashiwagi, 1980). As a result, socialization practices studied across a number of cultural contexts, and their relation to children's development, vary from one study to another considerably.

Summary of Mainstream and Cultural–Historical Activity Theory (CHAT) Adult–Child Interaction Research

The gist of the literature suggests a general, metacognitive distancing or assistance factor in adult–child interaction studies. It is associated with differences in children's development and task performance. Whether this metacognitive regulation factor is mostly a function of SES and is consistent across (schooled) cultural contexts or tasks remains an open question. Some evidence suggests that the assistance reflected in interaction patterns afforded by parents is associated with success across various tasks and school performance (Portes, 1991; 1996; Portes et al., 1998; Sigel, 1982). These studies show that certain interaction patterns covary with SES and account generally for roughly 10% of children's cognitive performance. Such patterns of interactions represent important continuities in forms of mediating culture through parent, teacher, and other interactions. Although interaction content may vary as a function of the task and the child's increasing representational competence from learning and maturation, evidence of continuity exists for such patterns (Sigel, Stinson, & Kim, 1993) and/or styles that may be partly independent of SES (Dunham, Kidwell, & Portes, 1988).

It seems plausible that some aspects of culture may influence the form and content of these scripts or styles of assisting young learners, such as SES, ethnicity, nationality, and related variables. Depending on family structure and function, more than one pattern of interaction or assistance may be involved in the family setting. In other cultures, parents do not concern themselves with providing metacognitive assistance in areas related to school readiness, and much is left up to siblings, peers, or teachers in school to do so (Tharp & Gallimore, 1988).

If cognitive assistance and strategies found in adult–child and peer interactions serve as mediational tools in development, we may ask "what sorts of means" are present in interactions between children and adults that actually result in SES differences in learning and development. At the group level, we may ask how sociocultural variables are organized in different activity settings in relation to the preceding question. How may certain patterns of interaction be identified and understood developmentally?

HISTORICAL CONSTRUCTION OF SOCIOECONOMIC STATUS

The topic before us requires not only a documentation of SES differences, but also the means for their historical and cultural construction. A systemic theory must be able to explain the origins of SES-based socialization differences and predict the impact on future development. We argue that such differences are tool-based, socially co-constructed, and susceptible to change in relative and historical terms. Tools from the cultural line of development (Vygotsky, 1978) and, of course, access to them play a major role in any explanation of developmental differences, particularly when they are linked to activities, forms of labor, or participation in certain social practices.

The history through which certain groups become subordinated[4] to others requires attention to patterns of mediated action to which some groups have access and the very means for socializing children intergenerationally. In addition, interactional patterns must be explored in terms of their compatibility with institution structures, such as schools. Those structures are the focus of research that is concerned with economic and educational gaps between groups. In CHAT, attention to sociogenetic influences on the development and status attainment of groups is fundamental and calls for dynamic analyses of agency that situate individual learning and development. For example, SES and gender differences in socializing children

---

[4] Here we are referring to subordination in terms of social status or position, both intranationally and internationally.

cognitively and emotionally just a century ago were mediated by social movements and laws that later altered forms of participation, as well as social and educational outcomes. The topic of mediated action and agency at the group level can be situated in recent initiatives to raise performance standards in schools.

The CHAT framework is unique in tackling broader individual–societal or psychological–cultural issues and the ways in which they are associated. Working from the first law of cultural development (Vygotsky, 1978), for example, we might propose two extensions: (1) to groups, rather than just individuals, and (2) to values, attitudes, and social expectations, rather than just the appropriation of higher-level mental functions. Middle-SES socialization practices and values may be grounded on theoretical knowledge (Karpov & Bransford, 1995) and include attitudes, complex operations, or reasoning. Low-SES socialization practices may not only be different on the surface, but reflect different goals, attitudes, and reliance on empirical knowledge. Under typical conditions (outside experimental interventions) we may describe and explain a social group's way of parenting in context with adaptation demands: Parenting practices appear first through engagement in everyday activities that are carried out in the family and community, before they become established in the next generation. The latter might involve various means of assisting development with one's children in most cases. In other contexts where different practices are observed, one would have to account for motivation, resistance (Anyon, 1980), conflict (Panofsky, 1999), personality (Valsiner, 1998), and other phenomena related to the other domains.

Interaction analyses of socialization can be enriched by employing a historical approach, one that is mainly theoretical and based on social practices. For example, the style of interaction observed around problem-solving tasks is not necessarily due to ethnicity- or SES-related socialization practices. It may be that members of a particular group employ certain socialization practices (sociocognitive and emotional) as an adaptive response to social conditions, often imposed by more powerful groups. Researchers may observe that the "delivery capacity" of the home environment, or what is increasingly conceptualized as cultural capital, is more or less effective in certain ethnic and SES groups than in others. The availability and delivery of certain type of capital, how it may be different or missing, how "profitable" certain interactions are, and when these are most critical are important questions for us to consider from a CHAT perspective. However, the "why" question is not often pursued. For us, this is a fundamental question to which the CHAT perspective not only affords access, but also requires attention.

When we consider adult–child interactions ahistorically and from a dominant perspective, explanations can become deficit-oriented (see Sigel et al., 1966, regarding "racial" differences). For example, one reason why low-SES African American parents were found to employ more controlling means was that they inadvertently adapted to the oppressive social conditions in the United States that became "natural" for that group after centuries of social injustice and discrimination (Portes, Dunham, & Williams, 1986). The hypothesis that providing the low-SES child with middle-class socialization directly and/or with parent education could bridge the achievement gap failed to be confirmed by the research documenting the "wash-out" effect (Lazar & Darlington, 1982). A number of variations that have been attempted since lead to a better understanding of socialization as a multidimensional culturing program. Research like this suggests that the assistance provided in terms of mediated action in the intervention may be necessary, but not sufficient in overcoming the structural obstacles that thwart low-SES children in school. In sum, interaction patterns may be a function of social conditions and the social structures that communicate them and reflect historical effects rather than simply "the cause" of children's current development.

Adult–Child Interaction Differences and Socioeconomic Status

Middle-class families tend to have a higher success rate in conveying the value of education and effort as a means to a better life. These beliefs are "communicated" through expectations, task demands, and scripts in ways that differ significantly from the everyday practices of low-SES families. In addition, many beliefs are supported and reinforced by the material conditions surrounding middle-class families, along with cultural notions of meritocracy and individualism that sustain a focus on individual goal achievement. For low-SES groups, the belief system may be quite the contrary (Kohn, 1977). Children's optimism in early schooling seems to dissipate by the end of elementary school. In terms of social cognition, messages regarding the value and worth of children from different SES groups seem to come through loud and clear by third grade (Comer, 1990) unless mediated otherwise.

From a CHAT perspective, low-SES "risk" behavior may be understood as a mode of adaptation founded on lived realities. The benefits of education (e.g., high school completion) are not as great for low-SES groups relative to those of majority middle-class individuals generally. Given the shift in social cognition during adolescence, it seems that low-SES youth begin to understand how SES generally moderates the effects of education on adult economic and career outcomes (Apple, 1989; Mickelson, 1990). Without support from family or other significant adults, work ethic attitudes and practices that lead middle-SES youth to success may not carry sufficient weight for low-SES students. The latter are subject to the influence of community and peer settings where reports that education does not pay off abound.

Knowledge about the structural aspects of SES is constructed gradually and semiotically by children as a function of operations and experiences found in various activity settings. The extent to which individuals become committed to schooling or other activities can thus be understood as a function of SES-differentiated relationships that concern the meaning and value of education, illegal activities, sexual activity, and others in their context. Low-SES children are indeed placed at risk, or in zones of proximal development that are perilous not simply because of group status, but rather, because of the constraints that limit certain forms of action and agency in low-SES family, peer, and community activity settings. The latter interact with other institutional and informal settings. Group membership not only associates children and youths with certain options, but also disconnects others. When low-SES youth drop out and work, join gangs, enter the drug trade, or run away, we label such actions negatively in terms of risk or actual individual psychopathological conditions. Actually, these actions may be interpreted differently as evidence of agency and adaptation to a given set of structured, unequal options. Certain family and group activity setting features (e.g., religion and sports) act as protective factors; others (e.g. conflict, violence, addictions) do not.

Mainstream developmental psychology has provided some insights and clues in understanding how distal status variables such as parental education and income translate into the cultivation of various zones of development and competence, which in turn may be integrated within the broad CHAT model. For example, comparative studies of child rearing and socialization patterns that have been completed suggest that low-SES families are more strict, punitive, and restrictive in language codes (Bernstein 1962; Jackson, 1956). Additional data are valuable yet require theoretical integration.

Cultural Capital as an Interdisciplinary Concept

Social structures have generally been given analytical primacy by social scientists, considered to play a greater role in determining human behavior than psychological factors. Analyses of cultural capital, both physical and symbolic, represent ways of understanding the sociogenesis of SES differences from a sociological view (e.g., Bourdieu, 1987). The flip side of that coin is more difficult, or perhaps slower in manifesting itself. Social structures are, in the final analysis, constructed by human agency. However, agency does not operate in a vacuum. The agency required to construct structures and institutions is interactive and collective in nature and power-based. Low-SES families may instantiate social structure properties by the values, routines, and scripts in their particular activity settings; they are also situated in a hierarchy that is largely based on the interaction between those structural properties and parental and group agency, the meaning of which is largely imposed by the dominant discourse (e.g. changing labels for the problem from *disadvantaged* to at *risk*).

As a person grows and ventures out to other settings, the effects of SES-related structures may have priority. The foundations of agency that were forged earlier become enacted and may be themselves transformed. Parental and group agency may become proximal variables, whereas social and educational policies and practices may remain distal for the person. For example, group forms of "social" capital reflect certain historical processes that create a hierarchy of social relations. It may be that tools and practices developed by members of certain groups commodify the participants in special ways, enabling them to interact in the marketplace differently or less advantageously. Perhaps as the result of such commodification, some participants accumulate more economic capital during the life cycle, something that in turn facilitates the development of psychological tools across generations. Socialization practices not only covary, but are implicated in the reproduction of SES structures. The notion of children as capital is less new than the perspective that children are commodified and/or empowered through patterns of adult–child interactions across stratified activity settings.

A Cultural–Historical Dynamic Model

A CHAT approach is interdisciplinary by nature (Kozulin, 1990; Wertsch, 1991) and adds to the sociological discussion the possibility of explaining the actual psychological processes of formation in terms of identity, agency, competence, and values, for example. A case in point, SES differences in academic achievement vary, from accounting for 5% of the variance in some research (White, 1982) to accounting for much more in other studies (Bryk & Thum, 1989), depending on the method and factors considered. Achievement motivation, delay of gratification, locus of control are some of the developmental outcomes subject to socialization practices (Portes, 1999; Wigfield & Eccles, 1992). Part of the answer to the question of how to level differences between social groups might be found in adult–child interactions after interventions that provide for greater or different cultural mediation and maximize learning (Portes et al., 1986). At the microlevel, Karpov and Bransford (1995); Tzuriel (1996); Portes, Smith, Zady, and Del Castillo (1997); and others show how learning can be mediated in ways that rouse new and more effective forms of individual agency, which is generally conceptualized in terms of task performance and development. However, as noted earlier, whereas these interventions are necessary, they are not sufficient to alter the influence of social structural factors.

Middle-class parents may be viewed as having both "more and different" cultural capital that in turn benefits the child's development cumulatively than parents with less cultural capital. If we view parent SES-based capital dynamically as it is enacted through activities in which children participate, then children's development of capital is understood as mediated by parents' and others' cultural capital through participation in a variety of activity settings. Mediated action is found in family interactions that may help co-construct values, dispositions, skills, and expectations for current and future forms of agency. What is being mediated and accrued across contexts? Physical capital, perhaps, but more important for our discussion, symbolic capital in the form of cultural tools: socially legitimated knowledge, social practices, cognitive and linguistic skills, and attitudes that drive development (see Anyon, 1980, for a discussion of the influence of physical and symbolic capital on instruction in schools).

One way cultural capital influences development is by exposure to and participation in various activity settings that help co-construct development, with an eye toward future agency (e.g., travel, museums, and mentoring). The agency concept may thus be related to motivation (e.g., achievement motivation, locus of control, persistence, effort orientation, learned helplessness, or conflict resolution skills) for future forms of activity. The latter may range from finishing school to abstaining from sexual relationships to making career choices. The CHAT perspective emphasizes the co-construction of psychological processes that underlie various forms of agency – given the availability and appropriation of cultural tools – contextualized by the value of the symbolic capital appropriated. This approach allows us not only to identify general trends, but also to understand the exceptions to those trends. For example, why do some low-SES groups or families produce children who are more highly motivated and successful than other low-SES and middle-SES groups or families?

Explaining within-group variations in development is as critical to any theory as explaining between-group differences. A CHAT model may be envisioned, in part, as an hourglass that can be inverted to see not only top-down forms of social agency that shape individual development over two or more time lines (see Figure 17.1), but individual and group agency that is propelled by social and cultural interaction and leads to the formation and reformation of past and present social structures. The figure suggests that the relation between individual and societal development changes as individual agency increases with tool acquisition and maturity. Hence, the individual's development is not totally determined by either society or biological traits as a "product," but is co-constructed jointly as cultural development progresses, playing a more influential role in its own right over time. Individuals with various culture kits (Wertsch, 1991) gradually influence social structures that change over time as well.

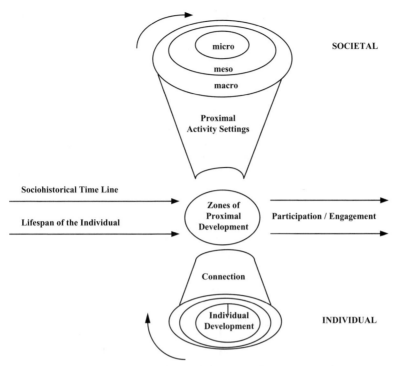

FIGURE 17.1 A cultural–historical dynamic model of development.

The way children's agency promotes changes in adult–child interaction has been studied to gain a better understanding of reciprocal change in human relations or activities. The role of agency at the larger collective level has received less attention in understanding the relation between SES and human development. Examples of this level of agency can be related to movements dealing with issues of oppression of various social groups, children's rights, and assertion of values through legal means. School reforms and accountability policies, at the sociogenetic level, may serve to change the relation between SES and school achievement over time. The point then is to understand the historical dance whereby the hourglass is seen slowly rotating over cultural and individual timelines and histories that constrain or promote development.

With tools, cultural groups have developed and maintained power, creating various social status groupings. The crucial point here concerns the role of SES-based cultural and conceptual tools in regulating development, as well as their own institutionalization in schools and beyond. One concern in this chapter is the way that the processes of access to and appropriation of symbolic capital becomes instrumental in understanding SES differences. For example, how do language, behavior, experience-based knowledge, and attitudes become the very means for establishing and sustaining compatibility with school and other institutions?

The relationship between SES and instructional approaches opens up at least two distinct questions: First, which instructional approaches are best used with students from different SES backgrounds? Second, and perhaps more important, which instructional approaches tend to be made available to students from different SES backgrounds? Given research by Anyon (1980) and Bowles and Gintis (1976), one way that the SES structure is reproduced is through the process of affording different instructional approaches, coupled with different forms of symbolic capital, to students from different SES backgrounds. If this is the case, then educators must ask themselves whether the activities they have created for their students are the kinds of activities that will best prepare them for a future filled with uncertain opportunities. Links between different methods of instruction across different SES school settings, as well as within schools in the form of ability grouping and tracking, provide the most obvious illustration. This discussion is reminiscent of the long debate in the United States between educators who advocate a liberal education for all students, and those who argue that tracking students into vocational and college preparatory coursework is more "socially efficient" and realistic.

A number of promising approaches have emerged in the educational research literature that are consistent with CHAT, including class size reduction programs and multiability, cooperative learning groups. Another example, reciprocal teaching (Palincsar & Brown, 1984), uses a structured form of participation that allows students to internalize strategies for reading and analyzing text. In a cooperative group format, a teacher leads a small group of students through a dialogue that asks students to form questions, identify confusing sections, summarize text, and make predictions about what occurs next. Over time, the teacher's role is reduced and the students take on the responsibility for leading the group through the process.

Academically oriented afterschool programs also help compensate low-SES students for the mediation often provided in middle-SES homes, including peer tutoring initiatives. On the teaching side of the school learning equation, teacher content expertise helps educators become more effective mediators, particularly when they use standards for effective pedagogy (CREDE, 2002) that have improved student outcomes. Efforts to transform the school culture in ways that assist educators to work collaboratively are also associated with high student achievement in schools with high proportions of students who are at risk. In those few exceptions, high expectations for low-SES students prevail, along with efforts to promote parent involvement. In sum, more effective socialization practices can be re-structured in traditional schools to support and promote the development of low-SES students with practices that remove them from the still present structured risks.

CONCLUDING THOUGHTS AND FUTURE RESEARCH

In the United States, approximately 20% of school-age children are stranded in a cycle of poverty with little hope of overcoming the barriers imposed by the task demands inherent in current schooling practices. For most African, Latin, and Native American children, the percentage is about three times as severe as that for dominant culture students (The Condition of Education, 1998). Poverty constrains development, particularly in areas that are most predictive of tool acquisition or literacy and achievement in school for those groups. Apart from the theoretical, practical, and ethical issues involved in altering the fates of these children, who are frequently sentenced to fail early, a solid theory-driven research base is urgently needed for understanding the ways in which SES impacts development and for guiding policy with respect to improving school contexts and changing institutionalized obstacles to equity.

It seems clear that SES-based interaction differences result in pervasive effects that generally are founded on a sustained gap in literacy-related variables, such as those inherent in parent involvement, time on task, adult–child ratio, and mediated activity. The effects of schooling on human development are typically not independent of the family–community culture. In fact, their interdependence grows over time, and before long, the consequences become further etched via "ability" grouping, vocational and college tracking programs, teachers' expectations, identities, and a host of nonacademic factors. Working toward a greater understanding as the basis for bringing about informed change for these children early is urgently needed.

It is evident that eliminating the disparity in SES-based adult–child socialization practices requires social restructuring and equitable access to a set of strategic mediated experiences. The latter implies the reorganization of institutional contexts and their social functions. Past research has identified certain interaction styles as defining SES differences, without recognizing the historical context that led to the development of social hierarchies and their associated characteristics. These differences are exacerbated when instructional approaches in schools are based on inaccurate perceptions of students and, therefore, magnify differences between them. The topic before us requires not only a documentation of SES differences, but also the means for understanding and improving their developmental and cultural construction. For example, a parental education curriculum for high school students is recommended for deconstructing SES-based differences in social and psychological knowledge and practices.

Finally, we need to remind ourselves that certain types of behavior and interaction styles may serve a functional purpose that reflects a coping strategy, rather than a "chosen" method of interaction. We should not assume that adult–child interactions are the result of oppression, lack of access to certain activity settings and social relations anchored to the mode of production and labor; nor should we assume that they are not. Rather, this is a call for research integration across genetic domains (Wertsch, 1991), employing a multilevel analysis of mediational means (Kozulin, 1990) and using the objective and subjective variables in the activity settings as the unit of analysis (Weisner, 1984). It is also a reminder, perhaps, of the motives behind the larger ethical project to which this science and research are aimed. As difficult as it was for Vygotsky to keep his science and politics separate in his time, today a praxis between the two seems not only emergent, but inevitable.

References

Anyon, J. (1980). Social class and the hidden curriculum of work. *Journal of Education, 162*(1), 67–92.

Apple, M. (1989). American realities: Poverty, economy, and education. In L. Weis, E. Farrar, & H. G. Petrie (Eds.), *Drop outs in schools: Issues, dilemmas and solutions* (pp. 205–224). Albany, NY: SUNY Press.

Baldwin, A. L., Kalhorn, J., & Breese, F. H. (1945). Patterns of parent behavior. *Psychological Monographs, 58* (3, Whole No. 299).

Bernstein, B. (1962). Linguistic codes, hesitation phenomena and intelligence. *Language and Speech, 5*, 31–46.

Bourdieu, P. (1987). *Distinction: A social critique on the judgment of taste.* Cambridge, MA: Harvard University Press.

Bowles, S., & Gintis, H. (1976). *Schooling in capitalist America: Educational reform and the contradictions of economic life.* New York: Basic Books.

Bryk, A., & Thum, Y. (1989). The effects of high school organization on dropping out: An exploratory investigation. *American Educational Research Journal, 26*, 353–383.

Caldwell, B., & Bradley, R. (1984). *Observation of the home environment.* Little Rock: University of Arkansas.

Carlson, E. A., Sroufe, L. A., Collins, W. A., Jimerson, S., Weinfield, N., Hennighausen, K., Egeland, B., Hyson, D. M., Anderson, F., & Meyer, S. E. (1999). Early environmental support and elementary school adjustment as predictors of school adjustment in middle adolescence. *Journal of Adolescent Research, 14*(1), 72–94.

Center for Research on Education, Diversity & Excellence (CREDE). (2002). *Five Standards for Effective Pedagogy and Student Outcomes* (Technical Report No. G1). Santa Cruz, CA: CREDE.

Cole, M. (1996). *Cultural psychology: A once and future discipline.* Cambridge, MA: Harvard University Press.

Cole, M., Gay, J., & Glick, J. (1968). A cross-cultural investigation of information processing. *International Journal of Psychology, 3*, 93–102.

Comer, J. P. (1990). Home, school and academic learning In J. Goodlad & P. Keating (Eds.), *Access to knowledge: An agenda for our nation's schools* (pp. 23–42). New York: College Entrance Examination Board.

The Condition of Education. (1998). Washington, DC: United States Government Printing Office.

Conroy, M., Hess, R., Azuma, H., & Kashiwagi, K. (1980). Maternal strategies for regulating children's behavior: Japanese and American families. *Journal of Cross-Cultural Psychology, 11,* 153–172.

Diaz, R. M., Neal, C. J., & Amaya-Williams, M. (1991). Social origins of self-regulation. In L. Moll (Ed.), *Vygotsky and education: Instructional implications and applications of sociohistorical psychology* (pp. 127–154). New York: Cambridge University Press.

Dunham, R. M., Kidwell, J. S., & Portes, P. R. (1988). Effects of parent-adolescent interaction on the continuity of cognitive development from early childhood to early adolescence. *Journal of Early Adolescence, 8*(3), 97–130.

Dunham, R. M., Kidwell, J. S., & Portes, P. R. (1995). Do the seeds of accelerative learning and teaching lie in a behavioral carrier wave? *Journal of Accelerated Learning and Teaching, 20,* 53–87.

Fine, M. (1989). *Framing drop outs: Notes on the politics of an urban high school.* Albany, NY: SUNY Press.

Gauvin, M., & Rogoff, B. (1989). Collaborative problem solving and children's planning skills. *Developmental Psychology, 25,* 139–151.

Hart, B., & Risley, T. R. (1992). American parenting of language-learning children: Persisting differences in family-child interactions observed in natural home environments. *Developmental Psychology, 28*(6), 1096–1105.

Heath, S. B. (1983). *Ways with words: Language, life, and work in communities and classrooms.* Cambridge: Cambridge University Press.

Henderson, B. B. (1991, February). Describing parent-child interaction during exploration: Situation definitions and negotiations. *Genetic, Social and General Psychology Monographs, 117*(1), 77–89.

Hess, R., & Shipman, V. (1965). Early experience and the socialization of cognitive modes in children. *Child Development, 36,* 377–388.

Isabella, R., & Belsky, J. (1991). Interactional synchrony and the origins of infant-mother attachment: A replication study. *Child Development, 60,* 103–118.

Jackson, P. W. (1956). Verbal solutions to parent-child problems. *Child Development, 27,* 339-349.

Kagan, J., Moss, H. A., & Sigel, I. E. (1963). Psychological significance of styles of conceptualization. In J. E. Wright, & J. Kagan (Eds.), Basic cognitive processes in children. *Monograph of the Society for Research in Child Development, 28*(2).

Karpov, Y., & Bransford, J. D. (1995). L. S. Vygotsky: The doctrine of empirical and theoretical learning. *Educational Psychologist, 30,* 61–66.

Kohn, M. L. (1977). *Class and conformity: A study of values* (2nd ed.). Chicago: University of Chicago Press.

Kozulin, A. (1990). *Vygotsky's psychology: A biography of ideas.* Cambridge, MA: Harvard University Press.

Kucznski, L., & Kochanska, G. (1990). Development of children's noncompliance strategies from toddlerhood to age 5. *Developmental Psychology, 26,* 398–408.

Laosa, L. M. (1981). *Parent-child interaction: Theory, research and prospects.* New York: Academic Press.

Lazar, I., & Darlington, R. (1982). Lasting effects of early education: A report from the consortium for longitudinal studies. *Monographs of the Society for Research in Child Development, 47*(2–3), 1–151.

Lytton, H. (1990). Child and parent effects in boys' conduct disorders: A reinterpretation. *Developmental Psychology, 26,* 683–697.

Mickelson, R. A. (1990). The attitude-achievement paradox among Black adolescents. *Sociology of Education, 63,* 44–61.

Murdock, T. B. (1999). The social context of risk: Status and motivational predictors of alienation in middle school. *Journal of Educational Psychology, 91*(1), 62–75.

Oakes, J. (1985). *Keeping track: How schools structure inequality.* New Haven, CT: Yale University Press.

Palincsar, A. M., & Brown, A. L. (1984). Reciprocal teaching of comprehension-fostering and comprehension monitoring activities. *Cognition and Instruction, 1,* 117–175.

Panofsky, C. P. (1999). Getting to the heart of the matter: Literacy as value commitments. In R. J. Telfer, (Ed.), *American reading forum* (vol. 19). Whitewater: University of Wisconsin.

Patterson, G. R. (1982). *Coercive family processes.* Eugene, OR: Castalia Press.

Piaget, J. (1954). *The construction of reality in the child.* New York: Basic Books.

Portes, P. R. (1988). Maternal verbal regulation and intellectual development. *Roeper Review, 11*(2), 106–110.

Portes, P. R. (1991). Assessing children's cognitive environments through parent-child interaction: Estimation of a general zone of proximal development in relation to scholastic achievement. *Journal of Research in Education, 24*(3), 30–38.

Portes, P. R. (1996). Ethnicity in education and psychology. In D. Berliner & R. Calfee (Eds.), *The handbook of educational psychology.* New York: McMillan.

Portes, P. R. (1999). Social and psychological factors in academic achievement of children of immigrants: A cultural history puzzle. *American Educational Research Journal, 36,* 489–507.

Portes, P. R., Cuentas, T. E., & Zady, M. F. (2000). Cognitive socialization across ethnocultural contexts: Literacy and cultural differences in intellectual performance and parent-child interaction. *Journal of Genetic Psychology, 161*(1), 79–98.

Portes, P. R., Dunham, R. M., & Williams, S. (1986). Preschool intervention, social class and parent-child interaction differences. *Journal of Genetic Psychology, 147*(2), 241–255.

Portes, P. R., Smith, T. L., Zady, M. F., & Del Castillo, K. (1997). Extending the double stimulation method in cultural-historical research: Parent-child interaction and cognitive change. *Mind, Culture, and Activity, 4*(2), 108–123.

Portes, P. R., Zady, M. F., & Dunham, R. M. (1998). The effects of parents' assistance on middle school students' problem solving and achievement. *Journal of Genetic Psychology, 159*(2), 163–178.

Radziszewska, B., & Rogoff, B. (1991). Children's guided participation in planning imaginary errands with skilled adult or peer partners. *Developmental Psychology, 27*(3), 381–389.

Rogoff, B., & Gardner, W. (1984). Adult guidance of cognitive development. In B. Rogoff & J. Lave (Eds.), *Everyday cognition: Its development in social context* (pp. 95–150). Cambridge, MA: Harvard University Press.

Roopnarine, J. L., & Carter, D. B. (Eds.) (1992). *Annual advances in applied developmental psychology* (Vol. 5). Norwood, NJ: Ablex.

Saxe, G. (1994). Studying cognitive developments in CHAT context: The development of a practice-based approach. *Mind, Culture, and Activity, 1,* 135–157.

Saxon, T. F., & Reilly, J. T. (1999). Joint attention and toddler characteristics: Race, sex, and socioeconomic status. *Early Child Development and Care, 149,* 59–69.

Scribner, S., & Cole, M. (1981). *The psychology of literacy.* Cambridge, MA: Harvard University Press.

Sigel, I. E. (1982). The relationship between parents' distancing strategies and the child's cognitive behavior. In L. M. Laosa, & I. E. Sigel (Eds.), *Families as learning environments for children* (pp. 47–86). New York: Plenum.

Sigel, I. E., Anderson, L. M., & Shapiro, H. (1966). Categorization behavior of lower- and middle-class negro preschool children: Differences in dealing with representation of familiar objects. *Journal of Negro Education, 35*(3), 218–229.

Sigel, I. E., Stinson, E. T., & Flaugher, J. (1991). Socialization of representational competence in the family: The distancing paradigm. In L. Okagaki & R. J. Sternberg (Eds.), *Directors of development: Influences on the development of children's thinking* (pp. 121–144). Hillsdale, NJ: Lawrence Erlbaum Associates.

Sigel, I. E., Stinson, E. T., & Kim, M. (1993). Socialization of cognition: The distancing model. In K. W. Fischer & R. Wozniak (Eds.), *Specific environments: Thinking in contexts.* Hillsdale, NJ: Lawrence Erlbaum Associates.

Stern, D. N. (1985). *The interpersonal world of the infant: A view from psychoanalysis and developmental psychology.* New York: Basic Books.

Tharp, R. G., & Gallimore, R. (1988). *Rousing minds to life: Teaching, learning, and schooling in social context.* New York: Cambridge University Press.

Tzuriel, D. (1996). Mediated learning experience in free-play versus structured situations among preschool children of low-, medium-, and high-SES. *Early Childhood Development and Care, 126,* 57–82.

Valsiner, J. (1984). Construction of the zone of proximal development in adult-child joint action: The socialization of meals. In B. Rogoff & J. Wertsch (Eds.), *Children's learning in the zone of proximal development* (pp. 65–76). San Francisco: Jossey-Bass.

Valsiner, J. (1989). *Human development and culture: The social nature of personality and its study.* Lexington, MA: Lexington Books.

Valsiner, J. (1998). *The guided mind: A sociogenetic approach to personality.* Cambridge, MA: Harvard University Press.

Vygotsky, L. S. (1978). *Mind in society: The development of higher psychological processes.* Cambridge, MA: Harvard University Press.

Weisner, T. S. (1984). Ecocultural niches of middle childhood: A cross cultural perspective. In W. A. Collins (Ed.), *Development during middle childhood: The years from six to twelve* (pp. 335–369). Washington, DC: National Academy of the Sciences Press.

Wertsch, J. V. (1991). *Voices of the mind: A sociocultural approach to mediated action.* Cambridge, MA: Harvard University Press.

Wertsch, J. V., Minick, N., & Arns, R. J. (1984). The creation of context in joint problem solving: A cross-cultural study. In B. Rogoff & J. Lave (Eds.), *Everyday cognition: Its development in social context.* Cambridge, MA: Harvard University Press.

White, K. R. (1982). The relation between socioeconomic status and academic achievement. *Psychological Bulletin, 91*(3), 461–481.

Wigfield, A., & Eccles, J. S. (1992). The development of achievement task values: A theoretical analysis. *Developmental Review, 12,* 265–310.

Wood, D. J., Bruner, J. S., & Ross, G. (1976). The role of tutoring in problem-solving. *Journal of Child Psychology and Psychiatry, 17,* 89–100.

Zinchenko, V. P. (2001). External and internal: Another comment on the issue. In S. Chaiklin (Ed.), *The theory and practice of cultural-historical psychology* (pp. 135–147). Aarhus, Denmark: Aarhus University Press.

18

Cultural Modeling

CHAT as a Lens for Understanding Instructional Discourse Based on African American English Discourse Patterns

Carol D. Lee

A continuing challenge is how we as educational researchers are to investigate learning and development as these occur in complex settings in an attempt to understand the ecological niches of practice in the real world. In many ways, these questions are the terrain of Cultural–Historical Activity Theory (CHAT). CHAT, as articulated by Cole (1996) and others (Rogoff & Lave, 1984; Rogoff, 1990; Wertsch, 1991), is an outgrowth of the Russian school of psychology represented by Lev Vygotsky (1978, 1981, 1987), Alexander Luria (1976), and Alexei Leontiev (1981). This orientation to the study of human learning and development places several core tenets at the center of inquiry. These tenets include the mutually constituting influences of social interaction in participation in jointly constructed activity across multiple settings and the functions of mediating artifacts. CHAT places culture at the center of human sense-making activities. Educational research rooted in CHAT has documented the centrality of cultural systems; much less attention has been paid to cultural systems of non–European or non-European-American ethnic groups. In this chapter, I will illustrate how multiple mediational resources have been drawn upon in culturally responsive ways to support discipline-specific learning.

I have an abiding personal interest in these questions. In the Cultural Modeling Project (Lee, 1993; 1995a; 1995b; 2001), we developed a curriculum intervention in response to literature that was implemented over a 3-year period in an urban, underachieving high school. The entire faculty of the English department of this high school participated in the intervention and implemented the Cultural Modeling curriculum. As part of that research, I also taught one high school English class each of the 3 years. I videotaped my teaching every day for each of the 3 years; we also videotaped classes of the other teachers in the department. In this chapter, I offer an analysis of a group of students preparing for a cross-class public debate on Toni Morrison's (1987) award-winning novel *Beloved*.

I will address in this analysis the following questions:

- What are the structures that undergird instructional discourse based on African American English discourse norms?
- What were the consequences for students of having this participation structure available to them as a resource?
- How does Cultural–Historical Activity Theory provide a framework for understanding how these students were able to participate in a complex activity system with improvisational, emergent characteristics?

VYGOTSKIAN ANALYTICAL TOOLS

Of particular interest to our work in Cultural Modeling is how we attend to patterns of cultural practices that are repeated across the settings of schools and community life and understand their consequences for student learning. Consistent with a Vygotskian perspective, concepts serve as tools for problem solving. Several constructs from Vygotsky proved useful for analyzing how African American cultural practices were taken up and with what consequences for student learning. First is Vygotsky's (1987) distinction between spontaneous and scientific concepts. Spontaneous concepts, he argued, represent the knowledge we develop through participation in everyday practices. It is largely intuitive. Vygotsky posited that scientific concepts represent the quality of knowledge most associated with learning in school. Such concepts tend to be taxonomic and abstract. Vygotsky said that spontaneous concepts provide a foundation for the development of scientific concepts. As has been the case in most Western studies of cognition in so-called developing non-Western nations, the knowledge certain peoples construct through participation in the routine activities of their daily lives has been denigrated as having little value for school-based learning. African American English, for example, has been viewed by some as a detriment to learning, an obstacle to be overcome (Bereiter & Engelmann, 1966; Orr, 1987; Stotsky, 1999). The Cultural Modeling framework, by contrast, takes seriously the interaction between spontaneous and scientific knowledge. Our analysis of the culturally responsive instructional conversations in Cultural Modeling classrooms documents how speech genres inherited from participation in everyday activity served as tools for working through complex discipline-specific arguments in the study of literature.

The second idea is that interdependent, co-constructed processes of joint activity are necessary components of what Vygotsky (1978) called the *zone of proximal development* (ZPD). The zone of proximal development represents what someone can do with help, in contrast to what he or she can do alone. Our analysis of culturally responsive instructional talk in these classrooms is an attempt to document the microlevel language structures through which these students were able to engage in sophisticated problem solving that their formal reading levels would not have predicted. Vygotsky's early work used dyad interactions as the basis for understanding a ZPD. As we attempt to adapt this analytical tool, the idea of a ZPD, to the study of classrooms, we must be able to take into account interactions across many individuals and across time. The ZPD has been explored widely in the research literature; much work remains to be done to understand the nature of microlevel interactions between novices and experts, the relationships between these interactions and disciplinary learning, and the range of cultural variation in patterns of mediation. We have chosen tools from discourse analysis to try to identify patterns of talk and interactions involving whole classes and small groups beyond dyads and across time (Lee 1995a, 2000, 2001; Lee & Majors, 2000).

The third is the idea that humans inherit cultural tools, which they adapt for problem solving (Vygotsky, 1978; Leontiev, 1981; Cole, 1996; Wertsch, 1991). This introduces the role of history in understanding how people learn. African American English is a repository of inherited worldviews, cultural models, and scripts that people of African descent in the United States have inherited from their African roots. The invocation of African American norms for talk represents a way that the past is carried forward and negotiated in the present.

Finally, Vygotsky was a Marxist. I do not share that political persuasion; however, I do share a commitment to education as a tool for social justice and community building. I believe that equity in education requires that learning environments in school respect and draw meaningfully on the resources that students across diverse backgrounds take from their everyday experiences. Our work in Cultural Modeling has been one attempt to articulate a framework for making such connections in ways that lead to deep disciplinary knowledge and that help students understand how such knowledge can be used as a tool for social justice.

AFRICAN AMERICAN DISCOURSE NORMS

There is an extensive body of literature documenting the features of African American English (Smitherman, 1977; 2000). There is a converging body of evidence documenting the West African roots of the phonology, syntax, prosodic features, and speech genres of African American English (Mufwene, 1993). I make this point because in discussing the relevance of speech genres to instructional discourse, in particular in the examples discussed in this chapter, connections between West African and Diaspora examples can easily be made.

Smitherman (1977) discusses at least three kinds of features: worldviews, rhetorical qualities, and modes of discourse. In the arena of worldviews, Smitherman illustrates how, often through lexicon, stock phrases, and proverbs, historically held belief systems are both communicated and sustained. These worldviews involve what Smitherman calls a *sacred–secular continuum*. On the secular end of the spectrum are language games such as playing the dozens. The dozens is a game of ritualized mock insult about someone's mother. On the sacred end are religious aphorisms and moral argumentation through storytelling. Rhetorical qualities include exaggerated language, use of proverbial and aphoristic phrasing, playing on words, use of indirection, and tonal semantics. *Tonal semantics* refers to the ways that meaning and point of view are communicated through the manipulation of tonal qualities in oral speech. Tonal semantics within African American English include, but are not limited to, strategic use of repetition and alliteration. African American English discourse modes include call and response and narrative sequencing. In the analysis of the culturally responsive instructional discourse in the class to be described, I will illustrate how students used all of these features in their talk, and with what consequences.

INSTRUCTIONAL DISCOURSE WITHIN A CULTURAL MODELING FRAMEWORK

Cultural Modeling is a framework for the design of curriculum (Lee, 1993; 2001) that explicitly links deep disciplinary knowledge and funds of knowledge of students, especially students of color, students from low-income backgrounds, and students who speak a language or language variety other than academic English. To date, the design work in Cultural Modeling has focused on the arena of literacy, specifically response to literature at the secondary level and narrative writing (Lee, Mendenhall, Rivers, & Tynes, 1999) at the elementary school level. The Cultural Modeling framework focuses the designer to analyze carefully what concepts, strategies, and habits of mind are most generative in the discipline. The designer then analyzes the routine cultural practices in which students engage outside school to look for linkages. Such linkages may be shared concepts, shared use of strategies, and shared habits of mind. They may also be naïve theories that if not interrogated will prevent students from developing deep conceptual understanding in the discipline. Such linkages are related to Vygotsky's (1987) distinctions between scientific and spontaneous concepts. Through the Cultural Modeling framework, we have attempted to provide a more detailed lens through which to consider such relationships.

In response to literature, we identified a core set of concepts, strategies, and habits of mind that are most generative. Generative concepts include satire, irony, symbolism, use of unreliable narrators, and specialized genres such as stream of consciousness. Strategies for recognizing that a text poses a problem of satire and strategies for constructing a reasonable interpretation of the satire are seldom articulated, especially in high school classrooms. However, there is research rooted in the cognitive sciences that documents the strategies that expert readers of literature, especially fiction, draw on to attack the ill-structured problems that literature poses (Graves & Frederiksen, 1996; Halasz, 1987; van den Broek, 1996). In terms of habits of mind, expert readers of literature take pleasure in word play and in indirection as aesthetically meaningful ends in themselves. From both personal experience as well as the sociolinguistic literature on African American English, I have documented that speakers of African American Vernacular English (AAVE) routinely in traditional speech genres interpret satire, irony, symbolism, and use of unreliable narrators (Lee, 1993, 1995a, 1995b). They also in the moment of ongoing conversational exchanges create satire, irony, and symbolism. I have argued, however, that the knowledge and concepts and strategies that AAVE speakers use in their everyday talk are largely tacit. Because this knowledge is tacit, when confronted with analogous problems in school-based literature classes, the students do not draw on relevant schemata to attack problems of interpretation that share meaningful attributes with the kinds of language interpretation and production in which they engage outside school.

Through what in Cultural Modeling we call *metacognitive instructional discourse* (Lee, 1998; 2001), existing prior knowledge is made public and open to analysis. This happens through both the topics of discussion, the text objects that are discussed, and the participation structures of talk.

STUDENTS' USE OF AFRICAN AMERICAN ENGLISH RHETORICAL TRADITION IN THE SERVICE OF LITERARY REASONING

Smitherman (1994, 2000) defines the following as features of the African American English rhetorical tradition:

1. Rhythmic, dramatic, evocative language
2. Reference to color–race–ethnicity (that is, when the topic does not call for it)
3. Use of proverbs, aphorisms, biblical verses
4. Sermonic tone reminiscent of traditional Black church rhetoric, especially in vocabulary, imagery, metaphor
5. Direct address-conversational tone
6. Cultural references
7. Ethnolinguistic idioms
8. Verbal inventiveness, unique nomenclature
9. Cultural values-community consciousness
10. Field dependency, involvement with and immersion in events and situations, personalizing phenomena, lack of distance from topics and subjects (pp. 86–87)

At the end of the fall semester, the senior class had completed reading Toni Morrison's novel *Beloved*. The Cultural Modeling Project decided to host a meeting across classes to entertain any remaining questions the students had about the novel. We also wanted to have the students debate one of the central questions of the novel: Was Sethe morally courageous and correct to kill her child in order to prevent the child from being enslaved? During the first 20 minutes, the talk looked like a traditional teacher-directed initiate–response–evaluation (IRE) sequence (Mehan, 1979; Cazden, 1988). One of the teachers asked students questions; students responded in sequence to the teacher's questions. Then students self-selected into one of three groups: (1) Sethe was not correct or courageous to kill her child; (2) Sethe was morally correct and courageous to protect her child from being returned into enslavement; (3) students were neutral on the question. Once the students broke into their self-selected groups, one teacher stayed in a separate room with each group. After the groups worked out their positions, everyone returned to the large room where the whole group had initially met. At that point, the debate turned into a raucous gathering that was virtually uncontrollable by the teachers: African American discourse norms at their most pristine moment in the service of literary debate. In this analysis I will focus on the debate constructed in response to position (1).

"It's WRONG ta Kill"

Group one took the position that Sethe was morally incorrect in killing her child. They co-constructed an argument supporting their claim by drawing on moral warrants rooted in the Bible. Jelani initiates the line of reasoning by articulating the warrant that would come to be the base of their evidence: "You should start with what the Bible say." One of the features that Smitherman discusses is narrative interspersion, in which an AAVE speaker begins to construct an argument and then appears to digress by telling a story. The story provides an analogy to the point the speaker is trying to make. African American preachers are known for use of this structure of argumentation. Jelani poses a narrative analogy of a woman's killing her child because life circumstances are difficult. Because African American verbal performance is often keyed by emphatic use of gesture, Jelani physically dramatizes the analogy. He walks across the room, steps behind a young woman sitting in her chair, and holds out his pick (Afro hair pick) above her neck as if he were going to slit her throat: "No, for real, I'm goin ta cut yo neck." In this way he constructs an analogy to Sethe's act in the novel; she slits her baby's throat. Later in the dialogue, what evolves is a nested argument. Toulmin defines a *nested argument* as one in which a larger claim is substantiated through a series of related subclaims. Each subclaim contains its own evidence and warrants.

Jelani goes on to reenact the drama of his analogy more emphatically:

JELANI: Look. Look. Let me show you something. I'm goin ta kill Megan because I think she's going to go through some pain at work tonight. So I should just kill her tonight.

MEGAN: Get me another job.

JELANI: Exactly, so why did she kill her baby?

Megan's comment, "Get me another job," is a form of signifying, the traditional ritual of verbal volleying based on ritual insult. She has placed herself in the narrative enacted by Jelani, in line with a field-dependent orientation. There is a certain humor in her response, "Get me another job," which also reflects a call and response motif. She affirms Jelani's claim–call embedded in his analogy through the humor of her response: If you are going to kill me because of the poor job I have, "Get me another job." It is clear the students share contextualization cues because they see no need to make explicit all that is implied, both by Jelani's narrativized analogy and by Megan's signifying response.

This co-constructed argument becomes a nested argument in which subclaims in support of the larger claim evolve. These subclaims are nested within other chains of reasoning being made simultaneously. This entire episode involves interspersed moments of multiparty overlapping talk. It is clear that students can all hear and follow the interspersed nested arguments as groups of students refer to an issue raised in an earlier segment of multiparty overlapping talk. For example, in line 6 of the transcript, Jelani says, "You should start with what the Bible say." In line 12, another student shouts out with great emphasis, "The HOLY Bible." Then in line 31, one girl asks, "How they gonna argue against the Bible?" This leads to a wonderful anticipation of possible counterclaims:

S1: How they gonna argue against the Bible?

S2: Some people probably don't even read the Bible

S3: || They got atheists.

S1: Well, that's why we come up with some atheist answers.

The phrase "atheist answers" could be seen as a lack of understanding that *atheist* is a noun rather than an adjective. It could also be viewed as an example of what Smitherman calls *verbal inventiveness* and *unique nomenclature*, characteristic of the African American Rhetorical Tradition. It also clearly shows that the students have anticipated the counterclaims that their peers might make against their line of reasoning. This anticipation of counterclaims represents a sophisticated form of reasoning according to Toulmin (Toulmin, Rieke, & Janik, 1984).

Interspersed between the argument by analogy rooted in biblical warrants and the common sense of everyday experience (i.e., a poor mother today could not be excused for killing her child only because life was hard) was another line of reasoning, a subclaim that demanded its own line of reasoning. Jason initiates this second line of reasoning as well, when he asks early on, "Why have a child if you gon ta kill it?" This leads to a flurry of comments about abortion. The students then begin to examine what they view as similarities and differences between physically killing a born child and having an abortion. This represents a very interesting and potentially tenuous line of reasoning. If the students among whom they will be defending their positions accept the proposition that abortion is morally acceptable, then this group's position potentially becomes less tenable. On the other hand, if their audience does not accept the right of a woman to an abortion on the basis that killing a fetus is like killing a baby, this group will have garnered a moral authority to warrant their claims that will be made more difficult to counter. This represents a sophisticated orientation to argument because, according to Toulmin, it involves crafting one's evidence and warrants in anticipation of the belief system of one's audience. The analogies they construct between what Sethe did in cutting her baby's throat and what happens in an abortion show the way they prune their examples to be consistent with the logic of their overarching argument. One girl argues that the two actions are the same. This proposition is then animated and elaborated by two other girls. Goffman (1981) defines *animator* and *elaborator* as roles to be carried out in conversational exchanges. According to Goffman, the animator gives voice to ideas but may not be the author of the ideas:

> AMOS: But that's the same thing though
> AISHA: Yeah, cuz they still cuttin the baby in pieces
> SYLVIA: but it's a living thing, it's a living thing.
>   . . . .
> KENYA: you doin it yo self; you the mother; you doing it to your
> LAINI: own kid
> TIRSHATHA: I wouldn't kill my kid.

When Sylvia adds, "It's a living thing," she makes emphatic the moral dimensions of the group's claim: That is, cutting a yet-to-be-born baby, who is a living being, into pieces is no different from Sethe's slitting the throat of her baby. The mother having the abortion and Sethe both felt they had good reasons for taking the life of a child, but in the light of the Bible and common sense (as they see it), both are morally wrong. Sylvia invokes a use of parallel structure to mark the formalism and importance of this idea. Further she uses a rhythmic prosody, "It's a LIVING thing, it's a LIVING thing," to communicate further how important this idea is to her. To make the point more emphatic and to make the connections between this analogy with Sethe more explicit, Kenya says, "You doin it yoself; you the mother." Further evidence of the fact that this is a co-constructed argument, Laini finishes Kenya's sentence for her. The entire argument is posed in a

TABLE 18.1. *Nested Argument, Evidence, and Warrants*

Claim	Evidence	Warranting
I. It is morally wrong to take a life.		Bible
A. Taking the life of a child is gruesome.	The act of aborting a child involves physical dismemberment.	Common human values would affirm that tearing apart human body parts is gruesome.
B. Difficult life circumstances are not a morally acceptable justification for killing a child.	By analogy, one would not believe it was morally appropriate to take the life of a child because the parent was extremely poor and had an extremely poorly paying job.	Killing a child because his or her parent is poor is morally offensive.
C. It is wrong to take such extreme action since you can not predict what the future will hold.		

narrative structure, with a coda given by Tirshatha to mark the significance of the narrative, "I wouldn't kill my kid." With this coda, Tirshatha, in line with a field-dependent orientation, places herself inside the story, as a kind of moral chorus representing the perspective of the community on the ethical debate. To reiterate, the discourse features of this part of the exchange – parallel structure, rhythmic prosody, narrative interspersion, and field-dependency – are features identified by Smitherman as characteristic of the African American English rhetorical tradition.

I have argued so far that these students use the mediational resources of AAVE to communicate their argument. I simultaneously assert that the inherent structure of the argument they construct reflects the principles of effective argumentation outlined by Toulmin (Toulmin et al., 1984) and Kuhn (1991). In Table 18.1, I have given a more abstract language to the organization of the group's argument. I illustrate in the table the overarching claims being made by the group and the nested subclaims on which the overarching claim is built. I also illustrate not only the evidence they use to support each claim, but, more importantly, the warrants they invoke to give authority to their evidence.

In my descriptions of their claims and subclaims, I have not used the exact language of the students. This is an important point for several reasons. I here take the position that their argument is structurally very complex and

TABLE 18.2. *Distributed Nature of Claims, Evidence, and Warrants*

Biblical Warranting	Abortion Analogy	Overarching or New Claims	Everyday Analogy
L 6			
	L 8–11		
L 12			
	L 13–17		
			L 19
	L 20–28		
L 31–35			
		L 40–41	
			L 44–53
		L 53–56	

well reasoned. However, it is still not communicated at a level of abstraction that reflects academic language. I must make clear here that it is not the AAVE syntax nor the rhetorical features of the discourse that prevent the students from using what some have termed the *decontextualized structure of academic discourse*. In this respect, I take serious objection to Bernstein (1970) and others (Bereiter & Engelmann, 1966; Orr, 1987; Stotsky, 1999) who posit that something inherent in the language functioning of low-income communities interferes with the appropriation of academic discourses. Rather, I claim that teachers need to understand the deep structure of this argument: that to understand the deep structure of the argument, teachers and educational researchers must understand the language of the student.

Besides delineating the structure of the group's nested argument, I want to point out that it is a distributed argument. Claims, subclaims, evidence, and warrants are distributed across members of the group. No one student carries the burden of constructing, elaborating, or extending the argument. Second, because these claims and subclaims are often communicated through multiparty overlapping talk, it is fascinating how students are able to enter and then reenter at much later points the evolving chain of reasoning. In Table 18.2, I list the line numbers where a claim, evidence, or warrant is introduced and then reintroduced.

I take the position here that it is the students' competence in AAVE discourse norms that allows them to hear multiple claims, evaluate them, hold them in short-term memory, and eventually respond by affirmation or elaboration, even when there is intervening talk in another direction. I have made similar observations in other Cultural Modeling classrooms (Lee, 2001).

In line 57, the teacher says, "So we're all agreed. We got her back." Whether intentional or not is unclear, but Mrs. Harrison's use of the stock phrase "We got her back" frames the event as a competition that assumes deep filial affiliation. You cover the back of dear friends or members of your team (i.e., basketball or football) when they are threatened. It is a vernacular phrase that one would not expect a teacher to use in a classroom space. Its use (she had made a similar comment before the groups dispersed to develop their positions) frames the event and defines not only roles for students but also a range of discourse and speech genres that are potentially acceptable. From the whole group debate that followed, it is very clear that the students had a shared vision of the event as a space in which you cover one another's backs.

APPLYING VYGOTSKIAN TOOLS IN ANALYSIS

In this final section, I want to discuss how I used Cultural–Historical Activity Theory (CHAT) and how my invocation of CHAT directed the methods I called on to analyze the data.

CHAT (Cole, 1996) served as a useful analytical tool for several reasons. Our interest in this analysis was to document the ways that argument structures and discourse norms rooted in African American English served as mediational tools in service of literary reasoning. Mediational tools carry knowledge accumulated across time. Because processes of mediation are always dialogic in nature, the invocation of historically inherited tools is also a more open process than the term *inherited* suggests. New users can imbue these tools with fresh meanings, adapt tools for new and unexpected uses, or significantly extend them, resulting in the construction of new tools. In the Vygotskian sense, tools may be physical artifacts or conceptual ideas. Which sources of knowledge (i.e., conceptual tools) can serve as resources for academic learning have been contested in the research literature. This topic has been particularly problematic in regard to populations in the United States who are not of Western European backgrounds. So-called nonmainstream language varieties of English, particularly African American English, have been a virulent target of such arguments.

In the case of the segment of instructional talk analyzed in this chapter, the argument structure employed by the students served as a mediational tool. Their shared understanding of this argument structure helped to organize their goal-directed activity to make relevant claims, consider the possible counterclaims that their peers might make, garner evidence to support their claim, and invoke real world norms to warrant the veracity of their claims. In this culturally responsive instructional environment, the argument structure was hybrid in nature (Gutierrez, Rymes, & Larson, 1995). On the one hand, it was grounded in an academic structure, as articulated by Toulmin (Toulmin et al., 1984) and Kuhn (1991). On the other hand, it was clearly reflective of African American English argument structures. The students' use of narrative interspersion (Ball, 1992; Smitherman, 1977) and distributed argumentation reflects these African American discourse norms. Narrative interspersion – that is, placing an illustrative narrative inside an expository argument – serves as a pointer to a specialized kind of analogical reasoning. In order to construct an illustrative story, the students needed to think of a narrativized analogy for a claim, a piece of evidence or a warrant. It led students consciously to make connections between their interpretations of the internal states of characters in the novel, specifically Sethe, and their own cultural models of how people should act and reason in similar circumstances. Their conscious invocation of issues related to abortion and to appropriate ways to struggle against adversity are examples of their analogical reasoning. Had they only drawn on the academic model of argumentation, that is, the Toulmin model, they might not have chosen to interrogate their life experiences as resources for tackling the interpretive problem on the floor. Kintsch (1998) makes the distinction between a text-based model and a situation-based model of reading. A text-based model comes into play when the reader has limited real world knowledge that is applicable to the text and is constrained by what the words on the page say, often in a literal way. A situation-based model involves the reader's using his or her knowledge of the world as a filter through which to make inferences, construct an understanding of themes, and use the text to do things in the world. He argues that the situation-based model is often a more sophisticated interpretation of a text as it calls for the reader to understand how the information and assertions of the text make sense in the world beyond the text. Thus in this case, I argue that the semiotic potential of both argument structures – the Toulmin model and the African American model – provided these students with important resources for literary problem solving.

CHAT has also been useful in its focus on local activity systems as well as interactions across multiple activity systems. Cultural Modeling designs classrooms as spaces in which community-based norms for talk and funds of knowledge are invited and privileged as resources for learning. For African American students, African American English is often the medium of communication through which spontaneous concepts in the Vygotskian sense are constructed. Learning the language and modes of reasoning in the academic disciplines is always challenging. In our work with the Cultural Modeling Project, we have consistently found that the use of what we call *cultural data sets* at the beginning of instruction results in students' engaging in very sophisticated literary reasoning before they have learned how to apply these modes of reasoning to canonical works of literature (Lee, 1995a; 2000; 2001; Lee & Majors, 2000). Cultural data sets used have included stretches of signifying dialogues involving ritual insult, lyrics from rap songs, rap videos, and media clips from television and movies. Students already have sophisticated interpretations of these texts, but their knowledge of the explicit processes they use to make these interpretations is tacit. Through what we call *metacognitive instructional conversations*

(Lee, 1998), the teacher helps students to describe their case-specific strategies at more abstract and taxonomic levels. This is the preparation the students reported in this chapter would have experienced before reading *Beloved*. It is through these interactions that Cultural Modeling attempts to bridge spontaneous and scientific concepts, in this case, in service of literary reasoning. I believe the power of this culturally responsive bridging is the reapplication of cultural norms across activity settings – in this case, school, home, and routine interactions in peer social networks. This bridging is a crucial design in a culturally responsive zone of proximal development. Conscious scaffolding in a zone of proximal development requires that the more expert member, in this case, the teacher and the curriculum designer, must understand what students take with them, including students' goals, prior knowledge, and cultural models of the world as they relate to the subject matter, in order to help the student learn to share norms for the work they are to do together. For the work described in this chapter, the question was how to help students with histories of low academic achievement who do not routinely read canonical literature outside school not only to share the value of reading a novel like *Beloved*, but to read it looking for multiple layers of meaning and for ways that it speaks to the human condition: that is, to engage in literary readings. The fact that in the example described these students were from different classrooms, engaging in a one-time cross-class debate on the novel, suggests even more strongly that they had internalized the value of literary reasoning. Such intense literary debates were routinely found across classrooms in the intervention.

A second important point is related to the mediational tools we have described, which are language-based. Human language, as are most symbolic systems (the language of mathematics, the patterned ways of visual representation in the visual arts, the notational systems of music), is inherently dialogic in nature (Bakhtin, 1981). That means that the argument structures and norms for interacting that the students drew upon not only helped to shape their goals and means for achieving those goals, but also were sufficiently open to be adapted creatively by each individual student. That creativity, however, was not so unique that other students in the group did not have cues as to how to make sense of one another's moves. For example, when Jelani physically got out of his chair and walked over to another student with his hair pick in hand and began to tell a story, neither the other students nor the teacher misinterpreted his actions as threatening. In fact, when Jelani says, "I'm goin ta kill Megan because I think she's going to go through some pain at work tonight," the students interpret this abbreviated narrative as a what-if story. They understand that the words are not intended to be interpreted literally. They use their knowledge of speech genres to place Jelani's words into an interpretive frame as part of an evolving argument regarding the internal state of the character Sethe in the novel. Megan's response "Get me another job" not only extends Jelani's narrative, but also adds an evaluative coda – I agree there is another option than killing because times are rough. Jelani understands the narrativized coda when he responds, "Exactly, so why did she kill her baby?" The use of narrative interspersion and co-constructed argumentation could not predict the unique statements of Jelani and Megan. Their statements represent unique adaptations of a cultural tool. However, it is the shared understanding of these cultural tools as parts of a dialogic, open system that allows others in the group to understand and contribute to the interchange. Vygotsky's descriptions of processes of internalization in dyadic interchanges illustrate the co-constructed and dialogic nature of internalization.

One of our goals as researchers is to unpack how patterns of interactions construct roles for participants and support them in carrying out those roles. In Cultural Modeling classrooms, participation structures included multiparty, overlapping talk. This was particularly evident when the students described in this chapter left the room where they were putting together the argument they would make and entered the larger room where all the groups debated one another. The room was often as loud as a basketball game. In this cultural participation structure of multiparty, overlapping talk, students knew immediately how to interpret subtle affirmations in call-and-response interactions, dramatic enactments, and prosody cues. Students heard one another, followed one another's lines of reasoning, and retorted to one another's claims with great intensity.

CHAT points to the need to understand how people, modes of talk, and use of tools structure opportunities to learn; it does not provide any explicit direction in terms of methods of analysis. Discourse analysis has provided our project with analytical methods that allowed us to understand patterns of participation and interrogate perspective taking or what Goffman calls *footing*. In this culturally responsive classroom setting, students shared norms for who could talk, about what, when, and how. Contextualization cues (Gumperz, 1982), such as the teacher's statement about covering one another's back, helped to shape a perspective that we are getting ready for a heated debate. Norms for debate here are fierce, dramatic, consequential, but fun. Because CHAT calls for attention to culture, history, and activity as mutually constituting, our analysis sought to learn the influences of culture – African American, disciplinary, and classroom – on what these students were able to do. Looking at language use also allowed us to consider relationships across participation in multiple settings – home, community, and school.

I have attempted to demonstrate specific features of culturally responsive instructional discourse based on African American English discourse norms. Part of what Cultural Modeling makes possible is the use of multiple mediational means for problem solving. These mediational means include structures for argumentation, participation structures that organize and distribute roles for students to play, and conceptual tools of the discipline. In Cultural Modeling, what gives leverage to these multiple mediating resources is that students get repeated opportunities to use them, not only in and across classrooms in a school using Cultural Modeling, but in their home and community life. Cultural Modeling helps students see the connections across the settings in which they participate. Brofenbrenner (1979) describes such overlaps as occurring within and across what he calls the *meso system* of the ecological–cultural niche in which people operate. The value of this synergy is captured in Bourdieu's (1990) concept of *habitus*. Duranti (1997) defines *habitus* as

A system of dispositions with historical dimensions through which novices acquire competence by entering activities through which they develop a series of expectations about the world and about ways of being in it. (p. 44)

I have begun to envision Cultural Modeling as sitting inside the matrix where microsystems such as family and community life meet in the learning trajectories of students.

CONCLUSION

I see one of the major challenges to the study of human learning and development in complex settings as understanding the interplay of routine participation across multiple settings. In the case of the students discussed, it means understanding what dispositions, competencies, and belief systems they construct across their experiences with their families, within their peer social networks, in their community lives, and in school. The field's intervention efforts have tended to place bets on one setting, or to assume that a heavy emphasis on one setting can compensate for or overcome perceived limitations in another setting. If only life were that simple. With Cultural Modeling, we have placed our bets on designing spaces in schools where students can use mediational resources they employ in other settings as tools to be extended in school. In many ways, understanding how participation in multiple activity settings and participation at different levels of context – home, school, within various social networks – work together in learning and development is the fundamental challenge that Vygotsky and colleagues posed. It remains a challenge, conceptually, methodologically, and from a design perspective in terms of affecting educational practices. My purposes in this chapter are to emphasize again the continuing need to understand how culture is the web that weaves human participation in activity together and to situate African American culture at the center of the learning and development of African American students. Just as Vygotsky wanted to contribute to the development of a society in which the needs of those not privileged with capital were addressed, so the work of those who try to build culturally responsive school environments aims to help youngsters become both culturally competent members of their home communities and effective participants in a civil democratic society (Ladson-Billings, 1994)

References

Bakhtin, M. M. (1981). *The dialogic imagination: Four essays by M. M. Bakhtin.* (M. Holquist, Ed.). Austin: University of Texas Press.

Ball, A. F. (1992). Cultural preferences and the expository writing of African-American adolescents. *Written Communication, 9*(4), 501–532.

Bereiter, C., & Engelmann, S. (1966). *Teaching disadvantaged children in pre-school.* Englewood Cliffs, NJ: Prentice Hall.

Bernstein, B. (1970). Social class, language, and socialization. In P. P. Giglioli (Ed.), *Language and social context* (pp. 157–178). Harmondsworth, England: Penguin.

Bourdieu, P. (1990). *The logic of practice.* (Richard Nice, Trans.). Stanford, CA: Stanford University Press.

Brofenbrenner, U. (1979). *The ecology of human development: Experiment by nature and design.* Cambridge MA.: Harvard University Press.

Cazden, C. (1988). *Classroom discourse: The language of teaching and learning.* Portsmouth, NH: Heinemann.

Cole, M. (1996). *Cultural psychology, a once and future discipline.* Cambridge, MA: The Belknap Press of Harvard University Press.

Duranti, A. (1997). *Linguistic anthropology.* New York: Cambridge University Press.

Goffman, E. (1981). *Forms of talk.* Philadelphia: University of Pennsylvania Press.

Graves, B., & Frederiksen, C. H. (1996). A cognitive study of literary expertise. In R. J. Kruez, & M. S. MacNealy (Eds.), *Empirical approaches to literature and aesthetics* (pp. 397–418). Norwood, NJ: Ablex.

Gumperz, J. (1982). *Discourse Strategies.* New York: Cambridge University Press.

Gutierrez, K., Rymes, B., & Larson, J. (1995). Script, Counterscript, and Underlife in the Classroom: James Brown versus Brown v. Board of Education. *Harvard Educational Review, 65*(3), 445–471.

Halasz, L. (1987). Cognitive and social psychological approaches to literary discourse. In L. Halasz (Ed.), *Literary discourse: Aspects of cognitive and social psychological approaches* (pp. 1–37). New York: Walter de Gruyter.

Kintsch, W. (1998). *Comprehension: A paradigm for cognition.* New York: Cambridge University Press.

Kuhn, D. (1991). *The skills of argument.* New York: Cambridge University Press.

Ladson-Billings, G. (1994). *The Dreamkeepers.* San Francisco: Jossey-Bass.

Lee, C. D. (1993). *Signifying as a scaffold for literary interpretation: The pedagogical implications of an African American discourse genre* (Research Report Series). Urbana, IL: National Council of Teachers of English.

Lee, C. D. (1995a). A culturally based cognitive apprenticeship: Teaching African American high school students' skills in literary interpretation. *Reading Research Quarterly, 30*(4), 608–631.

Lee, C. D. (1995b). Signifying as a scaffold for literary interpretation. *Journal of Black Psychology, 21*(4), 357–381.

Lee, C. D. (1998). Supporting the development of interpretive communities through metacognitive instructional conversations in culturally diverse classrooms. Paper presented at the Annual Conference of the American Educational Research Association. San Diego, California.

Lee, C. D. (2000). Signifying in the zone of proximal development. In C. D. Lee, & P. Smagorinsky (Ed.), *Vygotskian perspectives on literacy research: Constructing meaning through collaborative inquiry* (pp. 191–225). New York: Cambridge University Press.

Lee, C. D. (2001). Is October Brown Chinese: A cultural modeling activity system for underachieving students. *American Educational Research Journal, 38*(1), 97–142.

Lee, C. D., & Majors, Y. J. (2000). Cultural modeling's response to Rogoff's challenge: Understanding apprenticeship, guided participation and participatory appropriation in a culturally responsive, subject matter specific context. Paper presented at the Annual Meeting of the American Educational Research Association, New Orleans.

Lee, C. D., Mendenhall, R., Rivers, A., & Tynes, B. (1999). Cultural modeling: A framework for scaffolding oral narrative repertoires for academic narrative writing. Paper presented at the Multicultural Narrative Analysis Conference at the University of South Florida, Tampa.

Leontiev, A. N. (1981). The problem of activity in psychology. In J. V. Wertsch (Ed.), *The concept of activity in Soviet psychology.* Armonk, NY: M. E. Sharpe.

Luria, A. R. (1976). *Cognitive development: Its cultural and social foundations.* Cambridge, MA: Harvard University Press.

Mehan, H. (1979). *Learning lessons.* Cambridge, MA: Harvard University Press.

Morrison, T. (1987). *Beloved.* New York: Alfred A. Knopf.

Mufwene, S. (Ed.) (1993). *Africanisms in Afro-American language varieties.* Athens: The University of Georgia Press.

Orr, E. W. (1987). *Twice as less: Black English and the performance of Black students in mathematics and science.* New York: Norton.

Rogoff, B. (1990). *Apprenticeship in thinking: Cognitive development in social context.* New York: Oxford University Press.

Rogoff, B., & Lave, J. (Eds.) (1984). *Everyday cognition: Its development in social context.* Cambridge, MA: Harvard University Press.

Smitherman, G. (1977). *Talkin and testifyin: The language of Black America.* Boston: Houghton Mifflin.

Smitherman, G. (1994). The blacker the berry, the sweeter the juice: African American student writers. In A. Dyson, & C. Genishi (Eds.), *The need for story: Cultural diversity in classroom and community* (pp. 80–101). Urbana, IL: National Council of Teachers of English.

Smitherman, G. (2000). *Talk that talk: Language, culture and education in African America.* New York: Routledge.

Stotsky, S. (1999). *Losing our language: How multicultural classroom instruction is undermining our children's ability to read, write, and reason.* New York: Free Press.

Toulmin, S., Rieke, R., & Janik, A. (1984). *An introduction to reasoning.* New York: Macmillan.

van den Broek, P. (1996). Causal inferences in the comprehension of literary texts. In R. J. Kreuz, & M. S. MacNealy (Eds.), *Empirical approaches to literature and aesthetics*. Norwood, NJ: Ablex.

Vygotsky, L. (1978). *Mind in Society: The Development of Higher Psychological Processes*. Cambridge, MA: Harvard University Press.

Vygotsky, L. (1981). The genesis of higher mental functions. In J. Wertsch (Ed.), *The concept of activity in Soviet psychology* (pp. 144–188). Armonk, NY: M. E. Sharpe.

Vygotsky, L. (1987). *Thinking and Speech*. New York: Plenum.

Wertsch, J. (1991). *Voices of the mind: A sociocultural approach to mediated action*. Cambridge, MA: Harvard University Press.

19

The Relations of Learning and Student Social Class

Toward Re-"socializing" Sociocultural Learning Theory

Carolyn P. Panofsky

In his theory of mind, Vygotsky proposes three forms of mediation: tools, signs and symbols (semiosis), and social interaction. Most Vygotskian sociocultural research has focused on the semiotic form of mediation to address cognitive challenges in education. Whereas semiotic mediation relies on social interaction, and social interaction has often comprised the "unit of analysis," the mediation of social interaction itself largely remains to be unpacked. Even though some studies have investigated the processes of cooperation or collaboration in learning, the dynamics of those processes as social relations have not received extensive examination in Vygotskian research. The mediation of social relations – the dynamics of power, position, social location in the social interaction of learning – is of profound significance in education. Nowhere is the importance of social relations in learning more evident than in the dynamics of social class in schooling.

Yet the dynamic of social relations has been shown to be central in the experience of failure for many low-income students, although literature on these relations has only rarely informed sociocultural studies in education. As researchers concerned with students' learning, sociocultural theorists need to examine the matter of social relations of those we study, for these social relations are a key mediator of students' school learning. Ideally, the perspective of sociocultural theory is able to integrate levels of analysis from the macrolevels of culture to the microlevels of social interaction and individual thinking and speech. The research to be discussed here shows that the dynamic of social relations in the social interaction of learning comprises a critical piece in understanding the articulation and integration of levels. This chapter revisits the literature on the social relations of

Many thanks to the editors Vladimir Ageyev and Alex Kozulin, and to Carl Ratner, for comments on an earlier draft of this chapter.

411

schooling for low-income learners with an eye to ways that sociocultural theory may be informed by that work and to ways that sociocultural theory may inform the conception of low-income learners' experience of differential social relations in schooling.

BACKGROUND: VYGOTSKY AND "CLASS"

Researchers have theorized the workings of class in education in various ways, but sociocultural theory can offer an important new dimension. What is "class," and how does it operate in learning? The sociocultural approach of Vygotsky and others opens the way to answer such questions.

Vygotsky was influenced by a number of social theorists. In his work he refers to Durkheim, Hegel, Marx, and others (see Kozulin, 1990, especially chapter 4). In particular, Vygotsky's repeated references to Marx appear when Vygotsky's comments are particularly relevant to social or interpersonal relations. One key shared conception is the sociogenetic relation between the individual and society. In a discussion of consciousness, Vygotsky (1997b) wrote, "The social moment in consciousness is primary in time as well as in fact. The individual aspect is constructed as a derived and secondary aspect on the basis of the social aspect and exactly according to its model" (p. 77). In the following well-known quotation from Marx, which Vygotsky alludes to in his own work (e.g., 1993, p. 162), Marx emphasizes the *relational* dimension of society in the development of consciousness:

> The general result at which I arrived and which, once won, served as a guiding thread for my studies, can be briefly formulated as follows: In the social production of their life, men enter into *definite relations* that are indispensable and independent of their will, relations of production which correspond to a definite stage of development of their material productive forces. The sum total of these relations . . . correspond [to] definite *forms of social consciousness*. . . . *It is not the consciousness of men that determines their being, but, on the contrary their social being that determines their consciousness.* (Tucker, 1978, p. 4; emphasis added)

Vygotsky explored the significance of social relations to the formation of consciousness in an article translated as "The Socialist Alteration of Man" (1994). Commenting on the relationship between base and superstructure that Marx alludes to in the passage, Vygotsky wrote,

> The influence of the basis on the psychological superstructure of man turns out to be not direct, but mediated by a large number of very complex material and spiritual factors. But even here, the basic law of historical human development, which proclaims that human beings are created by the society in which they live and that it represents the determining factor in the formation of their personalities, remains in force. (p. 176)

Vygotsky goes on to emphasize that "class character, class nature and class distinctions...are responsible for the formation of human types" (1994, p. 176).

Although the connection here between class and personality may be stated too baldly, this passage is important for raising the issue of pluralism and the importance of considering class for developing a pluralistic perspective on learning and development. In his volume on *Educational Psychology* (1997a), Vygotsky writes that the "social environment is class-based in its very structure insofar as, obviously, all new relations are imprinted by the class basis of the environment.... Consequently, class membership defines at one fell swoop both the cultural and the natural orientation of personality in the environment" (pp. 211–212).

However, Vygotsky did not research the functioning of class in schooling; nor did he fully develop his conception of "the mediation by a large range of very complex and spiritual factors" that contribute to the formation of diverse forms of class character. He did, though, identify both the labor process and the institutional process of schooling as comprising social systems and sites that are significant in the production of personality and human psychology. This discussion aims to explore the school experience of low-income students as a site in the production of their identity as learners and to highlight ways that the interpersonal or social relations of the classroom mediate students' learning. Despite more than 20 years of Vygotskian-inspired research in education in the United States, little consideration has been given to the school per se as a site or a social system in which class mediates the formation of the personality and psychology of the learner. But just as Marx claimed the workplace as a key site in the production of the "social being" of adults, so the school may be considered a key site in the production of the social being of the young; and the student's social being has significant implications for her or his life as a learner. The discussion will explore the "definite relations" to which learners may be subject in schools and the implications those relations have for them as learners – and, in turn, for a Vygotskian sociocultural theory of learning. In particular, I address the issue of social class difference to examine students' social being and consciousness as learners, asking, "What is known about the 'relations of learning' for students from low-income backgrounds and how do these relations mediate their learning?"

I turn, for this discussion, to key ethnographic studies of social class difference in the lived experience of learners. Cole (1996) has encouraged workers in sociocultural studies of education to combine their research with that of researchers in other disciplines to study "the institutional settings of those activities-in-context.... [F]rom a cultural–historical perspective this level of analysis is important as a site where large-scale factors such as social class articulate with individual experience" (p. 340). In particular, a number of ethnographic studies of poor and working-class children in schools, elementary through high school, suggest the importance for a Vygotskian theory of learning of looking closely at issues of social relations, including power and conflict in the dynamics of institutional learning. I will use a few of these texts to illustrate the significance of these concerns for Vygotskian theory. First, however, I will clarify the ways culture and social class are used in this discussion.

FRAMEWORK FOR THE EXAMINATION OF
SOCIAL CLASS IN SCHOOLING

Vygotsky wrote that "children grow into the intellectual life of those around them" (1978, p. 88). In time, Vygotsky notes, the individual's environment undergoes change when "it expands to participation in societal production" (Vygotsky, 1998, p. 43). Children grow into the life of those around them, and those life spaces are multiple and varied. Of course, between the time that children grow into the life of the family and later into the life of "societal production," they also grow into the life of the school. As the environment expands, Vygotsky points out, the young also develop shared interests and life activity with a specific socioeconomic group: "The history of the school-age child and the youth is the history of very intensive development and formulation of class psychology and ideology" (ibid.).

Thus, Vygotsky noted the pluralistic nature of development and the importance of class in that variation. Leontev (1981), too, in discussing the concept of activity, identifies the relevance of social structures in all human activity:

> If we removed human activity from the *system of social relationships and social life*, it would not exist and would have no structure. With all its varied forms, the human individual's activity is a system in the system of social relations. It does not exist without these relations. The specific form in which it exists is determined by the forms and means of material and mental social interaction... [which depends on the individual's] place in society." (1981, p. 47; emphasis added)

Going further, Leont'ev argues that desires, emotions, motives are all produced in and through the system of social relations, just as are cognitive processes. He writes that desire is "a factor that guides and regulates the agent's concrete activity in the objective environment.... [The formation of desires] is explained by the fact that in human society the objects of desire are *produced*, and the desires themselves are therefore also produced.... We can say the same thing about emotions or feelings" (1981, pp. 49–50; emphasis in original). Leont'ev's conceptualization of the formation of desires and feelings becomes significant in attempting to understand students' lived experience in schooling and the formation of student identities, their ways of acting or forms of agency, and their transformation over time in the cultural processes of schooling. Although Vygotsky and

Leont'ev refer primarily to family and work settings as sites in the production of consciousness, the school is clearly also an important activity setting in the system of social relations.

The notions provided by Vygotsky and Leont'ev are important for providing a conception of cultural processes and their production and for alluding to the larger dynamics of power and conflict at play at the societal level. But more attention should be given to the specific ways that activity shapes psychological phenomena, especially because the workings of power and conflict in the macrolevel of social life and their reflection in the microlevel of social relations are so little discussed. Ratner (2000), however, has assembled the dimensions of Vygotsky's conceptualization of culture and added specificity in ways that can aid in the articulation of micro- and macrolevels of the analysis of particular examples. Ratner identifies five main kinds of cultural phenomena: cultural activities; cultural values, schemas, meanings, and concepts; physical artifacts; psychological phenomena; and agency. Because of the importance of Ratner's formulation in the analysis to follow, I will quote his discussion of the five main kinds in full:

1. *Cultural activities* such as producing goods, raising and educating children, making and enforcing policies and laws, providing medical care. It is through these activities that humans survive and develop themselves. They are basic to the ways in which individuals interact with objects, people, and even oneself.
2. *Cultural values, schemas, meanings, concepts.* People collectively endow things with meaning. Youth, old age, man, woman, bodily features, wealth, nature, and time mean different things in different societies.
3. *Physical artifacts* such as tools, books, paper, pottery, eating utensils, clocks, clothing, buildings, furniture, toys, games, weapons and technology which are collectively constructed.
4. *Psychological phenomena* such as emotions, perception, motivation, logical reasoning, intelligence, memory, mental illness, imagination, language, and personality are collectively constructed and distributed.
5. *Agency.* Humans actively construct and reconstruct cultural phenomena. This "agency" is directed at constructing cultural phenomena and it is also influenced by existing cultural activities, values, artifacts, and psychology. (Ratner, 2000, p. 4)

These five kinds of phenomena are clearly interlocking and interdependent, each embodying the distinctive character of the others within itself. For example, "Agency originates in, reflects, and facilitates activities, concepts, artifacts, and psychological phenomena" (p. 4). These five dimensions give specificity to the analysis of school contexts and activities.

In addition to a conceptualization of culture, a conception of social class is necessary for this discussion. A long history of sociological study of class has produced many conceptions and divergent views of social class. Here,

I take an approach offered by Pierre Bourdieu, who takes what he calls a "relational" rather than a "substantialist" or categorical approach to the conception of social class. He denies the existence of classes, in themselves, but argues that differences in social space are continually being enacted; hence "classes" are relational. Bourdieu asks, must we "accept or affirm the existence of classes? No. Social classes do not exist.... What exists is a social space, a space of differences, in which classes exist in some sense in a state of virtuality, not as something given but as *something to be done*" (1998, p. 12). Social space is an "invisible reality that cannot be shown but which organizes agents' practices and representations" (1998, p. 10). The practices and representations organized by social class construct distance or prox- imity between students and teachers and work through teacher–student interaction to differentiate students' experiences, as will be seen later.

Bourdieu's conception is especially well suited to sociocultural theory because he develops a theory of action and focuses on the analysis of prac- tices. His focus on differences that are enacted, rather than seen as static group characteristics, is particularly relevant to dynamics of class in school- ing. Although his writing is dense and complex, Bourdieu states that his perspective can be "condensed in a small number of fundamental con- cepts – *habitus*, field, capital – and its cornerstone is the two-way relation- ship between objective structures (those of social fields) and incorporated structures (those of the *habitus*)" (Bourdieu, 1998, p. vii). *Social space* is con- ceived as a kind of field, distributing and differentiating individuals by "economic capital and cultural capital. It follows that all agents are located in this space in such a way that the closer they are to one another in those two dimensions, the more they have in common; and the more remote they are from one another, the less they have in common" (1998, p. 6). The *habitus* represents the embodiment or incorporation of this relational structure. It is the

generative principle which retranslates the intrinsic and relational characteristics of a position [in social space] into a unitary lifestyle, that is, a unitary set of choices of persons, goods, practices.... [W]hat the worker eats, and especially the way he eats it, the sport he practices and the way he practices it.... But the essential point is that, when perceived through these social categories of perception, these principles of vision and division, the differences in practices, in the goods possessed, or in the opinions expressed become *symbolic differences and constitute a veritable language*. (1998, p. 8; emphasis added)

Here is the key to the analysis of school culture: The structures of differentiation and perception compose a language that everyone reads and understands, albeit out of awareness. Such readings function as what Bourdieu calls a "logic of symbolic violence... according to which domi- nated lifestyles are almost always perceived, even by those who live them, from the destructive and reductive point of view of the dominant aesthetic"

(1998, p. 9). When these structures of differentiation operate (as they culturally and historically have), they produce the sorting mechanism in schooling. The dominant lifestyle, in this way, enacts the "logic" of symbolic violence. Although *symbolic violence* may appear an exaggerated or overly dramatic term, it has real and specific meaning and is used to *denaturalize*, to specify the objectification through evaluation that differentiates opportunities (e.g., unquestioned hierarchies of high and low "ability" produced through identification of dialect or by testing). It is important to note that the cultural workings of the dominant aesthetic in schooling are largely invisible, appearing "natural," and are not to be understood as maliciously enacted by educators. Rather, the logic of symbolic violence is part of the out-of-awareness culture that analysis seeks to make visible. As Cole has suggested, the practices we study need to be located in a larger social field than they frequently are in our relatively microanalyses of activity. Bourdieu's concepts of field, *habitus,* and capital can help to do that, in conjunction with a conception of culture that seeks the unification of material, ideal, practice, subjectivity, and agency.

ETHNOGRAPHIC STUDIES OF SOCIAL CLASS DIFFERENCE IN SCHOOLS

Numerous studies by ethnographic researchers have focused on the issue of social class as a factor in schools and classrooms, and many of these are of significance here. Examples can be cited addressing all ages of learner populations, from preschool through college; addressing the full range of school settings, urban, suburban, and rural; considering all regions of the United States as well as other countries; and covering numerous subgroups across a range of ethnic, cultural, and racial identities. Rather than attempting to survey this literature, I choose to examine a few key studies in depth. The studies chosen here present important, revealing work, but the findings of each can be explicated in greater depth through application of the theories just summarized. Furthermore, applying these theories to a few classic studies illustrates how sociocultural theory can be articulated with sociological and anthropological studies of the workings of social class in schooling.

I will begin with consideration of two studies that examine children in the earliest years of public schooling. One study examines social class in a school where all students and adult personnel were Black; the other study compares classrooms in two schools in a community that was essentially all White. The similarity in findings across the two studies helps to clarify the relevance of social class difference to schooling. The first study to be considered was conducted by Ray Rist. Although Rist conducted the study more than 30 years ago, its influence has been long lived, and in 2000 the article was republished in the *Harvard Education Review* as a "classic" because of its ongoing relevance. The site of Rist's study was an "urban ghetto school" in which "all administrators, teachers, staff, and pupils [were] black" (1970/2000, p. 271) and more than half of the students had families who were receiving economic assistance. The study site and teachers were considered "as good as any in the city" (p. 271). Significantly, Rist found that class distinction was widely reflected in the adults' treatment of the students.

Rist identifies a profound pattern that was established before the end of the second week of kindergarten and appeared to define children's schooling from that time forward. On the eighth day of kindergarten, the teacher placed the children into three reading groups that she regarded as reflecting ability. The placement was based on no testing, as none had been done. In attempting to account for the way the placements were made, Rist identifies all sources of information available to the teacher. Before the beginning of school, the teacher had information about each child from parental registration forms (such as whether the child had attended preschool), from the social worker (whether the family received assistance, as did 55% of the school population), and from other teachers (such as whether an older sibling was "a trouble maker"). Once school began, the teacher appeared to begin favoring children who were dressed in newer and cleaner clothing and spoke in a dialect similar to standard. Even sooner than the children were placed in three groups of high, middle, and low ability, Rist noticed that a favored group had emerged – those the teacher called on to lead activities and to answer questions and who later all appeared in the high group. This is the logic of symbolic violence that Bourdieu refers to, reflecting the workings of the social space and the remoteness and proximity of agents and revealing the way an economic hierarchy of social relations is enacted in the classroom. The identifiable commonalities in the high group were material and class-identified: The children were dressed in newer, cleaner clothing, and their dialect of English more closely approximated the middle-class standard.

Over time, Rist found multiple levels on which the symbolic violence was manifested in line with the teacher's structuring of the three ranked groups and produced an economy in the class that represented a robust hierarchy of privilege within the classroom. The teacher gives her time and attention to the Table 1 "high-group" students and all but ignores students at Tables 2 and 3 during instruction. When the teacher does direct her attention to Tables 2 and 3, she delivers negative messages to the students; Table 1 never receives negative messages. Both the high- and lower-group students internalize the norms of value and privilege by treating each other according to a shared set of values: The Table 1 high-group students mistreat the Table 2 and 3 students, both physically and verbally. The Table 2 and Table 3 students also mistreat each other – but never the Table 1 students.

Rist accounts for the teacher's behavior in terms of a "normative reference group," by which she would identify individual students having characteristics she associates with being most like her own academically successful middle-class group, and least similar to those of the less privileged students. Bourdieu's notions of social field, *habitus*, and capital can give more specificity to the finding: The teacher appears to favor students who are located similarly to her in the social field, displaying a *habitus* that reflects similar cultural and economic capital. The student *habitus* includes "coming from a family that is educated [through high school], employed, living together.... demonstrating ease of interaction among adults; high degree of verbalization in Standard American English; the ability to become a leader; a neat and clean appearance ... and the ability to participate well as a member of a group" (Rist, 1970/2000, p. 276). Rist finds similar patterns of social relations between teacher and students and between groupings of children when he follows the children into Grades 2 and 3. In particular, he finds increasing disaffection from classroom activity among the Table 2 and 3 students, manifested either as "acting out" through verbal and behavioral resistance to school work or as apathy in the form of work not done.

Viewing Rist's findings through the lens of Ratner's (2000) five dimensions of culture highlights the potential formation of differential *habitus* in the experience of schooling itself. Rist's findings suggest that the lower-group children's lived experience of schooling differs substantially from that of those in the privileged group in terms of all five dimensions of culture identified by Ratner: (a) teachers engage the high-group children in more prestigeous *cultural activities,* and these activities offer greater opportunities for academic learning; (b) teachers endow the groups with different *values* through use of verbal and nonverbal messages so that subgroup identities of high and low social value are assigned; (c) lesser value is linked to *physical conditions* of tables and locations, as the lower-group tables are more distant from the teacher and the chalkboard, out of view of both, and more crowded; (d) the emotional and motivational experiences of rejection versus desirability construct differential classroom *psychologies;* (e) the different groups appear to reflect differential constructions of *agency,* as the privileged children conform to teacher and school values, whereas the stigmatized lower-group children enact either active or passive resistance in the forms of either oppositional behavior or disengagement. Over time, the development of increasingly different "durable dispositions" or *habitus* seems quite likely, with potential for diminished opportunities for some and diminished humanity for all.[1]

---

[1] In case the result of differential ways of acting may be thought simply to reflect differences in ability, Rist offers some telling details from visits to low-group students' homes: He discovers that children have actually learned material from classroom instruction either that

The point here, then, is not simply to revisit the literature on the effect of differential teacher expectations. Rather, this discussion seeks to explain the schooling of low-income children as a *cultural activity* with distinctive *social relations* because the character of such activity and of such relations is central to the development of children as learners, the development of their learners' *habitus* and school identity, which can powerfully mediate children's learning. If so, these dimensions are essential in the construction of a sociocultural theory of learning.

A second important study of social class as a factor in early schooling was conducted by Kathleen Wilcox (1988). Unlike Rist, Wilcox studied classrooms in two schools for 1 year in a controlled-comparison design. She, too, used ethnographic observation, here in two first-grade classrooms in the same district, one in an upper-middle-class (UMC) neighborhood school, the other in a lower-middle-class (LMC) one. Both the teachers and almost all the children were White. Wilcox's findings are very similar to Rist's (with African American teachers and children), and there are no discrepant findings between the two studies. Wilcox, however, uncovers further dimensions of differential expectations and treatment. Recall that Rist found more controlling behavior directed to children from less privileged backgrounds. Relatedly, Wilcox found qualitative differences in the ways teachers verbally controlled higher- (UMC) and lower- (LMC) status children. She identified "external control" language and "internal control" language. In *external control*, the teacher simply directed the child or children, for example, "I want that done now" or "You have an assignment; sit down and get busy" (Wilcox, 1988, p. 288). In *internal control* language, the teacher emphasized the children's internalizing of responsibility, as in "Will this misbehavior help you to become a better reader?" or "Be fair to yourself; use your time wisely to help you become a better reader" (Wilcox, 1988, p. 290). Wilcox found striking differences in the distribution of the teachers' uses of internal and external strategies and messages of control:

| UMC classroom | 39% Internal strategies | 59% Internal messages |
| LMC classroom | 9% Internal strategies | 10% Internal messages |

In order to determine whether such differences simply reflected individual teacher variation, Wilcox also separated each class into the top and bottom half of readers, with the following result:

Children in the top half of the reading groups in both classrooms received significantly more internal messages than children in the bottom half of the reading groups in the two classrooms ($p = .005$). They also received significantly more internal

their classroom performance does not display or that they are not given the opportunity to display. This information tends to belie an interpretation of ability difference and, even, to suggest the opposite: Despite being ignored during instruction, the low-group students were learning material that was being taught quite directly to others, but not to them.

academic messages ($p = .046$). Thus, an internal approach, particularly with respect to academic interactions, is associated in both classrooms with children who are perceived to have the highest ability level and future potential. (pp. 290–291)

In addition, Wilcox found that the higher-status children were given many more opportunities to develop what she calls "self-presentation skills" such as speaking and presenting before the group and that they received considerable guidance in and praise for doing so. The higher-status children were also given considerable focus on the future, "what you will become and therefore need to prepare for." The teacher of the higher-status children voiced her expectations eight times more frequently about their futures and emphasized going to college, whereas the teacher of the lower-status children was never observed referring to college. Of the teacher of the LMC children, Wilcox writes, "The most remarkable characteristic of Mrs. Jones' approach to the future of the children in her classroom was that she virtually ignored it" (p. 295).

Wilcox gives considerable attention to trying to place the pattern of identified differences into the larger sociocultural context in order to account for her troubling findings. She finds no evidence that the differential forms of treatment occurred *in response* to ways children acted; on the contrary, they were *initiated by school personnel*. Wilcox writes "Interviews with teachers themselves made it clear that they felt they were allowing and encouraging each child to develop and progress as far as each was able; they would have been shocked at any accusation of differential treatment based on social class" (p. 295).

What Wilcox finds is a *disconnect* between general commitments to equality and specific beliefs about the families and home lives of the children in the schools at the level of the school staff, the district staff, and the state educational apparatus. At the level of the school, she concludes that the "social class level of the neighborhood was a very salient characteristic in the minds of the staff at both schools. It generated general levels of expectations for children in each neighborhood which could be seen to influence the behavior of the teachers in the classroom" (Wilcox, 1988, p. 298). These differences appeared to have "strikingly different consequences in terms of the staff's reaction to individual learning problems on the part of individual children" (ibid.). A UMC child having a learning problem, for example, would receive multiple forms of assistance until the problem was solved, whereas an LMC child would receive no assistance because the problem was seen as "to be expected."

Wilcox's findings at the district and state levels reflected analogous patterns of differential expectations associated with social class.[2] Wilcox

---

[2] At the district level, the test scores of the UMC school were readily given out and shown off, whereas scores for the LMC school were withheld and the researchers were told that "the schools' achievement scores could not be given out" (Wilcox, 1988, p. 298), necessitating

concludes, "Most significant is the fact that all of the factors used to determine the level of expectations are factors *outside* the classroom walls. The implication is, unavoidably, that what is really important in terms of achievement are the characteristics a child brings from home rather than what takes place at school" (pp. 299–300). Ultimately, however, Wilcox does not indict the individual personnel at all levels of the educational system, but instead suggests that "the educational personnel observed in this study behaved no differently than one could expect any cultural beings to behave in the situation" (Wilcox, 1988, p. 302).

Wilcox's conclusion presents a significant challenge to educational innovation aimed only at the level of learning and instruction:

> The research findings suggest that many popular educational reforms are likely simply to rearrange the appearance of classroom interaction, leaving the substance of what takes place in the classroom largely untouched. This is because the reforms are conceptualized and introduced with little understanding of the powerful cultural influences at work in the classroom. (Wilcox, 1988, p. 303)

Employing Ratner's five dimensions again, as with Rist's study, there are signficant ways that Wilcox's findings add to conceptualizing the cultural production of student *habitus*. The differential focus on internal strategies and differential frequency of internal messages constitute specific cultural activities and cultural values (a and b); these, in turn, contribute to differentiation in psychology, particularly motivation (d), and produce significant differences in students' sense of agency (e). Similarly, the differential access to the activity of self-presentation (a) contributes to differential development of language, memory, and related cognitive processes (d), as well as to sense of agency (e).

The final investigation of first-grade classrooms to be discussed expands the significance of differential relations to specific curricular content. James Collins (1986) investigated the ways in which patterns of differential treatment such as those identified by Rist and Wilcox become translated into differential instruction in reading groups. Collins examined first-grade reading lessons in high and low groups of the same class, conducted by both a senior teacher and a regular teacher's aide, across the school year. The class was divided into four reading groups, considered low (1), mid (2),

---

extensive negotiation between the researchers and the district. Wilcox writes that officials gave the explanation that scores were not given out because parents complained about them. She adds, "A high-level district official said with considerable indignation that the parents simply did not understand that the scores were *a direct consequence of the average IQ and socioeconomic level of the neighborhood*" (Wilcox, 1988, pp. 298–299; emphasis in original). A similar attitude was reflected at the state level in the construction of a statistic that computed "an expected test score range for each district and for each school within the state" based on socioeconomic status and related factors (such as pupil mobility rate and percentage of bilingualism).

high (3), and extra high (4); Collins compared groups 1 and 3, the low and the high groups. "High-group readers were from white professional families, low-group readers from Black working-class families" (Collins, 1986, p. 122). Referring to the contrast between the groups, Collins writes, "Since the two groups were homogeneous with regard to ethnic group and social class membership ... we could expect maximal contrasts in community-based speech styles and in such things as implicit teacher expectations" (ibid).

Collins's findings follow a pattern that is similar to those identified by Rist and Wilcox. He summarizes his findings as follows:

Comparison of the groups revealed a two-tiered structure of differential treatment. On one level, the more general one of amounts of time spent at the various types of instructional activities, low-group readers were given extensive sound-word identification drill, with little attention paid to the meaningfulness of the reading task, while their high-group counterparts were given much more practice in passage reading and the answering of questions about the material being read. On the other level, that of specific instructional procedures, correction of oral reading errors for low-group readers focused on grapheme-phoneme correspondences and word recognition, while corrections for the high group readers focused more on the semantics and pragmatics of text comprehension – in short on meaning. (Collins, 1986, pp. 122–123)

Collins develops a more fine-grained analysis of transcribed lessons of the small groups than can be fully presented here. Of particular significance for this discussion is that the interactional process of teacher–student exchanges in the small groups leads to two differing conceptions of what counts as reading being learned by the two groups of students. By examining features such as pauses, points of interruption, and intonation, Collins shows that the *teachers respond differently to equivalent errors in the two groups*: "Numerous examples taken from the entire corpus of sixteen lessons had shown that identical miscues prompted either decoding-focused or comprehension-focused corrections" (Collins, 1986, p. 129). That is, teachers' responses differ not necessarily because children have different skills; rather, they differ even when the children in the different groups make the same miscues. This finding clarifies another dimension of the workings of social space as it "organizes agents' practices," as suggested by Bourdieu. The same academic "mistake" is interpreted differently, depending on the relative positioning in social space; the act of the more spatially distanced is interpreted as less meaningful and less skillful. Such findings raise the question of whether the same "correct" answer also may be interpreted differentially, depending on social location.

As with the Rist and Wilcox findings, Collins's study also suggests differentiation in the several dimensions of culture specified in Ratner's model: differentiated instructional *activity* (a) constitutes differential ways of reading as a linguistic and cognitive *psychological process* (d); the specific content difference of a mechanical vs. a meaningful task also carries implications for differing *values and meanings* students learn to give to reading (b), as well as for differential constructions of *motivations and feelings* about reading (also d), and sense of *agency* in relation to reading (e).

Like Wilcox, Collins (1986) is careful to note that his analysis

> should not be construed as a condemnation of individual teachers, however. When we study conversational interaction in multi-ethnic situations we are looking for the effects of unconscious habits of organizing talk (prosodically, lexically, syntactically) on the unfolding interaction. But a participant, as an actor present in the situation, either as a teacher or student, cannot be expected to employ the analyst's detached perspective. Instead, he or she is busy in the process of assessing and responding to another's contributions. (p. 129)

The reference to "unconscious habits" that Collins offers recalls Bourdieu's assertions about the functioning of social fields. Teachers' socially constituted perceptions of students who are positioned most distant from them enact the logic of symbolic violence because the students are given lesser opportunities to learn through differential and differentiating instruction, as well as differential and differentiating interaction.

Overall, the studies of Collins, Wilcox, and Rist all suggest that the process of differential expectations and differential treatment of low-income learners is both out of awareness of educational personnel in all dimensions that the researchers observed and, at the same time, integral to the cultural processes of schooling in U.S. society.[3] The findings of the three studies strongly suggest that differential treatment in the process of schooling itself is of central importance to the development of a learner's sense of identity and agency. If one accepts that a child does not begin formal schooling with a "student *habitus*" fully formed, then it is important to recognize that schooling is not a "null space" in the production of the child's sense of herself or himself as a learner and her or his sense of what the practices and processes of schooling are about. Teachers and other educational personnel at all levels go to work with their own social and cultural dispositions, their *habitus* highly developed over years of lived experience in a stratified and stratifying society. Considerable reflection is required to denaturalize resulting subjectivities so that they might be transformed and that the relations of learning for low-income students could be transformed, in turn.

---

[3] Of course, there are many educators, both teachers and administrators, who are aware of such cultural processes and successfully resist them. The reality, however, is that they remain in the minority and that differential expectations for low-income and minority learners remain a major challenge if education is ever to achieve the ideal of equal opportunity and social justice.

DISCUSSION

The three studies reviewed all examined the earliest school experiences of low-income learners. How might the lived experiences of the students in these studies be extrapolated over the long span of 12 years of schooling? Vygotsky's general law of cultural development offers a way to approach this question:

Any function in the child's cultural development appears twice, or on two planes. First it appears on the social plane, and then on the psychological plane. First it appears between people as an interpsychological category, and then within the child as an intrapsychological category.... [I]t goes without saying that internalization transforms the process itself and changes its structure and functions. Social relations or relations among people genetically underlie all higher functions and their relationships. (Vygotsky, 1981, p. 163)

The three studies help to suggest how children's "cultural development" is differentiated in the processes of schooling. Similarly, Bourdieu's concept of the *habitus* complements Vygotsky's notion. The *habitus* is that "system of lasting ... dispositions which, integrating past experiences, functions at every moment as a *matrix of perceptions, appreciations, and actions*" (Bourdieu, 1977, p. 82). It is "history made nature" (1977, p. 78). The *habitus* is "embodied history, internalized as second nature and so forgotten as history ... *the active presence of the whole past of which it is the product*" (Bourdieu, 1990, p. 56, emphasis added). Vygotsky and Bourdieu are explaining the same phenomenon on their respective levels of focus, the psychological and the sociological. Thus, for example, Collins finds a low- and high-group reader making the same oral reading error, but one is corrected with decoding facts and the other is corrected with a meaning-making strategy. For the former, reading is experienced as an activity of making sound–symbol correspondences; for the latter it is an activity of making meaning from printed text. Studies of adolescents who are nonreaders or poor readers bear out the suggestion that their reading instruction was not focused on meaning-making and they have not known reading as a meaningful and engaging activity (e.g., see Mueller, 2001).

If students' experiences are consistently patterned as the studies of Rist, Wilcox, and Collins suggest, consider how school history might become second nature. How might students' differential "interpsychological" experiences construct differential "intrapsychological" student *habitus* and identity? Referring once again to Ratner's (2000) cultural dimensions, the ongoing *cultural activity* (a) of schooling is a lived experience of significant failure and rejection for some, but one of success and affirmation for others. For some children, schooling and literacy come to be endowed with positive and desirable *meanings and values* (b), whereas for others they are endowed with negative and aversive meanings and values or at least boring and meaningless activities. Some children in school have access to valued *artifacts* (c) such as the "high table" and the "high books," and others receive less valued artifacts and placements. For some children, the lived experience of schooling constructs *psychological phenomena* (d) of negative emotions and motivations toward school and restricts access to experiences that can promote the development of language, memory, logical reasoning and intelligence; conversely, for others schooling is an activity that promotes the production and distribution of positive phenomena and highly developed cognitive processes. Finally, some children develop a strong and positive sense of *agency* (e) in school activity, whereas others either see themselves as weak and incapable learning agents or manifest agency in the form of rejection of school activity, whether actively as oppositional behavior or passively as disinterest. The suggestion, then, is that student–teacher relations of learning that diverge widely in terms of meanings, values, activities, artifacts, agency, and feelings contribute to the production of divergent student identities.

What might be imagined for the students such as those in the studies of Rist, Wilcox, and Collins when they get to high school? What kind of school participation might be expected after 8 years of unrewarding school relations? Many studies of low-income students in secondary schools bear out the hypothesis of a "school-rejecting" student identity (e.g., Everhart, 1983; McLeod, 1987; Weis, 1985). In a study of working-class high school students, Weis (1990) found commonalities across studies of low-income secondary students. In particular, there is "the often overt and sometimes covert rejection of school meanings and culture. There is an attempt on the part of working-class youth to carve out their own space within the institution – space that can then be filled with their own meanings which are fundamentally antischool" (Weis, 1990, p. 18). Ironically, Weis found that deindustrialization and the attendant loss of high-paying jobs had led students to aspire to higher education. But, contradicting their explicit aspirations, students' actions belied negative valuations of academic learning and dispositions. Students have learned to view schooling merely as work to be completed, which then translates as "a ticket" to a better job. As students who have effectively been "outsiders" to educational success, they do not see any substantive value in the schooling itself. In this understanding, "passing" one's courses is thought to be enough to get on to higher education, but of course such a view leads to later failure when they go to college. Not surprisingly, working-class students do not have access to the cultural knowledge – in Bourdieu's language, the "cultural capital" – to understand how higher education actually "works."

An interpretation of Weis's finding is that the school identity produced through years of subordinate experience is not easily transformed to support late-adopted aspirations. A long history produces a deep-seated "second nature" requiring substantially different social relations to achieve transformation: A new intrapsychological process can best be produced through a different interpsychological process. Such transformation is difficult and unlikely, though not impossible (e.g., see Rose, 1989). Some authors, however, identify family and community as sources of the kinds of commonalities identified by Weis and others, reflecting a "shop-floor mentality" available in working-class families and communities. Although such sources of influence cannot be discounted, compelling counterevidence has been found in studies of low-track classes in highly affluent high schools, where non-working-class students presented the same resistant, subordinated school identity. For example, Page (1987) studied "unofficially low-tracked" classes in a "dream high school." The students in the classes studied by Page were overwhelmingly middle-class and upper-middle-class and did not evidence working-class identifications. However, these students received differentially less-valued curricula and instruction, which the students themselves frequently referred to as "baby work." Like the low-income secondary students studied by Weis and others, the students in Page's study had become similarly school-rejecting agents, practicing absenteeism, tardiness, and classroom behavior characterized alternately by misbehavior or sullen withdrawal. Page's contrasting student sample adds weight to the argument that school itself is a significant source of the student *habitus*.

The point is that at a high-status school, just as at a working-class school, a social space constructs teachers as distanced from the low-track group, who it happens, receive a less-valued curriculum and less-purposeful relations with teachers. In Page's words, "Teachers distance themselves from the lower-track [teaching] role, mocking themselves, the students and the educational enterprise in which they are jointly engaged" (p. 450). In the end, "encounters in the [lower track] classes become caricatures of the excellent education provided the college-bound" (p. 472).

IMPLICATIONS FOR SOCIOCULTURAL LEARNING THEORY

The intentions of this discussion have been to construct an understanding of the experience of schooling of low-income students in terms of interpersonal relations that mediate their learning and their experience of schooling and to set the conception of the relations of learning in the larger context of culture and society. The discussion points to a need in sociocultural theory for an expanded definition of culture, such as Ratner's, and for an articulated theory of social space, such as Bourdieu's, to account for the dynamics of conflict and power in learning and development. The differential experiences of schooling reflect larger conflicts in society and constitute a form of symbolic violence suffered by low-income learners. It is not surprising that over time students who share the experience of being "losers" in this conflict, and the objects of symbolic violence in Bourdieu's sense, may develop opposition to school. If "social being determines consciousness," it is not surprising that negative interpersonal relations in schooling are connected to rejection of the meanings of school. Vygotsky recognized this when he wrote that the negativism of the adolescent "arises mainly as a reaction to a rejecting effect of the environment... [such as] oppressive effects of the school situation" (1998, p. 22). It is important to underscore that the rejection of the meanings of school is a collective act, not an individual one per se, corresponding to the shared experience of rejection. Rather than the deviant act of separate individuals, school rejection is the collective act of students who share institutional histories. Vygotsky has also commented on the development of collective psychology:

> [W]e must present class psychology not as suddenly arising, but as gradually developing.... The history of the school-age child and the youth is the history of very intensive development and formulation of class psychology and ideology.... Class cohesion is formed as a result not of external imitation, but by shared life, activity, and interests. (1998, p. 43)

The studies reviewed show that the school is a significant context in which students may collectively have a "shared life, activity, and interests."

Sociocultural learning theory has explored deeply the role of signs and symbols in mediation but must more fully consider the ways that interpersonal relations mediate students' school lives and the consequences of these social relations for learning. The zone of proximal development (ZPD) is a notion from Vygotsky's work that has been widely referenced in contemporary educational theory and practice. But discussions and applications of the ZPD have not taken up the qualitative or differential aspects of interpersonal relations. Kris Gutierrez and her colleagues (Gutierrez, Baquedano-Lopez, & Tejeda, 1995) indirectly address social relations in their use of the "third space" as a way of conceptualizing the achievement of real dialogue between students and teacher in a classroom that is almost exclusively monologic. Gutierrez and associates point out that real change for disenfranchised students requires more than merely new methods of instruction; the nature of relations between teachers and learners must change. Similarly, Alan Davis and colleagues (Davis, 1996; Clarke, Davis, Rhodes, & Baker, 1996) have studied classrooms where low-income learners are successful. These are classrooms where low-income students who elsewhere would be labeled as having *low ability* are succeeding. The researchers find no particular teaching method or approach (such as "whole language" or "phonics") to be common to the successful classrooms. Instead, they find each classroom to have "a highly coherent and inclusive social system.... What is 'culturally compatible' about the classrooms we have studied is not their underlying values or the nature of activities in which students engage, but rather the development of relationships in which each person is valued and able to participate successfully" (pp. 25–26). It is not simply that teachers are "nice" to students in these classrooms: Students are respected and expected to learn highly valued curricula and to engage in critical thinking. But opportunity for meaningful teacher–student *relationship* is precisely the characteristic that *mediates* access to academically demanding content and has been missing from classrooms examined in this discussion. There are two important questions related to the zone of proximal development here. First, what does the teacher take the student's ZPD to be? The answer here will depend on whether the teacher perceives the student to be able or not able and whether the teacher perceives the student to be open to learning or resistant to learning; a perception of able and open seems more likely to gauge the location of the student's ZPD appropriately. Second, what does the student take to be the teacher's intentions relative to his or her learning? The student who experiences a respectful and trusting relationship with the teacher will be more likely to want to learn from the teacher and, thus, to engage in his or her ZPD. Thus, the likelihood of a teacher and a student to "enter" a student's "zone" seems contingent on their relations. (Of course, productive relations may also be relative to a student's cumulative prior school experiences, for a student who has lived through many years of degrading relations of learning, for example, may be "hard to reach" and require considerable relational skill of a teacher. Sociocultural learning theory needs to address such challenges.)

In many studies that involve ZPD, the relations of learning are not problematic. For example, in studies of parent–children interaction, the parents finely tune their interaction to the needs of the child, and they are highly attentive and sensitized to those needs. However, when interaction moves from the intimate and private familial setting to the formal setting of public school, the relations of learning are different and require additional attention and theory. The dynamics of the social relations between teachers and students should be examined in fine-grained ways to understand the ways those relations mediate students' learning. Case studies of teachers who work successfully with low-income learners offer an important way to study the ways social relations mediate learning. It will be important to observe the ongoing interactions of those teachers and students, as well as to gather accounts of the teachers whose social relations with low-income learners establish productive learning environments and to gather accounts of the learners themselves.

FINAL WORD

Although social groups have long been the subject of Vygotskian-inspired research, as in Luria's early study of urban, rural, and homeless children (Luria, 1978), there has been little work on low-income learners as a social group *within* the activity context of the school, particularly with the school understood as a social field in which social relations mediate learning. As Dewey (e.g., 1900) began urging more than a century ago, educators must take more account of the social dimension in schooling, and a place to focus is on the social relations between students and teachers. Similarly, feminists and many social scientists have criticized the absence of social considerations in numerous domains of study (e.g., Geertz, 1983; Martin, 1992; 1994; Sampson, 1989; 1993). Although Vygotskian-inspired approaches aim to situate the individual in social, cultural, and historical context, I suggest that sociocultural approaches to learning give greater consideration also to the social conception of the learner and to the relations of learning if a fully adequate theory of learning is to be constructed for education.

References

Bourdieu, P. (1977). *Outline of a theory of practice*. New York: Cambridge University Press.

Bourdieu, P. (1990). *The logic of practice*. Stanford, CA: Stanford University Press.

Bourdieu, P. (1998). *Practical reason*. Stanford, CA: Stanford University Press.

Clarke, M. A., Davis, A., Rhodes, L. K., & Baker, E. D. (1996). *The coherence of practice in effective teaching*. Higher Achieving Classrooms for Minority Students (HACMS) Project, University of Colorado at Denver. Available at http://carbon.cudenver.edu/~wdavis/beyondmt.html

Cole, M. (1996). *Cultural psychology: A once and future discipline*. Cambridge, MA: Harvard University Press.

Collins, J. (1986). Differential instruction in reading groups. In J. Cook-Gumperz (Ed.), *The social construction of literacy*. Cambridge: Cambridge University Press.

Davis, A. (1996, April 9). *Successful urban classrooms as communities of practice: Writing and identity*. Paper presented at American Educational Research Association, New York.

Dewey, J. (1900). The school and society. In *The child and the curriculum* and *The school and society* (Combined edition 1956), p. 6159. Chicago: University of Chicago Press.

Everhart, R. (1983). *Reading, writing and resistance: Adolescence and labor in a junior high school*. Boston: Routledge & Kegan Paul.

Geertz, C. (1983). "From the native's point of view": On the nature of anthropological understanding. In *Local knowledge: Further essays in interpretive anthropology* (pp. 55–70). New York: Basic Books.

Gutierrez, K., Baquedano-Lopez, P., & Tejeda, C. (1995). Rethinking diversity: Hybridity and hybrid language practices in the third space. *Mind, Culture and Activity, 6*(4), 286–303.

Kozulin, A. (1990). *Vygotsky's psychology: A biography of ideas*. Cambridge, MA: Harvard University Press.

Leontev, A. N. (1981). The problem of activity in psychology. In J. Wertsch (Ed.), *The concept of activity in Soviet psychology*. Armonk, NY: Sharpe.

Luria, A. (1978). Speech and intellect of rural, urban, and homeless children. In *Selected writings*, pp. 37–71. White Plains, NY: Sharpe.

MacLeod, J. (1987). *Ain't no makin' it: Leveled aspirations in a low-income neighborhood.* Boulder, CO: Westview Press.

Martin, J. R. (1992). *The schoolhome: Rethinking schools for changing families.* Cambridge, MA: Harvard University Press.

Martin, J. R. (1994). *Changing the educational landscape: Philosophy, women, and curriculum.* New York: Routledge.

Mueller, P. N. (2001). *Lifers: Learning from at-risk adolescent readers.* Portsmouth, NH: Heinemann.

Page, R. (1987). Lower-track classes at a college-preparatory high school: A caricature of educational encounters. In G. Spindler & L. Spindler (Eds.), *Interpretive ethnography of education: At home and abroad* (pp. 447–472). Hillsdale, NJ: Lawrence Erlbaum Associates.

Ratner, C. (2000). Outline of a coherent, comprehensive concept of culture. *Cross-Cultural Psychology Bulletin, 34*(1–2), 5–11. Available at http://www.humboldt1.com/~cr2/culture.htm

Rist, R. (1970/2000). Student social class and teacher expectations: The self-fulfilling prophecy in ghetto education. *Harvard Educational Review, 70*(3), 257–301.

Rose, M. (1989). *Lives on the boundary.* New York: Penguin.

Sampson, E. E. (1989). The deconstruction of the self. In J. Shotter & K. J. Gergen (Eds.), *Texts of identity* (pp. 1–19). London: Sage.

Sampson, E. E. (1993), *Celebrating the other: A dialogic account of human nature.* Boulder, CO: Westview Press.

Tucker, R. C. (1978). *The Marx-Engels reader* (2nd ed.). New York: Norton.

Vygotsky, L. S. (1962). *Thought and language.* Cambridge, MA: MIT Press.

Vygotsky, L. S. (1978). *Mind in society.* Cambridge, MA: Harvard University Press.

Vygotsky, L. S. (1981). The genesis of higher mental functions. In J. V. Wertsch (Ed.), *The concept of activity in Soviet psychology* (pp. 144–188). Armonk, NY: Sharpe.

Vygotsky, L. S. (1993). *The collected works of L. S. Vygotsky.* Vol. 2. *The fundamentals of defectology* (R. W. Rieber & A. S. Carton, Eds.). New York: Plenum.

Vygotsky, L. (1994). The socialist alteration of man. In R. van der Veer & J. Valsiner, (Eds.), *The Vygotsky reader* (pp. 175–184). Oxford: Blackwell.

Vygotsky, L. S. (1997a). *Educational psychology.* Boca Raton, FL: St. Lucie Press.

Vygotsky, L. S. (1997b). *The collected works of L. S. Vygotsky: Vol. 3. Problems of the theory and history of psychology* (R. W. Rieber & J. Wollock, Eds.). New York: Plenum.

Vygotsky, L. S. (1998). *The collected works of L. S. Vygotsky: Vol. 5. Child psychology.* R. W. Rieber (Ed.). New York: Plenum.

Weis, L. (1985). *Working class without work: High school students in a de-industrializing economy.* New York: Routledge.

Wilcox, K. (1988). Differential socialization in the classroom: Implications for equal opportunity. In G. Spindler (Ed.), *Doing the ethnography of schooling* (pp. 268–309). Prospect Heights, IL: Waveland Press.

20

Vygotsky in the Mirror of Cultural Interpretations

Vladimir S. Ageyev

When Vygotsky's theory became accessible to American scholars, it was interpreted, understood, and further developed according to American cultural and intellectual traditions. American scholars contributed much to the creative development of his ideas on all levels: theory, research, and applications. They also played a crucial role in spreading his ideas throughout the world. In this chapter, however, I will be dealing, predominantly, with some cultural biases in understanding Vygotsky's ideas. As Alex Kozulin (2002, personal communication) recently noticed:

On one hand, American scholars were instrumental in acquainting English speaking audiences with Vygotsky's ideas, on the other hand, in the process of this acquaintance Vygotsky's ideas underwent a rather strong Americanization. This trend became clear already when the first (abridged) translation of Vygotsky's *Thought and Language* edited by Bruner appeared in 1962 (Vygotsky, 1962). While empirical aspects of Vygotsky's work were retained, almost all poetic, philosophical and historical images were purged from this edition.

I have been fortunate in having firsthand experience with Vygotsky's ideas both in Russia and in America, first as a student and professor in Russia, and then as a professor in the United States. Many years of teaching courses on Vygotsky in the School of Psychology at Moscow State University and several years of teaching Vygotsky-related courses in American graduate schools of education have provided me with excellent materials on how different interpretations of his ideas can be. These variations go far beyond any individual differences – however wide the scope of individual differences may be. In my opinion, these variations represent a very consistent cultural pattern, a few aspects of which are discussed in this chapter.

Differently from A. Kozulin's (1995) article with the similar title, in which the author provides an overview of the major developments of Vygotsky's educational ideas throughout the world, and differently from a number of other research-oriented publications on the cultural context of Vygotsky's work (Bruner, 1987; 1995a; 1995b; Kozulin, 1984, 1998; van der Veer & Valsiner, 1991), the present chapter focuses, mainly, on the perception of Vygotsky's theory in a typical American classroom.

By analyzing my students' responses to Vygotsky's ideas through cultural lenses, I hope to bridge Vygotsky's sociocultural approach with modern cross-cultural theory and research. A few particular dimensions of intercultural variability – such as collectivism versus individualism and high-context communication versus low-context communication – on which Russia and the United States seem to be so drastically different (Alexander, 2000) are especially relevant for this purpose, as are some important differences in general intellectual traditions in both countries. I will also share some of the creative pedagogies that help me to facilitate understandings of "culturally difficult" Vygotskian texts among American students.

BIOLOGICAL AND INDIVIDUALISTIC REDUCTIONISM

The first few chapters of Vygotsky's *Mind and Society* (1978), as well as many other of his works (1997, 1998), contain many references to the research on intellect and problem solving in higher primates. Vygotsky needed these data as a point of reference in order to prove one of his major theoretical advancements about the unique role that language plays in the process of mediating the higher psychological functions' development. My students are very often confused that one of Vygotsky's major assumptions, his insistence on the uniquely human ability of using symbols, seems to contradict directly what they see as modern scientific evidence to the contrary. It takes some time and effort to explain that Vygotsky was not and did not pretend to be an expert on animal intellect or primate behavior, though, ironically enough, not long before his death, and as a result of increasing political pressure and his deteriorating health, he seriously considered moving from Moscow to Sukhumi (Georgia) to work there in the National Ape Refuge (Feigenberg, 1996). It is also important to note that many modern branches of studies on primates did not even exist in his time.

The ability of higher primates to use symbols and tools is a serious research question (Kozulin, 1990; Tomasello, 1999), the whole issue of which goes far beyond the purposes of this chapter. My major aim here is simply, by using examples like this one, to describe what I should call a biological and individualistic reductionism tendency in explaining human mind and society that most of my students have either in its explicit or implicit form. In some cases, the very assumption that human mind is not limited to brain activity and can be described as a product of a variety of different social forces in action does present a big challenge for many of my students. As one of them stated in response to reading the early chapters of *Mind in Society*: "I'm a self-made man, and nobody ever shaped me, or constructed me, or brainwashed me for that matter." To my surprise, this confusion between the theory of social constructivism and the process of ideological brainwashing seems to be quite common among my students.

So, the question arises, does Vygotsky's theory, in its very essence, contradict some core values of American culture? In my view this question is too important to neglect asking, and I believe the answer is yes. The very idea that human mind is so deeply shaped and formed by social interaction seems directly to contradict many prominent American values and ideals, such as individualism, independence, and self-reliance. I believe this contradiction explains why some of Vygotsky's concepts and ideas, such as the zone of proximal development (ZPD) and its application in cooperative learning, are enthusiastically accepted and promoted, whereas others, such as his collectivist interpretation of the nature of social interaction and teaching–learning processes, are sometimes neglected or rejected.

Vygotsky's resolute rejection of individualistic reductionism in explaining the development of human mind and society constitutes an essential part of his theory. It went along with his rejection of biological reductionism. One of the most consistent ideas of Vygotsky's work is his rejection of any attempt to use either individualistic or biological reductionism to explain the genesis and functioning of the human mind. Whatever simple or complex psychological processes were in question, Vygotsky had a real gift for demonstrating that the most interesting part, or component, of it is not inherited biologically, but caused by and originated in a specific set of social interactions (Vygotsky, 1978; 1997; 1998).

This formulation also explains why he had so strongly disagreed with Piagetian developmental psychology – exactly because he saw it as biological and individualistic reductionism. It is interesting to mention that some Russian Vygotskians (Leontiev, 1978) in their struggle against any attempt to reduce a human being to his or her biological characteristics and to tear apart the individual and the society, have even coined a special term, *Robinsonade*, which is a Russian derivation from the name of Robinson Crusoe, a character in Daniel Defoe's novel. In Russia this term has been applied to any theory and research that portray psychological development in pure individualistic terms. This magnificent image of a loner, a single individual struggling to survive, alone, in social isolation on an uninhabited island, has been used as a metaphor for depicting the essence of many Western theories of child development, making a critique of individualistic reductionism convincingly palpable.

Are we still making Robinsonades? Are we still combining sociocultural concepts with individualistic contents? Do our implicit theories of psychological development and teaching–learning processes remain pretty much individualistic, deep inside, in spite of all sociocultural terminology we use? I believe these are very important questions to ask when we are talking about teaching sociocultural theory in American classrooms. My limited experience provides me with some insights into these questions. And even at the risk of being accused of overgeneralization, I am forced to admit that my answers, thus far, would be yes to all these questions.

MEASUREMENT AND QUANTIFICATION

The zone of proximal development (ZPD) is, probably, the most frequently investigated of all concepts ever introduced by Vygotsky (Tharp & Gallimore, 1988; Moll, 1990; see also Chaiklin, this volume). This is where some of my graduate school of education students, for the first time in their quest to grasp Vygotsky's complexity, find themselves on the more or less familiar terrain of the instructional applications and implications. However, matters do not necessarily go smoothly in relation to the zone either.

Where is the zone? Whom does it belong to? How can we measure the zone? These are but a small sample of the typical questions the students in my classes are often bothered with. Through the lens of these questions, culture speaks to me in its very loud and eloquent voice. One could almost physically feel the enormous pressure descending on my American students – the pressure to operate in clear, well-defined, and unambiguous terms, supported by reliable data and sophisticated statistics. The concept of ZPD is but one instance to illustrate how Vygotsky's way of experimenting and theorizing, in general, provides yet another serious challenge for most of my students: His samples are small, data are unclear and/or ambiguous, advanced statistics are absent, and it is not clear how he controlled the independent variables. In short, almost all modern standards of "proper scientific" objective investigation seem to be boldly violated.

One hundred years of a positivist–behaviorist dominance in education and psychology, with its focus on objective experimental methodology, reliable quantitative data, replicability of experimental designs, and so on, has not unfolded without the deepest cultural consequences. This dominance has left very deep roots in the American mentality and has become a culture in itself. And in spite of all recent trends to a paradigm shift (e.g., Fischetti, Dittmer, & Kyle, 1996), a movement toward more qualitative and intuitive approaches to studying and educating human beings, which has steadily gained popularity and strength during the last few decades, the old positivist stances are still too powerful: What cannot be measured does not exist or, at least, does not exist as a scientific entity or a sound object of scholarly investigation. Can Vygotsky's theory and research stand the scrutiny of such narrow positivistic requirements? This is one of the most difficult questions my students face, as soon as they read Vygotsky himself. To answer this question, one needs to look at Vygotsky's experiments more carefully.

The term *genetic*, used by Vygotsky to define the new brand of experiments he had invented, not only does not help but aggravates my students' confusion. Actually, this is one of the most misleading terms in the whole of Vygotsky's heritage. He used this term at the time when genetics, as a discipline, was in its cradle. Today, genetics is rightfully seen as one of the most advanced disciplines, with almost unlimited potentials and promises for ever growing progress in medicine and biology, and at the same time it is often viewed as a force threatening to change the very foundations of life on Earth. References to genetics are occupying a large part of daily political and public discourse (e.g., genetic engineering and cloning). In short, the word *genetic* today is automatically associated with something that cannot be further away from the meaning with which Vygotsky used it in the 1920s and 1930s (as in his struggle against biological reductionism, discussed earlier).

In many of my classes we have tried to find a better alternative to this misleading Greek derivative. The term *genesis* was helpful for some of my students: "So, it is about how this and that got started?" Almost anything would be better than *genetic* – possibly *genesis-like* or *generative* – but probably the best would be a plain term, *developmental experiments*. At least it would not automatically evoke those biological associations, which are so alien to the essence of Vygotsky's approach (for more detailed analyses of Vygotsky's experiments in cultural context, see Bruner, 1987; Kozulin, 1990; 1998; van der Veer & Valsiner, 1991).

What is even more difficult for my students to grasp is the big picture behind Vygotsky's experiments. In drastic contrast with most of his contemporaries and modern generations of researchers alike, Vygotsky always had a complex and authentic phenomenon as the object of his research, not a laboratory surrogate. Most important for him was always to draw a developmental path of a given phenomenon, for example, mediated memory, scientific concepts, or play. In every experiment he very carefully investigates the developmental phases of the phenomenon in question. Usually, one can discern at least five following phases in most of Vygotsky's research: (1) the phase in which the given phenomenon does not manifest itself yet; (2) the phase in which its initial traces seem to appear for the first time, always with corresponding analyses of the psychological tools and social forces that bring this phenomenon to life; (3) the phase in which the phenomenon reaches its climax, always linked to social interaction and usage of tools; (4) the phase of its gradual "interiorization" (see Lantolf, this volume); (5) and finally, the phase, in which it appears that the phenomenon in question has always been there, quite naturally, in our heads, resembling inherited individual property that was just waiting its time to be actualized.

Whereas mainstream experimental designs in psychology were increasingly eager to sacrifice the complexity, relevance, authenticity, and external validity of the phenomena they studied for the sake of internal validity, accuracy, reliability, and quantification, Vygotsky seemed to be intentionally moving in the opposite direction. If I may continue Toulmin's (1978) metaphor, calling Vygotsky "the Mozart of psychology," I would compare his experiments with long, complex, and elaborated musical pieces, such as operas, or symphonies, to the short and simple pop songs, however nice and worthwhile the latter might be, of most of his contemporaries.

DECONTEXTUALIZING THE SOCIOCULTURAL APPROACH

Another serious barrier my students bump into is the issue of Vygotsky's relationship to Marxism (for detailed analyses of this issue, see Bruner, 1987; Kozulin, 1984; 1990; Rosa & Montero, 1990). In my experience, an average student in an American graduate school of education knows very little about Marxism, and rarely has read any of Marx himself, not to mention the later Marxists. If most students have heard anything about Marxism at all (often Marxism is confused with communism), it definitely was not very positive. To connect Vygotsky's name (which many of them hold in high esteem even before entering the class and learning the sociocultural basics) with what they used to view as something old, negative, and outdated does present a challenge for many of my students. And, as the cognitive dissonance theory predicts, one of the strategies most frequently used in such circumstances is to avoid this connection altogether.

Ideological reasons for this figure of silence are quite obvious. It is only logical to distance oneself from the ideological background of a long-term political adversary that the former Soviet Union once was. To take a good theory and to use it without mentioning its "wrong" ideological roots, which could compromise it, seems a sound strategy, one that has been used, unfortunately, much too often in our highly politicized and polarized world. What is more important, however, is a more general tendency not only to avoid the connection of Vygotsky's theory to Marxism, but to avoid any contextual considerations of Vygotsky's work at all. One can see a great irony here: Cultural–historical theory tends to be interpreted and taught in a cultural and historical vacuum.

There are several reasons to why Vygotsky's work is being decontextualized besides the overtly ideological and political ones I have mentioned. Some of them are less evident than others. To understand those reasons, one has to go back several decades to the era of the new criticism of the 1940s and 1950s and of the structuralism of the 1960s and 1970s, which dominated social sciences, literacy, and education in the United States of America (e.g., Beach, 1993). According to these theoretical orientations, once very fashionable and very influential, the text is everything. Their position can be formulated in this way: "There is text, only text, nothing but text." All attempts to go beyond the text were declared not just irrelevant, but outright false. For instance, taking into account an author's intentions was labeled as an "intentional fallacy," considerations of any circumstances of the author's life and time as "affective fallacy," and so on (Rene & Warren, 1949).

Though the dominance, first, of new criticism and then of structuralism, gradually subsided, their influence can still be strongly felt in both scholarly texts interpreting Vygotsky and the university classrooms studying his work. In both cases, the readers and interpreters of Vygotsky alike seek to attain a full understanding of Vygotsky from his texts, and his texts alone. The simple idea of going beyond the texts and to consider the larger societal, political, cultural, and other contexts, which is, in my view, the only authentic way to understand his sociocultural approach, is not easily accepted. At first, many students see contextual analyses as irrelevant, or even troublesome, and keep trying to get all the answers from the texts. To use Vygotsky's framework, one could say in this case that contextualizing new information and ideas had not yet become a tool of the mind.

The last set of reasons, the ones I am actually most fascinated with, derive from the very basics of American culture. In the field of cross-cultural psychology, American culture is often defined as a low-context communication culture, or direct communication culture (Gugykunst, 1998; Ting-Toomy, 1999). "Say what you mean! Don't beat around the bush! Don't make me guess!" – maxims like these can be rightfully seen as the true communicative logos of American culture. The opposite tendency is seen in many other countries of the world, including Russia, in which communication patterns are often defined as a high-context communication culture, or indirect communication culture.

A *high-context communicative* pattern is one in which "most of the information is either in the physical context or internalized in the person, while very little is in the coded, explicit, transmitted part of the message" (Hall, 1976, p. 79). Thus, whereas "low-context communication tends to be direct, precise, and clear, high-context communication tends to be indirect and ambiguous" (Gudykunst, 1998, p. 57). There are many perfectly logical reasons for being indirect in high-context communication cultures, including specific cultural conventions, such as a generalized attitude of conflict avoidance and "saving face," numerous ideological constraints, and political pressure. This logic, though, may be evident and "logical" to high-context individuals only.

The differences between high- and low-context styles of communication have a huge impact on interpersonal interaction and are believed to be among the most frequent sources of intercultural misunderstandings, cultural blunders, culture clashes, and mutual frustration in interpersonal relationships (Hofstede, 1997; Fry & Bjorkquist, 1997; Gydykunst, 1998). The influence of high- and low-context communication cultures on academic writing is, no doubt, much smaller. Academic discourse tends to be more universal than patterns of interpersonal communication are. Yet, cultural variations definitely exist and should not be underestimated even in writing. Any college professor who has ever worked with international students from high-context communication cultures would immediately recognize what I am talking about: Special and sometimes significant effort must be made to help the high-context communication individuals' writings become more direct, explicit, linear, and precise. In short, we work hard to make their writing fit our low-context communication cultural expectations. Academic success of so many international students is the best proof that such a cultural change can occur, but it does not occur easily or automatically: It requires, as does studying a foreign language itself, a lot of time and effort.

Many specific cultural conventions, ideological constraints, and political pressures, contribute to the indirectness of academic writing in high-context communication cultures, as well. Therefore, though to a much lesser degree than in interpersonal communication, in academic texts produced in high-context communication cultures what is not directly said in the text is probably as important as, or even more important than, what is said. Thus, for all of us who deal with the academic writing of a person from a high-context communication culture, I would extend and slightly reformulate advice recommended by Miller (1998) for classroom conversations on multicultural topics: *Always keep in mind whose voice is silent, what we are not talking about, and why.*

Distinction between high- and low-communication cultures is highly relevant to cultural interpretation of Vygotsky's work. He is from a high-context communication culture, and his writing bears many typical features of such. All that was said previously about indirectness and ambiguity of high-context cultures' texts is applicable, to some extent, to Vygotsky's writings. English interpreters of his texts know this much too well (e.g., John-Steiner & Cole, 1978). Thus, however paradoxical and strange it may sound to some of my low-context communication colleagues, I would dare to say the following: When teaching Vygotsky's theory and reading Vygotsky's texts in American classrooms, it is highly advisable to keep asking, *What* is *not said* in his texts and *why*?

In further discussion, I will be focusing only on two issues that are not present in Vygotsky's texts in their explicit form, yet in my view are crucial in understanding his approach as a whole. One of these issues is related to the theoretical constraints and political pressure of his time; the other one is related to what I call *self-evidence* of one's own cultural conventions. The former is related to Vygotsky's relationship to modern multiculturalism; the latter touches on cultural specifics of social interaction, in general, and social mediation in the teaching–learning process, in particular.

VYGOTSKY AND MULTICULTURALISM

The word *culture* is one of the most frequently used in Vygotsky's writings. It is also one of the most frequently used words in modern educational theory and practice. Culture, cultural diversity, cultural sensitivity, multiculturalism, and many other derivatives have become a large part of modern theoretical and political debates on education. So it may appear that students should not have any difficulties, at least, with this part of Vygotsky's heritage. In fact, they do.

At first, my students see Vygotsky as a visionary, a forefather of modern multiculturalism, who talks about cultural aspects of development and education at a time when nobody else seemed to be interested in these issues. But as my students' acquaintance with Vygotsky's texts progresses, they invariably start asking the following uneasy questions: Did Vygotsky use the term *culture* in the same way as we use it today? Was he really a multiculturalist, or at least its predecessor? Was he really interested in cultures and cultural differences, after all?

These are very important questions, and comprehensible answers would require more space than the format of this chapter would allow. In order to answer them rather briefly, I need to touch on at least two different contexts. The first is related to the general theoretical relationship between Marxism and cultural relativism, which is being justly seen as one of the theoretical cornerstones of modern multiculturalism (Sleeter & Grant, 1999). The second is related to specific political and ideological circumstances in Russia during Vygotsky's time.

Cultural relativism, as a theory and ideology, emerged, first, within the field of cultural anthropology; it then spread to neighboring disciplines, such as linguistics and sociology. Psychology and education were, it seems, the last disciplines to be influenced by this paradigm. Cultural relativism radically contested almost all previous assumptions about history, social progress, and culture. It rejected linear, one-dimensional explanations of human civilization with their focus on social progress and cultural universals. Instead, it offered a detailed and profound analysis of cultural specificity (Cole, 1995).

According to Herskovits (1950), cultural relativism is "a philosophy which, in recognizing the values set up by every society to guide its own life, lays stress on the dignity in every body of customs, and on the need for tolerance of conventions, though they may differ from one's own" (p. 76). Cultural relativism insists that "all cultures are of equal value and the values and behavior of a culture can only be judged using that culture as a frame of reference" (Gudykunst & Kim, 1984, p. 97).

Cultural relativists saw Marxism as one of many "evolutionary" theories that try to fit all cultural diversity into a Procrustean bed of the universal, simplistic, and linear schemes, ill fitted to the empirical research of actual varieties of cultures ever existing on Earth. The question now arises, where did Vygotsky stand in this battle of cultural relativists against "evolutionists"? Where did he stand on this crucial dichotomy of cultural universals versus cultural specificity? There is no indication that Vygotsky was even aware that this battle was about to start. The forefather of cultural relativism, F. Boaz, was Vygotsky's later contemporary, and cultural relativism, as a new paradigm, was fully formulated only after Vygotsky's death (Herskovits, 1950; 1973).

Some insights on Vygotsky's overall position on this issue can be taken from his and Luria's research in Uzbekistan (Luria, 1976) on the role of literacy in mediating higher psychological processes. As ironic as it may sound, the fact is that Luria and Vygotsky did their best in trying *not* to investigate and *not* even to mention any of the peculiarities or specifics of Uzbek culture at all. The very reason Luria went to Uzbekistan was that it was easier to find a large sample of illiterate adults, which they needed for their study, there.

The reasons for the avoidance of cultural specifics in Vygotsky's work can be fully understood only in the broader political context, namely, in the light of political pressure on psychology, education, and the humanities in the former Soviet Union during Vygotsky's life. For Soviet scholars, the choice between cultural universals and cultural specifics was not only subject of academic debates, but more importantly, it was also a highly charged political issue. The former Soviet Union was one of the world's most culturally diverse countries. Soviet leaders saw many potential dangers in authentic interest in cultures and cultural diversity, which they used to equalize with the notion of "nationalism," used with an exclusively negative connotation.

An officially proclaimed political program was to build a new classless society without any traces of racism, ethnic inequalities, or discrimination. Soviet leaders saw the academic interest in cultural diversity, ethnicity, and ethnic identity as either an obstacle or a clear challenge and threat to this program. This is why, starting in the late 1920s, the term *culture* became less popular and less frequently used in psychology, education, and the humanities. This also explains, in my view, why Vygotsky's "cultural–historical theory" was replaced by Leontiev's (1978) "activity theory," the latter conspicuously losing the word *culture* from its title and, indeed, containing very few references to cultural issues altogether (for a more detailed and somewhat different interpretation of this issue, see Kozulin, 1984).

Therefore, any time Vygotsky uses the word *culture* or *cultural,* we have to keep in mind that he, generally, means its generic, universal connotation, not its specifics and particulars. That is why, in most cases, the words *culture,* and *cultural* can be so easily substituted with the words *society, social,* and *societal.* Actually, this substitution of *culture* to *society* works well as a tool in helping my students to understand better the meaning of Vygotsky's texts, whereas the word *culture* very often evokes its modern meanings, associated primarily with cultural specifics, and that can be very misleading. Just as misleading is the general tendency to modernize Vygotsky, to believe that all the answers about how to teach diverse learners today, at the dawn of a new century, can be taken directly from Vygotsky's texts written at the beginning of the last century, 70–80 years ago. Such a superficial modernization would do a disservice both to Vygotsky himself and to multicultural education.

At the same time, it is difficult to overestimate the importance of Vygotsky's approach to multicultural education, which, in its very essence, contains one of the best theoretical frameworks for educating culturally diverse learners. For instance, even if Vygotsky's contribution were limited to his work in special education, then already his impact on modern multicultural education would be very impressive. If we include learners who are disabled in the more general category of "culturally diverse learners," as is often done today, the contribution of Vygotsky to multicultural education would be very hard to overestimate. I cannot but agree with Gindis (1995): "Lev S. Vygotsky formulated a unique theoretical framework for the most comprehensive, inclusive and humane practice of special education known in twentieth century" (pp. 155–156).

Vygotsky's general theoretical framework is highly relevant to modern multicultural education for a number of reasons (see Kozulin, this volume). For instance, his fundamental interpretation of signs and symbols as mediators in the development of cognitive processes through social interaction has enormous potential for teaching culturally diverse learners. This potential derives from the mere fact that signs, symbols, and social interaction itself are, in large part, culturally specific, not universal. Increasingly, research has demonstrated this profound cultural specificity in many general and educational contexts (Moll, 1990; Rogoff, 1990; Martin, 1995; Cole, 1995). Such research has also demonstrated that a significant positive educational outcome can be achieved when this cultural specificity is taken fully into consideration in educational practice (McNamee, 1990; Au & Kawakami, 1991; Bruner, 1996; Shade, Kelly, & Olberg, 1997; Hollins, 1997; Gernsten & Himenez, 1998; Diaz, 2001).

Further research is needed, however, to understand fully the importance of cultural specificity to education of culturally diverse learners, including the cultural specificity of social interactions and interpersonal relationships. As Carolyn Panofsky (see Panofsky, this volume) stated, "Sociocultural learning theory has deeply explored the role of signs and symbols in mediation but must more fully consider the ways that interpersonal relations mediate students' school lives and the consequences of these relations for learning." In the last section of this chapter, I will discuss some issues related to the cultural specifics of interpersonal relationships and their mediational role in teaching–learning processes.

CULTURAL SPECIFICITY IN SOCIAL INTERACTION AND THE TEACHING–LEARNING PROCESS

Unlike the instances described, the notion of social interaction in Vygotsky's work does not seem to present any trouble for my students.

Are we not interacting more or less in the same fashion, after all? Yet, the notion of social interaction presents, probably, the major challenge and is the source of many cultural misinterpretations. And this is yet another example of something essential to Vygotsky's approach as a whole, which remains quite inexplicit in his texts. It is never addressed by Vygotsky directly, in my view, by simple reason of being just self-evident, as most of our cultural conventions are.

Are social interactions and interpersonal relations universal or culturally specific? As Alex Kozulin has noted (see Kozulin, this volume),

Though there is little doubt that certain forms of human mediation are universal and can be found in any culture; the question remains as to what constitutes this universal core of mediation and which forms of mediation are culture specific. It is also important to inquire whether the "same" aspects of mediation have identical meaning and importance in different cultures and for different social groups.

Thus, though general academic debates about the precise ratio of what is universal and what is culturally specific in human behavior continue, many specific aspects of cultural variability have become the subject of intense investigation in the fields of modern cross-cultural psychology and intercultural communication (Brislin & Yoshida, 1994; Triandis, 1995; Cushner & Brislin, 1997; Hofstede, 1997; Fry & Bjorkqvist, 1997; Ting-Toomy, 1999).

One of the most important dimensions of cultural variability that has attracted the attention of researchers is individualism versus collectivism. (Triandis, 1995; Hofstede, 1997; Gudykunst, 1998). I have already mentioned this dimension earlier, in discussing the tendency toward biological and individualistic reductionism in explanation of mind and society. At this point, I will discuss a broader range of implications related to this fundamental cultural difference.

There is a rare consensus among researchers in defining the North American culture as highly individualist and the Russian as much more collectivist (Brohfenbrenner, 1974; Hofstede, 1997; Landis, 1997; Alexander, 2000). Actually, a famous study of 53 countries and regions on all five continents by Geert Hofstede (1997) ranked the United States as the number one individualist country on the continuum of individualism versus collectivism. Differences between individualist and collectivist cultures seem to be numerous, profound, and encompassing. According to G. Hofstede, in collectivist cultures

people are born into extended families or other ingroups which continue to protect them in exchange for loyalty.... Identity is based in the social network to which one belongs.... Children learn to think in terms of "we."... Relationship prevails over task.... [In individualist cultures] everyone grows up to look after him/herself and his/her immediate (nuclear) family only.... Identity is based in the individual.... Children learn to think in terms of "I" ... and task prevails over relationship. (1997, p. 67)

Other researchers have added many other important distinctions between collectivist and individualist cultures. For instance, in individualist cultures, the goals of an individual prevail over the goals of a group; independence, self-reliance, and privacy are highly valued. In collectivist cultures, on the contrary, goals of the group prevail over the goals of an individual; interdependence is highly valued, and privacy is downplayed (Triandis, 1995; Brislin & Yoshida, 1994).

Interpersonal relationships in individualistic cultures tend to be short-term-oriented, whereas in collectivist cultures they tend to be long-term-oriented (Cushner & Brislin, 1997; Gudykunst, 1998).This last dichotomy means that collectivists tend to consider every social interaction as a living organism, as a long-term and developing process, slowly moving from a formal and conventional relationship to a personal and idiosyncratic one. Long-term cultural orientation means that the balance between the personal and the formal components of social interaction is a very dynamic process, slowly shifting toward the ever more personal pole. In other words, the ratio between the conventional, formal, and official aspects of social interaction and its informal, idiosyncratic, and personal components has a complex and intricate dynamic. Usually, every new social interaction starts in a rather formal and official way, and only as time passes does the ratio between formal and personal ingredients of a relationship change. Any successful interaction tends to become more personal, or at least this is an implicit cultural expectation in collectivist cultures.

Individualists, on the other hand, tend to establish the ratio between the personal and formal components in their interaction at the very beginning, and this ratio tends to remain more or less the same. What is more important here is not the future dynamic of this interaction on the continuum personal–formal, but rather the appropriateness of this ratio to the situation in which it takes place. Individualists seem to be more comfortable with short-term interactions defined solely by social roles, norms, and other constraints of a given social interaction that have been analyzed in great detail, for instance, in the theory of symbolic interactionism (Mead, 1934). That does not mean that social interaction in an individualist culture never changes at all, simply that the range of such change is much smaller, compared to that in collectivist interactions. In sum, collectivists tend to overemphasize the personal or interpersonal component of any social interaction, including teacher–student interactions, whereas individualists tend to downplay or to deemphasize it.

Diaz-Guerrero (1975) goes as far as directly juxtaposing the "Interpersonal" or subjective reality, which applies to behavioral, perceptual, and interactive patterns of collectivists, and the "External" or objective reality, which describe the behavior, perception, and social interaction of people from individualist cultures. As Tomoko Yoshida (1994) describes it, "Interpersonal reality refers to the feelings and impressions created during interaction between two or more people" (p. 256), whereas "external reality refers to measurable, verifiable, phenomena that exist in nature. These are often what people accept as 'facts'" (p. 258). According to Yoshida (1994), "Although many interactions enable the simultaneous considerations of both realities, certain situations force people to choose or to emphasize one over another. Culture is often the guiding force in making such decision" (p. 256). She concludes, "A society that values collectivism will obviously place a higher value on harmony and good interpersonal relationship while an individualistic society is likely to encourage behavior that brings merit to specific people" (p. 243). In her opinion, the reason numerous cultural blunders and clashes occur is the very existence of these entirely different realities, most often not recognized by either side.

This dimension of intercultural variability has an enormous impact on education of diverse learners, the importance of which, unfortunately, is not yet fully recognized. For instance, for an immigrant child who has recently arrived in the United State of America from a highly collectivist culture, the culturally familiar and successful way for her or him to interact with others (friends, peers, teachers, parents, other adults), thus, is to be indirect, interdependent, collaborative, noncompetitive, personal, and modest. Can we predict what will happen to a child with such a communicative attitude in a typical America classroom? As a growing body of data suggest, the tendency of collectivists to cooperate and collaborate spontaneously in and out of classroom (and not under a teacher's guidance within a narrow defined "cooperative learning" framework) is often perceived as dishonesty and cheating. Their modesty and nonassertiveness are very often perceived as a lack of ambition and low self-esteem. Their noncompetitiveness and orientation toward interdependent and long-term relationships are perceived as weakness and lack of character (Cushner, 1994; Goodman, 1994; Igoa, 1995; Shade et al., 1997; Diaz, 2001).

It is clear that much more concrete cross-cultural research of this sort is urgently needed to elucidate the intricacies and complexity of educating culturally different learners. At this point, however, we need to return to Vygotsky and to ask the following crucial question: When Vygotsky uses the terms *social interaction, social mediation,* and *interpersonal relationship,* which of the interpretations – individualistic or collectivist – does he have in mind? Or using Diaz-Guerrero (1975) and T. Yoshida's (1994) terminology, which reality does he imply – interpersonal or external?

I believe the answer should be quite evident. In spite of his enormous interest in Western culture in general (especially literature and theater), and his almost encyclopedic knowledge of Western psychology, philosophy, linguistics, and so on, in particular, Vygotsky had never lived in a foreign country and, thus, did not have an immediate, personal, firsthand experience of living in an individualistic culture. Without this personal experience, without a pressing necessity to adjust, to accommodate to a new culture that is so drastically different from one's home country, the main features of one's own culture, even the most basic of its values, assumptions, and conventions, remain implicit and self-evident. Another culture is a very powerful point of reference, a miraculous mirror, and only by looking into it can one clearly understand one's own culture, its most basic values and features.

We all take our basic cultural assumptions for granted. So did Vygotsky. Living in a collectivist culture, Vygotsky, in my view, attributed much more personal and interpersonal meaning to the notion of social interactions and social mediation, as his Russian colleagues and readers, no doubt, did as well. Such an interpretation did not require any references or special explanations because a collectivist style of social interaction was the only type they knew.

The conclusion I am going to draw on the basis of the previous analysis may start a new page in cultural interpretation of Vygotsky's work: Namely, I would argue that in order really to change our education in Vygotsky's sense or actually put his theory into educational practice, a more collectivist interpretation of his ideas is needed. And that would mean, in particular, among many other things, *making the educational process more personal*. Any time we eradicate, or just limit, the personal component in our interactions with our students, we are not approaching Vygotsky, but moving further away from him, no matter how often we quote him or how many of his concepts we use in our writings. No matter how important the reasons for limiting or eradicating the personal component in the teaching–learning process may seem – high-stakes testing, increasing pressure to use as much technology as possible, spreading popularity of distance learning, legal concerns – the absence of the personal component in teaching–learning processes always results in educational losses of one kind or another.

FINAL WORD

I have argued that there are several important reasons why contextual and cultural interpretations of Vygotsky's ideas are needed. In different countries, we see Vygotsky's approach through different cultural lenses, see his ideas reflected in different cultural mirrors. I believe the time has come to look carefully at these very lenses and these very mirrors, to reflect critically on our cultural values, assumptions, and conventions: Are they not somewhat warped or out of focus? I believe that the time has come, at last, when we need not only a good linguistic translation of Vygotsky's texts, but a good cultural interpretation of his ideas, as well. I believe, also, that now that all the political and ideological barriers that were so unsurpassable in Vygotsky's time have finally fallen, the time has come to start authentic intercultural dialogue on issues related to Vygotsky's theory and its application to educational practice.

As soon as my students accept this paradigm, as soon as they engage in intercultural dialogue, as soon as they start examining their own cultural lenses, as soon as they start their exploration of cultural and historical contexts associated with Vygotsky's life, work, and time, their relationship with Vygotsky is irrevocably changed: They start seeing a deep meaning where they used to see just a confusion, and they start to "fit" sociocultural ideas to their own life and their own teaching–learning process, instead of just talking about a set of unfamiliar concepts, the meaning of which they do not fully understand. Then, my role as a teacher is changed, as well. Instead of simply mediating their understanding of texts and decontextualized terminology, I am now engaging in a much more interesting and rewarding process. I am helping my students to discover some very profound personal and cultural meanings in Vygotsky's theory, without which it risks always remaining in what Jim Wertsch (1990) calls "decontextualized rationality."

References

Alexander, R. J. (2000). *Culture and pedagogy: International comparisons in primary education*. Malden MA: Blackwell.

Au, K. H., & Kawakami, A. J. (1991). Culture and ownership: Schooling of minority children. *Childhood Education, Annual Theme*, 280–284.

Beach, R. (1993). *A teachers' introduction to reader-response theories*. Urbana, IL: NCTE.

Brislin, R., & Yoshida, T. (Eds.) (1994). *Improving intercultural interactions: modules for cross-cultural training programs*. Thousand Oaks, CA: Sage.

Bronfenbrenner, U. (1974). *Two worlds of childhood: US and USSR*. London: Penguin Books.

Bruner, J. S. (1987). Prologue to the English eldition. In *The collected works of L. S. Vygotsky*. Vol. 1. *Problem of general psychology*. New York: Plenum Press.

Bruner, J. S. (1995a). Reflecting on russian consciousness. In: Martin, L., Nelson, K., & Tobach, E. (Eds.), *Sociocultural psychology: Theory and practice of doing and knowing* (pp. 67–88). Cambridge: Cambridge University Press.

Bruner, J. S. (1995b). Vygotsky: A historical and conceptual perspective. In James Wertsch (Ed.), *Culture, communication and cognition: Vygotskian perspectives*. Cambridge University Press.

Bruner, J. S. (1996). *The culture of education*. Cambridge, MA: Harvard University Press.

Cole, M. (1995). *Cultural psychology: A once and future discipline*. Cambridge, MA: The Belknap Press of Harvard University Press.

Cushner, K. (1994). Preparing teacher for an intercultural context. In R. Brislin & T. Yoshida (Eds.), *Improving intercultural interactions: Modules for cross-cultural training programs* (pp. 91–108). Thousand Oaks, CA: Sage.

Cushner, K., & Brislin, R. (Eds.) (1997). *Improving intercultural interactions: Modules for cross-cultural training programs*. (Vol. 2). Thousand Oaks, CA: Sage.

Diaz, C. F. (Ed.) (2001). *Multicultural Education on the 21st Century*. New York: Longman.

Diaz-Gerrero, R. (1975). *Psychology of Mexican: Culture and personality*. Austin: University of Texas Press.

Dixon-Krauss, L. A. (1995). Partner reading and writing: Peer social dialogue and the zone of proximal development. *Journal of Reading Behavior, 27*(1), 45–53.

Fischetti, J., Dittmer, A., & Kyle, D. W. (1996) Shifting paradigm: Emerging issues for educational policy and practice. *Teacher Educator, 31*(3), 189–201.

Feigenberg, I. M. (1996). *L. S. Vygotsky: The way he started: S. F. Dobkin's Memoirs*. Jerusalem: Jerusalem Publishing Center.

Fry, D., & Bjorkqvist, K. (Eds.) (1997). *Cultural variations in conflict resolution: Alternatives to violence*. Mahwah, NJ: Lawrence Elrbaum Associates.

Gernsten, R. M., & Jimenez, R. T. (1999). *Promoting learning for culturally and linguistically divers students: Classroom applications from contemporary research*. Belmont, CA: Wadsworth.

Gindis, B. (1995). Viewing the disabled in the sociocultural milieu: Vygotsky's quest. *School Psychology International, 16*, 155–156.

Goodman, N. (1994). Intercultural education at the university level: Teacher–student interaction. In R. Brislin & T. Yoshida (Eds.), *Improving intercultural interactions: Modules for cross-cultural training programs* (pp. 129–147). Thousand Oaks, Sage.

Gudykunst, W. B. (1998). *Bridging differences: Effective intergroup communication* (3rd ed.). Thousand Oaks, CA: Sage.

Gudykunst, W., & Kim, Y. Y. (1984). *Communicating with strangers: An approach to intercultural communication*. New York: McGraw-Hill.

Hall, E. T. (1976). *Beyond culture*. New York: Doubleday.

Herskovits, M. (1950). *Man and his works*. New York: Knopf.

Herskovits, M. (1973). *Cultural relativism*. New York: Random House.

Hofstede, G. (1997). *Cultures and organizations: Software of the mind* (2nd ed.). London: McGraw-Hill.

Hollins, E. (1996). *Culture in school learning: Revealing the deep meaning*. Mahwah, NJ: Lawrence Elrbaum Associates.

Igoa, C. (1995). *The inner world of the immigrant child*. Mahwah, NJ: Lawrence Elrbaum Associates.

John-Steiner, V., & Cole, M. (1978). Editors' Preface. In: Vygotsky, L. S. *Mind in society* (pp. IX–XI). Cambridge, MA: Harvard University Press.

Kozulin, A. (1984). *Psychology in utopia: Toward a social history of Soviet psychology*. Cambridge, MA: MIT Press.

Kozulin, A. (1990). *Vygotsky's psychology: A biography of ideas*. Cambridge, MA: Harvard University Press.

Kozulin, A. (1995). The learning process: Vygotsky's theory in the mirror of its interpretations. *School Psychology International, 16*, 117–129.

Kozulin, A. (1998). *Psychological tools: A sociocultural approach to education*. Cambridge, MA: Harvard University Press.

Leont'ev, A. N. (1978). *Activity, consciousness, and personality*. Englewood Cliffs, NJ: Prentice Hall.

Luria, A. R. (1976). *Cognitive development: Its cultural and social foundations*. Cambridge, MA: Harvard University Press.

Martin, L., Nelson, K., & Tobach, E. (Eds.) (1995). *Sociocultural psychology: Theory and practice of doing and knowing.* Cambridge: Cambridge University Press.

McNamee, G. D. (1990). Learning to read and write in an inner-city setting: A longitudinal study of community change. In Moll, L. (Ed.), *Vygotsky and education: Implications and applications of sociohistorical psychology* (pp. 287–303). Cambridge: Cambridge University Press.

Mead, G. H. (1934). *Mind, self and society.* Chicago: University of Chicago.

Miller, S. (1998, Winter). Entering into multicultural conversations in literature-history classes. *Arizona English Bulletin,* pp. 10–26.

Moll, L. (Ed.) (1990). *Vygotsky and education: Implications and applications of sociohistorical psychology.* Cambridge: Cambridge University Press.

Rene, W., & Warren, A. (1949). *Theory of literature.* New York: Harcourt.

Rogoff, B. (1990). *Apprenticeship in thinking.* New York: Oxford University Press.

Rosa, A., & Montero, I. (1990). The historical context of Vygotsky's work: A sociohistorical approach. In L. Moll. (Ed.), *Vygotsky and education: Implications and applications of sociohistorical psychology* (pp. 59–88). Cambridge: Cambridge University Press.

Shade, B., Kelly, C., & Oberg, M. (1997). *Creating culturally-responsive classroom.* Washington, DC: APA.

Sleeter, C., & Grant C. (1999). *Making choices for multicultural education.* New York: John Wiley & Sons.

Tappan, M. B. (1998). Sociocultural psychology and caring pedagogy: Exploring Vygotsky's "hidden curriculum." *Educational Psychologist,* 33(1), 23–33.

Ting-Toomy, S. (1999). *Communicating across cultures.* New York: Guilford Press.

Tharp, R., & Gallimore, R. (1988). *Rising minds to life: Teaching, learning and schooling in social context.* Cambridge: Cambridge University Press.

Tomasello, M. 1999. *The cultural origins of human cognition.* Cambridge, MA: Harvard University Press.

Toulmin, S. (1978, September). The Mozart of psychology. *New York Review of Books.* 25(14), 51–57.

van der Veer, R., & Valsiner, J. (1991) *Understanding Vygotsky: A quest for synthesis.* Oxford: Basil Blackwell.

Vygotsky, L. S. (1962). *Thought and language.* (E. Hanfmann & G. Vakar, Eds. and Trans.). Cambridge, MA: The MIT Press.

Vygotsky, L. S. (1978). *Mind in society.* Cambridge, MA: Harvard University Press.

Vygotsky, L. S. (1997). *The History of development of higher mental functions.* New York: Plenum Press.

Vygotsky, L. S. (1998). *Child psychology.* New York: Plenum Press.

Wertch, J. V. (1990). The voice of rationality in a sociocultural approach to mind. In L. Moll (Ed.), *Vygotsky and education: Implications and applications of sociohistorical psychology* (pp. 111–125). Cambridge: Cambridge University Press.

Wertch, J. V. (1991). *Voices of the mind.* Cambridge, MA: Harvard University Press.

Yoshida, T. Interpersonal versus non-interpersonal realities: An effective tool individualists can use to better understand collectivists. In R. Brislin & T. Yoshida (Eds.), *Improving intercultural interactions: Modules for cross-cultural training programs* (pp. 243–267). Thousand Oaks, CA: Sage.

Author Index

Subject Index

The Learning in Doing series was founded in 1987 by Roy Pea and John Seely Brown

THE LIBRARY
NEW COLLEGE
SWINDON

WITHDRAWN